THE
PHOENICIANS

This volume was first published
on the occasion of the exhibition
The Phoenicians
at the Palazzo Grassi,
Venice, 1988

Published in 2001 by
I.B.Tauris & Co Ltd
London & New York
www.ibtauris.com

ISBN 1-85043-533-2

Printed and bound in Italy

THE
PHOENICIANS

under the scientific direction
of Sabatino Moscati

I.B. Tauris *Publishers*
LONDON • NEW YORK

Contents

*The symbol • followed by page
number refers to color
illustrations*

Part I Phoenician Civilization

A Civilization Rediscovered
Sabatino Moscati

Our knowledge of Phoenician civilization has improved greatly in recent years. There have been very few cases like this, for not only has the body of our knowledge of this civilization increased in quantity, but the very nature of the people, their culture, and their heritage have been subjected to fresh thinking, fresh definition, and fresh assessment. It is true, of course, that an astonishing series of archaeological discoveries underlies this new state of affairs, but this is no coincidence: on the contrary, in certain cases, it reflects a carefully thought-out strategy of investigation; and in others, these discoveries have been followed by new evaluation.

It would be interesting to look at what we knew about Phoenician civilization about 25 years ago. First, we have to recall the complicated range of themes which that civilization shows. If we use the term "Phoenician" in its broadest sense, including evidence of the people both in its land of origin and in the Mediterranean diaspora, which extended to the limits of the then-known West, we have to distinguish the largest Phoenician colony, Carthage, and its people the Carthaginians, who built up a vast empire in the West. "Punic," a Latin adaptation of the word "Phoenician," was applied to those with whom Rome had the greatest contact: the Carthaginians.

Plaquette depicting scarab from Nimrud 8th century B.C. ivory 3.3 × 2.5 cm Brussels, Musées Royaux d'Art et d'Histoire

So is it all a question of terms? Not entirely. In the East, the situation is quite simple, since we have nothing but Phoenician evidence there. But in the West the situation is complicated, because one can distinguish an initial Phoenician phase and a subsequent Carthaginian or Punic phase, but there is not always a clear distinction between them. Whatever the case, our awareness of the various geographical, chronological and ethnic ramifications in which we place the civilization we call Phoenician is an acquisition of our times.

Returning to what we knew of the Phoenicians 25 years ago or so, the first fact is that there were very few direct literary sources: brief inscriptions in the Phoenician alphabet, with the names of sovereigns, dedications of monuments, and mention of divinities. One direct original source — but it has come down to us through classical mediation in the work of Josephus — was the Annals of Tyre, with historical records of that city in two periods, the 10th-8th and the 6th centuries B.C.

The situation was somewhat brighter as far as indirect historical sources were concerned. From both Egypt and Mesopotamia, we had chronicles on relations with Phoenician cities, and in particular, in Assyrian sources, on their subjection. And testimonies from the Old Testament were much fuller, espe-

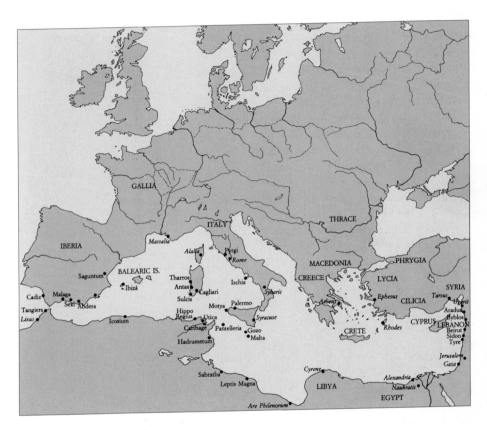

The
Mediterranean
at the time
of the Phoenician
expansion

cially when it came to relations with Tyre, and to Solomon's times, when the Tyrian king, Hiram I, had the temple of Solomon built in Jerusalem. Later, relations between the kings of Israel and the kings of Tyre extended to religious matters, such as the influence on Israel exerted by Phoenician polytheism.

As for archaeology, excavations in Phoenicia revealed rather large gaps, mainly because of the long span of the Phoenician people's existence. There was abundant evidence of earlier times, such as that from Byblos in Lebanon and Ugarit in Syria; and later evidence, mainly from the Graeco-Roman period. But very little was known about the Phoenician cities themselves, or rather the Phoenician phases of the cities: practically all we knew about Tyre, for instance, came from its Roman monuments. There was, however, a good deal of information about the surrounding regions, which revealed the spread of Phoenician craftsmanship: examples are the metal cups and carved ivories — definitely made by Phoenicians — found in Cyprus and Mesopotamia.

In the Mediterranean West, by far the most extensive body of knowledge covered Carthage. There was an abundance of epigraphical material, some thousands of inscriptions; most of them, however, were short votive dedications: while they repeated the more important names of gods and provided plentiful information in terms of the dedicators' names, they revealed little about beliefs and rites, or historical vicissitudes. It is probable that a Carthaginian historiography did exist; indeed, from what we read in classical authors, it definitely did. But nothing remains of it, so we actually had fewer sources in the West than in the East.

Statuette of male deity from Syria 8th century B.C. bronze and silver 20 cm, Paris Musée du Louvre • p.33

Classical literature, on the other hand, was and still is a rich source of information. Most of it concerns the clash between Carthage and Greece in Sicily and between Carthage and Rome all around the Mediterranean area. It is, of course, a somewhat partial historiography, for it was compiled by enemies who tended to cast shadows on the Carthaginians, stressing their cruelty and perfidy and the like. This did not apply to Hannibal, however, or at least not completely: along with hostility toward Rome's greatest enemy, there was a tendency to acknowledge and indeed exaggerate his valor, in order to justify the defeats Rome suffered at his hands.

The truth is that the shortcomings of classical sources do not lie so much in their partiality as in their limited horizons and interests, which give us only restricted information. Apart from accounts of wars, we have only sporadic data, such as what Aristotle says about the constitution of Carthage, the writings of Polybius on the revolt of the mercenaries, the account of Hanno's circumnavigation of Africa in the Greek version, and so on.

From the archaeological point of view, the destruction of Carthage drastical-

Aerial view of the archaeological area of Byblos

ly reduced the possibility of increasing our knowledge. Nevertheless, excavations in cemeteries have provided much evidence about the minor arts: terra-cotta figurines, amulets, carved ivory, scarabs, jewellery, and so on. And large numbers of inscribed stelae bearing figures have been recovered at Carthage and other North African centers (Sousse [Susah] and Constantine) from a special type of sanctuary, called *tophet*, in which children were sacrificed.

There was very little information about the colonies founded, first by the Phoenicians and then by the Carthaginians, on the western shores of the Mediterranean: along the African coastline, and on Malta, in Sicily, in Sardinia, the Balearic Islands and in southern Spain. Clearly such colonies existed, and some of them must have flourished, but the lack of interest in research led to a scanty body of knowledge and a superficial assessment of evidence.

At this point it is not difficult to understand how, until about 25 years ago, the very existence of Phoenician studies constituted a subject for debate. On one side, the specialists in epigraphy dealt with inscriptions with an eye to the language, literature and history of the Semitic peoples, showing no interest or competence in archaeology; on the other side, archaeologists excavating in the Punic world were more interested in classical evidence, for that was all they were competent in. Those who knew about language knew nothing about archaeology; those who knew about archaeology knew nothing of language.

Punic ruins
on the slopes
of Byrsa
Carthage

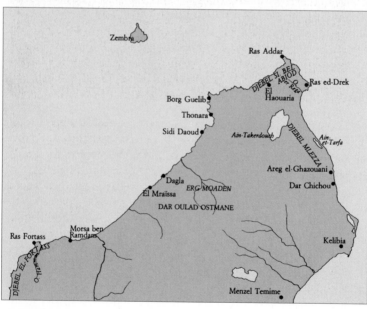

Zembra

Ras Addar

DJEBEL SI BEL
ABIOD

Abir Ksar

Ras ed-Drek

El
Haouaria

Borg Guelib

Thonara

Sidi Daoud

Aïn-Takerdouch

DJEBEL MLEZZA

Aïn-
et-Tarfa

Areg el-Ghazouani

Dagla

ERG MOADEN

Dar Chichou

El Mraïssa

DAR OULAD OSTMANE

Morsa ben
Ramdam

Ras Fortass

Kelibia

DJEBEL EL-FORTASS

Menzel Temime

The Cape Bon
area, site of three
Punic fortresses:
Kelibia,
Ras Fortass and
Ras ed-Drek

The great transformation of our knowledge of the Phoenician world that has taken place in the last quarter of a century is mainly due to archaeological finds. It might be thought that coincidence had a part to play, but that is not true, or at least only partly true. The fact is that the finds have been the fruits of renewed interest in the Phoenician world, of a new, painstaking methodology that has made it the object of exhaustive investigation. First of all, evidence of Phoenician civilization was searched for, and not casually encountered; then, research schedules were programmed; finally, ample space was created not only for actual excavations, but also for prospecting in order to define the archaeological areas, their characteristics and their consistency.

Ivory bed from tomb 79 at Salamis 8th century B.C. Nicosia, Cyprus Museum

It is sad that the recent war in Lebanon has reduced the chances we might have had of carrying out this work in the very heart of the Phoenician homeland. Surveys were proceeding satisfactorily, with the discovery of the Khaldé necropolis near Beirut Airport by the Lebanese Antiquities Authority, and the work of foreign expeditions such as the American one at Sarafand (Sarepta), which finally — if only locally — made up for the traditional scarcity of evidence about the Phoenician age. Work has proceeded only further north, and further south: to the north, with the Danish excavations at Tell Suqas (ancient Shukshu) in Syria; and to the south, with the Italian explorations at Akhziv, and the Israeli digs at various points along the coast.
Meanwhile, however, excavations on Cyprus by the local Antiquities Authority have been making great progress: in particular with the finds at Kition (Citium), an impressive Phoenician colony dating back at least to the 9th century B.C., that is, to the initial stages of the Phoenicians' expansion overseas; and the work at Salamis, which has brought to light a burial ground of the 8th-

*Plaquette depicting
crouching hare
and calf from Nora
5th century B.C.
ivory, 10 × 3 cm
Cagliari, Museo
Archeologico
Nazionale*

7th century B.C., with an abundance of funerary accessories, including some of the most highly prized ivory work of its kind ever found. We now know that the entire southern coast of Cyprus was penetrated by the Phoenicians.

There have undoubtedly been more important finds in the West as a whole than in the East. In Tunisia, excavations carried out by the National Institute of Archaeology and Art at Kerkouane, on Cape Bon, have brought to light the elements of a Punic city which it was thought would never be found again after the destruction of Carthage. Again on Cape Bon, Italo-Tunisian surveys have revealed a series of fortresses, evidence of the defensive system raised by Carthage at the exact point where Africa is nearest to Sicily. And at Carthage itself, international excavations sponsored by Unesco to salvage what remains of the Punic-Roman era are also giving us new information.

A series of Italian archaeological missions promoted by the University of Rome and then by the Italian National Research Council have revealed a good deal about the Phoenicians on the island of Pantelleria (Kossyra) and on Malta, where the discovery of the sanctuary at Tas Silg has yielded conclusive proof that several civilizations followed one another on the same site: prehistoric, Phoenician, Greek, and Roman. But the most significant Italian discoveries are without doubt those made in Sicily and Sardinia.

In Sicily, excavations at Motya by the two institutions mentioned above and the local Monuments and Fine Arts Service have brought to light a *tophet* with over a thousand stelae bearing figures that provide a great deal of information about Phoenician art. Again at Motya, other material has been discovered, while wall paintings and inscriptions of various periods have been found in the Grotta Regina, near Palermo; this rock sanctuary is the only one so far discovered in the Phoenician West.

In Sardinia, the 1962 discovery of Monte Sirai, a fortress built inland from the coastal town of Sulcis, provides evidence of military penetration on the island. In turn, the excavations at Antas show the encounter between a Roman cult and an earlier Phoenician cult: that of the god Sid, attested by over twenty inscriptions. More current finds are those being made at Tharros, the large Phoenician center near present-day Oristano, at the point where the ships

*Votive stele with
"sign of Tanit"
caduceus and
dolphin
from Constantine
3rd-1st century
B.C., limestone
46 × 23.5 cm
Paris, Musée
du Louvre*

14

Gold pendants showing various techniques from Tharros 7th-6th century B.C., 3-1.5 cm diam.1.92-0.9 cm Cagliari, Museo Archeologico Nazionale

coming in from Africa met the route for the Balearic Islands and Spain. Here, walls erected to provide a powerful defensive system have been discovered, along with a *tophet* and stelae of unusual size and form.

Tharros also exemplifies the attempt to integrate on-site research with muse urn research with the objective of publishing works on little-known objects. One example is jewellery: a very rich, fine-quality production examined and published in the Cagliari and Sassari collections. The same applies to other categories, which all together constitute an impressive body of knowledge about Phoenician civilization in Sardinia: the stelae of Nora and Sulcis, the terracotta statuettes of Bithia, the Cagliari and Sassari collections of scarabs, amulets, carved ivory and bone objects, and coins.

In Spain too, this new wave of knowledge has assumed considerable proportions. Spanish and German excavations on the Costa del Sol have provided us with ample, significant evidence of the Phoenician presence from the 8th century B.C. onwards, including necropoli like Almuñecar and Trayamar, and large inhabited centers such as Toscanos. The finds have led to a large-scale return to Phoenician studies, which has highlighted the encounter and interaction with the indigenous culture, and the development of production by local workshops of articles initially imported. This in turn has improved our knowledge of certain well-known collections, like the jewellery of La Aliseda, and the carved ivory of Carmona. We should also mention significant discoveries made in Portugal, the Sines jewellery being one good example.

This great renewal of interest has been supported by archaeological finds. At last, a number of questions are being answered. How can we define Phoenician civilization? What are the essential features of its history? How, why and when did the Phoenician colonization of the Mediterranean begin? How can we successfully integrate our former and present knowledge of their culture, religion and art? And at the same time, the Phoenician role in the Mediterranean world is being put into better perspective. The following pages will bear that out.

Who Were the Phoenicians?
Sabatino Moscati

There is no such thing as a clear-cut, broadly accepted definition of the Phoenicians as a people with an acknowledged territory of their own, a sufficiently homogeneous language, and a common historical and cultural background. On the contrary, debate on the subject runs hot, with a whole range of different theses. And these theses are frequently not so much expounded as assumed, which leads to confusion and to reciprocal misunderstandings among scholars. The main disagreements concern the origins of the people and their culture: some hold that the date goes back to the 2nd or 3rd millennium B.C., while others suggest the Early Iron Age, around 1200 B.C.

Confusion about their name probably helps to create confusion about their origin. *Phoinikes* for the people and *Phoinike* for the region are terms used by others, references having been found as far back as Homeric times. There is an obvious link between these terms and the common noun *phoinix*, which means "purple-red" and referred to the typical Phoenician industry of dyeing fabrics purple. But it could be that the name, in its common usage at any rate, was used earlier, in the 2nd millennium B.C.: in Mycenaean texts, one finds the feminine adjective *po-ni-ki-ja*, meaning "red" and referring to a chariot.

Now what name did the Phoenicians give themselves? We must remember first of all that the concept of national unity was hazy among the Phoenician

Main sites of the Late Bronze Age in the Near East

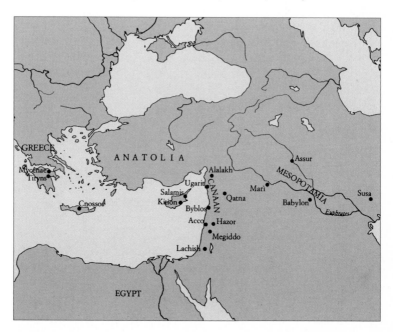

17

cities, so there are no established common terms that stand out above others. As early as the 3rd millennium B.C., the term "Canaanites" was used for the people and "Canaan" for the region, but this denotes the whole Syro-Palestinian area. The term is also used specifically for the Phoenicians, especially in the Old Testament, and it lived on in the Mediterranean diaspora, and later, too: Saint Augustine, talking about the population of Africa in his time, says that the peasants called themselves *Kena'ani*.

As cuneiform texts of the 2nd millennium show, the word "Canaan" is also linked with the concept of "purple-red." But in spite of this, one may conclude that the term "Canaanites" has a broader meaning than the term "Phoenicians": no doubt, it includes the Phoenicians, sometimes denotes them, but we cannot say that it meant them and them alone.

It is quite a different thing with another name, "Sidonians," which is actually too specific: both in Homer and in the Bible, it is used to denote the Phoenicians as a whole, but is seems obvious that this is because of the suzerainty at some time, in some place of the city from which the name derives, Sidon. In other words, it is an extended meaning, a linguistic phenomenon that once again emphasizes the lack of a unitary awareness among the Phoenicians.

Having dealt with the name, how do we define Phoenician unity? In the present-day concept we must refer to, a people is an aggregate of persons who may differ in race and origin but who share a common geographical area, language, and historical and cultural background. That being said, how and when can we say that these conditions were met?

The first answer is that, until the advent of the Iron Age, around 1200 B.C., Syro-Palestinian history does not differentiate the centers on the coast that were to constitute Phoenicia from centers inland. In the city-state system that characterizes the history of this region, there is no appreciable difference between the centers that were to be Phoenician (and which already existed, we should recall) and those that were not: in other words, there was no difference between coast and hinterland. Not even the language, or the religion, or craftsmanship are differentiated to any substantial extent: so here we have a "Syrian" civilization in the broad sense of the term (or "Syro-Palestinian" in the more customary usage) rather than a Phoenician civilization.

Anyone inquiring into Phoenician history must consider this "prehistory." And we will take all due account of it as we proceed.

Furthermore, one cannot underestimate the profound change that took place in the Syro-Palestinian area around 1200 B.C., one result of which was that the Phoenician cities emerged as quite independent entities. That time saw the invasion of the "Sea Peoples" (an invasion that may well have been more stratified in time and events than we have thought till now), which drove the great neighboring powers (Egypt and Mesopotamia) beyond the boundaries of the area, and witnessed the establishment in the hinterland of new peoples (the Hebrews and Aramaeans), so that the cities on the coasts were "negatively" differentiated, in that they played no part in either of the two events.

But it was obviously not only a negative phenomenon. For the very reason that they were isolated and concentrated together along the coastline, the cities that we can now rightly call Phoenician strengthened the links among themselves and worked more closely together in reciprocal affairs. Moreover, the closure of the hinterland, or the difficulty of expanding inland (we are obviously talking of commercial expansion, which was always typical of coastal cities) led to new paths being opened, paths toward the western Mediterranean. Thus began the great phenomenon of colonization: sporadic visits at first, and then true colonization, an outstanding feature of the Phoenician age, a phenomenon that was quite absent in pre-Phoenician times. And with it came encounters and clashes with the expansion of Greece, and therefore an interrelated Mediterranean situation.

The invention and diffusion of the alphabet, the appearance of new divinities, the affirmation of new linguistic elements in the complex development of the languages spoken in the area, and the increasing importance of Egyptian influence in craftwork were all factors that made Phoenician civilization autonomous from 1200 B.C. onwards.

But we have to remember and stress one important point: Phoenician civilization proper was the outcome of new events that changed contingent circumstances. Hence, paradoxical though it may seem, Phoenician civilization was the result of continuation, and not of the innovation that took place around it. It is in these terms that we may assess the complex phenomenon of the continuity and innovation from which the Phoenician nation emerged with total autonomy, though the people clung to the city-state structure and continued to prefer it to actual unity.

Territory and Settlements
Sabatino Moscati

The region in which Phoenician history was played out in
the East was the Syro-Palestinian coastal area, more or less
from Shukshu in the north to Acco in the south. These
points of reference are based not so much on regional characteristics as on the fact that no substantial Phoenician centers are to be found further north or further south. Further
north would be Ugarit, but its history had already unwound
by 1200 B.C., when real Phoenician history was beginning.
Further to the south would be Dor and Jaffa, which sources
say were conquered by Sidon in the Persian era, but neither
of these two centers has any typically Phoenician features.

*Sidon, example
of settlement
on headland
with inlets
on either side*

In any case, while we could debate the northernmost and southernmost limits of Phoenician settlement, there is no doubt about the homogeneity of the
region: it lies between the sea and the Lebanon mountain range, which
delimits it inland. It is a coastal strip of varying width, depending on how
much the Lebanese mountains project out toward the sea: at certain points,
they are 50 km inland, at others only ten, and in some places, mountainous
promontories actually touch the coast.

These promontories break the region up, hampering sea traffic, and making
certain areas independent of others. And the territorial division is accentuated by a series of rivers that come down from the mountains and flow into the
sea. In these areas, the land is fairly fertile, agriculture flourishes, and mountain timber is an important resource. It is no coincidence that Assyrian
inscriptions mention the desire to procure timber as one of the main reasons
for their expansion. In the 9th century B.C., for instance, Ashurnasirpal II
says in an inscription at Balawat: "I marched as far as
Mount Lebanon, and felled cedar, cypress and juniper trees.
With the cedar trunks, I made the roof of this temple; with
cedar wood I made the leaves of the doors, and covered
them with sheets of bronze, attaching them to the doors."

*Motya, example
of settlement
on island near
the coastline*

The main consequence of the geographical situation we
have outlined was political fragmentation, consisting of
numerous city-states. These were the greatest Phoenician
cities: Aradus, Byblos, Berytus, Sidon, Sarepta, Tyre. With
hinterlands of varying depth, these cities tended to be
autonomous, although there were many links among them,
and even though they took it in turns to prevail over one
another, Tyre and Sidon especially. This explains why the
Phoenicians as a whole were frequently called "Tyrians"
and, even more often, "Sidonians."

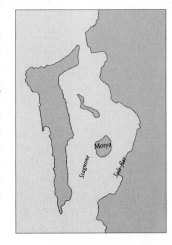

Aerial view of Motya island showing cothon *and the southern fortifications*

The urban settlements had their own characteristic nature. The cities were founded on rocky promontories that could use either of two ports, one to the north and one to the south, depending on the winds and the seasons. Alternatively, small islands lying off the coast were used for settlement: they were even easier to fortify and defend in case of siege. Aradus and Tyre were the major island settlements. We should recall that when Alexander the Great wanted to conquer Tyre, he had to build a causeway to get to it. Phoenicia's geographical situation meant greater or lesser separation from the hinterland, according to the vicissitudes of history. The coastal cities tended to develop independently. Byblos is a typical case: it flourished uninterruptedly from its foundation. After 1200 B.C., one consequence of the withdrawal, albeit temporary, of the great neighboring powers and the arrival of the Hebrews and Aramaeans from inland was that the cities of Phoenicia became increasingly separated, which explains why they developed so independently. The constitution of strong, self-contained states, however, discouraged the previously important trade inland. Seafaring activities therefore developed. Because of the position of their cities, the Phoenicians had always tended toward maritime trade, but it was mostly restricted — as far as we know — to the eastern Mediterranean, and Egypt in particular, which always enjoyed special privileges along the Syro-Palestinian coastline.

From 1200 B.C. onwards, then, the Phoenicians extended their seafaring activities. Two other factors were fundamental in this expansion early in the 1st millennium: on the one hand, the inland states were consolidating their positions, particularly Israel, and they tightened control over their commerce; on the other, Egyptian, and more particularly Assyrian expansion was resumed, leading to the search for other commercial outlets.

Thus was created the maritime outlook which, as we have seen, was typical of the Phoenician cities and which made their history a Mediterranean even more than a Near Eastern phenomenon. One outstanding feature of their expansion was the foundation in the West of colonies that had all the characteristics of the eastern cities: they stood on promontories, or on islets just off the coast; and they were spaced out fairly regularly along the coastline to provide convenient ports of call.

Hence the settlements on promontories, such as Carthage and Nora, and those on islands, such as Motya, Sulcis (on the island of Sant'Antioco), Cadiz, and Mogador. In all these the presence of shallow waters offered good anchorage and when necessary, an artificial dock called a *cothon* was built, as at Carthage and Motya. In turn, the shallow waters and their evaporation gave the Carthaginian settlements their typical salt flats.

So we can see quite clearly that there was a great difference between the ways the Phoenicians and the Greeks founded their maritime cities: while some Greek colonies were residential settlements and others were trading centers, all the Phoenician colonies were founded exclusively as commercial cities. If the Phoenicians did found residential settlements — and there were some in Sardinia — this was only during the imperial phase of Carthaginian expansion, when military necessity resulted in new developments in colonization.

The Origins in the East

Sandro Filippo Bondì

The essentially uniform body of political, linguistic, religious and artistic experiences that marks the Phoenician nation as an independent entity emerges clearly in the area roughly corresponding to present-day Lebanon only around 1200 B.C. This means that the period which can properly be called Phoenician, running from the end of the 2nd through most of the 1st millennium B.C., was preceded by a long historical, and before that, prehistoric stage, whose cultural manifestations cannot be assessed merely in terms of "Phoenician" and "non-Phoenician."

They belong, in fact, to a broader cultural unity embracing the whole area of Syria and Palestine. The analysis of the historical and cultural events of this earlier period, however, helps point up the continuity and the importance of the innovatory aspects that distinguished the Phoenician civilization from anything that preceded it. It is from this viewpoint that it is presented here.

The oldest archaeological evidence yielded by the Phoenician area comes from the city of Byblos. Here as early as the 5th millennium B.C. on the heights near the sea there existed an important Neolithic settlement described as the largest of its time in the Mediterranean area. The earliest inhabitants of Byblos engaged not only in farming and sheep raising, but in fishing as well, so that vital relation to the sea which was later to be peculiar to the whole history of the city already existed.

At the same time, the earliest evidence appears of the flourishing production of woven goods and yarns which was also to be typical of Byblos and all of Phoenicia well into the historical era. One of the most significant finds of this period is the characteristic pottery, decorated by incising with the back of a shell, or ornamented with rows of stippled triangles or with "herringbone" patterns. Also peculiar to the area of Byblos was the carving of pebbles into highly expressive, schematized figures of deities.

With the 4th millennium B.C. and the coming of the Copper Age, closer contacts were established between the Phoenician coast and Mesopotamia. Proof of this in particular are the strong resemblances between the wares produced in the two areas: the ivory carving of a four-footed animal in front of a jar that comes from Byblos is in fact very like a similar find from Ur. It is worth noting that this is the earliest example of a craft that was to be typically Phoenician, ivory carving.

A fundamental change occurred in Phoenicia with the 3rd millennium B.C. The "urban revolution" reached this coastal area, where for the first time a group of sanctuaries, dwellings and public buildings that could be called a city came into being.

The scene of this new experience was again Byblos. Favored by a geographical position that made it the natural trading station along the routes between the Syro-Palestinian coast and Egypt, Byblos was able to absorb and assimilate the innovatory elements coming from Mesopotamia, northern Syria and the Nile valley.

Byblos became a highly developed urban settlement. Served by two ports, the city was protected inland by a massive defensive wall which enclosed an extensive residential area. Two large sanctuaries, known as the "L-shaped Building" and the "Temple of the Lady of Byblos," were its principal places of worship. They yielded the most important artistic documents of this period, such as the characteristic zoomorphic pottery with geometric decorations.

With the intensification of international relations, the trade that made the city's fortune expanded. The most decisive contacts were with Egypt, which exerted an increasing influence on the culture of Byblos and largely conditioned its economy.

From the time of the 2nd Egyptian dynasty, at the beginning of the 3rd millennium, traders from the Delta area came to Byblos for supplies of timber, metals and valuable goods and around 2600 B.C. there was even an Egyptian temple in the city. The importance of Byblos for Egypt is confirmed by the fact that the city appears in the myth of Isis who comes there looking for the body of Osiris, cast into the sea by Seth.

Byblos in the 3rd millennium B.C. was a real economic power. The Ebla texts inform us that Byblos maintained very close commercial ties with that city, importing crude metals, textiles, perfumes, livestock and food products and exporting articles of linen and finished metal objects. Relations between the two cities were on a plane of absolute equality, as is proven by the fact that an Eblaite princess became the wife of the king of Byblos.

At the end of the 3rd millennium, a serious domestic crisis prevented Egypt from pursuing its policy of expansion in Asia Minor. Relations with Byblos itself were abruptly broken off, so that an Egyptian text of the time, known as *The Lamentations of Ipu-wer*, was forced to note: "Today no one sails north to Byblos any more. How will we get cedar for our mummies?"

But this was a period of great ferment throughout the Middle East, shaken by vast ethnic migrations which also involved the Phoenician area. At the beginning of the 2nd millennium, the arrival of the Amorite people introduced a phase of violent rupture, as the traces of destruction noticeable at Byblos attest, but it also brought innovatory influences, evident particularly in the field of language. These new elements now shed a clearer light on the independent cultural configuration of the Syro-Palestinian area and its essential inner unity.

Detail of dagger handle from the temple of the obelisks at Byblos gold and ivory Beirut, National Museum

The Egyptian revival which took place under the pharaohs of the Middle Kingdom made flourishing trade between Egypt and the cities of the Phoenician area possible again from the 20th to the 18th century B.C. The resumption of relations is well represented in the Egyptian narrative of the adventures of Sinuhe, who declared: "I made for Byblos and came to Qedem, and spent a year and a half there."

Byblos enjoyed another period of great splendor. Its rulers were the only ones in the East whom Egyptian sources refer to with the title of prince. The wealth of the city in the early centuries of the 2nd millennium B.C. and the still decisive influence of Egyptian culture are best testified by the lavishness of the tombs of certain kings, whose furnishings included a great many splendid Egyptian-style objects such as pectorals, medallions, crowns and scepters of gold, enamel and precious stones.

The buildings also attest the importance of the city. Dating from this period is the monumental systematization of the so-called "temple of the obelisks," a large four-sided enclosure containing various chambers and purification basins and a large number of pillar-shaped baetyls, aniconic symbols of the deity. The wares placed as offerings in the sanctuary anticipated the more typical categories of Phoenician craftsmanship. This applies especially to the numerous bronze statues covered with gold leaf representing male personages with short Egyptian skirts and cone-shaped tiaras, bare chests and arms by their sides (or

one arm bent forward and hanging straight). Egyptian models also inspired the large production of glass paste votive objects, representing among other subjects the lion-headed god Bes, sphinxes and dogheaded beings. Carved ivory combined with precious metals, which reappears in Phoenician products in the 1st millennium, is represented by the splendid ivory daggerhandle decorated with gold embossed deer, and gold is also to be found in the series of votive axes adorned with sacrificial and sacred images.

The temple of the obelisks at Byblos

Politically, as well, the Phoenician world of that period lay in the orbit of Egypt, whose influence extended over most of Syria and Palestine. There were already signs, however, of the subdivision into separate states based on single cities, which was to remain a constant characteristic of the political and administrative order of the area until the Hellenistic period. Among the towns that later became Phoenician, Acco, Tyre and Byblos were independent city-states, according to Egyptian texts.

The acceptance of Egyptian hegemony did not however prevent these towns from creating a wide web of commercial relations with Syria and Mesopotamia. According to the tablets of the Mari archives, in the 18th century B.C. there were relations between this city and Byblos, based on the trade in typical products (textiles, clothes) and on the exchange of envoys and gifts between their respective sovereigns.

But the 18th century B.C. also marked the accession of the Hyksos to the throne of the pharaohs, which marked a real rupture in the history of ancient Egypt and led to another period of distant relations between the Phoenician area and the Egyptian empire. It was a dark era that lasted roughly two centuries, for which no appreciable documentation exists regarding Phoenician centres and at the end of which the situation of the whole Syro-Palestinian area had completely changed.

Group of votive statues from Byblos gold-plated bronze, 16 cm Beirut, National Museum
• pp. 34-35

To the south, thanks to the military campaigns of Thutmose I (1525-15 B.C.) and his successors, the hegemony of Egypt was restored; to the north two large state structures grew up, the Hittite Kingdom in Anatolia and the Mittannian Kingdom between upper Syria and northern Mesopotamia. The history of the Phoenician cities became increasingly intertwined with the history of these great powers, for whom the Syrian area represented the natural battleground. On the whole, Egypt kept control of the coastal strip as far as Ugarit and therefore of all the Phoenician towns.

The situation remained fluid, however, for the whole period between the 16th and the 14th centuries B.C. As the international correspondence in the Egyptian archives of el-Amarna testifies, Egypt alternated moments of expansion and periods of withdrawal, while its alliances constantly shifted and changed. The Syrian cities themselves were involved in complicated intrigues, being drawn into the sphere of influence of the powers predominating at any given moment.

For the area that directly concerns us here, the most significant documentation comes from Ugarit in the north and Byblos in the south. The diplomatic documents of the Ugarit archive show the precarious situation of this city-state, which having submitted to Egyptian hegemony at the beginning of the 14th century B.C., after many ups and downs, eventually entered the Hittite orbit. Revealing in this respect is a passage from a treaty between the Hittite and Ugaritic sovereigns, in which the latter admits to being "deeply subject to the Sun, Great King, my lord," that is, to the Hittite ruler.

Stele depicting the god Baal from Ugarit 19th-18th century B.C., limestone 142 cm, Paris Musée du Louvre • p. 37

As to Byblos, our knowledge centers on the figure of the local king, Rib-Addi, who in his correspondence with the pharaoh, Amenhotep IV, attests the difficulties of safeguarding the customary allegiance to Egypt because of the activities of Abdi-aširta and Aziru (rulers of the nearby kingdom of Amurru), who were inciting his subjects to rebellion. Rib-Addi reports: "Abdi-aširta told the men of the city of Ammiya: 'Kill your lords and become like us! Then you will have peace'" and concludes: "So therefore, half the city loves the children of Abdi-aširta and the other half my lord."

Political dependence did not, in any case, imply the end of the city-states which in this period maintained, at least formally, the prerogatives of institutional independence. They were also centers of cultural phenomena of great importance, such as the search for a clearer and more practical system of writing than the scripts used in Egypt and in Mesopotamia, which were employed, with the relative spoken languages, in the Syro-Palestinian area too.

"The goddess of the wild beasts" engraving on pyxis lid from Ugarit 14th century B.C. ivory, 13.7 cm Paris, Musée du Louvre • p. 36

In Ugarit, an alphabet with cuneiform characters was invented (clearly because of the city's links with areas that used graphic symbols of this kind, namely Anatolia and Mesopotamia). To the south, after the experience of the so-called "pseudo-hieroglyphic" script of Byblos, obviously influenced by Egypt, a series of attempts were made that foreshadowed the great invention of the Phoenician alphabet, completed in the 13th-12th century B.C. Ugarit is the Late Bronze Age site that has yielded the most interesting documentation linking the craftwork of this period to the truly Phoenician production of the following age, providing concrete evidence of the Syrian foundations from which the later work developed.

27

So the typical Phoenician production of gold- or silver-embossed bowls can be traced back to the magnificent gold exemplar from Ugarit with a royal hunting scene, while the votive stelae, widespread in the Phoenicia of the 1st millennium B.C. and even more frequent in the Punic colonies of the West, are represented in Ugarit by the famous exemplar portraying the god Baal. Carved ivories, one of the most characteristic products of Phoenician artistry, are also to be found at Ugarit, with several examples of exquisite workmanship, such as the magnificent "goddess of the wild beasts" or the panels intended for the decoration of a bed.

Ivory plaquette depicting tribute scene from Megiddo 13th-12th century B.C. Jerusalem Rockefeller Archaeological Museum
• *pp. 38-39*

Ugarit provided an equally significant documentation of the continuity of religious life: the ritual texts discovered in the city attest the presence and in some cases the pre-eminence of a number of divinities that were to be particularly revered in the Phoenician world: the gods El, Baal and Reshef, and the goddesses Anath and Astarte. Ugarit is also an unquestionable forerunner of 1st-millennium Phoenicia with regard to long-distance trade: the close relations maintained by the city with the Aegean world and with Cyprus, in particular, may be considered the premise of the commercial, and subsequently colonial, expansion practiced by the Phoenician cities in the same direction from at least the 9th century B.C.

In other cases, the same cities which shortly afterwards were to call themselves Phoenician provide documentation of a notable continuity. We need only recall the ivories of the 14th-13th century B.C. from Byblos and Sidon, or that true masterpiece of the earliest Phoenician art, the sarcophagus of the king of Byblos, Ahiram, dating from the 13th-12th century B.C. Here Egyptian motifs (the king seated on a throne flanked by sphinxes; the lotus flower in his hands) are combined with others that are Syrian or Hittite in feeling (the features of the figures on the lid, the lions supporting the coffin). Influences and ideas from different sources, then, have been fused and reinterpreted freely, according to a procedure which was to remain typical of Phoenician art throughout its agelong development.

The sarcophagus of Ahiram dates from the eve of that great upheaval known as the invasion of the "Peoples of the Sea," which throughout almost the whole Syro-Palestinian region put an end to the political experiences of the Late Bronze Age. At the end of this change the Phoenician nation emerged fully independent and clearly defined. Nevertheless several of its most typical cultural traits appear deeply rooted in the preceding age: the political system of city-states ruled by kings, certain forms of craft production, impor-

tant aspects of religious thought, certain linguistic features. So while the Phoenician civilization appeared in its full expression only from the 12th century B.C., there can be no doubt that precisely its continuity with the period discussed here constitutes one of its most distinctive characteristics and ultimately allows it to be considered an autonomous formation.

The Course of History
Sandro Filippo Bondi

As has already been explained, a history that can rightly be called Phoenician started in the 12th century B.C. Barely touched by the great upheavals caused by the invasion of the "Peoples of the Sea," Phoenicia (the coastal region between Tell Suqas in the north and Acco in the south, corresponding roughly to modern Lebanon) from this period onwards shows a marked differentiation from the neighboring areas and a strong inner consistency as regards language, religious beliefs, artistic expression and political and administrative organization.

Our knowledge of the history of Phoenicia remains, however, largely conditioned by the available documentation. The virtually complete loss of Phoenician literature and the difficulties of archaeological research, due to the fact that the most important ancient sites are covered by modern buildings, mean that the reconstruction is based almost entirely on indirect sources. Particularly important among these are the references in the Old Testament, both because they originate in a world very close to that of the Phoenicians, and because they are usually almost coeval with the facts they record.

Other Near Eastern sources, Mesopotamian and Egyptian in particular, are also important for a knowledge of Phoenician history. The Mesopotamian sources are as a rule reports of military expeditions conducted by Assyrian rulers against Phoenician cities; they may be considered basically reliable, with the one reservation that they often exaggerate the importance of the successes obtained by the kings in whose praise the texts were written. Particularly noteworthy in the Egyptian sources is the account of the envoy Wenamon's journey, which throws a vivid light on the domestic situation of Phoenicia and its relations to Egypt in the 11th century B.C.

A significant contribution to our knowledge of Phoenician history also comes from the Greek historians, Herodotus, Diodorus Siculus and Arrian, to whom we owe most of the information about the period immediately preceding the conquest of Alexander the Great. Another Greek writer, Josephus, who lived in the 1st century A.D., cites numerous historical episodes of earlier periods, taking his information, as he states, from official documents in the Phoenician tongue, the so-called "Annals of Tyre."

This last point proves that a Phoenician historiography undoubtedly existed, although unfortunately nothing of it has survived in direct form. Little more than fragments of history can be gleaned, in fact, from the scanty Phoenician sources extant, consisting mostly of royal inscriptions. The record of a few episodes deemed important in the activities of the kings is preserved there, but very rarely do we find any of true historical events.

It is not surprising, then, that the first episode concerning the history of the

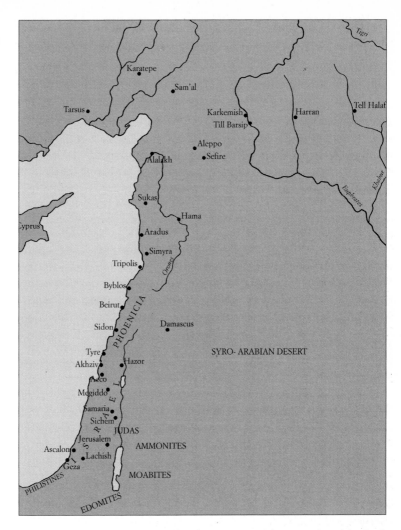

Phoenician cities immediately after the invasion of the "Peoples of the Sea" is known to us through an indirect source. This is the Roman historian Justin, who mentions that the inhabitants of Sidon founded Tyre when they fled after their defeat by the Ashkelonites (the Philistines, one of the "Peoples of the Sea").

We know that Tyre certainly existed long before the date to which Justin attributes the episode, around 1200 B.C., so the information can be interpreted to mean that Sidon contributed to the revitalization of Tyre. But the date is anyway significant, because it links up with other evidence pointing to a preeminence of Sidon in this early stage of Phoenician history: it should be recalled in this connection that the word "Sidonians" is used in both the Old Testament and in Homeric poems as a synonym for "Phoenicians."

Apart from the predominance of Sidon, the close of the 2nd millennium B.C. was marked by the beginning of the conflict with Assyria, destined to

31

condition the history of Phoenician cities for a long time. The first expedition to the Mediterranean seacoast by an Assyrian king, Tiglath-pileser I (1112-1074) is dated to around 1100 B.C. Although in his Annals he speaks of tribute received from Byblos, Sidon and Aradus, in fact his campaign was probably essentially commercial in character, since he mentions having obtained the highly prized timber of the Lebanese mountains. And the existence of far from hostile relations between Tiglath-pileser I and local kings is borne out by a curious reference to a fishing party offered him by his hosts.

Detail of the bas-relief in the palace of Sargon at Khorsabad depicting transport of timber from Lebanon 7th century B.C. Paris, Musée du Louvre • p. 40

In this phase the small Phoenician kingdoms along the coast enjoyed considerable independence and no longer acknowledged the supremacy of the major foreign powers. This was what the envoy of an Egyptian temple, Wenamon, was to learn to his cost, when he was sent to negotiate a shipment of timber. The account of his adventures mentions the disrespectful way he was treated (he had to wait days before being allowed to speak to Zakerbaal, the prince of Byblos) and the reiterated avowals of independence of the Phoenician ruler, who declared: "I am not your servant, nor the servant of him who sent you."

This independent attitude is all the more significant in that it contrasts with the deference that Zakerbaal's predecessors had shown toward the pharaohs and their messengers. In fact Wenamon, with reference to the permission to send timber to Egypt, challenged the prince: "Your father did it, the father of your father did it, you too have to do it." Evidently the influence of Egypt, forced by the invasion of the "Peoples of the Sea" to fall back inside its own borders, was no longer so strong.

Zakerbaal, who dealt with the Egyptian envoy from a position of independence, must have reigned over Byblos not long after 1100 B.C. Over the following centuries, the city monarchy seems to have remained strong, since a series of kings, almost all of them related to one another, is known from various inscriptions in Phoenician discovered in Byblos. The epigraphs cover a period of time from the mid-10th to the early 9th century B.C.

At all events, the most remarkable aspect of Phoenician history in this period is represented by the rising importance of the city of Tyre. Evidently freed from its former subordination to Sidon, Tyre now conducted an active foreign policy, especially under King Hiram, who reigned from 969 to 936 B.C.

The exploits of Hiram are recorded, from different angles, both by Josephus, who says he got his information from the Annals of Tyre, and by the Old Testament. Josephus refers to Hiram's activities in the religious field, and then mentions his action toward a city which refused to pay its tribute. If, as seems likely, that city was the Cypriot center of Kition, this is the first reference to a real military and political campaign against an overseas colony. In the Old Testament Hiram is mentioned for his relations with the kings of

Statuette of male deity
from Syria
8th century B.C.
bronze and silver, 20 cm
Paris, Musée du Louvre

Group of votive statues
from Byblos
gold-plated bronze, 16 cm
Beirut, National Museum

"The goddess of the wild beasts"
engraving on pyxis lid
from Ugarit, 14th century B.C.
ivory, 13.7 cm
Paris, Musée du Louvre

opposite page
Stele depicting the god Baal
from Ugarit
19th-18th century B.C.
limestone, 142 cm
Paris, Musée du Louvre

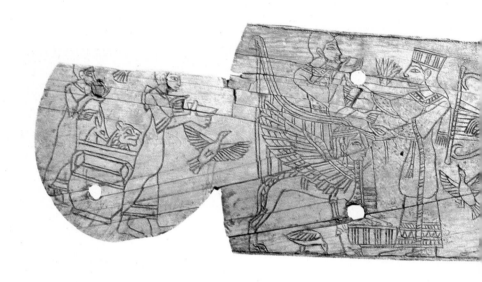

Ivory plaquette depicting
tribute scene from Megiddo
13th-12th century B.C.
Jerusalem
Rockefeller Archaeological Museum

Detail of the bas-relief
in the palace of Sargon
at Khorsabad
depicting transport
of timber from Lebanon
7th century B.C.
Paris, Musée du Louvre

Jerusalem, David and Solomon. The king of Tyre provided the raw materials and the specialized labor for building the royal palace and the temple of Jerusalem, receiving food supplies in exchange. This information is confirmed by the Annals of Tyre, and both sources also agree that the payment was completed by Solomon's cession of a number of cities to Hiram.

Even more interesting is some further information supplied by the Old Testament, regarding the sea trade undertaken jointly by the two sovereigns. It is reported as follows in *I Kings* (9,10): "And King Solomon made a navy of ships in Ezion-geber, which is beside Eloth, on the shore of the Red Sea, in the land of Edom. And Hiram sent in the navy his servants, shipmen that had knowledge of the sea, with the servants of Solomon. And they came to Ophir, and fetched from thence gold, four hundred and twenty talents, and brought it to King Solomon." Elsewhere it is specified that merchandise picked up during these expeditions, which went on for three years, consisted of gold, silver, ivory, sandalwood and precious stones, as well as apes and peacocks.

This information throws light on the politico-economic structure of Phoenician cities in this period. The palace held control over crucial economic sectors of the city: it distributed raw materials, had in its direct employ numerous skilled laborers and was in a position to engage in large-scale economic undertakings, such as highly demanding merchant trading abroad.

The basic principles of Tyrian foreign policy were apparently confirmed by Hiram's successors, whose names and reigns down to 774 B.C. have been recorded by Josephus. The good relations between the city kings and the Israelite rulers continued: King Ethbaal (889-856 B.C.) gave his daughter Jezebel in marriage to Ahab, son of King Omri. Ethbaal himself is credited with founding two colonies, one in Lebanon and the other in Africa. Commitment to a policy of expansion apparently deepened, while the fact that Josephus called Ethbaal, "king of the Tyrians and Sidonians" shows that the city of Tyre had succeeded in reversing its initial situation of subjugation to Sidon, and establishing a form of hegemony over it.

Precisely during the reign of Ethbaal, however, military pressure built up from Assyria, which was committed to a decidedly expansionist policy towards the Syro-Palestinian region. Ashurnasirpal II (883-859 B.C.) conducted several military expeditions there, forcing the rulers of many towns in the area into submission, including Tyre, Sidon and Byblos, and collecting considerable tribute. These include a number of characteristic products of Phoenician manufacture: bronze vases, garments of dyed wool and linen, ivory and timber.

The resumption of military action on the part of his successor, Shalmaneser III (858-824 B.C.), led the Syrian cities to join forces against Assyria. The participation in this alliance of the small Phoenician kingdoms, plainly not in a position to mobilize large armies because of their meager territorial base, was however in some instances little more than symbolic: for the first clash the Aradus contingent consisted of only two hundred soldiers. At all

Scene of tribute from the bronze doors of Balawat 9th century B.C. Paris, Musée du Louvre

events Shalmaneser III attained notable successes with a series of victorious campaigns conducted between 852 and 837 B.C., again forcing the most important center of the area into submission.

It was within this framework that the Phoenicians began a more systematic search for alternative markets for their trading activities. In 814 B.C., while in Tyre one of Ethbaal's successors, Pygmalion (820-774 B.C.), was in the seventh year of his reign, a number of Tyrian refugees reached the North African coast and founded the colony of Carthage, destined over time to take the place of the parent city at the head of the Phoenician world of the West.

The story of the founding of Carthage — the most extensive version is related by Justin and the essential outlines are confirmed on the Eastern side by Josephus — is too well-known to dwell on here. We need only recall that the story revolves around the figure of a Tyrian princess, Elissa-Dido, who was forced to flee from her homeland to escape the persecution of her brother, King Pygmalion, and in the end threw herself on a funeral pyre in order not to be forced into an unwanted marriage to the petty African monarch Iarbas. The modified version made famous by Virgil and centered on the love of Dido for Aeneas is simply a later poetic elaboration.

At this stage the political and economic prestige of the Phoenician cities, at least locally, did not appear to be endangered by increasingly difficult relations with Assyria. On the contrary, the 9th and the early 8th century B.C. represented a particularly happy period for Tyre and the other coastal towns. The opulence of Tyre in this period was to remain legendary as we see from Ezekiel's lamentation over the destruction of the city, which describes the wealth and vastness of Tyrian trade in the early 8th century B.C. The merchants of Tyre probed every corner of the eastern Mediterranean, from Anatolia to Egypt, and the typical products of Phoenician artisans were in great demand at the royal courts of Israel, Syria and even Assyria.

Phoenician prevailed as the international language of communication, while the Phoenician alphabet was adopted even by the Aramaic people and the Hebrews, so it has been possible to speak of a "cultural authority" exerted by the Phoenicians over neighboring populations for the period between the 9th and the first part of the 8th century B.C.

The attitude of Assyria, which still confined itself to collecting tribute without threatening the political independence of the Phoenicians, may have laid an economic burden on them but it did not hamper their overall development. On the domestic scene, the diminished enterprise of the city monarchies in those years was increasingly compensated by the activities of a class of private merchants and shipowners who ensured the continuity and vitality of international trade.

In the mid-8th century B.C., however, the situation changed swiftly and substantially. Under Tiglath-pileser III (745-727 B.C.), Assyria launched a campaign of annexation of Phoenician territories, which would be concluded in the course of a few decades. After a victorious campaign, Tiglath-pileser III annexed the cities of northern Phoenicia ("I brought them within the boundaries of Assyria," he states in his Annals) and out of their territories created a province, with several governors in charge. The southernmost monarchies, with Tyre and Byblos, remained formally independent, but were forced to pay tribute.

Fragment of ivory panel depicting Egyptian deity from Samaria 9th century B.C. Jerusalem Rockefeller Archaeological Museum

The work of Tiglath-pileser III was completed by Sargon II (721-705 B.C.), who seized the Tyrian possessions on the island of Cyprus, put down a revolt of several Phoenician and Syrian cities and consolidated Assyrian control over the region. The now very limited autonomy of the Phoenician monarchies, reduced to little more than formal expressions of their cities' independence, was testified by an episode of a few years later: the Assyrian King Sennacherib (705-681 B.C.), having crushed another revolt of the Syrians and Phoenicians, selected the new king of Sidon personally.

Probably the most violent suppression of Phoenicia's resurgent aspirations to independence took place under Esarhaddon (681-668 B.C.). Another revolt, with its center in Sidon, at that time ruled by Abdi-milkutti, was met by a harsh reaction from the Assyrian king, who wrote in his Annals: "I razed to the ground Sidon, the fortified city in the middle of the sea, destroyed and cast into the sea its walls and dwellings, annihilated the place where it stood. As to Abdi-milkutti, its king, who in the face of my armies had fled into the middle of the sea, I cut off his head. I deported his subjects, who were innumerable, to Assyria. I reordered the territory, placing one of my officials to govern over them."

A few years later it was Tyre which rebelled, with the backing of Egypt, but the attempt had no better luck and the limited independence which the city still enjoyed was virtually lost. This is vividly proved by a diplomatic document of exceptional interest, the treaty between Esarhaddon and Baal, the king of Tyre, which confirms that the Phoenician sovereign was stripped of power, and placed below the Assyrian governor.

Esarhaddon, in fact, orders Baal: "You are not to open the messages I send you in the governor's absence," and addresses him as "servant." The treaty also placed severe restrictions on the Tyrians' trading: their ships could move only within a limited area, whose boundaries were specified in the text: "These are the ports and routes which Esarhaddon, king of the land of Assur, has granted to Baal, his servant..."

So Assyrian domination also had a damaging effect on the Phoenicians' most traditional and remunerative activity: the loss of political independence in fact also meant the lost of freedom of trade. In these circumstances it was not surprising that over the following years the Phoenician cities should try repeatedly to throw off the Assyrian yoke.

Sargon II and a dignitary in a relief from the palace of Sargon at Khorsabad 8th century B.C. Paris, Musée du Louvre

Ashurbanipal (668-626 B.C.) had to face a rebellion first in Tyre, then in Aradus, then again in various cities. The defeat of these uprisings, put down with the usual brutality and deportations ("I defeated the rebel populace of Acco. Their bodies I hung on poles around the city. I carried away the survivors to Assyria," Ashurbanipal announced), marked the end of any possibility of throwing off the yoke of the Assyrian empire. The overthrow of that empire in 612 B.C. by the Medes must have been greeted with favor by the Phoenician cities.

The stage of relative peace following the overthrow of Assyria did not last long: a period of Egyptian supremacy in the closing years of the 7th century B.C. was followed by the Babylonian uprising, led by Nebuchadnezzar (605-562 B.C.). His victory over Egypt led the Babylonians to launch an immediate campaign against the Phoenicians. Tyre held out for thirteen years, but in the end was again forced to submit.

The Phoenician towns no longer seemed capable of expressing an independent policy and, as Josephus attests in his reconstruction of the dynastic succession of Tyre from 590 to 532 B.C., it was the Babylonians who frequently chose the local kings. The progressive crisis of the monarchical institution in this phase of Phoenician history is further confirmed by the fact that between 564 and 556 B.C., a republican form of government, led by magistrates known as "suffetes" (judges) was set up in Tyre itself.

The triumph of Persian hegemony at the end of the 6th century B.C. marked the beginning of a new period of political and economic expansion for the Phoenician cities. Among the Persian colonies Phoenicia was of particular importance as a strategic base for military operations against Greece and Egypt, so the emperors treated the inhabitants with considerable indulgence, fostered their commercial activities and granted a certain independence, at least on a domestic level, to the local city monarchies.

The larger Phoenician centers succeeded in profiting by their good relations with the Persian kings in territorial terms as well. Tyre considerably increased its dominions, which now extended from Sarepta to Mt. Carmel, and the king of Sidon, Eshmunazar (475-461 B.C.), was given the

Palestinian cities of Dor and Jaffa, as he himself records in an inscription: "The lord of kings has given us Dor and Jaffa, the mighty lands of Dagon, which are in the plain of Sharon, in proportion to the important things I have done. And we have added them to the borders of our land, so that they may belong to Sidon for ever."

The Phoenician fleets were an essential part of the armies equipped by the Persians against Egypt and Greece. The Phoenician kings commanded the naval contingents of their cities personally, thus demonstrating their complete agreement with the Persian policy of western expansion, which brought notable benefits to the Phoenician cities. Their ships started sailing the Mediterranean again, close relations were re-established with the colonial settlements, and in Cyprus, in particular, the Phoenician presence was consolidated (obviously with an anti-Greek aim). Here several dynasties with seats in Kition, Idalion and Tamassos, extended their rule to the interior of the island, rich in copper deposits.

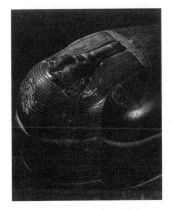

Detail
of sarcophagus
of Eshmunazar
king of Sidon
6th century B.C.
basalt, 235 cm
Paris, Musée
du Louvre

The preeminent Phoenician center during the Persian occupation seems to have been Sidon. The city was the seat of the Persian governorship and enjoyed a period of considerable prosperity, as is testified by important architectural remains. The political stability of the city is shown by the long series of kings who followed one another peacefully throughout the 5th century B.C. and in the early years of the 4th, and whose order of succession can be reconstructed on the basis of numerous literary, epigraphic and numismatic sources. A common characteristic seems to distinguish all the Sidonian kings of this period and that is their pro-Persian attitude, all the more remarkable in that it sometimes seems to contrast with the position taken by the kings of other cities or by part of the Sidonian population itself. It must in fact be observed that in the 4th century B.C., as the process of disintegration within the Persian empire became more marked and stirrings of revolt appeared in many provinces, a pro-Greek and anti-Persian spirit gradually took root in Phoenicia too.

This tendency explains the prompt submission of Tyre and other cities of the area to the Greek Evagoras after he conquered Cyprus in 392 B.C. The same explanation applies, a little later, to the change in Sidonian policy made by Straton I (375-362 B.C.), who earned the significant nickname of "Philhellene", and above all to the rebellion of another Sidonian king, Tennes (357-347 B.C.). In this instance, the uprising was violently suppressed by the Persian emperor Artaxerxes Ochus, who put Tennes to death together with 40,000 of his fellow citizens, ordered the destruction of the city and established a new pro-Persian dynasty.

In the conflict between Alexander the Great and the Persians, the defeat of the latter (decided by the result of the battle of Issus in 333 B.C.) was seen as a liberation by many Phoenicians: Byblos handed itself over to the con-

queror spontaneously, Aradus welcomed him with great honors. In Sidon an attempt at resistance by the pro-Persian king, Straton, was thwarted by his fellow-citizens, who forced him to surrender. Only Tyre, after an initial act of submission, refused to open its gates to Alexander but, besieged and lacking support of any kind, it was taken by storm and destroyed a few months later.

With the Macedonian conquest the history of Phoenicia as a free country in reality comes to an end. It is true that a number of original cultural expressions and moments of true independence remained, because up to the end of the 2nd century B.C. inscriptions were written in Phoenician and local independent dynasties reappeared in some cities. These were however flickers of life due more to the force of tradition than to the rekindled vitality of the Phoenician world, whose historical season finished against the background of the triumph of Hellenism.

Detail of inscription on Eshmunazar's sarcophagus

Colonization of the Mediterranean
Sabatino Moscati

There has been a great deal of discussion about why, how and above all when the great phenomenon of Phoenician expansion along the Mediterranean seaboard and the consequent foundation of colonial settlements actually took place.

As to why, a passage from Diodorus Siculus is of particular interest: it points to the precious metals to be found in the Iberian Peninsula as an essential reason for trade, in its turn a premise for expansion and colonization: "The country has the most numerous and excellent silver mines... The natives do not know how to use the metal. But the Phoenicians, experts in commerce, would buy this silver in exchange for some other small goods. Consequently, taking the silver to Greece, Asia and all other peoples, the Phoenicians made great earnings. Thus, practising this trade for a long time, they became rich, and founded many colonies, some in Sicily and on the neighbouring islands, others in Libya, Sardinia and Iberia."

So Diodorus Siculus says that the far West, with its wealth of metals, was the original objective of Phoenician expansion. This means that we should not think of it in terms of a progression in space, but rather as a network of points established to back up expeditions to the farthest destinations. As we shall see, discoveries made in recent years confirm this evaluation, revealing the antiquity and often the precedence of the settlements in Iberia.

The Phoenicians did not only obtain silver from Iberia: there was also copper and tin. As for gold, the most precious of all metals for processing and trade, the Phoenicians found it both in Iberia and in the African interior, whence it was sent to the coastal colonies and above all to Carthage.

As to how Phoenician expansion took place, there is no doubt that it followed the coasts, with ships that sailed mostly by day, seeking anchorage, in the West as in the East, beside promontories and small islands, at points where it was easy to land and find shelter from the winds. The Phoenicians also sought shallow waters so as to avoid damaging their ships: lagoons and their salt flats are typical of the Phoenician landscape.

The question of when the Phoenicians colonized the Mediterranean has been a matter of long controversy. In perspective, the relevant studies and theories may be divided into three stages and schools of thought.

The earliest gives credit to certain classical sources, according to which expansion began at the turn of the 12th century B.C. with the foundation of Gadir (Cadiz) in 1110, Utica in 1101 and Lixus (Larache) even earlier. Therefore Phoenician colonization must have come well before Greek colonization, which is attested only in the 8th century B.C.

The second school, prevalent at the beginning of the 20th century, radically criticizes ancient sources. Arguing that there is no archaeological evidence earlier than the 8th century B.C., this school not only refutes the early dates given in classical sources, but also the date of the foundation of Carthage in 814-813 B.C., also from a classical source. According to this view, then, Phoenician colonization ran parallel to or even followed Greek colonization.

Finally, in the last 25 years there has been a new series of studies, resulting in a reacceptance, albeit partial, of the early chronology. Increasing archaeological evidence for the 8th (if not of the 9th) century B.C., plus the fact that it is probably evidence of an ongoing process, leads us to believe that the classical dates are possible, and that at any rate the Phoenicians began their colonization before the Greeks.

This third school of thought still prevails today, and the present writer has recently put forward a series of considerations aimed at consolidating it, partly overriding it, and above all defining it in a new historical context. There is no doubt that archaeology today proves a solid Phoenician presence in the western Mediterranean during the 8th century B.C. (there is only supposition about the 9th, mainly based on inscriptions, but nothing definite), so 814-813 seems to be a perfectly plausible date for the foundation of Carthage. As for the previous centuries, however, at the present state of our knowledge we cannot speak of actual colonization. Certain evidence adduced so far has a different significance: it suggests, rather, that like the Greeks, the Phoenicians went through a period of "pre-colonization." That is, they sailed the seas simply to trade, not to conquer. What is already obvious in the case of the Mycenaeans, who preceded the ancient Greeks, can also be applied to the Phoenicians, thus clearing the ground of a few problems.

One piece of evidence is a small bronze of Phoenician, or rather Syro-Palestinian type, found in the sea off Selinus (Selinunte). It dates back to the 14th-13th century B.C., and at the most proves that the routes were being navigated (unless it was imported by Mycenaeans or someone else). The same may be said for certain elements of Sicilian culture in the 10th-9th century which correspond to the Phoenician milieu. Iberia, too, has yielded sporadic objects that could be dated earlier than the 8th century B.C., but the most they prove are isolated contacts or exchanges.

To conclude, we may accept 814-813 B.C. as the year when Carthage was founded, and we may set the beginning of Phoenician colonization in the 8th century B.C., taking earlier sporadic evidence as examples of pre-colonization. As for information from classical sources, critical analysis shows that it is all part of a single tradition, probably born in the Hellenistic period, in Alexandrian circles, which accepted Homer's poems as historical truth. Furthermore, since Heracles was considered the progenitor of the Phoenicians, his voyages in the West were assimilated to those of the Heraclidae.

What do we now make of the problem of relations between Phoenicians and Greeks in the history of the Mediterranean? Having eliminated the

Phoenician routes in the Mediterranean

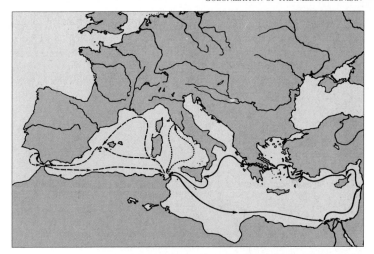

The southern route

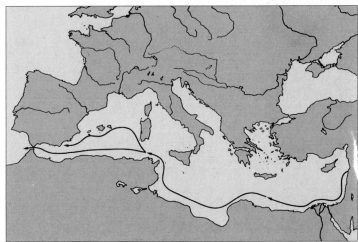

The northern route

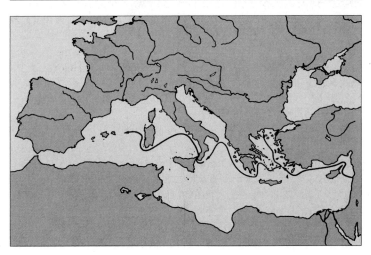

Map showing Greek and Phoenician settlements in Italy

idea of a long precedence of the Phoenicians, the fact remains that they seem to have begun colonization a few decades before the Greeks. Between the presumed foundation date of the oldest Phoenician colony, Carthage (814-813 B.C.), and that of the oldest Greek colony, Pithekoussa (Ischia) (775 B.C.), we have a gap of about 40 years, which is debatable but not totally deniable. Then there is the famous passage from Thucydides which describes a phenomenon in Sicily that must have been similar elsewhere: on the arrival in force of the Greeks, the Phoenicians gravitated toward them from their own more modest settlements.

The fact is that Greek colonialism had an interest in conquering the hinterland and in agricultural and commercial exploitation that was lacking in Phoenician colonialism (or anyway was far less important). This also explains how Phoenician colonization gradually adapted to the new situation in the Mediterranean. Finally one colony, Carthage, predominated over the others and an empire was founded which unlike that of the Romans was always to be characterized by the commercial, maritime origins of its early colonizations.

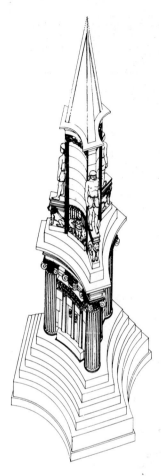

Axonometric reconstruction of the Neo-Punic mausoleum at Sabratha

When we come to consider the sites of Phoenician expansion in the Mediterranean, we have to begin with Cyprus, where recent excavations show a substantial Phoenician presence at least from the 9th century B.C. onwards. The main colony was undoubtedly Kition (Citium), on the coast facing the shores of Asia; other famous settlements were Golgoi, Idalion, Tamassos, Paphos, Marion and Lapithos. A colony from the point of view of its origins, like those in the West, Cyprus nevertheless seems intimately linked with the homeland, so much so that it is often difficult to distinguish its products from those of the homeland; indeed, Cypriot production was so abundant and striking that in many respects it is a greater source of knowledge than the Phoenician cities themselves.

The Phoenicians established colonies in the Aegean archipelago, although not much evidence of them survives. Greek tradition has it that the Phoenicians spread as far as Rhodes, and a number of inscriptions confirm this. Greek sources also tell us of settlements on other islands, and on Crete, where the city of Ithanos was said to have been founded by the Phoenicians. Then we should recall the cups found in Athens, Olympia and Delphi, which are at least the sign of solid trade, while the presence of Phoenicians in Attica is attested by inscriptions.

Along the African coast, there must have been restricted, sporadic appearances in Egypt: according to Herodotus, at Memphis there was a "Tyrian quarter" and a sanctuary dedicated to Astarte; and red Phoenician pottery has been found at er-Retabeh and other places in the delta of the Nile. Proceeding westward, there is Utica, whose foundation supposedly dates back to remote antiquity, as mentioned above: here the classical version is unacceptable but indicative. And as we have also said, the year 814-813 for Carthage's foundation is valid, at least as an approximation.

Following the colonies from east to west, we should note that in many cases we cannot distinguish between those that belong to the Phoenician stage, and those dating from the time when Carthage, having become a great power, began to found colonies in its turn. Auza, which has not yet been officially located, was founded by Ithobaal of Tyre in the 9th century B.C. according to the city's annals. Leptis Magna, which Sallust calls a colony of Sidonian refugees and others attribute to the Tyrians, has left us evidence of the 7th century, but definitely Phoenician documents only from the 3rd. At Oea, present-day Tripoli, a 3rd-2nd century necropolis has been brought to light, while numerous amphorae with Punic sealings have been found in nearby Bu Setta. As for the important center of Sabratha, the first settlement goes back to the 6th-5th century, while the necropoli abounding in Phoenician jewellery are of a later date.

In the area of today's Tunisia, we find, in order: Acholla (modern el-Alia), where an early *tophet* was discovered; Thapsus (Ras Dimasse), with its 4th-century burial ground; Mahdia (the modern name, for which we do not know the ancient equivalent), with a rich 5th-century necropolis; Leptis Minor (Lamta), with remains of wooden sarcophagi in pit graves; Hadrumetum (Sousse), a flourishing center from the 6th century, with a *tophet* that is particularly important for the stelae found there, and a necropolis.

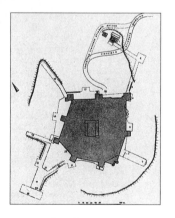

Recent exploration and excavation have revealed important archaeological remains on Cape Bon: firstly in the city of Kerkouane, the only one in Punic Africa that has preserved many of its original structures; and then in the nearby necropolis of Djebel Mlezza; and the better-known fortresses scattered along the coastline, of which Kelibia, Ras Fortas and Ras ed-Drek are the most important. Farther east, in the region of Hippo Acra (Bizerta), a number of tombs have been excavated at Cape Zebib.

We enter Algeria with Hippo Regius (Bone), where recent work has started to bring the Punic walls to light. At Cirta (Constantine), in the interior, a *tophet* has been found, with numerous stelae from the 3rd century B.C.

Map showing Punic fortifications of Kelibia

Map showing Punic fortifications of Ras Fortass

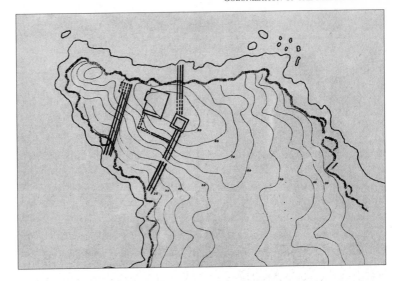

Map showing Punic fortifications of Ras ed-Drek

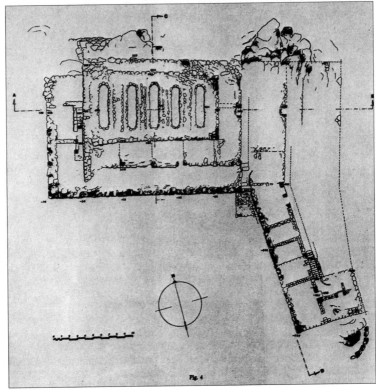

53

or later. Also from the 3rd century B.C. is the Chullu cemetery, while Igilgili (Djidjelli) has yielded tombs which some writers date to the 6th century B.C., others to the 3rd century B.C. The most important finds at Icosium (Algiers) have been coins. Tipasa has an important necropolis that can be dated to the 6th century.

Still in Algeria, to the west, we have, in order: Iol (Cherchel) and Gunugu (Gouraya), with fairly late necropoli (many of the characteristic painted ostrich eggs come from Gunugu); Les Andalouses, with a settlement and a necropolis dating back to the 4th century B.C.; the island of Rachgoun, with a burial ground rich in 7th-century remains; Mersa Medakh, with city walls and much pottery from at least the 6th century.

In Morocco we have, in order: Rusadir (Melilla), with a 4th to 3rd-century necropolis; Emsa, with remains of houses and somewhat later pottery; Sidi Abdselam of Behar, with levels of 5th-century habitations and pottery; Tamuda, a large but late settlement (2nd century); Tingis (Tangier), where jewellery and pottery found in necropoli are evidence of a much earlier settlement, around the 8th century. On the Atlantic coast of Morocco, we have Lixus (Larache), already mentioned for its legendary age, but presenting much 7th-century evidence (walls, temple, necropoli, inscriptions); Sala, with pottery from the same period; and lastly Mogador, with jewellery and inscriptions also from the same period.

Among the islands facing the African coast between Carthage and Sicily, Melita (Malta) has traces of the Phoenician presence from the 8th century B.C. onwards, as shown by pottery and finds in the Tas Silg sanctuary. Gaulus (Gozo) and Kossyra (Pantelleria) must have been occupied around the 7th century, but there seem to have been only modest settlements there. Phoenician colonization of western Sicily was early and intensive. The greatest center, and the best known, was Motya (Mozia), where the Phoenician presence is attested from the 8th century B.C. onwards. It continued to flourish until the early 4th century B.C., when the Greeks sacked the town. Especially important is its *tophet*, which, as we have said, has yielded more than a thousand figure-decorated stelae. The 7th-century set-

Plan of the acropolis at Monte Sirai

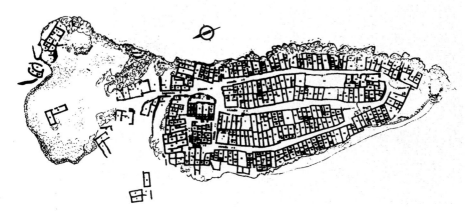

tlements of Soluntum and Panormus (Palermo) follow, but there is less evidence, in part due to subsequent superimpositions. Remains near the Greek centre of Selinus have long been known, and the discovery of a settlement at Monte Adranone, near Sambuca, is recent. Still more profound and widespread was Phoenician penetration in Sardinia, as has been revealed by exploration and excavations in recent years. Separate chapters have been dedicated to Sardinia and Sicily, but in the meantime it can be noted that the settlements of Sulcis (Sant'Antioco) and Tharros (Capo San Marco) are definitely 8th century, and Caralis (Cagliari), Nora and Bithia (Bitia) are at least 7th century.

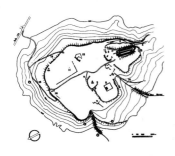

Map showing fortifications of the acropolis at Monte Sirai

Phoenician occupation was then extended to the north of Sardinia, where the chief center was Olbia; inland, there is evidence of military penetration at Monte Sirai, and of religious penetration at Antas. Furthermore, surveys have revealed a string of fortresses cutting transversally across the island, roughly from Padria to Muravera. If we add that a few modest settlements have been identified along the east coast, we see that the Phoenicians had control of the entire island during the maximum expansion of Carthage (4th century B.C.). It is once again to recent excavations that we owe our fuller knowledge of the Phoenician presence in Spain. In the past, the pillars of penetration were considered (and in part are still considered) Gadir (Cadiz) on one side and Ebusus (Ibiza) on the other. In the former case, traditional dating is not confirmed, but the center is undoubtedly impressive; in the second case, the necropoli have yielded large quantities of figured terra-cotta articles and other craft objects. Equally important for its necropoli is Villaricos on the south coast, where Spanish and German excavations have given us a new, comprehensive body of knowledge.

Besides the sites already known, settlements have been discovered at Cerro del Peñón, Toscanos, Alarcón, Chorreras, Guadalhorce and Aljaraque, which clearly prove that Phoenicians had arrived there by the 8th century. Furthermore, the necropoli of Almuñecar, Cortijo de las Sombras, Trayamar and Jardín, integrate our knowledge of the coastal areas. Inland, on the other hand, there are villages and necropoli that cannot be called Phoenician but which show considerable Phoenician influence. They offer large numbers of articles in gold and bronze in which Phoenician inspiration has been developed further and elaborated.

Seen as a whole, the spread of the Phoenicians along the Mediterranean coasts appears as an impressive phenomenon, the result of great initiative and great seafaring skills, undoubtedly fostered by prospects of trade, but later reaching well beyond the circumstances of history. If the Greeks blocked Phoenician expansion toward continental Italy, the Phoenicians in turn closed the routes to Spain and the Mediterranean West to the Greeks, thus clearing the way for the most extensive system of colonization known to the ancient world.

The Carthaginian Empire
Sabatino Moscati

Among all the information recorded in the Annals of Tyre, one fact stands out for its importance. In the seventh year of the reign of the Tyrian monarch Pygmalion (814-803 B.C.), his sister Elissa fled the city, and founded the colony of Carthage (*qart hadasht*, i.e. "new city"). Classical authors — Justin in particular, who seems to depend on Timaeus — confirm this, and give us a series of details: Elissa fled after the assassination of Pygmalion; she initially went to Cyprus, where the high priest of Astarte (Juno in the classical version) joined her; 80 maidens destined for sacred prostitution left with the fugitives. The voyagers landed on the site of the future Carthage. Elissa used all her shrewdness to ensure there would be enough room for her companions. She acquired a piece of land of a size that could be covered with an ox-hide, and then cut the skin into very narrow strips and laid them end to end around the hill the city was later to stand on. There is an obvious play on words here, and it is interesting that it should be of Greek origin: the acropolis of Carthage was in fact called Byrsa, the Greek version of which, *bursa*, means "oxhide." Once the area had been acquired and the city founded, the Phoenicians were paid homage by the local people, including their predecessors who already occupied Utica: this may not indicate an earlier date but does prove that this was the first settlement.

The personal story of Elissa came to a tragic end. Justin tells us that the local king, Iarbas, fell in love with her and asked for her hand in marriage, the alternative being war. Elissa took her time, but in the end decided she could not betray the memory of her lost husband and, to avoid another marriage, she threw herself onto a pyre. In tradition, her name was soon linked with that of Dido, and thus she appears in Virgil's poem.

For a long period of time we have no further information about Carthage. But the city did flourish and become powerful. We know this from archaeological finds and from the next historical fact provided us, that of the foundation of a colony at Ibiza (Ebusus) in the Balearic Islands. The information may not have been formulated properly, because the Ibiza colony was probably already Phoenician, but the mere mention of its foundation, implying that it was a subcolony, does at least indicate the presence of Carthage on the island.

Later sources tell us that somewhere around the year 600 B.C., the Carthaginians endeavored to prevent the Greeks from founding Marseilles: they were defeated at sea, but meanwhile had extended their interests and maritime power well beyond the African mainland. Subsequently we learn the Carthaginian general Malchus fought in Italy with his troops, first around 550 B.C. in Sicily, where he defeated the

Punic ruins on the hillside at Byrsa

Greeks and evidently subjugated the western part of the island, where the Phoenician colonies of Motya, Panormus (Palermo) and Soluntum had already been founded; and between 545 and 535 B.C. in Sardinia, but not even the presence of other Phoenician colonies (Caralis, modern Cagliari, Nora, Bithia, Sulcis, Tharros) saved him from defeat.

Malchus is an enigmatic name: it means "king", and might well have indicated the function rather than the person. In any case, sources go on to explain how the defeat in Sardinia had repercussions in Carthage, from which Malchus and his army were banished. Nevertheless the general fought back, laid siege to Carthage and took it. His rule lasted but a short time. Accused of tyranny he was executed. His successor was Mago, founder of a dynasty that was to reign over Carthage for a lengthy period. Its most outstanding personalities were Hamilcar and Hasdrubal. The history of Carthage was to resound with their names, plus that of Hannibal.

An important year for the foreign policy of Carthage was 535 B.C., when the Carthaginians and the Etruscans, as allies, defeated the Greeks at Alalia (Aleria) on the west coast of Corsica. It was the sign of a new dimension in Mediterranean politics, an anti-Greek alliance that gave rise to a division of spheres of influence: Italy, barring Magna Graecia, went to the Etruscans, and the great islands of the western Mediterranean went to the Carthaginians. The clearest evidence of the Etruscan-Carthaginian alliance comes from Pyrgi (Santa Severa) on the Tyrrhenian coast just north of Rome, where a king of Cerveteri had three gold plates inscribed — two in Etruscan and one in Phoenician — dedicating them to the Phoenician goddess Astarte (the Etruscan Uni).

Gold plates with inscriptions in Phoenician and Etruscan from Santa Severa 5th century B.C. Rome, Museo Archeologico di Villa Giulia
• *p. 73*

The Greeks made their comeback in Africa, where in 510 B.C the Spartan Doriaeus led them into battle and was repulsed. Doriaeus moved next to Sicily, another key area in the conflict between Carthaginians and Greeks. Here too he was defeated. At this point, Carthage turned to the growing power of Rome, and to reinforce its anti-Greek campaign, signed a treaty with Rome which defined their respective areas of influence: to the Romans went the Latin territory, while the Carthaginians retained part of Sicily and Africa. The details are recorded by Polybius: "On these conditions, there will be amity between the Romans and their allies, and the Carthaginians and their allies. Neither the Romans nor their allies may sail beyond the promontory named the Beautiful unless they should be obliged to do so by storms or enemy pursuit. Whosoever shall be forced there, will make no purchase on the market, nor shall he take more than is necessary for replenishing the ship or making sacrifices, and he shall leave within five days... Should a Roman go into the part of Sicily possessed by the Carthaginians, he will be treated on an equal basis with the others. In turn, the Carthaginians shall not offend the populations of Ardea, Antium, Laurentum, Circei, or Tarracina, nor any other city of the Latins subject to Rome; they shall also refrain from touching the cities of the Latins subject to the Romans, and should they lay hands on any of them, they shall restore them intact to the Romans. They may not build any fortress on Latin territory; and should they set foot in the country armed for war, they may not spend the night there."

In 480 B.C., a decisive event marked the recovery of the Greeks. At Himera, on the northern coast of Sicily, they inflicted a serious defeat on the Carthaginian army. Since in that same year the Greeks triumphed over the Persians in the East, in the battle of Salamis, certain ancient historians link the two events together, suggesting there was an anti-Greek alliance between the Carthaginians and the Persians. Modern historians ascribe this idea to Greek propaganda. At any rate, the victory of Himera marked the beginning of a long gap in our sources. But we have more information in 409 B.C., with a fresh round of clashes in Sicily.

The encounters had variable outcomes. In 409 and 406, the Carthaginians took the offensive, conquering Himera in the north and Selinus, Agrigentum and Gela in the south. The Greeks reacted by sending off an expeditionary force with Dionysius of Syracuse, who in 397 reached Motya and conquered it. On the death of Dionysius in 397, the frontier was established along the rivers Himera and Alico, so that the Carthaginians controlled the western third of the island and the Greeks the rest. Soon after this, a second treaty was drawn up between Carthage and Rome, and it contained an innovation: Carthage now controlled Sardinia, which is mentioned as one of its possessions, equal to that of Africa.

Punic silver coin from Sicily obverse: head of Heracles with lion's skin reverse: protome of horse and palm 4th-3rd century B.C. Parma, Palazzo della Pilota

The clashes between Carthaginians and Greeks in Sicily were resumed in the second half of the 4th century B.C.: between 342 and 339, on the initiative of Timoleon of Corinth, who was thrust back in the battle of the river Crimisus; between 318 and 305, on the initiative of Agathocles of Syracuse who, defeated and besieged in his city, put into practice the audacious scheme already conceived by Doriaeus: attack Carthage on its own territory.

One very important passage from Diodorus describes how the Greeks saw the region around Carthage, revealing the great prosperity of a land that had thus far been safeguarded by waging war abroad: "The intermediate territory, which had to be crossed, was scattered with gardens and orchards of every kind, because many streams had been channelled in to irrigate every part. There seemed no end to the country houses, built luxuriously and whitewashed, which attested the wealth of their owners. The villas

Aerial view of the port   *Ancient port*
of Carthage   *of Carthage*

were full of everything that contributes to the pleasures of life, since the inhabitants, during a long period of peace, had put aside large quantities of goods. The land was cultivated partly as vineyards and partly as olive groves, and also abounded in other fruit trees. In the remaining areas, herds of cattle and flocks of sheep grazed, and the neighboring pastures were full of grazing horses. In a word, there was much wealth in that region, because the more noble Carthaginians had their possessions there and, thanks to their resources, they could devote themselves to enjoying the pleasures of life."

Agathocles, armed with the element of surprise, scored victories at first: he conquered a number of African centers, and formed an alliance with the successors of Alexander the Great in Egypt. But events turned against him in Sicily, and he was forced to withdraw and sign a peace treaty in 305 B.C. that brought the frontier back to the rivers Himera and Alico. Meanwhile the Carthaginians had entered into a third treaty with the Romans, in 306; and a fourth treaty was drawn up in 279, for mutual defence against the latest Greek assault, that of Pyrrhus, king of Epirus, who in 276 had to abandon Sicily. Now the very fact of Greek absense created the premises for the clash between Carthage and Rome. It began in 265, when the Carthaginians moved in on Messana (Messina), and the Mamertines who were occupying it sought help from the Romans.

It is not possible here to provide a detailed account of the Punic Wars, well documented by the Romans. Regarding the first of the wars (264-241 B.C.), one interesting problem is whether and how far the Romans foresaw the development of the clash, or had actually prepared it. This was not the case, it seems: the appeal of the Mamertines greatly embarrassed the senate, which anyway expected a brief, restricted war. It began with a series of victories for the consul Appius Claudius Caecus, who disembarked at Messana and reached Agrigentum in 262.

The Romans then had to tackle the problem of preparing for war at sea, where the Carthaginians were extremely skillful. Polybius gives us a lively account of this: "They were far superior, both in the speed of their ships and in the way they built them, and also in the experience and skill of their seamen. If some of them were driven back by the enemy, they withdrew without running any risk, because they could move with agility and make off easily. The enemy would sail forward to pursue them; and they [the Carthaginians] would turn and sail around them, or come in to their flank and ram them, while the Roman ship had difficulty in turning round, because of its weight and the lack of experience of the rowers. This led to numerous boats being sunk..."

But the Romans did not take long to adapt to the requirements of war at sea. They built a fleet featuring a number

Poculum depicting elephant fitted with war harness from Capena 3rd century B.C. Rome, Museo Archeologico di Villa Giulia • p. 74

Obverse of Punic silver coin depicting portrait identified by some as being Hannibal 237-218 B.C. 22.5 g Barcelona Gabinete Numismático de Cataluña

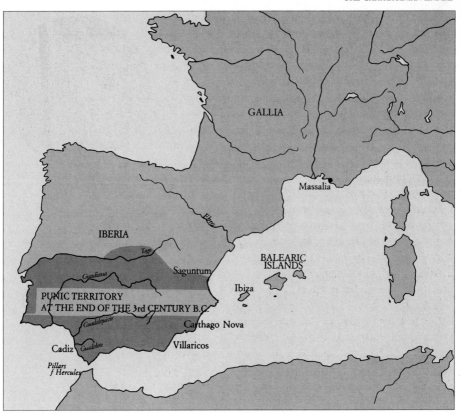

GALLIA

Massalia

IBERIA

BALEARIC
ISLANDS

Saguntum

Ibiza

PUNIC TERRITORY
AT THE END OF THE 3rd CENTURY B.C.

Carthago Nova

Cadiz

Villaricos

Pillars
f Hercules

*Carthaginian
dominion
in Spain during
the Barca period*

of innovations, such as the *corvus*, a kind of gangway for boarding parties that could be thrown across like a grappling iron and hooked on to the enemy ship. The victory in the bay of Mylae (Milazzo) in 260 B.C. was the first success in these new circumstances, and the Cape Ecnomus victory in 256 consolidated it. There followed an attempt to take the war to Africa, with M. Atilius Regulus, but it failed tragically. In the meantime, from 247 onwards, the Carthaginians conducted successful campaigns in Sicily under the leadership of Hamilcar Barca. The war was concluded at sea, with the victory of the consul Lutatius Catulus at the Aegates in 241. The peace terms were very harsh for the losers: the Carthaginians had to relinquish Sicily, hand back their prisoners, swear to renounce any hostility towards the Romans and their allies, and make very large reparations.

At this point that the gradual decline of Carthage began, for the empire was now reduced to such an inferior condition that it would never again be able to rise. The first signs of the crisis were felt instantly, in Africa. The mercenaries revolted, helped by the Libyans, and a four-year war began, during which the revolt spread to Sardinia (238 B.C.). Here the mercenaries sought assistance from Rome, which stepped in and occupied the island, along with neighboring Corsica. This was another blow to the power of Carthage in the Mediterranean, and only in 237 did it manage to put down the revolt in Africa. Just one path toward expansion remained, and that was the Iberian Peninsula, where the Barca family was imposing Carthaginian dominion. In 229 Hasdrubal founded Cartagena, and in 226 he drew up a treaty with Rome that made the river Ebro the dividing line between their spheres of influence.

In 221 Hasdrubal was assassinated, and was succeeded by Hannibal, one of the most brilliant military commanders of antiquity. Lauded for his genius by the Romans themselves, in their eyes he was their predestined enemy. Politically speaking, we may say rather that Hannibal inherited the pan-Mediterranean vision of Alexander the Great, and made one last attempt to fulfill it.

The Second Punic War began at Saguntum in 218 B.C. Hannibal conquered the city and moved overland toward Italy, crossing the Pyrenees, Gaul, and the Alps. After his epic crossing of the mountains — which leaves us with a deep impression, partly on account of the elephants that went along with the Carthaginian army — Hannibal descended into the interior of the peninsula, and marked up a number of victories: in 219 on the Tessin and on the Trebbia, in 217 at Lake Trasimene, and in 216 at Cannae. His strategy on land and not at sea is indicative of his genius, but also of a certain necessity, for Carthage no longer reigned over the seas.

One problem historians have tackled repeatedly is the relationship between Hannibal and the homeland. Was Carthage always agreeable to his enterprises, and did it always back them up without restraint? There must have been suspicions about the general, but there is no evidence that he acted against the opinions of the governors of Carthage, or that they opposed him. As for the policy implemented in Italy, Hannibal's design was evidently to cut the peoples of the peninsula off from Rome. This is borne out by certain clauses in the treaties drawn up with various peoples and cities, which always guaranteed them autonomy, namely a form of federation with Carthage, and that made no mention of dominion. Particularly outstanding was his attempt to make Capua the "capital of Italy." On the whole, we may say that the results of his efforts were meager, and herein lies the major reason for the failure of his enterprise. No less significant, and equally fruitless, was Hannibal's agreement with Philip V of Macedonia, in which we see the great Mediterranean design he inherited from Alexander the Great. Polybius says that the Macedonian plenipotentiaries expressed themselves as follows: "We commit ourselves to setting no traps or ambushes for one another, but rather to fight, with all vigour and dispatch, with no trickery or envy, against the enemies of Carthage, with the exception of those kings, cities and peoples that are bound to us by peace treaties." And the Carthaginians: "We shall be the enemies of anyone who should wage war against King Philip, with the exception of kings, cities and peoples that are bound to us by peace treaties. You will help us in the war against the Romans until such a time as the gods grant victory to us and to you, and you will succour us in our needs, and in whatever we shall ask you. If the gods grant us victory in the war against the Romans and their allies, and the

Romans wish to come to a treaty, we shall sanction it on condition that they conclude the same friendship with you, and that it shall be unlawful for them to wage war at any time."

So Hannibal's overall political vision was indeed grandiose, but also unsuccessful. The failure of his endeavors both domestically and abroad allowed Rome to gradually gather fresh strength. The Romans conquered Syracuse in 212 B.C., Capua in 211, Cartagena in 209. Thus the war was now taken to the very bases of Hannibal's expedition, and no attempt to help him succeeded. Finally the Romans moved over to Africa. Scipio landed there in 204 and made an alliance with Massinissa, king of the Numidians. Hannibal returned in great haste, and was defeated in the decisive battle at Zama in 202 B.C. The peace conditions were extremely exacting: Iberia and the territories occupied in Africa had to be given up, the fleet had to be destroyed, there were heavy reparations, and Carthage was prohibited from waging war without the consent of Rome. For a while Hannibal tried to raise Carthage to its feet again by means of reforms. But these involved powerful interests, so Hannibal was forced into exile, and in the end he took his own life rather than be handed over to the Romans. Meanwhile the provocations of Massinissa led to the third war with Rome (149-146 B.C.), which ended with the final destruction of Carthage.

Seen as a whole, the defeat of Carthage seems to be linked with its inability to create a solid empire such as that controlled by Rome. Neither dominion of the seas nor the genius of Hannibal could compensate for this grave political shortcoming. The heritage of Carthage lingered on for a long time in Africa and the occupied territories, in the form of language, beliefs and customs. Paradoxically, one might say that it was Rome itself that kept it alive, so that it disappeared completely only when the Roman Empire came to an end.

Hannibal's Expedition
Giovanni Brizzi

The Family

Hannibal was born in 247 B.C., presumably in Carthage itself, the eldest of three brothers, although there is a legend which gives Malta as his birthplace. His family had a large and solid patrimony (the ancestral estates in what is now the Tunisian Sahel are well-documented) and descended from ancient nobility. While some modern scholars believe that the family came from Phoenicia much later, Silius Italicus — who draws his information from often excellent sources — claimed that it came with the foundress Elissa and traced its origins back to Belos, mythical king of Tyre.

The first to style himself Barca ("Lightning") was his father Hamilcar, who had been the hero of the war against Rome and the victor in the bitter conflict against the rebel mercenaries in Africa; his brother-in-law, Hasdrubal, *enfant prodige* of the Punic political world, was the favorite of the people of Carthage. Both recognized leaders of the democratic-nationalist faction, these two leading exponents of the family had promoted a thoroughgoing reform of the city institutions that certainly weakened the oligarchy and even, according to some, represented an authentic popular revolution; and they had been at one time among the most enlightened and sensitive supporters of Hellenism in the debate on Greek culture, still very lively in Carthage.

Votive stele featuring male bust from the tophet at Carthage 3rd century B.C. limestone 72 × 18 cm Carthage, Musée de Carthage

This approach, however, only prepared the ground for what was probably a much wider and more complex design. For more than a century the Mediterranean world had witnessed the rise of men who followed the example of Alexander the Great, by claiming a superiority of divine origin over other men; and of princes and commanders placed by their armies above the law. The Barcae took their inspiration from such models. Their political reform, which started with the systematic weakening of the city's oligarchic structures, was intended to continue with a reordering of the Punic Empire, through the conquest of enormous dominions overseas; the final aim was probably to establish personal power in Carthage after the inevitable war with Rome.

The most characteristic figure in the Barca pantheon, the divinity under whose protection all the family's plans were placed, was Melqarth, the hero traveller and leader of armies who according to the legend had crossed the Alps coming from Spain. Revered in the Iberian, Celtic and Magna Graecia worlds, this divinity was closely associated with Heracles and from Alexander onwards became one of the universal symbols of Hellenistic sovereignty. A precise political and ideological choice on the family's part emerges from later Greek and Latin anecdotes: Fabius Pictor explicitly reproaches Hasdrubal for his ambition, but concedes to Hannibal, in particular, the stamp of regality. For the Barcae the preliminary to every future development was the conquest of the Iberian Peninsula. The possession and direct working of the Spanish mines would have compensated Carthage, defeated and deprived of its maritime dominions, for the loss of its agricultural resources in Sicily and Sardinia and its commercial monopoly in the western Mediterranean. More importantly, it would also have allowed strong contingents of mercenaries to be maintained. Spain would have offered a secure base, at a safe distance from Roman interference, and would have provided a valuable terrain for the recruitment of excellent troops. From 237 B.C. onwards, therefore, Hamilcar undertook its conquest; military operations were continued after his death, first by his son-in-law Hasdrubal, who organized the Iberian colonies in admirable fashion and founded its capital, New Carthage (Cartagena), and later by his son Hannibal, who in 221 assumed command of the Carthaginian army when he was just twenty-five years old.

Tactics and Strategy

Removed from his native city before he was ten years old and brought up in his father's army camp in Spain, Hannibal grew up in a very special environment. He came to Hellenism through family tradition and education, but also through personal inclination. Perhaps it was Hamilcar's memory of a man he had much admired, the strategist Xanthippus (who some years before, at the head of the Punic forces, had destroyed Regulus' army in Africa *non virtute sed arte*, thanks not to courage but to skill), that led him to choose the Lacedaemonian Sosilus from Sparta as tutor to his son. Carefully instructed, especially in all things military, Hannibal thoroughly studied the campaigns of Alexander, on whom he was to model himself, as well as works of later military history, and became familiar with the most recent developments in the field of tactics and strategy.

Superior both to Pyrrhus and to Alexander himself, to whom ancient tradition often compared him, the commander being formed in these years was without doubt the greatest exponent of the Hellenistic military school: on the battlefields of Italy he several times applied the encircling tactics typical of the school, bringing them to incomparable perfection. Hannibal, however, was one of the rare military geniuses of history and therefore cannot be considered simply as the product of a particular school. The changes he effected in the structure of the Punic army represent an original contribution to the military science of his time.

Although, like all his predecessors, he was obliged to make use of heterogeneous contingents recruited from the vast dominions of Carthage, Hannibal was the first to realize that in order to transform a rabble of mercenaries often of barbarian origin into an efficient fighting force, it was necessary to exploit the native characteristics of these different ethnic groups to the full, if possible combining their action on the field of battle. To achieve this, the equipment and manner of fighting of the Libyan heavy-armed infantry, backbone of the Punic armies, would have to be adapted taking other troops' capabilities into consideration. Until then the Libyan force had been armed and deployed in the Greek manner with often far from brilliant results. Both the hoplite and, even more, the phalangite tactics, which depended for their effectiveness on the perfect cohesion of serried ranks, required long training, tight discipline and the ability to handle suitable weapons such as the lance and the long Macedonian sarissa.

Vice-versa the western warriors, including the Libyans, were more used to man-to-man combat and saw battle as a series of individual duels. Discarding the pike — typical of the Hellenistic armies and the strongly Hellenized Carthaginian forces — Hannibal equipped all his heavy infantry contingents with the sword as their main offensive weapon. Besides the Iberians and the Celts, who already had swords, the Libyans were immediately provided with a more suitable weapon for close combat: this is shown by the fact that after the victories at Lake Trasimene and Cannae they exchanged their arms for those of the Roman dead, superior in quality but evidently similar to their own.

This was undoubtedly Hannibal's most outstanding innovation. Apparently less powerful and compact than the Hellenistic armies, which were based on the massive block of the phalanx, Hannibal's army was however far more elastic and flexible; divided into *speirai*, minor tactical units comparable to the Roman *manipuli*, it had considerable maneuverability; less tied to the necessity to maintain a rigid formation at all times, it was also much less conditioned by the nature of the terrain it had to fight on; and finally, although it had to know how to operate in compact formation, it encouraged in its men the native ferocity and individual fighting spirit which were their true prerogatives. Thus both in equipment and in ethnic composition, the army that Hannibal led into Italy was in some respects an anomaly in its epoch: in its ranks the "Western" characteristics of the peoples composing it were maintained and at the same time perfectly fused.

Endowed with features which perhaps made it superior to any other, Hannibal's army had nothing Greek about it any more. Only the maneuver that it was called upon to execute in the field remained Greek: as in the Hellenistic armies, the outflanking was carried out by the cavalry, but it might be initiated by formations of heavy-armed infantry which were much more agile than their Greek counterparts. Hannibal has the merit of having been the first to devise an original tactical scheme for the West, freed from the allegiance to Hellenistic models which still at times afflicted even the Roman armies. His army represents the link between the Roman armies of the second period of the Republic, still slow and severely hampered by

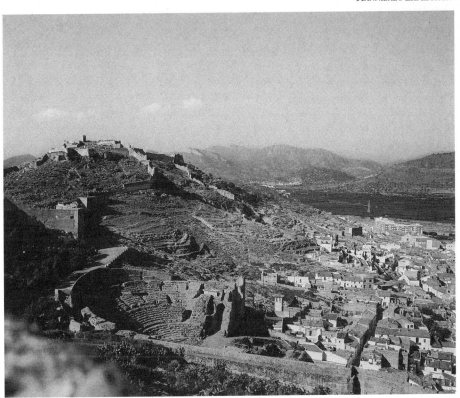

Saguntum Roman theatre and citadel

their repetitive and mechanical tactics, and those organized after Scipio's reforms, which in the decade following the battle of Zama were easily able to win the day against the outdated Hellenistic forces.

Against the enormous resources of the Roman state (according to the *formula togatorum*, the list of men fit for military service, in the year 225 B.C. Rome could mobilize more than 600,000 men in case of need) Hannibal was to lead only a small force of chosen veterans into Italy. He was well aware of not being able to compete numerically with the Republic's conscripts, whose number exceeded that which the Punic state as a whole could have mobilized. In a war of attrition Carthage would have had no hope, but Hannibal had evaluated the intrinsic weaknesses of an Italian federation divided by conflicting interests. Perhaps on the basis on his own experience as a Carthaginian, he believed that an action from inside, aimed at the heart of the enemy state, would show its imbalances and bring out latent discord, breaking up the structure of the confederation and depriving Rome of much of her strength.

Most of the Gallic peoples of north Italy were openly hostile to the Republic; their survival had been threatened by the recent offensives of Flaminius and Marcellus so they received Punic emissaries and sent their ambassadors to Hannibal's camp in Spain, offering to lead him toward Italy. Discontent and revolt had also been in the air ever since the Roman conquest in the Osco-Sabellic and Italian worlds, some of whose cities proposed themselves as potential allies. The situation of Capua, the second city of Italy, was also delicate, since it was threatened in its economic primacy.

Hannibal was convinced that the compactness of the Italic confederation relied essentially on the strength and prestige of an army that he counted on being able to defeat with ease. Very few allies were likely to remain loyal to Rome when her armies, defeated on the field, proved incapable of defending Italian territory from destruction and pillage. In order to dismantle the system of alliances on which Rome's strength rested, Hannibal would have to attack her first of all in Italy, destroying the reputation of invincibility of her legions, humiliating her before her allies and, at the same time, luring away by whatever means — with promises or threats — those *socii* who provided her armies.

Lake Trasimene

Hannibal's was not an unviable plan. He believed that Rome, once she was isolated, could be forced to negotiate: he probably remembered how she had been on the point of making peace with Pyrrhus, and as a Carthaginian he thought — rightly perhaps — that only the offer of help from Mago had prevented the successful conclusion of the negotiations at the time. He counted on obtaining this result very quickly. An often overlooked passage of Livy gives an insight into Hannibal's hopes and plans. During the crossing of the Alps, in order to encourage his demoralized troops, Hannibal halts the march on a high plateau and tells his men to look down to the valley below; when they have reached it, he promises, the difficulties will be over, one or two battles at the most and Rome herself, *arcem et caput italiae*, will be in their power. A proper programmatic declaration this, in which Hannibal shows that he was planning a real "blitzkrieg" against the enemy. Although he had sworn eternal hatred of the Romans, Hannibal was not planning to exterminate them: his object was to reduce Rome's power and return her to her original status as a simple Latin city.

The War Against Rome

In 226 B.C., with Hasdrubal, the Carthaginians had given their word that they would not cross the Ebro river. Acting once more as protector of western Hellenism, with this pact Rome meant to respond to the appeals of her ally Marseilles, worried about the fate of Emporiae (Ampuria) and Rhode (Rosa), its last colonies on Spanish soil.

It was the Treaty of the Ebro that finally caused the war. South of the river, Saguntum, an indigenous city which tradition said was of Greek origin, was still free. Both sides claimed the right to decide its fate: Rome, because the city had been under her protection for a long time; the Carthaginians, because it was within their sphere of influence. When, despite Rome's warnings, Saguntum was destroyed, conflict was inevitable. The juridical controversy over the responsibility of the clash has been discussed, fruit-

*Map
reconstructing
Hannibal's route*

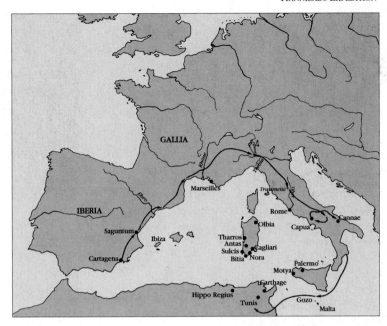

lessly for the most part, by many scholars. What is certain, however, is that it was only at the last minute and not without hesitation that Rome went into a war that was dictated by reasons of prestige, but for which she was not adequately prepared, and which was also against the interests of a large and influential part of the senate.

Convinced that Hannibal would want to defend his colonies in the Iberian Peninsula, the Romans prepared to send P. Cornelius Scipio there, while they entrusted another consul, Ti. Sempronius Longus, with the task of organizing a landing in Africa; but Hannibal's lightning departure at the beginning of the summer of 218 B.C. frustrated their plans. Held back by the insurrection in North Italy of the Boii Gauls, who had perhaps been incited by Punic agents present for a long time in that region, Scipio reached the Rhône only after the enemy had already moved toward the Alps. After a long and difficult march, during which he overcame the opposition of some of the Celtic peoples — such as the Allobroges — Hannibal crossed over the mountain range probably either at the pass of the Traversette or that of Col de Clapier, and finally reached the Po valley.

While Sempronius was hurrying northwards as fast as possible in order to counter the threat, Scipio was facing the enemy, but he was defeated and wounded in a cavalry skirmish beside the Ticino river, perhaps near modern Lomello, and forced to withdraw to Piacenza, while the Insubres in revolt joined forces with Hannibal. Sempronius was no more successful at the command of the united consular forces. Near the Trebbia, to the west of Piacenza, the Romans were first attacked and overwhelmed on wing and flank by the superior Punic cavalry and then attacked from the rear.

71

Although about 10,000 men managed to get out of the pocket, another 15,000 were killed or taken prisoner. North Italy, in full revolt, was by now completely lost.

The consuls of 217 B.C. tried in vain to block the enemy. Having emerged in late spring onto the plains of Etruria, perhaps through the Porretta pass, Hannibal paraded in sight of Arezzo where Gaius Flaminius was waiting for him, and then proceeded along the Val di Chiana. In the hollow of Tuoro, Hannibal lured the enemy into a lethal trap: with fewer men and surrounded on all sides with Lake Trasimene behind it, the Roman army was rapidly annihilated. About 15,000 men died during the battle and the consul himself fell heroically, killed by a Gaulish lance. Shortly afterward the cavalry of the other consul, Servilius, marching from Rimini, was surprised by the forces of Maharbal: another 4,000 men dead or taken prisoner were added to the list of victims.

The nomination of Q. Fabius Maximus as dictator also turned out to be of little help. By an unusual procedure the people elected his political adversary, M. Minucius Rufo, *magister equitum* (master of the cavalry), making him more or less equal to the dictator, but his disagreement with the delaying tactics of Fabius prevented a combined action. In the meantime, having crossed the Piceno, Hannibal had reached the South, leaving devastation and pillage in his wake; and here, having cleverly avoided Fabius' attempt to block him in the Falernian plain, he withdrew to winter in the citadel of Gereonio.

Cuirass in gilt bronze from Ksour es-Saf 3rd-2nd century B.C., Tunis Musée du Bardo • pp. 76-77

The unanimous desire for a decisive battle as soon as possible led Rome towards the worst defeat in her history. On 2 August 216 B.C., led by the consuls L. Aemilius Paulus and G. Terentius Varro, an 80,000-strong army, brought together to crush the enemy, met with Hannibal's forces near Cannae, in the plain of the Ofanto. Encircled in what was a perfect maneuver, the great Roman army was completely destroyed: during the battle the consul Paulus fell and with him 45,000 foot-soldiers, 2,700 cavalry, both quaestors, 29 military tribunes, 80 senators and a large number of *equites*. More than 19,000 men were taken prisoner, less than 15,000 managed to escape from the enemy.

Between early November 218 and early August 216, then, Hannibal had virtually concluded his lightning war: honoring the family nickname, he had crossed the peninsula winning all the way, destroying any army that dared to meet him and bringing the Italic federation near to collapse. At the final, most terrible blow it finally began to crumble and the losses soon appeared very serious. The Italian world deserted en masse: in less than two years, a number of cities, including Capua, Syracuse, Taranto, Turi, Metaponto and Eraclea went over to the enemy. So did Atella, Calzia, the

Gold plates with inscription
on Phoenician and Etruscan
from Santa Severa
5th century B.C.
Rome, Museo Archeologico
di Villa Giulia

Poculum *depicting elephant fitted*
with war harness
from Capena, 3rd century B.C.,
Rome, Museo Archeologico
di Villa Giulia

*Phoenician warship
in a bas-relief from the palace
of Sennacherib, Nineveh
7th century B.C.
London, British Museum*

*Bas-relief depicting
Phoenician trading ship
2nd century B.C.
w. 80 cm
Beirut, National Museum*

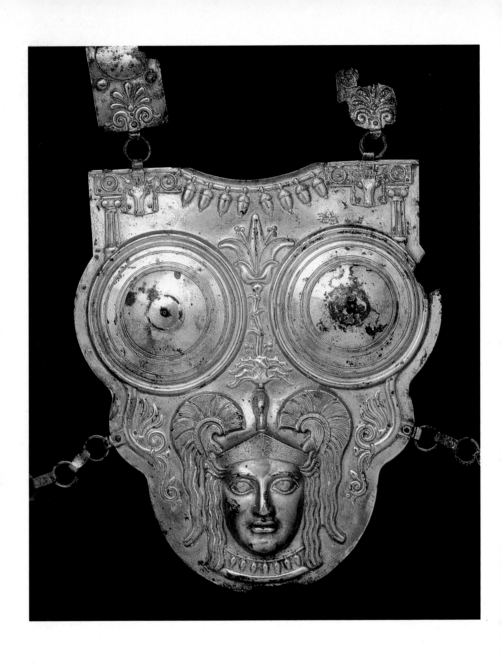

Cuirass in gilt bronze
from Ksour es-Saf
3rd-2nd century B.C.
Tunis, Musée du Bardo

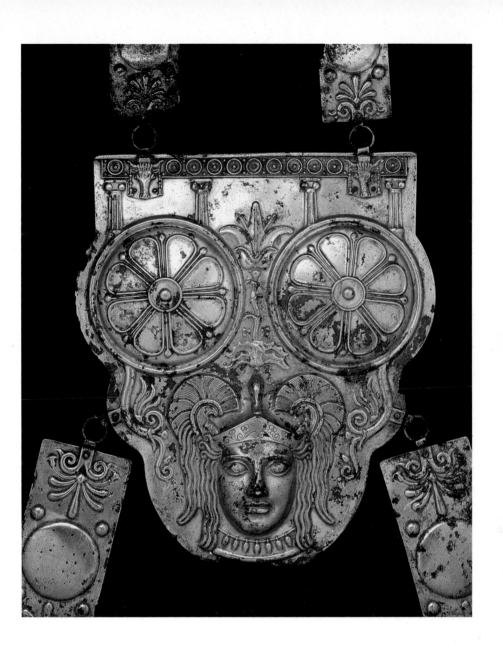

Necklace with beads
and pendants of various kinds
from Carthage
7th century B.C.
electrum, 22 cm
Carthage, Musée de Carthage

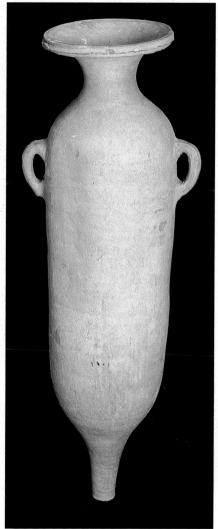

Amphora for transportation
from Carthage
4th-3rd century B.C.
clay, 18 cm
Tunis, Musée du Bardo

Amphora for transportation
from Carthage
2nd century B.C.
clay, 110 cm
Carthage, Musée de Carthage

Askos *in the form of a dolphin*
from Carthage
4th-3rd century B.C.
terra-cotta, 10.5 cm
Tunis, Musée du Bardo

Askos *in the form of a ram*
from Carthage
4th-3rd century B.C.
clay, 15 cm
Tunis, Musée du Bardo

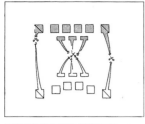

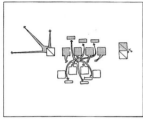

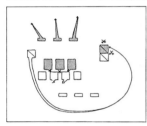

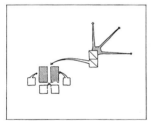

▨ Roman infantry

◩ Roman cavalry
▭ Roman light infantry

☐ Carthaginian infantry

◩ Carthaginian cavalry
▭ Carthaginian light infantry

Troops formations at the battle of Cannae

Irpini and most of the Apuli, all the Samnites except the Pentri and all the Bruzzii except the Uzentini — the whole of southern Italy was in revolt.

Despite this, Rome obstinately refused to surrender: the *perfidia* and *crudelitas* which in the eyes of the Romans characterized Hannibal's methods ruled out the possibility of negotiations. The senate objected to Hannibal's propensity to an indiscriminate use of trickery and expediency — the result perhaps of his particular upbringing — and they censured him and his unconquered army for the barbaric nature of the peoples who composed it. The ancient aristocratic ethos of the Roman nobles led them to refuse every recourse to deceit *inter pares* and although they saw war as pure violence, they rejected the savage and alien nature of the enemy's warfare and the instinctive ferocity that Hannibal, far from repressing, seemed to tolerate and even actively encourage. The Romans could not forgive Hannibal for having put himself at the head of a barbarian rabble, leading it from one victory to another. It was probably this aspect that led to a grouping around Rome of Latins, Etruscans, Umbrians and Sabines (that is, almost all of Tyrrhenian Italy, whose oligarchies were most deeply linked politically and had already managed to conquer the peninsula). The Roman senate could ask them for an immense effort in view of what was seen as a real holy war. Hannibal, on the contrary, was supported only by the scattered forces of allies who had as little loyalty toward him as they had previously had toward Rome: allies that fought in isolation, with no respect for a common strategy and no longer linked together in any way. Hannibal's army was not much strengthened by their contribution: the Greek cities, for example, used mercenary troops and could not be forced into mass mobilization, while the Samnites could not be pressed into regular discipline so as not to give them the impression that they had simply changed masters. Moreover, the *socii* who had gone over to Hannibal proved clearly incapable of measuring themselves against the forces of Rome; and even Philip of Macedonia, who had offered his help, was soon reduced to stalemate.

Hannibal might still have been able to win if the enemy had allowed him another pitched battle in which large contingents were deployed, but the Roman generals had by now aligned themselves with the doctrine of Fabius Maximus and were avoiding any direct confrontation. Even though there were still more of them (during the second phase of the war Rome kept 20-25 legions under arms), the armies of the Republic no longer offered the enemy a single center of resistance, but operated instead with increasing

81

*Cannae
the archaelogical
area*

success while Hannibal was far away, and gradually deprived him of his bases.

Hannibal continued to have some successes. In 212 B.C. the praetor Ti. Gracchus fell in battle, probably while leading his *volones*; and shortly afterwards, not far from Ordona, the forces of another praetor, Cn. Fulvius Flacchus, were annihilated. In 210 near the same city, the proconsul Cn. Fulvius Centumalus perished along with almost all his men, and in 208 there was the last consulate of M. Claudius Marcellus, who fell along with his colleague T. Quinctius Crispinus in a clash with the Numidian cavalry. In 211 Hannibal's thrust toward Rome could not prevent the fall of Capua, while in Sicily Syracuse was taken by storm. In 210 the Romans ended operations on the island and a year later Taranto also fell. When the head of Hannibal's brother, Hasdrubal (defeated and killed at the Metaurus) was thrown in front of his trenches, every last hope of victory disappeared. Gradually forced down toward the southernmost tip of Italy and then surrounded near Crotona, in the autumn of 203 B.C. Hannibal finally abandoned the peninsula.

Waiting for him was P. Cornelius Scipio (Africanus), son of the Scipio defeated near the Ticino. After having demolished the Barca empire in Spain, the young general had become consul; despite opposition from Fabius' party, he took the war into Africa and was now impatient to measure his forces against Hannibal. On the field of Zama Hannibal achieved his last masterpiece, giving his rival a fine lesson in tactics and very nearly managing to win. Perhaps only one other battle, Waterloo, has shown as much as Zama the superior ability of the losing side, but, like Napoleon, Hannibal could not avoid defeat. The man who had most wanted the war with Rome now resolved to favor as the lesser of two evils the acceptance of a very hard peace.

Exile and Death

Able in only six years to raise exhausted Carthage and exploit its enormous agricultural potential by starting the cultivation of specialized crops throughout the African territory, and able then as *suffete* (judge) to suppress the abuses of the oligarchy, Hannibal, like his father and brother-in-law, had also aimed at a political transformation of the Punic state. Hated for this by his peers no less than by the Roman senate, in 195 B.C. Hannibal was forced to go into exile. He spent the last years of his life wandering from Syria to Bithynia, where in 183 he committed suicide to avoid being given up to the Romans.

More than for their nostalgic plans for revenge and more than for his participation in some of the eastern conflicts, the years of exile were important for the spiritual "homecoming" of the person himself. Freed at last from contingent circumstances, Hannibal discovered an authentic Hellenistic dimension. Forced to leave his native land, he accepted his new situation as a stateless person with great naturalness, turning out to be just as much at his ease in distant, unknown Bithynia as in Carthage or among the savage tribes of Iberia. From Hellenism he finally took not only the heroic superhuman nature of its commanders, but also its essential matrix — that culture which alone ennobles man and calls him to be part of a much wider, universal reality.

He had learned to love that reality through his readings and his upbringing without ever experiencing it directly. He was perhaps disappointed by the serious political weaknesses it displayed, and certainly by the narrow-mindedness and short-sightedness of some of its rulers. The "heritage" he left to Italy and to the world would start off economic and social processes which, much later on, were to lead to the collapse of the structures of the Roman Republic: of this he could have no inkling. He did realize, however — and this was to embitter the last years of his life — that he had involuntarily put into motion, without then having known how to stop it, a ruthless machine destined to dominate the whole inhabited Mediterranean world.

Ships and Navigation
Piero Bartoloni

The seafaring skills of the Phoenicians greatly impressed their contemporaries, infallibly arousing much admiration or deep envy. The fact is that their mastery of ships and navigation and their sound knowledge of the seas, and atmospheric elements, plus their custom of trading on the seas, allowed the Phoenicians to distinguish themselves among others in the Mediterranean area. Hence their reputation as cruel pirates or accomplished merchants, shrewd, swindling traders or great, intrepid navigators. Whatever the case, driven by the desire to acquire new and more remunerative sources of raw materials and to sell their products to markets other than in the homeland, the Phoenicians covered enormous distances, being the first to trace routes to the western Mediterranean and beyond the Pillars of Hercules toward the Atlantic coasts of Africa and Europe. In doing this they opened the western basin of the Mediterranean to history.

Phoenician warship on the obverse of a coin from Byblos silver, 340 B.C. Beirut, National Museum

On the basis of ancient written sources and archaic settlements, it is possible to deduce the various systems of navigation used in those times. There were two fundamental systems: the first, short-haul coastal navigation, was used to sail from one village or town along the coastal regions to another, always within sight of the coasts themselves; the second, deep-sea navigation, was used when sailing over the open seas toward places that were often very far from the port of departure.

Short-haul coastal navigation was mainly a daytime activity carried out close to the coasts, on routes that linked settlements no more than 25-30 nautical miles away from one another, with no real problems of visibility and direction. For this purpose, alongside the large merchant ships, smaller vessels were also used, depending on the route and cargo.

In deep-sea navigation, on the other hand, the ships would take routes farther away from the coastline, usually on the open seas, but probably always in sight of land. During the night, whenever it was not possible to berth, the ship was kept in the right direction by observation of the Ursa Minor constellation, which the ancient world called the "Phoenician Star." But whenever possible, depending on weather conditions, deep-sea ships would make temporary stops for supplies and repairs. For the night, or in bad weather or unfavourable winds, they would choose protected waters behind some promontory or island, while smaller vessels could easily be beached when necessary.

Looking carefully at a map of the Mediterranean, it is easy to see that there are not really many stretches of open water where it is necessary to navigate without reference points on the coastline. Then, bearing in mind that the speed of commercial shipping was around 2-3 knots, it emerges that a craft could cover more than 50 nautical miles a day, so except for particularly long crossings, it was always well within the reach of land. The longer voyages, without reference points along the coastline, included the Channel of Sardinia, from the African coast to that island, or the Balearic Sea, from the African coast to the Balearic Islands, or from these to the western shores of Sardinia.

All the other routes frequently used by the Phoenicians could have been along the coasts, as in the great crossings between East and West. Definite information on the maximum sea-speed achieved is provided by Polybius, who tells us how a Carthaginian captain in a warship, a certain Hannibal "of Rhodes", covered the stretch between Carthage and Lilybaeum (present-day Marsala), a distance of 125 nautical miles, in twenty-four hours, at an average speed of over 5 knots.

Commercial navigation took place almost exclusively between March and October, in the more clement season, and the first departures were celebrated with special ceremonies invoking protection for seafaring activities.

The Mediterranean basin was definitely no easy sea to navigate for long distances, given the type of sails used in those times. On the other hand, while the Mediterranean winds were irregular and often changed direction, frequently obliging shipping to lay to for a couple of days, they did allow freight ships to move in all directions regardless of the season, and to undertake unscheduled and very long voyages.

Warships, on the other hand, travelled all the year round, to patrol the coasts and suppress piracy, or in the event of wars already being waged, for whatever military operations were opportune. Very often, however, the outcome of such undertakings, dependent as they always were on the weather, was disaster. One example is what happened during the first war between Rome and Carthage: losses in the Carthaginian merchant fleet, including troop and supply ships, caused by storms and shipwrecks amounted to around 700 vessels, while the Roman fleet actually lost 1,000 of its ships.

The voyages of discovery made by the Phoenicians and Carthaginians as they searched for precious metals and new, profitable markets greatly impressed the ancient world. Of outstanding interest is the voyage, related by Herodotus, which the Phoenicians undertook on behalf of Pharaoh Necho around the end of the 7th century B.C.: it lasted three years, and included circumnavigation of the African continent. Then there was the voyage of the Carthaginian Hanno in the late 5th century B.C. from Carthage into the Atlantic, past the Pillars of Hercules, and on as far as the Gulf of Guinea.

Another voyage well worthy of mention was the one undertaken some

Bas-relief depicting Phoenician trading ship 2nd century B.C. w. 80 cm Beirut, National Museum
• p. 75

time in the 5th century B.C. by the Carthaginian Himilco along the Atlantic coast of Europe to Brittany and possibly as far as the Cassiterides Islands (Great Britain and Ireland) in search of tin, and in the endeavor to open a new trade route for this mineral, as an alternative to the continental route across France to the Gulf of Lions and Marseilles. Certain archaeological finds attest the presence, albeit temporary, of Carthaginians in the Azores, and other ancient authors recount legends of the voyages the Phoenicians made in regions beyond the Atlantic.

In order to implement their commercial activities, the Phoenicians used ships specially fitted out for the purpose, exploiting all the most advanced shipbuilding techniques and devices available at the time, which were not really very different from the construction criteria still applied today.

The first type of Phoenician ships considered here are transport vessels, called *gauloi* ("round") by the ancient authors because of their rounded hulls. They had ample cargo space and were four times as long as their width: between 20 and 30 m long and 6 or 7 m wide. Their draught was about one and a half meters, as was the height of the ship above the waterline. These measurements applied to most of the Phoenician fleet, but there were probably larger vessels as well. The stern was rounded and culminated in a fishtail or spiral decoration. The bows were also curved, and ended with the *aplustre*, a representation of a horse's head. Depicted on the hull just aft of the prow were two eyes, which were intended to allow the ship to see the route it was following and must have aroused great fear in enemies.

These ships had a mainmast bearing a rectangular sail set on a yard that

Phoenician
warship
in a bas-relief
from the palace
of Sennacherib
Nineveh
7th century B.C.
London
British Museum
• p. 75

changed direction with the wind. The shape and position of the sail allowed the ship to move only with aft winds. The ship was steered by the rudder, an oar with very broad, asymmetrical blades, that was attached on the port side near the stern. Also toward the stern was the quarterdeck, which provided shelter for the crew and contained equipment and the ship's galley. There were rarely more than twenty men in any one crew, including the captain-owner and the pilot, because no more than this number were needed for sailing.

Moving on to the warships of the Phoenicians and Carthaginians, the first thing to note is that they were narrower than the merchant ships. In order to house a larger crew and the greatest possible number of oarsmen, the ships were seven times as long as their width. A description of the different types of ships used during the various stages of Phoenician maritime history follows; first let us illustrate their appearance and describe the components of a warship.

The stern was very similar to that of the merchant vessels, while the prow was very different, because it was the most important part of the vessel. In fact it was also a weapon, since on the very tip of the bows was lodged the rostrum: this was a bronze beak with various shapes that was used to ram and shatter the flanks of enemy craft. At the sides of the prow were the usual eyes and, above them, apertures for the anchor cables. On the deck, again at the bow end, was the forecastle, a wooden structure occupied by bowmen or catapults during battle. The aftercastle, refuge and quarters for the captain and officers, was at the stern end. The ship was steered by two rudders on the sides at the stern.

The sails of the warship were more complicated, because it had to be able to veer and turn very rapidly in order to ram enemy ships with the rostrum, and to avoid being damaged. Thus, there were two masts, one in the center, bearing the mainsail, and one at the prow, bearing a small sail that allowed the craft to be maneuvered in crosswinds. During battle, if a ship happened to be unmasted, it was propelled by oarsmen stationed along the inner sides of the hull.

Alongside the merchant vessels and warships, there were minor ships, sloops used for short-haul voyages, and fishing boats. Their hulls were similar to those of the merchant vessels, with the same length-width ratio. Their decorated sterns were roundish, while the bows were pointed and surmounted by a beam. They were propelled either by sails on small masts, or by oars, and were steered by rudders on the port side of the stern.

Itinerary of the African *periplus presumably undertaken by the Phoenicians on behalf of Pharaoh Necho*

Coming back to the war fleet, mention should first be made of the types of craft used from the beginning of the Phoenicians' history to the fall of Carthage. The oldest and most elementary ship was the penteconter, which means a ship with 50 oars. Indeed, it was about 25 m long and was crewed by 50 oarsmen, 25 on each side, plus the captain, the first mate, the pilot and the team for manoeuvring the sails, a complement of no more than ten. The rowing pace was set by a flute-player.

Queen of the Mediterranean, uncontested mistress of the seas between the 7th and 4th centuries B.C., was the trireme, the invention of which ancient authors attribute to the seafaring Phoenicians. The ship had a crew of about 180 men: 80 oarsmen on each side, and the rest handled the sails and worked on deck, plus a small contingent of assault infantry. The fundamental innovation of this ship was that: since the craft was no more than 36 m long, the oarsmen were not arranged in straight lines, but in three staggered rows or banks, thus accomplishing the threefold aim of a) not hampering rowing operations, b) not needing excessively high sides on the vessel, and c) limiting the craft to a reasonable length.

Hanno's voyage

The next kind of ship, the tetreme, which was in service with the Carthaginian fleet from the 4th century B.C. onwards, is also attributed by ancient historians to the shipbuilding skills of Carthage. The innovation of this ship, and of the next, the quinquereme — the classic ship of the Punic Wars — was that they had respectively four and five oarsmen on the same bench plying the same oar. Thus, the sides of the ships did not need to be too high, which would have jeopardized their stability. Both the tetreme and the quinquereme were about 40 m long and little more than 6 m wide, with a draft of no more than 2 m. They had crews of around 240 and 300

men respectively, working on the 30 oars per side — plus the sail team — and their maximum speed with the simultaneous use of both forms of propulsion, and only for short periods, was 5 or 6 knots. Their cruising speed, using just one of the two means of propulsion, was about half that.

Only sails were used to approach the battle area. Once the enemy was sighted, the sails were lowered and the mast was removed and, where possible, laid flat, to free the deck completely for fighting. Only oars were used for deployment in battle and the actual encounter, so that the ships could be as maneuverable as possible.

Ancient sources become extremely interesting when they mention that, while the Carthaginian armies were composed mainly of mercenary

Himilco's voyage

troops recruited from various regions around the Mediterranean, the ships' crews were exclusively Carthaginian citizens. During the clash with Rome, the fleets ranged from several squadrons of 12 ships each to fleets of 120 craft and, in special cases, over 300.

There were basically two forms of naval battle tactics. The first, called the *diecplus*, consisted of the simultaneous, fast departure of all the fleet deployed in a straight line, breaking through gaps in the enemy line, turning sharply toward the enemy's rear, and delivering the final blow into their sterns. The second strategy, the *periplus*, involved heading toward the side of the enemy ship and ramming it. If an enemy ship was not fatally struck, it was towed to some dry dock on the coast to be repaired and reused.

The discovery in a stretch of water north of Marsala of two Punic ships of the 3rd century B.C. has told us a great deal about the carpentry and construction techniques used in those times. Both craft are in a fair state of preservation considering how long they have been under water. They have been classified by their discoverers as warships, but since they have no rostrum and are no more than 30 m long, there is every reason to conclude that they were reconnaissance or escort craft, not used for battle, but for liaison.

Whatever the case, how they were built is the most important thing. It can be seen that both craft were fully built of wooden components prefabricated separately and assembled later. This can be deduced from the presence of letters from the Punic alphabet on single parts, and guidelines that must have been drawn for the ships' carpenters. It is assumed that the various structures were made separately with the help of standard patterns, and were assembled at a second stage, after seasoning and according to need. Thus, having stored the essential components of the ship in very little space, it was possible to assemble a large number of craft at the same time, and make them seaworthy very rapidly.

Reconstruction of a small boat used for coastal trade viewed from prow 3rd century B.C.

Outline reconstruction of a Carthaginian quinquereme 3rd century B.C.

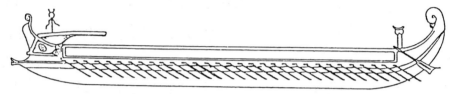

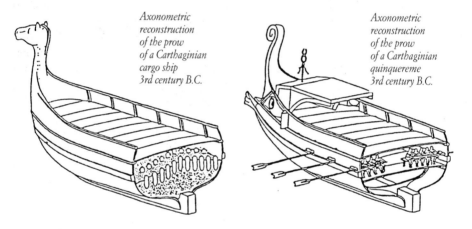

Axonometric reconstruction of the prow of a Carthaginian cargo ship 3rd century B.C.

Axonometric reconstruction of the prow of a Carthaginian quinquereme 3rd century B.C.

The same discovery also helps to shed light on the famous episode nar-rated by Pliny (*Nat. Hist.*, XVI, 92), when he tells how the first Roman fleet was constructed in only sixty days. Polybius (I, 20, 9-10) has this to say: "On this occasion, the Carthaginians had assaulted [the Romans] in the Straits [of Messina], and a covered ship, having driven too far for-ward in the heat of battle, had gone aground, and had fallen into the hands of the Romans; these latter used it as a model for building the whole fleet."

It is fairly obvious that if the Carthaginians used the construction meth-ods we have discussed, the Roman carpenters had no problem at all in discovering how the ship had been built once it had been dismantled, and therefore were able to set up a fleet in a very short time. On the other hand, since Carthaginian supremacy at sea in this period was undeniable, it was natural that their ships should be taken as models of the utmost in naval techniques, functionality and maneuverability throughout the entire western basin of the Mediterranean.

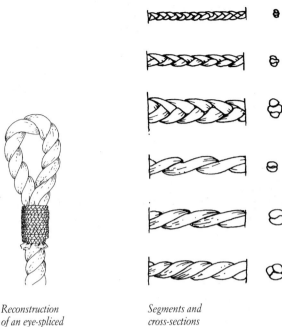

*Reconstruction
of an eye-spliced
line used on
Phoenician ships*

*Segments and
cross-sections
of twisted and
plaited lines
of various sizes
used on
Phoenician ships*

To conclude, let us say that what we can gather from surviving remains of the structure of ancient Phoenician and Punic ships and their components reveals that they were very similar to the fishing boats still being used in our times along the Mediterranean coasts. They were a complex of wooden planks laid on edge or partly overlapping — the planking — which was supported on the inside by a ribwork of beams — the frame — at right angles to the keel. There are also traces of an exterior lining that covered and protected the planking: it consisted of sheets of lead spread with pitch on the underside and fastened to the planking with copper nails.

Commerce and Industry
Piero Bartoloni

To fully understand the particular commercial inclination of the city-states of Phoenicia, mention must first of all be made of their specific geographical position and the historical situation that existed at the close of the 2nd millennium B.C. along the coastal strip of Syria and Palestine. This region, which throughout the 2nd millennium was bitterly contested by the great empires of the East and Egypt, received from these "contestants" influences and cultural incentives which enabled it to evolve an artistic culture of its own, enhanced by the different ingredients and in great demand by buyers both in the Near East and, later, in the West. Moreover, the city-states, squeezed as they were into the narrow passageway between the mountain range of Lebanon and the Mediterranean coast, thus meagerly endowed with agricultural and mineral resources, necessarily turned their attention in the direction of trade and handicrafts. In fact for the proto-historical West they represented the gateway to the East.

In the second half of the 2nd millennium B.C., historical circumstances stemming from a series of often devastating episodes, such as the invasion of the "Peoples of the Sea," the sudden fall of the Hittite empire, the no less sudden demise of the Mycenaean thalassocracy and of the city-states of the northern Syrian coast, created the premises for the commercial expansion of the Phoenician cities. On the other hand, even before a Phoenician cultural identity had come into being, the inhabitants of the Syro-Palestinian region were known throughout Egypt and the Near East

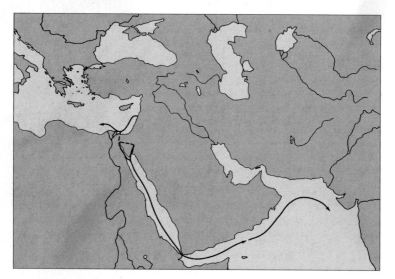

The Phoenician navigation route to Egypt and the Red Sea

Plaque with enthroned figure from Nimrud 7th century B.C. ivory, 7.1 cm London British Museum

for their undoubted ability in the techniques of shipbuilding and for their skill as navigators.

The earliest commercial activities of the Phoenician cities, in the last two centuries of the 2nd millennium B.C., were carried on primarily in the eastern basin of the Mediterranean and consequently involved neighboring regions such as Egypt, the southern coast of Anatolia and Cyprus, in the exchange of products and manufactured articles and in the necessary search for raw materials for production. Not much later intense and significant commercial relations were initiated with the nearby kingdom of Israel and long voyages undertaken by Phoenician ships toward distant Tarshish, according to what has come down to us in the Old Testament. Trade with the kingdom of Israel took on special importance with the agreements between King Solomon and Hiram, king of Tyre, for the construction of the temple of Jerusalem. The biblical account tells how, for the building of this monument, materials and skilled workmen were imported from the cities and inland regions of Lebanon; trade centred primarily around the cedar and fir needed in those days for building, sold in exchange for wheat and olive oil, and the sending of Phoenician laborers who helped in the building as specialized craftsmen.

The profitable commercial intercourse between the two kings, according to the Bible, also took the concrete form of joint ventures. Mention is made, in particular, of the fitting out of an Israelite fleet equipped with Phoenician crews which, setting sail from the Israelite port of Ezion-geber on the Red Sea, headed south to the land of Ophir, very likely modern Ethiopia, and also of the goods carried back home: sandalwood, precious stones, ivory, apes, peacocks and, above all, gold and silver.

Not long after this, the nearly annual forays of the Assyrian armies began. These Assyrian kings, who in their annals recounted the main events of each year of their reign, mentioned conquests of Phoenician cities and the imposition of tributes, which for the most part consisted of the materials and objects cited above, along with *exotica* that aroused the curiosity of the Assyrians. At any rate, these were probably not so much out-and-out conquests of the Phoenician city-states, which would have inevitably weakened the commercial potential of their inhabitants, as periodic impositions of tributes or, in certain cases, maybe even of trade. From the materials traded or imported, it is easy to establish the confines of the Mediterranean East within which the Phoenician cities operated in this period and what articles were manufactured in their workshops and exported as precious wares. Imports included, along with the aforesaid materials from Ophir, copper ore from Cyprus, tin from Anatolia, linen from Egypt and iron from Tarshish. Among the articles for export, mention is made of household furnishings of ivory-inlaid cedar, finely chased bronze or silver bowls, sandcore glass vessels and purple cloth. Phoenician trade, in any case, was not confined to importing raw materials or exporting finished wares and products; by taking aboard their ships materials from different places, the navigators served as carriers and go-betweens to various areas without necessarily touching ports along the Phoenician coast. This was the case, for example, with the slave traffic, in which slaves were picked up in the West and shipped to Near Eastern markets.

At the same time, around the beginning of the 1st millennium B.C., the Phoenician cities turned their attention and their economic potential to the commercial prospects of the Mediterranean West, where, for that matter, they had already looked in previous centuries, if the mythical land of Tarshish is to be identified as strong circumstantial evidence indicates with Tartessus, a city in southern Spain. Non-Phoenician commercial enterprises in the Near East also took part in the western ventures, at least in the early period, as emerges from several existing inscriptions. The financing of these undertakings, which were extremely costly given the long distances to be covered and the remote countries to be reached, was provided by public shipowners, such as the reigning house itself, or the treasuries of the temples of the powerful priestly caste.

Partners, at least in certain respects, of this westward commercial expansion were the Greeks of Euboea, widely active from the 9th century B.C. in trading up and down the Syro-Palestinian and Cypriot coasts. Interesting in this sense was the mixed settlement of Pithekoussa, the present-day island of Ischia, which represented, as far as is known today, the oldest Euboean and Phoenician colony in Italy, founded around the mid-8th century B.C.

In any case, with the change in commercial prospects, the main aspects of Phoenician trade would also change. In fact, while in the eastern Mediterranean Phoenician commerce had dealt with the great Near Eastern kingdoms or already firmly-established cities, adapting itself to these conditions, in the West it came into contact with local petty kings or princes or with ethnic communities of a pre-urban tribal sort, lacking a national conscience and with limited territorial control, except perhaps for the kingdom of Tartessus in the far west Mediterranean. Thus, while in the Near East inevitably the Phoenicians quickly became integrated into the different countries, setting up districts of their own, exclusively

Seal with
inscription
in Aramaic
7th century B.C.
agate
2.7 × 1.4 cm
Paris
Bibliothèque
Nationale

commercial in character (this occurred at Memphis and then Naucratis in Egypt, or Corinth in Greece), in the West they soon settled into enclaves served by a hinterland, however meager, and absorbed indigenous elements. Good examples are Utica and Carthage (its foundation commemorated in a significant legend) in North Africa, the centers of Sulcis and Tharros in Sardinia, the island of Motya in Sicily, and Cadiz, Huelva and Sexi along the southern coast of the Iberian Peninsula.

This territorial expansion, while embryonic and revealing no political aims, expressed the obvious desire of the Phoenicians to function as a permanent conveyor of raw materials for the Eastern market, in partnership with the local populations which, as was the case in Sardinia, held control over the mines and the ores extracted.

Another particularly interesting aspect of Phoenician trade is related by the historian Herodotus. "The Carthaginians also recount this, that there is a region of Lybia and men dwelling there, beyond the Pillars of Hercules. When they reach the place and unload the wares, laying them out neatly on the shore, they climb back on the ship and give a smoke signal. At which the natives, seeing the smoke, come to the sea and then in place of the wares put down gold and withdraw far from the goods. And the Carthaginians going ashore observe and if the gold seems worth the wares, they pick it up and leave; if instead it does not seem worth it, going back aboard they wait again; and the natives, coming forth, put down more gold, till they are satisfied. And they do not wrong each other, for neither touches the gold before the other has equalled the value of the wares, nor do the latter touch the goods before the others have taken the gold" (IV, 196).

From this account what emerges most clearly is an exchange based on mutual trust, which contradicts the rather unflattering, or even downright villainous image of the Phoenician merchants that has generally been handed down by ancient sources. But that is not all. The particular way in which the exchange was carried out, as well as the ore that was used as money, points back to a North African origin, but applies in any case to a general western environment, in the period in which the Greek historian wrote his account.

In conclusion, one can see from this that Phoenician trade was not inspired by territorial conquest (as was the case a little later with the Greeks, the Dorians in particular, compelled by an unexpected population increase). The search for raw materials to produce the wares in particular demand in the Near East and central Mediterranean area represents the driving force behind Phoenician sea trade. Over the following centuries, the embryonic trading stations or settlements were built up into great urban centres that grew also thanks to the inevitable demographic increase of the local populations. These, in turn, especially in the case of Carthage, themselves became conveyors and purveyors of goods, replacing the Phoenician cities on the Lebanese coast which were temporarily under pressure from the renascent Mesopotamian empires. With its rising fortunes in the making during the 7th century B.C., and prevailing in the following century over the western markets, Carthage changed its policy which, once commercial, now became territorial. Eloquent proof of this are the great military campaigns which, starting in the mid-6th century B.C., invested Sicily and Sardinia, and the treaties with Rome. So for the North African metropolis, whose political goal was total hegemony over the former Phoenician cities of the West and the surrounding territories, the search for raw materials was no longer the primary concern. This Carthaginian tendency can be seen clearly in the fact that a policy of widespread exploitation of agricultural resources now prevailed, together with an increasingly bitter conflict with coastal towns.

As far as industrial activities are concerned, mention has already been made of the Phoenicians' special skills in craftsmanship. There was a constant need to seek out new overseas markets in order to supply the workshops back home with the raw materials required for production. Particularly interesting in the area of craftsmanship was the ivory work used for ciboria, amulets and, in particular, decorations of high artistic quality for inlaying wooden chairs, beds or cabinets, and articles for export to the Near Eastern courts. There was also intaglio carving of precious or semi-precious stones, such as lapis lazuli and cornelian, for making pendants or signets, the latter particularly important for seals on official documents or sailing papers.

The production of purple dye was of the greatest historical, as well as economic importance (the colour of the dye — *phoinix* — gave the Phoenicians their name). The substance was indelible and for this reason particularly prized, and used in the dyeing of linen or woollen goods woven locally or imported from Egypt. Making the pigment needed for impregnating the cloth involved the harvesting of a special kind of univalve mollusc which abounded in the shallow waters along the coasts of the Mediterranean basin, molluscs of the *Murex* genus and, more specifically, of the *Brandaris*, *Erinaceus* and *Turnculus* species, as well as some examples of the *Purpura* genus, which was however much less widespread.

The final product was obtained as follows: the molluscs were gathered, probably with traps baited with pieces of fish, then emptied into large pools located on the outskirts of the town. The molluscs were left to stand for a short period, during which the shells were broken. Later, after the calcareous residue of the shells had been extracted, sea water was added to dilute the pigment that had been obtained by soaking the molluscs, in a quantity depending on the shade of color desired, which

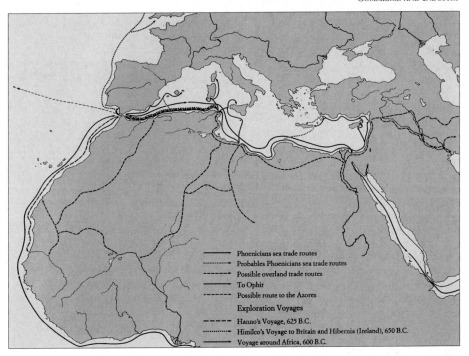

Phoenicians sea trade routes
Probables Phoenicians sea trade routes
Possible overland trade routes
To Ophir
Possible route to the Azores

Exploration Voyages

Hanno's Voyage, 625 B.C.
Himilco's Voyage to Britain and Hibernia (Ireland), 650 B.C.
Voyage around Africa, 600 B.C.

The main Phoenician trading routes

ranged from dark red to violet. Remains of this industrial activity are still to be found in the huge piles of broken shells situated outside the ancient urban centers, because of the bad odour emitted during the early stages of the manufacturing process.

Another typical industrial activity of the Phoenician world was glass, though they did not so much invent it as spread it abroad. Discovered in ancient Egypt and produced in considerable quantities around the middle of the 2nd millennium, glass was widely manufactured and exported by the Phoenicians. Ignoring the aetiological myth of the Phoenicians inventing glass, advanced by the ancient writers, it is easy to understand why they were able to take over the technique of manufacture and become the primary producer of glass in the Mediterranean. Glass paste was made by fusing together, at high temperatures, sodium and calcium silicates, particularly abundant in the sand of Lebanese beaches. The fact that the raw materials were so easy to find undoubtedly encouraged the growth of this industry and the making of objects such as ampullae and unguent flasks, gaudily colored with metal pigments, which well deserved the label of valuable goods, whose unquestionable worth was further enhanced by the virtues of minimum space occupied and maximum profits earned in shipping by sea.

Along with the manufacture of glass, and offering similar advantages, was the working of precious metals and in particular gold, the scale of which can be seen, as mentioned earlier, in the constant request for gold and silver by Phoenician cities. In this case, the novelty introduced by

97

Phoenician craftsmen consisted in perfecting the techniques and artistic levels already to be found in the Near East. Among them should be mentioned the beating of gold into thin sheets and the consequent gilding of jewellery made out of base metals, bronze in particular, or the large-scale introduction of gold granulation, through the fusion of minute drops of gold in charcoal which were then applied with special solders. In addition mention must certainly be made of the embossing of silver- or bronze-plated bowls by hammering the sides into special small moulds of perishable materials such as wood or leather, set on pitch bases.

As for the other nonprecious metals, such as copper, iron and lead, it may be remembered that copper, always alloyed with precious tin, was used to make objects of a practical sort, such as hairpins, razors or tweezers, or of value, including, apart from the above-mentioned bowls, receptacles primarily produced for export, such as jugs, amphorae and incense-burners, mounted out of separately worked parts. Ironwork is mainly documented, directly and indirectly, in a wide range of domestic implements, such as shears, ploughheads, chisels and knives, and of weapons, including, especially in archaic times, lances, javelins and among small arms, daggers

and spearheads. The use of lead, however marginal, is attested by small objects, obviously not for domestic use, like inlaid ciboria and, in the Phoenician towns of southern Sardinia, by thick layers of slag left over from the smelting of silver-bearing lead ore.

The quarrying of stone was closely related to construction activities. It should be noted, first of all, that in general the Phoenicians, at least in the archaic period, always preferred using local stone, while only later were quarries used that were at times very far from the town sites. For example, limestone from Malta and Cagliari, trachyte from Sulcis and Monte Sirai, sandstone from Motya and Tharros. At any rate, the kind of stone preferred by the Carthaginians was most certainly sandstone, by virtue of its relative lightness and the ease with which it could be cut. Limestone and tufa were also widely used, at least for private building, but basalt, granite and trachyte are less frequently found, used primarily for foundations and fortifications.

Sandstone, mined from quarries widely spread and still visible along the shores of the Mediterranean, was sawed into blocks and carried to the building sites, mostly by boat. Particularly important and impressive are the great sandstone quarries of El Haouaria, at the tip of Cape Bon in Tunisia, which, utilized in Punic and Roman times, were essential to the building of Carthage and centers nearby.

Information regarding woodworking is naturally scantier, but of the greatest interest. There is, to be sure, the question of shipbuilding, pride

Pair of earrings with basket pendants from Carthage 6th century B.C. gold, 4.4 cm Carthage, Musée de Carthage

Necklace with beads and pendants of various kinds from Carthage 7th century B.C. electrum, 22 cm Carthage, Musée de Carthage
• p. 78

Small amphora with a jug on right from Carthage 7th and 3rd centuries B.C. clay, 8 cm, 9 cm Tunis Musée du Bardo

Askos in the form of a dolphin from Carthage 4th-3rd century B.C., terra-cotta 10.5 cm, Tunis Musée du Bardo • p. 80

and glory of the Phoenician navy, but that will be discussed elsewhere. Regarding the use and processing of wood, highly indicative are the references above to the cedars and firs of Lebanon, so famous in antiquity that their timber was in constant demand by neighbouring countries. There are references both to the exporting of logs, mostly towed by ships, and to the sale of finished products, like the ivory inlay-work mentioned above. Furniture was built without nails (also rarely used in shipbuilding) using only dovetailing and not always with the addition of bronze cotters; doors, if any, were hung on bone hinges.

Pottery is one of the most important areas of Phoenician craftsmanship because of the sheer quantity produced; these were articles of everyday use, widespread and inexpensive. There is no material evidence of a commercial exchange of pottery between the various centers, but it may be assumed that at least in the early periods of the oldest settlements, imported vessels were used. For the rest, there is practically no documentation regarding the commercialization of these wares, which were usually manufactured by individual towns exclusively for local use, so that every production site can be identified by its potter's clay, and the color and shapes of its ware.

Askos in the form of a ram from Carthage 4th-3rd century B.C., clay, 15 cm Tunis Musée du Bardo • p. 80

Ceramic manufacture was at least to a certain extent closely related to Phoenician trade through the amphorae used for carrying provisions. These large receptacles terminating in a point and for this reason adapted primarily to sea transport, changed shape according to the time or place of production, but their capacity was always between 20 and 25 litres. They were used to carry grain, fish and bits of meat preserved in wine, as is testified by the archaeological finds. Less easy to document is the transport of oil and wine because of the difficulty of hermetically sealing vessels without a neck.

Lastly, there was the fishing industry, practiced on a large scale, espe-

Amphora for
transportation
from Carthage
4th-3rd century B.C.
clay, 18 cm
Tunis
Musée du Bardo
• p. 79

Amphora for
transportation
from Carthage
2nd century B.C.
clay, 110 cm
Carthage
Musée de Carthage
• p. 79

Amphora for
transportation
from Carthage
3rd century B.C.
clay, 56 cm
Carthage
Musée de Carthage

Amphora for
transportation
from Carthage
3rd century B.C.
clay, 132 cm
Carthage
Musée de Carthage

cially the catching of blue fish, like tuna, mackerel and sardines. The catch, mackerel in particular, was used in making a sauce called *garum*, highly valued in antiquity, which consisted of morsels of fish pickled in vinegar. An idea of the importance of these fish can be gathered from the fact that they appeared on the coins of ancient Cadiz.

The Question of the Alphabet
Giovanni Garbini

Pliny the Elder, the learned Roman admiral who died in the eruption of Mount Vesuvius in the year A.D. 79, wrote: "To the Phoenician people is due great honour, for they invented the letters of the alphabet" (*Nat. Hist.*, V, 12). These words show that Pliny shared in an ancient assumption, voiced by Herodotus five hundred years earlier: "These Phoenicians who came to Greece with Cadmus... also introduced among the Greeks... the alphabet, which up to that time, I believe, was unknown to the Greeks" (*History*, V, 58). Not all the people of antiquity were of this opinion, however. In the 1st century Diodorus Siculus quoted the Cretans on the question: "Contrary to those who affirm that the Syrians invented the letters of the alphabet, and that the Phoenicians, having thus learned them, passed them on to the Greeks (these are the Phoenicians who sailed toward Europe with Cadmus, and this is why the Greeks call the letters 'Phoenician'), they [i.e. the Cretans] say that the Phoenicians were not the original inventors, but merely changed the form of the signs" (*Bibliotheca historica*, V, 74, 1).

Urn with inscription in Egyptian hieroglyphs from tomb 16 in the Laurita-Almuñecar necropolis 9th-8th century B.C., alabaster, 47.5 cm Granada, Museo Arqueológico

These quotations prove that while everyone acknowledged the importance of the Phoenicians in the history of the alphabet, opinions differed as to the role they had actually played in the matter: inventors and propagators of the alphabet to some, to others the Phoenicians were mere conveyors to the Greeks of someone else's (the "Syrians'") invention. To the Cretans, they represented something more, having contributed to the final shaping of the alphabet they brought to Greece.

Modern studies have in a sense confirmed the three contradictory theses propounded by ancient writers, and have added a fourth: that the Phoenicians had nothing to do with either the invention or the propagation of the alphabet. This state of affairs is paradoxical only in appearance, for it rests on a terminological ambiguity: who exactly are the "Phoenicians" and the "Syrians," both to us and their contemporaries? For those who, like Pliny and Herodotus, believed that only one phase of the alphabet preceded its introduction to Greece, the alphabet could only be "Phoenician", as Greek tradition held (the letters of the alphabet were called "Phoenician"), but Herodotus considers even the inhabitants of the coastal towns of Palestine "Phoenicians" (I, 105).

Those who differentiated between "Phoenicians" and "Syrians" concerning the origins of the alphabet probably gave the former term a narrower meaning, not unlike the one accepted among modern researchers — that is, they

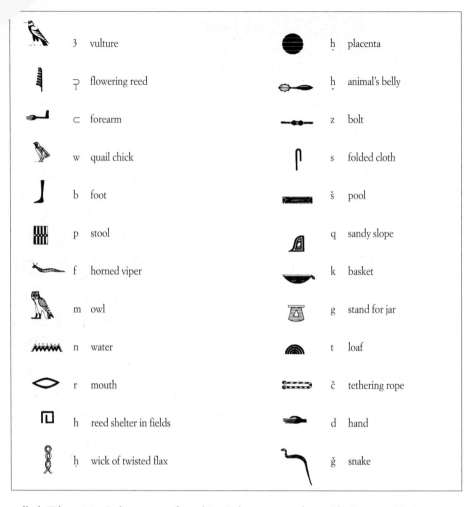

	3	vulture		ḥ	placenta
	ꜣ	flowering reed		ẖ	animal's belly
	c	forearm		z	bolt
	w	quail chick		s	folded cloth
	b	foot		š	pool
	p	stool		q	sandy slope
	f	horned viper		k	basket
	m	owl		g	stand for jar
	n	water		t	loaf
	r	mouth		č	tethering rope
	h	reed shelter in fields		d	hand
	ḥ	wick of twisted flax		ǧ	snake

The Egyptian alphabet is based on originally pictographic symbols referring to one-consonant words used as phonetic values

called "Phoenician" the towns of modern Lebanon, together with Acco, while the towns further south were referred to as "Syrian" (in the passage mentioned above Herodotus speaks of "Syrian Palestine"). If this is really so, modern research has confirmed both a distinction of roles between "Syrians" and "Phoenicians" and the further specification added by the Cretans, who were obviously well informed on the subject. In the final analysis, a too limiting identification of the Phoenicians in time and space (such as the one currently prevailing) leads to the conclusion that the alphabet was not really invented by them, they merely altered the form of a few signs and perhaps did not even introduce the alphabet to the Greeks. But now the time has come to tell this strange tale from the beginning.

Around 1700 B.C. the great civilizations which already flourished in the Mediterranean, or gravitated toward that area, used three main types of script. Egypt had a system which used several hundred pictographic signs (men and women in different attitudes, animals, plants, various objects),

right
*Foundation
inscription
at the temple of
Eshmun at Sidon
5th century B.C.
stone, 82 × 62 cm
Paris, Musée du
Louvre*

under
*Pseudo-hieroglyphic inscription
from Byblos, 1st half of the
2nd millennium B.C.
This inscription includes 52
different symbols of a total 202.
The pseudo-hieroglyphic writing
has not yet been decyphered but
it is certain that it has a syllabic
nature. Presently 120
different symbols are known.*

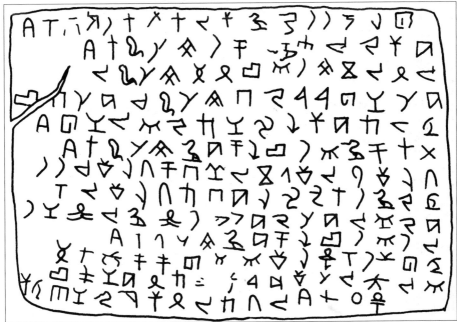

some with ideographic value only (like our numerical figures and road signs), others with both ideographic and phonetic value, but limited to consonants only (between one and three). This is how it was done: "lion" in Egyptian was roughly *arwe*; the sign which depicted a crouching lion could mean either the word "lion" or the consonant grouping *rw* in any other context. This Egyptian script was used largely for monuments (such as obelisks), therefore it was called "hieroglyphic" (i.e. sacred writing), while a cursive form used on papyrus was called "hieratic" (i.e. sacerdotal). In Mesopotamia a system was used which was structurally analogous to the Egyptian one (derived from the one invented through a lengthy process on the banks of the Two Rivers). The main difference was that the signs, which initially had been pictorial in Mesopotamia as well, had become simplified into combinations of short, wedge-shaped lines (the word "cuneiform" derives from the Latin *cuneus*, wedge) with no relation to the original form. This change was due to the need to write with a stylus on unfired clay. As

103

far as phonetic values are concerned, the Mesopotamian signs indicated syllables (and not only consonants as did those of the Egyptians) since the cuneiform script had been invented by the Sumerians, whose language had vowels and consonants of equal value. The cuneiform script also had several hundred signs.

Lastly, in Crete a mainly phonetic script was invented in which single signs had a syllabic value of the *ba, bi, do, ke*, etc. type. This is the so-called "Linear A" which consists of some hundred signs and has not been completely deciphered to date.

The Syria-Palestine region, to which Phoenicia belonged, is left out of the overall picture. Geographically placed between Mesopotamia and Egypt, this area has always been exposed to cultural and political influences from its two great neighbors. It is not surprising, then, that documents written in Egyptian and cuneiform script exist in this land dating from as early as the 3rd millennium B.C. In the first centuries of the 2nd millennium B.C., however, Syria-Palestine showed signs of wanting her own graphic system, following the emergence of politically important regional states. Although Babylonian continued to be the language (and script) used for cultural purposes and international relations, a need was felt for a certain degree of autonomy in the matter of writing as well, especially since the Egyptian and Babylonian systems were exceedingly complex and difficult to master. Political and linguistic fragmentation, however, rendered the creation of a "Syrian" script impossible, so various attempts were made, at different times and in different places, to invent autonomous simplified scripts. Evidence of these efforts does exist, but in documents that are so brief and sporadic that no evaluation is possible. There is, however, one notable exception.

At an indeterminate time, which some believe was in the 3rd millennium B.C., but for various reasons can be more properly set in the first centuries of the 2nd millennium B.C., a new type of script, documented by a dozen monumental inscriptions in stone and bronze, was invented in Byblos (which perhaps we could say was already Phoenician). It uses about a hundred signs, which suggests a graphic syllabic system analogous to the one used in Crete. The form of the signs varies; some are inspired directly by the Egyptian hieroglyphs (hence the name "pseudo-hieroglyphic" for the Byblos script), others have fairly simple forms. In spite of various attempts at decipherment (one of the most recent by the American G.E. Mendenhall) this script remains mysterious. Were it not for the fact that it gives various hints in a negative sense which are very useful for the reconstruction of the early history of the alphabet, this script would represent a simple, self-contained chapter in the prehistory of the subject.

The "pseudo-hieroglyphic" script of Byblos tells us first of all that the oldest Phoenician script (invented in the city which in the 2nd millennium B.C. boasted the finest cultural tradition of the Mediterranean coastal towns) was not alphabetic in type and was influenced more by the Cretan than by the Egyptian script, despite the close relationship that had existed between

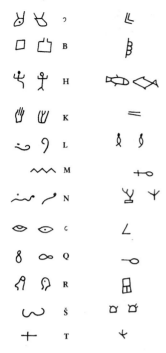

left
Symbols (with graphic variations) the phonetic value of which has been ascertained
right
Symbols with uncertain or unknown value

Byblos and Egypt ever since prehistoric times. It is also worth recalling that "pseudo-hieroglyphs" were used until the 13th century B.C., i.e. until the establishment of the Phoenician alphabet; significant evidence is provided by a bronze spatula, found in Byblos, whose faces bear two inscriptions, one in Phoenician and the other in "pseudo-hieroglyphic". Lastly it must be remembered that this ancient Gublite script evolved to a certain extent towards linear writing and that one of the objects which bear this more advanced kind of writing was found in Palestine, in a Megiddo tomb, also of the 13th century B.C. (a gold ring with an inscription falsely held to be "proto-Canaanite"). While "pseudo-hieroglyphics" were being invented and used in Byblos, in Palestine, which was under direct Egyptian rule, an attempt was made to create a new script, directly inspired by the Egyptian model, but much simpler. The scanty material (a stone slab from Shechem, a shard from Gezer and a sword from Lachish), datable between 1700 and 1550 B.C., which bears this script does not allow a proper evaluation of the writing itself or its relationship to the one we are about to discuss.

A relationship does exist, but whether it is one of affinity or identity we do not know. It is in fact certain that there is continuity between this Palestinian script of the Middle Bronze Age and the one which appeared in the Sinai region in the 15th century B.C. The latter is known to us from some forty inscriptions engraved on votive statuettes, stelae and rockfaces, found near a turquoise mine and a temple in the Serabit el-Khadim area. The mine had been worked for centuries by Egyptians, who had left behind numerous inscriptions, and the temple was dedicated to the Egyptian goddess Hathor; the "proto-Sinaitic" inscriptions (as they have been called) were written by Semitic speakers. Since they were literate and able to compose official dedications they were clearly not simple miners.

Although not all the signs have yet been firmly identified, the known ones have made it possible to read words written in a language similar to Phoenician; that the reading is correct is confirmed by a resemblance to the contents of the Egyptian inscriptions. These are dedications to the goddess Hathor, called in Semitic "Lady" (*bʻlt*) by "the head miners" (*rb nqbn*), who sometimes refer to themselves as "beloved of the Lady" (*mʼhbʻlt*). It is pointless to reiterate that this script could not have been invented in the desolate wastes of mountainous Sinai; its origins must lie in a Palestinian city where culture, nurtured by Egyptian influences, enjoyed a lively expansion. Since this is the most ancient of alphabetic scripts, let us see what led to it. We have already said that the Egyptian script presents phonetic signs whose value is exclusively consonantal and which correspond to the word indicated by the sign itself: from arwe, "lion", derives the phonetic sign *rw*;

from *ad*, "hand", a *d* sign; from '*ay*, "sparrowhawk", the '*aleph* sign (');
from *bo*, "foot, to walk", comes *b* and so on. By assembling 25 monoconsonantal signs one arrives at a complete alphabet, which the Egyptians
already possessed. It could then be argued that the true inventors of the
alphabet were the Egyptians, except for a small detail: in reality the
Egyptians had an alphabet but they never used it. To them writing was
linked to an ideology other than that of mere practicality and simplicity —
which to us are the first prerequisites of a graphic system. That the
Egyptians had very good reasons for not using their "alphabet" is proved
today by those very efficient people, the Japanese, who in spite of their
knowledge of the alphabet prefer to use their own syllabic script and the
thousands of Chinese ideograms. Let us now see the reasoning behind the
invention of the Semitic alphabet.

The Egyptian "alphabet" was the point of departure; some Canaanite
scholar, endowed with a "secular", pragmatic perception of the potential of
writing, understood how revolutionary it would be to use single monoconsonantal signs, eliminating all ideographic traces and the useless labour of
writing a phonetic biconsonantal accompanied by its two monoconsonan-
tals, as often occurred. However, he was unable, or unwilling to reach ultimate abstraction by employing any single graphic sign as mere visual support for a sound. At least in principle, the inventor of the Semitic alphabet
did not want to discard the Egyptian relationship between the phonetic

Egyptian		Semitic			*From the Egyptian to the Semitic*
	k³		ᵓ(alp)	ox	
	pr		b(ayt)	house	
	Ḥᶜᵓi		h(alal)	to rejoice	
	n		m(aym)	water	
	ǧ		n(ahaš)	snake	
	ᵓir.t		ᶜ(ayn)	eye	
	tp		r(aᵓš)	head	

Alphabet table from Ugarit 14th century B.C. A small terracotta tablet bears the alphabet used in the Syrian city of Ugarit. More evolved than the Phoenician alphabet the successive order of the symbols similar to our own, is as follows: (read from left to right)

*'A B G H D H
W Z H̱ Ṭ Y K Š
L M Ẕ N Z S 'P
Ṣ Q R Ṯ Ġ T 'I
'U Š*

value of a sign and the object depicted, more or less schematically, by that same sign.

The ideal would have been to find as many monoconsonantal Semitic words as the monoconsonantal signs in the Semitic alphabet, but since Semitic has very few monoconsonantal words, the difficulty was avoided by using only the first consonant of longer words (the acrostic principle). In Egyptian a quadrilateral indicated a house and had the phonetic value *pr*; in Semitic, "house" was *bet*, therefore the quadrilateral sign was adopted to express the corresponding Semitic word, but only in relation to the first consonant, i.e. *b*. Another example: in Egyptian a wavy line represented "water", *nu* and had a phonetic value *n*; in Semitic "water" is *mem* (*maym*); at this point the wavy line adopts the value *m*. This procedure was applied to all the consonants; as far as possible, Egyptian signs with the new Semitic phonetic value were used and examples were drawn — this is worthy of note — from the whole Egyptian graphic system rather than from the Egyptian "alphabet".

Thus was born the first Semitic alphabet — the one we know from the proto-Sinaitic inscriptions — but this Semitic translation of Egyptian signs could only have taken place in a Semitic region dominated by Egyptian culture such as Palestine. One wonders why this simple but brilliant idea of creating a Semitic alphabet did not occur to the scholars of Byblos... unless the choice of a Cretan model was dictated by a conscious rejection of Egypt for political reasons.

On the basis of our present knowledge we must therefore recognize the correctness of the tradition of the ancient peoples who (from Acco onwards) refused to ascribe the creation of the alphabet to the Phoenicians. This achievement was attributed instead to the Syrians (of Palestine), whom today we prefer to call Canaanites, excluding the Phoenicians (although they in fact referred to themselves as Canaanites). It must however be added that this is only the beginning of the history of the alphabet and that very few proto-Sinaitic signs were called "Phoenician letters" by the Greeks.

The fate of the first Semitic alphabet, invented in Palestine and documented in an area as unlikely as the Sinai mining region, at present remains shrouded in mystery. It certainly disappeared as such, and was replaced later by a similar system which cannot, however, be considered a simple graphic evolution of the proto-Sinaitic script as some scholars would have it.

The Syrian town of Ugarit overlooked the Mediterranean. During the period of intense international exchanges in the 15th-13th centuries B.C., Ugarit was involved in a number of political events and struggles for supremacy amongst the then major powers — Egyptians, Hittites, Babylonians, Mittannians. The *lingua franca* in the city was Babylonian, but since different peoples with their own linguistic and graphic traditions settled there during the 14th century, Ugarit sought to create a graphic system to express its own language, which was similar to Phoenician. The news of the discovery of the easy alphabetical script had of course reached Ugarit. It seemed a good idea to adopt it, but since the local scribes were accustomed to, and equipped for, Babylonian script (wedge shapes impressed with a stylus on unfired clay), use of the same writing means had to continue.

The alphabet was acceptable, but not the signs, often curvilinear and suited to papyrus. They needed to be replaced by others with very simple cuneiform shapes. This resulted in the formal abstraction in which graphic signs are completely disconnected from their phonetic value. The Ugaritic cuneiform characters, rightly called "alphabetic", are a transposition of the alphabet into cuneiform script — a writing created specially to receive the new graphic structure. This was an *ex nihilo* invention which occasionally glanced at the Phoenician alphabet, copying the shape of a few signs. We have said Phoenician, not Palestinian or proto-Sinaitic alphabet, because the one adopted in Ugarit had a sign, the *samek* (*s*), which is found in the Phoenician but not in the proto-Sinaitic script. The Phoenician alphabet known in Ugarit differed from the one known to us; it had several extra signs because it reflected a language with more consonants than the Phoenician, as was the case with Ugaritic. Owing to the lack of documentation, we know nothing of what happened between the creation of the first alphabet in Palestine and the time when a Phoenician model reached Ugarit (a span of time that can reasonably be estimated as two centuries or a little less).

From the Ugaritic data we can however deduce that the Palestinian alphabet probably also made up of about thirty signs, was adopted by a Phoenician city where the form of the signs was partially modified. The most decidedly pictographic forms (the ox's head, the human head, the fish, the man with raised arms, the snake) were abolished and replaced with more schematic ones. The new alphabet met with remarkable success, for by the 14th century B.C. it had already reached not only Ugarit but Palestine as well, where it replaced the preceding proto-Sinaitic alphabet, as is shown by a Lachish cup datable to that century.

Inevitably one wonders where this change occurred. It seems natural to relate it to the statements of the Cretans recorded by Diodorus tally with

Phoenician inscription on a stele found at Nora 9th-8th century B C. sandstone 105 × 57 cm Cagliari, Museo Archeologico Nazionale

	Proto-Sinaitic	Ugaritic 14th century B.C.	Canaanite or Palestinian 13th century B.C.	Phoenician 13-11th century B.C.	Phoenician inscription (Ahiram of Byblos)	Phoenician inscriptions 10th century B.C. (Yehimilk of Byblos)
ɔ						
B						
G						
D						
H						
W						
Z						
Ḥ						
Ṭ						
Y						
K						
L						
M						
N						
S						
ʿ						
P						
Ṣ						
Q						
R						
Š						
T						

Comparison of the most ancient alphabets. The empty spaces correspond to a lack of evidence

the Cretan tradition according to which the signs were altered by the Phoenicians. It is harder to single out a particular site: on the one hand Byblos seems a likely candidate, on the other there is the fact that Byblos is excluded from the documentation. In fact at the time Byblos was using its own "pseudohieroglyphic" script and the most ancient inscriptions found there, the very oldest Phoenician inscriptions in the strict sense, show a "reduced" alphabet. In fact a curious phenomenon occurred during the 13th century: while the Ugaritic cuneiform alphabetical script began to

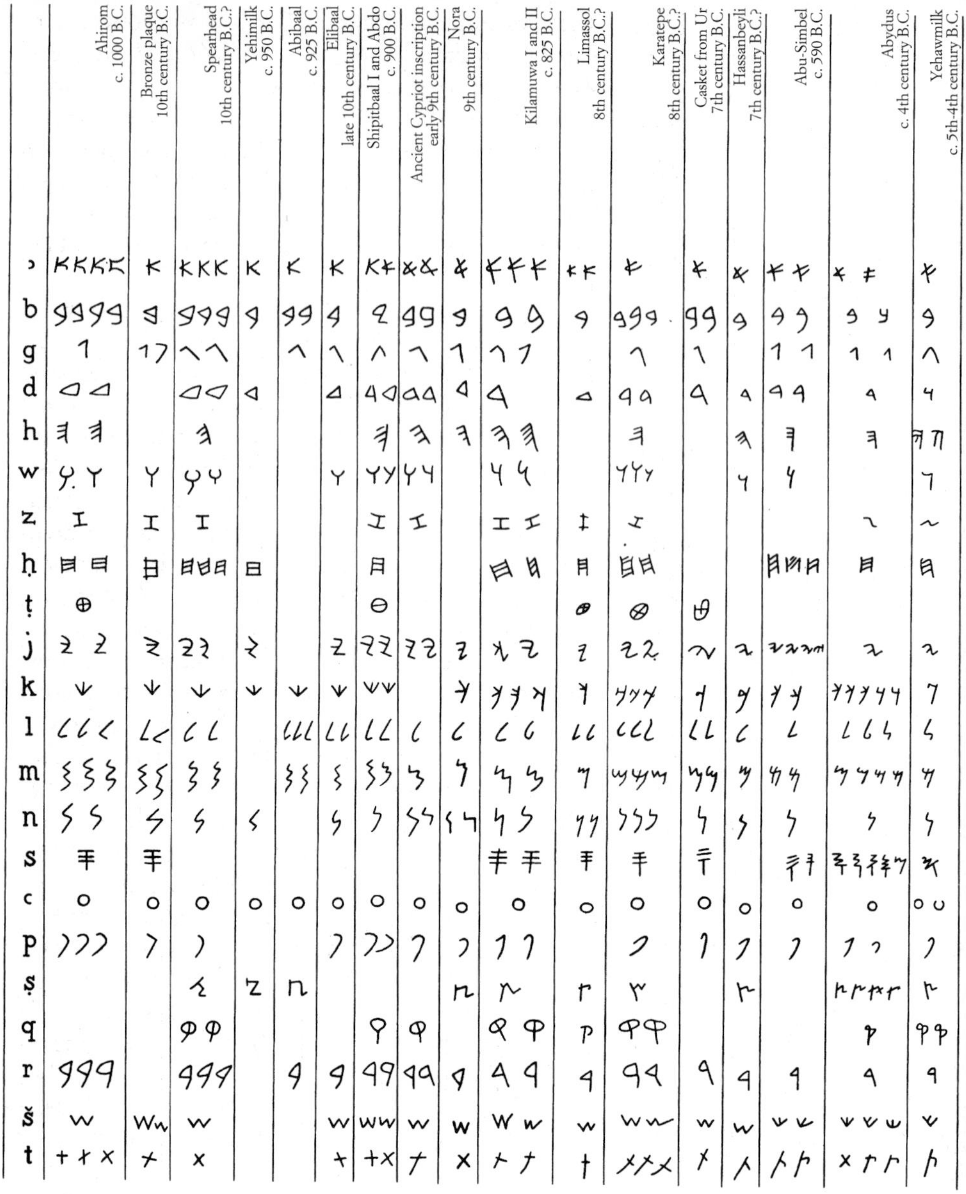
Ahirom c. 1000 B.C.
Bronze plaque 10th century B.C.
Spearhead 10th century B.C.?
Yehimilk c. 950 B.C.
Abibaal c. 925 B.C.
Elibaal late 10th century B.C.
Shipitbaal I and Abdo c. 900 B.C.
Ancient Cypriot inscription early 9th century B.C.
Nora 9th century B.C.
Kilamuwa I and II c. 825 B.C.
Limassol 8th century B.C.?
Karatepe 8th century B.C.?
Casket from Ur 7th century B.C.
Hassanbeyli 7th century B.C.?
Abu-Simbel c. 590 B.C.
Abydus c. 4th century B.C.
Yehawmilk c. 5th-4th century B.C.
ʾ
b
g
d
h
w
z
ḥ
ṭ
j
k
l
m
n
s
ʿ
p
ṣ
q
r
š
t

The Phoenician writing from the 11th to the 4th centuries B.C.

Shipitbaal III 4th century B.C.	Batnoam late 4th century B.C.	Inscriptions on *ostraka* from Elephantine 5th-4th century B.C.

spread from the Syrian town through Syria, Phoenicia and Palestine, in this diaspora and in Ugarit itself the script showed a decrease in the number of signs — the consequence of a phonetic evolution of north-western Semitic which obviously affected the whole area. Thus the 13th century B.C. saw the birth of a reduced alphabet (22 signs) familiar to us from the Phoenician alphabet, but cuneiform in shape: Phoenicia continues to be oddly absent.

It seems strange that the Phoenician alphabet should be absent, or appear late in the very place where it was, if not invented, at least elaborated, but there are two explanations for this. First of all one must bear in mind that the Phoenician towns (with the exception of Byblos — an unfortunate exception considering the absurd way the excavation was carried out) have yet to be explored archaeologically, since they are buried under modern cities. The whole of Lebanon is as yet relatively unknown on the archaeological level. Secondly, one cannot ignore the decidedly biased attitude shown by epigraphists in dating the most ancient documents of Phoenician script: these are invariably assigned to a more recent period than analogous objects of Palestinian origin. The brief texts inscribed on arrowheads are a typical example: all the Lebanese inscriptions are considered more recent than the Palestinian ones. Even more significant is the dating of an inscription on the sarcophagus of Ahiram, king of Byblos, discovered in the twenties and ascribed to the 13th century B.C. Twenty years later, for reasons that are now not worth recalling, the date was moved forward to the beginning of the 10th century B.C. Although arguments of various kinds support the earlier dating, most scholars still incline to the more recent date. When Byblos inscriptions were found which were graphically more archaic than the Ahiram inscription, and therefore datable to the 11th century B.C., these were unhesitatingly called non-Phoenician, i.e. "Canaanite." It is therefore clear that the stated lack of Phoenician documents relating to the 14th and 13th centuries B.C. could be the result of a simple error in dating on the part of the scholars.

In conclusion, our present knowledge of the origin of the alphabet could be summed up as follows: using the Egyptian monoconsonantal signs as a point of departure, a Semitic alphabetic graphic system was created in Palestine which made abundant use of Egyptian signs but with phonetic values taken from Semitic. Probably after a few false starts, by 1500 B.C. it was totally operative. In one of the Phoenician cities (Byblos seems to be

The evolution of Phoenician writing, showing letter forms across sites and periods:

	Sidon 4th-3rd century B.C. Tabnith Eshmunazar	Sidon 4th-3rd century B.C. variations	Masub 222 B.C.	Umm-el-Awamid 2nd century B.C.	Tyre 2nd century B.C.	Malta 2nd century B.C.	Cyprus 4th-2nd century B.C.	Greece 4th-1st century B.C.	Delos 1st century A.D.?	Byblos Roman period 1st century A.D.?	Medallion 7th century B.C.?	Ben Isa (Malta) 3rd-2nd century B.C.?	Gozo (Malta) 3rd-2nd century B.C.?	Sardinia 3rd-2nd century B.C.	Marseille 3rd-2nd century B.C.	Carthage
ʾ																
b																
g																
d																
h																
w																
z																
ḥ																
ṭ																
j																
k																
l																
m																
n																
s																
ʿ																
p																
ṣ																
q																
r																
š																
t																

The evolution of Phoenician writing
from the 4th century B.C. to the 2nd century A.D.

Magic Tablet 2nd century B.C.?	Ibiza 2nd-1st century B.C.	Massinissa 140 B.C.	Dougga 1st century B.C.?	Constantine 1st century B.C.?	Bithia (Sardinia) c. 170-180 A.D.		Leptis around the birth of Christ	Hadrumetum 2nd-1st century B.C.	Variations 2nd-1st century B.C. 1st-2nd century A.D.

excluded) some of the signs of this Palestinian alphabet underwent a slight change in form; the revised form is documented directly in Palestine and indirectly in Ugarit in the 14th century B.C.

Pared down to 22 signs, this alphabet continues to appear in Palestine between the 13th and 11th centuries (writers on the documentation of this

Ivory plaquette with inscription in Aramaic mentioning Hazael king of Damascus found at Arslan Tash 9th century B.C. Paris, Musée du Louvre
• *p. 145*

period prefer to speak of "Canaanite" rather than "Phoenician" script). Concerning Phoenicia, we find a range of dating and opinions, according to the position adopted by the specialists: those who believe in a continuity between proto-Sinaitic and the alphabet imitated at Ugarit consider the Lebanese inscriptions before Ahiram (dated around 1000 B.C.) to be "Canaanite", and those who assign Ahiram to the 13th century believe that the Palestinian writings dated between the 13th and the 11th (or perhaps l0th) centuries B.C. are a phenomenon of provincial backwardness. These two positions agree however on one point: with the Ahiram inscription, the Phoenician script appears slightly different from the preceding one. The first group of scholars see it as the birth of the true "Phoenician" alphabet, around the year 1000 B.C., while the second group consider it a reform (made around 1300 B.C.) of a Phoenician alphabet which was itself a re-elaboration of the proto-Sinaitic Palestinian script.

Whether we call it Canaanite or Phoenician (the old conflict between Syrians and Phoenicians again...), the shortened alphabet is the one that was transmitted to the Greeks and later introduced by them in Italy. But who transmitted it? Perhaps the fact that some of the upholders of a Palestinian origin for the "Canaanite" alphabet date the Greek alphabet back to the 11th century B.C., is no mere chance; and if we date Ahiram to 1000 B.C., then the mythical Cadmus would have been a Canaanite, not a Phoenician. This extremely early date for the transition of the alphabet to Greece does not however meet with wide agreement. Most researchers lean toward a date around the 9th century B.C.; this would guarantee a genuinely Phoenician matrix, validating the opinion of the ancients.

However, a document published only a few years ago may bring about some revisions. A Palestinian *ostrakon*, datable between the 11th and 10th centuries B.C. (even though the editor, without justification, claims an earlier date) shows a script of the "Canaanite" type with a few signs which in form and position are strikingly similar to the Greek ones. Since the southern provenance of the document (Qubur el-Walaydah) reveals its Philistine origin, we may have to get used to the idea that the Phoenicians who took their script to Greece were in fact Phoenician-speaking Philistines — either Phoenicians or Syrians.

*Fragment
of Phoenician
inscription
scratched into a
red slip jug
found at Kition
clay, diam. 25 cm
9th century B.C.
Nicosia, Cyprus
Museum
• p. 145*

Having assumed its classical form at the time of Ahiram, the Phoenician script evolved slightly in the form of its signs — a decidedly slow evolution compared with that of the other scripts derived from it, such as Aramaic and Greek. At first Phoenician signs were, at least in tendency, all of equal height (a few seem slightly shorter); at some point, however, part of the documentation (extremely exiguous regarding Phoenicia itself) shows a lengthening in the vertical lines. Since this phenomenon occurred in areas like northern Palestine and Kition, on the island of Cyprus, which were politically or culturally dependent on Tyre, it is probably safe to assume that it was from this city, predominant in the 1st millennium B.C., that the new script, born toward the 9th century B.C., spread. Over time, this writing became a very elegant script with long, slightly slanting vertical lines, minuscule loops and flat letters.

This was the script that gradually took hold in the whole of the Phoenico-Punic world, emphasizing the dominant role played by Tyre. An entire papyrus and several *ostraka*, discovered in Saqqarah and Elephantine in Egypt, acquaint us with the cursive script that was being used towards the 6th-4th centuries B.C. This script does not differ greatly from the monumental one, at least in the form of the signs, but a cursive *ductus* could not fail to bring about fairly substantial changes in the long run. Apart from the inevitable transformations in the later part of the documentation, the most noticeable change in the Phoenician script was the monumentalization of the cursive, which made way for a new script called "Neo-Punic". This happened in the colonial world only, and following a period of transition the new script took permanent roots after the destruction of Carthage in 146 B.C. In the Punic town of Bithia, in Sardinia, a script derived from the Punic, rather than from the Neo-Punic, was still in use in the 2nd and 3rd centuries A.D., but this is an isolated instance.

Having discussed the invention of the Phoenician alphabet and the evolution of its signs, we should turn our attention to the nature of this alphabet. As has already been mentioned, in the Phoenician alphabet only con-

Table of Punic and Greek writing

	Phoenician					Greek (8th century B.C.)			
	Shipitbaal inscription (c. 925-900 B.C.)	Mesha inscription (c. 830 B.C.)	Kition inscription (c. 850-800 B.C.)	Karatepe inscriptions (8th century B.C.)	Cyprus bronze bowl (c. 730 B.C.)	Cretan (Herpetidamos)	Attic (Dipylon oinochoe)	Euboean (Pithekoussa, Lefkandi)	
ꜣAlep									Alpha
Bēt									Beta
Gimel									Gamma
Dalet									Delta
Ḥē'									Epsilon
Wāw									Diagramma
									Upsilon
Zayn									Zeta
Ḥēt									(H)eta
Ṭēt									Theta
Yēd									Iota
Kapp									Kappa
Lamed									Lambda
Mēm									Mu
Nūn									Nu
Samek									Xi
'Ayin									Omicron
Pē									Pi
Ṣadē									San
Qop									Qoppa
Resh									Rho
Šin									Sigma
Tau									Tau
									Phi
									Chi

Table of Punic and Greek writing

sonants were expressed. There were no signs for vowels, although these were part of the Phoenician language. The systematic introduction of vowels was an important contribution made by the Greeks. For their vowels the Greeks chose the signs used for Phoenician consonants which they themselves did not possess, or did not think it necessary to express. Thus the consonant *'aleph*, a laryngeal sound pronounced but not written by the Greeks, was used for the vowel *a*; the sign for the consonant *h* was used for *e*; the pharyngeal *'ayn*, a typically Semitic sound, became the vowel *o* and so on.

Since the Phoenician alphabet did not record vowels (these had to be supplied by the reader, as happens nowadays for short vowels in Arabic, whose script includes only long vowels), a few scholars have wondered whether it is legitimate to call the Phoenician example an alphabet. The answer to this question depends on our definition of the word "alphabet." If a simple and purely phonetic script, i.e. without ideograms, is intended, the answer is positive. But if a script that has signs for each sound, and viceversa, is intended, the answer must be negative, because the Phoenician sign *b* can correspond to four sounds — *b, ba, bi, bu*.

On the strength of this, a number of scholars have argued that Phoenician writing is a syllabic, compendiary script rather than an alphabet; this means

Marble votive cippus with bilingual dedication in Phoenician and Greek to the god Melqarth-Heracles from Malta 2nd century B.C. Paris, Musée du Louvre

that the single signs represent syllables which the reader has to complete each time. This way of writing would be absurd as an expression of our Indo-European languages (one sees why the Greeks immediately emended it) but is suitable for Semitic languages, both because of the structure of their syllables (in which two consecutive consonants are unknown) and because their roots are almost exclusively consonantal. If we were to write *spr* in English, we would not know whether it referred to "spire," "spare," "spore", "sphere," "spar," "spear," "spry," "spur" and perhaps others. *Spr* in Phoenician, however, can only refer to "writing" or at most "counting". It is impossible to speak of the alphabet without alluding to the problem of the name of the single letters (our own word "alphabet" is made up of the names of the first two Greek letters, *alpha* and *beta*). Although the direct Semitic tradition relative to the names of the signs is not anterior to the Greek translation of the biblical Psalms (around the 2nd century B.C.), the names are certainly much older, since they passed to the Greeks together with the signs. The correspondence between the phonetic value of the sign and the first consonant of its name must be considered a mnemonic device (in the Greek alphabet the first letter can be vocalic), so it is highly proba- ble that the names were born together with the signs.

On the other hand the thesis, favoured by some, that the name of the sign always refers to the object originally depicted in the sign ('*aleph* is an "ox," *beth* is a "house," *mem* is "water," *samek* is a "fish," '*ayn* is an "eye," etc.) is more debatable. Undoubtedly it did happen in many cases and it was after all in this way that the Semitic alphabet was created; the fact that sev- eral Semitic names of signs have no meaning and that often there is no rela- tionship between an object and the name of the sign shows the secondary origin, logically if not chronologically, of the names as opposed to the signs. No satisfactory solution has been found so far to the problems posed by names of Greek letters. There is no doubt of their Semitic origin, at least in the case of real names; but in spite of the presence of typically Phoenician vocalic instances (*iôta* with the vowel *o*, *rhô* with the vowel *o*) the -*a* ending of many names is an un-Phoenician characteristic that could be called Aramaic (enter once again the Syrians!).

I would like to end this brief discussion of problems connected with the alphabet by touching on a question that has long remained unexplained, although recently an unexpected and interesting solution may have been found: the order of succession of the signs. The order followed by our own letters (*a, b, c, d, e...*) is extremely ancient: it is directly documented in the 14th century B.C. in a primer found in Ugarit. Why are the signs in this order and not another?

The reasons are certainly not phonetic (phonetically similar sounds such as *t* and *d*, *s* and *z* are placed far apart) or graphic (graphically similar signs such as '*ayn* and *tet*, *gimel* and *lamed*, or *gimel* and *pe* are not close togeth- er); on the other hand it is difficult to believe in a casual grouping, totally devoid of guiding criteria, knowing the mentality of the ancient Near East civilizations. In 1978 Alessandro Bausani, the brilliant orientalist who went

*Phoenician
inscription
on the base of a
bronze statuette
of Astarte
found at
El Carambolo
7th century B.C.
Seville, Museo
Arqueológico
• p. 146*

on to specialize in History of Oriental Astronomy, suggested a new solution: on the basis of a study of lunar stations in Arab, Indian and Iranian astronomy, which have sometimes been related to the signs of the Arab alphabet according to its ancient order (corresponding to the Phoenician one), Bausani came to the conclusion that the Phoenician alphabetical order depicts a sort of calendar where the signs *'aleph, tet, 'ayn* and *taw* represent, in that order, the autumn equinox, the winter solstice, the spring equinox and the summer solstice. All this in an astronomical situation where the full moon of the autumn equinox occurred near the Pleiades, that is, around 2000 or 1600 B.C. The latter date corresponds exactly to what we have said about the beginnings of the alphabet. In its traditional order, the alphabet would then amount to a sort of primitive calendar, however approximate, which was worked out in a region like the Near East where summer, with its attendant drought, was felt to be especially inimical.

The hypothesis of the calendarlike nature of the alphabet as a whole, and in particular the order of the signs which, as Bausani says, "probably symbolized the days of a complete lunation felt to be more benevolent than others," has been significantly confirmed by Syro-Palestinian epigraphic documentation dating from the 1st millennium B.C. Numerous vases and seals, as well as various stands, present more or less complete alphabetical series, which are sometimes preceded by the preposition l, "for". Since these objects are always connected with religious ritual (votive or funerary), the religious character taken on by the alphabet in this context is evident. The presence of the above-mentioned preposition makes it probable that the expression "for *'bgdh*..." (this is the beginning of the Phoenician alphabet) corresponds to the expression *l'lm* "for always" — a well-wishing formula addressed to both the living and the dead. When in the *Apocalypse* God introduces Himself with the words: "I am the Alpha and the Omega," using the first and last letters of the Greek alphabet to signify His eternity, we again meet the ancient Phoenician concept of the alphabet as symbol of cyclic time, and we understand perhaps why the inventor of the alphabet wished to keep that relationship between sound and graphic sign which to us appears entirely superfluous.

Beliefs and Religious Life

Sergio Ribichini

Sources

When in the early 19th century scholars began to study the history of religion and to attribute an important place within it to the religion of the
Phoenicians, it immediately became clear that sources were a major problem. The enthusiasm of archaeologists embarking on successful missions
and excavations in Cyprus, Phoenicia and the whole of North Africa, was
counterbalanced by the scepticism of scholars who regarded with suspicion
the variety of documentation available, which offered a picture of
Phoenician religion that was full of contradictions and gaps. Historians in
the 19th century, in fact, could only rely on a few archaeological findings
and indirect sources, such as the writings of classical authors and of the
Fathers of the Church, or the Old Testament: sources not to be accepted
literally and certainly simplified.

Unfortunately, the situation has only slightly improved as a result of the
extraordinary progress of archaeological exploration, which has proved fundamental for the understanding of certain phenomena, but shows its limitations since we must still rely largely on indirect sources. Useful as the
numerous archaeological findings are, comparison with the texts remains a
fundamental step in order to interpret them correctly and to provide precise
definitions of iconographical or architectural elements that are often used
acritically to describe the character, life story and functions of the divinities.
Although Phoenician epigraphic sources at present amount to a total of
over 6,000 inscriptions, for the most part they provide no information on
religion. Except for a few rare documents, such as the sacrificial tariffs
practiced in Carthage or the list of expenses of some temples, almost all the
documents offer only laconic information on the worship of certain divinities. Primarily, what is lacking are liturgical and mythological texts, which
alone could give us sufficient insight into the gods, the ideology and religious sentiment, and the forms of worship.

In other words, we are still forced to resort to indirect sources, which
always require attentive preliminary criticism. The Bible, for example, frequently provides information on the worship of Tyrian or Sidonian deities,
against which the prophets and priests of Yahweh cast their invectives. But
the writers' perspective must always be kept in mind: that is, as followers
of the religion of Yahweh, they were committed to presenting as idolatrous
all forms of worship except the monotheistic faith, even though these cults
were extremely widespread and considered by many not at all irreconcili-
able with the worship of Yahweh. Thus, deities and rituals presented in the
Hebrew Bible as Phoenician and foreign should in some cases be considered rather as genuine manifestations of the more general religion of the

Votive stele with "sign of Tanit" from Carthage 5th-4th century B.C., sandstone 74.5 × 18.5 cm Carthage, Musée de Carthage

people of Israel. We are provided with relatively abundant information in the writings of several Greek and Latin authors, who mention deities, myths, and rites of the Phoenician religion in a more or less incidental way. Texts that provide us with a great deal of information are the works of Herodotus, Polybius, Diodorus Siculus, Plutarch, Lucian, Strabo, Appian, Josephus, Titus Livy and Silius Italicus. But special importance and value must be granted to Philo of Byblos's *Phoenician History* (1st-2nd century A.D.), which the author claims to have translated into Greek from the original Phoenician written by Sanchoniathon of Berytus, a priest who lived at the time of the Trojan War.

Only some fragments of this work have come down to us, quoted by Bishop Eusebius of Caesarea in the 4th century A.D.; these fragments are one of the most important sources for Phoenician mythology, but they must be used with great prudence. This caution is called for by the very way in which these texts have come down to us, making it difficult to distinguish the genuine Phoenician traditions from the critical interpretation and the literary or apologetic aims of those who transmitted them. The same kind of difficulty appears, for instance, in the references to the Phoenician cosmogony made by the Neo-Platonic philosopher Damascius (5th century A.D.), who mentions Phoenician traditions using a terminology which makes it quite clear that he has made a personal adaptation.

All the classical sources raise this problem of fidelity to Phoenician religious facts. Although these sources must not systematically be considered suspect, it should be kept in mind that, in recording the information, the Greek or Latin author performs a mediation-alteration of the facts, due to his own cultural patterns. A myth which appears to be thoroughly "Phoenician," the founding of Carthage by Queen Dido, must therefore be read bearing in mind that in classical mythology it also served the purpose of emphasizing Carthaginian otherness.

Another example of the difficulties encountered in using classical sources is the impossibility of attributing a specific name to the Phoenician "Poseidon-Neptune," mentioned by so many authors and several inscriptions as being of primary importance in the religion of the Phoenician merchants and sailors. The Greek and Latin interpretation may identify not just one god, but various Phoenician deities similar to the "Lord of the Sea" in classical mythology.

Some further elements can be derived from the study of Syrian epigraphical documents of the 2nd millennium B.C., in particular the inscriptions found at Ugarit, which provide us with very precise and abundant data on the religious beliefs in this area in the period before the formation of the Phoenician states; they also offer elements of comparison for the origin,

121

permanence and development of various cults. But these are merely elements of comparison, not data which come to us directly from the religion in question.

Elements of Phoenician Polytheism

While we know of no Phoenician word to indicate what we call "religion," the term *qodesh* was probably the equivalent of our concept of "sacred," in its widest semantic sense. This term meant both "to consecrate" and "consecrated," "holy" and "sanctuary," and referred to persons involved in the worship, offerings, sacred places and deities. But it is probable that the Phoenicians made no conscious distinction between the religious phenomenon and other aspects of human existence. As in the majority of historic civilizations of the Mediterranean area, in the Phoenician religion the system of beliefs and rites is polytheistic, that is, characterized by the veneration of a plurality of superhuman beings, indissoluble from reality, who represent as a whole (the "pantheon") the totality of man's and society's interests and needs. We therefore find some important deities, around whom the fundamental experiences of reality revolve, and other divine beings who are "minor," in that the society's interest in the aspects expressed through them is minor.

The generic term for a deity is *el* (or *il*), which becomes *elat* in the feminine gender. But this is also the proper name of a god (El), whom we know primarily from the myths of Ugarit as the supreme being, the father of the gods, the guarantor of all institutions. The whole body of deities, that is, the pantheon of each city or of each mythological tradition, is defined by specific expressions, such as "the assembly of the holy gods of Byblos," or "the whole family of divine children," or more simply "the gods." They are considered lords or kings, saints, wielders of power, and they exercise a positive action on man, nature and society; in the inscriptions the faithful declare that they have received benefits, favors and protection from the gods and they qualify themselves as servants or slaves to the gods.

In some cases, for example in the pantheon of Byblos, but also in Sidon and in Carthage itself, we find that certain female deities hold a preeminent position: Astarte, Baalath, Tanit. Anath probably also played an important role, as in the religion of Ugarit, but there is little mention of her in Phoenician inscriptions. These female deities are probably to be connected with fertility, prosperity, love and war; but we cannot establish with certainty, not even on the comparative level, whether there existed a relationship between the role attributed to them and the social position of women at the time these cults developed, for we do not have sufficient data.

For the most part Phoenician goddesses are surrounded by an aura of ambiguity: their morphology is not always clearly defined, nor are the distinctive features between one and the other. Tanit, for example, is easily confused with Astarte, who can easily be mistaken for Anath and Baalath. This may of course simply depend on the limitations imposed by the nature of our

*Statuette of
enthroned deity
from Meniko
6th century B.C.
painted terra-cotta
18.5 cm
Nicosia, Cyprus
Museum*

documentation, but we cannot rule out that it may reflect an actual functional fluidity, which made the morphological features of each goddess interchangeable with those of other female deities.

This fluidity in the definition of the superhuman beings is also to be found in the personal names of the deities used as epithets or common names. We have seen this already in the case of El, but we find it particularly in the case of Baal, which is used quite normally as a generic term meaning "lord" or "master" and applied to various male deities, but is also the personal name of a god and also, accompanied by a variety of specifications and attributes, the designation of autonomous and distinct superhuman personalities. Thus we find Baal Saphon, Baal Malage, Baal of Lebanon, Baal Addir, Baal Marqod, Baal Hammon, the Baal of Tyre and the Baal of Sidon, Baal *mgnm* and others still, each identifying an autonomous deity, distinguished by a reference to a place, city, or a specific aspect of the form of worship.

Characteristic of Phoenician religion is also the attention given to particular places or natural phenomena, considered sacred because of their exceptional position or importance. In the Old Testament there are frequent references to sacred woods, sacrifices on hilltops, mountains, stones and trees as objects of veneration. And this is confirmed in inscriptions and in the classical sources. The Baal of Mount Lebanon, for example, was the recipient of a dedication made by the governor of a Sidonian colony on Cyprus, in a Phoenician text of the 8th century B.C., and in a Greek inscription found on the Janiculum in Rome he is invoked with the name of Hadad.

Similarly, on Mount Tabor, also in Roman times, there was a widespread worship of a mountain Baal identified with Zeus; and Tacitus states that the name Carmel indicated both the mountain and a god, perhaps the very same Baal that Elijah, in the Book of Kings, mocked here on this mount, and whose prophets he killed. The worship of Baal Saphon, which was already widespread in the 2nd millennium B.C., is also documented in Tyre in the 7th century B.C. and in Carthage in the 3rd century B.C. From inscriptions we also know of sanctuaries built near springs or rivers and of woods consecrated to the worship of various deities.

And, lastly, we also find evidence of the worship of these local Baals in the writings of Philo, who confirms the important position held constantly by another Baal, seen as the dominator of the sky and the master of lightning, perhaps the heir of an ancient celestial being of a primitive type. This is Baal Shamaim, the "Lord of the Heavens," considered one of the main gods of Byblos as early as the 10th century B.C. We find him again at Tyre, Cyprus, Carthage and in Sardinia, always in a very exalted hierarchical position. Although infrequently, we do have evidence of the worship of

123

other astral deities, such as the moon-god Yarih and the sun-god Shamash, both extremely popular among the Semitic peoples of the 2nd and 1st millennia B.C.

Alongside deities connected to specific places or elements of the universe, Phoenician polytheism also included divine beings whose sphere of action involved the whole of human activities and the dangers that threatened them. Outstanding among them is the god Reshef, connected to lightning, war and the plague, worshipped primarily in order to ward off the calamities that his wrath might cause. Reshef, mentioned already in the texts of Ebla, Mari, Ugarit, in the Bible and in several Egyptian documents, reappears in Phoenician inscriptions in Sidon, Tyre, Karatepe, Cyprus, Carthage and Spain, with a very complex divine personality.

Another Phoenician god, inherited like Reshef from the Canaanite tradition of the 2nd millennium B.C., is the smith and craftsman god Chusor, for whom we have very little epigraphical documentation, but whom both Philo and Damascius portray as important in the origin of the world and in the history of inventions. There is also very little information concerning Horon, a god of the Syrian tradition, invoked at Ugarit against snake poisonings, and later documented throughout the 1st millennium B.C. always as a benevolent deity. The recurring presence in the Phoenician religion of superhuman beings common to the Semitic religions of the Syro-Palestinian region of the time, or earlier than the Phoenician civilization, must not mislead us in establishing the origins and the distinctive elements of this polytheism. It would, in fact, be a mistake of both judgement and method to believe that the Phoenician religion is a simple evolution or a continuation of the Canaanite cults of the Syrian region, maintaining the millennial worship of deities like El, Baal, Astarte or Reshef. For the mention of the same divine name in documents that are very distant from each other, both in time and place, certainly cannot be accepted as proof that the morphological and functional features of the deity of that name remained unchanged.

This observation, therefore, does not allow us to use our biblical, classical, Ugaritic, etc. documentation indiscriminately in order to reconstruct artificially and outside history the characteristics of the Phoenician deities. On the contrary, it encourages us to keep to the chronological, typological and geographical distinctions provided by the documentation itself, and to suggest an overall vision of Phoenician forms of worship. And, in fact, it is possible to trace, in the case of Iron Age Phoenician polytheism, some elements of autonomous evolution and some innovations that are quite distinct from the developments of the religion of ancient Syria. In particular, it appears that after the political upheavals resulting from the invasion of the "Sea People", each city-state along the Phoenician coast decided to become distinctive from the religious point of view as well, and this was achieved both by creating new forms of worship and by the importance assigned to certain traditional values. A consequence, or at any rate a religious parallel, of the political subdivision of Phoenicia in the 1st millennium B.C. is therefore the new constitution or the reorganization of the local city pantheon. Each city organized its public forms of worship in a totally autonomous way; each also had its own feasts and celebrations, its own traditions, its own deities, in forms which might be common to other towns, but which would not be given the same importance. The most significant example is the rise to a position of supremacy of certain "city" deities, perhaps placed at the summit of the local pantheon as the gods of the various reigning dynasties. These deities embodied almost all powers and functions, and were the result of the evolution of the worship of deified sovereigns in Syrian religion in the Bronze Age.

This tendency towards religious autonomy remained dominant for a long time in Phoenicia, even after the region had been conquered by the Assyrians and the Persians, and still later, after the Hellenization and the Romanization of the Orient, despite all the inducements to syncretism determined by these events. It also spread to Cyprus and the colonies, at the same time as the traditions of the motherland were modified by their contact with other forms of religion.

The City Pantheons
In Byblos, among the first religious institutions in the city already towards the end of the 3rd millennium B.C., we find two sanctuaries. One is dedicated to a deity about whom we have no epigraphical documentation, but who has traditionally been identified as Reshef. It was a large temple, built on the city's acropolis; at the time of the Romans an even larger sanctuary was built on the same site, with a central tripartite nucleus, courtyards and arcades. This temple probably dated from the first quarter of the 2nd millennium B.C. the period when Byblos was ruled by an Amorite dynasty. The other sanctuary, which was older, was consecrated to the worship of a goddess called Baalath, "mistress" and "sovereign" of the city of Byblos, mentioned in Akkadian and Egyptian documents of the 2nd millennium B.C. and still famous in the 2nd century A.D. with the name Aphrodite. From the early 1st millennium B.C. until the 5th century B.C., a series of royal inscriptions are evidence of her supremacy and her role as the protectress of the reigning dynasty.

In the 10th century B.C. King Yehimilk dedicated a sanctuary to her and called upon her, together with Baal Shamaim and all the gods, "to grant long life to himself and his kingdom"; this formula is repeated in inscriptions by his successors Abibaal, Elibaal and Shipitbaal, and even at the time of the Persians, King Yehawmilk declared that he owed his throne to her, and begged her for protection, long life and vengeance against violators.

The Baalath of Byblos was portrayed with all the symbolic attributes of the Egyptian Hathor-Isis, with whom for centuries she was identified; in King Yehawmilk's votive stele she has horns on her head and bears the disc and a crowned uraeus (headdress in the form of the sacred serpent), while Egyptian texts from the Middle Kingdom equate Hathor, "Lady of Byblos," with the Egyptian "Lady of Dendera."

Reflecting the political and cultural influence of Egypt over Phoenicia, in the pantheon of Byblos we find other identifications with Egyptian deities. El, portrayed on Hellenistic coins with two pairs of wings, according to an iconography also familiar to Philo, was considered identical to Ra, the pharaoh's god; Reshef is probably to be identified with the god who in certain texts of the Old Kingdom is given the name Khai-Tau ("He who appears surrounded by flames"), while Baal Shamaim is probably called Seth, the name which the Egyptian account of Wenamon attributes to the main god of Byblos.

Among the gods recorded in the Phoenician inscriptions in the city we must also mention Baal Addir, the "powerful Lord": this name appears in a Phoenician text from the Persian period and later, in some Punic and Neo-Punic inscriptions in North Africa. This is probably a chthonic divinity, and is perhaps the same figure as the African Pluto, invoked in numerous Latin dedications as lord of the underworld and of agricultural fertility.

Our documentation then leads us to the 2nd century A.D., when the treatise *De Syria Dea*, attributed to Lucian, describes an enormous celebration held in Byblos in honour of Adonis, whose story takes place in the city. The name of the character is obviously Semitic (*adon* or *adonai*), and is frequently used to refer to male deities with the generic meaning of "lord"; it never appears in Phoenician inscriptions used as a proper name. Greek and Latin sources tell the story of a young hunter of great beauty, born of incest; the beautiful Adonis is loved and fought over by two goddesses, Aphrodite and Persephone. In classical mythology Adonis dies while hunting, killed by a wild boar, and Aphrodite and her followers create the mourning ritual that characterized the celebration of the Adoniad festival.

Votive scene, detail from the stele of Yehawmilk from Byblos 5th century B.C. Paris, Musée du Louvre

In the Greek and Roman world this was celebrated by the women in a private way, on the rooftops, with lamentations, sexual license and the creation of small "gardens" made up of short-lived plants. In Byblos the celebration took place in the sanctuary of Aphrodite, with public mourning ceremonies, tonsure of women or ritual prostitution, the liturgy of the "awakening" of Adonis, who was considered alive even after his experience of death. In Byblos, therefore, the worship of Adonis was very different from the ritual veneration of the god in Greece from the 7th century B.C. onwards. We have further evidence of this in a lengthy Greek inscription from the 4th century B.C. It is a decree allowing Cypriots resident in Athens to celebrate their own Adoniads "according to the customs of their homeland": the ritual was part of the worship of Aphrodite of Cyprus and was celebrated in forms that are directly reminiscent of what we know about the Adoniads of Phoenicia.

And so behind the Adonis of Byblos, beyond the interpretations of the classical world, we can recognize one of those city deities not present in

Aerial view of Byblos

earlier Syrian traditions, but somehow derived from them as a development of eschatological beliefs on the "life" after death of the ancestors of royalty.

Going from Byblos to our documentation on Tyre, the first observation concerns the extreme poverty of direct epigraphic documentation. The best document we have is the list of deities invoked as guarantors of the treaty signed in 675 B.C. between Baal, king of Tyre, and Esarhaddon, king of Assyria. Transcribed in Akkadian, we find here the names of Anath and Astarte, Baal Shamaim, Baal Malage (possibly the "Lord of Plenty" or maybe a sea god), Baitylos (probably a deification of the baetyl, the stone in which the divinity dwelt) and Baal Saphon. There are also two new names: Eshmun and Melqarth. In Tyre, Melqarth was the main city deity, for his name means "King of the City"; in a bilingual Maltese inscription his name is accompanied by the definition "Baal of Tyre" and by the Greek epithet *archegetes*, i.e. "founder" of the Tyrian dynasty.

Melqarth appears for the first time in an Aramaic inscription of the 9th century B.C., in which Bar Hadad, king of Damascus, dedicates a votive tablet to him. But the cult of Melqarth in Tyre dates back at least to the 10th century when — according to Josephus, who quotes Menander of Ephesus — King Hiram had a sanctuary built in his honour, and another in honour of Astarte, on the ruins of some earlier temples; Hiram was also the first to cel-

127

ebrate festivities in honour of Melqarth. This was probably an actual religious reform, in line with what we saw about the origins of Phoenician polytheism.

There is, in fact, no trace of Melqarth in our documentation from the 2nd millennium B.C., while during the Iron Age we can follow his gradual rise in popularity and importance. Clearly this was a deity who expressed a sort of mythicized hypostasis of the ideal of the Phoenician sovereign, interpreted originally as the founder and master of the city of Tyre, and then increasingly as the protecting divinity and inventor of the fundamental interests of society, from purple dye to westerly navigation. Dedications to Melqarth thus appear also in Cyprus, Carthage, Sicily, Sardinia, Malta and Spain, and his sanctuaries accompanied the overall Phoenician expansion and marked the navigation routes.

Votive stele with baetyl from Carthage 6th century B.C. sandstone 50 × 35.5 cm Carthage, Musée de Carthage

Melqarth was very early on identified with the Greek Heracles and a much of the information we have on this god and his worship has come down to us with that name. He was the son of Zeus (perhaps a Baal of the heavens) and of Asteria (Astarte in an astral translation); another version, given by Philo of Byblos, has him as the son of Hadad-Demarus and a descendant of Uranus. Athenaeus and other Greek language authors give an account of his resurrection, brought about by his friend Iolaus who made him smell a fragrant roasted quail. This episode must be related to other stories of the death and resurrection of the Tyrian Heracles and also to the important yearly celebration of Melqarth's "awakening," first organized by King Hiram, which took place not only in Tyre but also in other centres until the advent of the Romans, and was always held in the active presence of the king or of the highest city magistrates.

Despite the spread of his worship throughout the Mediterranean region and the fame of the sanctuary dedicated to him in Tyre (even Alexander made a sacrificial offering there), the portrayals of Melqarth are very few and uncertain. Some Greek sources tell us that in the god's sanctuaries there were no statues or effigies at all; the Bar Hadad stele portrays him with the features of a Baal Lord of Tempest, but this is probably derived from iconographies that are not original to this deity; some Carthaginian portrayals on razors reflect the developments connected to his identification with the Greek Heracles.

In Tyre, alongside Melqarth there was a widespread worship of Astarte, to whom, as we saw earlier, King Hiram also dedicated a temple: in the treaty of Esarhaddon she is the deity called upon to punish whoever shall dare to violate the clauses of the agreement, by "breaking his bow in battle." This goddess, who was very well-known among the Semitic peoples of Syria-Palestine but had only secondary roles in Ugarit, was first mentioned in Egypt as a warrior deity ("Lady of the Battles, Goddess of the Asians"), whereas in the Bible she is connected to fertility and love, a connection which explains why she is frequently identified with Aphrodite. In the fragments of Philo's text Astarte is the wife of her brother Cronus and the mother of many children; in Tyre she is called "the highest" and is worshipped with astral connotations.

Astarte appears to be predominant also in Sidon, where the sovereigns themselves were among the goddess's priests. But the main god in this city was Eshmun, whom we have already come across in the Esarhaddon treaty with the king of Tyre. He is the "Baal of Sidon" mentioned in the inscriptions, also called the "holy prince." The texts which document his cult date from the late 6th century B.C. and the 5th century, and for the most part come from the excavations of a temple dedicated to him by the dynasty of which Eshmunazar is the most famous representative. The dedications are to Eshmun and Astarte, who were worshipped together in a sanctuary with many canals, a pool and other channels for the waters of the Yidlal spring, which presumably played an important role in the cult.

Like Adonis and Melqarth, Eshmun is not documented before the 1st millennium B.C., and it seems likely that his origin is similar to theirs, as an evolution of earlier Syrian traditions. This god's name, in fact, seems to derive etymologically from the Semitic word for "oil," which in both Ebla and Ugarit we find used as a divine name in the cult. This hypothesis is supported by archaeological findings and by the classical interpretations, all of which identify Eshmun with Asclepius, the god of medicine.

Like Adonis and Melqarth, Eshmun is portrayed in our classical sources as a god who dies and then returns to life. According to Pausanias, who quotes a Sidonian source, the Phoenician Asclepius is the son of a sun god and an immortal woman and has a specific health-giving nature. Damascius, on the other hand, speaking of the Asclepius of the city of Berytus, recounts a hunting myth which is partly similar to the myth of Adonis, and which ends with the violent death of the protagonist and his elevation to the level of immortal god.

The identification of the pantheon of Berytus is more complex. According to Philo, in this city were preserved the relics of the god called Pontos in Greek, while the divine supremacy had been entrusted to the god Poseidon

Statue of Heracles-Melqarth from Idalion 5th century B.C. limestone, 44 cm Paris, Musée du Louvre

by Cronus. The veneration of a sea deity is also confirmed by sources from the Hellenistic and Roman periods. A dedication in Greek, for example, would seem to equate with Poseidon, "the shaker of the earth," a local god called Baal Marqod, which presumably represents the ancient name of the city's deity, identified in the Latin inscriptions with Jove Optimus Maximus.

The Baal of Berytus, frequently portrayed as a sea god with a trident and

Votive razor with seated figure and Heracles-Melqarth with leonté from Carthage 3rd century B.C. bronze, 17.5 cm Carthage, Musée de Carthage

riding in a chariot, was accompanied by a Baalath-Aphrodite, the protectress of sailors (identified with Juno Regina) and by the god (or goddess) Sima. Our information, however, dates from a period in which the widespread Greek and Roman syncretism had altered the city's Phoenician forms of worship.

Byblos, Tyre, Sidon and Berytus give us an idea of the wide range and specific character of the cults in the more important Phoenician cities. But we can also see their variety from the epigraphical and archaeological evidence from other locations. For example, not far from Tyre, in the ancient village on the site of present-day Umm el-Amad, the main cult in the 3rd and 2nd centuries B.C. was that of the god Milkashtart, who was probably a particular hypostasis of Melqarth associated with Astarte; other gods worshipped were Baal Shamaim, El, Astarte and the Egyptian Osiris. In Amrith, the inscription on a 5th-century B.C. votive tablet mentions the name of the god Shadrapa ("Shed, the Healer"), which also appears on an ostrakon from Sarepta and in Punic, Palmyrene and Greek inscriptions from Syria; anoth-

er inscription at the end of the 5th century B.C. records the offering of a statue to the god Eshmun. Greek dedications from Delos mention, among the
Phoenician gods of Ascalon, the Palestinian Astarte and a marine Baal.

A group of inscriptions of the 9th-8th century B.C. from Zinjirli, in
Northern Syria, and Karatepe, in Cilicia, show how widespread Phoenician

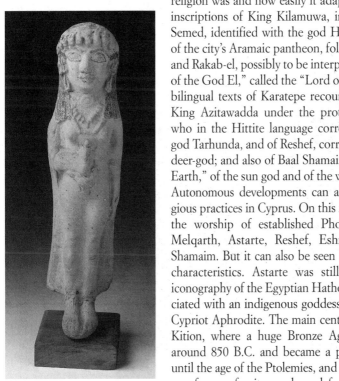

religion was and how easily it adapted to local needs. The
inscriptions of King Kilamuwa, in Zinjirli, mention Baal
Semed, identified with the god Hadad, the supreme lord
of the city's Aramaic pantheon, followed by Baal Hammon
and Rakab-el, possibly to be interpreted as the "Charioteer
of the God El," called the "Lord of the Royal House." The
bilingual texts of Karatepe recount the feats of the local
King Azitawadda under the protection of Baal *krntrys*,
who in the Hittite language corresponds to the tempest
god Tarhunda, and of Reshef, corresponding to the Hittite
deer-god; and also of Baal Shamaim, of El "Creator of the
Earth," of the sun god and of the whole family of the gods.
Autonomous developments can also be observed in religious practices in Cyprus. On this island there are traces of
the worship of established Phoenician gods, such as
Melqarth, Astarte, Reshef, Eshmun, Anath and Baal
Shamaim. But it can also be seen how they acquired local
characteristics. Astarte was still worshipped with the
iconography of the Egyptian Hathor, but she was also associated with an indigenous goddess and identified with the
Cypriot Aphrodite. The main centers of her worship were
Kition, where a huge Bronze Age temple was restored
around 850 B.C. and became a pilgrimage center in use
until the age of the Ptolemies, and above all Paphos, which
was famous for its oracle and for its sacred prostitution

*Female statuette
from Lapithos
6th century B.C.
terra-cotta, 23 cm
Nicosia, Cyprus
Museum
• p. 147*

rites. Reshef, too, was very popular on Cyprus, but in new forms: associated
with other deities, such as Mikal and Shed, and assimilated to the god Apollo
in two Cypriot variations (Reshef *'lyyt* and Reshef *'lhyts*, which in the bilingual inscriptions correspond to Apollo of Helos and Apollo of Alasia).
Carthage preserved the cults of the motherland, but beginning from the 5th
century B.C. the city seemed to make a theological and liturgical choice
which many scholars have interpreted as a reformation. But first let us look
at the elements that show continuity. The oldest inscriptions mention
Astarte and a god of Cypriot origin, Pygmalion. Melqarth had a temple in
the city and his worship was undoubtedly official. The same can be said of
Eshmun, who was also worshipped together with Astarte. Other gods were
Reshef, Baal Saphon and Shadrapa, mentioned in inscriptions by their
priests or ministers.

Any analysis of the structure of the traditional Carthaginian pantheon is
extremely complex. Some believe that the position of supremacy was held
by Baal Shamaim, and there appears to be evidence for this in the Greek

adaptations of Punic deities (mentioned by Polybius) in the treaty signed in 215 between Hannibal and Philip V of Macedonia. In it appear the names of Zeus, Hera and Apollo, followed by the *genius* of the Carthaginians, Heracles, and Iolaus, Ares, Triton and Poseidon. Zeus could therefore correspond to Baal Shamaim, Heracles to Melqarth and Apollo to Reshef; yet this might well not be the city's pantheon, but simply a group of deities corresponding to the Carthaginian general's religious preferences.

Tablet with Latin inscription dedicated to Sardus Pater from Antas 3rd century A.D. bronze, 6 × 9 cm Cagliari Museo Archeologico Nazionale

It seems certain that there was a definite break with the traditions of the past around the beginning of the 5th century B.C., when a divine couple, Tanit and Baal Hammon, gained a position of supremacy within the pantheon. The phenomenon was probably connected with the political upheavals resulting from the Carthaginian defeat at Himera in 480, which led to the breaking off of relations with Tyre and also had repercussions on religious life. This new divine couple, mentioned in thousands of inscriptions, was not unknown to Phoenicia, but only in Carthage was it given such preeminent importance. Tanit, or Tinnit as she is called in some Greek transcriptions, is a goddess of Phoenician origin, even though in the eastern Mediterranean her worship appears to have been of secondary importance and limited to the area around Sidon. In Carthage she is never mentioned before the second half of the 5th century, but an inscription mentions Astarte and Tanit "of Lebanon" together, and there is a 7th-6th-century B.C. dedication from Sarepta to "Tanit-Astarte." In some texts the goddess is called "mother," but she is more frequently referred to as "Mistress" or as "Face" or "Revelation of Baal." In Roman times, worship of Tanit was associated with the worship of Juno Celestia, perhaps with an accentuation of the astral connotations which must have been present in the morphology of this deity from the origin of her veneration. The worship of this Carthaginian goddess spread throughout the Mediterranean area, with characteristics which were very similar, and in some cases identical, to those of Astarte.

Baal Hammon, her companion and the best-known god of the Carthaginian pantheon, has a name of obscure origin. Some have suggested a connection with a Libyan god, but this theory is disproved by the presence of his name in one of the Kilamuwa inscriptions and on a small amulet found in the region of Tyre and studied recently by P. Bordreuil, which confirm his Phoenician origin. He may have originally been the god of a small town near Tyre, in other words the "Baal of Hammon." But the name can also be interpreted as the "Lord of the Perfume Altar," or even as the "Baal of *hmn*," a term which in the ritual texts of Ugarit denotes a place of worship. Despite our uncertainties about the meaning of Baal Hammon's name, we do know that he was worshipped in all Punic centres of the West, alone or together with Tanit, primarily in the dedications which state his importance as the main recipient of *molk* sacrifices. In Carthage, Tanit usually had supremacy over him, whereas the inscriptions from el-Hofra invert this order, and those from Motya, in Sicily, do not even mention the goddess at all.

This survey of the religion of Carthage ends with a mention of the presence of Greek forms of worship: from the 4th-3rd century B.C. onwards there is a progressive Hellenization of the city's religion, from sacred iconography to specific forms of veneration, from the sacrificial typology to the worship of Greek gods. In the year 396 B.C. the worship of Demeter and Kore was introduced officially, and a special priesthood was instituted for this purpose. Coming to the religion of the colonies, we can start with Malta, where we know there was a sanctuary of Heracles-Melqarth (not yet identified) and the most famous temple of Astarte, excavated at Tas Silg. To build this temple the Phoenicians used some prehistoric wall structures; the sanctuary was then altered several times, and continued to be used until Roman times for the worship of Astarte, identified first with the Greek goddess Hera, and later with the Roman Juno Regina.

As well as the dedicatory inscriptions to Baal Hammon in Motya and others to Tanit and Baal Hammon found in Lilybaeum, epigraphical documents and classical sources inform us that the Punic religion was represented in Sicily also by the sanctuary at Eryx dedicated to Astarte-Aphrodite-Venus, famous for its wealth and its sacred prostitution rites. Another Punic sanctuary, carved out of the rock, has been discovered near Palermo, in the Grotta Regina, and has inscriptions invoking Shadrapa and the Egyptian Isis.

Votive stele with "sign of Tanit" caduceus and crescent on solar disc from Constantine 3rd-1st century B.C. Paris, Musée du Louvre

In Sardinia we know that Tanit was worshipped at Sulcis, Tharros and Nora, and Melqarth at Tharros; there is also a cult of Eshmun, as we know from a trilingual inscription from San Nicolò Gerrei which mentions him as a healer, with the obscure epithet "Merre". Baal Shamaim was venerated on "the island of hawks," the present-day Carloforte, while at Nora, in the earliest Phoenician inscription found in the West, the name of Pumay seems to be attested, identified in a Carthaginian inscription with the Cypriot Pygmalion. Particularly interesting are the inscriptions found in the excavations of the temple of Antas, which date from the 2nd-1st century B.C.: they show that the Phoenician god Sid corresponded to the Latin Sardus Pater and perhaps to the highest indigenous deity of pre-Phoenician Sardinia.

Among the votive offerings to Sid we also find effigies of Horon and Shadrapa, whose functions were probably to act as intermediaries in the contact with a god who was considered the colonizer of the island and also its healing divinity. Among the few inscriptions ftom Phoenician Spain, there is first of all the dedication of a sanctuary in the 5th century to the pair Reshef-Melqarth, in the Cueva d'es Cuyram (Ibiza). The votive inscription is incised on a bronze plaque which around 180 B.C. was reused for a dedication to Tanit "Power" and "Fortune." The name of this goddess also appears, coupled with Astarte, on the base of a female statuette of Egyptian type, dating perhaps from the 8th century B.C. The name Milkashtart is incised on the setting of a 2nd century B.C. ring, which was probably used as a seal in the sanctuary of Cadiz. The writings of classical authors help us particularly in reconstructing the worship of Heracles-Melqarth in this sanctuary, famous throughout the classical world for its beauty and wealth, as well as for its oracle, which was still consulted at the time of Caracalla.

Lastly, we must mention the presence of Astarte in an Etruscan sanctuary at Pyrgi, on the coast of Latium. In the 5th century B.C. Tefarie Velianas, king of Caere, erected in this sanctuary a bilingual dedication tablet for Astarte and her Etruscan equivalent, Uni. Recent excavations have shown that the worship of the Phoenician goddess was not considered secondary to the veneration of Uni, and that sacred prostitution rituals were practised in the temple. So far religion has been discussed in terms of what we know about the official forms of worship and beliefs, in other words the religion belonging to the class that governed political life, and administered the economy and society in general. This is why the gods have so far appeared in their public and institutional functions, whereas the popular aspects of their worship have not been dealt with at all. Some light is shed on this by the Phoenician onomatology, normally consisting of expressions like "son," "brother" or "servant" of one god or another. In the way these proper names are formed, a certain distinction between family worship and public religion can be noticed, as well as a degree of explicit archaism. Tanit, for example, does not seem to be popular at all, whereas the Egyptian deities and Baal and Astarte are quite widespread. Another way of studying popular religion is to examine the gradual development, particularly after the middle of the 1st millennium B.C., of some healing cults: the worship of Eshmun, for example, and also of Shadrapa, Horon and Sid, and even Sasm (a practically unknown deity active in the field of magic), and of Bes, a pygmy god of Egyptian origin. These were public cults, frequently celebrated by the state with the care and organization given to official cults: this fact must not be seen as a matter of chance, but rather related to the breakup of the official forms of worship caused by the Hellenization of Phoenician cities. What survived from this breakup, and even increased in importance, were those deities, or those aspects of the traditional deities, which were most closely connected to the people's immediate needs.

A further aspect of popular religion was the widespread use of apotropaic and devotional objects such as amulets, scarabs and other small sacred items, frequently of Egyptian origin; this indicates that the people were turning their attention towards interests and gods quite different from those of the official state cult, but which offered protection against the dangers of everyday life.

Statuette of Bes from Phoenicia 6th-5th century B.C. terra-cotta, 21 cm Paris, Musée du Louvre

Mythology

When speaking of Phoenician mythology we must break away, at least in part, from the definition of myth and mythology we have learned from the classical tradition. As far as we know, in fact, Phoenician mythology was not oral but written, collected and chosen by theologians, preserved in the archives of the temples and used for official ceremonies.

Philo claims to have gleaned his information from this kind of canonical source when he wrote his *Phoenician History*, so that he could contradict the false accounts that the Greek tradition was transmitting orally, from poet to poet. And he certainly did obtain material from the archives of Byblos and Tyre, among others, for in his time they still preserved a great number of ancient documents. But frequently he puts various pieces of information together in haphazard combinations regardless of their provenance and placement in time. This, for example, is the case of his long story of Cronus and Uranus, in which he elaborates on the Phoenician myths using what he knows of similar characters from Greek mythology.

The events which Philo recounts as having occasioned the origin of the universe are perhaps more faithful to Phoenician traditions. According to this account, before the existence of the world, in the primordial chaos there was just a dark and windy air, a swirling blowing gale who fell in love with his own origins and set in motion the whole creation process. Wind and chaos as the origins of the universe also appear in the fragments of Phoenician cosmogonies mentioned by Damascius, who also speaks of Cronus as the creator and of the existence of a huge cosmic egg, which opened up into two pieces and gave rise to the primordial separation of heaven and earth.

Fragment of stele with male figure from Umm-el-Awamid 3rd-2nd century B.C., stone 47 × 30 cm Paris, Musée du Louvre

If we move on to the traditions concerning the origin of arts and crafts, we find a great number of characters in Philo's text: Usoos invented the idea of clothing made of animal hides and was the first to venture onto the seas; Aion discovered that trees can provide nourishment, while Agraeus and Halliaeus invented hunting and fishing. Then there is Chusor, the smith who was an expert in magical practices and wise sayings. These characters are followed by the inventors of the building arts and by others who taught the organization of villages, agriculture and animal husbandry, writing and navigation.

According to Philo, at the summit of the genealogy of the gods there are Eliun, the "supreme" god, and the Baalath of Berytus; from them descends Uranus who begot El (Cronus), Baitylos, Dagon ("wheat"), Astarte and other children, who later engage in a bitter struggle for the conquest of sovereignty over the whole world. The war ends with the victory of Cronus, the death and deification of their father Uranus and the division of the cities of Phoenicia among the gods allied to the winner.

Philo's *Phoenician History* also reports on some deities

135

representing specific qualities or functions (such as Sydyk and Misor, Justice and Rectitude), who also appear in other Semitic mythologies.

Private and Public Worship

Our study of the Phoenician pantheon of the East has shown that the kings of Sidon, Byblos and Tyre were also high priests of Baalath, Astarte and Melqarth. In fact, for Phoenician kings at the time of the Persians, their religious role was more important than their royal title: in the Tabnith inscription the title "priest of Astarte" comes before the attribute "King of the Sidonians" in the description both of the king and of his father Eshmunazar.

In the Punic world, the higher ranking priestly positions were frequently the privilege of the oligarchical aristocracy and sometimes even hereditary. From a funerary inscription from Carthage, for example, we learn that one family held the position of high priest for at least five generations. We also know that the Carthaginian state, and the political authorities of the Phoenician cities before it, exercised direct control on all religious matters through specially appointed magistrates, even though the Phoenician priesthood always enjoyed considerable political and economic prestige.

Plaquette depicting scene of adoration 5th century B.C. terra-cotta 13.5 × 8 cm Paris, Musée du Louvre
• p. 148

The Phoenician kings, and the Carthaginian suffetes and generals later, personally celebrated the liturgical ceremonies at festivals or at important times in the social, political or military life of the community. Normal religious ceremonies, on the other hand, were officiated by professional priests, who, as we learn from various inscriptions, were rigidly structured into several different hierarchical levels. At the summit there was a high priest, who presided over a number of priests and priestesses; below them there was a whole range of minor functionaries, from butchers to perfume masters, from scribes to slaves. An important document which provides a great deal of information on life inside the sanctuaries is a mid-5th-century B.C. inscription from Kition, with a list of the expenses incurred by the management of a temple over two months, including salaries paid to the staff: among these are priests, choristers, butchers, bakers, servants, barbers, a "water master" and also sacred prostitutes of both sexes.

Two offices seem to have been particulary important: that of the "sacrificer," who was probably publicly appointed and whose duties were perhaps similar to those of the *mageiros* in Greek religion; and that of the more obscure *mqm 'lm*, who may have been the priest who "resurrected the deity," frequently mentioned in inscriptions from Carthage, Cyprus, Rhodes and Tripolitania. We also know that there were councils of the priesthood and religious associations. Among these, one of the most interesting is the *marzeah*, a term used in inscriptions also to indicate a festival. This word was also used in Ugaritic, in the Bible and in some Aramaic texts to indicate a ritual symposium, a sort of sacred banquet which was part of the divine cult and of ancestor worship.

Probably the word had the same meaning in Phoenician religion.

We have already mentioned the practice of sacred prostitution in the worship of Astarte. This is undoubtedly one of the elements which contributed most to the celebrity of the goddess's sanctuaries at Byblos, Paphos, Eryx, Pyrgi and Sicca Veneria; and it is also one of the aspects of Phoenician religion most fiercely attacked in the Old Testament. As some of the distinctive signs of Astarte's prostitutes, the Bible mentions a special type of clothing and emblems on the forehead, face and breast; the Bible further absolutely forbids the introduction into the temple of Yahweh of any money collected in this way. Herodotus states that in Babylonia and Cyprus all women had to submit to this ritual at least once in their life: they had to go to the goddess's sanctuary and wait until a foreigner had enjoyed their favors, leaving an appropriate sum of money in the temple's treasure chests.

In the treatise *De Syria Dea*, too, the Byblos ritual of sacred prostitution is presented as an exceptional event, intended only for foreigners. In Paphos, on the other hand, and in Eryx and other sanctuaries of the West, prostitution was practised by the temple slaves, who performed the ritual as a profession, on behalf and in honor of the goddess.

Plaquette with woman at window from Nimrud 8th century B.C. ivory 10.8 × 8.6 cm London British Museum

In the past this custom was frequently interpreted as an act aimed primarily at fostering plant and animal fertility, or as a rite of passage. Today we tend to stress other aspects of the matter: the practice of sacred prostitution in strongly commercial centers, for example, or the fact that our sources speak of foreigners as the privileged category with access to the practice, or that the sum paid by the client always went to the sanctuary coffers. Sacred prostitution, in other words, was used as a mechanism for raising money in coastal sanctuaries, which were considered custodial places for huge quantities of riches; politicians frequently made use of these riches in exceptional circumstances, taking them over by public decree or simply by force.

This mention of the wealth of the sanctuaries leads to consideration of the typology of Phoenician places of worship. The temples of Astarte we mentioned above and those of Melqarth in Lixus, Cadiz, Malta and on the Nile Delta were cosmopolitan sanctuaries in busy port towns, real centres of cultural and economic, not just religious development; they were maritime sanctuaries, possessing huge deposits in money and in precious votive offerings, and were probably very much involved in the Phoenician trading expeditions from the time of the first expansion to the West.

Also a coastal sanctuary, intended for navigators and traders, was the temple near Palermo, Grotta Regina, in use from the 5th or 4th century B.C. to the 2nd century A.D. But in this temple there is little trace of official forms of worship, and the sanctuary appears to have been devoted solely to popular cults and the worship of healing deities.

Public worship took place primarily in the urban sanctuaries which were

137

financed by the income from sacrifices and votive offerings and which, at least in some cases, also owned large amounts of land.

View of the ruins of the sanctuary dedicated to Astarte at Tas Silg, Malta

The cult of the various divinities culminated in periodical feasts and celebrations, but we only have a vague idea of them, since our information is very meagre. The Karatepe inscription refers to three sacrificial offerings instituted by King Azitawadda: the sacrifice of a bullock, perhaps connected to a celebration of the New Year, and the sacrifice of a sheep, to take place at the time of ploughing and at harvest time. In the Phoenician text from Pyrgi there is mention of the "day of the burial of the divinity," probably a feast in honor of Melqarth, and of the "month of the sun sacrifice (sacrifice to the sun-god)." This last festival is mentioned again in 370 B.C. in an inscription from Kition and may perhaps indicate a celebration coinciding with the winter solstice.

More famous festivals are the Adoniads of Byblos, the feast of the "awakening" of Melqarth and the *marzeah* celebrated by the Sidonian community in Piraeus, all mentioned above. We can add to these a fragment of a Carthaginian inscription from the 3rd century B.C. which mentions a (spring?) festival that lasted at least five days and included the offering of fruit, perfumes, honey and incense. Still at Carthage, a number of inscriptions mention the *mayumas* feast, similar to the Hydrophoria of Greece and the Hellenized East. The epigraphical sources are more useful when it comes to the reconstruction of the sacrificial offerings. In fact we have several lists of the tariffs practised in Carthage in the 4th-3rd century B.C., with information concerning the victims, the terminology and typology of animal

Votive stele with walking animal from Sulcis 3rd century B.C. tufa, 17 × 14.8 cm S. Antioco Museo Comunale

Votive stele with female figure holding disc to breast from Sulcis 4th-3rd century B.C. tufa, 21 × 13 cm S. Antioco Museo Comunale • p. 149

sacrifices, and the taxes to be paid. These texts were drawn up by the magistrates who administered the cult, and were then posted up at the entrance to the temples, in order to inform the faithful of the regulations governing each rite. The victims listed are oxen, calves, rams, lambs, birds, poultry and game, and they could be sacrificed in different ways, according to the various rites, which also determined the division of the victim's meat between the offerer and the celebrant, and the fee levied by the latter. The priests were given a sum of money and a small share of the meat; some pieces of the animal were then burnt in honour of the deity and the rest of the meat was given to the offerer. If the animal was killed by the offerer himself, then the share due to the priests was much smaller, almost symbolic; in the case of sacrifices of birds, since the animals were so small, all the meat went to the offerer. These tariffs regulated sacrificial offerings by private citizens and not official rituals, governed by the calendar of festivals; the tributes due were calculated so as to allow individuals to offer regular sacrifices of animal meat and at the same time ensure that the sanctuaries had a regular income, proportional to the importance of the rites and the victims. As in Greece, the sacrifice was important from a nutritional point of view as well: and actually it may be that each meal that included meat was also a sacrifice, just as each animal sacrificed was also a meal.

To many, the most charateristic rite of Phoenician and Punic religion became human sacrifice, more specifically the sacrifice of children. In fact this ritual was probably reserved for exceptional circumstances, when the seriousness of the situation demanded more powerful religious intervention.

In classical sources we can read numerous accounts of the use made by Phoenicians and Carthaginians of this practice, considered barbarous and stigmatized as disgraceful. According to Diodorus Siculus, when Carthage was besieged in 310 B.C., hundreds of children from the highest families were immolated in the fire in honour of Cronus. In the Bible, as well, there is mention of raised areas built in a place called a *tophet*, where the sons and daughters of the idolatrous Israelites were "passed through fire." The rite is also mentioned by the Fathers of the Church, who in their commentaries and translations of the Old Testament call the deity who received this offering Moloch.

Thus, when excavations in Punic cities brought to light a series of open-air sanctuaries with thousands of terracotta urns containing the ashes and burned bones of young children, literally "passed through fire" before burial, it was thought to be a sad and precise archaeological confirmation of the written information about the *tophet* and Punic

child sacrifice. At Carthage and in other North African cities, at Motya in Sicily, and at Tharros, Sulcis, Monte Sirai, Nora and Bithia in Sardinia, excavations have in fact revealed vast consecrated areas, generally located outside the city walls and designed to receive not only cinerary urns, but also other offerings, particularly stone stelae with votive images and inscriptions.

Punic stelae from the tophet *at Carthage*

The urns contain the bones of children and small animals (lambs, birds), sometimes mixed and sometimes separate; there are also remains of fetuses and of more than one child in the same urn. The stelae commemorate a rite called *molk*, offered to Tanit and Baal Hammon, separately or as a couple, by private citizens, men and women alike, as an expression of gratitude or in the hope of having a prayer answered through divine benevolence.

The *tophet* as described seems to be characteristic of the whole Punic world, over several centuries; in fact still under the Roman Empire, in North Africa dedications were offered to Saturn, and lambs were immolated to safeguard a child's life. It must however be added that our certainties about the existence and diffusion of child sacrifice in the Phoenician and Punic religion, and hence also about the specific function of the area reserved for the remains of immolated children, are today no longer so certain. Recently there has been a global reconsideration of the subject.

The classical sources, in fact, do talk about human sacrifices, but as an exceptional practice, with a wide variety of rites, victims and deities to whom

140

they were addressed. None of this information, however, finds exact corre-spondences in the archaeology of the Punic *tophet*. In other sources, the descriptions of child sacrifices (not mentioned by the most important historians) often include crude details that clearly reflect anti-Carthaginian propaganda aims. It must also be noted that the Phoenician East appears practically silent on the subject, with the sole exception of the biblical references. These might however allude to initiation rites, so that "passing through fire" could have the meaning of a purification with no sacrifice of life.

Concerning the characteristics of the *tophet*, it must be said that this was undoubtedly a sanctuary with a public, community function; the deposits, however, do not seem to have been a collective rite, nor reserved for particular classes of citizens. Moreover Tanit and Baal Hammon are not characterized as bloodthirsty gods; from the little we know about them they appear as benevolent beings, with a positive role in the destinies of children. As for the *molk* rite, while it is certain that it had a sacrificial value, it is less certain that the ritual implied the immolation of human victims. At least to a certain extent, it appears to have been aimed at preserving the life and ensuring the survival of children through the risks of birth and the dangers of infancy.

We may therefore conclude that among the uses recognized for the sacred area defined with the name *tophet*, there was certainly also the function of a child necropolis, designed to receive the remains of infants who had died prematurely of sickness or other natural causes, and who for this reason were "offered" to specific deities and buried in a place different from the one reserved for the ordinary dead; and that this was combined with an effort to ensure the benevolent protection of the same deities for the survivors. It is also likely that according to a specific religious conception, the children buried in the *tophet* were destined to a glorious (or at any rate special) afterlife.

As for the ritual killing of human victims, and children in particular, this seems to have been a rather limited phenomenon in the Phoenician and Punic religion, not included in the ordinary forms of worship, but reserved for particularly serious situations. Phoenicians and Carthaginians probably had recourse to this solution only when disaster threatened, according to a practice widespread throughout the ancient world.

Death and Afterlife, Magic and Divination

From what Philo tells us and from our knowledge of the myths of Ugarit, we can assume that in Phoenician mythology death was conceived of as a supernatural being (personified as Mot or Muth), whose role was one of a chaotic and threatening force in the early times of creation, and later reduced to limited powers over man. Mot, quite obviously, is not part of any form of worship, for Death cannot be venerated: but his powers were recognized and the last moment of human life was ritualized accordingly in forms, however, that we have only partially been able to reconstruct.

The ritual followed during the early part of the ceremony in honour of the deceased, for example, is hardly known to us. Vague allusions in the Bible and carvings on the sarcophagus of Ahiram, king of Byblos have led us to conclude that, at least in Phoenicia, the family's "leave-taking" of the dead was marked by lamentations and other forms of ritualized mourning. From the excavation of many Punic tombs we also know that, after a special preparation, the body was wrapped in bandages and buried, in some cases in a sarcophagus, more frequently just laid out on the rock of the funerary cell.

In the case of kings or nobles, there is occasional evidence of embalming and the use of aromatic substances. We also know that both burial and cremation were practised, even in the same tomb, and we have not been able to find any distinction in the eschatological ideas behind the two practices. The ritual of cremation, used more widely than burial in the earliest times, later appears to have been abandoned for a few centuries; it came back into use in the Hellenistic period, probably because of the influence of Greece. In any case, the body was always accompanied by pottery, jewellery and ornaments of different kinds to which the Phoenicians probably attributed symbolic and apotropaic properties, for example to indicate a belief in the afterlife or to ensure that the deceased would be granted protection after death.

Urns in the tophet at Sulcis

What survived of human beings after death according to Phoenician eschatology we cannot say; but it is difficult to imagine that there was a distinction and a separation between body and soul. Information from archaeological finds lead us to suppose that the tomb was considered the deceased's eternal dwelling-place; from those same sources we learn that there was widespread concern about violation of the burial place and that death was seen as a long sleep. The dead were called *rephaim*, a term which probably indicated a sense of the languor of non-life, but also meant "gods" or "deities", much in the same way as the Greeks called all deceased "blessed."

As to the existence of a worship of the dead, there are only a few references made by classical authors (Arrian, Lucian and Cicero) to rituals performed at the burial places. Lastly, it is interesting to note that, although individual salvation appears to be foreign as a concept to Phoenician polytheism, it did probably include positive eschatological beliefs, derived from foreign salvation cults, especially those of Isis and Osiris and of Demeter and Kore.

As far as magic is concerned, there are two Phoenician magic spells dating from the 6th century B.C., found at Arslan Tash, in Syria. The first is an amulet in the form of a pendant containing a long exorcism, with two distinct and parallel texts, in which Sasm and Horon are invoked against the "Flyers" and "Stranglers," evil forces lurking in the night. The second one is aimed against the serpent demon *mzh*: his negative force is neutralized by Baal and the magic spell recalls the mythical powers of the god, who can destroy the evil eye cast by the "Serpent who dwells in the steppe."

Another magic spell comes from Carthage and dates from the 3rd century B.C. This is an exorcism calling on the goddess Hawwat, never mentioned elsewhere, for an operation of black magic against a woman with whom the

The tophet
at Sulcis

dedicator has a disagreement on money matters. The text suggests that there was in Carthage a specific set of formulas and actions used outside regular religious practices, and derived from foreign influences. In this particular case, the dedicator was following the ritual called *defixio* (from *defigere*, to nail), widespread in classical times. But we know that Carthaginians followed many Egyptian models as well, for they had a wide range of amulets,

talismans, scarabs and other apotropaic objects, imported from Egypt or simply imitated. One final aspect of religious practice leads us back to the official religion: the consultation of oracles and the practice of divination. On this matter the only information we have is indirect evidence from classical sources, but we can safely say that these activities were widely performed. In some cases they appear to have been conducted between private citizens, but normally they were connected to the institutions of the state.

There were oracles in many major sanctuaries, such as the temple of Astarte at Paphos and that of Melqarth in Cadiz; and others about which we know less, such as the oracle on a small island near Cadiz, in a cave consecrated to the worship of a sea goddess (Astarte?). At Paphos, as at Cadiz and elsewhere, the prophecies were drawn from the examination of the entrails of an animal sacrificed especially for this purpose; those who requested the prophecy were normally merchants and politicians, before embarking on trading or military expeditions. We also know of other forms of divination, where the will of the gods was interpreted from dreams or from unusual natural phenomena, such as lightning or the miraculous movement of the holy baetyls. Lastly, soothsayers and diviners always accompanied the Carthaginian armies on their expeditions, to ensure that the commanding general and his troops constantly followed the dictates of the gods of their native land.

Ivory plaquette with inscription
in Aramaic mentioning Hazael
king of Damascus
found at Arslan Tash
9th century B.C.
Paris, Musée du Louvre

Fragment of Phoenician inscription
scratched into a red slip jug
found at Kition
clay, diam. 25 cm
9th century B.C.
Nicosia, Cyprus Museum

145

*Phoenician inscription
on the base of a bronze statuette
of Astarte, found at
El Carambolo
7th century B.C.
Seville, Museo Arqueológico*

opposite page
*Female statuette
from Lapithos
6th century B.C.
terra-cotta, 23 cm
Nicosia, Cyprus Museum*

opposite page
*Plaquette
depicting scene
of adoration
5th century B.C.
terracotta
13.5 × 8 cm
Paris, Musée
du Louvre*

*Votive stele with
female figure
holding disc to
breast from Sulcis
4th-3rd century B.C.
tufa, 21 × 13 cm
S. Antioco, Museo
Comunale*

Funerary mask from Phoenicia
6th-4th century B.C.
gold, 16.6 × 13.8 cm
Paris, Musée du Louvre

Cippus with bilingual inscription
in Latin and Neo-Punic
found at Sulcis, 1st century B.C.
Cagliari, Museo Archeologico Nazionale

Statuette of armed horseman
from Byblos
8th-6th century B.C.
terra-cotta, 33.5 × 24 cm
Brussels, Musées Royaux
d'Art et d'Histoire

Political and Administrative Organization
Sandro Filippo Bondì

The Phoenician cities of the East were monarchies in which the transmission of power normally took place through dynastic succession. The only, not particularly important, exception concerns the city of Tyre, during a short period in the 6th century B.C. when it was governed as a republic, headed by elective magistrates known as "suffetes" (judges).

This political format was undoubtedly inherited from earlier times, since it is documented throughout the Palestinian area from at least the 2nd millennium B.C. Compared to the earliest period, the prerogatives of the kings were less clearly drawn and certainly not as far-reaching. The Phoenician sovereigns left no historical or memorial epigraphs, and what information we have mostly refers to religious activities. Many kings mention having built sanctuaries to the gods and call themselves priests, sometimes even placing this attribute before their royal titles.

This has been seen as a consequence of the material limits within which the Phoenician monarchies were forced to operate. Due to the restrictions imposed by the various foreign powers that ruled them, or by certain classes of the city population itself, the Phoenician kings did not as a rule enjoy real decision-making independence in the political field. Their authority in the civic sphere was based primarily on their sacred and priestly function.

Several elements, distributed over almost the whole span of Phoenician history, would seem to confirm this supposition: Ethbaal, who reigned in Tyre in the 9th century B.C., was described by Josephus as a "priest of Astarte." The same title was taken over by Eshmunazar and Tabnith, king of Sidon in the 5th century B.C., while in Byblos, as late as the 4th century B.C., King Ethbaal was called in an inscription "priest of the Lady." It is interesting to note that the kings were already connected with the most important deity of their cities, which suggests a theocratic conception, where power was held by a god who administered it through a high priest.

In the actual wielding of power, moreover, the king was flanked, and in fact checked, by a series of officials and representative bodies. The Ahiram inscription in Byblos, which dates back to very ancient times, already refers to a "governor" and a "field commander." It is possible that these figures were high civil magistrates, with respectively administrative and military functions. Still another official, called "port supervisor," appears in the Egyptian Wenamon's story of events in 11th-century Byblos.

As to representative legislative bodies, this is probably what is referred to in the Biblical passage of Ezekiel mentioning the "ancients of Gebal," and above all in the text of the treaty between Esarhaddon of Assyria and Baal of Tyre where, in an unfortunately mutilated passage, there is a reference to the "ancients of your town [i.e. Tyre] in council." Here too the institutional

organization of the Phoenician cities borrowed well-known
features from the Late Bronze Age, when an assembly of
elders with the functions of a collective deliberating body is
documented at Ugarit and elsewhere.

Administrative districts of Punic North Africa

Certain evidence provided by classical writers regarding
Phoenicia in the 4th century B.C. has sometimes been
taken as proof of the existence of an actual city council in
various centres (Sidon and Tyre in particular), but recent
research has shown the flimsiness of this thesis. It is instead
possible to presuppose, on the basis of a passage from Arrian, the existence
of general city assemblies. The Greek historian mentions that ambassadors
were sent to Alexander the Great, who was preparing to conquer Tyre, "on
behalf of the community." This phrase may well refer to an assembly of citizens endowed with deliberative powers.

Though the main features of the institutions of the Phoenician cities of the
East are in many respects still elusive, information about Carthage and the
Phoenician colonies is much more complete, since we possess considerable
Punic epigraphic material and a great deal of data provided by Greek and
Latin writers.

The second part of this documentation, however, presents a serious draw-
back: the classical sources usually make use of a terminology that is peculiar to Greek and Roman institutional organization and this gives rise to
faulty interpretations and misunderstandings. It is precisely this state of
affairs that makes it so hard to solve one of the essential issues in reconstructing the history of the Phoenician world of the West and its institutions: the existence of the monarchy.

It is well-known that the origin of Carthage is linked, in the foundation
myth of the city, to the figure of a royal princess, Elissa-Dido. Along with
this element, which seems to suggest the existence of the monarchical institution in the earliest times of Carthage, there is the fact that Punic epigraphic sources always mention republic-type magistracies, whereas classical literary sources are extremely undecided, endowing the highest representative of the Carthage governmental system with titles of a monarchical
type, or alternatively, magisterial functions.

Taking the various sources available today all together, it seems reasonable
to conclude that the republican system was typical of the Phoenician cities
of the West from the beginning of their history. This, after all, is a logical
consequence of the central role played, in their founding and early development, by the mercantile aristocracy, which was responsible for the enormous boost given to the expansionist movement.

In any case, such an institutional order was certainly in force from the end
of the 6th century B.C., that is, from when epigraphic and literary sources
provide clear enough documentation, centered mostly on Carthage. And it
is worth noting that the governmental system of this city was spoken highly of by ancient writers: according to Strabo, the Carthaginians, precisely
because they were well governed, were not to be considered barbarians,

*Detail of carved
inscription on the
sarcophagus of Ahiram
king of Byblos
13th century B.C.
Beirut, National Museum*

*Detail of the bas-relief on the side
of Ahiram's sarcophagus with scene
of subjects rendering homage
13th century B.C.
Beirut, National Museum*

and for Polybius the Carthage constitution was simply one of the best in the world and the best outside of Greece. To another Greek writer, Aristotle, who deemed the Carthaginians "governed, from many points of view, in a way superior to other people," we owe the most complete description of their political and administrative institutions.

At the head of the Carthaginian constitutional order were two chief magistrates, the "suffetes" (a title already met with in Tyre). These magistrates, who remained in office for one year, were chosen from among the aristocratic families and had to have at least a small income. Aside from administering justice (in Phoenician, the word "suffete" means "judge"), they presided over the senate, convoked it and established the working agenda. But the suffetes were apparently not entrusted with military responsibilities, which were delegated to influential public figures, chosen according to circumstance.

The Carthage senate, consisting of representatives of the noble families of the city, was the true hub of legislative activity: it was up to this assembly, whose members remained in office for a given period of time, to promulgate laws, to lay down the course of foreign policy, decide whether to wage war and under what conditions to call it off, receive delegations of foreign states and keep watch over the conduct of the military commanders.

Within the senate, subcommittees were set up, consisting of five members (Aristotle calls them "pentarchies"), which were probably put in charge of special sectors of the legislative activity. Among the duties delegated to the pentarchies (whose members remained in office longer than ordinary senators) was that of appointing the members of an important body, a restricted council of 100 or 104 Carthaginians, chosen from among the senators in office.

This council dealt with particularly delicate aspects of Carthaginian public life. It originated in the 5th century B.C. as a high court of justice whose primary duty was to keep a check on the conduct of the generals, but it subsequently expanded its prerogatives to the administration of civil justice and by the 3rd century B.C., ended up wielding enormous power, practically escaping the control of the other magistrates. Membership of the court, in fact, became irrevocable, because the appointment was for life. By then in a position to condition every other state office, this council, expression of the most uncompromising Carthaginian oligarchy, ruled the public life of the city, so that the Latin historian, Livy, could speak of the "reign" of its members.

Within this institutional framework, the prerogatives and decisional independence of the people's assembly, the most broadly representative body in Carthage, were obviously limited. As to the functioning of this assembly, it is Aristotle again who informs us in detail: it had to be consulted in case of disagreement between suffetes and the senate, but otherwise there was no obligation to take its advice. At any rate, it was up to the assembly to appoint generals and suffetes. It is not clear who had the right to be a member, but certainly slaves, foreigners and people without at least a small income were excluded. In the closing phase of Carthage's history, the pow-

Punic inscription found at Carthage 2nd century B.C. Carthage, Musée de Carthage

ers of the people's assembly greatly increased, most of all at the hand of Hannibal who, having become a suffete, lay the foundations of what was described as a true "democratic revolution" by extending the prerogatives of that body. He had a decree approved only by the assembly, without submitting it to the senate, limiting the duration of membership in the Court of the Hundred to one year. This law put an end to the abuse of power of that council, upon which the Carthaginian aristocracy in particular had for centuries based its undisputed control of the senate.

The same administrative system which is known in such detail with regard to Carthage must have been adapted by other Phoenician cities of the West, but what information we have is incomplete and fragmentary. Suffete magistracies existed up until Roman times in many Punic cities of North Africa, and the epigraphic sources attest the presence of this sort of public institution both in Sicily (Eryx) and in Sardinia (Bithia, Sulcis, Tharros and probably Cagliari).

For Malta and Spain (Cadiz), the existence of suffetes is deduced from, respectively, a Greek inscription mentioning two "archons" (the Greek equivalent of a suffete magistrate) and a passage from Livy. The city senate is known not only from Carthage but also from Utica, Sulcis and Malta, whereas the people's assembly is documented both in North Africa (at Leptis) and in the overseas territories (Gozo in the Maltese archipelago, Bithia and Olbia in Sardinia).

This data leads us to assume that even when Carthage extended its hegemony over the whole Phoenician world of the West, the individual centers maintained their traditional forms of civil independence (which for that matter were not even denied to the Greek cities of Sicily subjugated by the Punic metropolis, according to the indirect evidence of classical literary sources). In any case, Carthage, by now responsible for a huge territorial state, had to cope with unquestionably complex administrative duties, which it performed by realistically parcelling out its responsibilities in the different areas under its control.

The administration of the African territory that stretched from Algeria to the border of Cyrenaica was based on a subdivision into districts (called "lands" in Punic), which were put in the charge of officials appointed from the capital. The individual cities governed themselves independently, at least as far as domestic affairs were concerned, while Carthage exerted its authority mostly in terms of taxation, since the whole metropolitan territory lay under tribute. These tributes included both farm produce, where under exceptional circumstances taxation could amount to up to half of the harvest, and customs duties, which brought in a sizeable revenue, especially in the port towns. A sort of united governorship could be set up during wartime: the general designated assumed the title of "commander of all Lybia" and took over both military and civil powers.

Cippus with bilingual inscription in Latin and Neo-Punic found at Sulcis 1st century B.C. Cagliari, Museo Archeologico Nazionale
• *p. 151*

As far as war events are concerned, we also know that military call-ups were announced publicly in the metropolitan territory, but conscription was obligatory only for native subjects (the "Libyans"), that part of the population deprived of civil rights which was surely the most oppressed by Carthaginian domination. For instance, only the Libyans were obliged to pay rents and taxes, while the Carthaginians and Libyan Phoenicians (Punic citizens with full rights resident in other cities of North Africa) were normally exempt.

As to the administration of the overseas territories, Sardinia was subjected to a juridical organization similar in every way to the North African area. Mentioned in international treaties together with Libya, it was also the only other region in which there is evidence of a centralized military command, held by an officer with the title of "boetarch." Carthage exerted its administrative hegemony with the customary collection of taxes, but also with forms of direct intervention in the island economy: a part of the harvest remained at the disposal of the military command, and the metropolis could moreover intervene to lay down certain operational guidelines for the local economy, forbidding for example the planting of certain crops.

Spain, at least in the Barca period, was governed along lines similar to those followed in North Africa and Sardinia, with unified military commands, obligatory conscription among native tribes and state intervention in certain economic sectors (in particular mining, the proceeds of which went directly to Carthage).

Carthaginian policy in Sicily took a wholly different form. There the Carthaginians collected taxes, as usual, on behalf of the Punic cities, but otherwise their interference in the internal affairs of the region was very much milder. The cities in the Punic part of Sicily remained completely independent as far as local administration and management of the territory were concerned, acknowledging Carthage's authority in the conduct of foreign policy and military expeditions.

In conclusion, it can be stated that in its administrative territories, Carthage showed an indubitable capacity for coordination and control in the fields of tax collection and military organization. What it lacked was a unified grasp of the problems of empire and with it the ability to create a really homogeneous body of people, bound by the common conviction of being an integral part of a state that allowed free political rights and opinions.

This lack probably arose from the fact that Carthage always remained, in its structure and in the conception of its governmental system, a city-state, whose ruling class (with some exceptions, including above all the Barca family and its most illustrious member, Hannibal) never budged from a metropolitan, or at most "North African" political perspective. This must undoubtedly be considered one of the crucial factors of Carthage's weakness and, in the final analysis, one of the reasons that led to its defeat in the conflict with Rome.

Army, Navy and Warfare
Piero Bartoloni

Information on the armies of the Phoenician cities on the Syro-Palestinian coast is very scarce, whereas a good deal is known about the armies of the empires of the Near East. This is mainly due to the political and territorial status of the Phoenician cities, which lacked inland holdings and were therefore unable to equip themselves with large permanent armies. It is therefore more than likely that when the need arose — coinciding usually with an attack by the Assyrians — the city-states arranged for the recruitment of mercenary troops, many of whom came from Anatolia. From the limited sources at our disposal, most of which relate to the annals of the kings of Assyria, we know that infantry troops were supplemented with scythed chariots which were used to break through and disrupt the enemy lines.

In addition, contemporary representations and archaeological finds suggest the use of infantry soldiers armed with spears, daggers, axes and maces, but relatively ill-equipped when it came to their own defence (helmets, armour and shields appear very rarely in reliefs or sculptures); finally, there were teams of archers.

Data concerning the armed forces belonging to the Phoenician cities on the western Mediterranean coast before the conquest of Carthage are equally limited. Historical sources are almost completely silent regarding the composition and organization of the Phoenician armies. It is clear, however, that particularly in the early stages of the colonization process, large armies were both inappropriate and unnecessary since the Phoenicians based their relationship with the peoples of the western Mediterranean coast principally on trade.

It is also obvious that in the early days the Phoenicians did not have enough colonists to permit them to expand politically and commercially through aggression.

The earliest archaeological evidence of Phoenician military activity was discovered in Sardinia and dated from the last years of the 7th and the

Bronze arrow-heads found at Cagliari 3rd century B.C. 2.1-2.8 cm Tunis, Musée du Bardo

Statuette of armed horseman from Byblos 8th-6th century B.C., terra-cotta 33.5 × 24 cm Brussels Musées Royaux d'Art et d'Histoire
• p. 152

first decades of the 6th century B.C. Archaic tombs have revealed, besides pottery, numerous weapons suitable for light infantry. Amongst the weapons, mostly made of iron, are spear-points with serrated edges, spear-butts, short daggers with curved blades and fine lances with bronze points and shafts. The daggers and lances had been placed in sheaths made of a perishable material, probably leather.

Evidence regarding the following centuries is much more ample and detailed. This was the period when Carthage first fought the Greek cities for control of the islands of the central-western Mediterranean and then turned her attention towards Rome. As far as the composition of the Carthaginian armies is concerned, it is most probable that, at least at the outset, the nucleus of the army was made up of citizens in arms, backed up by tributary allies and mercenaries who over time became the main component of the force. Carthaginian coinage came to be widely distributed throughout Sicily in the first instance, and later throughout the North African provinces and Sardinia, not only to check the Greek cities' economic power but also to pay for these large numbers of troops.

The national contingent of the army was made up solely of native-born Carthaginians — foreigners resident in the city did not qualify — and was kept in reserve during battles, moving into action only in times of great danger when there was a possibility of defeat. These battalions of citizens were sometimes protected by ostentatious armour and pieces of jewellery indicating the number of campaigns they had taken part in (for example the young soldiers brought together in the "sacred legion" for the battle of Crimiso fought in 339 B.C. against Syracuse). The citizen-soldiers were involved in the main events of the wars against Sicily, tasting both victory and defeat.

With the passage of time and according to the geographical location of military operations, the use of national troops was gradually phased out in favour of mercenaries, who sometimes formed the core of the Carthaginian armies. The Carthaginians enlisted most of their mercenaries from areas under Carthaginian rule, such as North Africa, or from places with which Carthage had extensive trade links, such as Iberia. Often mercenaries were also recruited from areas which were renowned for the war like character of their peoples, such as Gaul, Campania or Sannio, or where training and discipline formed the basis of military prowess, such as Greece.

The mercenaries from the Balearic Islands were used as light infantry armed with slings; their role was to open the hostilities, and then to irritate the enemy during the various stages of the battle. The remainder of the light infantry consisted of Iberians, who were armed with sabers, and Celts, who used long slashing swords. The phalanx was formed by the Greek mercenaries who were armed with very long spears, particularly during the Hellenistic period. The cavalry squadrons were made up of Celts and Numidians, traditionally highly skilled in horseback warfare. For a better understanding of the composition of the Carthaginian armies, their strategy and their behaviour in the field of battle, it is useful to quote the main points of the account of the battle of Cannae written by the historian Polybius:

"Hannibal brought his slingers and pikemen over the river and placed them in the front line. He stationed the Celtic and Iberian horsemen on the left flank, opposite the Roman cavalry, and next to them he placed half of the African heavy infantry, and then the Iberians and the Celts. Next to them he placed the other half of the African infantry and finally on his right wing the Numidian cavalry. Having drawn up his army in a straight line, he moved forward with the central contingents of Celts and Iberians, creating a crescent-shaped bulge... When the advance guards moved into action, the outcome of the battle between the light infantry looked uncertain, but as soon as the Iberian and Celtic cavalry on the left flank engaged the Roman cavalry, the struggle became fierce... the Carthaginians finally prevailed... and then the infantrymen, finding themselves surrounded, engaged battle with the enemy. For some time the Iberian and Celtic troops bravely held out against the Romans, but then, overwhelmed by the sheer weight of the legions, they were forced back and the convex center of the Carthaginian line was driven in. The Roman forces... easily pierced the enemy's front... and advanced so far forward that they found the African heavy infantry on either side of them... Thus, the Romans, pressing too far ahead in pursuit of the Celts, were trapped between the two African divisions, exactly as Hannibal had planned... the Numidian cavalry on the right flank, attacking the allied cavalry lined up on the Roman left, neither inflicted nor suffered heavy losses... but merely immobilized the enemy... However, when the Carthaginian cavalry on the left flank, after crushing the Roman cavalry... came to the assistance of the Numidians,... the allied Roman cavalry retreated. Hasdrubal... sent the Numidians in pursuit of the retreating cavalry and led his own squadrons to the aid of the Africans, who were still involved in the infantry battle... The Roman legions therefore came under attack from the rear... which served to revive African morale and weaken the Romans... the latter, finding themselves totally surrounded in a small space, were slaughtered to a man... The Numidians managed to slay the majority of the fleeing allied cavalry" (Polybius, III, 113-16).

The reason for quoting Polybius' account of this tragic battle is to show that in addition to Hannibal's genius, there are several other very clear

*Helmet and jamb
from Sant'Antioco
6th century B.C.
bronze
22 cm, 31 cm
Cagliari, Museo
Archeologico
Nazionale*

reasons why the Romans suffered such a crushing defeat. The use of cavalry and the allocation of troops by nationality were important and decisive factors in the outcome of the battle. It should be observed that these military strategies owed very little to contemporary Greek military theory. While it is certainly true that Hannibal was a child of his time and derived some of his inspiration as a military leader from the armies of the Hellenistic age, it is clear that he was equally influenced by the military heritage of the Near East, which used massed horsemen for their great tradition and disruptive qualities, rather than as elite troops, which was how the Greeks and Romans tended to consider the cavalry. The makeup of Carthaginian armies was largely the same as that of contemporary Hellenistic armies, but the methods favoured in the home country were not neglected. As pointed out above, this was particularly evident in the use of heavy contingents of cavalry and, in early times, of scythed chariots, later replaced by battle elephants.

As far as the scythed chariots were concerned, these vehicles probably had one axle only and were usually drawn by a pair of horses. The body held the charioteer and one soldier, usually an archer. Sharp blades were mounted on the rear of the chariot and the wheel hubs. The obvious purpose of this vehicle was to break through the enemy lines and throw them into disarray. However, in order to function with maximum efficiency and reach the required speed, the scythed chariot needed large flat expanses of land, such as the great Mesopotamian plains, for example. Probably for this reason the vehicle was not so often used in the West, where the required amounts of space were few and far between.

The scythed chariots seem to have been soon abandoned and were replaced by battle elephants, which were able to move easily even over rough ground and could cover the same strategic functions as the scythed chariots. These animals belonged to a breed native to North Africa which has since become extinct, and were smaller in size than the Central African elephants of today. It appears that they did not carry the small towers containing archers shown in representations of the battle between Pyrrhus and the Romans, but only their drivers. These drivers, who were probably brought especially from India in the early days, rode on the elephants' necks and carried only a special hook which they used for guiding the animals.

The Carthaginian armies were sometimes particularly large, with up to 90,000 light and heavy infantrymen and 12,000 cavalry. The army with which Hannibal set about crossing the Pyrenees from the Spanish side would have been this size, although this is still a matter of some dispute. Normally, however, the number of men did not exceed 28,000-

30,000, about one sixth of these being cavalry. As for the individual units that made up the army, it appears that each infantry squad consisted of 500 men, while for the cavalry this number was reduced to 50. Three hundred elephants were housed in the special stables built for them within the thickness of the city walls of Carthage. The number of elephants used in battle varied considerably. For example, Hannibal used a line of 40 in the battle of the Tagus but at Zama he deployed twice that number. Hasdrubal used about 200 during his Spanish campaigns. A description of the composition of the Carthaginian armies would be incomplete without some mention of the generals and the officers under their command. The commander of the army was usually a Carthaginian nobleman, appointed by the Assembly in Carthage. He was assisted by a small number of senior officers, all native Carthaginians, who commanded the different units. The general had complete autonomy in his conduct of military campaigns but was personally responsible to the Assembly for the progress and outcome of the war, to the extent that several generals paid for defeats with their own lives. On at least one occasion, however, the command of a Carthaginian army was handed over to a Spartan, one Xanthippus, who introduced certain Hellenistic practices into part of the forces under his command.

Stele with elephant from Carthage 2nd century B.C. limestone 44 × 13.5 cm Carthage, Musée de Carthage

The subalterns, on the other hand, came from the ranks of the foreign or mercenary troops and gave orders in their native language, with interpreters beside them to act as intermediaries with the commander.

The navy was the second but not least important part of the Phoenician and Carthaginian war machine. The Phoenicians boasted a long naval tradition which was held in great respect by the peoples of the Mediterranean. It may be recalled that the naval battle of Salamis was fought for the Persians chiefly by the joint Phoenician fleets. The Phoenician cities on the Syro-Palestinian coast were equipped mostly with fleets of warships, which had one or more banks of oars. The older warships, from the beginning of the 1st millennium B.C., had only one bank of oars, but these were very soon superseded by more sophisticated designs with two or even three banks. According to some historians it was the Phoenicians of Sidon who invented the trireme, but others, in particular Thucydides (I, 13, 2) attribute this development to the city of Corinth around the 8th century B.C. In fact there had been a Phoenician trading station in Corinth for many years and the Corinthians may well have taken their inspiration from the Phoenician ships.

*Scarab depicting
warrior
from Tharros
5th century B.C.
green jasper with
gold mount
1.4 cm
Cagliari, Museo
Archeologico
Nazionale*

Classical sources attribute the development of the quadrireme or *tetera* to Carthage, around the 5th century B.C., and later of the quinquereme or *pentera*, which became the main warship used during the war against Rome.

The crews of these warships, from the officers to the deckhands and oarsmen, were all Carthaginians. We do not know whether the shipowner (who sometimes had to fit out the ship against his will) also became the commander, as happened in ancient Greece, but given the rapid development of war fleets in the Hellenistic age, with often dramatic results, it is likely that the vessels were owned and fitted out solely by the state power of Carthage.

The ships were commanded by at least three officers, the chief of whom was in charge, the second was *proreuta*, or second in command, while the third was the pilot, held in great esteem because of his experience. No more than 30 sailors handled the sails and worked on deck; while the number of oarsmen varied according to the type and size of the ship. For a trireme, we know that around 150 men manned the oars, while a quadrireme required about 240 and the quinquereme 300. To this number must be added between 10 and 20 infantry soldiers who became operative during battle or landings.

The warships were propelled using both sails and oars, usually alternatively. The ship had two masts, one at the bow and the other amidships, on which were hoisted the sails, fixed to yards. The central sail, the larger of the two, provided the lift, while the bowsail was used for steering. The sails were used for normal travelling and for approaching the battle area, then during battle the masts were removed and the ship was propelled using only the oars.

Each squad was made up of 12 ships, supplemented by several smaller craft, swift and easily maneuverable, used mainly for passing communications between the ships themselves and between the ships and dry land. The fleet was composed of several squads usually totalling 120 ships, although some sources have reported the existence of even larger fleets with 180-200 ships.

As far as the pattern of battles was concerned, these took place primarily near the coast where it was possible to find relatively calm stretches of water which allowed the ships to be steered with ease and provided greater safety to the crews of ramming ships. Before the conflict, the ships were arranged either in a straight line or in a convex formation. The signal for the advance was communicated to the fleet by raising a red flag or by means of the smaller ships mentioned earlier. Since the principal aim was to sink the enemy ships or make them uncontrollable through use of the ship's rostrum, it was essential to reach maximum speed as soon as the order was given to advance. Two tactics were used, according to the amount of space between the enemy

165

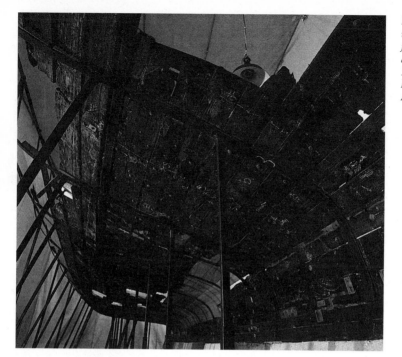

ships. If there was a sufficient gap, the ship moved alongside the enemy vessel and, turning swiftly, aimed a rostrum thrust into the hull. If space was limited, the ship passed by the enemy, turned and hit it in the stern. In the meantime the smaller craft moved around the battle area to offer help to damaged ships or tow away captured enemy vessels.

Part II   The Great Areas

Phoenicia
Antonia Ciasca

The density of the population and settlements along the Phoenician coast is one of the main constants underlying the entire history of the region. It is also a limitation which has negatively conditioned the possibility of on-site research. Subsequent building over the ages, from the large Hellenistic and Roman cities down to the crusader castles and Arab towns, created far-reaching upheavals that have badly damaged the earliest phases, often eradicating the evidence of whole centuries of history.

Byblos, Roman buildings on earlier Phoenician settlement

The Phoenician cities of greatest historical importance are the ones most severely compromised by the superimposition of monumental structures, which prevent even an outline evaluation of the buildings and urban layouts for which they were famous, in fact models which the Phoenician kings exported to neighboring kingdoms together with the skill of their craftsmen. In the case of Tyre, it is highly improbable that the "Church of the Crusades" will be torn down to allow investigation of the famous temple of Melqarth, as the director of the Department of Antiquities in Lebanon, Emir M. Chéhab, has observed. Though the problems elsewhere may be less obvious, they are substantially the same for many of the ancient settlements of Phoenicia. The sheer compactness of these places, especially the citadels and the island towns, also limits the chances of unearthing intact layers of settlement. Those parts of the necropoli which have survived ancient and modern acts of destruction and depredation are better known than the towns themselves, but at present offer little evidence for the centuries preceding Persian dominion.

The dearth of archaeological data is particularly serious in the case of the Iron Age (c. 1200-555 B.C.), which represents the central stage of the history of the city-states. During this period, the elements typical of Phoenician culture emerged and the colonial expansion toward the West took place.

In addition to the paucity of the evidence yielded by the Phoenician cities, a further limitation to our knowledge lies in the nature of the objects found in the neighbouring regions (Palestine, Assyria). This material is not fully representative, since many of the finest products of Phoenician workmanship (apart from the celebrated purple-dyed fabrics, obviously perishable) were made specifically for export, or on commission, such as ivories and metalwork. Consequently their stylistic and iconographic features are only marginally representative of Phoenician figurative culture. Even in the case of material culture, and its most widespread and modest evidence, pottery, there is still much uncertainty, not only in distinguishing between imported

items and local manufacture (for instance between Phoenicia and Cyprus) but also in correctly ascertaining which very common types and forms really originated in the Phoenician cities. This uncertainty is even stronger in the case of the earliest examples of the western colonies.

The ruins of the larger Phoenician cities, then, do not furnish a very reliable map of their layout and shed relatively little light on their specific cultural characteristics. Better possibilities are offered by centres of minor political importance, such as Sarepta, where excavations have been carried out using modern archaeological methods, and an abundance of material has come to light. This material has yielded a rich fund of data relating to an unbroken history of habitation between the 13th and 6th-5th centuries B.C., which provides a solid basis for the development of the work on other sites. Excavations in some of the minor or more remote inhabited sites have supplied (and continue to supply) important information for our knowledge of the Phoenician world. These include Tell Suqas, on the northern border, the site at Ras Ibn Hany, even further north, and the series of excavations along the coastline south of Carmel. All these sites have provided rich evidence of the contacts established between the Phoenicians and outside cultures, especially those of Syria, Palestine, and the Aegean. The current tendency among scholars is to consider this as evidence of the simultaneous presence of people of diverse cultural origins in these centers.

Byblos
Byblos is situated on a headland about 37 km north of Beirut, bounded by two small water-courses to the north and the south. The preserved area of the city is of approximately five hectares and is bordered on the east by an outcrop of calcareous rock sloping gradually towards the sea. A spring rising in a deep cleft in the rock was a crucial factor throughout the history of the settlement. Excavation work carried out over many years has exposed traces of at least fifteen main stages or periods of habitation, stretching from prehistoric times to the Arab conquest. Carbon-dating tests have set the age of the earliest settlement at around 7000 ± 80. The Phoenician settlement, of the 1st millennium B.C., however, still lies outside the excavated area. The superimposition of remains and the upheaval caused by the construction of large buildings in Roman times have made it difficult to reconstruct complete ground plans of the various settlements, but the fragmentary data recovered offer an historical view of exceptional importance and breadth. As in the case of Palestine and southern Syria, the development of Byblos

Byblos
Roman ruins

*Byblos
aerial view*

as a city probably dates back to the beginning of the 3rd millennium B.C., during the Early Bronze Age. The settlement expanded rapidly, especially after c. 2700 B.C. Proof of trade links with Egypt exists in the form of a fragment of an alabaster vase bearing the name of Khasekhem, the last pharaoh of the 2nd dynasty. Its urban character is underlined by the stone perimeter wall, punctuated inside by a series of square buttresses, with a main gateway at the northeast accessed by a huge ramp. The settlement's main thoroughfare is a broad street cutting across irregularly from north to south. The houses have a regular floorplan with a spacious central courtyard and rooms off either side, and are built with a mixture of materials: stone blocks, mud bricks, wooden facing, and mud plaster on the walls. The roof was held up by rows of wooden columns against the walls and down the centre of the room. Two doors were used, facing north and south. The central area around the spring was rebuilt and assigned a strictly sacred function which it retained. Also dating from this period is the conversion into a temple of a complex dedicated to the "Lady of Byblos," on foundations dating back to the Chalcolithic period, including a wide courtyard with rooms leading off it on at least three sides. In front of the altar in the courtyard rose five colossal statues (their fragments have been found), representing three divinities and probably two pharaohs in the role of devotees. The sculptures are certainly of local manufacture, although strongly

Egyptian in iconography and style, and the whole layout of the temple is considered to be an adaptation of Egyptian and Asiatic types. Another large-scale sacred complex is dedicated to a male divinity.

Like many other Phoenician and Palestinian cities, around 2300-2200 B.C. Byblos was destroyed during the invasion of the Amorites; many such towns were never rebuilt, but ports such as Byblos and Ugarit (Ras Shamra) quickly regained their former prosperity.

Byblos experienced a fresh burst of urban vitality during the Middle and Late Bronze Ages, when many large-scale works were undertaken, including the reconstruction of the Baalath temple and the erection of new sanctuaries. The temple dedicated to the male deity (temple of Reshef or of the Obelisks) took on the form it was to keep until the period of Persian dominion. It consisted of a square cell and an antechamber or portico, in a sacred enclosure accessed from a large courtyard or from outside, where service buildings stood. In the center of the courtyard was the great obelisk, surrounded by a series of cult shrines and a number of smaller obelisks or obelisk-chapels. The influx of offerings, which had waned considerably, picked up again, indicating the renewed prestige that the city and its temples were enjoying.

This intensification of activity is amply attested by the votive repositories under the Reshef and the Baalath temple floors, including the *Montet Jar* containing about one thousand objects of varying origins, which was placed around 2130 B.C. or shortly afterwards. The Byblos workshops produced votive offerings for the temples (bronze statuettes covered in gold leaf, gold model or votive axes in Mesopotamian style with filigree work, etc.). The frequent gifts from the pharaohs bear witness to renewed relations with Egypt. The tombs of the kings of Byblos also contain sumptuous goldsmiths' work, such as a casket in obsidian and gold inscribed with the name of Amenemhet IV, and jewellery of local manufacture echoing Egyptian motifs and techniques. One of the burial areas designated for civic use stands to the northeast of the city (necropolis K) and contains dug-out tombs with access shafts.

Besides Egypt, the city's trade relations included the Aegean coast (a Kamares-style vase was found in one of the tombs) and, to the east, Mesopotamia (Byblos is mentioned in a text of the 3rd dynasty of Ur) and Syria.

Between the 18th and 16th centuries B.C. (the Hyksos period), the central part of Byblos was still reserved for worship and the residential area probably spread outside the fortified walls. Five tombs in the royal necropolis, kept in continuous use, attest to great affluence and thriving contacts with the outside world, particularly with northern Syria and the Aegean.

Male statuette with silver and gold leaf from Phoenicia late 3rd-early 2nd millennium B.C. bronze, silver and gold, 14.9 cm Beirut Archeological Museum American University

Byblos, view of the "temple of the obelisks"

Around 1200-1100 B.C., Byblos was probably involved in the waste and destruction that followed the invasion of the "Peoples of the Sea." Relatively little information has survived concerning the period between the end of the Late Bronze Age and the beginning of the Iron Age, partly due to the erosion and progressive landslip of the whole western sector of the promontory. There are however no traces in Byblos of any settlement of the invading peoples. We have very little archaeological evidence for Byblos during the period of Phoenician independence (11th-8th century B.C.) and the subsequent period of Assyrian and Babylonian domination. We do know that the city's defences were rebuilt and strengthened a number of times. In the eastern section of Byblos, a sturdy wall with a glacis was erected near the city gate (9th-8th century B.C.); to this was later linked a watch tower (7th century B.C.). Between the late 7th and early 6th centuries, advanced defences were added.

The royal necropolis remained in use until at least the end of the 9th century B.C.; it was tomb V of this necropolis that yielded the sarcophagus of Ahiram, king of Byblos, dedicated by his son according to the Phoenician inscription engraved on the lid. On the same occasion a message was also carved into the wall at the top of the access shaft to warn away tomb robbers. The upper part of the shaft was fitted with a wooden floor over embedded beams and used for funerary rites. Fragments of vases dating from the 9th century B.C. are evidence of the last burial here. In addition to Ahiram's sarcophagus, the funeral chamber itself contained another two chest-shaped sarcophagi, clearly shifted to one side to allow room for the next. Among the earliest grave goods (fragments of a carved ivory plaquette, pottery, objects in alabaster) is an alabaster vase bearing the name of Rameses II (1301-1234 B.C.).

The period of Persian domination undoubtedly witnessed a surge in the economy of Byblos attested by the building activity under King Yehawmilk, who undertook restoration work on the city's public buildings, and in particular on the ancient sanctuary of Baalath; the king's contribution is solemnly recorded on the commemorative stelae on which he appears kneeling before the goddess in the attitude of a devoted gift-bearer. A monumental entrance with a gateway is cited as being decorated by a winged sun; the bulging column bases found in the area may have been part of it. According to some scholars, also belonging to this period are certain architectural features in a decidedly Egyptian style, such as the architrave with its uraeus frieze. In the last decades of the 6th century B.C. an imposing rectangular platform or terrace was built in the northeast sector of the city walls, with towers at each corner. The solidity and engineering skill of this work are complemented by an isolated decorative feature, a lion protome in Syrian style. Crowning the terrace was a rectangular building (50 × 25 m), with a double row of pillars. The floorplan puts the structure in the same category as the *apadana* type of building (for example, Pasargadae) common in Iranian imperial architecture. While the fortified structures were reinforced and completed over time (for instance, by the inclusion of a glacis at the east corner of the towered perimeter wall), it was not until the late 5th or early 4th century B.C. that the defense system towards the northeast was further extended into the plain, with the addition of another fortified line equipped with seven solid square towers. The result was a series of progressive lines of defence built on different levels, linked by ramps leading to the uppermost platform dating from the 6th century. This system was already in disuse by the 3rd century B.C.

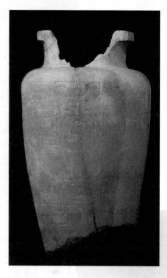

Vase with Pharaoh Pepi I cartouche from Byblos 24th-23rd century B.C., alabaster 26 cm, Beirut Archeological Museum American University

As in other Phoenician cities, the Roman buildings at Byblos included features typical of Assyrian and Babylonian architecture such as tiered battlements (such features had already been assimilated into the local building tradition in the previous centuries and are also found in Susah and Persepolis). The memory of Egyptian religious symbolism remained, however, blended with standard classical solutions, as in the architrave with a winged sun.

Sidon

The city of Sidon is situated on a small promontory amid a line of islets following the coastline. There are two small rivers to the north and south (El Kamlé, El Barghout). The oldest surviving remains of the settlement date back to mid-way through the 4th millennium B.C. A little further to the south (Dakerman), traces of a Chalcolithic settlement have come to light in an area later used as a necropolis. This village belongs to the end of the 4th millennium, and has oval huts built of rough-hewn stone blocks covered with a thick mud plaster. The village was surrounded by a wall over two metres thick with a carefully built outer face. Eight tombs containing inhumed adult remains in jars have been unearthed in the village area. The area immediately inland from Sidon has supplied a profusion of tombs dating from the Bronze Age. These throw light on the context in which the city developed, since almost nothing has come to light in the urban area itself. Roughly 10 km east of Sidon is the site of Kafer-Giarra. Here a great many Middle and Late Bronze Age tombs have been located, dug out of the rock-face and complete with shaft and burial chamber. The grave goods include Egyptian scarabs, socketed bronze axes, Syrian style cylinder seals, weapons, objects in faience, etc. Locally made vases are linked to the pottery production of southern Syria and differ considerably from traditional Canaanite earthenware of the Early Bronze Age; a number of painted fragments have been traced back to Cypriot workshops of the same period. The site of Lébé'a has yielded similar material, with occasional evidence of Early Bronze Age habitation.

Northeast of Sidon, in the town of Majdalouna, a tomb of the usual type (in use between the 16th and the early 15th centuries B.C.) has yielded a considerable amount of Cypriot pottery, scarabs made of faience, bronze weapons, and pottery from local workshops with Syrian characteristics. A cave at Qrayé adapted for funerary use contained jewellery and beads made from various materials, and also 15 scarabs dating from the 18th dynasty (two bearing the name of Thutmose III), amphorae for transporting goods, Cypriot pottery and other material. A small flasklike amphora imported from Mycenae and others of local origin indicate renewed contacts with the Mycenaeans after the break caused by the arrival of the Hyksos.

The cemetery areas of Iron Age Sidon before the start of the Persian period have been steadily emerging, thanks to the efforts of the Lebanese Department of Antiquities especially in the last few decades. Dakerman, in the south, is a vast necropolis that was in use from the 14th century B.C. up to the 1st century A.D.; it has already yielded several hundred tombs of varying types — simple cists in the sand (Late Bronze Age), stone cist tombs or burial chambers (7th-6th century B.C.), and terracotta sarcophagi (Late Hellenistic and Early Roman periods). The simplicity of the tombs identifies this necropolis as the burial ground for the middle and lower classes of the population. The grave goods include a large selection of late Mycenaean, Cypriot and local pottery, together with ware imported from Egypt, and are of fundamental importance for an understanding of the relations between the eastern Mediterranean countries during the last quarter of the 2nd millennium B.C. The discovery of pottery comparable to the classic black-glazed Greek vases provides a useful point of reference for establishing the chronology of the Phoenician world in the Late Iron Age.

The necropolis of Tambourit to the southeast probably also belonged to Sidon. The discovery of the remains of a tomb containing cremations carved out of the rock has yielded local vases and a Greek geometric pyxis (dating from the end of Early Geometric and start of Middle Geometric around the third quarter of the 9th century B.C.) and a locally made amphora with a brief painted inscription in Phoenician characters.

Ain el-Helwé, south of the Barghout river, was undoubtedly in active use around the 8th-7th century B.C., it has yielded a number of artifacts typical of Phoenician workshops (including a fragment of an ivory statuette of a female figure and a "palette" for cosmetics). The sector called Sheikh Abaroh on the southerly beach is of the same date.

The temple of Eshmun at Sidon

The "royal" necropoli are distributed along the line of hills inland of Sidon. The tombs are rock-carved and usually include a shaft. The Mogheret Abloun sector has yielded the sarcophagus of Eshmunazar, while the sarcophagus of Tabnith comes from Aya. The typology of the tombs found here, defined by E. Renan and G. Contenau after the excavations started in 1887, is still substantially applicable: a) chamber-and-shaft (the oldest were in use in the 7th-6th century B.C.); b) tomb with vaulted ceiling and niches; and c) large funerary chambers with plastered walls bearing painted decorations. At least some of the shaft tombs may have originally been surmounted by a small monument, for example Eshmunazar's tomb, of which only a deep vertical access shaft survives. During the Persian and Hellenistic periods the area was intensively used, but the burial chambers were often reopened down to Imperial Roman times. Whole sections of these necropoli were virtually obliterated by quarrying activity (for example at Abloun, semi-destroyed by 1867). The control enforced today by the Lebanese Department of Antiquities, however, allows important finds still to be made and ensures the continuation of work according to modern criteria. In 1963 Abloun was the site of the discovery of a typical single shaft tomb, with two chambers and burial niches carved out of the rock, containing a number of anthropoid sarcophagi and also wooden caskets, particularly rich in personal ornaments.

Ain el-Helwé also yielded the anthropoid sarcophagi now preserved in the National Museum in Beirut. A single underground complex with several rooms contained sarcophagi with Graeco-Ionic reliefs — the "Lycian" sarcophagus (c. 400 B.C.), the "satrap's" sarcophagus (380-370 B.C.), the "weepers'" sarcophagus (360-350 B.C.), Alexander's sarcophagus (after 332 B.C.), and an anthropoid sarcophagus.

Sidon was undoubtedly one of the production centers of anthropoid sarcophagi (a number of unfinished sarcophagi have come to light), with high-quality workshops where Greek sculptors carved marble from their own country. Production probably ended before the destruction of the city in 350 B.C.

The site of the Phoenician citadel, identified on the promontory now occupied by the St. Louis Castle near the southern port, has remains dating from the second half of the 2nd millennium B.C., plus other evidence of Hellenistic-Roman buildings; a number of scholars have suggested the existence of an official Assyrian residence in Sidon following the discovery of a column base with the enlarged, torus moulding and floral decorations commonly found in northern Syria. This column might belong to the period immediately following Esarhaddon's punitive expedition against the Phoenician cities.

Detail of the temple of Eshmun at Sidon

What is certain, however, is that Sidon was the seat of a Persian governor, whose palace was built in typically Achaemenid style, probably by imported labor — a fragment of a capital with double taurine protome found on the site shows close parallels with the architecture of Persepolis. The excavations conducted by G. Contenau in 1914 in the southern outskirts of Sidon brought to light one of the industrial districts of the city, reserved for fabric dyeing, and in fact the mound of refuse dumped there is still 40 meters high.

Situated not far from Sidon, the temple of Eshmun spreads out over a series of split-level terraces along the southern side of the Nahr el-Awali valley, just where the river runs out onto the coastal plain. To the period of Neo-Babylonian domination (first half of the 6th century B.C.) belong the remains of a section of terracing on a pyramidal base. Its construction was a remarkable feat of building skill; its shape links it to Mesopotamian ziggurats. Also connected with this phase of the city's history are fragments of torus mouldings for column bases, faceted columns, etc., and a chamber with sculpted bucrania, dedicated to Hadad. The votive offerings include a number of sculptures in the Cypro-Phoenician manner. The large-scale alterations carried out on the sanctuary have also been attributed to the Achaemenid period. The chief work was the construction of a massive podium (60 × 40 m) built out of huge blocks near the river bed at the foot of the valley. Work on a marble temple constructed on the podium has been dated around 500 B.C. (all traces of this building have been lost owing to the lime-kilns installed in the area in a later epoch). The immense podium draws on the Achaemenid style of architecture, which has also been found elsewhere in Phoenicia, including at Byblos, while the temple was probably built by Ionic artisans, known to have been active in Phoenicia and at Persepolis, in a style that has been defined by M. Dunand as "Graeco-Iranian." From the 5th to midway through the 4th century B.C. the sanctuary was enlarged with a series of new structures richly decorated with reliefs. The so-called "tribune," set against the podium wall, has a parapet embellished with twin sculpted registers (depicting various divinities, maenads, satyrs, etc.) in a style that recalls the school of Halicarnassus. During the Hellenistic period, the sanctuary was extended from the foot of the podium across the valley. The new constructions included a large building encircling the original chamber, the pool of the goddess Astarte, decorated with sculpted friezes, and another building put up alongside. The area has yielded a great many stone votive objects, including statues of athletes or of children, symbolic urns, etc. The presence of Hellenistic pottery, including imported ware (Rhodes, Pergamon), confirms the intensity of trade contacts. The sanctuary continued to be altered. The structures added over the centuries include a colonnade, covering part of the preceding buildings along the bottom of the valley (3rd century A.D.), a nymphaeum, a hypocaust, a chapel, a Christian church, and so forth.

Tyre

Virtually every trace of the Phoenician city of Tyre has been eliminated. Extensively reconstructed as a Hellenistic city, its relatively limited surface area was subsequently covered over by major Roman, Byzantine and crusader buildings. In addition, some parts of the city are now below sea level.

Recent excavations have confirmed that the site was settled from at least the 3rd millennium B.C., with a permanent settlement being established in the Early Bronze Age. The correlation between the archaeological evidence and the tradition of the priests of Melqarth, reported by Herodotus, which claimed that the city and its temple were established around 2750 B.C., is satisfyingly close. There is no reference to Tyre in the Egyptian texts of the Old Kingdom. Moreover, a thick layer of sand provides archaeological evidence of the fact that between the years 2000 and 1600 B.C. the site was abandoned. This would appear to invalidate the theory that Tyre was referred to in the Egyptian Execration texts. The first definitive references appear in the El-Amarna letters while Mycenaean pottery finds (Myc III A-C) and Greek ware from the late Proto-Geometric period supply evidence of contact with the Aegean.

Plan of the area of Tyre

Historians and geographers have furnished written accounts of the city. Built on a series of islets and rocks along the coast about 600 meters from the mainland, the city had two ports, the northern "Sidonian" port, which corresponds to the present-day port, and the southern "Egyptian" port, which was abandoned after the Byzantine period. Detailed underwater and air archaeological investigations carried out around the site of the south port between 1934 and 1936 analyzed remains probably dating from the Hellenistic and Roman periods. These comprise a series of breakwaters and piers enclosing the inner harbor, with towers commanding the entrances. Inside the harbour, quays with man-made embankments enclosed variously shaped bays which were often interlinked (a paved dry-dock for repairs, etc.). The external pier is linked to the city walls by an enormous tower measuring 17 × 7.5 m.

Tyre present-day port which corresponds to the ancient northern port

Josephus tells us that the city's main temple, dedicated to Melqarth, was built by Hiram I in the 10th century B.C. on the northernmost and largest island, after razing the remains of a previous temple. In front of the façade stood two stelae or columns, one of gold and the other of emerald. It has not proved possible to uncover the temple itself but it is probably located under the basilica built by the crusaders, where M. Chéhab's excavations brought to light the remains of large Phoenician public buildings. In the immediate vicinity was found an altar with a dedication in Greek to Heracles Haghios, dated to A.D. 187-188. It is reasonable to suppose that there were close similarities between the temple of Melqarth in Tyre and the temple in Jerusalem, which

Hiram's craftsmen helped to build. Its longitudinal plan, with a vestibule, antechamber and long room set along the main axis, is derived from a temple design developed in Syria during the Middle Bronze Age and used over a long period of time (Ebla, Tell Fray, Meskene-Emar, Alalakh, Tell Ta'yinat) not only in Syria but also in Palestine (Hazor). According to Palestinian evidence from the Solomonic era the façade made great use of stone and wood, and had tiered merlons and a variety of capitals, including some with double volutes. There is no evidence of the use of any Egyptianizing elements.

The southernmost island that made up Tyre, and which today forms the southwest tip of the peninsula, was the site of another of the city's main temples, dedicated to a god whom the Greeks identified with their Zeus Olympus. The sources also mention the existence of other temples in the city, such as the one dedicated to Astarte which some scholars believe was located on the mainland. Another temple to Melqarth also stood on the mainland, which according to some sources (Justin, Curtius Rufus), was even more ancient than the one already mentioned on the island.

Tyre's urban fabric was enhanced by a number of other works carried out

Throne with dedication to Astarte from Khirbet et-Tayibeh, Tyre 2nd century B.C. limestone, 47 cm Paris, Musée du Louvre

during Hiram's reign. These included the reclamation of the land between the two islands, giving the city an extensive open space which was probably used as a public square and marketplace. Hiram has also been credited with the construction of the ports. However, it has been estimated that the entire surface area of the city never exceeded one square kilometer.

The mainland sector of the city of Tyre (called Ushu in Egyptian and Assyrian texts and Palai-Tyros in classical sources) was situated 6 km (30 stadia) further south, probably corresponding to the modern Rashidiyeh-Ras el 'Ain. The causeway built by Alexander the Great to reach the besieged city, and the gradual silting up around this line, contributed towards extending the artificial area which emerged (and was later inhabited), creating the land configuration that we see today, that of a peninsula jutting into the sea.

The city must have been very heavily fortified from as early as the 9th century B.C. On the reliefs of the bronze doors of Balawat, Tyre is shown as a city encircled by a crenellated wall with towers and two gates. The reconstructed fortifications brought to light by excavations over the last few years belong to the Persian period, and include a double set of dry stone walls, 4 m thick, with towers at the water's edge. Outside the walls, the beach on the landward side between the two ports probably accommodated shipyards and functioned as a berth for the ferry that plied to and from the mainland. Of the necropolis in use from the Middle Bronze Age, only a very small part has been found south of Tyre along the coast, at Rashidiyeh, but the remains of tombs have been discovered in the countryside around the city. Another part of the necropolis extends inland at the site of Joya. The tombs found at Rashidiyeh are of the shaft type. Archaeological evidence has revealed that cremation was practiced in the 9th-8th century B.C. The most frequently found type of pottery has a light background with a painted decoration of concentric circles, comparable in style to the contemporary ware of Cypriot workshops. Tyre is the site of a tomb of unusual design. It is shaped like a large chest-sarcophagus, set on a pedestal of three massive rows of stone blocks; a stylistic connection with the tomb of Cyrus at Pasargadae has been suggested.

Sarepta
Thanks partly to epigraphic finds, the ancient center of Sarepta has been definitely identified at a coastal site near the modern village of Sarafand, about 15 km south of Sidon. In addition to evidence dating from the Roman and Byzantine periods, scattered over an extensive area, the hill that formed part of the city has provided a clear, although incomplete, picture of the main features of a Phoenician town, and of its economic activity.
There is proof of an earlier settlement in the remains of tombs dating from the end of the Middle Bronze Age, but archaeological evidence of dwellings starts at the beginning of the Late Bronze Age (c. 1600 B.C.). Development then continued apparently uninterrupted until the height of the Hellenistic period. The reference to Sarepta in a text from Ugarit dating from the 14th century B.C. and the discovery on the site of an amphora handle with a Ugaritic inscription demonstrate that commercial relations existed with the northern coastal towns, while the mention of the city's name next to those of Sidon and Tyre in an Egyptian 13th-century text shows that it was an important city, at least in the southern sector of the Phoenician area.
The extensive surveys made in different parts of the city, on the top of the hill and on the slopes leading to the sea, have produced evidence which can easily be integrated and compared to existing documentation. The buildings discovered belong to neighbourhoods which seem to have been industrial and residential at the same time, apparently a typical feature of life in this city. The main industries were the production of purple dye, metalwork, and food-crops, especially olives. Some particularly significant similarities with the metalwork of Enkomi in Cyprus have been noted, and Mycenaean imports are associated with the 14th and 13th centuries B.C. For subsequent periods there is particular evidence of the production of pottery — mainly large containers designed for transporting food-stuffs — fired in bilobate kilns.
The delicate red-slip pottery which is typically Phoenician makes its first appearance in an archaeological stratum that is considered to be fully Phoenician, although its general context provides no signs to distinguish it from the preceding settlement and manufacturing output. Contact with Cyprus continued during this period, and there is a fragment of the imported Greek pottery most commonly found in the Near East (Proto-Geometric cup with semicircular motifs). The features that can be considered typically Phoenician become more pronounced between the late 9th and early 8th centuries B.C., not only in the pottery, but also in the particular building techniques which involved the use of square blocks and "frame walls."
In the lower part of the city, a road separated the industrial zone that housed

the pottery works from an area allocated to a different use. Two small shrines were built here, one on the ruins of the other, with different floor plans.

The older shrine (which has survived better than its successor) was in use from the 8th to the 6th century B.C. Its small size and the unexcavated remains of adjacent buildings have led experts to the conclusion that this chapel belonged either to a larger religious complex or to a palace. It has a rectangular floor plan (6.4 × 2.5 m) on an east-west axis with the entrance near the corner of one of the longer walls. This door was later bricked up in favour of another opening on the short east side, probably to make access easier from the road that ran alongside. Typical features found in the chapel include a raised platform built in stone along three of the walls, the altar for offerings, placed against the shorter wall opposite the entrance, and a socket in the floor for inserting a pole or standard before the altar (for a baetyl or an incense burner).

The plan of the building and the cult installations bear similarities to other buildings found in Palestine and Cyprus. A great many of the objects discovered around the altar are undoubtedly votive offerings that comprise typical examples of Phoenician artifacts and iconography (including various items in terracotta, ivory and pottery), and faience amulets and a phial for cosmetics in Egyptian alabaster. Several inscriptions in Phoenician have also been found in the shrine, one of which is carved on a small ivory plaque and refers to a statue dedicated to Tanit-Astarte.

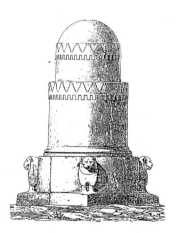

Design in perspective of a restored funerary monument from the necropolis at Amrith as interpreted by Ernest Renan

Amrith

Located on a narrow coastal strip, the site of Amrith was bounded on the east by a rock face, and enclosed between the courses of two small rivers, Nahr Amrith and Nahle el Kublé. It was fed by two perennial springs. Higher up in the rocky area to the east of the city are two archaeological sites, one to the north, where remains of a settlement called Tell Amrith have been found, and a second to the south, with the necropolis. The corresponding coastline has no inlets and hence was unsuitable for use as a port. The lowland bounded by the coastal dunes (which would have been flooded especially during the winter and spring seasons) was the part of the city designated for religious practice. In fact two groups of sanctuaries at some distance from each other — Ain el Hayat to the south and the so-called *maabed* to the north — have been discovered immediately below the slopes of the inhabited area. Archaeological finds have revealed that there was a period of settlement during the Early Bronze Age (towards the end of the 3rd millennium B.C.) and the city may be mentioned in the lists of Pharaoh Thutmose III relating to his Asian campaign, and also in the texts from Ugarit and from Assyria. During the Phoenician period Amrith must have had particularly close ties with the adjacent island city of Aradus, and may well even have been its mainland extension.

181

The northern sanctuary, already known from E. Renan's explorations, was the subject of extensive study in the post-war period. A series of excavations and detailed surveys brought to light hundreds of architectural fragments, which are still being studied with a view to reconstruction, but which have in the meantime been described in various publications. As a result of this archaeological research, a monument of outstanding importance has been rediscovered. The general layout has been traced back to Egyptian designs and it must have been built during the Persian period. It was built in part by carving out the rock face to a depth of 3-3.5 m, and in part by the addition of stone blocks. The most unusual feature of the sanctuary is a rectangular basin (c. 47 × 39 m) carved out of the rock. In the center a square dais was left standing, which formed the base for a small chapel (3.5 × 3.8 m). Water gushing from the spring nearby would have flooded this basin to form an artificial pool around the chapel. The pool was enclosed on three sides by porticoed passages at water level, their roofs supported by rows of closely spaced heavy rectangular pillars. On the northern side was a monumental entrance, flanked by a pair of towers, between which were two symmetrical altars. The reconstructed plan provides some very interesting details. The central chapel with flat roof was decorated with Egyptian mouldings on all sides, surmounted by a band with a relief design of tiered merlons. The dais had a similar ornamentation at the top. The three wings of the portico, also decorated with a running band of merlons, were probably covered over with a roof (possibly coffered), made of stone blocks resting horizontally on the pillars at the front and the rock walls behind. In the two towers flanking the monumental entrance (perhaps the only constructions visible from the land side) the dividing line between the two floors was decorated with merlons, while on the roof terrace the same decorations appeared on the parapet. A spout in the form of a lion's head carried rainwater into the basin below. The sanctuary was dedicated to a healing god (Shadrapa or Eshmun). A nearby repository contained votive offerings, particularly stone and terracotta statuettes in Phoenician style. The necropolis at Amrith is one of the few to have intact examples of the funerary monuments built over the usual burial chambers carved out of the rock. One of these monuments could be considered a "tower mausoleum," of the type that spread from the coast of Asia to the Punic regions of Northern Africa. It has a concave moulding crowned with an obelisk (late 4th-early 3rd century B.C.). The obelisk is a distinctive feature of another tomb, built in the shape of a cube with loculi, probably dating from the 3rd century B.C. Another funerary monument has a cylindrical shape, with a series of sculpted lions emerging from the stone, tiered merlons, and dentils.

Amrith's Maabed in a graphic interpretation by Ernest Renan

Fragment of female statuette with hands to breasts from Amrith 6th-4th century B.C., terra-cotta 9.1 cm, Beirut Archeological Museum American University

The tombs at Amrith have yielded a number of anthropoid sarcophagi, including one made of terra-cotta.

Suqas

Archaeological research on the site of Tell Suqas (probably the Shukshu of the Late Bronze Age, a city at the southern extreme of the territory under Ugaritic rule) has provided evidence of the presence of different cultural groups living in the area, inferred from the variety of religious practices. The stretch of coast below the southern port and the hill containing the remains of the city were used as a religious site from the Late Bronze Age and certainly served this purpose until the 2nd century B.C. During this period the site underwent a number of alterations (sometimes very radical) in relation to the different religious practices of the different groups of residents, Phoenicians and Greeks. An extensive votive depository consisting of small groups of vases together with the remains of cremated bones has been dated to the period between the end of the Bronze and the start of the Iron Age (late 13th-first half of the 10th century B.C.). These finds may be remains from cremation tombs or represent a burial ground of the *tophet* type, very common in western Phoenician colonies.

In the later Iron Age the sanctuary consisted of a sort of raised terrace with a trench for sacrifices of the "high place" type. Nearby was found a small temple with a porch and external altar, built in the Greek style with a tiled roof, where Greek pottery (from the 8th century B.C.) came to light. In one part of the open space near the temple a series of tombs were found containing Greek ware next to Phoenician-style cinerary urns. During the 6th century B.C. the temple and the buildings around it were rebuilt and expanded, and the quantities of Greek pottery increased. In the necropolis a chapel open to one side was built, containing a baetyl and two altars with different functions.

Tell Dor

Eshmunazar's inscription suggests that the centre of Dor (traced to modern Khirbet el-Burj) was under the sovereignty of Sidon and it is reasonable to suppose that during this period it was an important Phoenician port city. The strata of the 11th and 10th centuries B.C. contain fragments of painted Cypriot pottery. Recent archaeological research has brought to light a stretch of the city wall which includes remnants of a monumental entrance gate with rooms inside and two towers flanking it outside; the construction is of mud bricks on a stone base. Considering its distinctive features, this complex, in use from the 9th to the 8th century B.C., has been attributed to the Phoenicians and it is therefore considered the only known example of Phoenician monumental architecture from the pre-Assyrian period.

Two deposits of votive material found in different areas of the city but from the same period are of some interest. One contained terra-cotta and stone votive statuettes of a kind often found in sanctuaries in central Phoenicia and on the Palestinian coast; the other contained terra-cotta figures of a Greek type together with Greek pottery.

Tell Mevorakh
The site of Tell Mevorakh shows evidence of the continued use of Phoenician masonry and building techniques, which are first attested in the 10th century B.C. and reappear in the Late Persian and Hellenistic periods. These are the quite distinctive walls attributed ever since the time of Solomon to the work of Phoenician craftsmen in Palestine, made with massive blocks of stone dressed in a particular way and laid head to edge. In the important buildings of the city this technique is found in conjunction with other walls in which vertical lines of blocks alternate with rubble ("frame wall"). In the Persian and Hellenistic periods these techniques are attested in many Phoenician settlements, from Suqas on the northern border as far as Jaffa. Another peculiarly Phoenician architectural feature found at Tell Mevorakh is the use of tiered merlons at the top of important buildings, also frequent in the Solomonic cities of Palestine.

Atlit
The best-known find from the Iron Age at Atlit is the necropolis, in use from the 7th century B.C. until the Hellenistic era. The most ancient tombs show that the cremation rite was in use, as at other Phoenician sites, particularly the earliest necropoli of the Mediterranean colonies. The Atlit tombs contain pottery similar in style to the ware found in Phoenician settlements in the Levant and in Cyprus; the most recent (6th-4th century B.C.) are of the dug-out shaft type, also well known in many Phoenician settlements.

Cyprus
Vassos Karageorghis

The island of Cyprus, situated in the eastern Mediterranean at the point where the cultural spheres of the Aegean and the Near East intersect, has been throughout her history a "stepping stone" or "melting pot" where these great cultures met and intermingled. Furthermore, the rich copper resources of the island attracted the powers that dominated the Mediterranean from the Late Bronze Age onwards.

From Cape Andreas at the easternmost tip of Cyprus on a clear day the continental coast opposite is visible. Those who sail from the Lebanese seaboard westwards encounter first the southeastern coast of the island, a fact which in recent years has been tellingly demonstrated following the tragic events in Lebanon. This was also the case in antiquity when the first Phoenicians set sail on their westward journey: they landed at Kition (modern Larnaca), as did the first Lebanese refugees of our own days.

The question as to when the Phoenicians first appeared on the political and cultural scene of the Mediterranean has long been debated. If the Canaanites of the Syro-Palestinian coast of the Late Bronze Age are to be considered "Proto-Phoenicians," then relations between these people and Cyprus already began in the second half of the 2nd millennium B.C. These relations were both commercial and cultural. Following events initiated by groups called the "Peoples of the Sea" in contemporary texts, Cyprus and the Syro-Palestinian coast experienced a very similar history through to the 12th century B.C. The Aegean element in the character of the "Peoples of the Sea" is generally accepted and in this respect their link with both

*Phoenician
settlements
in Cyprus*

185

Cyprus and the Near East is worthy of note. In Cyprus, however, the continued influx of colonists from the Aegean caused different political developments until the 11th century B.C., and kept the island within the Aegean orbit, whereas in the Near East the "Peoples of the Sea" of Philistia and other regions were absorbed by the local populations. Nevertheless, contact between Cyprus and the Syro-Palestinian region continued even in the 11th and 10th centuries B.C. As well as importing goods, the Cypriots also adopted Syro-Palestinian forms in their own production of pottery. Recent excavations at the necropolis of Palaepaphos-Skales have yielded strong evidence for this early contact. Lentoid flasks and "Canaanite" amphorae, imported for their contents, are frequently found in tombs of the 11th and 10th centuries B.C. and Cypriot pottery of the same period has been discovered in the Levant.

These relations are echoed in mythical tradition. All the 11th century B.C. (Early Iron Age) towns of Cyprus have foundation legends which link them with great heroes "who came to Cyprus and built cities after the end of the Trojan War", except for Kition, the Phoenician colony par excellence in Cyprus. Instead of a foundation legend there is a myth that Kition was founded by King Belos of the Sidonians, who helped the Achaean Teukros take possession of Salamis. In the Bible reference is often made to Kittim, which may designate either the whole of Cyprus, or the town of Kition; in any case it refers to an island, region which was the last stop of the Phoenician ships sailing back home, before reaching the Levantine coast.

There is ample archaeological evidence of the Phoenicians' presence at Kition; already in the 19th-century inscriptions and other material remains were unearthed and published as the result of excavations carried out beneath the modern town of Larnaca, which is built on the ruins of ancient Kition.

When should the initial stages of the Phoenician presence at Kition be dated? There is literary evidence that at the start of his reign Hiram I, king of Tyre, had to suppress a revolt of the people of Kiti(on) on the island of Cyprus. If this information is correct then we have to accept that Kition was already under Tyrian rule at the beginning of the 10th century B.C., during the reign of Hiram's father Abibaal.

An early date for the presence of Phoenicians in Cyprus is suggested by inscriptions on bronze bowls said to have been found near Amathus, and which were dedicated by the governor of Khartihadasht to Baal of Lebanon. The governor is referred to as "servant of Hiram, king of the Sidonians." The king is Hiram II of Tyre, who reigned during the latter part of the 8th century B.C. Khartihadasht is now widely accepted as being Kition. It has been convincingly argued that after 707 B.C., when Cyprus came under Assyrian domination during the reign of Sargon II, relations between Kition and her parent city Tyre changed, though Kition must also have had a king and was no longer called Khartihadasht ("New City"), having reverted to its former name, Kition (Kittim). From the end of the 8th century B.C. onwards the name Khartihadasht was reserved for

Aerial view of the temple of Astarte at Kition

Carthage, but not surprisingly, the city is referred to by both names even after this date.

Recent excavations at Kition have shown that the town flourished in the Late Bronze Age and in the northernmost area of the site there is evidence that it was destroyed sometime in the first half of the 11th century B.C., probably by a natural phenomenon, and was rebuilt soon after. The new town was inhabited for only about fifty years and the northernmost part of it at least was abandoned. This abandonment may have been a result of the silting up of the old harbor. A new harbour, probably a *cothon*, and therefore man-made, was built to the south of the old one, and the new town developed around it.

In the northernmost part of Kition life began again sometime at the end of the 9th century B.C. when a large temple was built on the foundations of a Late Bronze Age predecessor. It retained the dimensions of the earlier structure (33.5 × 22 m) as well as the interior arrangement. The roof of the new temple was supported on four rows of seven wooden pillars. The original Late Bronze Age stone bases with rectangular sockets for the wooden pillars were reused and have survived to the present day. The construction of temples in Phoenician colonies was common: they served to stimulate the economy of the colony and also to provide refuge.

*Red slip-coated
bowl with
Phoenician
inscription
from Kition
9th century B.C.
clay, diam 25 cm
Nicosia, Cyprus
Museum*

On either side of the central opening to the "holy of holies" or *sancta sanc-
torum* there are traces of two rectangular free-standing pillars which recall
the biblical pillars of the temple of Solomon in Jerusalem, known as Jachin
and Boaz. The date of this early temple as well as of two other smaller temples which also had Late Bronze Age predecessors may be determined by
the Phoenician and imported Greek pottery found in level 3, the earliest:
they point to the end of the 9th century B.C., a date that corresponds to the
massive Phoenician expansion to the West.

There is evidence that the above-mentioned Great Temple was dedicated to
a goddess; a red slip Phoenician bowl found in the earliest level and dating
to the time of the first temple destruction (c. 800 B.C. or soon after) bears
an engraved Phoenician inscription, unfortunately fragmentary, which mentions a certain *ML* from Tamassos who went to Kition and made sacrifices
in honour of Astarte. That it was Astarte who was worshipped in this temple is not universally accepted, as different readings of the Phoenician
inscription have been proposed.

There is also a possibility that the temple of Astarte was located further
south, where an *ostracon* (now in the British Museum in London), which
mentions the accounts of the temple of Astarte in the classical period, was
found during levelling operations at the end of the 19th century. We know
that in this area there was also a temple of Heracles Melqarth. Even if the
Great Temple is not that of Astarte, it is nevertheless the most magnificent

temple of the Phoenician period so far discovered. The cult of the goddess Astarte must have been accepted as official by the new colonists of Kition. We know that the cult was initiated by King Ethbaal who reigned between 887 and 856 B.C. and was high priest of the goddess before he ascended to the throne of Tyre and Sidon.

Finds on the floor of the Great Temple provide further information concerning the cult of the goddess at Kition. There were clay masks and bull's masks which were worn during ritual ceremonies, as was the custom also during the Late Bronze Age at Kition and Enkomi. The fragmentary inscription on the red slip bowl mentioned above says that *ML* dedicated his hair in the temple. This custom is known from Lucian's description of the Great Goddess at Hierapolis in Syria (*De Dea Syria*). He informs us that young worshippers going to the temple for the first time cut their hair and dedicated it to the goddess. The classical *ostracon* mentions sacred barbers among the personnel of the temple of Astarte. There were also sacred prostitutes. Another famous temple of Astarte which succeeded a Late Bronze Age temple is that at Palaepaphos. It is interesting that Late Bronze Age religious customs survived for so long in Cyprus despite new cultural and religious influences. This, however, is perhaps not so surprising in small communities where people could preserve many features of the ancestral cults.

The temple at Palaepaphos was used without interruption through to the end of the classical period. It was subsequently pillaged for construction materials and is very poorly preserved.

Lamp-holder plaque with deity and bull protomes from Famagusta 9th century B.C. painted terracotta, 70 cm

Representations of Astarte (successor to the Great Goddess of fertility who had been worshipped earlier in Cyprus for over six millennia) sometimes show a remarkable continuity in style with those of the Cretan "Goddess with uplifted arms" who was introduced to Cyprus in the 11th century B.C. On a "wall-bracket" found in the Famagusta district (which until 1974 was part of the Hadjiprodromou private collection in Famagusta, then stolen and illicitly exported from the now occupied Famagusta), the goddess is represented nude in relief, with arms raised upwards and outwards; she wears a tiara and has red spots on her cheeks like the Cretan examples.

The wall-bracket dates to the 9th century B.C. Above the head of Astarte there are two bull's heads, another holdover from the ancestral religion when the bull was the symbol of the god of fertility. Indeed, bull figures with the same symbolic significance continue to appear in sanctuaries through to the end of the archaic period. This shows how strong the indigenous Cypriot cultural tradition was, even at a time when Phoenician influences were widespread. Terra-cotta figurines representing the same goddess with features similar to those on the wall-bracket are also known from Palaepaphos.

Phoenician products imported by Cyprus vary considerably. They include fine pottery, in particular the well-known dishes with thin walls and engraved circles on the base, sometimes painted black. One remarkable vase, which was found recently in a tomb at Amathus, is a chalice-shaped vessel 15.5 cm high with a wide pedestal foot. The exterior is decorated with a red slip; there is a black slip around the middle and two finely engraved horizontal lines. This vase has been identified as a presentation stand, probably for an ostrich egg, and is datable to the 8th century B.C.

There are also numerous types of terracottas dating from the 8th to the 6th centuries B.C. which may have had Phoenician prototypes. One is a female tambourine-player from Amathus which is paralled almost exactly by figurines from Tel Shiqmona in Israel and from Tyre. These terra-cotta figurines may be dated to the 8th century B.C.

It has been argued that Amathus was a Phoenician "resettlement" of the 8th century B.C. and even that Amathus may claim the name "Khartihadasht." Even if we accept the truth of this, we cannot overlook the very fine taste of its inhabitants for eastern Greek, Proto-Corinthian, Cycladic and Late Greek Geometric pottery. No other site in Cyprus has produced so much ware from the Aegean region. This taste continues in the 6th and 5th centuries, as is obvious also from the character of the so-called "Amathus style" pottery (see below).

Of particular importance are a series of metal bowls of bronze and silver, usually called "Cypro-Phoenician." They are found throughout the 7th century B.C. and are richly decorated in repoussé or with engraved designs arranged in various zones around a central medallion. The designs are in the pictorial style, with animal or human figures or both, and are occasionally of a narrative character. The style is both Cypriot and Phoenician, hence the term Cypro-Phoenician, and their decorative motifs are strongly Egyptianizing.

Ivory carving flourished in Cyprus during the latter part of the Late Bronze Age. In the 8th-7th century B.C., however, carved ivory objects were most probably imported from the Levant. The Phoenicians may have been responsible for this trade. This refers especially to ivory furniture, like that found in the "royal" tombs of Salamis, and dated to the early 7th century B.C.

The style of this ivory-carving is Phoenician with a strong Egyptian influence in the iconographical repertory. One of two plaques decorating the ivory throne from Salamis Tomb 79 represents a sphinx wearing the crowns

Late Geometric Euboic krater from Amathus 8th century B.C. painted clay 45 cm Limassol, District Museum
• *p. 217*

Chalice-shaped vessel with wide base from Amathus 8th century B.C. painted clay 15.5 cm Limassol, District Museum

of Upper and Lower Egypt; the other depicts a composite lotus flower. The two plaques are carved on both sides in the *à jour* (cut-out) technique. There are areas of cloisonné inlaid with enamels of various colours and whose walls are lined with thin sheets of gold. This technique is known from the carved ivories from the palace of Nimrud.

The headboard of a bed from the same tomb at Salamis is decorated with various carved ivory plaques, some with relief representations, others with

blue paste cloisonné. The former represent sphinxes and the Egyptian divinity Heh in front of a "tree of life" from which hangs the *ankh*, the Egyptian symbol of life.

The "royal" tombs of Salamis have produced an abundance of bronze plaques used to adorn chariots and horses. They are richly decorated in repoussé with motifs taken from Phoenician iconography, though elements from other art styles, e.g. Urartian, may often be detected.

The role of the Phoenicians in the formation of an artistic *koinè* in the eastern Mediterranean and the Levant (c. 700 B.C.) must have been decisive, not only because they traded luxury goods of bronze, silver, ivory, faience, etc. very widely (their merchandizing activities were known to Homer), but also because they were themselves skilled craftsmen.

Political conditions in Cyprus at the end of the 8th century and in the 7th century B.C. were favorable to the island's prosperity. Assyrian rule was "benevolent" and the Cypriots were allowed to conduct their own cultural and religious life in a climate of independence, as long as they paid their tribute regularly to the Assyrian king. The Phoenicians readily acknowledged the rule of Assyria in

Bowl decorated with hunting scenes and inscription in syllabic Cypriot from Paphos 7th century B.C. bronze diam. 15 cm Nicosia, Cyprus Museum
• *p. 218*

Cyprus and thus were able to trade freely.

The 7th century B.C. must have been characterized by artistic exuberance, wealth and pomp. The kings of Salamis were buried with gifts which were rivalled only by those of the Assyrian kings. In their palaces there was not only mythical wealth but an atmosphere of intellectual activity, complete with bards and musicians. The Homeric poems were widely recited and epic poetry flourished, including among its most esteemed exponents a well-known Cypriot, Stasinos. This Greek tradition on the one hand and Levantine luxury on the other constituted the mixed atmosphere in which the orientalizing culture flourished and expanded throughout the Mediterranean. The Phoenicians played an important role in its diffusion.

A rich religious ritual accompanied by musical and other types of performances must have been practiced in the sanctuaries of Astarte both at Kition and Paphos. Dancers holding flowers or walking through a wood are depicted on vases of the 7th century B.C. and on metal bowls. These dancers may have been performing in honour of Astarte in sacred gardens. We know that there were gardens dedicated to the goddess in Paphos; a vil-

Headboard of bed with panels in carved ivory from tomb 79 at Salamis 7th century B.C. Nicosia, Cyprus Museum

lage near Palaepaphos, now called Yeroskipoui, was known to Strabo as "the sacred garden." On certain occasions ritual sexual practices must have taken place there, as is attested by scenes on vases both of clay and metal, following the custom of sacred prostitution as described by Herodotus.

At Kition, our main source of information about the activities of the Phoenicians in Cyprus, the Great Temple was destroyed by fire sometime in the early years of the 8th century B.C. The Kitians rebuilt the temple, having made sacrifices and offered a "foundation deposit" consisting of miniature jugs and bowls, many of which were Phoenician imports. The wooden pillars which supported the roof and which must have been destroyed in the fire, were replaced by two rows of rectangular masonry pillars. Objects such as vases and terra-cotta figurines dedicated in the temple during the first period were removed and placed in shallow cavities (*bothroi*). The rich finds from these deposits provide much information on the quantity of Phoenician imports as well as the nature of the cult. Most of the terra-cotta figurines are related to Astarte. The new temple remained in use for nearly two centuries.

A votive stele from Pyla (east of Larnaca) surmounted by a large limestone mask of a local divinity (h. 68 cm) has recently been reexamined by A. Hermary. The stele bears a Phoenician inscription which reads: "Made by Eshmounhillek, the sculptor, for Reshef Shed." The mask is that of the divinity Reshef Shed who has the attributes

Plaquette with sphinx from the throne found in tomb 79 at Salamis 7th century B.C. ivory, 16 cm Nicosia, Cyprus Museum
• *p. 219*

Bronze harness from tomb 79 at Salamis 7th century B.C. 58 cm Nicosia, Cyprus Museum • p. 220

Illustrations of two harnesses found in tomb 79 at Salamis 7th century B.C. Nicosia, Cyprus Museum

of the Egyptian Bes: leonine ears, flat nose, large eyes, wrinkled face. This Semitic god is also mentioned at Ras Ibn Hani in Syria in an Ugaritic text. The Pyla stele and mask date to the mid-7th century B.C. and is one of the earliest pieces of Cypriot sculpture made by a Phoenician artist.

Apart from the major sanctuaries in the main centres of Kition and Palaepaphos, the 7th and 6th centuries in particular are noted for rural sanctuaries, many of which have already been sites of excavation. An example is the sanctuary of Baal Hammon at Meniko in central Cyprus, not far from a copper-mining area, which dates to the 6th century B.C. and was closely associated with the Phoenicians. (The Phoenicians had already appeared in the mining area in the 9th and 8th centuries B.C., as demonstrated by the inscription found in the Great Temple.)

The architecture of the sanctuary indicates that it was of a dual character. In the main cella a terracotta figurine of a seated, bearded and horned Baal Hammon was found, as well as large *thymiateria* (incense burners) of clay and limestone. It has been suggested that the latter items may be directly related to the specific attribute of Baal Hammon as god of the incense-burners (*hammanim*). Other votive offerings from the sanctuary include terra-cotta figurines of bulls, rams and so forth, suggesting that this new god of the Phoenician pantheon was assimilated by the rural community of Meniko with the ancestral fertility god of the Bronze Age, the god of cattle, the patron of shepherds and farmers. Of particular importance is a terra-cotta group representing a large ox flanked by two human figures. Similar representations are known in Cyprus from the Late Bronze Age, both in clay and in bronze.

The theory of the dual character of the architectural remains is further supported by the discovery of a large limestone slab in the form of "horns," previously identified as "horns of consecration"; it is quite possible, however, that they may be associated with the symbol of Tanit. Documentation from Sarepta has now proved that Tanit was already known in Phoenicia in the 6th century B.C. at least.

There was a cult of Baal Hammon in Libya and it is significant that King Evelthon of Salamis had particular links with that country in the mid-6th century B.C. In the 5th century B.C. at Carthage the god was worshipped in association with the goddess Tanit Pene Baal, and in the 4th century B.C. on Monte Adranone in Sicily there was a double temple dedicated to these two divinities. It would therefore not be surprising to find in Cyprus a similar cult, knowing that Tanit had the same qualities as Astarte.

Large amphora of the IV Bichrome with figures dancing in sacred garden 7th century B.C. clay, 93 cm Nicosia, Cyprus Museum
• *p. 221*

A sanctuary dating to c. 500 B.C. was excavated at Limassol-Komissariato. Few architectural remains were uncovered but there were large numbers of votive offerings, mainly terra-cotta figurines. The character of these offerings suggests that a divinity of fertility was worshipped in the sanctuary. The male terra-cottas are of a phallic nature and an actual clay phallus was among the offerings. There were also many stylized bull figurines. The female companion to the male god is suggested by several female figurines. The male figurines are turned on the potter's wheel and have a cylindrical body, with applied genitals clearly in evidence. Other figurines closely paralleling these have been found in large numbers in Carthage, Spain, Motya and elsewhere. They cover a period from the 8th to the 1st centuries B.C., with an apogee during the 6th and 5th centuries. Whereas all the Cypriot figurines have their arms beside the body, the Punic figurines have their arms indicating a part of the body (head, eyes, genitals, etc.); this has led to the theory that they point to an ailing part of the body which the offerer asks the god to whom the figurine is dedicated to heal. The Punic figurines

Black slip jug and cups from foundation deposits of the Kition temple 9th century B.C. Larnaca, District Museum

Thymaterion
*incense burner
from the Baal
Hammon
sanctuary
at Meniko
6th century B.C.
terra-cotta, 38 cm
Nicosia, Cyprus
Museum*

are either male or female, and in both cases the sex is well indicated. The similarity between the Cypriot figurines and those of the Punic world is striking, not only in the general type but also in the facial characteristics, which are crude and simplified.

There is evidence that there were various open-air sanctuaries, with only a small cella for the image of the divinity or for the ritual vessels. Though only a few rural sanctuaries have been excavated so far, we know their various architectural forms from small terra-cotta models which have been found in tombs, usually of the 6th century B.C. They consist of one cella, resembling a niche, often with a pilaster on each side. The upper part of the cella is decorated with a crescent moon and a disc (symbols of Astarte) and small globes representing roses. Two fairly large models were found at Idalion. One depicts a "woman at the window" on both sides, recalling the oriental Astarte in the form of sacred prostitute as she appears, for example, on ivory-carvings from the Assyrian palaces and before that, on Late Bronze Age bronze stands from Cyprus. The second model represents a portico in front of the main entrance to the cella, flanked by two pilasters topped by capitals in the form of a lotus flower. Inside the cella a winged siren appears through the door. It is noteworthy that similar pilasters have been found in stone at Palaepaphos.

Small models of sanctuaries (*naiskoi*) with a human figure inside also appear at the top of Hathoric capitals dated to c. 500 B.C. They are in the form of a framed window, recalling the "Punic" stelae. It should be mentioned that such capitals gradually lost their architectural significance and were used as freestanding stelae. Independent "Punic" stelae as they appear in the West are very rare in Cyprus. There are only very few examples from Palaepaphos. Models of *naiskoi* are known in the Levant from the Late Bronze Age (as at Kamid el-Loz).

Phoenician elements also appear in tomb architecture. The two 6th-century B.C. "royal" tombs of Tamassos have a stepped *dromos* and their opening is flanked by two pilasters topped by "Aeolic" capitals. These, like the Hathoric capitals, soon lost their architectural significance and developed into freestanding stelae, with the upper part of the Aeolic capital decorated with a lotus flower.

Another Phoenician element is the disc-and-crescent symbol of Astarte which appears on the tomb façades (e.g. at Salamis) and the anthropomorphic sarcophagi, mainly of the classical period. The origin of these sarcophagi is Egyptian and they appear quite early in the Levant, but their wide diffusion dates from the 5th and 4th centuries B.C. They have been found mainly in the Levant, and in Cyprus at Kition and Amathus.

Though it is clear that there are various "Punic" elements in Cypriot culture, there is a basic difference. In Cyprus no evidence has been found so far of *tophets*, not even at Kition. The cruel Punic custom of child sacrifice does not seem to have been practiced in Cyprus.

The Phoenicians consolidated their position in the island, having enjoyed the favour first of the Assyrians to whom they showed faithful allegiance and later of the Persians. The forests of Cyprus provided ample timber to build the ships with which they plied the Mediterranean in the trade of Cypriot copper. It is not surprising that Cyprus appears in the list of thalassocracies mentioned by Eusebius. The objects found in the deposits of the Kition temples are indicative of their wealth and the range of their commercial activities: vases from the Aegean, faience, amulets and scarabs from Egypt and ivory objects.

After the failure of the Ionian revolt against the Persians in 499 B.C. (in which the Cypriots participated as well), the Persian rulers of Cyprus relied on the Phoenicians for the administration of the various kingdoms of the island. In this way the Persians, whose military presence in Cyprus must have consisted mainly of mercenaries, could keep the rebellious Greek cities in check. Kition, with its Phoenician dynasty, must have been particularly favoured by the Persians. In order to subdue the pro-Greek city of Idalion, the Persians conquered it in 470 B.C. and annexed it to Kition. The Phoenician rulers of Kition gradually extended their influence, both political and cultural, over other towns such as Amathus, Golgoi, Tamassos and Lapithos. The legends on the coins of Lapithos are in Phoenician. Phoenician inscriptions have been found in large numbers not only at Kition and in surrounding areas (e.g. at Pergamos), but also in places such as Tamassos, Golgoi, Lapithos, Chytroi, Palaepaphos. Isokrates mentions the name of a Phoenician king at Salamis, Abdemon, who was dethroned by Evagoras in 411 B.C. Under the reign of the pro-Greek King Evagoras even the Phoenicians of Salamis had to succumb to his Hellenic policies. Thus, the epitaph on the façade of a tomb of a certain Phoenician called Abdubalos in the Salamis necropolis is written in the Cypriot syllabary and the Greek language.

Amathus must therefore have been within the cultural orbit of the Phoenicians, though trade with the Greek world was brisk and had started already in the 8th century B.C. We know that the Phoenicians themselves had developed a taste for the fine Greek vases of the Late Geometric and subsequent periods. Phoenician objects found in tombs at Amathus are numerous: pottery, jewellery, objects of faience, etc. Vases and terra-cotta figurines imitate Phoenician prototypes. This influence is attested as far west as Kourion and Palaepaphos. At Amathus, however, there is a strong

Group with bull flanked by two human figures from the Meniko sanctuary 6th century B.C. terracotta 28.5 cm Nicosia, Cyprus Museum

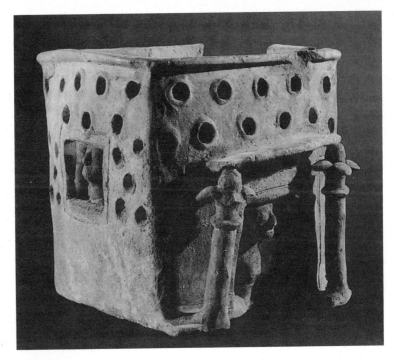

Naiskos with inside winged "siren" from Idalion 6th century B.C. terra-cotta, 21 cm Paris, Musée du Louvre

Entrance to "royal" tomb at Tamassos flanked by pilasters with "aeolic" capitals 6th century B.C.

element of the Greek combined with the indigenous culture, which is epitomized in the so-called "Amathus style" of pottery.

The involvement of the Phoenicians in the internal political problems of the Cypriot kingdoms and their opposition to the pro-Hellenic policies of some of these states manifested itself frequently and in many ways during the 5th century B.C. When the Greek army under Kimon tried to liberate Cyprus from the Persians, the Greek general attacked the Phoenicians in their main stronghold, Kition. But in 449 B.C., when the Greeks were about to defeat the Phoenicians, Kimon died and the Athenian army was forced to withdraw.

At Idalion, which was occupied and annexed to the kingdom of Kition, the Phoenicians symbolically destroyed the temple of Athena in 470 B.C. An attempt was made to introduce Phoenician gods, or to assimilate the cult of Greek gods with that of the Phoenician equivalents: Athena-Anath, Heracles-Melqarth, Apollo-Reshef, and so on. The Athenians made their final attempt to oust the Phoenicians from Kition when they sent Chabrias with ten ships to dethrone Melekiathon, the Phoenician king of Kition, and to enthrone an Athenian, Demonikos, in his place; but in 386 B.C. an agreement between the Athenians and the Persians known as the "Peace of Antalkidas" left Cyprus under Persian rule and the dream of freedom thus had to be abandoned.

The political scene changed with the expansion of Alexander the Great. Both Greeks and Phoenicians tried to win his favor. The Phoenician king

Poumyathon of Kition even sent him a special sword which is described by Plutarch, but this did not save him. When Ptolemy I sent his army to subdue the four kingdoms allied with his opponent Antigonus, Poumyathon, who resisted the forces of Ptolemy, was killed. With his death the Phoenician dynasty of Kition came to an end, and in 312 B.C. the Phoenician temples of the city were burnt down. On the once famous sacred grounds in the northernmost part of the city thermal baths were built over the remains of the Phoenician temples. Thus ended a Phoenician presence in Cyprus which had lasted for nearly five centuries.

Detail of anthropoid sarcophagus from Amathus 5th century B.C. marble, 221 cm Limassol, District Museum

Hathoric capital from Paphos 6th century B.C. limestone, 80 cm Parigi, Musée du Louvre
• p. 222

Chronology

Geometric or Cypro-Geometric

I	1050-950 B.C.
II	950-850 B.C.
III	850-750 B.C.

Archaic or Cypro-Archaic

I	750-600 B.C.
II	600-475 B.C.

Classical or Cypro-Classical

I	475-400 B.C.
II	400-325 B.C.

Hellenistic

I	325-150 B.C.
II	150-50 B.C.

North Africa

M'Hamed Fantar

Who Were the Punic People?

A distinction is usually made between the Phoenician and the Punic peoples when speaking of the various areas of North Africa and the other countries of the western Mediterranean. For a long time it was thought that the differences were purely geographical; Punic people were confused with the immigrant Phoenicians who had settled in parts of the western Mediterranean such as Sicily, Sardinia and North Africa. As studies have progressed and new data have been analyzed, scholars have realized the shortcomings of this geographical division.

Specific cultural differences have emerged not only between the cities of the eastern and those of the western Mediterranean, but also between the Punic peoples of Sardinia and those of North Africa. The stelae found in Sardinia and at Tharros, for instance, are unlike those found in the *tophets* of Carthage and Sousse (ancient Hadrumetum). Here, however, we shall focus on the differing local characteristics that appear within a single area. In fact the basic aspects of Punic culture in Carthage are not the same as those of Sousse, or Utica; they differ even more from those of Kerkouane on Cape Bon, of Thapsus in the Tunisian Sahel, Cirta in Algeria, or Lixus and Mogador in Morocco. At all events, the Punic people of North Africa are the result of an ethnic and cultural union of peoples coming from the eastern Mediterranean, with the autochthonous races known as *LWBM*, i.e. the *Libous* cited in the ancient Egyptian and Libyan texts. This fact is inferred from Punic inscriptions in Carthage bearing the names *LBY* and *LBT*, and is corroborated by other historical and epigraphical data. Without going

The Phoenician and Punic expansion in Africa

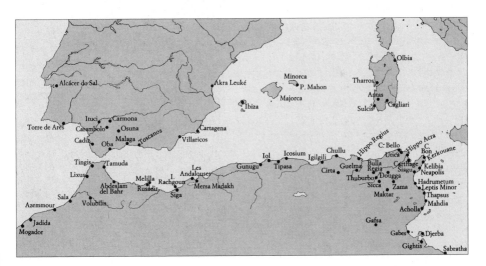

199

ch detail, let us look at the various analogies arities in relation to dates and areas, bearing in le issue of Punic identity is complex and hard in order to isolate the substratum of extrinsic influences we therefore need to sort very carefully through the information we have.

Chronology

What was the purpose behind this meeting of races in North Africa and when did it take place? The Phoenicians seem to have reached the lands of the *LBM* or *FRM* (which the Romans knew as the *Ifri* or *Afri*) at the close of the 2nd millennium B.C., certainly by 1100 B.C. For Lixus in Morocco, we know from a text by Pliny that a number of historians of that period dated the city's foundation at about 1180 B.C. It may well have occurred a few years earlier; what is certain is that the temple of Heracles-Melqarth at Lixus precedes the sanctuary erected by the Phoenicians at Cadiz towards 1110 B.C. "We have an example," writes Pliny, "of a mallow tree in Mauritania, in the estuary where the town of Lixus stands, in the place where it is said that once the gardens of the Hesperides grew, two hundred paces from the ocean, beside the temple of Heracles which is thought to be more ancient even than Cadiz" (*Nat. Hist.*, XIX, 63).

Votive stele with "sign of Tanit" and figure in a frontal niche from the tophet *of Carthage 2nd century B.C. limestone 4 × 17.5 cm Carthage, Musée de Carthage*

A few years later, in 1101 B.C. the city of Utica was founded in the northeast of Tunisia, where the valley of the Bagradas (modern Majardah) meets the sea. The date is taken from a text by Velleius Paterculus (1, 2, 4), who, fixing the period of the return of the Heraclidae to Peloponnesos eighty years after the fall of Troy, writes, "In that epoch, the Tyrian fleet, which commanded the seas, founded Cadiz, on the outermost tip of the Spanish mainland and at the edge of our world; Utica too was founded by the Tyrians a few years later." Referring to the time in which he wrote Book XVI, i.e. the year A.D. 77, Pliny states that "tke cedar beams used for the roofing of the temple of Apollo are the self-same beams laid there at the time of the foundation of the city, 1178 years ago" (*Nat. Hist.*, XVI, 261). These keys to the chronology tie in with the date given by the *De mirabilibus auscultationibus* (134), in which we read: "It would appear that Utica was founded by the Phoenicians 287 years before Carthage, as is recounted in the Phoenician histories." Although this text, which must date from the 2nd century A.D., is relatively late, it is nonetheless a valuable source of information. The data seem to have been culled from Phoenician sources, most likely from temple archives and from texts which could be consulted in the libraries in Carthage or in Utica itself.

Despite the general dearth of material testifying to such remote times (i.e. the close of the 2nd millennium B.C.) the archaeological finds include a number of objects of great value. One particular treasure is a bronze figure found in the sea not far from Selinus. Originally the figure was called the "Melqarth of Sciacca"; later it was identified with the Babylonian god Hadad, but today experts believe that it originated in Ugarit or another Semitic city of the Late Bronze Age. Basing their calculations on technical and iconographical data, a number of art historians have dated the statuette to the 14th-13th century B.C. Whatever its origin, according to Sabatino Moscati it must have been transported by the Phoenician navy in the 12th century.

The archaeological evidence relating to the Phoenician presence in the western Mediterranean (and particularly North Africa) around the 12th and 11th centuries B.C. may also include certain other pieces, such as "a bronze figure in the Babylonian manner dating from the mid-2nd millennium," as Guy Bunnens defined it in his paper on Phoenician expansion through the Mediterranean, published in 1979 in Rome. Also of note is a cylinder seal which at the time of its discovery in the last century did not gain the attention it deserved — in fact the seal is one of the earliest pieces of evidence attesting to relations between the Near East and the Iberian peninsula, dating back to midway through the 14th century B.C. According to the Spanish scholar J.M. Blázquez, "The cylinder seal of Vélez Malaga seems to confirm the date given by the ancient authors on Phoenician presence in the Straits of Gibraltar; midway through the 2nd millennium B.C."

It should be noted however that as far as our present state of knowledge goes, excavations in the countries of North Africa have not touched strata earlier than the 8th century B.C. It might be possible to push beyond this time barrier by using systematic surveying methods and modern technological means.

Factors Favoring Navigation

In their effort to reach the farthest lands of the West and settle in Africa and on either side of the Pillars of Hercules, the Phoenicians seem to have been helped by a series of favorable conditions. One was the increased accessibility of the Mediterranean itself — around the year 1200 B.C. this world was caught up in ethnic, cultural and technical turmoil, caused by the invasion of the Dorians, the decline of the Aegean powers and the arrival of the "Peoples of the Sea."

Due to these factors, the waters of the Mediterranean became altogether less hostile and more accessible to those who had a fleet able to navigate them. Metalworking skills improved considerably in this period, and craftsmen were able to shape iron and bronze tools that were useful to the ship builders.

During the Iron Age, iron nails were used in ship building for fixing the various pieces together, which by then were more finely made — the flat hull of the vessel of the previous age was replaced by a proper keel, which acted as a backbone onto which the skeleton of the ship was anchored.

Furthermore, we should also consider specific skills and the level of evolution achieved by the Phoenicians, who enjoyed an open and liberal society which fostered a high degree of self-expression, encouraging self confidence, a spirit of initiative, enthusiasm for action and even for adventure.

Why Did the Phoenicians Navigate?

The physical characteristcs of the Phoenicians' homeland did not allow them to establish a lasting settlement in the area. The terrain was indeed fertile, but tightly wedged between the mountains and the sea. In order for their society to thrive and develop, they had to look elsewhere, exploring even as far as the land of Tarshish, mentioned in the Bible.

The main objective of their maritime exploits seems to have been to trade metals — gold, silver, copper, lead, and above all tin. The Phoenicians did not hesitate to leave the ports of Tyre, Sidon or Byblos, and sail out past the Straits of Gibraltar to land in Cadiz in Spain, or in Lixus on the Atlantic coast of Morocco, to find the metals that were sought after by the major powers of the day such as Egypt and Mesopotamia.

In order to make this trading activity on the high seas efficient, it was vital to have trading posts or ports-of-call where the sailors could take shelter from storms, repair any damage, rest, and replenish their food and water supplies. In addition to trade, the Phoenicians had other objectives, not least the desire to broaden their knowledge of distant lands — a desire that had spurred on the Mediterranean peoples for centuries — and the settlements which grew up in these lands were an outcome also of this spirit of curiosity.

The presence of the Phoenicians in North Africa continued to expand, spreading and multiplying in all directions. For whole centuries the Phoenician culture grew increasingly diversified, reaching a peak at the end of the 9th century B.C. with the foundation of Carthage.

Phoenicians and Carthaginians in Tunisia

Evidence suggests that a great many cities of ancient Tunisia were in fact founded by the Phoenicians or the Carthaginians, or at least were deeply influenced by the Phoenician and Punic civilization. The facts that emerge from historical accounts, epigraphy and archaeology seem to confirm that the whole of Tunisian territory was under the sway of Punic authority. A number of Punic and Neo-Punic inscriptions indicate how strong this cultural imprint was on the indigenous society: it is manifest in the architecture, in the way physical spaces are organized, in religious activity, and in the art and the writing.

Stele featuring figure inside niche with foliate motifs from Maktar 1st century B.C. limestone 57 × 38 cm Tunis, Musée du Bardo • p. 223

Punic sites have come to light along the coastline and also inland; locations include Carthage, Utica, Hadrumetum (or rather *HDRM*), Kerkouane, Korba, Ta Fekhsite near Menzel Temime, Cape Bon, Leptis, Thapsus in the Sahel, Gabes, Gigthi and Djerba in the southeastern regions (the latter was

the home of the Garamantes tribes who acted as go-betweens for the Punic
people and the tribes in the Sahara and the other side of the desert).
Even inland, far from the coast, at Maktar, Medidi, Dougga, Sicca (modern
Kef) and Althiburos, relics have come to light testifying to Punic influence.
In the southeast, Neo-Punic inscriptions have been found in Tataouine and
Remada, on the edge of the desert. In the case of Tunisia, it is clear that
Punic culture had worked its way into every corner; the evidence for this
continues to mount — stelae, architectural details, capitals, fragments of
cornices, texts carved on stone or other materials. But the bulk of hard data
is afforded by the necropoli. Since archaeological investigations started in
Tunisia, thousands of Punic tombs have been located and excavated.

Carthage
Despite the extent of the Punic presence throughout Tunisia, Carthage
remained the most prestigious city, the capital of a thriving empire and the
hub of a brilliant civilization. The year of the city's foundation has been set
at 814 B.C., on the basis of the writings of ancient authors starting from
Timaeus of Taormina, who lived in the 3rd century B.C., an epoch during
which it was still possible to draw directly on Punic sources for information.
Stéphane Gsell subjected the texts relating to the foundation of Carthage to
the most exacting analysis and exegesis, and the results are still valid. We
know that some contemporary historians have suggested that the date widely recognized should be altered and set around 673-663 B.C., considering
the lack of archaeological remains dating from the 9th century B.C.
However, this hypothesis, based largely on the archaeological "silence," was
considered fragile by those who sustained the validity of the earlier, traditional foundation date; and indeed, today the earlier date is accepted by all,
and has been corroborated by archaeological evidence, which continues to
grow with the increase in the number of excavations and of studies made of
existing museum collections. A number of Punic tombs in the necropoli at
Carthage have been attributed to the 8th century B.C., and likewise some
of the deeper strata excavated at the large sanctuary known as the *tophet*.
In the excavations carried out in the context of the international campaign
for the reclamation of Carthage, the German team led by F. Rakob seems to
have worked its way down as far as the 8th century B.C.
We are still short of the traditional foundation date, but it must be observed
that the soil of the Punic capital has never been subjected to systematic,
detailed and exhaustive excavations. Furthermore, the earliest signs of occupation of a given terrain are often hard to identify. Light constructions, perishable materials, the early and hesitant occupation of an area by people
homesick for their native land, the destruction and reutilization of dismantled
structures — these are all factors of development which tend to cover up the
first signs of settlement. At all events, literary and archaeological sources seem
to concur in setting the foundation date for the Punic metropolis towards the
end of the 9th century B.C.; in fact there has been no evidence to contradict
the traditional belief that this great event preceded the first Olympics by 38

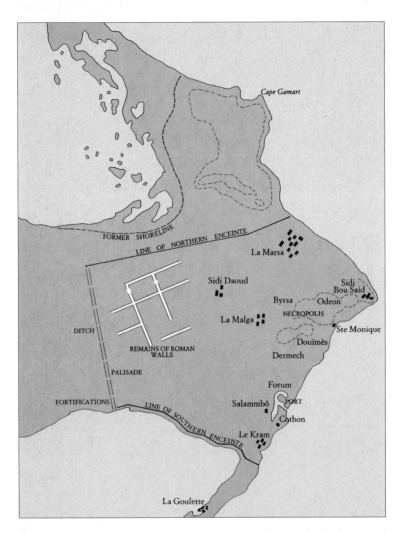

years. Thus, in the year 814 B.C., the Phoenicians dispensed with their usual policy of setting up temporary settlements in favour of a permanent one.

Leaving aside an in-depth discussion of the factors leading to Carthage's foundation, the fundamentally legendary nature of the accounts handed down to us by such ancient authors as Virgil and especially Justin should be born in mind. They give credit to a princess of Tyre, Elissa-Dido, for the city's foundation. It is, rather, the growing menace of the Assyrians and Greeks that can be identified as one of the basic motives; by the close of the 9th century B.C., the Phoenician shipowners were fully aware of the need to procure a station for themselves in the heart of the Mediterranean, far from Assyria, a base that would enable them to guarantee the safety of "Phoenician waters," and thus establish zones in which their vessels could dominate free from all competition.

Carthage was born from this need, and undoubtedly the Phoenicians found-

Ruins on the Carthaginian coast

ed the city as a result of long reflection and a legacy of experiences — their reconnaissance of the coastlines, their exploration of the inland regions, and association with the indigenous peoples. All this can only mean that the city was to be an "official colony," whose creation was decided upon in ruling Tyre, with the consent and approval of a king who was in a position to warrant and authorize the outlay required. The foundation of a new city was a costly enterprise, as we can infer from the historians of antiquity.

What Remains of Carthage?

After being plundered and burned to the ground by the soldiers of Scipio the Younger in 146 B.C., Carthage vanished beneath a thick layer of ash which has been investigated at intervals by archaeologists. The site has yielded metal objects, coins, and local and imported pottery, but all in very poor condition. The reconstruction attempted later by the technicians of Augustus Caesar wreaked greater damage than the original sacking and burning. To "rebuild" Carthage, Augustus had the ground levelled and filled in, huge platforms erected, and works commenced on a mammoth scale, as attested by the huge piers at the foot of the Byrsa hill, in the heart

205

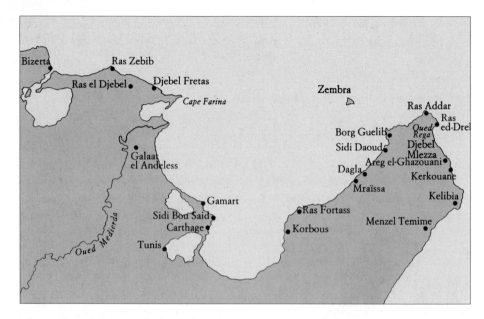

of a residential district which in all probability dates back to the time of
Hannibal, during the Second Punic War (219-201 B.C.). Either way,
whether at the hands of Scipio's vandals or the architects of Augustus, it was
Carthage's destiny to be laid waste by the Romans.

The area of Carthage and Cape Bon

In order to write his novel *Salammbô*, Gustave Flaubert decided to "confer
with the Muses on Carthaginian soil." The year was 1857, and his visit coin-
cided with the first systematic excavations led by the archaeologist Beulé.
Apart from a number of stelae, Flaubert saw nothing of Elissa's Carthage, but
he made good use of the magic properties of the texts. Melpomene and Clio
were forced to yield to the spells of Diodorus Siculus, Justin, Thucydides, and
the authors of the Bible. Flaubert's opus was a poetic one. But since the end
of the 19th century, archaeologists and historians have tried to unravel the
mysteries of Carthage. Some progress has been made —

Remains of a Roman street at Carthage

something more is known (though still not enough) about
the city, its inhabitants, their names, their work, their political and administrative responsibilities, the beliefs they held,
how they lived inside their homes, their tastes; we are also
better informed now about their links with the eastern
Phoenicians and with the other peoples of Africa, Sicily,
Sardinia, Italy, Greece, Egypt, and so on.

To get back in touch with Carthage and mingle with its people, we have the tools of archaeology and epigraphy at our
disposal. Thousands of inscribed stelae have come to light,
and their texts have been compiled in the *Corpus
Inscriptionum Semiticarum* — a vast compendium of information on the people and the gods, the society and economy, not to mention facts about the language ranging from

simple vocabulary to the labyrinths of grammatical form and syntax. In some cases, these texts carved on the stelae commemorate religious rites carried out in the sacred confines of a temple; in others they are simple epitaphs recalling the names of the dead at the entrance to the tomb.

The Necropoli at Carthage

On April 7, 1878, during excavation work, Father Delattre happened upon the Punic necropolis of Carthage. Excavations soon multiplied, thousands of tombs came to light and were subjected to thorough examination, though exactly how many were found is not known: there were clandestine excavations, and excavations condemned to remain unknown because they were not published at the right moment; the excavations were then forgotten, and the traces gradually faded and disappeared altogether. Meanwhile the material lodged in the site storerooms and museums was also forgotten, and the mountain of objects continued to grow as the years passed.

Punic walls at Byrsa

Be that as it may, our acquaintance with the Punic necropolis of Carthage is guaranteed by the array of treasures on display in the museums of Tunisia or visible on the site of the discoveries themselves. Particularly at the Musée du Bardo there is a vast exhibition of the material gathered from the tombs investigated by foreign archaeological institutions or expedition teams (permits to dig were available until 1956). The material at hand affords a compelling view of the "elaborate simplicity" of this funerary architecture.

There are pit and shaft tombs, at times running far underground (tomb no. 55 at Borg Djedid is 31.86 metres deep); access is by a set of "steps" cut out of the large facing side-walls. The tomb chamber itself is set in one of the walls, usually facing the entrance, and contains the deceased along with sundry grave goods. Occasionally the chambers are set one above the other like a multi-story house, and open onto the access shaft. This kind of construction is mainly found in the so-called S.te Monique necropolis, excavated by Father Delattre. In the Rabs necropolis close by, a whole series of marble sarcophagi were discovered in tomb chambers several metres underground. These large sarcophagi (which sometimes weigh several tons) occasionally have painted or sculpted ornaments. The most striking belong to the type generally defined as "anthropoid," where the lid is shaped like a human figure. It is hard to tell whether this is a reference to a deity or simply an evocation of the deceased. At all events, these objects are a rich source of knowledge for our understanding of the aesthetic and religious values of Carthage: the portrait on the sarcophagus, the costumes, ornaments, colours, gilding, jewellery, poses — all this provides valuable information about the world of the Carthaginians, their gods and men, living or dead.

Sanctuaries

In Carthage, great importance was given to religion. This is quite evident from ancient texts, Punic inscriptions, and of course archaeological finds. A

Punic buildings at Byrsa

temple is said to have been erected to the god Eshmun on the summit of the Byrsa hill, reached by a monumental flight of steps. This was where the last of the Carthaginians fled, holding out despite their failing hope in their own strength and in their gods. Here, the wife of the general Hasdrubal, with her children, joined the others who refused to give in and, as though to vindicate the honor of Carthage, chose fire and death rather than be taken prisoner. The cycle was complete — a woman had presided over the birth of the city, and a woman witnessed its demise. This seems to have been the city's destiny in the minds of the Carthaginians and of their successors.

The writers of antiquity speak of other temples, one dedicated to Juno (undoubtedly identifiable with Tanit or Astarte), and one to Apollo, with a chapel decorated entirely in gold leaf which the soldiers of Scipio gouged from the walls with their swords, according to Appian, who was perhaps inspired by the tales of Polybius.

The Punic inscriptions speak of temples dedicated to various deities — Astarte, Tanit of Lebanon or Tanit of the Grotto, Sid, Baal Saphon, and so on. Usually these are just passing references, but the linguistic and terminological contribution is important, since the inscriptions tell us the names by which the temples were known.

The archaeological finds also provide useful information. Several chapels have been brought to light in Carthage, and have been successfully identified. Unfortunately there are no traces left on the sites, but the Carthage and Bardo museums have put on display part of the material collected during excavations, including terra-cotta figurines and fragments of painted stucco.

Detail of a votive stele from the tophet at Carthage with figure holding youth to his breast 4th century B.C. Tunis, Musée du Bardo

The Tophet of Salammbô

There is no doubt that this area was the site of the central religious area — a "natural" sanctuary, consecrated to the two main deities of Carthage, Baal Hammon and Tanit. The site, which has yielded a rich crop of urns and stelae, was discovered in 1921 by a workman who chanced upon the famous stele of the "priest and child." Excavations followed, and thousands of urns and stelae came to light: shapes, images, dedications, promises and hopes. But though the dedications associate Tanit with Baal Hammon, the prayers are nearly always to Baal, patron of the *tophet*. In Carthage and throughout the Punic world, the sanctuaries were open to all, without discrimination — to the rich and poor, to men and women alike. Even slaves were permitted to offer sacrifices in conformity with the set rituals. The inscriptions cut into the stelae confirm that Carthaginians of all social classes left a token of their visits to the *tophet*.

The Punic Seaports

Carthage was conceived as a hub of trade and exchange. As a marine base

ready to defend the city's interests and maintain a deterrent policy where competitors were concerned, it was equipped with suitable port facilities — two docks excavated from the rock, well-protected by the coast and cliffs surrounding them and screened from the winds and from all possible surprises. One of the ports was rectangular, and was allocated to trading activity; the round one was for the navy, and in its center was a small island as the base for the admiralty, which included the administration buildings and service areas that ensured the full working order of the port. There were also a series of breakwaters and docks to harbour 220 ships, with warehouses built along the docks.

The two lagoons near Carthage (which are still easily recognizable) seem to tie in with the description left us by Appian and the excavations opened up in the context of the international campaign for reclaiming Carthage definitely confirm the identification of the Punic ports of the city with the two lagoons. Archaeological evidence shows that these ports were used during the Punic wars — traces have been found of several sloping dry docks. As for the other port facilities, there were ramps built with earth brought to the site; in them sockets spaced at roughly 60 cm intervals have been found. These held wooden poles and crossbeams, above which are the remains of the structures they supported; articles recovered include copper nails for use in shipbuilding and terra-cotta moulds used in metalcasting that indicate that founders worked at the ports. We thus have a complete picture of the port facilities dating from the last centuries of Carthage described by Appian, but the ports relative to the earlier, original city have not as yet come to light.

Dwellings

The excavations begun as part of the international campaign for the recla-mation of Carthage (sponsored by Unesco) have made it possible to explore the dwellings of the citizens whose names appear in the *tophet* stelae and on the epitaphs. The remains of two residential districts have come to light beneath the earthworks built up during Roman times. One of these districts is situated at the foot of the Byrsa, and the other is along the seafront, with elegant houses built with peristyles.

The more modest dwellings found at Byrsa have the advantage of being easy to interpret. Both the structure and the arrangement of the dwellings are quite clear — the long, narrow entrance corridor turns a sharp corner before leading into the courtyard, which supplies plenty of light and air to the surrounding rooms. Particularly interesting is the engineering of the water supply and drainage system. The system consists of a supply from cis-terns, and a series of gutters and cesspools. Decorations also appear: mosaics on the floors, mouldings in stone and stucco, capitals, cornices or Egyptian cymae, etc.

Although these remains are important, we are still a long way from the glory of Carthage, queen of the Mediterranean, world-famous for its stature, splendor and the impact it had on civilization in its day. To fill this gap in our knowledge we have to consider other sites such as Utica, Hadrumetum, Leptis, Thapsus, and Gigthi.

Kerkouane

Of all the Punic world, Kerkouane is the city of which most seems to have survived. The earliest remains brought to light date back to the 6th centu-ry B.C., attested beyond any doubt by an Ionic cup of the B2 type. This find means that already at that early stage the population was sufficiently advanced to import costly pottery from distant lands. Numerous archaeo-logical clues (architecture, pottery, etc.) and inscriptions (mainly onomastic examples) seem to indicate the existence of a Libyan village that burgeoned due to its contacts with the Carthaginian world.

The town fell victim to two invasions (one by Agathocles about 310 B.C., and the other by Regulus during the First Punic War), and was probably abandoned toward 253 B.C. What has remained is easy to interpret. The urban layout consisted of a set of ramparts and a grid of crisscrossed streets, neighbourhoods equipped with all the facilities of the period, including a proper bath on a plinth, a working plumbing system, carved or painted dec-orations on fragments of columns from porticoes. In addi-tion to those built round a courtyard, there are also row houses, a style of prevalently Libyan origin.

Kerkouane is also the site of the largest Punic sanctuary discovered in the western Mediterranean. Here the plan of the western Semitic temple is complete — the two frontal pillars of the entrance, which leads straight to the main road of the town, the vestibule that opens onto an oblong

Kerkouane, detail of the dwellings showing plumbing facilities

room containing two benches; the spacious courtyard divided into two by the cella — the forward section complete with an altar for worship, and the rear section organized for feasts. There are also outbuildings and a complete workshop for terra-cottas, including the store for clay, wells, tubs and a kiln. The ashes in the kiln have been carefully sifted and fragments of figurines were found, notably two male heads and the foot of a goddess.

The excavations at Kerkouane have yielded a wide range of material, affording us a picture of the everyday activity of the inhabitants. Knowledge of the city is complemented by the necropolis of Areg el-Ghazouani, where a great many tombs have come to light dating from the 6th-3rd centuries B.C. The types found here differ from the purely Carthaginian form — the access shaft is longer, and the tomb chamber is built into the thickness of the wall opposite the steps leading down. This kind of design was probably quite foreign to the Carthaginians. On occasion, the architrave of the tomb chamber bears an epitaph, such as the one found in the tomb of Ramel Ben Gath or that of Yzbeq, the foundry-man. Inside one of the tomb chambers there is a signature painted with red ochre, left by a stone-mason.

After the destruction of Carthage, Punic civilization continued to survive in Tunisia, achieving great splendour in the cities of Maktar, Teboursouk, Medidi, Gigthi, Bulla Regia, Chemtou and others. There are many remains testifying to this, including sanctuaries, mausolea, stelae, and institutions, in which it is common to come across the names of suffetes of Rabs and Baalim, i.e. dignitaries. At Maktar, inscriptions carved in the cursive writing commonly termed Neo-Punic mention the "dignitaries of Maktar."

*Kerkouane
dwellings with
central courtyard*

The Phoenico-Punic Presence in Morocco

For plotting the traces of Phoenician and Punic peoples in Morocco, there is a wealth of evidence already available, coming from diverse and plentiful sources. Apart from the much-quoted Homer, whose heroes probably entered Libya, i.e. North Africa, another important reference is Herodotus, offering a picturesque account (IV, 126) of Carthaginian merchants with their vessels loaded with a bounty of assorted goods, and telling how they sailed out past the Pillars of Hercules to reach the inhabitants of the Atlantic coastlands and nearby mountains.

There is no way of establishing in which zone the silent barter of Carthaginian wares for the gold of the indigenous people, described with picturesque realism, actually took place. Some contemporary historians have suggested that it was the Atlantic coast of Morocco, and more precisely Mogador, where traces of fires discovered in the area have been ascribed to bonfires lit by the Carthaginians to announce their arrival to the local tribes.

Other authors refer to the ancient cities of Morocco and their Phoenician origins. Regarding Lixus, which the *Periplus of Scylax* defines as "city of the Phoenicians," Pliny gathered traditional stories about its origins and the temple dedicated to its founder. Pliny also recorded information on other cities, such as Tingi, Rusadir, Rusibis and Zili, cited also by Ptolemy and Strabo, in the *Itinerarium Antoninum*, and in the works of the Geographer of Ravenna. Tingi is also mentioned in the writings of Hecataeus of Miletus, Silius Italicus, Pomponius and Plutarch.

Strabo ascribes to Eratosthenes a tradition according to which the

213

Phoenicians founded 300 colonies along the Atlantic coast of Morocco, all of which were totally razed by natives. While recognizing the historical foundation of the claim, the ancient authors (Artemidorus and Strabo in particular) consider it an exaggeration.

This disputed history could tie in with the lost cities of Cotte, Lissa, Thrinke, Exilissa and others, all mentioned in the works of Hecataeus of Miletus, Pliny, Strabo and Ptolemy. This is rather a bold supposition, especially if we consider the obstacles to identifying even more historically important sites such as the colonies founded by Hanno during the time of the famous circumnavigation, which continue to excite great discussion, despite the fact that most modern historians agree that they did exist.

It is clear, then, that the Phoenico-Punic presence in Morocco did not escape the notice of the Greek and Latin historians. Drawing on written and oral sources of varying origins, some authors invoke Punic traditional beliefs or writings. The work *Le Maroc chez les auteurs anciens* by R. Roget (Paris, 1924) is a highly useful tool for those who wish to quantify and assess the historical data relative to the Phoenico-Punic cultural presence in that country. The data is, however, insufficient, and at times verges on myth and legend rather than chronicled historical facts. Without excluding them altogether, the historian must refer to more direct sources.

The Contribution of Archaeology

During the colonial period, archaeological research took on extraordinary momentum, but it was not until the end of World War II that proper missions were set up and programmes were realized, like the one at Lixus, in which Spanish and French archaeologists took part. The example of Mogador, a relatively recent excavation site, is indicative of the burgeoning interest manifested by the independent Moroccan authorities for their archaeological and historical heritage. Moroccan archaeologists are now participating in surveying and excavation work throughout the country, especially along the Atlantic and Mediterranean coasts from Tangier to Lixus and out beyond Mogador, with outstanding results in terms of the quantity, diversity and significance of the finds obtained.

Numerous necropoli have been located and excavated at Tangier, Lixus, Melilla, Tit near el-Jadida, Azemmour, and many other places that have been subjected to systematic investigations. In addition to their structure and type, the tombs of these necropoli, rock-cut, stone-built, or grouped together in grottoes like mausolea, have offered abundant material for study, including plain and high-quality pottery (the latter often imported from Greece or Italy), jewellery, amulets and scarabs — all objects which add to our knowledge of the Phoenico-Punic presence in Morocco. These tombs include a group of chambers carved out of the sandstone in the neighbourhood of Azemmour, of Sidi Slimane, and the tomb of Cape Achakar.

These funerary structures, whether isolated or arranged in clusters, imply the presence of a residential setting. Surveying and excavation work have revealed urban remains notably at Lixus and Tamuda, where houses and sanctuaries have been identified. For military architecture, the walls surrounding Lixus and Volubilis are of interest. On the other sites, the Phoenico-Punic presence can be traced in the various finds, including shards, tools, jewellery, amulets, coins and so forth.

The coinage is a great help in evaluating the Punic presence and the extent of Punic influence. The right to mint coins was granted to many cities, for example Rusadir, Sala, Tingi, Tamuda, Lixus and Mqom Shemesh. Legends in Neo-Punic characters engraved on the coins enable us to establish the links between the cities and the Phoenician or Punic peoples, as well as the influence exercised by Phoenico-Punic civilization on a particular region of Morocco or a particular urban agglomeration. The toponyms give a clue as to the place of origin, and occasionally even the contents. This way we can confirm that the place-name Rusadir, mentioned by Pliny, is written *RŠ'DR*, which in Punic means "Cape Powerful", modern Cap des Trois Fourches. The iconography also provides useful information. The obverse of the coin carries a portrait of a beardless youth; it is still undecided whether the image is of a prince or a deity. But the reverse, with its sheaths of wheat and a honeybee, is easier to interpret — on another series of coins, the bee is seen between a bunch of grapes and a sheath of wheat. This is clearly an allusion to the agricultural wealth of the city and its region, and to the fact that the place-name Melilla seems to derive from the Latin word for honey. A sweet coincidence! It appears that the Greek version of the *Periplus* designates the same city with the name "Acros," a simple translation of the Punic *RŠ*, meaning "cape." This rich archaeological and philological tradition has been inherited by modern Melilla in Morocco.

The city of Lixus also had two names. The first was *MQM ŠMŠ*, a Phoenician expression meaning "Abode of ŠMŠ," the sun god venerated by the Phoenicians; we should not forget that, according to Herodotus, the Libyans carried out sacrifices to the sun and the moon, and so this *ŠMŠ* could be either a purely Semitic deity or a Libyan one whose name we do not know. The other double name found on coins from Lixus could correspond to the transcription in Neo-Punic characters of a place-name written as *LKŠ*, which the Latin scripts translate either as *LIX* or *LIXS*.

Punic Epigraphy
In addition to the legends in Punic and Neo-Punic script impressed on the coinage of some ancient Moroccan cities, whose contribution in terms of economy and religion has already been discussed, it is important to recall the texts carved on stelae and fragments of pottery. The Punic inscriptions of Morocco have interested epigraphists for a long time; already in 1892, in the *Bulletin Archéologique du Comité*, Philippe Berger published an article on a Phoenician inscription of the 2nd century B.C. discovered at Lixus.

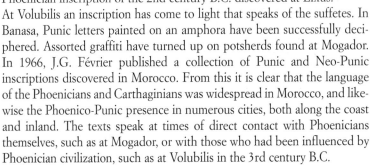

Island of Mogador

At Volubilis an inscription has come to light that speaks of the suffetes. In Banasa, Punic letters painted on an amphora have been successfully deciphered. Assorted graffiti have turned up on potsherds found at Mogador. In 1966, J.G. Février published a collection of Punic and Neo-Punic inscriptions discovered in Morocco. From this it is clear that the language of the Phoenicians and Carthaginians was widespread in Morocco, and likewise the Phoenico-Punic presence in numerous cities, both along the coast and inland. The texts speak at times of direct contact with Phoenicians themselves, such as at Mogador, or with those who had been influenced by Phoenician civilization, such as at Volubilis in the 3rd century B.C.

On the basis of this rich and varied evidence, historians are in a good position to assess the impact of the Phoenico-Punic presence in Morocco. As for the Phoenician centres, it seems that Lixus and Mogador were the most prominent, and are certainly the ones most amply covered by Greek and Latin historical accounts, and by direct sources (archaeology, epigraphy and numismatics). On the other hand, Phoenician culture was very widespread and exerted a strong influence on every aspect of daily life — language, religious practices and even beliefs concerning the land of the dead and the world beyond the grave.

Chronologically the accounts of the ancient authors attest to the presence of the Phoenicians in Morocco already in the 2nd millennium B.C., when Lixus was probably founded. But the oldest archaeological evidence that has reached us goes no farther back than the 7th century B.C., as in the case of the tomb at Cape Achakar, or the material recovered at Mogador. From the 6th or 5th century B.C. onwards, the Punic people of Carthage took over from the Phoenicians of eastern origin, and Phoenico-Punic culture continued to predominate until the period of the last kings of Mauritania, leaving a deep and lasting imprint.

From a cultural point of view, the Phoenico-Punic presence is most strongly felt today in some of the ancient sites in Morocco, notably at Lixus,

Late Geometric Euboic krater
from Amathus
8th century B.C.
painted clay, 45 cm
Limassol, District Museum

*Bowl decorated with hunting scenes
and inscription in syllabic Cypriot
from Paphos, 7th century B.C.
bronze, diam. 15 cm
Nicosia, Cyprus Museum*

*Plaquette with sphinx
from the throne
found in tomb 79 at Salamis
7th century B.C.
ivory, 16 cm
Nicosia, Cyprus Museum*

Large amphora of the
IV Bichrome
with figures dancing
in sacred garden
7th century B.C.
clay, 93 cm
Nicosia, Cyprus Museum

Bronze harness from tomb 79
at Salamis
7th century B.C., 58 cm
Nicosia, Cyprus Museum

opposite page
*Hathoric capital
from Paphos
6th century B.C.
limestone, 80 cm
Parigi, Musée
du Louvre*

*Stele featuring
figure inside
niche with foliate
motifs
from Maktar
1st century B.C.
limestone
57 × 38 cm
Tunis, Musée
du Bardo*

Motya, the so-called "house of mosaics"
detail of pebbled pavement

Walls at Lixus

Tamuda and Volubilis. Anything that can be removed has been transported for display in the museums, the most important one being at Rabat. But in order to understand the impact of this Phoenico-Punic presence, there is still a great deal of work to do, both on the sites of the excavations and in the organization of already existing material.

The Phoenico-Punic Presence in Algeria

The Phoenicians must have come to know the Algerian coast at the time when their ships sailed to the biblical Tarshish. The accounts of the ancient authors are confused and rarely go beyond conjecture. The city of Auza, that Menander of Ephesus spoke of, has still not been tracked down. Stéphane Gsell rejected the hypothesis of a city named Auza (modern Aumale) in the hinterland of Algiers but in an inaccessible area. Hippo, mentioned by Sallust, is still the subject of debate. The choice lies between Hippo Regius (modern Annaba in Algeria), and Hippo Dyarrhytus, now Bizerta in Tunisia. Both cities have the same toponym, and both sites have yielded evidence of Punic civilization, but much later than the early Phoenician navigation.

The period corresponding to Carthaginian domination is documented more explicitly (and more credibly) by classical historians. Several large cities are mentioned in the chronicles of the voyages that coincide with the period of Punic dominion — for example in the famous *Periplus of Scylax*, probably written in the 4th century B.C., and notably in the texts that cover the kingdoms of Numidia and Mauritania and their links with Carthage and the other Mediterranean countries. Thanks to Polybius, Livy and other Greek and Roman historians, we have references to Syphax, Massinissa, Micipsa, Jugurtha and other princes in the tents and palaces of Siga or Cirta. As for Hippo, Silius Italicus describes the city as the "favorite of the ancient kings." Other towns were Hebdomos, Maes, Akion, Chalca and Arylon, none of which have as yet been identified, although the *Periplus* locates them between the cities of Iol and Siga. Since the texts refer to towns in contact with Carthage and with Punic civilization generally, the information is vague and does not allow us to establish their whereabouts.

Sometimes the place-name itself is a key, especially where philological analysis makes it possible to trace a Semitic or even Phoenician root. Rusicade (now Skikda) retains the memory of the Phoenicians or Carthaginians who founded or perhaps colonized it — the letters *RUS*, meaning "head," dispel all doubt. The same applies to Rusucurru (now Dellys), Rusippisir (now Takdebt), Rusguniae opposite Algiers, Rusasus, Azeffoun, south of Cape Corbelin, and Rusubbicari (now Menzel-Hajej). Other place-names along the Algerian coastline seem to derive from a period preceding the Numidian and Mauritanian kingdoms. The city of Iol (Caesarea in history, now Cherchell) may take its name from a Phoenician deity, though this is only a hypothesis. The same could be said for the name Iar, which Gesenius ascribed to Phoenician origins; the site of the city is thought to have been beyond Gunugu, somewhere between Cartili and Cartennas — two other place-names in which we can trace the root cart, which means "city" in Phoenician and Carthaginian. Similarly, the place-name Cirta is still in doubt, as on coins it appears in Neo-Punic script with the initial letter "Q". We should also remember that some philologists contend that the initial letter "I" in place-names such as Iol, Iar, and Icosium (now Algiers) is actually the Phoenician letter designating an island. At all events, it is certain that the study of place-names supports the idea of a Phoenico-Punic presence in Algeria.

Archaeological Evidence

Since the end of the last century, archaeologists have drawn attention to relics related to the Phoenician presence, to the dominion exerted by Carthage, and to the widespread penetration of the Libyan world, and even Numidia. Besides chance or sporadic discoveries, there have been extensive systematic searches at Gouraya, the ancient Gunugu, at Cirta (in the sanctuary of el-Hofra), at Iol, at Tipasa and further west at Siga, Rachgoun, Mersa Medakh, Les Andalouses, Bemi Ghenane, and other sites along the coast and inland. The archaeological evidence thus far accumulated relates to aspects of daily life, religion and death. A series of necropoli have been identified and explored at Gouraya, Tipasa, Igilgili, Hippo, Mersa Medakh, and on the island of Rachgoun. The excavations have yielded an abundance of information on the tomb structures, their typology, the grave goods found in them, the burial methods, funerary practices, and so forth.

Deserving special attention among all this evidence are the Punic and Neo-Punic inscriptions. The stelae of el-Hofra attest to the existence of a place consecrated to the chief Punic deities, the goddess Tanit ("face of Baal") and the god Baal Hammon. Other inscriptions have come to light at Iol, where the famous epitaph of Micipsa was unearthed, while at Hippo a number of Neo-Punic dedications have been found. In his *Punica*, J.B. Chabot presented an assortment of Punic and Neo-Punic texts, votive dedications and epitaphs, all discovered at Algerian sites, mainly in the region of Constantine, not far from the western borders of Tunisia.

One of these inscriptions is of particular interest: it appears on a stele marking a tomb and the name of the deceased. Using a little imagination, the late J.G. Février deciphered the following appeal to the passerby: "O you who pass — Pause here and read!" The stele was recovered in the countryside of Guelaa Bou Sba, not far from Guelma; it testifies to the fact that in the 1st century A.D. a considerable part of the population still knew how to read and write in Punic. We might even go so far as to assume that schools existed where, during the period of Roman dominion, the language of Carthage was taught. The excavations at Les Andalouses have brought to light a fine stele with a triangular top and a crescent moon over a sun disc, a divine symbol underlining the religious nature of the monument. In a rectangular frame bordered by a flat band, the votary stands with a raised sceptre; in his left hand is a gift which he is about to place on the altar. The soft,

Aerial view of the Tipasa settlement

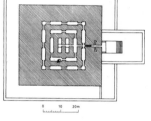

Plan of the southern tumulus at Tiaret

weather-worn sandstone of the stele has suffered from being buried so long under the rubble, and only a vague outline of the image remains. Below the votary, in Punic script the word *MTNT* is inscribed, which in Carthaginian means "offering"; the giftbearer is called *WRTGRS*. The stele from Les Andalouses is convincing evidence of Punic presence in the region of Oran, which after being occupied by the Phoenicians and Carthaginians reverted to the authority of the kings of Massaeyles. Syphax, the most renowned of these kings, minted coins in Siga with legends in Neo-Punic script rendering the place-name, *ŠG'N*, and the name of the king himself, *SPQ*. Permission to mint coins with Neo-Punic writing on them was granted to other Algerian cities, namely Gunugu, Iol and Cirta (which ought to read Cirtha according to the Neo-Punic letters).

Finds include a variety of other historically valuable objects, such as pottery from local workshops, or imported from Carthage or elsewhere; the plain wares were evidently for everyday needs and the finer ones reserved for ceremonies. The jewellery and amulets are also of great interest — the museum at Cherchell possesses a series of scarabs, while the necropolis at Les Andalouses has yielded jewellery and amulets in faience or cornelian. The tombs at Rachgoun contained an assortment of scarabs, seals with swivel mounts, earrings and *nezems*, or nose ornaments. One of these earrings represents the Egyptian symbol of life, the *ankh*.

As far as public and private buildings are concerned, various remains of domestic architecture have come to light at Tiddis, and also at Les Andalouses, Mersa Medakh and Rachgoun, where survey work has led to the discovery of traces of Punic dwellings datable between the 7th and 5th centuries B.C. The walls are built from rough-hewn stone held together with clay; the partitions are made from mud-brick, and the floor of plain earth.

Among the sanctuaries discovered, the *tophet* at Cirta, with its wealth of urns and stelae with or without inscriptions, provides the strongest evidence of the Phoenico-Punic religions in Algeria. The language of the inscriptions and the images on the stelae show predominantly Semitic and Phoenician components, but without excluding elements from native cultures or Greece and Egypt. The area around el-Hofra, which has yielded most of the Punic stelae found so far, was first discovered at the end of the last century.

The rock-cut temple of Tiddis, which seems to be of predominantly Libyan design, was probably a Punic sanctuary. The architectural details are typical of a sacred place — fragments of columns, capitals, a piece of a grooved cornice, and two small pyramid-shaped obelisks. G. Vuillemot, who drew up the inventory, writes, "It is possible that these ruins are the remains of a traditional Punic temple, with a Hellenistic façade and Egyptian-style dec-

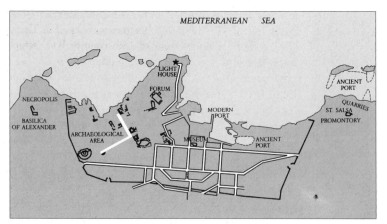

orations." The stelae of Hippo also suggest an ancient sanctuary, despite their later date.

Among the various Phoenician deities worshipped in Numidia were Baal, Tanit and Baal Addir, whose name is carved on stele no. 27 from el-Hofra. Some scholars have ruled out the possibility that this is a different deity from Baal Hammon, because the term "Addir" can be used as an adjective, an epithet to Baal, lord of the *tophet*.

Melqarth seems to have been part of this pantheon in Algeria. An ancient tradition mentioned by Solinus attributes the foundation of Icosium (now Algiers) to companions of Heracles: "On their way through the area, twenty of Heracles' retinue left him, decided to found a town, and erected the perimeter walls. So that none of them could claim to have given his own name to the city, they assigned it a name which would evoke the number of its founders" (Solinus, XXV, 17). On some coins minted in Icosium, bearing inscriptions that prove the Punic origins of this place-name, there is an image that could be identified as Heracles-Melqarth.

Although Melqarth undoubtedly replaced a Libyan god of a much earlier date than Heracles, the fact remains that in African mythology the latter is cited as a founder of cities. The name of Heracles is linked to the foundation of Tingi in Morocco, Iol in Algeria, Capsa (now Gafsa) in Tunisia, and Lixus. A terracotta statuette in the museum of Oran shows that in the ancient city of Les Andalouses worship of the goddess Demeter was also widespread. It is not yet clear, however, whether this was a cult introduced to Numidia under the direct influence of Carthage, or the result of an infiltration of cults encouraged by the kings of Numidia. The indications point to Massinissa and his philo-Hellenic followers.

According to the evidence available today, the oldest traces of the Phoenico-Punic presence in Algeria go back to the 7th century B.C. — a *facies* currently under investigation on the island of Rachgoun, in the vicin-

*Detail of votive
stele from
Cheffia Tal
1st century A.D.
sandstone
135 × 92.5 cm
Annaba, Museum
of Annaba*

Design in perspective and plan of the mausoleum at Es-Soumâa

ity of Oran. The finds at Gouraya include Greek pottery from the 5th century B.C. while the excavations at Tipasa have yielded material from the 6th century B.C., which may be the period of the town's foundation. It is certain that by the 6th century B.C. the inhabitants of Tipasa had already reached a high level of development and were in contact with the outside world, since they were able to import and appreciate luxury wares manufactured and decorated in foreign workshops, and brought over in ships that made long and dangerous voyages.

In conclusion, we can safely state that the Phoenico-Punic presence in Algeria dates back to the very beginnings of the Phoenician involvement with the western Mediterranean. The navigators who headed toward the realm of Tarshish doubtlessly came to know the Algerian coastal regions, and exploited them for their human and natural resources. After the Phoenicians came the city-state of Carthage, and it is difficult to ascertain exactly when the Numidian rulers took over the Carthaginian ports. We know that in the 3rd century B.C., during the reign of Syphax, this had already occurred.

The change in government was by no means negative for Punic civilization. The kings of Numidia, who were already imbued with Punic culture, did not hesitate to adopt the Punic language and mint coins using the Semitic language and characters. The institutions were probably also influenced by Carthage; a similar form of "suffetate" or magistrature was adopted, tailored to suit the needs and customs of the Libyan kingdoms and communities. It has been noted that beliefs in certain Numidian circles were also deeply affected, as can be seen in the sanctuary and stelae of el-Hofra.

The impact of Phoenician culture was clearly felt everywhere, but it is most evident in the monumental mausolea — the Medracen mausoleum near Batna, the Somaa of Khroub close to Constantine, the tomb of Bemi Ghenane near Siga, and the so-called "tomb of the Christian woman" near Algiers.

The structure and layout of these specimens of funerary architecture are strong evidence of the presence of the Phoenicians and Carthaginians in Algeria and show the process of osmosis that took place between the indigenous peoples and those who came from afar, first from Phoenicia and then from Carthage — to set up trading posts and contribute to the development of the existing towns and villages.

Despite the abundance and variety of the evidence of the Phoenico-Punic presence in Algeria, the material remains are found mainly in the showcases and storerooms of the museums. Little survives of the splendor of great cities such as Cirta, Siga and Iol, and the material garnered from the sanctuaries and necropoli certainly does not reflect their original grandeur.

This rapid overview shows how extensive the influence of the Phoenicians and Carthaginians was in North Africa, starting from the 2nd millennium B.C. In the first instance, the colonizers built trading ports along the coast to ensure the best possible travelling conditions for the ships that "sailed for Tarshish," meaning those vessels equipped for the high seas which could undertake long and dangerous voyages between the Phoenician cities of the East and the coastlands of the western Mediterranean, venturing out beyond the Pillars of Hercules. These temporary trading posts were followed by a colonial policy which had its greatest realization in the birth of Carthage around A.D. 814. From the end of the 7th century B.C. onwards, the new Punic metropolis ensured the survival and safety of all the Phoenician bases in North Africa, and the peaceful penetration of Punic culture. This feat was not accomplished through a policy of annexation by power, but through the Phoenicians' unparalleled knowledge of the sea, their monopoly of the markets, their economic clout, their marked technical superiority, and their superior solutions to material and spiritual problems, including agriculture, urbanization, religious practices, written documents, institutions, and so forth. Neither directly planned nor the result of a systematic policy based on an ideology, the penetration of the Phoenician and Punic influence throughout North Africa, and the introduction of these cultures in every corner of the Libyan world, was the spontaneous outcome of the foundation of Phoenician or Punic cities. This Semitic influence was a valuable stimulus for the existing Libyan culture, and opened the way to development and riches. Such acquisitions are timeless and remain manifest in the daily behaviour of the people — the farmer's attachment to his land, the housewife attending to her bread-oven. The spirit of Carthage has been animating the reaches of the Maghreb for thousands of years — the past nourishing both present and future.

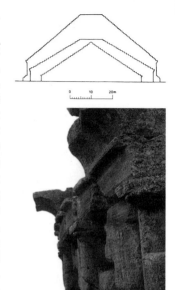

Outlines of the mausoleums at Tipasa Medracen and Djedar

Architectural detail of the monumental mausoleum at Medracen Algeria

Sicily
Vincenzo Tusa

A discussion of the Phoenicians in Sicily should start by considering their first impact on the island. I shall not deal with this in terms of the wider picture of "Phoenician expansion in the Mediterranean" (as it is generally called), recently a subject of much heated debate among scholars, but merely touch briefly on it as the essential introduction to the Phoenico-Punic presence in Sicily. Until a few years ago most scholars believed, on the basis of various facts and observations which are here briefly set out, that the presence of the Phoenicians in the Mediterranean and hence in Sicily could reasonably be dated to between the late 12th and early 11th centuries B.C. The most interesting information we have, forming the starting-point for this aspect of Phoenician studies, is a passage in Thucydides (VI, 2). Its value and accuracy are becoming increasingly evident, and its importance makes it worth quoting:

"The Phoenicians then also dwelt along the whole coast of Sicily, having occupied the promontories on the seacoast and islands just offshore, because of their trade with the Siculians. But then when the Greeks came there from across the sea in large numbers, after giving up most of the island they dwell at Motya, Soluntum and Panormus (having formed of them a confederation) close to the Elymians, relying on an alliance with them and also on the fact that from this point Carthage is only a short sea-crossing from Sicily."

Map of Sicily
★ Phoenician and Punic sites

This passage from Thucydides, despite its brevity, tells us a number of

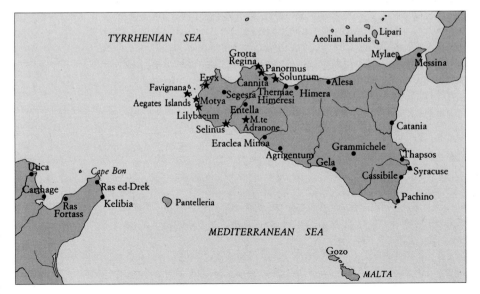

231

things which have been partly substantiated by historical and archaeological documents: the foundation of settlements at Motya, Soluntum and Panormus (Palermo); the prior settlement of western Sicily by the Elymians. This passage is also geographically accurate: the relatively short distance from Carthage, which having been founded in 814 B.C., by the middle of the 8th century B.C. (the first period of Greek colonization in Sicily) had become the main point of reference for Phoenicians scattered around the Mediterranean.

Thucydides also states clearly that the transfer of the Phoenicians from eastern Sicily was not caused by their expulsion, as some scholars have held, but was a voluntary decision on their part, or at least one made in agreement with the newly-arrived Greeks. Thucydides does not refer to the use of force, much less struggles or battles: he uses an expression which can be accurately translated as "having abandoned that which was overmuch," i.e. "the superfluous." This was because the kinds of places that Thucydides mentions — "promontories on the sea and islands just off-shore" — were not the sites of permanent and fully functioning Phoenician towns but rather "landing stages along the great sea-crossing, trading stations, corresponding offices for the purchase and disposal of goods" (Pace).

Posts of this kind were scattered all over the Mediterranean, including Sicily: a small island such as Ortigia would have been ideal as a link with Sicily. (The possibility that the Phoenicians were present in eastern Sicily, if only culturally, has yet to be investigated; clues, however, do exist.) Evidence that is worth bearing in mind in this regard is provided by a passage in Diodorus Siculus (an author often distrusted by historians and archaeologists but who is proving to be a source of some value). He says: "And so for this trade for many years [practised] by the Phoenicians, who had acquired great wealth, they sent out many groups of colonists, some to Sicily and the nearby islands, others to Libya, Sardinia and Iberia."

Since they were not towns but ports of call, as stated above, it is logical that nothing should remain on the site and hence nothing of archaeological interest is to be found. The kind of trade the Phoenicians engaged in did not call for permanent structures but perhaps merely a few tents at the various ports they called at to trade with the local populations. This is what Herodotus tells us in a noted passage which may sound like legend but has a basis of truth. Herodotus's passage also provides further evidence that permanent settlements did not exist in the early period of Phoenician expansion in the Mediterranean, between the late 12th and early 11th centuries B.C.; the formation of towns belongs as we now know to the second half of the 8th century B.C. These permanent settlements or towns, mentioned by Herodotus (and others), must also have been trading stations in the sense suggested above, in places with which the Phoenicians were already familiar from their trading voyages across the Mediterranean.

In light of these observations, the term "pre-colonization" is acceptable to indicate the Phoenicians' presence in various parts of the Mediterranean

*Aerial view
of the island
of Motya*

before the establishment of permanent settlements in the second half of the
8th century B.C., the date which is taken as the starting-point of so-called
"colonization." In my opinion, as I have explained elsewhere, these are
terms of convenience, which may sometimes be useful but have no real significance in the historical-archaeological picture summarily sketched out
here.
Examination of the Phoenicians' permanent settlements in Sicily can begin
with those named by Thucydides.

Motya
Motya is a small island with a surface area of about 45 hectares lying almost
at the center of the lagoon off Marsala known as the "Stagnone." As
Thucydides says, this island was ideal for the Phoenicians as a station for
trade with the native inhabitants of the Sicilian coast lying opposite and perhaps also those of Motya itself, as recent finds seem to confirm.
The town wall is the first impression of the archaeology of Motya upon
arrival on the island: it is completely surrounded by a wall washed by the
sea at some points and having a total length of 2,375 m. It is very simply
built of largish undressed blocks of local limestone, except for a few short
stretches of tufaceous stone, not found locally, which must have been
brought from the Sicilian mainland. These brief stretches are laid in an
isodomic structure in the Greek manner. At fairly regular intervals the wall
is reinforced by square towers, some flanked by steps communicating with

the outside. Access to the outside was also provided by smaller gates, or posterns, of which one, to the north, is well-preserved but now bricked up.
Four gates probably linked the city with the outside; two remain today, to the north and the south. The former is the more interesting; it is set at an angle to the road leading from it into the town. The doors can be seen, and the local museum has a bronze hinge found on the site. The road-way shows clear signs of the passage of carts.

Motya, the cothon

The gate is flanked by two large quadrangular towers set at an angle. The two towers bounding the southern gate are also quadrangular, but built differently: they are set along the axis of the entrance and made of small fragments of rock instead of the large blocks of the north gate. The wall, probably built (as stated above) in the early 6th century B.C., was worked on extensively over the centuries, perhaps through to the 4th century B.C., until the threat of Dionysius loomed large on the horizon.

Motya, details of the walls

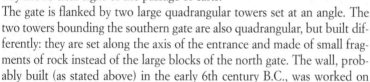

Close by the south gate there is a small inlet (51 × 37 m) that was once considered the port of Motya. However, it seems very strange, indeed highly unlikely that such a small inlet could have served a town which required a harbor adequate to its flourishing commerce. The problem was solved by excavations conducted by the British Mission, which ascertained that the inlet was used as a dry dock (*cothon*). The port of Motya may have comprised the whole of the Stagnone.

Moving on to the "Cappiddazzu" shrine: the strange Sicilian name refers to the old hat propped on a stick in the vineyard which once covered the site of Whitaker's excavations. What remains there today is primarily a rectangular wall (27.40 × 35.40 m). To one side, facing northwest, are inset the foundations of a building with a nave and two side-aisles running lengthwise, with a transverse nave at the northwest end. This inset structure is frequent among Phoenico-Punic shrines (a typical example being the Astarte Paphia sanctuary in Cyprus, later dedicated to Aphrodite, in its third phase). The dedication of this site to a divinity (perhaps Baal Hammon) took place in the first period of the formation of the town, and may have included a sacrificial pit which came to light during excavations in recent years. A building under construction with low walls of small, rough undressed stones, with a round well for lustral water, it can be dated to no later than the second half of the 7th century B.C., while the enclosure was built midway through the following century. The enclosure was perhaps erected at the same time as

Motya, aerial view of archaic necropolis and the industrial zone

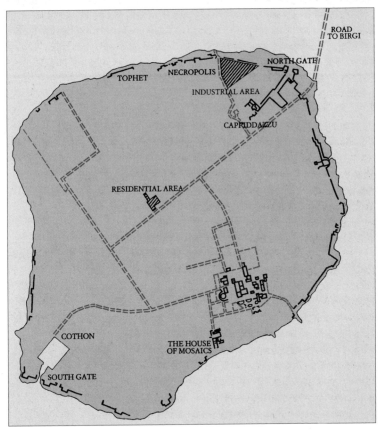

Map of Motya

a new building which included architectural elements from the Syro-Palestinian area and North Africa: Amrith, Utica, Dougga, Medracen, etc. The construction as seen today belongs, however, to the last phase of the shrine's activity, perhaps after 397 B.C., as is borne out by the above-mentioned architectural elements, used as building material for the later structure.

In front of the main building stands a typical small structure comprising a rectangular stone slab pierced through by a large hole in the centre and two semicircles — one might say "demi-holes" — at both ends, set within a small enclosure, also rectangular, made of a number of roughly shaped stones. It was most likely meant to contain three cone-shaped baetyls indicating the sacred edifice: *bet el* in Punic means "house of God". Inside the enclosure there are traces of other buildings whose materials were utilized for the construction of edifices of a later date.

Motya, remains of the road now underwater that linked the island to the mainland

The *tophet* was the sacred place where, according to tradition, children were sacrificed to the divinity. (Recently the function of this place has been questioned, with some justification.) The *tophet* of Motya, identified by Whitaker and recently excavated, consists of various levels of small urns containing the burnt remains of sacrifices, ranging from the early 7th century to well into the 3rd century B.C. Together with the urns, the deposits include terra-cotta statuettes of various kinds, and in particular a group of figures wearing female protomes and one male face with a sardonic smile, presumably having an apotropaic function.

In the terra-cottas and especially the masks the eclectic taste of Punic craftsmanship is evident; alongside forms reflecting Greek taste there are Egyptian influences and occasional Phoenico-Punic elements. This eclecticism, typical of all Phoenico-Punic art, is evident in particular in the more than 1000 stelae, most of them decorated with figures, also found in the *tophet*, which show that in the 6th and 5th centuries B.C. local craftsmanship must have been flourishing. Some stelae bear dedicatory inscriptions to Baal Hammon.

The so-called "industrial zone" is an almost square area covering a little more than 500 m², its boundaries clearly marked by low walls. Upon excavation, this rocky space appeared studded with holes, mostly elliptical in shape, hewn out of the rock and about two metres deep on average; they were lined with unbaked clay. There were also a few wells placed at different points of the area, plus two ovens, elliptical in shape and of considerable size.

The discovery here of quantities of shell fragments, especially of murex, famed as the source of the purple dye used by the Phoenicians, suggests that this area was used for dressing and dyeing leather (as is still done in Algeria and Tunisia) and perhaps also textiles. It is possible that part of the area was used for brick-making. This zone was in use from the early 7th century, if

*Detail of depositions
in the* tophet *of Motya*

not earlier, down to the early 4th century B.C., when Motya was destroyed.

The archaic necropolis appears as a large, rocky, flat space, almost at the sea's edge, strewn with holes or small quadrangular containers in which jars with the ashes of the deceased were placed. The tombs excavated so far number about 200, mostly holding cremated ashes. Only a few served for inhumation. The necropolis is traversed by the town wall, which cuts through it leaving most of the tombs outside but some inside the town itself. Since the oldest tombs can be dated to the late 8th-early 7th century B.C., it may be reasoned that — as mentioned above — the wall did not exist when the necropolis began to be used, but was built in the early 6th century B.C., the date attributed to the most recent burials. Subsequently the Motyans buried their dead on the mainland opposite the island, at Birgi, building a causeway that still exists.

Motya the so-called "house of amphorae"

The tomb furnishings usually consist of two or three typical Phoenico-Punic vases, one of which contained the ashes of the deceased. Corinthian vases have been found in some, making it possible to date these tombs to the period suggested above. There is a certain monotony in the furnishings, perhaps indicating a lack of interest in them unlike the Greek custom. One tomb containing fifteen items is somewhat of an exception: six of the items are imported Corinthian jars and there is a Phoenician figurine, a unique find belonging to the well-known oriental iconography of a female figure pressing her breasts, interpreted as a symbol of fertility and fecundity.

The residential area is still little-known, despite excavation work recently carried out. Only two dwellings had come to light before the latest excavations: the so-called "house of the mosaics" and the "house of the amphorae," both datable to after 397 B.C. and with only part of each remaining. Of the first we have an atrium with a peristyle and ambulatory which must have been covered. This building rests on an earlier edifice, whose function is unknown, built with the so-called "frame" walls typical of the Punic world. The ambulatory still has a mosaic pavement made of white, black and grey pebbles from the riverbed. It is bordered by three bands reproducing a Greek fret pattern, lotus flowers and a stylized wave curve. Within this frame are designs which are common in the oriental tradition, representing fights between animals and individual animals. This is the only such pavement in Sicily. Of the other house, all that remains is one room which contained a number of torpedo-shaped Punic amphorae. This must have been a storeroom and may also have been used as a selling point for amphorae, as is suggested by a roughly made rectangular counter.

Headless statue in volcanic rock found in the Stagnone di Marsala 6th-5th century B.C. 127 cm Palermo, Museo Archeologico Regionale

Two recent excavations have shed light on the town centre, revealing a cluster of seven structures along a broad dirt road. It is likely that this was a sacred area, similar to those at Soluntum and Selinus which belong to the last period of Punic rule. The complex can be dated to the second period of activity in Motya, following its destruction in 397 B.C.

A joint mission sent recently by the Department of Punic Antiquities of Palermo University and the Archaeological Superintendency of Western Sicily has uncovered another building, also later than 397 B.C., containing a pottery workshop with two bilobate kilns of Phoenician type, and other installations for pottery-making. Nearby was found the well-known statue of Anatolian marble, perhaps brought here to provide lime, as suggested by the presence of the kilns and the common practice of using marble statues for this purpose. The statue is a work of art of outstanding importance and real beauty. It shows a youth of above-average height, clad in a long tunic with a broad band perhaps of purple cloth or leather round his chest. It can be dated to the first half of the 5th century B.C., the period of the severe style, though some scholars hold that certain details around the head and the rich garments make it more probably a work of a much later period. This, I feel, is very unlikely. My belief is that this statue is one of the best examples of Graeco-Punic cultural exchange: a work commissioned by a wealthy Motyan from a Greek artist, or at least one familiar with Greek culture. The client may have required the statue to be clad in this dress, with the band round his breast, as symbols of his office as magistrate or priest.

Motya, the so-called "house of mosaics" detail of pebbled pavement
• *p. 224*

The material Whitaker assembled for the island's museum is a remarkable collection, indispensable for the study and understanding of Phoenico-Punic civilization in the Mediterranean. It contains all the material found on the island (it is to be hoped that the articles now in the museum of Marsala, including the statue, will soon be brought back here), in part coming from ancient Lilybaeum, and in part given to Whitaker or acquired by him on the antiquarian market. Some of this material is presented in this catalogue.

Soluntum

About 20 km east from Palermo on a hill called Monte Catalfano lie the fairly numerous remains of Soluntum (*Soloeis* in Greek, *Kfr* in Punic), the second city mentioned by Thucydides after Motya. This could suggest that it belongs to the same age as Motya, but this is not so. Its layout is Hellenistic, typically Hipodamean, with the distinctive characters of a township designed on paper and accurately transferred to the site.

The streets running east-west are broad and cross the narrower north-south streets in a grid pattern; the various quarters are differentiated according to the social status of the inhabitants; shops line the main street; the public buildings, both religious and civil, are all clustered in the same western section of the town; the industrial zone is in the southwest; there were private and public cisterns for collecting rainwater, and drains and conduits for carrying off waste which still function today.

All this seems to indicate that it was a Greek city, but Punic elements appear not just in various objects (stone stelae, terracotta heads with Punic symbols on them, etc.) but above all in the religious edifices; that is, in the aspect that best reflects the spirit of the townspeople. Three are known so far. One is at the highest point of the town (irresistibly bringing to mind the "high places" of the Bible), consisting of a group of rooms reminiscent of a labyrinth, with a niche in the last room which most probably contained a symbol of the divinity. On another spot, sheltered by the hill, there once stood a bipartite edifice with cross- and barrel-vaulting which housed two divinities, one male and one female. The male divinity is most probably Zeus (or perhaps Baal Hammon in the guise of Zeus) represented in a statue of a seated figure discovered nearby early in the last century. Finally, on the main street, where the public buildings start, there is an altar with three baetyls which are a symbol of the Phoenico-Punic religion. Judging from remains found in a trough at the foot of the altar, animals (sheep, fowls and rodents) were sacrificed here.

The more ancient Soluntum mentioned by Thucydides has not yet been found. It may well lie near the city we have described, considering the fur-

View of the Soluntum Hellenistic-Roman settlement on Monte Catalfano

Map of Soluntum

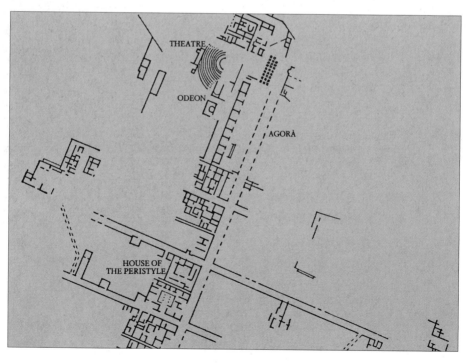

*Remains of a monumental
building of the
Hellenistic-Roman
settlement at Soluntum*

241

nishings found in certain tombs close to the ones belonging to the Soluntum active from the 4th century B.C. until late in the 2nd century A.D., as shown by coins of Commodus found on the site.

The material found here is kept partly in a collection *in situ*, and partly in the Palermo Archaeological Museum.

Palermo

This is the third city mentioned by Thucydides in the famous passage. The name Panormus ("all port") was given to it later by the Greeks; its Punic name is unknown to us. It is very unlikely that it can be assigned the Phoenician name *Ziz*, which is found on a coin.

We have little archaeological information about the ancient city. It lies under the modern one and it is almost impossible to study it as a whole, as we can with Soluntum, which has not been built over since the end of the 2nd century A.D. At points in the modern city stretches of the old wall have come to the surface, providing support for G. Columba's topographical reconstruction of the ancient city. He proposed that the ancient city lay within the boundaries of what is now the "historic inner city," the four districts of central Palermo, with the sea to the north and the *cala* (inlet) at the centre, which may have functioned as the port of the Punic city, Piazza Indipendenza to the south, and the two waterways of the Papireto and the Kemonia, respectively to the west and east.

Black-painted skyphos from tomb 63 in the Palermo necropolis 4th century B.C. clay, 10 cm diam. 10 cm Palermo Museo Archeologico Regionale

On the other hand we do know the Punic-Roman necropolis that stretches a long way south of Piazza Indipendenza. It has yielded up hundreds of graves (many dug open in the Arab period), some with highly interesting contents including Phoenico-Punic pottery, but mostly imported or locally imitated Greek wares, as well as objects of silver. The tombs are often marked by sandstone cippi of various forms. The material from the site is in the Palermo Archaeological Museum. A section of the museum is devoted to items from western Sicily, mainly oriental in origin.

Lekythos in the form of aryballon decorated with red figures from tomb 63 in the Palermo necropolis 4th century B.C. clay, 6.4 cm Palermo Museo Archeologico Regionale

Marsala

This was the ancient Lilybaeum founded by the Motyans after the destruction of their city in 397 B.C. The name is Punic in origin. Lilybaeum was the only city Pyrrhus failed to capture when he invaded Punic Sicily, including Panormus (Palermo), in 267 B.C. But it was conquered by the Romans in 241 B.C., after a long siege lasting nine years. Sections of the city wall, recently discovered, remarkably strong and six metres thick, explain the difficulties encountered by the Romans in the conquest of the city.

The vast necropolis (4th century B.C. to 2nd century A.D.) spreading out to the west of the city has yielded a great deal of material which has been

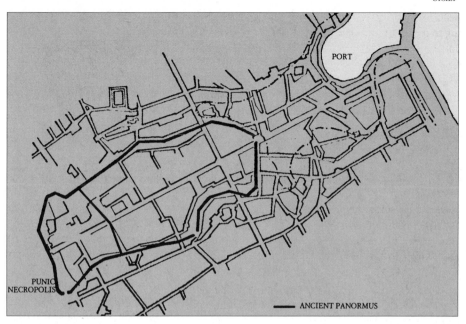

Map of Palermo

dated with some certainty. It presents the usual Punic tomb types: excavated in the rock (like those of Soluntum and Palermo), with a vertical shaft, or a chambery with an access corridor (*dromos*), or a rectangular pit. Again in this necropolis the two burial rites of cremation and inhumation co-exist. The grave goods consist of typical Hellenistic pottery: unpainted vases and black glazed pottery, Punic pottery and small vases typical of this area, of different shapes with white slip and painted floral decorations.

There is a remarkable group of funerary stelae, including one in so-called *lattimusa* (a white limestone found near Palermo) from the 4th-3rd century B.C. with a Punic inscription to Baal Hammon and various symbols connected with Punic religion. Others, dated to the lst-2nd century A.D., are in the form of stone aediculae covered with plaster and shaped like small houses, with columns at the sides or in front, painted in vivid colours with feast scenes, and bearing the sign of Tanit with caduceus: this detail makes it clear that the Punic religion was practised at Lilybaeum until the Roman Imperial period.

Cannita

In this locality about 10 km east of Palermo, along the course of the Eleuterio, a number of archaic Phoenician objects have been found, including two notable sarcophagi discovered in the late 17th and early 18th centuries and kept in the Palermo museum. They can be dated to the 6th-5th century B.C. and are the only Phoenician sarcophagi found in Sicily. The features of the dead depicted on the lids and their garments clearly point to their derivation from Greek models.

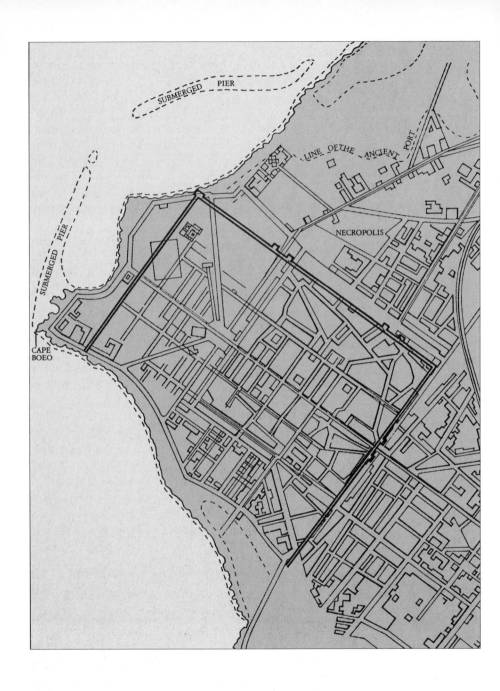

Map of Lilybaeum

Selinus (Selinunte)

The last period of this flourishing Greek city, founded by the Megarians of eastern Sicily in the middle of the 7th century B.C., was spent within the orbit of the Punic eparchy after the city was destroyed by the Carthaginians in 409 B.C. Punic remains have been found at Selinus especially in the last two decades. There are also remains from the period before its destruction in 409 B.C.: an outstanding example is the statuette found in the waters off the city, the image of a Phoenician male divinity, Hadad or Reshef, of a clearly Ugaritic type and datable to the 13th-12th century B.C. From the same period there are also remains of various kinds, including faience amulets, oriental motifs on two archaic metopes from the early 6th century B.C. and so forth.

After 409, following a chequered period (Selinus lay on the border between the Greek and Punic towns) the city passed definitively into the Punic orbit. To this period belongs the conversion of the acropolis into a residential quarter for the citizens, as the Greek city had been destroyed and was used as a necropolis.

The buildings were adapted to the new needs: a new district was built to the north of temple C; the Doric temples that were the most outstanding buildings in the city were left derelict and largely destroyed. The pronaos of some of these temples (e.g. temple A) were used as places of worship, as is shown by the symbols of Tanit and the sun: the latter was

Selinus acropolis area south of temple C with pavement of sherds with marble inlay showing "sign of Tanit" and caduceus

depicted as a bull's head surrounded by a circle of rays. Another sign of Tanit with the caduceus has been found on the pavement of a section of the acropolis. These are the only symbols of Tanit found on pavements in Sicily.

Selinus acropolis pronaos of temple A with pavement of sherds and marble inlay showing a bull's head

The suburban sanctuary of Selinus, the so-called shrine of Malophoros, formerly dedicated to Zeus Meilichios, was adapted to new forms of worship. The twin stelae from this later period are famous. They represent a male and female figure, perhaps Baal Hammon and Tanit. Punic symbols and letters are found on many of the *cretulae* dug up around temple C, which may have been used as an archive in the Punic period. Altogether, the Punic remains from the 4th and 3rd centuries B.C. at Selinus are among the most noteworthy in Sicily.

Map of the Selinus acropolis

Pantelleria

The ancient name of this island was Kossyra; for this reason the hypothesis of a Phoenician component is not to be excluded. There are no substantial remains of Phoenico-Punic culture. There are a number of terracotta models of a female head or protome with a *klaft* or headband, found according to Paolo Orsi at Bagno dell'Acqua, where presumably a shrine from the 6th century B.C. was located. At all events, the possibility that a Phoenico-Punic cultural *facies* existed on Pantelleria is not to be ruled out.

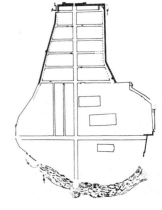

Favignana

Similarly restricted in scope are the Punic remains on Favignana, the largest of the Aegates. The typical Punic torpedo-shaped amphorae have been found in its offshore waters, where the famous battle of 241 B.C. put an end to the First Punic War. On the island there are only a few tombs of the Punic type with access often by a corridor. On one of these tombs there is a Neo-Punic inscription dating from the 2nd-1st century B.C.

Eryx (Erice)

This town was in the Elymian zone, as Thucydides tells us (VI, 2). The Elymians and Phoenicians had a close, continuous alliance and Eryx illustrates it best. The most interesting fact in this respect is the phase of wall-building around the city (following an earlier phase which was presumably the work of the Elymians) carried out in the Punic period, perhaps in the 4th century B.C., as borne out by the Punic letters carved in the wall itself.

Monte Adranone

Excavations and studies conducted in recent years by the Archaeological Superintendency of central-southern Sicily (Agrigento) have revealed the Punic aspect of an inhabited centre along the Belice valley, on Monte Adranone. Here, bounded by an imposing wall, there is a sanctuary of Punic type, as well as various objects related to the same cultural world.

Excavations still in progress have recently brought to light a Punic quarter within the ancient town of Agrigentum dating from the Hellenistic period. The Phoenico-Punic presence in western Sicily can be summed up as having mainly commercial objectives, with any territorial interest being subordinated to trade. Perhaps the Phoenicians engaged in agricultural activity, but it is strange that they should have imported grain from Agrigentum, Libya, and Sardinia when Sicily in the Roman period was considered the granary of Rome. They also carried out certain industrial activities, manufacturing pottery and dyeing fabrics and perhaps leather, as at Motya.

With their neighbors the Greeks they enjoyed a necessarily privileged relationship, at times even one of friendship. This appears, for example, in the

Map of Eryx

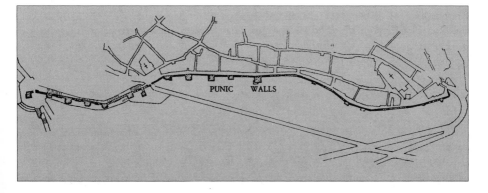

pro-Punic element at Selinus that was allied with Carthage in the battle of Himera in 480 B.C. and which offered hospitality to Gisco, the son of Hamilcar, after his defeat at Himera, and it was there that he died. Trade with the Greeks flourished; this appears in the numerous Greek products that have been found particularly in the tombs; but the relationship between the two peoples had various aspects. Soluntum was actually built by Greek architects, and the now famous statue from Motya was executed by a Greek, or at any rate by a person familiar with Greek culture. This did not prevent the Phoenico-Punic world from achieving an expression of its own, as in the sacred buildings of Soluntum. Noteworthy products also include their characteristic gold work, the so-called "Bithia" figurines, pottery, etc.

Head of Demeter found at Monte Adranone 4th century B.C. limestone 17.4 × 11.5 cm Agrigento Museo Archeologico Regionale

We have reason to believe that there was no centralized and unified administration of Punic territory in Sicily, since the various towns were autonomous. This, however, did not prevent them from uniting, and also forming an alliance with the Elymians, whenever the danger of invasion threatened. Indeed, this repeats a pattern established in Phoenicia, where the cities of Sidon, Tyre, Byblos and others were autonomous units: the Phoenicians were actually called "Sidonians" or "Tyrians," according to their respective cities.

Graphic reconstruction of the entrance side of the sanctuary located in the acropolis of Monte Adranone

*Monte Adranone
detail of public
buildings
in the acropolis*

*Locally crafted jug with trefoil rim
decorated in geometric patterns from Monte Adranone
6th-5th century B.C., clay, 28.5 cm
Agrigento, Museo Archeologico Regionale
• p. 289*

*Locally crafted jug with trefoil rim
decorated in geometric patterns
from Monte Adranone
6th-5th century B.C., clay, 26 cm
Agrigento, Museo Archeologico Regionale*

Ruins of the acropolis at Monte Adranone

Appendix: Coins in the History of Punic Sicily
Aldina Cutroni Tusa

Drawing of coin minted in Sicily 320-300 B.C.

The numismatic evidence from Sicily suggests that the Greek victory there in 480 B.C. led to an acceleration and diffusion of the process of Hellenization on the island, involving the Phoenico-Punic settlements as well. The coinage offers the most immediate expression of this process, and is documented by the issues at Motya, Palermo and later Soluntum. That is, there was the assimilation of a cultural and conceptual element such as currency, which by that time had gone beyond the experimental phase and matured within the Graeco-Siceliot culture. This process of participation in the island's monetary economy established a wider and structurally more unified monetary picture, favoured by a tendency towards integration and aggregation with the emergence of new sociopolitical hegemonies.

Motya and Palermo organized their coinage according to the Euboean-Attic metrological system, at that time well-established in the main Siceliot cities that had grown up from the ancient Greek colonial settlements. The first denomination to appear was the didrachm of about eight grams, which had already been the basic coin of the island's western Greek zone, i.e. Selinus, Agrigentum, Gela and Himera. The use of Greek-language inscriptions, at first exclusively, and the adoption of the Siceliot coin typology correspond to the assimilation of the system and the selection of the denomination itself. The inscription ṢYṢ, which initially appeared sporadically, became an established feature of the coins beginning from 409 B.C., when production of the tetradrachm started. The latter achieved a very high rate of production while at the same time in the Syracuse mint, under Dionysius, striking of the didrachm was reduced and then finally halted. Between the end of the 5th century B.C. and Agathocles's reign (in the course of which Syracuse resumed mintage of this denomination) the growing scarcity of the Syracusian tetradrachm was accompanied by an increase in the minting, circulation and accumulation of the ṢYṢ series and then of a new series of the same type bearing the inscription RŠMLQRT. This new inscription could be the Punic name for Selinus, destroyed in 409 B.C. and reestablished by the Carthaginians. In the archaeological deposits, the Punic tetradrachms are very often found beside coins with an international circulation, Athenian tetradrachms and Corinthian staters.

This new situation upset the 5th-century monetary picture, tipping the balance of production in favor of the Punic area, to Syracuse's loss. The question arises as to whether this was simply a result of the ascendancy of Carthage which by the end of the 5th century was exercising its prerogatives as a new political power in the field of coinage as well, or if it was not also the result of a monetary peace deriving from the treaties drawn up between the Punic power and Syracuse. In other words, I believe that the adoption of Syracusian models and prototypes should not be considered simply as evidence of a competition related to an emerging political power, but rather as the consequence of a monetary agreement between the Carthaginians and Dionysius on a level of juridic parity: on the part of the Carthaginians, a concession to the local economic situation, and on the part of the Greeks, recognition of a right acquired by its rival. The tetradrachms bearing the inscription ŞYŞ would thus have had an official character recognized by Syracuse.

An analysis of the currency of the original Phoenico-Punic settlements (Motya, Palermo, Soluntum, Thermae and Eryx) under Carthaginian influence, and of the ŞYŞ and RŠMLQRT production centers (the name of the former is still unkown, while the latter could be Selinus), indicates a gradual intensification of monetary production parallel to Carthage's expansion of influence and territorial control. Coinage continued to evolve throughout the 4th and 3rd centuries B.C., until the Roman conquest. The repertory was enriched with new types displaying a typically Punic iconography accompanied by increasingly complex legends that often followed the pattern set by the Greek issues, by specifying their purpose of maintaining military troops, made up primarily of mercenaries, deployed throughout the island. The style of these new issues, like the prior ones, is inspired by Greek models, suggesting that Siceliot and Punic engravers trained by Greeks worked in the mints established on the island by Carthage.

Drawing of coin minted in Sicily 320-300 B.C.

However, it is necessary to distinguish between the coinage struck by the stable Punic settlements and by centers located in areas under Carthaginian rule, and issues of a territorial type. Belonging to the first group is the production of the mints of Motya, Palermo, Soluntum, Eryx, Thermae, ŞYŞ, and RŠMLQRT; and to the second group coinage bearing the inscriptions QRTḤDŠT, MḤNT, 'MMḤNT, S'MMḤNT, 'MḤMḤNT and MḤŠBM, produced either by itinerant workshops or in secondary mints.

The issues of the first group testify to Sicily's status in the Carthaginian state, a special legal status of fundamental autonomy for officially recognized cities, all at an equal level: this situation precludes therefore the possibility that Palermo was the capital of the Punic eparchy, recognized as the leading city. It was Carthage that, in its involvement in the island, gradually took on the role of the new capital of a territory considered an extension of the metropolitan territory.

The issues of the second group suggest that functionaries were sent to the Sicilian province by the central government for military reasons and tax collection. The inscription Š'MMḤNT, translated as "the people of the encampment," could allude to the particular juridic status of the island's resident Carthaginians, as distinguished from that of the citizens of Punic Sicily.

The Carthaginians who made up the island's expeditionary camp maintained a juridic position separate and distinct from that of the councils of the individual cities making up the eparchy, and while respecting the municipal autonomy of those cities had their own decision-making powers and the right to mint coins.

Carthage's acceptance of coinage was a sign of her cultural and political broad-mindedness and marked the onset of lively contacts with the Greek world. In fact the inclusion of the Demeter and Kore cult in the Carthaginian pantheon, amply demonstrated by the monetary iconography, would not have been possible in a milieu that was completely foreign or hostile to Greek culture.

The Punic coinage experience in Sicily, and later in Carthage, highlights and gives order to a series of connecting elements that range from the integration of Carthage into the already mature culture of Hellenic Sicily and continual interaction on a regional level, to the autonomy of political and administrative structures guaranteed by Carthage, the new political capital, as attested by the legends on coins alluding to controlling bodies, citizens' assemblies and the supreme magistrature.

Thus, the numismatic documentation gives the impression that Carthage's rule over the island was not simply that of a regime primarily interested in military occupation; the metrological continuity, the figurative repertory and the stylistic elements all imply that the coins were minted for contingents used to this means of payment, which in turn indicates that the Carthaginian army was primarily made up of mercenaries recruited in loco. This dual situation shows that the towns controlled by Carthage could govern according to their own traditions, without Punic regulation, that their subjection to Carthage was of a fiscal nature, and that the territory of the eparchy did not have a unitary administration. For the Carthaginians, Hellenic Sicily remained a different political and economic world against which to measure themselves, in a relationship which ensured their cultural strength.

Malta
Antonia Ciasca

The geographical position of the Maltese archipelago and its cultural history, dating from at least the 3rd millennium B.C, are essential factors for understanding its particular features in the Phoenician period.

Extremely flourishing periods of local pre-history, particularly in the Late Stone Age (c. 2400-1600 B.C.), characterized by impressive religious buildings, connect the islands to the phenomenon of Mediterranean megalithic construction and highlight Malta's considerable wealth. The absence of mineral resources and the limited land available for agricultural development led to an economy projected towards the outside world, via the sea, with activities that included trade and forms of piracy. For the last part of the Bronze Age there is evidence of a variety of overseas relations. Despite the small size of Maltese territory, communities of foreigners (probably from South Italy) lived around Bahrija. Conversely, pottery and perhaps also groups of people from the islands reached sites in eastern Sicily (Thapsos, Ognina, Milocca, Cozzo Pantano). Mycenaean pottery (Mic. III A) has been found in Malta.

Cippus with inscription from Rabat 7th-6th century B.C., stone 23.5 × 8 cm La Valletta National Museum of Archaeology

As in the case of many other Mediterranean countries, modern building has largely covered over the Phoenician sites. However the necropoli survive, with shaft and chamber tombs or rock-cut chambers. The chronology of the grave goods and the locality and size of the cemetery areas allow us to reconstruct the basic outline of Maltese topography in the Phoenician and Punic period. The nature of the Phoenician presence in Malta is immediately apparent when we observe that their settlements often coincide with sites intensively inhabited by natives at the end of the Bronze Age, when the colonists arrived. Finds of red-slip pottery together with local wares in contexts relating to native life point to a probable cohabitation between the two groups.

The geographer Ptolemy mentions two main towns in Malta, and the concentration of the archaeological evidence defines two main areas of settlement: one linked to a port on the southeast coast of the island, around the large bay of Marsaxlokk and numerous nearby inlets; the other inland with the natural defence of a high hill completely isolated from the sea (Rabat-Medina). The latter was the main settlement in Malta. The surrounding necropoli are the largest of the island and pottery finds include wares imported from Grecian Sicily from the 7th century B.C. onwards. On the smaller island, Gozo, this dual type of settlement is evident as

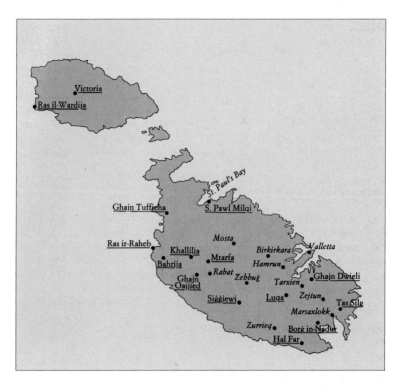

well; the main center seems to have been the inland plateau site of Victoria.

The juxtaposition between local and Phoenician culture is also confirmed by the remains of religious buildings. The great extra-urban sanctuary of Tas Silg near the south port zone — one of the two cited by Ptolemy as existing in Malta — is dedicated to the Phoenician Goddess Astarte.

In reality it dates back to the Late Stone Age, but its buildings continued to be used throughout the Phoenician and Punic period until at least the 1st century B.C. The large temple with an oval plan and concave facade was still in use in the Byzantine period, transformed into a baptistry.

The Phoenician rites must have been amalgamated with the local religious tradition. The latter is reflected in the prolonged use of particular constructions for votive offerings and the presence of a large, Late Stone Age relief depicting a (female?) figure, found near the entrance to the historic temple; the Phoenician Astarte perhaps took on chthonic connotations like the native divinity. Near Eastern architectural tradition is reflected in the few alterations made, for example the addition of pilasters on the façade, and in the general layout of the sanctuary, where open spaces predominate with a series of large courts containing chapels, ex-voto offerings, altars, wells and so on.

Over the centuries, and particularly from the end of the 4th to the 1st century B.C., the sanctuary surrounding the ancient prehistoric temple underwent alterations. The new architecture combined Egyptianizing, Phoeni-

cian and Greek elements. This places Malta in a Hellenistic-Punic context known to us particularly from a series of well-preserved, mostly funerary monuments, found on the north coast of Africa between Libya and western Algeria and also in Sardinia (Tharros).

Tas Silg, the northern sector of the sanctuary dedicated to Astarte

This is a cultural horizon in which scholars have recognized the influence of Alexandrian Hellenism. The minor temples, as well, built outside the towns or rock-cut — for example, Ras il-Wardija (Gozo) and Ras ir-Raheb (Malta) — kept their walls and layout dating from the Late Stone Age until the Hellenistic period.

The later stages correspond to a period of particular vitality in the life of the islands. There may have been a considerable increase in population, the systematic use of agricultural resources — with farms of the type found at S. Pawl Milqi — and the emigration of groups or individuals toward Carthage, Lilybaeum and Ibiza.

Altogether, the particular conditions described above explain why the Phoenician colonization of Malta has left traces very different from those found in other regions. There were only loose ties with Carthage, which in its expansionist policy looked first toward Sardinia and Spain and later aimed at the agricultural exploitation of large areas. Apart from the archipelago's possible strategic function in the earliest period of colonization (late 8th-7th century B.C.) for controlling shipping routes in the Channel of Sicily, and its subsequent involvement in war events — Malta's part in the First and Second Punic Wars is mentioned by ancient historians — it seems evident that the most vital relations of the archipelago were naturally directed toward regions on the fringes of the Phoenician colonial area.

Papyrus with inscription found inside the case from "Tal-Virtù" near Malta 6th century B.C. 4.85 cm, 7.39 cm La Valletta National Museum of Archaeology

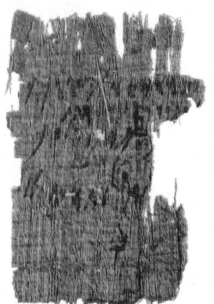

Bronze amulet case in the form of a falcon's head from Tas Silg (Malta) 6th century B.C. 3.8 cm La Valletta National Museum of Archaeology

In the course of the 7th and 6th centuries B.C. there were certainly contacts with Greek Sicily and with Phoenician colonial towns on the African coast east of Carthage. There may also have been regular exchanges with Egypt, in particular with communities of foreigners living in the Nile Delta. The multiplicity of influences may explain the peculiarities of most expressions of Phoenician and Carthaginian culture in Malta. As an example from the archaic period, we may take the exceptional terra-cotta anthropoid sarcophagus from the Rabat area, with Rhodian-Ionian stylistic features; and for the later period, the strongly Egyptianizing or Cirenaican iconography of the coins minted in Malta.

Funerary customs also seem to be very different from those in the southern Mediterranean. For example, archaic tomb hoards include only very few terracottas (masks, protomes, statuettes), while the Hellenistic period has yielded vases which repeat foreign types, probably Egyptian, used as cinerary urns instead of the small limestone ossuaries familiar to us from Carthage and Lilybaeum. Forms typical of the Asiatic Phoenician tradition appear in locally manufactured limestone cult objects with relief foliated decoration, from tombs in the Rabat area and the Tas Silg sanctuary. A bronze torch-holder or incense-burner with similar decoration probably comes from a Phoenician or Cypriot workshop in the West and may have belonged to the category of objects exported to non-Phoenician communities (nuraghic Sardinia, Cerveteri). The relatively frequent use of Egyptianizing amulets relates Malta to Carthage, where we know that Egyptian examples were imported in quantity and frequently copied.

Some of the written evidence of the Hellenistic period includes proper names not found elsewhere, for example in the bilingual inscriptions in Punic and Greek on the bases of two conical marble cippi with foliated decoration (these may not have been locally made). The great international sanctuary of Tas Silg has yielded varied evidence, with inscriptions on stone, bone and ivory. The normal use of writing in local potteries working for the sanctuary is also testified by the very extensive series with cursive script, and by a number of carefully made pieces with lettering in relief.

Phoenician pottery made in Malta also follows particular lines of development — always with a marked tendency toward the imitation of foreign forms — which differentiate it from the culture of the South Mediterranean colonial world.

Imported food supplies in all probability came from regions outside the Phoenician colonial world: this can be deduced from the frequent appearance of Greek amphorae of various regions — found particularly at the Tas Silg sanctuary — compared with the scarcity of Punic amphorae made in non-Maltese workshops.

S. Pawl Milqi Phoenico-Hellenistic and Roman farm

Sardinia
Enrico Acquaro

Among the most rewarding Phoenician ventures in the Occident, Sardinia yielded longterm fruits. Its trading posts along the southwestern coast quickly outgrew their status as provisional ports of call, and a Near Eastern urbanism was introduced into the traditional nuraghic cantonal system. The Near Eastern city-plan is typical of the first towns in Sardinia.

The Proto-Sardinian use of land and buildings did not fail to influence the first prestigious colonies of Cagliari, Nora, Sulcis and Tharros. The island was already familiar with the Near East, having benefited from technological and cultural stimuli coming mainly from the pre-Hellenic Aegean. The Phoenicians gathered and transmitted this first Aegean stimulus which clearly bore the mark of Cypriot intervention and contributions, and turned the Sardinian trading posts into colonies. And the colonizers' natural pride had to reckon with a well-developed local reality.

By the end of the first colonization period (9th century B.C.) a certain fusion between the two cultures seems to have taken place. Ineradicable differences also remained, for instance in urban development. Both large and small Proto-Sardinian "villages" consisted of groups of round huts which were casually arranged. The Phoenicians, on the other hand, tended to create settlements in which rectangular buildings faced onto streets or squares, creating communal spaces.

Only on a very minor scale, usually in rural areas, pre-existing nuraghic structures were adapted by the Phoenicians. The colonists preferred to build in their own rectilinear style, although often over curvilinear Proto-Sardinian remains, since the sites of the early villages corresponded to their own needs (harbors, roads, etc.).

One aspect of nuraghic architecture seems to have been preserved: the surrounding walls which gave collective strength to the earlier villages. In Phoenician hands these walls retained some of their function in terms of layout and reflection of the area's topography. Their line, which cuts and follows the curves and gradations of the terrain, served as a guide for the fortified ramparts of the colonial installation. However, in most cases the implementation of other technologies and different strategic schemes is evident.

The settlers entrusted the expansion and upgrading of the existing Proto-Sardinian harbors to the Phoenicians' proven technical ability in port construction. Nature helped as well: these harbors were created around natural

Fortification systems and road networks in Phoenician and Punic Sardinia

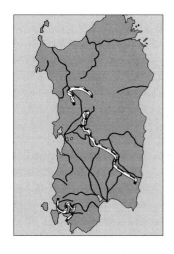

ᑎᑐ *Fortifications*

⎯ *Main access routes*

lagoons. The Sardinian coastline has many characteristics typical of Phoenician coastal cities: a promontory which extends into the sea (as at Nora and Tharros), or an island a short distance from the coast (Sant'Antioco and Bithia), and salt flats (Cagliari). Other characteristics shared with Phoenician cities are the availability of lagoon products to integrate the urban economy, and access to rich and fertile hinterlands (as at Cagliari and Tharros, among others). When this urban type had to be adapted to inland settlements, particularly in the time of Carthage, the choice fell on hills, valleys and tablelands fed by rivers with a more or less seasonal flow, near the most frequently used channels of communication and transhumance. In such cases the structure of the Proto-Sardinian villages served as a guideline since it reflected the same requirements of military defence.

The greater the effort in military improvement, both structural and defensive, the more evident is the influence of Phoenician expertise, with complex fortifications which transform imported plans into functioning units (as can be seen at Monte Sirai). Both the Phoenician colonization and Carthage's successive territorial venture, which in some cases upgraded and in others reorganized or redeveloped the economies of the island's first Phoenician colonies, took advantage of affinities or similarities between local "national" divinities and the colonists' gods. This can be seen at the sanctuary of Antas, where the god Sid was proposed as the heir to the previous nuraghic cult divinity (and was then perpetuated in the form of the Roman Sardus Pater). Given the period and the cultural orientation, the political strategy here seems to have been that of Carthage.

In the urban layout of Phoenician colonies most temples are constructed within the city walls. The 6th and 5th centuries B.C. seem to have been the period, when there was most religious construction, while the 4th and 3rd centuries B.C. show a systematic effort at restoration, renovation and transformation which would see many buildings through to the period of late Roman occupation. There was a continuing desire to maintain over time the sacredness of the city *tophets*, which are found in colonial life from its beginnings up to the first Roman occupation. Similar care was reserved for cult objects, including monuments and pottery reflecting the Eastern tradition. Also noteworthy are the thousands of votive stelae carved in each colony, gauges of the sanctuaries' presence over many centuries, reflecting in their style the development of the material culture of the various centres. Thus at Nora we see western conservatism and at Sulcis an acceptance of Hellenized designs (still mediated however by the Phoenician tradition), and later, the interpretation of nonspecialized craftsmen as in the stelae of Monte Sirai, and finally the sandstone monuments of Tharros which echo nuraghic work.

The ability to conceive large structures of complex archi-

Ruins of Nora with the Tower of Sant'Efisio on the cliff of Coltellazzo in the background

*Sardinia in the
Phoenician
and Punic period*

tectural design and sculptures demanding significant skill is confirmed by objects from Sulcis and Tharros. In the former city, the pair of crouching lions which once flanked the city gate has the Cypriot component of the first colonial period through to the end of the 5th century B.C.; the latter city is the home of the sandstone "monumental temple", partly dug out of the rockface and partly of ashlar masonry making up the façade, suggesting comparisons with Phoenician structures. The use of the Phoenician cubit (46 m) confirms links with a wide range of monuments of the Punic West. In the vast hypogean necropoli of Cagliari, Nora, Sulcis and Tharros, there is a renewed link with Near Eastern tradition in the decorations in

261

bas-relief and painting. As remarked above, this culture was not entirely foreign to the Sards. In its new western environment, this link finds a series of original applications which on the one hand relate the reliefs to the flourishing production of sandstone stelae for the Sardinian *tophets*, and on the other confidently reinterpret themes from the Greek tradition. Nearly all the information we have on the material culture of the Phoenicians and Carthaginians in Sardinia is provided by tombs, monumental and otherwise, containing cremated and inhumed remains. An appraisal of the artistic value of the finds depends in part on their function as funerary accessories, since systematic study of the sites has only recently begun (particularly in Cagliari, Sant'Antioco, and Tharros). One example serves for all: until a few years ago the presence of imported Greek and Etruscan pottery was considered exceptional in view of the few finds of this sort in the tombs. This led to a series of studies which tended to see in the Greek and Etruscan contributions the reflection of particular conditions and evidence of favoured cultural relations with single centers.

Intensification of research in the urban areas has given the problem a different perspective — confirmed by classical sources — which sees Sardinia as fully integrated into a vital central Mediterranean *koiné*, whatever the axis of transmission (Etruscan, Punic, Graeco-Oriental). This was a common market which Carthage, with the territorial gains of the 6th century, guided firmly to the North African vector; there is a quite notable presence of Attic imports which Carthage traded throughout the Punic Occident, but the koiné maintained the Tyrrhenian relations established with the first settlements on the island. The Punic local output as well as the colonies' absorption of luxury products of the nuraghic culture are part of this complex picture.

The early influence of the Phoenician homeland and successively the reversion to narrower North African circuits, gives Punic material culture in Sardinia archaizing tendencies.

Thus, the archaeological finds — of statues (the Monte Sirai statue, the lions and funerary high-relief of Sulcis), figurines (the terracotta of Monte Sirai and the Castagnino statuette), and small bronzes (Flumenelongu) — bear witness to the presence of Near Eastern connections along with the converging effects of insularity, which ensured the upholding of tradition. Certain archaic ivories of Tharros (7th-6th century B.C.), of a decidedly Phoenician type, may have been direct imports.

Female protomes and grinning or Silenus masks in terracotta are more decidedly western and show close links with the Motya-Carthage-Ibiza triangle. In the former, alteration by the natives of the common moulds is limited, while in the latter, local influence is greater. The Sard versions of the grinning masks give more human attributes to the aging faces, while the Silenus masks adopt two forms: one is massive and square, comparable to Ibizan models and to the representation of the god Bes (Sulcis); the other is oval and closer to the Punic type of the satyr (Tharros). The absence of

Map of Cagliari

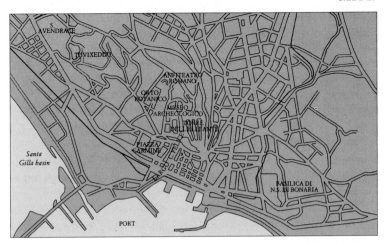

negroid-type masks on the island, together with the designs of Silenus masks similar to those from Ibiza indicate a certain autonomy of artistic expression in this category.

Parallel to the western terra-cotta production, but with Phoenician precedents, appears a series of wheel-made votive statuettes which in the offerings of Bithia make a uniquely direct reference to specific infirmities for which a cure is invoked.

Past and recent excavations of the necropoli have yielded amulets, scarabs, jewellery, ostrich eggs and bronze razors in great quantity, now scattered throughout Italy and Europe in public and private collections. Some of this material was locally produced and some was imported, while in a number of cases its origin remains unclear.

The single cultural provenance of these objects indicates an overall homogeneity throughout the island, with increasing evidence in the north as well, an area up to now little investigated. In recent years the luxury grave goods have been more correctly considered in the single urban context of their provenance, which however they only partially reflect. Therefore characterization of the cultural material of the single centres is still incomplete; Cagliari, the first center taken into consideration, amply demonstrates this.

Cagliari (Caralis)

Here, the favourable convergence of geographical factors, with the accomodating and accessible platform of the western shore of Tuvixeddu's chalky promontory, and the surrounding calm and safe waters of the Santa Gilla basin opening out to the sea, lies behind the Phoenician settlement active at least from the 7th century B.C.

Prehistoric Cagliari has been discovered only recently in all its richness in cultural strata and evolution ranging from the 6th to the 1st millennium B.C. There is evidence here of a vast trade area whose traditional centrality must have been a beacon for the first Phoenician settlement. This function as an important trade centre from the time of the pre-nuraghic culture of Ozieri (late 4th to mid-3rd millennium B.C.), is reflected in the vastness of the Punic necropolis and in the wide radius of outlying towns (Settimo San Pietro, Monastir-Monte Olladiri, San Sperate).

Characterized by a material culture with North African connotations, Cagliari at present seems devoid of the older "Tyrrhenian" evidence which distinguishes other centers such as Sulcis and Tharros. Whenever some autonomy is given to local craftsmen, they are able to produce objects, especially terra-cotta figurines, in which Sicilian themes of the Punic *koiné* are re-interpreted, also using Cypriot iconographic traditions transmitted by Greeks and Phoenicians. Should this documentation be increased and confirmed, it would demonstrate the Phoenico-Cagliaritan hetero-Punic context which in all probability was equal in volume of trade to the other centres of the island's first Phoenician colonization.

Santu Teru-Monte Luna

The foundation of Santu Teru-Monte Luna, in Trexenta, serves as an example of Carthage's penetration into the interior. The centre is situated on a plateau bounded by the Riu Santu Teru and the Riu Craddaxius, on the roads linking the Campidano and the interior regions, Gerrei and Sarrabus. It occupies and controls an extensive area characterized by the presence of farmsteads already active during the Punic era.

Probably originally settled for Punic military purposes (late 6th century B.C.), the centre enjoyed a significant economic development based on agriculture up to the 3rd century B.C. The material culture reflected in the rich array of grave goods found in the necropolis of Monte Luna indicates a fully Carthaginian context, which must have had as its point of reference nearby Cagliari. Trade in products from the marketplaces of North Africa, Attica, Latium and Magna Graecia is the best and most eloquent testimony to the results achieved by Sardinia's Punic economy, which seems to have found unexpected openings and opportunities in the interior.

Nora

Greek and Latin mythological sources indicate Nora, on the Pula peninsula, as the earliest Phoenician settlement in Sardinia. These sources plus the famous inscription discovered there more than two centuries ago assign a key role in the Mediterranean network to Phoenician Nora. They also indicate early relations with Iberia and Cyprus. The available archaeological evidence, however, indicates a less important role and in any case not before the first half of the 7th century B.C.

The *tophet* stelae in fact reveal the activity of a minor crafts center, largely dependent on Punic models. Reexamination now in progress of the Punic material which sporadically

Map of Nora

264

Nora, the residential area

reemerges among the Roman buildings, particularly in the necropoli, attenuates the restrictive judgment deriving from the stelae. It is the pottery which suggests a reevaluation, since it shows Greek and Etruscan influences and a local production based on imported forms.

The existence of a Phoenician centre already active in the late 8th century B.C. has been determined from the remains of buildings discovered near the Chia basin. The selection of the site hinged on the lagoon. The settlement, which must have been important, consisted of distinct quarters lining the lagoon shore all the way around to another lagoon to the west, the "Su Stangioni de su Sali."

Bithia

Yet again it is the necropolis discovered in the sandy shore of the Chia basin that has yielded the most significant data on the centre of Bithia. This centre fits naturally into a deliberate plan which provided for a series of landing stations along the southwest coast of Sardinia for the purpose of distributing products from Iberia, North Africa, Tyrrhenian Italy and the cities of Phoenicia and its immediate diaspora. Especially in Bithia, this opening to trade competed with a local production of votive statues echoing the nuraghic tradition, such as wheel-made figurines with appliqué arms which indicate the afflicted area of the body. Punic culture

265

accompanied and gave formal content to the more explicit reemergence of this tradition until the Late Roman era, confirming the complete interpenetration of the Punic and nuraghic elements on an ethnic level as well.

Map of Bithia

Sulcis

The location of ancient Sulcis, whose settlement can be traced back as far as the second half of the 8th century B.C., is particularly interesting. Probably a loading port for the argentiferous lead found in Iglesiente, it rose on the island of Sant'Antioco out of the foundations of a previous Late-Neolithic settlement of the Ozieri culture, successively a Proto-Sardinian village of the Early Iron Age.

The centre's geographic position is important. The small island was linked to the mainland by an isthmus, partially man-made: its accessibility, made possible by the alignment of a few alluvial islets of the Rio Palmas, is an engineering feat generally attributed to the Phoenicians. The remains of the Phoenician and Punic settlement have been identified in the whole coastal area of Sant'Antioco. The city grew up from the ports, with a line of fortifications along the backlying hills, the Monte de Cresia and the Fortino heights; other fortifications must have been built on the seafront. There are two necropoli, one northeast of the Fortino heights, and the other on the western slopes of the Monte de Cresia. The *tophet* has been located in "Sa Guardia'e is pingiadas," a district lying to the north.

There are two ports: a southern one facing the Palmas gulf, and a northern one formed by the Sant'Antioco basin. The Palmas gulf, closed at its ends by the Teulada and Sperone promontories, offers deep waters all the way to the shore: sheltered from the principal winds, the *Maestrale* (northwest), the *Greco* (northeast), the *Scirocco* (southeast) and the *Libeccio* (southwest), throughout time it has provided safe anchorage. The Sant'Antioco basin, protected and secure as well, is nevertheless not as navigable for large ships because of its shallow waters.

A stretch of trachytic stone masonry is still preserved on the Monte de Cresia; in the area of the present-day Fortino Sabaudo, older remains have been uncovered, with stretches of medium-sized trachytic masonry. The Fortino lies over a structure of squared blocks, made up of two rectangular elements emerging from an earlier nuraghe: these are probably the remains of a tower, also part of the enclosing wall, dating from the 4th-3rd century B.C.

The contour of the wall leads north in a nearly straight line. It has two supporting faces, the external one of large, sometimes roughly hewn stones, and the internal one of smaller stones; construction rubble fills the space between them. At one point there is a trachytic node where foundation lines reveal the existence of a small tower and the wall turns toward the sea. The defensive potential of this area, devoid of any natural topographical relief, was enhanced by a ditch carved into the tufa.

Punic ruins at Sulcis

A vast building complex, partially sunk into the ground, has been discovered within the walled enclosure. The structure, in which two phases are discernible, can be interpreted, at least in the initial phase, as a large city gate with antechamber, probably the northern one leading into the city. The northeastern burial ground lies on the slope below the Fortino heights. There are numerous tombs at various levels in the tufaceous rock, from the deeply sunk Punic hypogea, the first use of which can be dated to the 6th-5th century B.C., to the loculi of Roman times. The typology of the Punic graves is worthy of note.

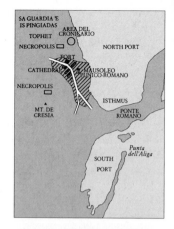

The *tophet* lies outside the city walls, north of the northeast necropolis. The sanctuary occupies a rocky trachytic promontory and, as seen today, shows a large rectangular wall of dressed blocks of the same rock, enclosing a cistern, and another wall parallel to it. The urns holding the sacrificial ashes were deposited in the natural cracks in the ground together with the many stelae found. The size of the wall blocks, quite unusual for a sacred area of this type, suggests that this could have been a military structure to defend the northern approaches. The urban defensive line continues beyond the wall installation. The *tophet* was in use for a very lengthy period, from the 8th century B.C. to Roman times.

The hypogea that were dug into the tufaceous rock of the Monte de Cresia seem to be from an altogether later period than those of the eastern necropolis, and were converted to catacombs by the first Christian community of Sulcis.

A building called "Sa Tribuna" or "Sa Presonedda," a mausoleum of Punic design dating not before the 1st century B.C., is to be found east of the town's main square, surrounded by modern constructions. From its very beginnings the centre shows a wide range of Mediterranean pottery including Euboean and Proto-Corinthian imports as well as wares from Phoenicia. The colony seems to have had a special relation with Cypriot craft traditions, so that some scholars have suggested a participation of Cypriots in the foundation of the settlement.

Map of Sulcis

Detail of the necropolis of Sulcis

In fact the connection with Cyprus is the leitmotif and distinguishing element in the craftwork of Phoenician and Punic Sulcis. Even the Near Eastern and Greek influences which appear in sculptures and bas-reliefs from the 6th century B.C. on, seem to have originated or at least undergone important modifications in the Cypriot milieu, from the figures of devotees with stole on the votive stelae from the *tophet* to the sculpted lions unearthed in 1983.

This Cypriot mediation in which Phoenician and Graeco-Oriental traditions merge and intermingle as in no other environment, explains the receptivity to Hellenizing typologies which characterizes the mediation stelae. It also explains the diffusion of these typologies even before the appearance of the Hellenistic *koiné*, and its penetration throughout the Occident, including the areas of Punic occupation. The formation *in loco* of such intricately derived designs proves the existence at Sulcis of a highly developed craftsmanship which could modify and reinterpret other classes as well. This is demonstrated by the terra-cotta Silenus masks, where the Sulcis version is partly independent of both Carthaginian and Ibizan features.

In substance, one gets the idea that present and future studies must show in Sulcis the mark of an urban experience that in no other case, except possibly Cagliari and Tharros, was so tied to a direct knowledge of the Near East. This is the basis of a craftsmanship which was familiar with the Greek models by virtue of the mediation of the Phoenician or Cypriot Near East, and thanks perhaps precisely to this was able to reformulate these models in designs which were to become typical of the Punic West.

Necropolis of Monte Sirai

Monte Sirai

The Monte Sirai fortress is situated behind Sulcis on a small plateau overlooking the roads running along the coast and inland to the Campidano. It offers a fine example of the evolution of an interior centre of Punic Sardinia. The hill, covered by a wide spread of lava, shows signs of nuraghic presence and was the seat of a community of Phoenician colonists from the second half of the 7th century B.C. The site was then fortified and militarily occupied by Carthage, which placed its own garrison in defence of Sulcis and the strategic routes identified from the plateau. When its function as a fortress became less important, apart from a brief period of use by Rome during the civil war maneuvers, the center lived the modest existence of a village in which the Punic population blended with the Sardinian.

The few artifacts of material culture so far yielded by Monte Sirai show an obvious link with Sulcis, and an equally predictable share of imported materials from the areas covered by Sulcis's trade circuits. Where dependence on the coastal city is less, the local element adopts extrinsic designs creating works which demonstrate the extent of the integration between the two ethnic groups in the period lasting until Roman occupation.

The artifacts which merit careful analysis (the votive stelae, the bone plaques with the god Bes and sphinx, the wheel-made clay figurines) show a dependence on models all well represented in the Punic Occident, with a few novel elements as far as the female statuettes, and small bronzes are concerned. However, it is highly unlikely that these works were of local Punic craftsmanship, both because of their specific characteristics and their general context.

269

Antas

The Antas valley in the Iglesiente yields important evidence on the way in which Punic religious culture was able to converge with the existing Proto-Sardinian tradition, and in turn influence the Romans. In all probability, the Phoenician presence here took the same form as at the Tas Silg sanctuary in Malta. The site of a nuraghic village already visited by the Phoenicians at the start of the Iron Age, in the 6th century B.C. Antas witnessed the foundation of a sanctuary dedicated to Sid. Heavily rebuilt to render it more monumental around the 3rd century B.C., during the Roman occupation it underwent further alterations and renovations in honour of the god Sardus Pater, achieving its present architectural form.

Antas therefore appears as a prestigious "national" center of worship in which first the Carthaginians and later the Romans proposed equivalent deities. In this dynamic, where politics and religion blend to ensure territorial control and occupation, one can observe the recovery in Roman times of Proto-Sardinian elements which emerge with a new vitality, together with elements of the early Phoenician presence, after the parenthesis of Punic domination. The archaeological evidence of the votive offerings confirms the prestige enjoyed by the temple over a long period of

Acropolis of Monte Sirai residential area

time, especially during the Punic period. The numerous dedications by the Punic communities of the island to the health-giving hunter god Sid, with works in marble of the Argive-Attic and Alexandrian schools, confirm the importance of the sanctuary.

Tharros

A series of studies dedicated to Tharros and its material culture have for some years been the leading archaeological literature on Punic Sardinia. The publication of previously unknown works from Tharros, preserved in

Antas, south side of the temple dedicated to Sardus Pater

Site plan of the temple of Sardus Pater showing the remains of the sanctuary dating from Punic times

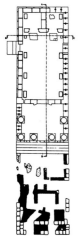

the museums of Cagliari, Sassari and London, has provided important data on the Phoenician and Punic *facies* of the city.

The documentation is substantial, particularly if compared to that of the other Punic centers of Sardinia, and has greatly contributed to make Tharros a useful point of reference for analyzing the phenomena of importation and local production in the Western Phoenician world.

Around the 8th century B.C., the Phoenicians, following a trade relationship that had enabled them to assess the economic potential of the site, founded the colony, rebuilding the Proto-Sardinian village.

The site overlooks the Sinis and Oristanese coasts and the two main arteries to the interior — the Campidano to the southeast and the Tirso valley to the northwest. This fortunate position guided the Phoenician colonists in their settlement strategy. In the 6th century B.C. Carthage became interested in the area because of its key position on the Iberian and Tyrrhenian trade routes.

To what degree the Tharros community actively participated in Carthage's consolidation of sovereignty is unknown. What is certain is

271

that under Carthaginian control, Tharros took on a new urban aspect suited to a centre with primary administrative and strategic responsibilities in the Sinis area.

The residential centre of the first colonists must have faced south on the "Su muru mannu" hill, protected to the west by the Torre San Giovanni hill. Hypogean tombs were excavated to the south, on the western slope of the San Marco promontory.

In this initial phase, in which the colonists' main intention was to create a trading post, the Proto-Sardinian structures concentrated on the promontory (Baboe Cabitza nuraghe, "Su muru mannu" village) were partly taken over and put to different use. The remaining foundations of the western district of the Proto-Sardinian village were used for the *tophet*, the rampart served as defence of the hinterland and the lagoon port was expanded.

In the 6th century B.C. the center outgrew its entrepot form and new sandstone constructions gave it the urban aspect that was to characterize it for centuries to come. To the north was a defensive wall of barely roughed out sandstone blocks, with at least two monumental gates, posterns and towers. This wall picks up and completes the fortified line from east to west already suggested by the western rampart. New tombs were excavated in the northwest coastland; with a skilled technique the first canals were opened to drain off effluent waters. The problem of water supply was solved by digging new wells and installing tublike cisterns.

The "monumental" temple dates to the end of the same century. The foundations carved into the rockface in the eastern coastal area bear witness to the religious dignity with which the city desired to invest itself. Later the Roman city spread out over this sandstone framework, covering the entire urban area up to the northern fortifications with buildings and "cyclopic" structures in basalt.

The monuments from Punic Tharros, though scarce, can be traced back, on the basis of the excavation and construction techniques and their measurements, to a key period in the city's urban history: the 6th-5th century B.C. A primary characteristic of the buildings is the way in which the sandstone is cut, sometimes hollowing out the rockface, as in the monumental temple foundation and the hypogean tombs of the southern necropolis. The three monuments or monumental complexes that best exemplify this unified effort in Punic Tharros's urban development are the temple in the southern district, the *tophet* and the northern fortifications of "Su muru mannu."

Of great interest are the excavations under way on the "Su muru mannu" hill, the northeast side of which was the main center of a sprawling Proto-Sardinian village with a nuraghe located at the extreme northeast point and

Tharros map of the archaeological area

Restoration scheme for "temple K" at Tharros

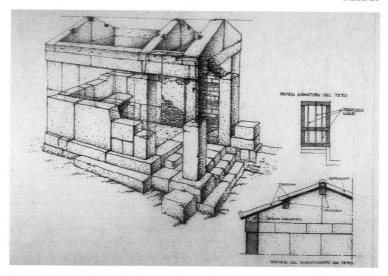

Tharros, "temple K"

a port access from the northern slopes. The circular basalt dwellings of the Late Bronze Age were protected to the north by a rampart, also in basalt blocks. A period of abandonment and sanding up left the entire area at the disposal of the first colonists towards the end of the 8th century B.C. They established their *tophet* in the eastern sector, and there it remained in use until the Christian period.

In the 6th century B.C. the northern stretch of the walls was modified over the remains of the village ramparts; what is left standing today of a turret at Torre San Giovanni marks its westernmost point. The wall was completed in sandstone with posterns to the east and west of a monumental gate, which today remains as a stretch of rubble, and two other fortified lines on the slope overlooking the port, which was probably also extended and reinforced. Also in this period an effort was made to provide the area with a water source, unsuccessful because the water-bearing stratum was not reached. A well was dug three meters wide, and was left incomplete at a depth of approximately fourteen meters.

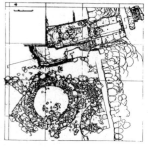

That Tharros invested the resources of the rich and varied economy of its own territory in trading activity in the Mediterranean is by now well-known, and it was also notably open to the Tyrrhenian markets. Less well-known, but increasingly evident in the light of new research, is the link to the Near East, which lasted through to later periods.

From an analysis of the material culture of Phoenician and Punic Tharros as yielded by the rich necropoli, and recently also by buildings and *tophets*, it is clear that in more than one instance the centre must have been an active participant in the trade movements of the western Mediterranean. Tharros workshops, probably under Tyrrhenian masters, started a characteristic production of scarabs in green jasper and cornelian with Egyptian, Near Eastern and Greek designs.

In the votive stelae of its *tophets* Tharros demonstrated an original vein, borrowing designs directly from the Near East and executing them in the local sandstone. An example of this are the unoccupied stepped cubic thrones. This receptivity recalls the established Proto-Sardinian practice of transposing to stone cult figures originally made of wood. Tharros provides an example, therefore, of a fruitful cultural encounter in which foreign designs were commissioned and carried out by accomplished local craftsmen, of the sort that created the statuary of Monte Frama.

At Tharros, therefore, a broad issue which affects most of the Punic Occident is particularly clear: the alternative between local production and importation. Analyses conducted up to now on various classes of material tend to favour the theory of local production, identifying Tharros as a sup-

Tharros, the dry moat around the northern fortifications with the Tower of San Giovanni in the background

Tharros: ground plan of the eastern postern and the nearby wall showing the foundations of the nuraghic village on the hill of Su Muru Mannu

opposite Necklace element from Tharros 6th-5th century B.C. gold, 3.9 × 1.9 cm Sassari Museo Nazionale G.A. Sanna

The hill of Su Muru Mannu with remains of the nuraghic village

ply centre for most of the Punic Mediterranean, dealing in both jewellery and trinkets in general. To what degree this role was exclusive is still difficult to establish in the complex context of Punic commerce, where the market demand was met from multiple supply sources.

In contrast with the series of centres dotting the island's southwestern shore, up to now only a sporadic presence on the northeastern coast has been noted. With Olbia as the focal point and, until recently, meager evidence, the Punic presence appeared extremely limited, determined by a policy that had to reckon with the local and Tyrrhenian inhabitants. As a result of the latest research efforts, involving topographical reconnaissance and systematic recovery of all signs of man in the area, the general picture will probably be updated and reinterpreted. However, the overall impression is that in northeastern Sardinia the predominant influence was Carthaginian, and therefore the dissimilarity between the northeast and southwest is bound to be confirmed, at least in relation to the first Phoenician colonization.

The main source of information on the cultural presence of Phoenicia and Carthage in Italy, Sardinia has up to now yielded an impressive body of evidence which however is still far from being exhausted. Future studies should approach a definition of Phoenician urban culture and of Carthage's administration of territory, with a comparative analysis that should be integrated with the analogous Mediterranean experiments carried out in Sicily, North Africa and Spain.

Appendix
Coins in the History of Punic Sardinia
Enrico Acquaro

Drawing of coin minted in Punic Sardinia with head of Kore on obv. and 3 sheathes of wheat and disc with crescent moon on rev. 241-238 B.C

Drawing of coin minted in Punic Sardinia with head of Kore on obv. and equine protome on rev. 264-241 B.C.

Carthaginian bronze coins of the 4th century B.C. and their massive circulation on the Punic Sardinian market represent the completion of the final phase of Carthage's economic and administrative takeover of Sardinian territory. This action left the island's ancient Phoenician colonies no possibility of asserting themselves independently in the new monetary market adopted by the entire Punic world. Nor did the colonies seem to assume a role of more importance when in 300 B.C. the island was authorized to issue a first bronze series in two denominations, with the head of Persephone and on the reverse an equine protome.

The first Sardinian issue of Punic currency was followed by another seven series; the last two were struck after the Roman occupation in 238 B.C. The historical events of the last century of Punic Sardinia are reflected in the succession of Sardo-Punic issues, in their denominations, technique, types, and values assigned by weight. Carthage was engaged during this period in various theatres of war and encouraged the ancient Phoenician colonies' natural desire for autonomy.

It is true that the second, third and fourth series reiterate the Carthaginian coin types (head of Persephone and standing horse with or without palm tree, facing forward or not) in a version of poorer quality which justifies every hypothesis of the provisional nature and emergency status of the mints. However, the fifth series shows a change in the relation between Sardinia and the North African city. The series, whose innovation lies in the three ears of corn depicted on the reverse, was minted in bronze in two denominations between 241 B.C. (year of the Aegates battle, the peace treaty between Carthage and Rome and the arrival of the mercenaries in Africa) and 238 (the year in which Carthage lost control of Sardinia). It is thus quite possible to see in the series with ears of corn an explicit recognition of the island's role as the granary of Carthage. It is not without significance that the first "national" economic affirmation of Sardinia as grain supplier, which took place under the rule of Carthage, was reiterated in the new context of a Mediterranean dominated by the Romans.

The following (6th and 7th) series, depicting a bull, in bronze or electrum, and in rare examples gold, sheds light on an epoch in Sardinian history to which some of the classical sources and tradition have imparted a truly epic consistency. This period, from 216-215 B.C., is marked by the battle of Cannae, Capua's defection and the Hampsicoras revolt. The new coin's link to Proto-Sardinian tradition, plus its reference to a well-known Campanian tradition, reflect the new political impetus and far-reaching Mediterranean strategy that the Barcae brought to the renewed conflict with Rome.

The great quantity of coins minted in a period when Sardinia was formally under Roman rule and Hannibal was conducting his campaign in Italy bears witness to how uncertain the outcome of the conflict was and to the breadth of the strategic theatre of war. Sardinia must have had a significant role in Hannibal's scheme, barely hinted at by the classical sources. The coins with the bull call attention to this role and its economic and political importance. How much the urban culture of the ancient Phoenician cities contributed to this will probably be revealed by the coins themselves, once the much debated question of the site of the mint or mints has been resolved.

Spain
Maria Eugenia Aubet Semmler

Maria Eugenia Aubet Semmler

View of the present port of Cadiz

The Iberian Peninsula represents the westernmost point of the Phoenico-Punic expansion in the Mediterranean. Although this was then the furthest known frontier, both classical historians and archaeological material show it to have been one of the first destinations chosen by the west-bound Phoenicians.

The study of the Phoenico-Punic past in Spain is divided into three important phases of historical-archaeological research. These have conspicuously enriched the existing store of knowledge, which only a few decades ago was limited almost exclusively to information transmitted by Greek and Roman historians and to some late archaeological remains found in necropoli and sanctuaries. The first phase of this research came to an end at the beginning of the sixties and on the basis of discoveries mostly made in the early years of this century, acquainted us with the great Punic necropoli of Cadiz, Ibiza, and Villaricos, whose remains dated back to around 500 B.C. The island of Ibiza has also revealed the existence of important centers of worship such as the well-known sanctuaries at es Cuyram and Isla Plana where Carthaginian influence was evident.

The second phase of research, which belongs roughly to the years 1965-1980, focused the interest of both archaeologists and historians on southern Spain, especially Andalusia, where a whole series of Phoenician colonies had been traced. From these, one could deduce the existence of an archaic colonial period, during the 8th-6th centuries B.C., associated with the arrival of contingents of eastern Phoenicians who continuously inhabited (over a period of 200 years or longer) the eastern coast of the Straits of Gibraltar. The spectacular nature of the archaeological discovery of the necropoli and settlements at Almuñecar — Phoenician Sexi — Toscanos, Chorreras, Mezquitilla and Guadalhorce diverted the attention of scholars from the old colonies of Ebusus (Ibiza) and Gadir for some time.

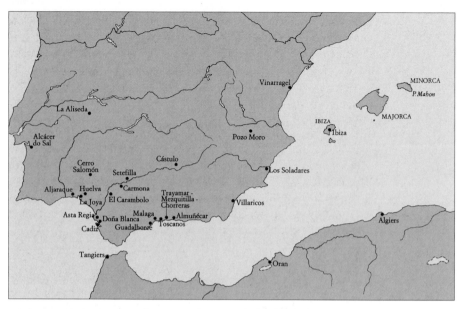

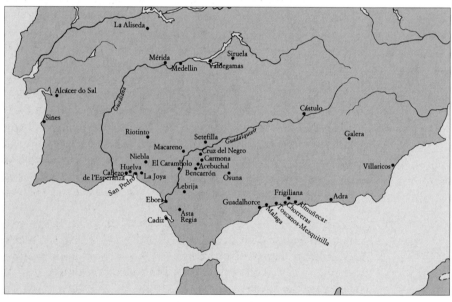

The Phoenician settlements
of the Iberian Peninsula

Map of Phoenician colonies
of Spain and the main
Tartessian settlements

Meanwhile the discovery of an indigenous culture at Tartessus, in the low Guadalquivir valley, whose inhabitants had made contact with the Phoenicians living in Cadiz in the 8th and 7th centuries B.C., allowed an analysis of the economic and cultural influence of Phoenician Gadir on the indigenous communities in the Andalusian interior. A cultural horizon, the so-called "orientalizing" Tartessian, was defined which had developed between 750 and 580 B.C.

The third and last phase of Phoenico-Punic research in Spain began in the eighties. In a sense it involved a return to the origins of the studies. The rediscovery of Cadiz and her bay in 1980 and the discovery of Phoenician Ibiza in 1982-86 have opened new avenues for archaeological inquiry into an era which is crucial to the past of the Iberian Peninsula. It is an era that witnessed the end of prehistory as Spain made her way into the eastern Mediterranean circuits of commerce and culture.

Gadir and Her Sphere of Influence
The classical historians Strabo and Velleius Paterculus date the Phoenician foundation of Gadir, or modern Cadiz, to c. 1100 B.C. This means that as one of the colonies of Tyre, Gadir was among the early centres of Phoenician expansion in the Mediterranean.

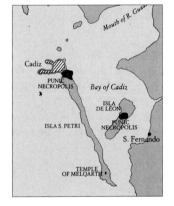

Plan of Cadiz

Excavations in Phoenician Gadir have not been possible, since the ancient town is situated under modern Cadiz. Only occasionally when building has taken place, has it been possible to gain access to the deeper levels of the town and discover archaeological remains of the Phoenico-Punic era more than five meters below ground level. However, the archaeological material found in the neighbourhood of the town, in the adjoining regions and in the indigenous or Tartessian villages dotted along Gadir bay, such as Torre de Doña Blanca, Asta Regia and Huelva, proves that Phoenician or eastern influences did not appear in the Cadiz area before 770-760 B.C.

The date transmitted to us by a few classical historians, who place the origins of this Tyrian colony around the end of the 2nd millennium, comes from Hellenistic historians, whose tendency was to lower the foundation dates of the remote cities of the West and to link their mythical origins to Heracles' legendary voyages or the Trojan War.

Nevertheless Cadiz became the most important Phoenician colony in the farthest West. Its economic and cultural sphere of influence spread as far as the Atlantic towns of Morocco — Lixus, Mogador, Oran-Rachgoun, and also Ibiza. Its foundation was due to a purely economic need: to obtain silver, which the Phoenicians could get with relative ease from the Tartessian region and particularly from the mines in the mountains in the provinces of Huelva and Seville. It was a time when in the East, especially in Assyria, silver was in great demand, so the founding of Gadir is to be seen as the immediate response to a particular market situation, which would certainly immensely enrich the kings and merchant princes of Tyre. The recent discovery of mineral-metallurgic installations of the 8th and 7th centuries B.C. near the famous silver mines of Riotinto and Aznalcóllar, in western Andalusia, as well as a quantity of gold and silver slag found in smelting ovens, show that the Phoenicians of Cadiz, in more than 200 years of intense industrial activity, were able to obtain tons of ore which were shipped as ingots from the port of Gadir to Greece and the East. The archaeological excavations carried out in the mining areas of the interior of the Guadalquivir region have shown that the Phoenicians used local labor for the mining and smelting of the silver.

The historian Diodorus has written on this subject, emphasizing the fact that the Phoenicians exchanged merchandise of little worth for Tartessian silver. The Tyrian merchants were so acquisitive that they went so far as to replace their lead anchors with silver ones in order to exploit fully the carrying capacity of their ships (Diodorus, 5, 35, 4-5). According to Diodorus, this typically colonial disparity in commercial exchanges enabled Tyre to increase her power in the Mediterranean and to found new colonies in Africa, Sicily, Sardinia and Spain itself.

Thymiateria
*from Lebrija
near Seville*
6th century B.C.
gold, 70.5 cm
*Madrid, Museo
Arqueológico
Nacional*

Archaeological studies document the intense exploitation of Tartessian silver by Gadir, and also the cultural influence of the Tyrian colony on the indigenous communities of the low Guadalquivir region, i.e. the Tartessians. This is known as the "orientalizing" influence.

There is evidence of this progressive influence, or acculturation, in the Tartessian material culture, particularly in the pottery output, and in architecture and technology. It is significant that in western Andalusia the 8th and 7th centuries B.C. witnessed a spread of the use of iron, and of the potter's wheel. But Phoenician influences made themselves felt most of all in the fields of ideology and social structure.

Thus the Tartessian princes and lords, grown wealthy through commercial exchanges with Gadir and control over the access to the inland mineral and agricultural resources and stock-farming, around the 7th century B.C. adopted a whole series of funerary rites of oriental and Phoenician character in their monumental tombs. These indigenous princes also enriched their tombs with decorated ivory, gold jewellery and vases of silver and bronze, specially made for them in the workshops of Gadir. The "princely sepulchres" of La Joya at Huelva, of Carmona and Setefilla in Seville, and of La Aliseda at Cáceres are famous.

A study of the Tartessian-orientalizing period discloses one of the most significant aspects of Phoenician trading in the West. In exchange for gifts of prestigious and luxurious objects — ivory, jewellery, metal bowls — which the indigenous leaders used for their sumptuous burials, the Phoenicians were granted a sort of right of transit to the territories that were richest in silver and agricultural produce. In the long run this system benefited some minority groups in the indigenous population — those who controlled routes — putting an end to the egalitarian regime that had prevailed in the area up to the arrival of the Phoenicians. In the last analysis, Phoenician colonization led to the first hierarchical social systems in Andalusia.

Gadir was responsible for all this. The Tyrian colony was perched on the summit of a promontory at the center of a small island, in the middle of a bay that dominated the estuary of the Guadalete. The town, called *Gdr* in Phoenician, therefore rose on a site that was highly advantageous from the economic, strategic and naval point of view. It was also fairly close to the natural entry to the rich and fertile Guadalquivir valley, then considered the main artery of communication for the whole of southern Spain. Recent paleo-topographic studies reveal that in ancient times an archipelago existed in the area, consisting of three main islands which later became joined to the mainland, forming the peninsula at Cadiz. The Tyrian colony, apparently fortified, stood on the smallest island, called Erytheia

Elephant tusk with inscription from Bajo de la Campaña 5th century B.C. ivory, 7.10 cm diam. 9 cm Cartagena Museo de Cartagena

by classical historians, site of the modern Cadiz. Marine erosion, ocean waves and the inroads of the sea have gradually reduced the size and modified the shape of this small island, today joined to its larger neighbour. Underwater archaeology has brought to light remains of ancient Gadir in the vicinity of the town, including vestiges of monumental architecture, such as capitals and plinths, which suggest the religious and political importance achieved by the ancient eastern colony.

At the end of the largest and narrowest of the islands nearest to the town, named Kotinoussa by Pliny, was the necropolis of Gadir, dating from the Punic era and already known at the end of the 19th century for its spectacular finds and marble sarcophagi. At the other end of the island rose the town temple, dedicated to the god Melqarth, and known in the Hellenistic era as Herakleion. The third island, the Isla de León, corresponds to the site of modern San Fernando on the mainland.

The existence of this ancient archipelago explains why early historians and geographers used the plural in describing the zone: *Gadeira, Gedeiroi, Gades.* The temple at Cadiz enjoyed fame and prestige throughout ancient times. The sanctuary was consecrated to Melqarth, patron of Tyre, and represented the most important political-religious institution of the entire Phoenician colony, from which Tyre watched over her economic interests in Spain. There are references to the economic function of the temple, which operated as a bank or branch office for the temple of Melqarth in Tyre, in addition to ensuring protection and asylum for the eastern navigators.

Subsequently the cult was associated with Heracles-Hercules, but the temple at Gadir retained all the characteristics of oriental worship until

the Roman era, causing astonishment to Greek and Roman visitors. According to the testimony of some historians, the Herakleion at Gadir preserved an oriental rite priesthood up to a late epoch. As in other Phoenician temples of the eastern Mediterranean, women were not allowed in the enclosure. This temple assumed such political and economic importance throughout the West that its oracle was consulted by such illustrious men of that time as Hannibal, Fabius Maximus, Polybius and Julius Caesar. It must also be mentioned that the Roman emperors of Hispanic origin — Trajan and Hadrian — gave the cult of Heracles-Melqarth imperial status.

Phoenician Gadir owed her prosperity to the silver trade. But documents exist which attest that Punic Gadir (6th-3rd century B.C.) was also a flourishing town, which controlled a lucrative naval traffic from her port. This enabled her to maintain regular commercial exchanges with Morocco, the Atlantic, Oran and the Mediterranean coast of Spain. We know of powerful shipowners and merchants who made this port the centre of communications between the Atlantic and the Mediterranean.

In the Punic era Tyre gave up her trade with the Tartessians, while Gadir continued to maintain close ties with the East, especially with Sidon, where the wealthy citizens of Cadiz purchased valuable anthropomorphic sarcophagi to furnish their tombs. Some of these have been discovered in the Punic necropolis of Cadiz, situated at Puente de Tierra and Punta de la Vaca on the ancient island of Kotinoussa, which was reserved for burial from the 6th century B.C. to the Roman era.

The Roman conquest of Gadir in 206 B.C. and the founding of Roman Gades, not far from the Phoenico-Punic town, only widened and length-

Iberian female statuette from Santa Elena, Jaen 6th-5th century B.C. bronze, 8.3 cm Madrid, Museo Arqueológico Nacional

Iberian statuette of warrior with dagger from Santa Elena Jaen 6th-5th century B.C. bronze, 11.5 cm Madrid, Museo Arqueológico Nacional

Iberian female statuette with outstretched arms from Santa Elena Jaen 6th-5th century B.C. bronze, 9.3 cm Madrid, Museo Arqueológico Nacional
• p. 291

*Iberian female
statuette with
raised arms
from Santa
Elena, Jaen
6th-5th
century B.C.
bronze, 12.7 cm
Madrid, Museo
Arqueológico
Nacional
• p. 290*

*Iberian statuette
of horseman
from Santa
Elena, Jaen
6th-5th
century B.C.
bronze, 6.3 m
Madrid, Museo
Arqueológico
Nacional*

ened the orbit of commercial influence of this ancient Tyrian port in the West and in the Atlantic.

The Colonies of Eastern Andalusia

The Costa del Sol, running through the provinces of Malaga, Granada and Almería, contains one of the most spectacular and archaic Phoenician archaeological complexes in the western Mediterranean area. This is a coastal strip about 170 kilometers long, bounded on one side by the river Guadalhorce, which flows into the sea near the modern town of Malaga, and on the other, by the river Adra in the Almería province. This coast has a large concentration of Phoenician settlements, organized as small harbor-towns dominating the deltas of the main rivers of the area.

We know from archaeological sources that sizeable contingents of eastern settlers were present on this coast between 750 and 550 B.C. According to recent reckoning, the foundation of some of these colonial enclaves, such as the Morro de Mezquitilla (Malaga), might date back to the beginning of the 8th century B.C. The colonists did not create large urban centres, such as Gadir or Ibiza, but remained in small coastal settlements, whose shape and distribution corresponded to the geographical and economic conditions of an essentially agricultural zone. Unlike Cadiz, this coastal stretch needed the relatively scattered type of settlement we see today.

All of these Phoenician colonies were built on a low coastal promontory near a river delta (Toscanos, Morro de Mezquitilla, Chorreras), on a peninsula dominating a river plain (Almuñecar) or on an islet in the middle of an estuary (Cerro del Villar del Guadalhorce). This situation gave the colonies a double strategic advantage: on the one hand it ensured excellent harbor conditions, since ships were able to moor in sheltered spots, protected from winds and currents, and on the other, colonists could be sure of an easy exploitation of the alluvial land near the rivers, which to this day remains well irrigated and extremely fertile. In Guadalhorce, for example, uninterrupted large-scale cultivation of wheat has been documented from ancient times up to the 18th century.

In Toscanos, Mezquitilla, Chorreras and Almuñecar numerous archaeological remains have been found, enabling us to reconstruct the history and the activities of the western Phoenicians in the 7th and 6th centuries B.C.

Research places the arrival of the Phoenicians within the first decades of the 8th century B.C. although most of the colonies emerged between 750 and 720 B.C. Before long, these people were erecting imposing buildings of considerable architectural merit on hilltops, marking out wide roads and creating well-planned towns. Towards the end of the 8th century B.C. a remarkable demographic growth was recorded for the whole area, due certainly to the arrival from Tyre and Cadiz of a second wave of Phoenician colonists. At this time there appeared in Mezquitilla and Toscanos industrial districts intended for the working of iron and copper and the production of pottery. Such structures encouraged the growth of industrial autonomy in these centers.

The topography of Toscanos

Towards 700 B.C. the first appearance of defence installations is documented in the Phoenician colonies. They were probably built in response to a new need to control the coast and protect the agricultural areas, as was the case in Toscanos. But only between 700 and 600 B.C. did all the settlements reach a level of true economic prosperity. In southern Spain, Phoenician trading reached its peak of development in the 7th century B.C., while the "orientalizing" phenomenon was at its most brilliant among the indigenous communities of Andalusia.

○ *settlements*
□ *necropoli*

It was then that a vast two-story building with three aisles, intended as a central deposit for goods and warehouse, was built on the summit of the Toscanos hill. The warehouse became the center of all economic activities in the colony and the surrounding land — the river Vélez valley. Its architectural characteristics and the archaeological material found inside — amphorae and jars for wine, oil and wheat — suggest the existence of a relatively complex and well-coordinated administrative structure among the Andalusian Phoenicians. The organization of the Toscanos colony recalls the great mercantile ports and commercial centres of the Middle East, such as al-Mina in the Orontes region, and Hazor.

During the entire 7th century B.C. goods were delivered to Phoenician ports from the East, from Cyprus, eastern Greece, Pithekoussa and even Etruria, probably in exchange for wheat, oil and wine. The many archaeological remains found in Toscanos include Attic, Rhodian and Corinthian pottery, some of it made in the Greek colonies of the West, such as Ischia-Pithekoussa.

A few aspects of the social organization of these colonial groups are known to us through the discovery of their necropoli, which are of particular interest being the most archaic of all Phoenician burial places found to date in the Iberian Peninsula. The most famous are at Almuñecar, Mezquitilla and Toscanos.

They were all near the settlements, on the other side of the river which flowed at the foot of the colony. The rite of cremation predominated, associated with a very homogeneous oriental ritual. A number of red-painted jugs, intended perhaps for libations or purification rites, an oil lamp, a plate with food on it and objects for personal use — jewellery, ivories, rings, etc. — were always placed next to the cinerary urn. Sometimes, after the tomb was closed, a few pieces of pottery were deposited or intentionally broken on the burial site. However the most significant aspect of these Andalusian necropoli is that luxurious alabaster or marble urns of Egyptian make were sometimes used to receive the ashes of the dead. For example, in the Phoenician necropolis at Almuñecar a number of urns bore inscriptions and emblems of various Egyptian pharaohs who reigned in the Nile valley between the 16th and 8th centuries B.C. However, most of the vases bore royal inscriptions relating to the pharaohs of the 22nd dynasty, such as Osorkon II, Takelot II and Sheshonk III, who ruled Egypt in the years 874-773 B.C. Alabaster vases of the same type, originally intended for precious wines, have been discovered, although in fewer numbers, in the royal palaces of Assur and Samaria in the East acquired as war booty or presents exchanged between royal houses.

The topography of Almuñecar

The topography of Chorreras Mezquitilla and Trayamar

How such exceptionally fine objects ended up in Phoenician tombs of the 7th century B.C. in the far western regions remains to be explained. Perhaps the Phoenicians plundered royal Egyptian tombs on Egyptian soil, or the pharaohs may have given these alabaster objects as gifts to the citizens of Tyre. Whatever their origin, the fact remains that the Phoenicians of eastern Andalusia reused these ancient and precious vases as cinerary urns. This denotes a high social and economic level and the presence in this colonial society of people at the top of the hierarchy with notable purchasing power.

Similar conclusions can be drawn from the archaeological finds made in the Phoenician necropolis at Trayamar, on the banks of the Algarrobo river. A few years ago, large underground tombs were discovered at Trayamar, made of dressed stones, with access through a long corridor leading to a chamber where Phoenician family groups or clans were buried. During the second half of the 7th century B.C., these tombs were reopened and reused, initially for cremations and then, toward the end of the century, for inhumations.

287

The furnishings, consisting of pottery, alabaster urns and objects for personal use were similar to those found in the necropoli at Almuñecar and Toscanos. In this case, however, what stands out is the typically oriental monumental architecture, the size of the burial chambers and their use by one or two generations of Phoenician colonists. Trayamar presupposes the presence on the Malaga coast of high-ranking family groups firmly rooted in the West.

Towards the beginning of the 6th century B.C. there was a crisis or a reorganization of most of the Phoenician settlements in eastern Andalusia. In Toscanos, the large warehouse fell into disrepair, the houses were rebuilt and renovated and commercial intercourse with other Mediterranean countries came to an end. This crisis reached its peak around 550 B.C. with a general exodus from the area, in some cases temporary and in others final. The Toscanos hill, for example, was not to be inhabited again until the age of imperial Rome.

Alabastron
*in alabaster
trefoil rim jug
mushroom-lipped
jug, and clay
kotylai
found in tomb 19
of the necropolis
of Laurita
Almuñecar
7th century B.C.
alabastron 50 cm
trefoil rim jug
17 cm
mushroom-lipped
jug, 21 cm
kotylai 8 and
7.8 cm
Granada, Museo
Arqueológico
• p. 292*

The origin of the crisis can be attributed either to the fall of the city of Tyre to Nebuchadnezzar (586-573 B.C.), or related to internal problems deriving from the crisis and fall of Tartessus in western Andalusia. As chance would have it, archaeological research has discovered that an inrush of Greek-Phocaean trade started in the Huelva area at the same time. This activity probably filled the temporary void left by the Phoenicians in Andalusia. It seems that the crisis affecting the Phoenician colonies around the second half of the 6th century B.C. was felt more acutely in Spain than in the Phoenician centres of Sardinia and Sicily. Not only were all activities interrupted in the Phoenician centres of eastern Andalusia; we know from archaeological sources that in the Gadir area silver was no longer mined in the interior and that Tartessian civilization fell into decline, having been the main beneficiary in the past of the trade exchanges with the Phoenicians.

Classical sources give us no information on the history of the small colonies of Malaga, Granada and Almería. Owing to this, and to the lack of inscriptions of the Phoenician era, we do not know the names of all the coastal towns in the 8th-6th centuries B.C. Late sources and numismatics have provided only three original Phoenician names: Malaka, which corresponds to modern Malaga; Sexi, the modern Almuñecar on the Granada coast and Abdera, which is now the village of Adra, near Almería.

At the end of the crisis most of the centres of eastern Andalusia formerly inhabited by Phoenicians were repopulated. This new settlement went side by side with a general reorganization of the area and the inhabited centers, which shifted to neighboring areas, such as Toscanos, or else became populated again after a brief interval, as happened in the region of the river Guadalhorce. At all events there was a general cultural transition to the Punic period of the 6th-3rd centuries B.C., and in southern Spain

Locally crafted jug with trefoil rim decorated
in geometric patterns from Monte Adranone
6th-5th century B.C., clay, 28.5 cm
Agrigento, Museo Archeologico Regionale

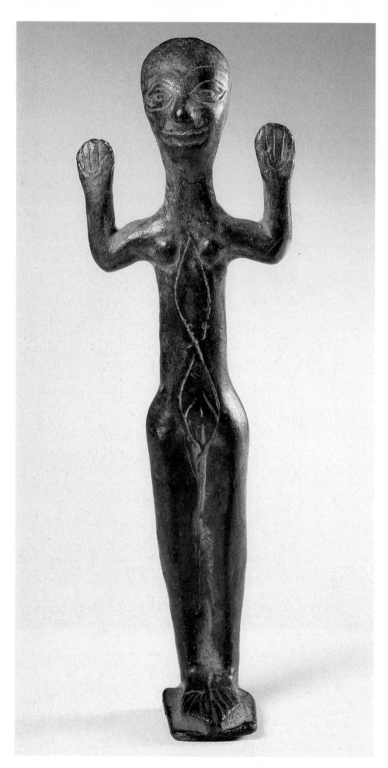

*Iberian female
statuette
with raised arms
from Santa Elena
Jaen
6th-5th
century B.C.
bronze, 12.7 cm
Madrid, Museo
Arqueológico
Nacional*

*Iberian female
statuette with
outstretched arms
from Santa Elena
Jaen
6th-5th
century B.C.
bronze, 9.3 cm
Madrid, Museo
Arqueológico
Nacional*

Alabastron *in alabaster*
trefoil rim jug
mushroom-lipped jug, and clay
kotylai *found in tomb 19 of the*
necropolis of Laurita, Almuñecar
7th century B.C.

Alabastron *50 cm*
trefoil rim jug 17 cm
mushroom-lipped jug 21 cm
kotylai *8 and 7.8 cm*
Granada, Museo Arqueológico

*Alabaster urn and clay plate
found in tomb 17
of the necropolis of Laurita
Almuñecar, 7th century B.C.
Urn 45 cm, plate diam. 27 cm
Granada, Museo Arqueológico*

Female statuette on plinth from the Puig des Molins necropolis 4th-3rd century B.C. terra-cotta, 40 cm Ibiza, Museo Arqueológico

opposite page
Bust of deity from the Es Cuyram cave sanctuary at Ibiza 3rd century B.C. terra-cotta, 13.2 cm Ibiza, Museo Arqueológico

Necklace pendants from Olbia
4th-3rd century B.C.
sand-core glass
approx. 0.7 × 0.5 cm
Cagliari
Museo Archeologico Nazionale

Alabaster urn and clay plate found in tomb 17 of the necropolis of Laurita Almuñecar 7th century B.C. Urn 45 cm, plate diam. 27 cm Granada, Museo Arqueológico • p. 293

this was characterized by the arrival of elements of Carthaginian influence which were adopted by a Semitic-speaking people, heir to the preceding ethnic group.

The appearance of large necropoli with inhumations in graves or in hypogea dug in the rock is typical of the Punic-Andalusian world. This indicates changes not only in the funerary rites but also a considerable population increase in formerly outlying districts. This is evident at Villaricos (the ancient Baria), near Almería where at that time work began in the nearby silver mines of Herrerias, perhaps already under Carthaginian control, or at Malaka, which around the 6th century B.C. became the most important harbor-town of that region. On the other hand the Punic Toscanos, known to us chiefly through its necropolis — Jardín — declined considerably from the position it held in the archaic colonial era.

The Punic period reflected a new socio-economic situation in which the old Phoenician mercantile ports were replaced by urban centres such as Gadir, Malaka and Ebusus. The most striking novelty of these is represented by the appearence of the cult of Tanit or other gods of the Carthaginian pantheon, which replaced the more centralized oriental cults of Melqarth or Astarte.

Ibiza

The strategic importance of the island of Ibiza, inevitable port of call for all navigators through the western Mediterranean area, could not escape the notice of the Phoenicians of the West.

In fact they seem to have discovered very early on the remarkable advantages offered by the bay of Ibiza and the navigation route through the Balearic Islands, as anchorage that would ensure control of a crucial zone in the West. From here, they could call at the ports of the Spanish Mediterranean coast and establish commercial relations with the northeastern Mediterranean regions.

Archaeological studies show that in the second half of the 7th century B.C. various groups of Phoenicians coming from the Gadir area settled gradually along the southern coast of Ibiza. The most ancient Phoenician settlements seem to have been on this island where the Punic town of Ebusus rose, and a few kilometers to the west, Sa Caleta.

It seems that initially only a small contingent of colonists landed in the island, which archaeological studies show to have been uninhabited at the time. Colonization coincides with the time when the Phoenician colonies of Andalusia were at the height of their economic prosperity. Probably around 630 B.C. these colonies sought to expand their sphere of commercial activities by venturing to the north, the Balearic Islands and the Gulf of Lions in search of tin and other raw materials. Judging by the earliest kind of Phoenician pottery found in Ibiza, the initiative for this enterprise came from Gadir.

Bronze piece with deity among animals called the "Carriazo bronze" found at Punta de la Vaca near Cadiz 6th century B.C.

Bronze piece with protome of winged divinity found near Seville 6th century B.C.

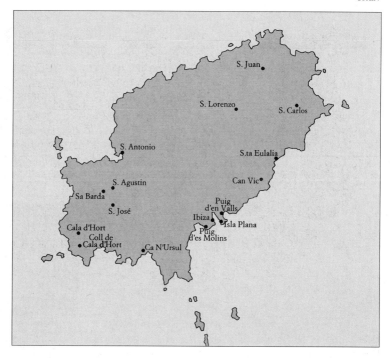

Plan of Ibiza showing main Punic settlements

Among the early Phoenician settlements in Ibiza was a part of a necropolis situated in the northeastern area of the hill of Puig des Molins, known to us because around the 6th century B.C. the urban necropolis of Punic Ibiza was created on the same site. This archaic necropolis, dating back to the 7th-6th centuries B.C., is made up of modest tombs with cinerary urns deposited in holes or pits dug in the rock. It is obvious that these Phoenicians, originally organized in small family groups — sailors, merchants — had nothing in common socially with the wealthy Phoenician society of Malaga and Granada.

The presence of Phoenician imports dated between 630 and 580 B.C. in the delta of the river Ebro (southern Catalonia), in western Languedocq, along the coast of Castellón (Vinarragell) and in indigenous villages of the Alicante province (Pe-a Negra de Crevillente, Los Saladares) proves that once in Ibiza, the Phoenicians lost no time in establishing a network of regular trade with northwestern Spain and southern France. These regions probably supplied them with tin from the Atlantic area, which reached them through Aquitaine. Toward the end of the 6th century B.C., however, this commercial circuit was interrupted by the crisis of the Phoenician colonies in southern Spain and by the arrival and consolidation of Phocaean commerce in these areas. In fact, starting from the two most important Phocaean colonies in the northeastern Mediterranean — Emporion (Ampurias) and Massalia (Marseilles) — the Greeks took over control of the commercial routes to Catalonia and southern France.

Owing to an incorrect reading of a famous passage by the historian

Diodorus (5,16), for many years it was thought that the colony of Ibiza had been founded by Carthage around 650 B.C. Diodorus relates that in Ibiza there was a town called Eresos, a Carthaginian colony, inhabited by barbarians, most of them Phoenicians. According to him, this town was colonized 160 years after the foundation of Carthage (Diodorus, 5,16, 2-3). However, archaeology reveals that Ibiza was absorbed into the orbit of Carthaginian political influence only during the second half of the 6th century B.C., and it is to that era that the beginning of the economic development of the island belongs. Between 540 and 500 B.C. Ibiza became a large urban center, paving the way for the golden age of Punic-Ebusean culture, datable to the 5th-2nd centuries B.C. The best-known monument of Punic Ibiza is unquestionably the necropolis of Puig des Molins, about 500 m from the fortified walls. The modern town rises on a hill overlooking the bay and the harbor, on the site of the Punic colony whose original name was Iboshim. The necropolis of Puig des Molins occupies an area of over 50,000 m² and has yielded between 3,000 and 4,000 tombs up to now, so it may certainly be considered one of the largest Punic necropoli of the West. Three different types of tombs are to be found in the necropolis: hypogea dug in the rock, simple rectangular graves dug either in the rock or in the earth and child burials inside amphorae. As in all known Punic cemeteries, inhumation is the prevailing funerary rite.

Interior of a tomb in the Puig des Molins necropolis at Ibiza

The most spectacular tombs are unquestionably the hypogea, subterranean chambers dug in the rock, used as communal graves until the Romans conquered the island in 123 B.C. These are large chambers with a well and an entrance door, generally rectangular in shape and between two and six metres in length. They have yielded stone sarcophagi and rich furnishings consisting of votive terra-cottas, pottery of Greek importation, razors, Egyptian or imitation Egyptian amulets made of faience, jewellery and other ornaments. The necropolis posed serious problems to archaeologists, who began excavating as early as 1903, when it came to dating and recognizing the Punic tombs. This is because most of the hypogea were used by a number of consecutive generations over centuries, so that tombs and furnishings of different epochs intermingle within the enclosure.

It has nevertheless been possible to distinguish three different ways in which the necropolis of Ibiza was used. The first corresponds to the archaic cremations of the 7th and 6th centuries B.C. mentioned above; this is a part of the necropolis somewhat damaged by the excavations for the more modern Punic hypogea. A second phase, dated between the 5th and 4th centuries B.C., corresponds to the period that saw a consolidation of the inhumation rite and the number of hypogea excavated is higher. This is the time of greatest development in Ebusus, where the Punic population must have amounted to about 4,000. The third and last phase, around the 3rd and 2nd centuries B.C., represents a period of crisis and regression in the

Puig des Molins
necropolis at Ibiza

Interior of tombs
in the Puig des Molins
necropolis at Ibiza

necropolis, where the ritual of cremation briefly returned. During the Roman era the population of Ibiza reused the old Punic hypogea as communal graves.

The impressive quantity of tombs dating from the 5th and 4th centuries points to a considerable increase of the population of Punic Ibiza during that time. This suggests not only a growth in prosperity but also the possible arrival of North African colonists. For Ibiza those were years of thriving commercial relations with numerous countries of the western Mediterranean area.

An analytical study of Punic pottery, as well as of other handicrafts, has shown that the island had become a center for the production of vases for export to the Greek colonies of Ampurias and Marseilles, to Andalusia, to Sicily and to Sardinia. Together with this development went the exploitation of the salt pans and an increase in agricultural production in the interior. In fact around the 6th century B.C. we find traces of rural settlements dedicated to the cultivation of grapes and olives, whose necropoli are well-known. Among these rural centers Cala d'Hort, Can Roques, Cala Vedella, Cala Tarida and Sa Barda are of particular archaeological interest. From there oil and wine were carried in amphorae to the port of Ibiza and shipped overseas.

One can guess at the range of the Ebusean trade in those years from the circulation of a Punic-Ebusean coinage, which toward the end of the 3rd century B.C. spread to the entire Mediterranean area. Coins from the Ebusean mint have emerged in Roussillon, Languedocq, Majorca, the Spanish Levant, Andalusia, North Africa, Campania (Pompei), Sicily and Sardinia. Two great sanctuaries belong to Punic Ibiza: one at Isla Plana and the other in the Es Cuyram cave. The former rose on a small island, now a peninsula, in the center of the bay and so was a necessary transit point for all ships arriving in the port of Ibiza. The sanctuary of Isla Plana, discovered in 1907, has become famous for the quantity of votive terracottas found in a well, or sacred enclosure, which probably was part of a building attached to a temple. These are male and female figurines in an attitude of prayer which reproduce a model also known in other Punic centers of the West, such as Carthage, Bithia and Motya—grotesque clay statuettes which the faithful of Ibiza deposited at regular intervals as offerings to the deity from the 6th century B.C. onwards. They were probably votive gifts to the god Eshmun, placed on sacred ground to entreat a cure, fertility, health.

The position of the Isla Plana sanctuary on an island, facing the port of the Punic town, suggests that it was one of the earliest places of worship in Ibiza. The second great sanctuary on the island is the cave of Es Cuyram, used between the 4th and 2nd centuries B.C. This is a rock sanctuary situated on the northwestern side of the island in a craggy, isolated spot, ideal as a place of worship for navigators and sailors. Hundreds of votive terracottas have been found there so far, mostly female figures.

The cave of es Cuyram was discovered in 1907. On the ground, mixed

opposite page
Female statuette with tunic and outstretched arms from the Puig des Molins necropolis 4th century B.C. terra-cotta, 39 cm Ibiza, Museo Arqueológico

Bust of deity from the Es Cuyram cave sanctuary at Ibiza 3rd century B.C. terra-cotta 13.2 cm Ibiza, Museo Arqueológico
• p. 295

Female statuette on plinth from the Puig des Molins necropolis 4th-3rd century B.C., terra-cotta 40 cm, Ibiza Museo Arqueológico
• p. 294

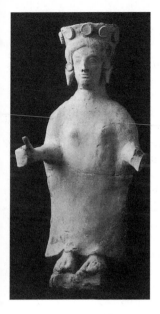

with a great quantity of ash and a number of bronze inscriptions, votive terra-cottas were found. The characteristics of the archaeological finds and the placing of the offerings indicated that as the faithful deposited votive gifts inside the cave, the priests in charge of the sanctuary would periodically remove the contents, so it has been impossible to establish a clear stratigraphy of the deposits. The structure of the cave shows the existence of water in the area. This helps to explain why the place was chosen, since a great many Punic sanctuaries owed their existence to the cult of water.

Over six hundred terra-cotta statuettes, originally polychrome, and about a thousand fragments belonging to terra-cottas, ceramics and ivory and bronze figurines, constitute the archaeological material found in Es Cuyram. It was mixed with a thick layer of ash and burnt bones, which suggests the custom of animal sacrifices in the enclosure.

The most significant discoveries consist of clay statuettes representing a female bust with two large wings folded over the breast, bearing symbolical motifs such as a lotus flower, crescent moon or a solar disc. This is the winged depiction of the goddess Tanit, symbol of life and protection, which shows that the cave was dedicated to the cult of the most important divinity in the Carthaginian pantheon, in a place that was obscure but at the same time strategically sited along the Punic navigation routes.

Other terra-cottas are local copies of Greek models of the Hellenistic period and recall the images used for the cult of Demeter and Kore in Sicily. Probably some of the moulds used to produce these pieces are of Sicilian importation. One of the most significant finds from the cave is a bronze plaque discovered near the entrance, inscribed with two Punic dedications dating back to different epochs. The earliest, dated to the 4th century B.C., is dedicated to the god Reshef-Melqarth by a citizen of Ebusus named 'Š'DR. The second is more recent (2nd century B.C.) and was offered to the goddess Tanit by one Abdesmun, son of Azarbaal, probably a resident of Ebusus.

The position and characteristics of the Ebusean sanctuary recall other places of worship in caves, also consecrated to the goddess Tanit, such as the one discovered in the Gorham cave on the Rock of Gibraltar, which would have served to protect the route of Punic navigators bound for Cadiz. The island of Ibiza was in general a propitious spot for religious cults and popular worship. Numerous legends on the sacred virtues of the island are recorded by classical authors. Some refer to the absence on the island of any type of snake, scorpion or other noxious animal, so that the land of Iboshim was thought to be sacred. According to Pomponius Mela (2, 125-126), for example, carrying some Ebusean soil would ensure protection against any danger.

The Roman conquest of Ibiza did not suddenly interrupt a cultural development, a language and a way of thinking which had been profoundly rooted among the inhabitants since the Phoenician era.

Part III The World of Art

Arts and Crafts
Sabatino Moscati

The Phoenicians' main contribution to art in the Mediterranean world was small-scale craftsmanship, mostly of precious objects they sold or exchanged along their maritime routes. Can this production be defined as art? Obviously the comparison with coeval Greek work highlights the problem. Further, there is the anonymity of the Phoenician craftsmen, which gives their output collective mass-production connotations.

This does not only apply to form, but also and even more to substance: that is to say, substantially the same typologies and iconographies were repeated unchanged in time and space, so that very often we may wonder, without finding an answer, where a certain work was produced (because where it was found does not necessarily coincide with where it was made) or when (since the archaism and poor state of preservation of the artifacts often make an evaluation impossible).

In reality, the judgment as to whether or not this is art cannot be based on a distinction between art and craftsmanship which did not exist before the Renaissance. If it is true that craft is distinguished by a strictly practical and functional purpose, then one can hardly deny that Phoenician production as a whole is in fact art. We may take jewellery as an example: it is clear that the goldsmiths intended not only to make useful objects, but also to create a sense of beauty and rarity in order to give their work more prestige. From the point of view of use, there would certainly have been no need to employ gold for a cup, ivory for a box-lid, much less fashion the materials with such care and elegance, often making unique pieces.

So what one sees in at least some of the Phoenician artifacts is a "will to art" that distinguishes them from craft. It is true that the repetitiveness of many iconographic motifs prevents the emergence of individual artists, but that was an intrinsic aspect of the workshop. As for the absence of names, the same can be said of much of the Graeco-Roman output, to which nobody denies a "will to art." Moreover, the fact that Phoenician production has been little studied has prevented the discovery of individual styles that might emerge from a more careful examination despite the anonymity of the craftsman.

We should now consider a particular feature of Phoenician work, its tendency to fall into types or classes that at least appear to be very solid and limiting: stelae, terra-cotta figurines, busts and masks, jewellery, etc. The constant practical function of Phoenician artifacts, their observance of traditions and models, and even their religious and magical connotations emphasize these divisions according to type; and the typical characteristics of archaism and a return to ancient tradition undoubtedly consolidate them.

Necklace
pendants
from Olbia
4th-3rd
century B.C.
sand-core glass
approx.
0.7 × 0.5 cm
Cagliari, Museo
Archeologico
Nazionale
• p. 296

Art critics, who for a long time had denied the autonomous validity of production types, have recently rediscovered at least their functional reality, as models or designs consciously or unconsciously present in the craftsmen's work. The truth is that these types can be better understood if they are considered not as "containers" into which the creative process had to be fitted, but rather as directions or trends within the creative process, in relation to the conditions in time and space of a production which, while it felt the desire for beauty and value, did not (apparently, at least) feel any desire for change and innovation.

So there is no reason to discount the role of types in this production. Rather, there exists the problem of their definition, especially in the framework of the "minor" arts. And this is where we see just how inadequate certain traditional classifications are. For example, jewellery is distinguished by its precious material decorative function, but scarabs can also be made of precious material and used as ornaments. Vice-versa, scarabs and jewels alike can be used as amulets, and the same may be said of carved ivory and bone objects, classified by their material while their functions may be extremely varied.

In fact, conventional classifications do not suit these "minor" arts, which the Greeks (referring specifically to the Phoenicians) called *athỳrmata*, "knickknacks" or "trinkets." There is no doubt that this definition, or a similar all-embracing term, fits the group of objects under discussion.

It is interesting to note that at Tharros, the main centre where these articles were made, a 16th-century proclamation speaks of *jocalia*, forbidding the inhabitants to search for them in the area of the ancient city: this word, derived from the Latin *iocalis* (the adjective of *iocus* = "play", "game") which is the root of our word "jewellery", is the exact equivalent of the Greek *athỳrmata* — though the equivalence is unintentional — and expresses very well the basic homogeneity of these artifacts.

Coming back to the problem of history, it may be observed that the continuity of a large number of products was a feature not only of the Phoenician age, but also of the one that preceded it. As I have said elsewhere, Phoenician culture is characterized by its continuity with the past, while circumstances changed the cultures of neighboring regions. It is a fact that the more we know about Phoenician products, the more links appear with the preceding artifacts in the Syro-Palestinian area. But it is also true that our growing knowledge often reveals how deceptive this homogeneity is: for instance, there was undoubtedly an increase in Egyptian influence in the Phoenician age. The choices and preferences of product types also show a definite evolution in time and space when we look at them more carefully. In fact some types appear drastically reduced when they move to the West: sarcophagi, for instance, and embossed cups. Conversely, the West sees a great increase in the number of stelae compared with the East. And in certain cases, the metal razors, for example, there seems to be no Eastern precedent. In others, East and West are independent: terra-cotta masks and scarabs exemplify this, since they are partly inspired by Egyptian models, without the mediation of Phoenicia, and partly originally made in Sardinia.

The case of the scarabs testifies to a fact that recent excavations have corroborated: in reality the colonies were not only areas of passive reception, but also of original production. This is true not only of Carthage and North Africa, but also of Sicily, Sardinia and Iberia. Besides the scarabs, one may recall Sardinian jewellery, Iberian ivories and so on. In some cases, the originality of the colonies' work stems from outside influences that they, and not the homeland, received: examples are the large-scale production of terra-cottas inspired by Hellenic Sicily, and the indigenous substratum evident in Iberian ivories.

Another factor in the differentiation of Phoenician production according to place and time is the progressive emergence of definite local characteristics, which often lead beyond a superficial grouping by geographical area. Sardinia is a case in point: thanks to recent finds and studies, it has become possible to subdivide the material into centers of production: Bithia specialized in terra-cotta figurines, Sulcis in stelae, Tharros in *athỳrmata*. It is also possible to differentiate within types: the stelae from Sulcis, for instance, reveal a strong Greek influence that is not found in Nora or Tharros.

So there are many ways in which a geographical differentiation can become evident in a craft (or art) production that at first sight seems to be inflexible and homogeneous. It must be added that exterior investigation cannot

Amulet featuring head of Bes from Aghios Georghios Larnaca 6th century B.C. faience diam. 5.5 cm Nicosia, Cyprus Musem

give us a full understanding of this sort of work; a study from the inside is also needed to explain certain results and bring out differences. That is to say, besides iconography we also need iconology to appreciate what the craftsman wanted to express, and why. This form of enquiry is even more essential in the case of a cultural world deeply permeated by religious values, since if we do not understand these it becomes difficult to understand that culture.

Let us take a few examples. Iconographic motifs like the "sign of Tanit" or the "bottle idol" can be found on stelae, but what do they really mean, and what do they express there? We may ask the same about the human images on the stelae: are they gods or priests, or sometimes one and sometimes the other? Then there is the fact that iconic and non-iconic designs coexist, so that alongside human figures and animals we find motifs such as baetyls, lozenges, etc., probably used as symbols alluding to the divine. The question becomes different with the advent of Greek influences, for we then find figures of offerers rather than deities.

The secondary motifs are no less important than the primary ones for the purposes of iconological enquiry. In the early phase, of Eastern inspiration, we find the disc of the sun and the crescent moon, the hand raised in prayer, the palm-tree, the Egyptian *ankh* (which was probably so popular because it was considered the "sign of Tanit"). In the later phase of Greek influence, attested on stelae in Carthage especially, we find the caduceus, the dolphin, birds and flowers. Finally, the later stelae bear various animals, liturgical

309

instruments, offertory tablets and ships: we are now close to Phoenician iconography (and iconology). It cannot be denied that these motifs were often used out of *horror vacui*, but that does not exclude the need for research to find out why they were chosen.

Along with problems of iconological interpretation, we have to deal with another phenomenon typical of Phoenician art: the fact that iconographical motifs tended to be used for ornamental purposes, with the result that the contents were gradually lost. In other words, the figures undergo a process of reduction and schematization, i.e. stylization. The images lose their meaning: the original content is subordinated to a rhythmic function, leading to near-abstraction. In short, representation is neglected in favor of decoration.

The most typical example here are the metal cups on which motifs taken from Egypt, Mesopotamia, and the Phoenician repertoire are arranged in bands with an alternating rhythm, manifestly for decoration. However, the choice of motifs could not have been purely casual, or at least not to start with, so the decorative reduction occurs at the end and not the beginning of the process. The sphinx, symbol of pharaonic power, the sacred plant, symbol of the earth's fertility, the winged scarab, symbol of the sun and life: these and other motifs were certainly not originally haphazard choices.

Given these results, can we think that the meanings inherent in these images were still realized? Perhaps not by all, and not specifically, but it seems unlikely that the people who used these products should have been unaware of their religious and magical implications. We have some significant evidence for this: the figured scarab motifs, taken as a group, show that their choice from the Egyptian repertoire was by no means casual; in fact there is a deliberate selection of motifs with magical rather than funerary connotations. Be that as it may, the constant reappearance of the same motifs shows that their adoption was a matter of importance for both craftsmen and users.

City Planning and Architecture
Sandro Filippo Bondì

The body of evidence regarding city planning and architecture in the Phoenico-Punic world allows the identification of certain constant features that combine to delineate a typical "settlement culture." One of the basic aspects of this culture consists of the topography of the town-sites, whose peculiarities have made it possible to extract a real "Phoenician cityscape," that is, a compendium of distinguishing elements to be found in a great many colonies in the East and West.

Phoenician settlements were generally sited on promontories, or on islets not far from the coast, facing rather shallow or lagoon-like stretches of water, to meet the demands of the ships of the day, equipped with short keels unsuited to great depths. A settlement of this kind offered the best conditions for protecting its sailing vessels (both sides of the promontories could be used for berthing), and considerable defensive advantages, since islets were less vulnerable to attack than mainland settlements, and promontories were naturally well-protected sites suitable for accommodating a citadel.

On the other hand, the Phoenician colonists do not seem to have been much concerned with finding large, flat in inland areas near the chosen sites, as most of the cities were oriented towards the sea and towards economic activities connected with the sea (trade, fishing, etc.). With few exceptions, a real strategic dominion over territory can be documented only starting from the 6th century B.C., as the result of the more marked commitment of Carthage towards the exploitation of the agricultural resources of North Africa and Sardinia.

So in these two regions numerous rural communities, often of limited size, sprang up, revealing the pervasiveness of the Punic penetration and the variety of economic activities that supported it. Connected primarily with the Carthaginian undertaking was the construction of large fortified works, such as the coastal fortifications of Cape Bon and the district of Bizerta in Tunisia, and the inland forts of Algeria and Sardinia.

The different typologies of settlements obtainable from the mass of archaeological evidence thus established, it is worth stressing that, in any case, the large coastal cities have yielded most of the evidence regarding the city planning of Phoenician centres, and their relative architectural structures. These centres show a morphology that is rarely contradicted by the evidence in our possession: at their heart was a walled citadel, around which other quarters sprang up containing private houses, religious buildings, and premises for commercial and industrial activities.

Sanctuaries in some cases were located in special sections of the city,

*Remains of Punic
dwellings
at Byrsa*

*Level of Roman
structures
over Punic
settlements:
the foundations
of the Roman
Forum at Byrsa*

Main types of Punic shaft graves

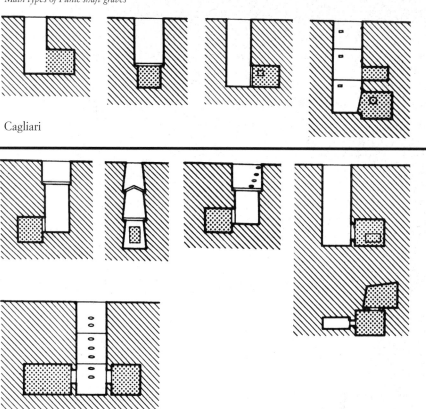

Cagliari

Lilybaeum

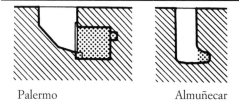

Palermo   Almuñecar

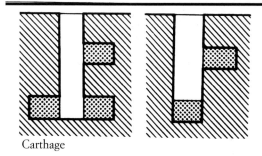

Carthage

*Partial view
of the necropolis
at Utica*

*Necropolis
at Kerkouane
entrance to a
dromos tomb*

Main types of Punic graves: dromos *and shaft tombs*

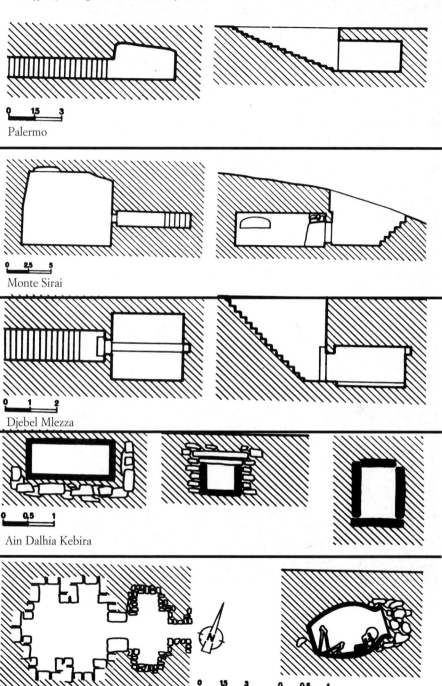

Palermo

Monte Sirai

Djebel Mlezza

Ain Dalhia Kebira

Mogogha es-Srira

Florinas

which thus took on the function of real "sacred grounds." The whole city was often encompassed by walls, sometimes consisting of several curtain walls, following the typically Carthaginian principle of in-depth defence. Near the walls was usually found the sacred area most characteristic of the Phoenician world, the *tophet*, the enclosure set aside for the celebration of infant sacrifices. Archaeological evidence of this exists only in the West, but various sources testify to its existence in the Phoenician homeland as well.

Also lying outside the city walls were the necropoli where the deceased were buried intact or after cremation in one of the basic types of underground tombs: pit, shaft (one or more burial chambers opening off the side or at the bottom of a vertical entrance shaft) and *dromos* (with a sloping passage leading into the cella).

As to ports, the specific skill of the Phoenicians in this field of engineering is apparent in the complexity of the installations that served their cities: natural mooring places were often supplemented by wharves and breakwaters. Typical of several western settlements was the presence of a drydock (*cothon*), documented at Carthage and Mahdia in North Africa and at Motya in Sicily.

Cothon at Motya

Phoenicia
The vast urban and architectural evidence mentioned above varies greatly from area to area. Though the constant elements just examined recur in all the regions touched by Phoenician expansion, only in the Punic West is it possible to reconstruct clearly the general characteristics of the individual centres.

In Phoenicia archaeological investigation has been hindered by the fact

Ruins of the city of Byblos that the sites are occupied by modern buildings, so tracing the city planning of major centers is a difficult undertaking. The best method here is to proceed by known types rather than by individual sites, extracting in this way the basic features of the architecture even when the various constructions are not included in an urban fabric that is legible in all its essential parts.

317

The existence of defensive curtain walls in Phoenician cities of the homeland is documented by illustrations on several Assyrian monuments. The fortified walls of Tyre are portrayed on the bronze gates of Balawat, dating to the time of Shalmaneser III (858-824 B.C.) and on reliefs of the time of Sennacherib (705-681 B.C.). The city walls are marked by the presence of jutting towers, between which are several arched gateways. Battlements run along the top of the whole circuit of defenses.

On an archaeological level, the existence of similar fortifications is confirmed by the remaining sections of the walls of Byblos and, above all, by clues from the fortified cities of the West, recently brought to light through regular excavations.

The temple of Eshmun at Sidon with the votive throne of Astarte

The Assyrian sources also show interesting evidence of private dwellings. In a Sennacherib relief, the residential quarter inside the walls of a Phoenician city is seen, in which the individual houses are all crowded together. These houses are several stories high and have elegant touches: columns stand on either side of the front doors and the upper-floor windows have balustrades with scroll-like decorations.

This form of decoration is also known from several examples unearthed at Ramat Rahel, in Palestine, and its diffusion in Phoenician culture is corroborated by its frequent appearance in carved ivory miniatures. Further documentation regarding Phoenician domestic architecture comes from the Greek geographer Strabo who observes that in Tyre and Aradus houses were several stories high and Tyrian palaces taller than Roman ones.

As to constructions for industrial uses, a recent archaeological find has made it possible to draw important conclusions about the size and location of these complexes. At the Sarepta site a full-blown industrial quarter was identified, that is, a neighbourhood of the city reserved exclusively for workshops and small establishments, an area of about 800 m², where artifacts, implements and remains of raw materials were found, proving the existence of various manufacturing activities there.

Numerous pottery kilns attest to the production of amphorae and pottery, while a sizeable deposit of murex shells which produced the characteristic purple dye point to the industry of textile dyeing. Furthermore, slag and some well-preserved olive-presses indicate that workshops for processing metals and making olive oil were in operation in the city.

As regards religious architecture, Phoenician sanctuaries were normally not particularly monumental in appearance. The sacred areas, called "high places" in the Bible and typical of the Phoenician world, for example, were modest enclosures open to the sky where the deities were worshipped by putting up cippi or stelae. However, in or near the larger cities places of worship of greater structural complexity also existed.

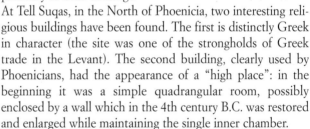

Detail of ruins of Byblos

Reconstruction of plan of the temple of Solomon in Jerusalem by C. Watzinger (1935)

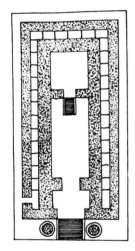

The most typical example here is that of the sanctuary of Eshmun, which stood on the outskirts of Sidon, in the locality of Bostan esh-Sheikh.

A type of place of worship that may be considered peculiar to the Phoenician area and which also developed in the colonies, is that of the small cubic shrine copied from Egyptian models, two monumental examples of which are known at Amrith and Ain el-Hayat.

The sanctuary of Ain el-Hayat, in particular, consists of a couple of Egyptianizing sacella, the architraves trimmed with a row of sacred snakes (uraei) and a solar disc, set inside an enclosure where, as at Amrith, there is a small pool. The diffusion in the West of this temple type, proved mainly by representations on votive stelae, was significantly confirmed by the discovery of a similar place of worship at Nora, in Sardinia.

Further information about Phoenician religious architecture has come from recent excavations at several sites.

In Sarepta (the modern Sarafand) the remains have appeared of a small religious building from the 7th century B.C. that, with various alterations, went on functioning up until the 4th century B.C. The temple, with handsome ashlar masonry, consisted of a single chamber, roughly 16 m² in size. Set up against one of the short sides was a small altar with a freestanding column in front of it, while stone benches ran all around the inside walls, probably to hold offerings.

At Tell Suqas, in the North of Phoenicia, two interesting religious buildings have been found. The first is distinctly Greek in character (the site was one of the strongholds of Greek trade in the Levant). The second building, clearly used by Phoenicians, had the appearance of a "high place": in the beginning it was a simple quadrangular room, possibly enclosed by a wall which in the 4th century B.C. was restored and enlarged while maintaining the single inner chamber.

A specific category of sanctuary, the *tophet*, used for infant sacrifices, certainly existed in Phoenicia, though there is no archaeological trace of them in the area. Biblical and literary sources agree, in fact, in attesting the practice of human sacrifice there and the existence of places of worship set aside for it.

The Old Testament mentions that Joshua "defiled the Tophet, which is in the valley of the children of Hinnom, that no man might make his son or his daughter pass through the fire," and remarks that the practice was alien to the customs of Israel. As can in fact be read in Jeremiah: "They have built the high places of Baal, to burn their sons in the fire for burnt offerings unto Baal, which I commanded not, nor spake it, neither came it into my mind."

So while the practice may go back to the Canaanite part of the popula-

tion, the classic sources specify that it is to be ascribed more specifically to the Phoenicians. Porphyry and Eusebius of Caesarea, quoting Philo of Byblos, record in fact: "The Phoenicians in the gravest dangers, whether of drought or of plague, would kill some of their own children, sacrificing them to Saturn."

But biblical sources preserve above all the first-hand report of what must have been one of the major Phoenician achievements in religious architecture, the temple of Solomon in Jerusalem, built by Tyrian workmen. The temple was preceded by a spacious courtyard with a lustral basin and an altar, and entered by a doorway flanked by bronze columns. It was divided inside into a succession of three rooms: a square vestibule, a central rectangular chamber containing a gold altar and a table for offerings and lastly a "Holy of Holies" where the Ark of the Covenant was kept. The building was completed by outside service rooms on three stories.

As to Phoenician funerary architecture, more or less extensive necropoli have been brought to light near almost all the major centres, where tomb types of different monumental and structural importance coexist. The main burial grounds are to be found near Tyre, Sidon, Akhziv and Beirut. The tombs of Tyre are mostly shaft tombs, but there are also burials in simple pits. In Sidon the shaft type also prevails and the plans of the tombs are often quite complex, with several burial chambers opening off at the bottom and along the sides of the entrance shaft, which can be up to 5 m deep.

Dating from between the 9th century B.C. and the Persian occupation are the burial grounds of Akhziv, where the shaft type alternates with the stone cist type, while the cemetery of Khaldé, near Beirut, probably served a rather poor community: used from the beginning of the 1st millennium B.C., it has about 400 graves in which the bodies were as a rule buried directly in the ground. True funerary monuments, the only exceptions to the rule of underground chambers, are the Amrith tombs, known by the Arab name of *meghazil* (moulede). They are mausolea several stories high, consisting of a base, circular or polygonal in plan, crowned by a cupola or an obelisk. In one instance, two lions flank the foot of the building. The dates of these monuments are between the beginning of the Persian occupation and the first Hellenistic period.

The remains of ancient harbour works bear out the particular skill of the Phoenicians and the care they gave to the planning and maintenance of their ports. The city of Tyre was served by a northern "Sidonian" port and a southern "Egyptian" one.

*Proto-Aeolic
capital
from Cyprus
6th century, B.C.
limestone
91.5 × 102 cm
Paris, Musée du
Louvre*

Sidon was fitted out with only one port, while the city of Aradus possessed complex harbour works, consisting of at least two docks and possibly an inner lagoon, which was compared to the *cothon* of Carthage.

Cyprus

Among the Mediterranean areas touched by the Phoenicians in their expansion, the one closest to home was Cyprus, where elements of a Phoenician culture have been found from the 10th century B.C. The Phoenician settlement of the island did not lead to the founding of new colonies, but rather to the exploitation of existing towns, where the local culture always remained prevalent.

So Phoenician influence was to be seen not so much in the overall layout of the cities as in certain specific buildings. Among these, the most remarkable is without question the great temple of Astarte at Kition, which was founded in the 9th century B.C. and remained in use until the end of the 4th.

The temple was built on the site of an earlier Mycenaean sanctuary and its perimeter walls were made of finely dressed and rusticated blocks of stone. Two entrances, south and east, gave access to a large rectangular hall which led to the cella at the far end. The bigger room was divided into aisles by four rows of columns.

Starting in the 8th century B.C., the temple underwent a number of alterations, the most extensive of which involved cutting down the number of aisles (from five to three) and placing stone benches for offerings along the walls. The importance of the Kition sanctuary, founded by Tyrian Phoenicians, is proved not only by its long life, but also by the richness and variety of the votive offerings, which include, alongside Phoenician materials, Greek pottery and terra-cottas and a great many Egyptian amulets and scarabs.

North Africa

In the Phoenician world of the West, the great amount of archaeological data and the thorough exploration of many settlements, whose basic architectural and urban features have been traced, mean that they can be presented here city by city, placing the description of the monuments within the logical framework of their respective urban structures.

Starting with North Africa, the presentation can begin with the most important of the western colonies of Phoenicia, Carthage, whose urban format can be reconstructed both from the descriptions in literary sources and from the results of archaeological explorations, in particular those recently undertaken as a part of the international programme for protecting the remains of the ancient city.

Phoenician Carthage was spread out on the promontory between the lagoons of Sebkret er-Riana to the north and Tunis to the south. The early port must have been at the southernmost part of this area, but this was then replaced by the *cothon* complex, consisting of two communicating docks. The outer, rectangular one was reserved for merchant vessels, the inner, circular one for the fleet.

Not far from the harbor district was the *tophet*, where burials took place from the 8th to the 2nd century B.C. Connected with the earliest use of the sanctuary is the so-called "Cintas shrine", a small chapel preceded by a courtyard with an altar and several concentric surrounding walls. At present, the *tophet* consists of two adjoining enclosures where thousands of urns were discovered containing the ashes of sacrificial victims, and with the stelae that accompanied them.

The Carthage area is dominated by three hills (Juno, St. Louis and the Odeon), which according to the traditional reconstruction formed the acropolis of Byrsa. Excavations conducted recently on the hill of St. Louis, however, have revealed that in the oldest phase it contained a burial ground and after that workshops for forging metals, while residential quarters were laid out only in the Hellenistic age, with *insulae* formed by streets intersecting at right angles. So the location of the acropolis of ancient Carthage is still an unresolved question.

Another residential area was recently brought to light between the hills and the sea, a sizeable group of private houses, built initially in the 6th-5th

*Ruins of Punic dwellings
at Byrsa*

323

century B.C. and subsequently altered up to the eve of the city's destruction. The large symmetrical *insulae* contained rather spacious homes, adorned, in the phase of greatest prosperity, with typical mosaic floors. These results seem to bear out what Appian says about the grandeur of the private houses of Carthage between the acropolis and the sea. He mentions buildings up to six stories high, arranged along three main streets which sloped up to the acropolis from the forum situated in the lower town. According to Appian again, another residential quarter existed in a less central position, in the Megara district, and its houses were all surrounded by gardens and orchards.

Tombs in the necropolis at Utica in background walls dating from Roman times

Nothing remains of the public buildings and temples of Carthage. According to the literary sources, the senate must have been near the forum, while we know that on the acropolis stood the temple of Eshmun, last stronghold of the defenders of Carthage during the crucial Roman attack. As for the necropoli, they were spread out over the sides of the hills without any apparent planning. The oldest burial sites were in Dermech and Douïmès, dating from the 8th-7th century B.C., but then increasingly extensive areas were set aside for burials and the last cemeteries reached the district of S.te Monique, much further north. Carthage necropoli document the use of pit, *dromos* and shaft tombs (the latter the most frequently used in the last phase). As for burial rites, inhumation prevailed over cremation until the 4th century B.C., then the situation was reversed.

Literary sources agree in stating that Carthage, at least from the 3rd century B.C., was completely surrounded by walls. The existence of defensive curtain walls by the sea, mentioned by the sources, has now been

Kerkouane courtyard of dwelling with perystyle

borne out by the above-mentioned excavations in the "Magonid" quarter, which have turned up a line of fortifications along the coast. Inland, the fortifications of Carthage consisted of three lines of walls, up to 17 m high according to Diodorus, and reinforced by square protruding towers which, in Appian's description, were set at regular intervals of about 60 m.

Polybius affirms that the perimeter defences also included a moat and a palisade. The defensive walls to the north and south of Carthage must have been simple curtains, but from the remains in the field it is impossible to get an exact idea of the whole fortified works. Nor have appreciable traces been found of the inner defensive walls which, according to the description of various ancient writers, surrounded the acropolis of Byrsa. After Carthage, the Punic settlement in North Africa which most lends itself to a complete survey of its urban and architectural features is Kerkouane, on the east coast of Cape Bon. Founded in the 6th century, and occupied through the 3rd century B.C., the city did not undergo successive destruction and reconstruction; it remained fairly integral and this allows for an accurate reading of its urban context.

Kerkouane was protected by two curtain walls. Two main gates and several side gates were set into the outer wall, separated from the inner one, which was reinforced by numerous square towers and by a moat some 10 m wide. A road ran round the outside of the fortifications, which encompassed the city completely on the inland sides for about a third of a mile.

Inside these walls the city was planned in an extremely clear and logical way: a gridiron of streets formed a series of residential *insulae* which have so far yielded the richest evidence for domestic Punic building. The

houses usually consisted of a narrow entrance passage leading to a central courtyard, often decorated with floor mosaics where the "sign of Tanit" appears. In the courtyard there were one or more basins, a well and possibly a flight of stairs leading to the upper floors. Around it were arranged the different rooms, according to the disposition typical of Punic town houses.

Kerkouane pottery kiln

The main public building of Kerkouane is the so-called "house of columns," which served as a temple and consists of a large central hall measuring 7 × 10 m, containing the columns which give the building its name and surrounded by a series of rooms. The necropoli are located outside the walls, on a hilly ridge west of the town. Most of the burials were in *dromos* tombs, several hundreds of them, covering the whole period of the city's existence (6th-3rd century B.C.).

Aside from Carthage and Kerkouane, no other Punic town in North Africa, in the present state of knowledge, allows an organic reconstruction of its urban and architectural features. The Punic occupation is mostly documented by the necropoli, while the habitation sites are usually buried under modern buildings.

Kerkouane, well for storing lime

Thus Sousse, the ancient Hadrumetum, one of the most important Punic cities in North Africa, is known only from its cemetery and *tophet*, while of Utica, which sources indicate as the oldest Phoenician colony in the

Kerkouane floor of sherds and marble inlay with "sign of Tanit"

region, nothing remains except a few scattered traces of dwellings, aside from the tombs. Outside the urban context, of particular importance is the evidence of military architecture recently unearthed both in Tunisia, in the area of Cape Bon and Bizerta, and in Algeria, on the banks of the Seybouse river. The fortifications erected by Carthage to protect its metropolitan territory have been located both in the coastal region most exposed to possible attack and along what must have been the western *limes* of its possessions.

On Cape Bon the three Punic forts of Djebel el-Fortas, Ras ed-Drek and Kelibia have been identified. The first consists of a double curtain of defensive walls with a fort wedged in between them. The second includes two blocks joined to form a sort of L, both containing numerous rooms which were used as quarters and storage chambers, while the necessary water supply was guaranteed by five capacious "tub" cisterns.

The stronghold of Kelibia was a polygonal fort defended by several projecting towers from which led numerous branch walls for keeping every possible approach under control. The main passage into the fort was moreover blocked by an outpost consisting of a quadrangular rampart.

In the Bizerta area an imposing fortress has reemerged on the Djebel Touchela, an oval structure measuring approximately 200 × 60 m, preceded by a smaller building that served as an outpost. Another small fort, also fitted with an outer rampart, has been brought to light in nearby Djebel Fratas, between Cape Zebib and Cape Farina.

*Kelibia, the Turco-Hispanic
fortress built on the ruins
of Punic structures*

In Algeria, in the neighborhood of Hippo, several military installations have been identified, set at intervals along the right bank of the Seybouse. They are large square or oval forts, sometimes preceded by the usual outposts, on the sites of Ksar el-Ashur, Henshir Torba and Ksar el-Kebsh. Since the district is wholly lacking in non-military settlements of the Punic period, it is clear that with these fortified complexes, Carthage was interested not so much in protecting specific towns as in controlling the western border of its metropolitan territory.

Sicily and Malta

Outside North Africa the most striking evidence of Phoenician town planning and architecture comes from the larger Italian islands, mostly as a result of the systematic field research conducted there for over twenty years. Regarding Sicily, the most thoroughly explored site is Motya, a small, roughly circular islet in the Stagnone (lagoon) di Marsala, less than half a mile from the mainland.

The island was surrounded by a massive perimeter wall, carefully planned from the moment it was built in the 6th century B.C. This wall, which in some places was nearly 2 m thick, was reinforced by a series of projecting towers set at regular intervals. Two monumental gates, as well as several lesser entrances, were set into the curtain walls, linked by a road that ran across the whole island.

Another road led from the north gate connecting the islet of Motya to the mainland coast at Birgi. Near the south gate was situated the *cothon*, measuring about 51 × 35 m, joined to the sea by a channel some 30 m long. Inland, part of the residential area has been identified, with houses facing onto wide streets, datable mostly to a late period.

More substantial evidence exists regarding the industrial works: aside from a few pottery kilns and two ceramics workshops, unearthed in various parts of the island, a true industrial quarter was discovered near the northern coast. It is an area of some 600 m^2 where tanning and dyeing of hides and manufacture of bricks and other fired clay products must have taken place. Most interesting is the evidence of the island's places of worship. The principal one was certainly the *tophet*, which occupied a triangular area beside the northern walls of the city. Founded in the 7th century B.C., it was enlarged halfway through the 8th by filling in a depression in the rock just east of the area originally used. The fill-in was retained by a wall made from the votive stelae gradually removed from the sacred site. The only building inside the *tophet* enclosure was a small quadrangular cella with a built-in altar. On the front were Greek architectural elements (Doric columns), a characteristic that is also to be found in another religious building discovered at Motya, a little shrine outside the north gate, with Doric columns in the first phase (6th century B.C.) and foliated capitals of Hellenistic inspiration in the second. This is a clear indication of the deep assimilation of Greek cultural models which distinguished Motya in the period of its greatest development.

329

Another important place of worship at Motya was the sanctuary of "Cappiddazzu", located in the northeast part of the island. In its most monumental phase, datable to the 4th century B.C., it consisted of a large building with a nave and two aisles, surrounded by a vast circuit of walls. But fragments of Egyptian cymae discovered on the site point to the existence of an earlier version with typically Punic structural features.

The Motya necropolis extends from the *tophet* to the north gate. It was used only during the archaic phase of the city, since from the 6th century B.C. the burial grounds were moved to the mainland, on the Birgi coast. The tombs for the most part contain cremated remains placed in jars, stone cists or monolithic sarcophagi, buried in shallow pits in the ground. When in 397 B.C. Motya was destroyed by the army of Dionysius the Elder, the population moved to the new colony of Lilybaeum on the site of present-day Marsala, and this town soon became the chief Punic stronghold in western Sicily. This settlement, served by three gates, was protected on all sides by massive defensive walls, which were reinforced on the land side by several towers and a moat under which ran a long tunnel.

Archaeological excavations within the walls have brought to light several residential areas, whose Punic *facies* is testified by the adoption of the characteristic "framework" technique (i.e. upright orthostats alternating with spaces filled in with rubble). Also dating from the Punic period is the square grid layout of the wide, straight streets. Outside the fortified city walls lay the broad necropolis zone, where over a thousand tombs have been discovered, both of the shaft and pit types, most of them containing cremated ashes.

The urban aspect of the other Punic centres in Sicily is, at the present state of knowledge, much less perspicuous. At Eryx, for example, the Phoenician factor is apparent chiefly in the thick city walls which Phoenician workers helped to build in the 6th century B.C., as is proved by the letters of the Phoenician alphabet used for assembling the stone blocks.

At Palermo, which was one of the largest and most prosperous cities of Punic Sicily, the outlines of the city plan can be traced, but architectural remains worthy of its real importance have not been brought to light. The city was enclosed by walls up to 6 metres high, with at least four gates, one on each side. A vast necropolis has yielded shaft and *dromos* tombs, datable between the 7th and the 2nd centuries B.C.

Undoubtedly linked to the Palermo site is the rock sanctuary discovered near the city in a natural cave called Grotta Regina, on the slopes of Monte Gallo.

The occupation of the grotto in Carthaginian times, borne out by numerous pottery finds, is eloquently confirmed by a series of Punic

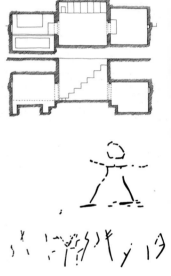

Plan and section of a dromos tomb in the necropolis at Palermo

"Sign of Tanit" and Punic inscription in the Grotta Regina near Palermo

Ruins at Motya showing the North Gate

inscriptions and several charcoal drawings on the walls. Among the figures are two "signs of Tanit" and various boats which resemble the military vessels of Carthage. In the inscriptions mention is repeatedly made of the name of Shadrapa, a health-giving deity invoked by Punic worshippers.

Evidence of the greatest interest is provided by the town of Soluntum, on Monte Catalfano, which in the Hellenistic period replaced an earlier settlement nearby, destroyed during the wars between Carthage and Syracuse and not yet explored archaeologically. The importance of Soluntum lies mostly in the fact that it testifies to the adoption in the Punic world of Hippodamus's concept of town planning. The city is in fact laid out at the top of the hill around a strictly rectilinear central axis with several streets branching off it at right angles, while the public buildings are concentrated in a special area in the middle of the town. In this urban context, so clearly influenced by Greek models, elements exist that can be traced directly to the Punic style and which sometimes testify to the persistence of this up to until the Late Roman age.

A sacred area near the main square, consisting of two connected buildings, contains a three-baetyl altar of clearly Carthaginian origin. Another sanctuary, at the center of the public area, is distinguished by the existence of two adjoining chambers. Lastly, at the top of the hill, a religious building extremely complex in its plan, set around a maze-passage, suggests the existence of Punic architectural influences.

The meeting of Greek and Punic elements, so apparent in Soluntum, also characterizes the Carthaginian *facies* of Selinus, which between the end

of the 5th and the middle of the 3rd century B.C. was a part of the Punic province of Sicily. From an urban and architectural point of view, the Carthaginian contribution can be detected above all in the new organization of the city acropolis, where a quarter of modest dwellings was formed on streets intersecting at right-angles.

Buildings alongside the city walls to the south of Motya

The houses show the characteristic "framework" technique and the typically Punic arrangement of rooms around a central courtyard. Mosaic floors with "signs of Tanit" and caducei bear out the Punic character of the dwellings. Also to be ascribed to the Carthaginian reorganization of the acropolis are a sacred site made up of twelve rooms, in some of which animal sacrifices took place, and a little sacellum fashioned inside Temple A, where mosaic floors are again to be found, with a bull, a caduceus and a "sign of Tanit." Finally, there are unquestionable Punic elements outside the acropolis, in the sanctuary of Demeter Malophoros; in the enclosure an Egyptian ogee altar with three baetyls, clearly Carthaginian in origin, stands out.

The discussion regarding Sicily can finish with the unique documentation offered by the site of Monte Adranone, in the province of Agrigentum. A Greek settlement situated near the eastern border of the Punic eparchy and conquered by the Carthaginians in the 4th century B.C., it preserves architectural remains related to the period of Punic domination.

The Carthaginian *facies* of the centre is noticeable especially in the two most important places of worship. The first, set on the acropolis, is a rectangular construction measuring 31 × 10 m and divided inside into three chambers.

The central one, open to the sky, contained two baetyls, or votive stones,

Buildings alongside the city walls to the south of Motya

Motya, detail of wall built with the "framework" technique

on special sandstone bases, while a large cistern existed a short distance from the temple. The façade of the building was a combination of Greek elements, such as the Doric columns and the triangular pediment, and Punic ones, such as the Egyptian ogee cornices.

The second sanctuary is a rectangular building measuring 21 × 8 m consisting of two adjoining chambers, in the larger of which were found baetyls on sandstone bases and a small altar for sacrifices. Near the sanctuary were a cistern and two wells. Also dating from the Punic phase of the city is the double circuit of walls with bastions, buttresses, and an outer rampart, obviously built according to the Carthaginian principle of in-depth defence.

Architectural evidence of Phoenician and Punic colonies in the Maltese archipelago is provided primarily by evidence of a non-urban kind. Our poor knowledge of the towns (which on the other hand the Phoenicians never built from scratch using instead pre-existent native settlements) is only partly made up for by the over 500 tombs discovered in various parts of Malta, which at any rate attest to a concentration of Phoenician elements in more densely inhabited areas like Zejtun, Pawla and Rabat.

The most significant nucleus of evidence today is the sanctuary of Astarte at Tas Silg, near the bay of Marsaxlokk. This sanctuary enjoyed a vast popularity in ancient times: Cicero cites it in his orations against Verres as *fanum Iunonis* and mentions the veneration it had received for centuries and the richness of its embellishments and furnishings.

The Phoenician site made extensive use of the megalithic walls of a previous place of worship dating back to the 3rd millennium B.C., and especially a large horseshoe-shaped structure which formed its central nucleus. Its walls were straightened and two rooms created inside; furnishings and articles of worship already in use in the preceding phase continued to be utilized.

The central nucleus of the sanctuary was reached through a vast open space with various shrines, wells and reservoirs opening off it, and containing a large monolithic lustral basin flanked by a baetyl. A *temenos* wall ran around the whole sacred area, which with time underwent a number of changes: the entrance to the central body was given a moulded architrave, the enclosed area was enlarged, and later a portico with an *opus signimun* floor was added to one part of the courtyard.

Another important place of worship, of the Hellenistic period, has been brought to light on the second largest island of the Maltese archipelago, Gozo, in the locality of Ras il-Wardija. The sanctuary consists of a double enclosure open to the sky, at the foot of a rocky knoll into which a chamber has been carved with niches in the walls. A basin and several small wells discovered outside this chamber can be related to purification practices and libation rites according to a custom coming from the local prehistoric tradition.

Returning to the island of Malta, interesting evidence of the diffusion of Punic people on its territory comes from excavations in the locality of St. Paul Milqi. The architectural structures brought to light belong to buildings that were part of a farming community, whose inhabitants lived off the utilization and transformation of the resources of the land, as is evinced in particular by the reservoirs, the canals and the plastered basins. It is a striking example of the presence of Punic elements not only in the large urban centers, but also in the countryside, in a period around the 3rd century B.C.

Sardinia

Knowledge of the Phoenician and Punic centres in Sardinia has greatly improved over the last twenty years, thanks to systematic excavations, so the island today offers a complex set of coastal, insular and inland settlements, concentrated mostly in the southwestern part.

One of the chief coastal centers was Cagliari, founded by Phoenician settlers at least as early as the 7th century B.C. The town-plan comprises a citadel, situated on the hill of the Castle, and a lower town on the shores of the basin of Santa Gilla, where the port was located. The citadel, from at least the 4th century B.C., was protected by fortifications which are still visible beneath the Pisan walls.

Most of the vestiges of the Punic settlement come from the lower town. Probably here, in the locality of San Paolo, was the *tophet*; remains of private houses have been unearthed near the basin of Santa Gilla, while Punic elements continue to be found in dwellings dating from Roman times, with "framework" walls and floors decorated with "signs of Tanit."

Punic religious architecture is represented in Cagliari by two late sanctuaries discovered in Via Malta and near Largo Carlo Felice. The former consists of an enclosing wall incorporating a chapel with four columns on the side of the entrance, which was accessed by a flight of steps. The remains of the second sanctuary are confined to another enclosing wall and traces of a colonnade and pavements. Neither place of worship dates from before the Hellenistic age. Two separate necropoli served the town of Cagliari in Punic times. The first, on the hill of Tuvixeddu, was in use from the 6th century B.C.; the more than 300 tombs discovered there are mostly of the shaft type and contain inhumed bodies. A number of burial chambers were decorated with religious symbols in relief or painted scenes. On the opposite edge of town, on the slopes of the Bonaria hill, another necropolis, similar to the one described, started to be used in the 4th century B.C. when the other was nearly full.

Plan, cross-and through sections of a shaft tomb in Cagliari

In the hinterland of Cagliari recent excavations in the territory of Senorbì have revealed the existence of a large rural settlement dating from Punic times. This is the town of Santu Teru-Monte Luna, founded in the 5th century B.C. in order to utilize the considerable agricultural resources of the Trexenta. It consisted of a citadel encircled by massive defensive walls and several outposts, and a lower town, outside the fortifications, which contained houses and artisan workshops. The necropolis was located on another hill nearby, with about a hundred tombs whose rich contents bears witness to the wealth of the Punic inhabitants. Most of the tombs are shaft-and-chamber, but there are also trench graves, alcoves and stone cists.

A typical promontory settlement is Nora, on Capo di Pula, whose appearance in Punic times can be reconstructed from various elements that can be made out beneath the presently visible Roman remains. The promontory, with its jagged coastline, made possible the utilization of three different ports on the various sides of the peninsula, the entire perimeter of which was defended by fortified walls. The highest point of the promontory formed a sort of natural citadel. Here a nearly square building measuring 10 × 11 m, known as the "temple of Tanit," served a defensive purpose, at least in the earliest period, before being used as a temple in Hellenistic times. The town was set out on the slopes of the headland, while the commercial district was probably situated behind the main port, where the Romans later placed their forum. The southwestern spur of the promontory, called "Sa punta 'e su coloru," was developed into a sacred area, while the *tophet* and the necropolis were located on the other side of the peninsula, near the isthmus connecting it to the mainland.

Thus the town of Nora was very functional in its organization and the architectural remains connected with the Phoenico-Punic occupation

confirm both its size and importance. Private houses are well known from the identification of two residential areas: the oldest, behind the strand to the southeast, is recognizable only by the beaten earth of the floors. The more recent, on the slopes of the "hill of Tanit," is a group of buildings jumbled together, suggesting the effect of a *casbah*.

As to religious architecture, the structures of the *tophet* no longer being identifiable (it has been swallowed up by the sea due to a slow shifting of the sea level), the most interesting evidence is found in the "Sa punta 'e su coloru" area. Here an architrave was found decorated with uraei and the winged solar disc, belonging to an aedicula of the Phoenician type existing in Amrith and Ain el-Hayat.

Not far away is the most important sanctuary of Nora, the so-called temple of Eshmun. In the phase visible at present, not earlier than the 2nd century B.C., it consists of a rectangular courtyard with a mosaic pavement leading into a central hall, with a curvilinear apse at the far end containing two small adjoining cellae.

In the same area, less visible traces point to the existence of another sanctuary, dating from Roman times but Punic in its architecture.

As to the necropolis, evidence of the ancient cinerary urnfield is almost completely lost, while the remaining tombs, dating from the 5th-3rd century B.C., are of the shaft type, or more rarely, rectangular pits covered by stone slabs. An example of a coastal settlement apparently lacking a central nucleus and haphazard in its growth is Bithia, on the promonto-

Ruins at Nora:
residential district

Capo di Pula
the jutting rock
at Coltellazzo
now joined
to the mainland

ry of Torre di Chia. The remains of the city are in fact scattered over a vast area, so it is difficult to reconstruct its layout in detail. The most useful elements for establishing its boundaries are the remains of defensive walls on the promontory and the surrounding heights, and the numerous traces of private dwellings unearthed in various places inland, between the coast and the hills.

The *tophet* of the city has been discovered on the islet of Su Cardulinu, but it was evidently used only in archaic times. The most important place of worship in Bithia was the temple of Bes, near the Chia promontory. It consists of three adjacent rooms set lengthwise, with various shrines or service areas along their sides, and dates originally from the 4th century B.C.

The necropolis extends along the shore west of Torre di Chia and contains tombs datable to between the 7th century B.C. and Roman times. From the oldest period there are pits with ashes of the dead, substituted in the mid-6th century by stone cists with inhumations; in Hellenistic times, as was the norm, cremation burials came back into favor.

Among the Phoenico-Punic towns of Sardinia, the one that best exemplifies the typology of insular sites is Sulcis, founded in the 8th century B.C. on the island of Sant'Antioco, which already in antiquity was connected to the mainland by an isthmus, with two ports set along the sides.

The Phoenician town that grew up behind the port area was encircled by casemate walls built on the hills behind it. Double-faced, with huge blocks on the outside and small stones on the inside, the walls were reinforced by projecting towers (a couple are still visible) and finished off to the east by a moat. A large vestibuled gate, near the present-day museum, was set into the northern section of the walls.

Remains of the walls in the tophet *area at Sulcis*

Entrance to a dromos tomb *in the Sulcis necropolis*

The necropolis of the city, undoubtedly the most monumental in all Punic Sardinia, was spread out over the same area. The burial ground, used from the mid-6th century B.C., contains shaft tombs or more frequently tombs with *dromoi*, whose burial chambers consist of two or more very spacious rooms (up to 7 m long), nearly man-size in height.

The *tophet* of Sulcis is situated to the north of the city, outside the walls. It stands on a trachytic hilltop and consists of a large rectangular enclosure and several smaller ones, where the urns and related stelae were set in natural hollows in the ground. The original layout of the sanctuary dates from the 8th century B.C., the same period as the remains of the Phoenician town which very recent excavations have brought to light in the area between the cemetery and the sea.

Architrave from an aedicula from Nora 6th century B.C. Cagliari Museo Archeologico Nazionale

Ruins of Nora a Punic "tub" cistern

The tophet
at Sulcis

*Details of the
Punic walls
of Sulcis*

In the 7th century B.C., the Phoenician settlers of Sulcis also founded the outpost of Monte Sirai, which stands about 14 km from the city, on a hilltop near modern Carbonia. This site still represents the best-known example of an inland settlement built for primarily military purposes.

In the southern part of the plateau running along the top of the hill (whose steep sides made it a natural stronghold), a citadel was located, defended by a circuit of massive walls up to 4 m thick, which, in keeping with a typically Phoenician technique, contained several casemates. Inside the citadel, the central element of defence was represented by the keep, a massive construction some 16 m long, built on the remains of a ruined nuraghe. In the 6th century B.C., following Carthaginian occupation, the whole complex was reinforced by restructuring the keep, putting up two towers by the main entrance (a tenaille gate leading into a tapering passage), and adding outposts in the flat space in front of the citadel.

Inside the citadel, as of the 3rd century B.C., stood a vast residential centre, laid out in *insulae* created by the grid plan intersection of three wide longitudinal streets and smaller side-streets. The houses usually consisted of several rooms, often plastered, set around a central courtyard. Some single rooms facing directly onto the street may be interpreted as shops.

Outside the citadel, following the principle of a strict functional division of the various zones of the plateau, were the necropolis and ex-urban sacred area. The former, situated in a narrow valley northwest of the citadel, consists of several pits with ashes of the dead, from the period between 600 and 525 B.C., and a dozen *dromos* tombs, sometimes decorated with funerary reliefs (demonic heads, a "sign of Tanit"), in use between the end of the 6th and the 3rd centuriers B.C. and containing inhumations.

The sacred area, which occupied a rocky slope in the northwest corner of the plateau, consisted of the *tophet* and an adjoining chapel. The *tophet*, which was used between the 4th and 2nd centuries B.C., was a vast open area preceded by extensive sacred grounds. On the upper part of the slope several enclosures were built. Here were massed the urns with the ashes of the sacrificial victims, some 300 of which have been discovered, often accompanied by stelae.

A ramp led from this area to a raised platform upon which stood the temple's shrine, a rectangular structure measuring 6 × 8 m, with a spacious central vestibule and several rooms along the sides and at the far end. In the north corner of the building the altar was found, covered with ashes and burnt bones (obviously the remains of sacrifices carried out there).

Architectural evidence of great interest, even if limited to the field of religious buildings, emerged from the finds at Antas, a site in the hills north of Iglesias. It was here that the Carthaginians built a Punic temple in the 6th century B.C., when they penetrated into this area, rich in ore deposits.

The most impressive aspects of the temple date from the Late Roman period (3rd century A.D.), but some of its peculiarities, such as the twin cellae and the small lustral basins, suggest Punic precedents. This precedent was abundantly substantiated during the excavations carried out in 1967 in front of the podium of the Roman temple. What emerged were the remains of a Punic sacred site, consisting originally of a rectangular room with a smaller room inside containing the holy rock. Later, in the 3rd century B.C., the plan was enhanced: the entrance was ornamented with a pair of Doric columns and an Egyptian moulding and, without touching the cult cella, three consecutive rooms were made out of the rest of the building. A large enclosure, some 68 m long, surrounded the whole area.

A significant peculiarity of the temple of Antas lies in the fact that it was not connected with any specific settlement. Set on the metalliferous hills around Iglesias, in a zone devoid of important Punic centres, it appears to have been a great regional sanctuary; it was dedicated to Sid, a god identified with Sardus Pater in Roman times, the national deity of the Punic people of Sardinia. In fact the inscriptions discovered there include dedications to this god by worshippers from centres such as Cagliari and Sulcis.

View of the acropolis at Monte Sirai

Returning to the city settlements, the most important centre of Phoenico-Punic colonization in Sardinia was certainly Tharros, set at the tip of the Sinis peninsula in the Gulf of Oristano. A typical promontory settlement, it was founded no later than the 7th century B.C. and, thanks to its trade and its hold on a vast hinterland, grew to be the richest city on the island. The first Phoenician settlers probably occupied the southernmost tip of the peninsula, on Capo San Marco, but soon the whole peninsular area must have been taken over, all the way to the isthmus which marked its northern limits.

The settlement had a very orderly layout, with a small sanctuary and a necropolis in the southern ex-urban area, a considerable residential quarter further north, the *tophet* towards the northern part of the peninsula, immediately inside the fortifications that protected the city inland. Another burial site lay outside the walls, near the modern village of San Giovanni di Sinis. Analyzing the various areas separately, the chief port

The temple of Antas dedicated to Sardus Pater

of Tharros was located in the northwestern sector of the promontory, in the locality of Porto Vecchio, where underwater exploration has identified two parallel wharves some 20 m in length. Smaller landing places for seasonal use must have existed, however, in other smaller coves of the peninsula.

The fortifications of Tharros, some of the most impressive in the whole Punic world, consisted of an outer curtain wall over 6 m high and about 2.5 m thick, into which a tenaille gate was set, a moat and a second wall, at present preserved up to a height of 3 m. A crosswise retaining wall closed off the moat and a third external wall completed the defensive system. Other remains of fortified walls, with a tower and a postern, have been found on the slopes of the hill of San Giovanni, which has been suggested as the site of the citadel of Tharros.

Traces of Punic private buildings are hard to make out from the Roman *facies* now mostly visible. They are discernible especially in the "framework" type walls, in the dwelling places set around a central courtyard, or in the so-called loggia plan, with a court occupying the whole forefront of the buildings. Also the numerous "tub" cisterns, typically Phoenician in form though mostly Roman in date, seem to have been built originally in the Carthaginian phase of the city.

Numerous temples and sanctuaries served the Phoenico-Punic settlement, as was fitting for a centre of the importance and size of Tharros. The most important among them is the so-called "monolithic temple,"

341

consisting of a great plinth measuring 19 × 8 m, cut out of the rock, with Doric semicolumns carved on the side and rear faces. These were crowned by Doric capitals and a cornice with an Egyptian moulding.
According to the usually suggested reconstruction, the podium held an aedicula entered by a staircase, probably flanked by two sandstone lions at the bottom. A wall measuring 34 × 16 m enclosed the area around the temple.

The "temple" must have been built in the 4th-3rd century B.C. In Roman times, however, the sanctuary was considerably modified: the floor was raised by a cast of concrete, upon which a small temple with Doric columns was built. Dating from this renovation is a large "tub" cistern built into one of the long sides.

Adjoining the monolithic temple is a construction described as a "temple with Semitic-type floor plan", which takes the form of a large open rectangular space with a wall and traces of small chapels or shrines. The religious function of the complex, the visible part of which dates from Roman times, is still very much open to question.

The Punic architectural tradition reappears very distinctly in "Temple K," a small religious building with two columns on the front and a rectangular cella, reached by a flight of five steps. At the rear end of the cella, which was roofed over, was a bench-altar with Egyptian moulding, the same decorative motif returns on the inside walls. The temple is datable to the 2nd-1st century B.C. Outside the residential quarter, at the tip of Capo San Marco, another place of worship has been unearthed which could date back to the 7th-6th century B.C., and therefore be the oldest sanctuary in Tharros. It is a rectangular structure measuring 12 × 7 m, with an entrance set into one of the longer sides, leading to a vestibule. This opens on one side into a chamber with an altar and on the other into a penetralia preceded by a row of six columns. The succession of rooms has been identified, though with some modifications, as the three-cellae plan typical of Phoenician sacred architecture.

Postern in the Punic walls at Tharros
• *p. 393*

Punic covered cistern at Tharros

The *tophet* of Tharros, close by the northern walls of the city, was founded in the 7th century B.C. on the ruins of an existing nuraghic town, the remains of which were largely utilized in adapting the area to its new function; urns with the ashes of the sacrificial victims were in fact frequently placed in the thickness of the remaining walls. The stratigraphy of the Phoenico-Punic phase shows four levels, whose dates run from the 7th to the 2nd century B.C.

The dry moat and counterscarp of the fortifications at Tharros

Late Roman structures in the precinct of the monumental temple of Tharros

The construction work dating from Punic times consists in the laying of a basaltic cobblestone paving in the 4th century B.C., the creation of a system of communication between the *tophet* and the moat, and the building of platforms and low walls for which, as of the 3rd century B.C., the stelae and altars formerly deposited in the consecrated area were widely used.

The sanctuary was thoroughly modified in the early Roman period (2nd century B.C.), during the reconstruction of the whole Su muru mannu hill, on which the *tophet* stands. Traces of subsequent occupation appear there, with building modifications and pottery, up to late Roman times.

Tharros, as mentioned above, was served by two separate necropoli, at the northern and southern outskirts of the city. In the southern necropolis, in the locality of Torre Vecchia, one finds the sequence of an archaic phase (7th-6th century B.C.) with cremation burials in pits and stone cists, and a more recent phase (late 6th-3rd century) with inhumations in pit, shaft or *dromos* tombs. Some pit tombs have gabled lids, while the outside of some *dromos* tombs are decorated with baetyls, free-standing or in threes. The second burial ground of Tharros is not so easy to decipher because most of the tombs have sunk into the sea. But generally speaking they confirm the alternation of types and burial rites found in the southern cemetery.

The only large Carthaginian colony on the northeast coast of Sardinia was Olbia, founded in the 4th century B.C. The city structures from Punic times are little in evidence, because the area has been built up uninterruptedly from Roman times down to the present day. The Punic citadel is thought to correspond to the later medieval village and the most important landing-place to the Roman port area.

The clearest traces of the Punic occupation have been yielded by the necropoli, which grew up west of the town. The several dozen tombs identified are mostly of the shaft type, where the entrance shafts are often covered by large upturned amphorae. This custom is to be found in the burial districts of Abba Ona, Fontana Noa and Joanne Canu, whereas in the Acciarodolzu necropolis the tombs are primarily *dromoi*. The burial grounds of Olbia date to between the 4th and the 2nd centuries B.C.

Spain

Our knowledge of Phoenico-Punic settlements in Spain has greatly improved in recent years, due particularly to the archaeological excavations conducted on the southern coast of the Iberian peninsula. The results of these excavations have not made it possible to completely reconstruct the fabric of the individual towns, but have supplied precious and quite new information about the extent of the earliest Phoenician occupation and its precociously urban character.

Moving from west to east along the coast, one first comes upon the city of Cadiz, just northwest of the Straits of Gilbraltar, which was probably the largest Phoenician center on the peninsula, a typical insular settlement concentrated on the two islands (today joined together) of Gadir and San Pedro. The waters surrounding the site allowed for easy landings, especially on the side facing the mainland. The town was situated at the northern tip of Gadir and served by two separate necropoli, the most important of which, Punta de la Vaca, has yielded numerous chamber tombs dating from no earlier than the 5th century B.C.

Literary tradition ascribes two important sanctuaries to Cadiz, one dedicated to Cronos (Baal Hammon) inside the town-site and one to Heracles at the southern tip of the island. The latter was one of the most celebrated places of worship in antiquity; according to the testimony of Strabo, it contained a pair of bronze columns and two lustral basins. The existence of wooden structures is attested by Silius Italicus.

Detail of semi-columns from the monumental temple at Tharros

Passing through the Pillars of Hercules into the Mediterranean, the Phoenicians founded a group of neighbouring settlements, occupied for the most part between the mid-7th and the end of the 6th century B.C., which formed a functional chain of control and assistance along the metal trade-route. The westernmost of these centres was Guadalhorce, situated a little over a half a mile from the sea near the mouth of the river of the

345

same name, which has yielded remains of dwellings and a large building, interpreted as a warehouse for commercial products. It is possible to date these constructions from the 7th-5th century B.C.

The most important Phoenician site brought to light in this district is Toscanos, on the coast not far from the final stretch of the Vélez river. The most significant yield of the excavations has been the discovery of numerous private dwellings, with the lower walls of stone and the upper of brick. The houses are generally rather small (no more than 6 m long), but their dates, 730-720 B.C., offer important proof of the great antiquity of the Phoenician settlement in this area.

Proto-Aeolic capital from Cadiz 7th century B.C. limestone 28 × 30 cm Cadiz, Museo de Cadiz

The most interesting building discovered in Toscanos is a large warehouse (which confirms the commercial role of the city), measuring 15 × 11 m, with three inside rooms and a cellar. Another public building measuring 11 × 7 m, divided inside into three aisles and equipped with a flight of steps, probably served the same purpose.

The Toscanos settlement was protected to the rear by the fortified outpost of Alarcón, located 450 m from the city. It consists of a stone socle and a wall of unbaked bricks, preserved to a height of about 4 m. Problematic is the dating of a large wall of squared stone blocks that closely encompasses the residential area; in its present state it should date back to Roman times, but a similar construction probably existed in the Phoenician period.

The necropolis associated with the city of Toscanos was discovered in the locality of Finca del Jardín. The more than twenty tombs that have come to light are cists, monolithic sarcophagi or pits, and contain both cremated and inhumed remains. It is possible to date them to between the 6th and the 5th centuries B.C.

Nothing remains at present of the town of Morro de Mezquitilla, 7 km east of Toscanos, except a few ruined walls datable, judging by the pottery, from the 8th century B.C. Particularly outstanding is the evidence afforded by the adjacent necropolis of Trayamar, where several tombs of monumental appearance have been discovered: a *dromos* entrance leads to a burial chamber with gabled roof. Inside the chambers, the richness of the grave goods is documented by several fine pieces of gold-work, and by the fact that the ashes of the dead were placed in alabaster urns.

The site of Chorreras, only half a mile from Morro de Mezquitilla, has yielded traces of another town dating from the 8th-7th century B.C., with large groups of buildings set along wide straight streets. The buildings reveal a painstaking construction technique, with large rough-hewn blocks or squared stones at the corners and near the entrances. Wide empty spaces separate the single buildings inhabited, as in Toscanos, by people who practiced farming and trade.

The settlement of Almuñecar (the ancient Sexi) is so far known almost exclusively from its necropoli. That of Cerro de San Cristóbal has yielded about twenty shaft tombs, round or oval in shape, characterized by the constant presence of alabaster urns containing the ashes of the dead. They date from between the 8th and the 7th centuries B.C.

More recent is the funerary complex of Puente del Noy, whose tombs can mostly be dated from the 5th to the 2nd-1st century B.C. In the main period of use they were pit or *dromos* tombs for inhumation; from the 2nd century B.C., deposits of ashes appear, placed in urns or directly in crevices in the rocky ground.

Entrance to a shaft tomb in the necropolis of Ibiza

While the Spanish sites examined so far reached their apex of prosperity in the first phase of Phoenician expansion, the settlement of Villaricos (the ancient Baria) had its decisive development in the Carthaginian period. The size of this centre is attested by the cemetery, containing about 2,000 tombs whose finds include the most important group of painted ostrich eggs in all the Punic West.

It is interesting to note that the alternation and often the co-existence of the different tomb types and the various funerary rites in this burial ground, has suggested that between the 2nd and the 1st centuries B.C., groups of native inhabitants lived in the city side by side with the Punic majority.

The largest Carthaginian colony in the Spanish area was unquestionably Ibiza, in the Balearic Islands, which according to tradition was founded in 654 B.C. No appreciable evidence remains of the inhabited center, which must have been very large and which Diodorus called the abode of "barbarians of different countries." What does remain, however, testifying to Carthaginian presence inland as well, is evidence of several "rural" complexes, such as those discovered at Cala d'Hort and Puig d'en Valls.

Two sacred areas of unclear structure, but in any case from Punic times, have been unearthed in Ibiza. The first is the rock sanctuary of Cueva d'es Cuyram, whose plan at present cannot be reconstructed, but which has typological similarities to the sacred sites of Grotta Regina and Gozo. The site was occupied from the 5th to the 1st century B.C. and dedicatory inscriptions mention the deities Reshef-Melqarth, Tanit and Gad. Numerous terra-cotta figurines left by visitors provide the most important documentary evidence.

The other sacred area, unearthed in the locality of Isla Plana, is more precisely a pit, which has yielded some thirty terra-cotta votive offerings datable to the 6th-5th century B.C. As can be seen, the architectural evidence from Ibiza is not, in its present state, commensurate with the importance the Carthaginian colony had in antiquity.

The most remarkable source of documentary evidence in Ibiza remains the great necropolis of Puig des Molins, which contained over 3,000 tombs and was occupied from the 6th to the 3rd century B.C.

Lastly, as regards another important Carthaginian colony in Spain, Cartagena, founded by Hasdrubal in 221 B.C., no meaningful archaeological remains are to be found today: only a few stretches of wall can possibly be ascribed to the Punic city, which according to ancient sources was protected by a fortified girdle of walls 4 km in length, with a natural harbor set in a particularly favorable position, sheltered from almost all winds.

Statuary
Sabatino Moscati

The outcome of the Phoenicians' general custom of making small craftwork objects that could easily be transported and traded is that we have very little evidence of statues carved in stone in their world, and what we do have consists of single pieces which do not add up to an organic tradition. Egyptian influence can be seen in the earliest stage, and Greek influence later; this is the general pattern of Phoenician artifacts, which is all the more evident in the categories for which no independent tradition existed.

Funerary statue of bearded figure from Gammarth 3rd century B.C. limestone 115 cm Tunis, Musée du Bardo

A torso of a male figure in a forward-moving posture discovered at Tyre has been dated to the 8th century B.C., but it more probably belongs to the 7th-6th century. The figure is wearing a broad breastplate on his naked chest and a pleated kilt edged at the top and bottom by bands and also divided by a vertical band. The tops of the legs remain, and only one arm, the left one, which hangs down the side and ends in a clenched fist holding a scroll or a "handkerchief." The iconography is typically Egyptian, and has its major counterpart in the East in a torso from Sarepta (Sarafand) and in the West in a statue from the Stagnone di Marsala. The Sarepta statue is very similar to the Tyrian one. It too has a breastplate over a naked chest, and a pleated kilt. Hanging from the breastplate is a crescent moon, holding a solar disc. The kilt is embellished with a uraeus decoration. In this case, too, the tops of the legs survive (more on one side because the statue is broken crosswise), but both arms are missing. The statue has been dated to the 6th-5th century B.C.; although it is difficult to judge, because it might have been a late product, it is probably more correct to attribute it to the 7th-6th century, like the Tyrian torso.

Noteworthy discoveries of works revealing Greek influence but datable to the archaic period (around the 6th century B.C.) have been made in the temple of Eshmun at Sidon. In particular, there is a head and bust in limestone: the wig, with its sinuous lines, is Phoenician in style, but the treatment of the face, with its almond eyes, straight nose and slight smile, fully fits the Greek *kouroi* model.

The temple of Eshmun at Sidon has also yielded a number of statuettes of boys standing, squatting, or playing with an animal or some small object. The style is fully Greek, with a probable Cypriot influence that might explain the point of departure or transit of the artisans or the products. The Phoenician inscriptions on the bases of the statuettes suggest a dating to the 6th-5th century B.C. The decorative head of a lion and a

349

few fragments of limestone statuettes come from Tell Suqas (ancient Shukshu) in Syria. They can be dated to the 6th century B.C. Amrith has yielded other fragments: male heads and busts with lion-skins and close-fitting tunics, in which the Egyptian influence is again evident. Particularly interesting is the use of a kilt similar to the one on the Tyre and Sarepta torsos. However, the Egyptian features are handled in a way that brings us down to the 4th-3rd century.

There is the same shortage of statuary in the West as in the East, and the documentation is again sporadic. From Carthage, we have a woman's head in stone: its features and hairstyle recall the Egyptianizing terracotta protomes. This is an example of the transposition of iconographies from one artisan category to another that can be defined in terms of the "image culture" and definitely reflects a sophisticated level of work. Also from Carthage, we have a few small female heads in stone bearing traces of paint. Like the previous case, they can be dated around the 6th century. There is also a baetyl, a sacred stone, freestanding and about one and a half metres high, found at Mogador, which is very interesting as the iconographic precedent of the relief stelae.

Votive statuette of youth with inscription from the Temple of Eshmun at Sidon 4th century B.C. marble, 35 cm Beirut, National Museum
• *p. 394*

Crouching lion from Byblos 6th-4th century B.C., basalt 42 × 68 cm Paris, Musée du Louvre
• *p. 395*

All the works we have discussed so far belong to the early period. A second stage, during the Hellenistic era, shows a predominating Greek influence, so that the Phoenician work seems to be no more than a provincial variant. Carthage has given us a veiled female figure on a throne, flanked by sphinxes, known as the "great lady of Carthage" and dating from the 3rd-2nd century. Again from Carthage are two male figures in short tunics (preserved from the neck to the knees) and a few funerary statues representing the deceased in an upright position. From Korba, between Tunis and Kelibia, come two fragmentary statues: the left hand holds a perfume casket to the chest.

Leptis Magna has given us two male torsos wearing short tunics clasped at the waist by a broad belt: the posture of the figures is Greek, but the right arm folded across the chest and the clothing take us back to the East; they should be dated as late as the 2nd-1st century B.C. Also from Leptis Magna are two male heads, one beardless, the other wearing a beard, with the hair stylized into a cap and crowned by a *kalathos*: in this case, too, the Greek models have been considerably reworked in provincial style; these two heads can also be dated to the 2nd-1st century.

From Sabratha, we have a number of torsos and fragments of sculpture, more or less contemporary with the pieces from Leptis Magna. They are in local sandstone, plastered and painted, and are life-size. Outstanding is a torso with the arms stretched along the sides and exaggeratedly large hands: the *peplos* gathered at the waist immediately recalls the Sicilian terracottas of similar style. In fact, apar,t from Greek inspiration and its provincial reworking, the influence of Sicily is very probable in this production.

Of the islands near Carthage, Malta has given us the fragment of a male statuette found at Tas Silg. It represents an upright figure wearing a straight, smooth garment with short sleeves and a triangular neckline at the back. The arms, only partly preserved, were probably stretched forward. The statuette is similar to Cypriot works depicting the standing worshipper, and like them, must be from the 6th-5th century B.C.

In Sicily, the male torso found in the Stagnone di Marsala is interesting because it immediately recalls the example from Tyre and also has links to the stelae. The bust and two arms of a person moving forward survive: the right arm (not the left, as in the Tyrian torso) is stretched down along the side, the hand clenching a scroll or "handkerchief"; the left hand is folded across the chest. The upper part of the body is apparently totally naked (while the torso from Tyre is wearing a breastplate), and the lower part is covered by an Egyptian-type kilt, seemingly similar to the Tyrian one. This outstanding work, which can probably be dated to the 6th century B.C., reflects Egyptian-inspired eastern models in the West.

Other noteworthy pieces of Phoenician statuary have been found in Sicily. Of special interest is an enthroned female figure, possibly from Pizzo Cannita, seriously damaged on the upper part and sides, where the throne was flanked by two sphinxes. The iconography is widely documented in the Phoenician world, although the fine folds of the dress suggest Ionian influence. Equally outstanding is a group from Alesa representing a lion and a bull in combat. The head and front part of the bull are well preserved. In this case, too, the iconography is Phoenician, but the treatment is unusual, reflecting a local taste imbued with Greek culture. Both works are datable to around the 6th century B.C.

Sardinia has yielded notable examples of Punic statuary, including an outstanding representation of a female divinity found at Monte Sirai. The body is dealt with very summarily: there is only a suggestion of the breasts and sex, the right arm is folded at the side and the left one reaches forward toward the pudenda. The head, on the other hand, is carefully modelled: the full cheeks and chin reveal a fine sense of

Female statue from Monte Sirai 7th century B.C. sandstone 40 × 20 cm Cagliari, Museo Archeologico Nazionale • p. 396

mass, the arched eyebrows converge over the protruding nose and include deep eye sockets, the mouth is heavy and well-cut. The hair on the low, receding forehead forms a cap and falls in stylized parallel lines behind the large ears, also stylized into a double circle, below which it becomes two big curls that develop in parallel lines.

Some kind of model for this exceptional work has been sought in the East, ranging from a statue from Tell Halaf to a relief work of Zinjirli. More recently, echoes in the Etruscan world have been pointed out: from the Vulci centaur to various pottery pieces. If this is correct, the statue would reflect orientalizing tendencies and its dating would be around the 6th or 5th century B.C., and not the 7th, as has been suggested.

Other Sardinian examples are later and more questionable. A bust in grey granite minus head and arms and bearing Egyptianizing reliefs on the front has been found in Cagliari, but in all probability it was imported from Egypt. Definitely of local origin, on the other hand, are the six statues found in various sites representing the obese, bearded figure conventionally called Bes. However, connections with works from the age of the Roman Empire produced elsewhere suggest that these statues date from that period and are the outcome of the diffusion throughout Sardinia of Egyptian-inspired cults of Isis.

Connected with these same cults, we have a sphinx in pink granite found in

Statue of enthroned deity between two sphinxes from Pizzo Cannita 6th century B.C. tufa, 77 cm Palermo, Museo Archeologico Nazionale

the Cagliari Botanical Gardens alongside fragments of similar works. The crouching figure has a face with soft features, a mane stylized in curved parallel lines, breasts, short back legs, and the tail curled to the left. In this case, too, an origin in the Hellenistic era was presumed, but now, by analogy with the Bes statue, it seems we have to go down to Roman times.

The lions discovered at Tharros and Sulcis, on the other hand, are undoubtedly Phoenician. The two Sulcis lions, found in 1983, are nearly life-size: they stand on bases with Egyptian mouldings and are framed at the top by a kind of straight architrave that continues behind with a skaped pilaster, both of these elements being devices for anchoring the work to a city gate. The lions are crouching, their front paws forward and their tails curled elegantly in a spiral over their bodies. The manes are fashioned into a series of triangular curls that end in volutes on their flanks.

There is an obvious connection here with the lions which were stationed beside city gates and palaces in the Near East. However, the slimmer bod-

*Statue of Bes
found at Bithia
2nd century B.C.
sandstone
155 × 75 cm
Cagliari, Museo
Archeologico
Nazionale*

*Crouching sphinx
from Cagliari
2nd century B.C.
pink granite
70 × 90 cm
Cagliari, Museo
Archeologico
Nazionale*

ies and the treatment of the manes suggest the influence of Ionian animal statuary. As for their date, the initial suggestion of the 6th-5th century should probably be lowered to the 4th, the time of walled cities. The same applies to the two Tharros lions (one of which, however, survives only in a very fragmentary state).

A full-relief baetyl similar to the Mogador example but much smaller, only 50 cm, has been found at Monte Sirai. It is a truncated pyramid and has a projecting foot that fits into a square base with a central recess. It therefore precisely resembles the model developed in relief stelae.

A few small examples of figures and heads could be added to the repertoire of Sardinian statues found at Antas, but it seems certain that they were imported from Greece.

Iberia does not offer much in the way of Punic statuary. A female divinity

353

enthroned between two sphinxes, 18 cm high and carved in alabaster, has been found near Galera. The head of the goddess is covered by a three-piece lace veil held on the forehead by a band and falling over the shoulders and back. Her dress is a closely pleated ankle-length tunic; the feet are bare. She is holding a large bowl in her arms, between the heads of the two sphinxes. The pierced breasts, resting on the rim of the receptacle, are connected to a hole in the top of the head, indicating that this is a representation of the goddess of fertility.

Its elegance and refined workmanship, with the full, soft modelling of the figures, suggest an imported work, probably from the East, where the closest echoes are to be found in the carved ivories of the so-called Syrian group. But another enthroned divinity discovered near Granada in 1971, is of typically Punic-Phoenician type: measuring one and a half metres in height, the goddess is wearing richly decorated garments, and bears traces of pigment.

Pair of crouching lions from Sulcis 6th-5th century B.C., limestone 156 × 170 cm S. Antioco Museo Comunale

Statuette of enthroned goddes between two sphinxes from Granada 7th century B.C. alabaster 18.5 × 12 cm Madrid, Museo Arqueológico Nacional

Statue of Bes found at Cagliari 2nd century B.C. sandstone, 85 × 48 cm Cagliari Museo Archeologico Nazionale

Sarcophagi
Sabatino Moscati

Sarcophagus of Tabnith king of Sidon 6th-5th century B.C., basalt Istanbul Archaeological Museum

The Phoenician stone sarcophagi are a genre of Egyptian origin, not only in their inspiration but often also in the models used. However, at a certain moment during their history, between the 5th and the 4th centuries B.C., Greek influence intervened, leaving the typology intact but radically altering the iconography.

The oldest and most famous Phoenician sarcophagus, that of King Ahiram (as its inscription states) belongs to the Syro-Palestinian area. The work dates back to the 13th-12th century B.C., while there is some doubt as to whether the inscription is contemporary or later. The sarcophagus is shaped like a box supported by crouching lions. On the long sides are depicted processions: one shows the sovereign (or a god) on a throne flanked by sphinxes before a table spread for a banquet towards which seven offerers and worshippers proceed. On the other side, there are eight offerers and worshippers. On the shorter sides are portrayals of women beating their breasts or tearing their hair. On the lid lie two outstretched lions flanked by two figures bearing a lotus flower. The main scene on the sarcophagus, the offering made to the enthroned sovereign (or god), is directly linked with an iconography from the Syro-Palestinian tradition, which reappears, for example, in a strikingly similar form on a Megiddo ivory. This sarcophagus is a unique case since no others have appeared prior to the 6th-5th century: from this period we have two black basalt coffins dedicated to the Sidonian kings Tabnith and Eshmunazar. The dedications are documented by inscriptions, but that does not mean that the sarcophagi were made locally: on the contrary, investigation suggests that they were brought from Egypt and reutilized in Sidon.

The Tabnith sarcophagus has the form of a large mummy roughly shaped to the lines of the body: the head, or rather, the funerary mask covering it, is recessed into the shoulders: it is very large, surrounded by a broad band of hair and the conventional beard. The head of Eshmunazar sarcophagus is similar to that of Tabnith. A necklace with several strands ends at the sides in falcons' heads, according to a design already present on the gold breastplates of the oldest tombs in Byblos. It should be noted that a third sarcophagus was found along with these two: containing a woman's body, it was unfinished and not decorated, maybe on purpose.

The Greek-inspired stage of sarcophagus production developed with numerous examples between the 5th and 4th centuries B.C. There are a few dozen pieces, most of them from Sidon. The shape of the body is only hinted at or is not there at all, while the head is handled in a completely Greek way: see particularly the male heads with thick hair and stylized curly beards. In this case, too, some of the sarcophagi may have been imported, but the stone often seems local, and the inscriptions in Phoenician characters do not suggest reutilization, as had been the practice in earlier times.

The production of sarcophagi at Carthage was remarkable. One group comes from the S.te Monique necropolis and can be dated to the 4th-3rd century B.C. Outstanding in this group is a small example which must actually have been a funerary urn. On the front, in low relief, we see a representation of a Carthaginian *rab*, Baalshillek. The man, wearing a long beard and an ample garment that falls in folds to his feet, is holding a pyxis or ciborium to his chest with his left hand, while his right hand is raised in the customary sign of benediction. All the connotations of this figure are Phoenician: there is no trace of Greek influence yet.

Sarcophagus of Eshmunazar king of Sidon 6th-5th century B.C., basalt 110 × 225 cm Paris, Musée du Louvre

The same cannot be said of two other sarcophagi found in the same burial ground. They depict two bearded priests with long, pleated robes, bearing cups: one has a covered head and a stola hangs from his left shoulder, like the one that reappears in Sardinian stelae. There is no doubt that Greek influence predominates in these figures.

This also applies to another figure which is however interesting because it also retains Egyptian features. The statue represents a woman wearing a tunic and wrapped in two large overlapping wings, a motif obviously taken from the Egyptian iconography of Isis and Nephthys. The head is covered by a scarf on which the head of a falcon emerges, also an Egyptian design. The right arm hangs by the side of the body and the hand carries an incense-burner in the shape of a dove. The left arm is bent forward and the hand carries a cup. There are another nine sarcophagi in the S.te Monique group and all confirm the predominance of Greek influence, visible already in the actual shape of the sarcophagi, with double-sloping lids and *acroteria*, unlike their flat-topped predecessors from Phoenicia.

Tunisian excavations at Kerkouane have revealed the existence of wooden sarcophagi alongside stone ones. There is a sarcophagus from the 4th-3rd century B.C. with an anthropoid lid depicting a woman wearing a short-sleeved tunic and a wide cloak or veil. The hair on the head is arranged in curls, with a central parting and a tiara on top. There are numerous traces of paint.

Sarcophagi made with materials other than stone are obviously more perishable and hence less well preserved, but none the less interesting for purposes of comparison. In Malta, three terra-cotta sarcophagi have been

*Sarcophagus
of Ahiram
king of Byblos
13th-12th
century B.C.
limestone
152 × 305 cm
Beirut, National
Museum*

*In foreground:
two sarcophagi
one in Greek
style from Sidon
the second
in Egyptian style
from inland
Lebanon
4th century B.C.
Istanbul
Archaeological
Museum*

found. While one of them repeats the shape of the wooden chests on high feet and reflects modest local craftsmanship, the other two are anthropoid in form and therefore linked to the Phoenician models. The strong Rhodian-Ionian stamp of one of the two reflects the convergence of diverse influences in Phoenician civilization on the island.

Two important stone sarcophagi have been found in Sicily at Cannita, near Soluntum. The first has a female figure on the lid, with the head in full relief, framed by hair that falls at the sides to ear-level. The face is broad,

357

the chin and mouth accentuated. The body, wrapped in an ample pleated garment from which the feet on high soles emerge, displays prominent breasts, the right arm extended along the side, and the left arm slightly bent to carry an unidentified object. Like the other, this work dates back to the 6th-5th century B.C. and reveals Ionian influence in the hair and clothing, while the face has local connotations.

The second sarcophagus displays a perfectly smooth body, but it must be clothed since the feet emerge. The head, that of a woman, is typically Greek, with long wavy hair falling over the chest in broad bands. The fleshy lips and chin, however, suggest a certain provincial conno-tation. For this reason, even though the close connection with Phoenician models is obvious, the sarcophagus was probably not imported, but rather made locally.

While no sarcophagi have as yet come to light in Sardinia, we do have evidence in Iberia, where one example from the Punta de la Vaca necropolis at Cadiz has long been known. The typology is decidedly Greek, as we see from the male head with abundant curly hair and a thick, equal-ly curly beard. On the body, the right arm is stretched out and the left arm folded across the chest, while the feet project. Here, too, the question has arisen as to whether this is an imported work or a locally made example. Whatever the case, a second sarcophagus has recently been discovered in Iberia: it is the female type, and looks more archaic, so there seems to be no doubt about its local origin.

Sarcophagi with lids bearing male and female figures from Carthage 4th-3th century B.C. painted marble 72 × 193 cm Carthage, Musée de Carthage

Detail of male sarcophagus from Cadiz 5th century B.C. alabaster 91 × 235 cm Cadiz, Museo de Cadiz

358

*Female sarcophagus
discovered
near Amrith
4th century B.C.
roseate marble
55 × 210 cm
Paris, Musée
du Louvre
• p. 397*

*Detail of female
sarcophagus
from Cadiz
5th-4th century
B.C., alabaster
83 × 218 cm
Cadiz, Museo
de Cadiz
• p. 398*

*Detail of female
sarcophagus
from Sidon
4th century B.C.
marble
68 × 205 cm
Paris, Musée
du Louvre*

Stone Reliefs
Sabatino Moscati

There were two major types of stone carving in the Phoenician world: stelae and sarcophagi. Outside these categories relief work on stone appears only infrequently and sporadically. The typical character of the area and its local politics precluded the great development of the historical relief that took place in Egypt and Mesopotamia.

We may recall first a small alabaster panel from Aradus, probably from the 7th-6th century B.C., which depicts a large-winged sphinx crouching on a low podium set in a rectangular frame. The sphinx has the double Egyptian tiara, while the podium displays the Egyptian-style moulding and torus. Above the frame is a chequered strip, and above that, several rows of palmettes, a decorative motif that was to enjoy wide popularity.

The same palmette decoration in several rows above a frame can be seen in a relief in the Geneva museum representing two rampant griffins on either side of a sacred plant, stylized to include palmettes. The image is framed above and below by a fishbone pattern frieze.

The same central scene appears in another relief from Aradus, similar in other respects to the first one discussed. Evidently there existed repeated prototypes. Palmettes also appear in a vertical strip in a relief from Adlun, near Tyre. All that survives of the subject is the head of a sphinx belonging to the throne of a god, of whom one knee and one hand remain. The hand is supporting a stele in front of an incense burner.

Parallel to the iconography of the stelae — which we will discuss later — is a relief from Fi, south of Tripoli, depicting an enthroned female figure seen in profile. The goddess is crowned with a sun disc over Hathor's horns and wears a long garment on which she is resting one hand, while the other reaches out to a person standing in front of her, arms outstretched in prayer. The high-backed throne is flanked by two winged sphinxes and accompanied by a stool on which the goddess rests her feet. Two small animals walking towards each other are depicted below the scene.

In Carthage, stone reliefs which do not fall into the other monumental categories are even scarcer. One example is a large, grey-granite pebble on which a heavily stylized human face is engraved. Interpreting this as a baetyl, or sacred pillar, does not concur with what we know of the baetyls from stelae. In reality this is an item closer to folk art, which may be considered Punic on the basis of a few signs of the alphabet engraved on the

Fragment of a panel featuring a crouching winged sphinx from Aradus 6th-5th century B.C. alabaster, 61 cm Paris, Musée du Louvre
• p. 399

Incense burner with winged sphinx bearing dish from Cyprus 4th century B.C. painted limestone, 16 cm Paris, Musée du Louvre

back. Any further classification or dating is a matter of conjecture.

In Malta, stone relief work is documented by a small monument with an aedicula and a stylized human figure on the front. The aedicula is framed by two rectangular pillars bearing an architrave with Egyptian moulding and a winged sun disc in the center. Above the architrave are three overlapping horizontal strips, convex in section. This is obviously a model for a sacellum, but it is also important because it gives us a front view of a stele in Malta, which is quite devoid of stelae. That the origin of this monumental class can be traced to the sacellum is thus clearly documented.

In Sicily, Motya has yielded a relief depicting a fight between a bull and two lions. It must have been part of the decoration of a door. The heraldic layout of the composition is striking, with the two lions flanking the mauled bull. Also found at Motya, but smaller in size, are two sphinxes carved in relief on blocks of sandstone. The animals are in a crouching position and are depicted from the side, so that only one outstretched wing of each is seen, whereas the head is seen in a three-quarter profile, which is unusual. The work can be dated to around the 5th century B.C.

Still leaving aside the stelae, in Sardinia Tharros stands out for its production of relief work. First we have the so-called "horned altars," moulded monuments with four projections at the corners, possibly reproductions of capitals. Also typical of Tharros are stone cippi made up of three pillars projecting from the same base. The central and tallest pillar bears the sym-

Three-sided stele with figures surmounted by winged disc from Aradus 1st century B.C. stone, 60 cm Paris, Musée du Louvre

Head of sphinx from Sidon 4th century B.C. stone, 40 cm Paris, Musée du Louvre

bol of the sun and crescent moon on the front, and is surmounted by a pyramidal roof. The side pillars end in listels and an Egyptian moulding with a hollow suggesting that the object may have been used to contain incense or libations. These monuments are a freestanding version of the stelae with three baetyls.

Again from Tharros, we have two sandstone cippi, with relief scenes all around. One of them shows four dancing figures: three female nudes seen from the back, and one kilted man seen from the front. At the top of the cippus, as the focal point for the dance, there is a protruding ox-head. Considering the realistic dancing and the way the nude figures are handled, we can conclude that this work is from the Late Hellenistic period.

The other cippus, conical in shape, bears a relief scene of a man killing a winged monster with a spear. It was first interpreted as a Punic transposition of the myth of Bellerophon killing the Chimaera; later, with no real foundation, it was thought to represent the god Sid with a griffin. This very unusual work for the Punic environment must also date from the Late Hellenistic age. Still in Sardinia, an outstanding high-relief work has been discovered at Sulcis on the wall of a tomb. It depicts an advancing figure, wearing only a kilt, his left arm folded over his bare chest and the right arm hanging by his side. The design, which also exists in a rougher, less well-preserved example at Monte Sirai, is an obvious parallel of the statues in the round of Tyre and the Stagnone di Marsala.

Typical of Monte Sirai are two very schematized heads carved in relief on tomb walls. The outline is triangular, with a long, straight nose, slit eyes, and obliquely cut mouth. Their presence on tombs suggests an apotropaic func-

Phallic cippus showing ritual dance, from Tharros
5th century B.C.
sandstone, 41 cm
Cagliari, Museo Archeologico Nazionale

Fragment of a group with bull fighting a lion from Alesa
6th-5th century B.C., stone
66 × 48 cm
Palermo, Museo Archeologico Regionale

tion, similar to that of the earthenware masks placed inside the tombs to ward off evil. Another interesting relief work on a tomb from Monte Sirai displays a reversed version of the "sign of Tanit." We can assume that the local craftsman received the "cartoon" (probably a wooden model) and reproduced it without grasping its full significance. The last example from Sardinia is an isolated case: a voluted capital with a human head in the centre, found at Nora. The type of capital is widely attested in the Phoenician East, but the head is unknown there. Its inclusion in this case suggests a late period, under classical influences.

Since Iberia offers no stone evidence outside the traditional categories (stelae and sarcophagi, and even these are rare), this chapter may be concluded, and its salient point summarized as the sporadic, occasional nature of Phoenician stone relief work as compared with the organic development of other genres.

Egyptianizing statue found incomplete in a tomb at Sulcis now restored 6th century B.C. trachytic tufa 200 cm Cagliari, Museo Archeologico Nazionale

Cippus featuring three pilasters with solar disc and crescent moon from Tharros 5th century B.C. sandstone 130 × 100 cm Cagliari, Museo Archeologico Nazionale

Stelae
Sabatino Moscati

The most widespread products of craftsmanship in the Phoenician West are the stelae, long ago discovered in large quantites at Carthage and also found in equal numbers in recent years in Sicily and Sardinia. There is no doubt that this genre had its roots in Phoenicia, but there is equally no doubt that stele production in the West far surpassed production in the East, in both quantity and quality.

Among the examples found in Phoenicia, we should recall first a stele from Amrith depicting a man riding on a lion. The figure wears Egyptian headgear and an Egyptian kilt, and is brandishing a club in his raised right hand, while his left arm holds a lion cub. The lion he rides is proceeding toward a rocky mountain. The stele is rounded at the top and the crown bears a winged sun disc, below which are another disc and a crescent moon. The work can be dated between the 9th and 6th centuries B.C.

The stele of Yehawmilk from Byblos is from the later Persian age, as its inscription tells us. With the same sort of upper part as the Amrith stele, this one depicts a king standing and offering a cup to an enthroned goddess. The king is wearing the low, cylindrical headgear typical of the Persian period. His beard and hair are long, and he is dressed in full-length robe with a large shawl over it. The goddess is seated on a cubical throne with a low back, her feet resting on a stool. She wears a long, tight dress and on her head is the Egyptian disc with two horns. In one hand, she holds a long scepter shaped like a papyrus stem, while the other hand is raised in blessing.

The divine iconography of the Yehawmilk stele is repeated in a number of fragments from other sites. One from Tir Dibba depicts a female bust with the sun disc and horns on her head, a uraeus on her forehead, hair falling in locks, papyrus stem in her hand. Her face is turned to the right, while another fragment from the same place is exactly the same except that the face is turned to the left. A variant of this iconography can be seen in a fragment of a relief with a female figure wearing a long garment and turned to the left, wearing no symbols on her head but carrying a lotus flower. Finally, from Beirut comes another Persian-period relief, with a female figure seated on a high-backed throne flanked by lions: she wears a small cylindrical tiara and is holding a lotus flower and a papyrus.

The most direct antecedents of the Punic stelae of the West are a monument

Stele featuring male figure found in Syria 4th-3rd century B.C. limestone 52 × 20 cm Paris, Musée du Louvre

right
Stele of Yehawmilk
from Byblos
5th century B.C.
limestone, 130 × 56 cm
Paris, Musée du Louvre
• p. 400

Fragment of stele
with female figure
and winged disc
from Tyre
2nd century B.C.
limestone
49 × 22 cm
Paris, Musée
du Louvre

from Sidon and another from Burg esh-Shemali. The Sidon aedicula stands on a base with Egyptian moulding and is framed between two pillars decorated with palmettes. Above it is an Egyptian moulding with a large winged sun disc, and above that a uraeus frieze in relief. Inside the aedicula are two animals seen from the front, sphinxes probably, that once bore a throne. The Burg esh-Shemali aedicula stands on a high base, and inside it are two baetyls surmounted by an architrave with an Egyptian moulding. In the centre of this is the disc with crescent surmounted by a uraeus frieze. Both stelae must date before the advent of Greek influence.

A particularly interesting case is a stele from Akhziv depicting an aedicula with several frames one inside the other, in the centre of which is an image very similar to the so-called "bottle idol" so common in the West.

Finally, documentation on stelae in the East has recently improved with the discoveries made by a German mission on the site of ancient Paphos, in Cyprus. According to preliminary information, finds include the multiple receding frames and male figures in profile, with conical headgear and long, open robes, bearing a floral element.

Carthage has yielded thousands of stelae, linked as everywhere in the West with the *tophet*, the sacred place where sacrificed children were buried. Two main stages can be distinguished in their production. The first, around the 7th-6th century B.C., consists both of cippi (rectangular in section and plain or else shaped into a throne at the top) and of true stelae (rectangular in section, flat-topped and with one decorated side predominating over the others). The second stage, from the 5th to the 2nd century B.C., consists exclusively of stelae, this time with triangular tops.

The articles of worship depicted in the niches in the centre of the stelae from the first period are mostly baetyls or pillars, single, double, triple or quintuple, sometimes surmounted by the sun disc with the crescent moon. There are also lozenges and "bottle idols," so-called on account of their shape. These are the geometrical patterns. As for human representations, we have the naked figure with arms by the sides placed between two baetyls or on an altar; rarer are the passant male figure and the woman with hands on her breast.

The beginning of the 5th century B.C. marks the appearance, still on flat-topped stelae, of the most famous symbol of the Punic world, the "sign of Tanit." Its origin has been much discussed. The most reliable hypothesis is that it represents a schematized version of a female figure, although its subsequent development was towards both male and female figures. Then, with the advent of triangular-topped stelae, the repertoire of figures was greatly enriched, while the technique became simple engraving. Among the iconographies of the new stage, which have sometimes a primary and sometimes a secondary function in a figurative field that tends toward increasing complexity, are the hand raised in prayer, the Aeolian capital, the palm-tree. The human images are the sacrificing priest and the worshipping devotee.

At the same time, however, Greek inspired motifs began to appear: the Ionic or Doric column, the caduceus, the dolphin, birds and flowers. A taste for symbols and allusions predominates in these designs, which tend to be in a coded language with a typically religious purpose combined with a decorative function, receptive and not selective towards every possible influence.

The phenomenon intensified at the end of this second stage, between the 3rd and the 2nd centuries B.C. Among the human figures, we have the

Votive stele featuring priest and child, found at Carthage 4th century B.C. stone, approx. 118 × 15 cm Tunis, Musée du Bardo
• *p. 433*

Stele featuring male figure and winged disc from Umm el-Amed 3rd-2nd century B.C., marble 85 × 22 cm Paris, Musée du Louvre
• *p. 433*

offerer and the so-called "temple boy," a youth sitting on his left leg with his right leg folded under him. At the same time, animal iconography flourished (bulls, rams, doves, cocks, swans, fish, elephants, rabbits, horses, panthers and others), together with images of liturgical articles (offertory tablets, caskets vases, knives, etc.), and also geometrical patterns (the fishbone, rings, ovules, lattice-work, etc.). In this veritable outbreak of minor iconographies, which intermingle and throng the decorated space, there is a real *horror vacui*, along with an evident desire to be complete and representative, omitting none of the symbols of faith and, now, also of everyday life.

The stelae are not always connected with the *tophet*. In the last period of Carthage, funerary stelae became widespread independently of infant sacrifice. In the 4th century B.C., and even more between the 3rd and the 2nd, the iconography of these stelae portrays the deceased standing frontally, with an arm raised in salute and prayer. The style is simple and homogeneous, hardly touched by Hellenistic influences.

Still in Africa, but away from Carthage, an important centre of stele production was Hadrumetum (Sousse). Its stelae date back to the 6th century B.C. and bear motifs similar to those from Carthage, with one or two differences: grooved columns framing the baetyls, double baetyl triads, bottles with bell-shaped bottoms. Certain iconographies typical of Carthage are missing here: the lozenge, the hand, the palm-tree. But the main features of Hadrumetum are a number of autonomous stelae directly derived from Phoenician models. One of these monuments shows a worshipper before an enthroned god. The god wears a tall conical tiara and a full-length robe, the high-backed throne is flanked by winged sphinxes. The whole takes us back to Phoenician reliefs without any evidence of mediation by Carthage. The same can be said of two similar stelae, both depicting a woman enveloped in a long garment and seated on a stool: she holds a sphere in her hands which she proffers toward an incense burner.

A few hundred stelae have been found at Cirta (Constantine), all rather late since none of them go further back than the 3rd century B.C. Many of them bear the sign of Tanit, in relief in the centre of the field, frequently flanked by the caduceus and surmounted by astral symbols. Below is a frame containing the inscription. Production then had local ramifications: a very humanized sign of Tanit holding the caduceus or a branch; various kinds of arms, such as helmets, often stylized; geometrical and astral figures, like the disc, the upturned crescent moon, and stars; animal figures, such as dolphins, rams, bulls and horses; while human figures are very uncommon.

Other groups date from much later, to the Roman period, including the Dougga stelae. Some of the latter, of the 2nd-1st century B.C., still display

traditional Punic motifs, like the sign of Tanit, in an altered form, however: the disc is detached from the dividing line, or replaced by the upturned crescent moon, or again, it takes on a human face while the arms become threadlike and long.

View across the tophet *at Carthage*

From the peak of the Roman period we have the stelae from Ghorfa, dated to the 2nd century B.C. The dedicator is depicted in the lower part, in a temple, while the upper section displays a series of divine figures arranged in an ascending order, converging towards the top. Contemporary with these are the Maktar stelae, which show the dedicator at the centre, draped in a toga or wearing a cuirass and a chlamys, accompanied by diverse symbols, such as the pine-cone and the peacock, fish and birds, or a human-headed sun disc. With these examples, however, we have left the realm of Punic art, since the stelae retain only their elementary typology.

A true revelation for the history of Phoenician stelae are the discoveries made at Motya in Sicily. Over a thousand pieces have been brought to light, and they are rich in new, characteristic features that often have no parallel in Carthage, but can rather be traced back to the Phoenician homeland. In other words, they are the outcome of the independent innovations or developments of a high-level craftsmanship. In their technique, the Motya stelae show an autonomous use of paint, which was applied elsewhere only to complete the relief. As for typology, there are some double stelae, like the one representing two Egyptianizing figures

Carthage tophet *stele with "sign of Tanit" and baetyl*

*Votive stele with
column and
pomegranate
from Carthage
2nd century B.C.
limestone
42 × 26 cm
Paris
Bibliothèque
Nationale*

*Votive stele
showing figure
in profile and
large open hand
from Carthage
2nd century B.C.
limestone
33 × 14 cm
Paris
Bibliothèque
Nationale*

*Votive stele from
Carthage
with caduceus
between open
hands 3rd-2nd
century B.C.
limestone
58 × 18 cm
Carthage, Musée
de Carthage*

*Votive stele with
"sign of Tanit"
and rabbit, from
Carthage
2nd century B.C.
limestone
31 × 11 cm
Paris, Musée
du Louvre*

*Stele from
Ghorfa
featuring figure
in small temple
and symbols
2nd century B.C.
limestone
138 × 35 cm
Paris, Musée
du Louvre*

Double votive stele with male figures facing each other from Motya 6th century B.C. limestone 39 × 38 cm Motya, Museo Whitaker

walking towards each other. But the major innovations are obviously in iconography.

Compared with Carthage, there is a prevalence of human figures. Some of these are characteristic: the frontal female figure with hair falling to the chest in locks, arms folded under the breasts and wearing a long, smooth, flared garment from which the feet emerge; the male figure, also seen from the front, naked and advancing, decidedly Egyptian in feeling; and the profile male figure, with a tall, pointed headdress, arms outstretched, wearing a robe that falls on the back leg. These iconographies are not found at Carthage (the only doubt concerns the woman), and they are handled with an elegance and refinement unknown elsewhere. There are also variations, as in the case of the female figure with her arm raised in benediction.

Motya has also yielded a few examples of the type of female figure with a disc on her breast, a design practically unknown in Carthage but which was to become predominant at Sulcis in Sardinia. At Motya, the figure is found not only in the frontal position, as elsewhere, but in profile as well.

Among the geometrical designs are the baetyl and the bottle idol, frequently elegant and refined. We do not find the sign of Tanit, but that is simply because stele production in Motya was broken off when the Greeks invaded Sicily in the early 4th century B.C., just when the new iconography was spreading. One series of designs can be described as an intermediate stage

Votive stele with open hand "sign of Tanit", caduceus and ram above from Carthage 2nd century B.C. limestone 26.5 × 15 cm Paris, Bibliothèque Nationale
• p. 434

370

*Stele featuring female figure
with arms across the breast
from Motya
6th-5th century B.C.
limestone, 45 × 30 cm
Motya, Museo Whitaker*

*Stele with two heads
from Selinus
4th century B.C.
limestone, 25 × 20 cm
Palermo, Museo
Archeologico Regionale*

*Votive stele with stylized
female figure
from Motya
6th-5th century B.C.
limestone, 50 × 27 cm
Motya, Museo Whitaker*

*Votive stele with walking figure
from Motya
6th-5th century B.C.
limestone, 30 × 27 cm
Motya, Museo Whitaker*

*Votive stele with "bottle idol"
from Motya
6th-5th century B.C.
limestone, 36 × 25 cm
Motya, Museo Whitaker*

*Votive stele with baetyl
from Motya
6th-5th century B.C.
limestone, 47.5 × 24 cm
Motya, Museo Whitaker*

between the human and the geometrical, for two reasons: first, the human figure is simplified and reduced to essentials, and secondly, the geometrical figure is integrated with details that "humanize" it. The first phenomenon is particularly common, as we see from certain human figures that are only outlined. In these cases the stelae may be unfinished works, roughly sketched in while waiting for further details to be decided by the clients. But it is equally possible that the craftsmen were intentionally working toward abstract forms. It may be added (and this is another question) that the level of the workshops varied, some being extremely refined, others somewhat rudimentary.

Located on the coast south of Motya, Lilybaeum (now Marsala) was a refuge for the island's inhabitants when the Greeks sailed in to conquer Sicily in 397 B.C. The craft of stele-making continued here with an evolution that was primarily the result of the gradual affirmation of Greek influence, missing in Motya. Some of the older examples, from between the 4th and the 3rd centuries B.C., show relief scenes of worship and libation typical of the Hellenistic repertoire, although their composition also includes typical Punic motifs like the sign of Tanith and the caduceus.

Votive stele with "bottle idol" from Nora 6th-4th century B.C. sandstone 84.3 × 39.2 cm Cagliari, Museo Archeologico Nazionale

The other stelae, from between the 2nd and 1st centuries B.C., are of the funerary type and use abundant stucco and various tints of watercolour to depict the funeral banquet of the deceased, now a hero, in a simple or elaborate niche framed by Tuscan columns which support a pediment with tympanum. One special case, important on account of the parallel we shall see with the Selinus stelae, is an anthropomorphic example, in which the roughly stylized body fits the shape of the stele. This is a funerary monument, as we see from the surviving traces of an arm raised in salute. All the stelae made at Lilybaeum are of Carthaginian and not Graeco-Sicilian inspiration; any new features derive from independent local development.

A very important group of stelae from Selinus has quite original characteristics. They are pieces with the unfinished body ending at the top with one or two human heads (one male, the other female). The heads have elements of the Greek style, but are much more a folk development, strongly stylized, with almost triangular faces and the basic features (eyes, mouth, nose) marked by simple deep cuts. Since it is now certain that the Carthaginians were at Selinus at the time when these stelae were probably made (4th century B.C.), the prevalent theory is that they are Punic, or Punicized at a folk level. But we cannot exclude the possibility that the popular ingredient was local, fostered by the Greek influences that are evident in certain examples.

Votive stele with female figure holding a lotus flower from Monte Sirai 4th-3rd century B.C. tufa, 55.5 × 35 cm Cagliari, Museo Archeologico Nazionale
• *p. 435*

Finally, Sicily has yielded a number of sandstone stelae, about 50 cm high, found in the Soluntum area and dating back to the 4th century B.C. They are square in shape and decorated with small pediments displaying the image of the crescent moon, a typically Phoenician motif. In the center is a horseman turned towards the left, his body often covered by a large, round shield. Behind the rider is a figure with stylized lines. Taken together, these stelae reveal an awareness of the Punic tradition together with a strong development and differentiation.

After Carthage, Sardinia saw the largest output of Punic stelae. From Nora, about eighty examples remain of double that number found. The first obvious impression is the predominance of geometrical over human designs. The Carthage repertoire is fairly faithfully repeated here, with variants in the details: the single and triple baetyl predominate, the double or quintuple ones are rare. The most frequent is the triad with a higher central element, sometimes surmounted by the sun disc and crescent moon. Also consistently present are the lozenge, the bottle idol and the sign of Tanit.

Among the human images, fewer in number and poorer in quality, we note the standing male figure seen from the front and the advancing male in profile, the female figure with hands on breasts and the female figure with disc on chest, mostly frontal but also in profile. There is a notable trend towards intermediate forms between the geometrical and the human, created on the one hand by completing the lozenge with a projection on top, two lateral appendages and a small base, or by giving the bottle a neck and rounding its shoulders; on the other, by reducing the human figure to a geometrical outline, as in the case of the sign of Tanit depicted as a cruciform image.

Also characteristic of Nora is the tendency to vary details which gives the works a certain autonomy. Thus, for instance, the baetyl is rounded or its squat base broadened; the lozenge is also rounded; minor elements are added, as we have noted, to make geometrical shapes more human and vice-versa. Taken as a whole, Nora seems to have been a moderately important centre of stele craftsmanship, outside the commercial and cultural mainstream — hence the emergence of variants — and closely connected with Carthage throughout the period documented by finds, between the 6th and 4th centuries B.C.

opposite page
Votive stele with three baetyls from Nora 6th-4th century B.C. sandstone 74.4 × 36.4 cm Cagliari, Museo Archeologico Nazionale

A major centre of Phoenician stele production in Sardinia, and more generally in Italy, was Sulcis (Sant'Antioco), with over 1,500 examples. The typology includes flat-topped, pointed and triangular-topped stelae (often bearing acroteria). Characteristic is the inclusion of a number of tufa or marble stelae in sandstone blocks. The triangular pediments are already a clear demonstration of a special feature of Sulcis: the advent of Greek influence. This is confirmed by the supporting columns, which are Doric (rare), Ionic, and above all Tuscan, with entases and often grooves.

In the iconography, the prevalence of human (and animal) figures over

Votive stele with figure holding ankh from Sulcis 4th-3rd century B.C. tufa, 24.2 × 17.3 cm S. Antioco Museo Comunale

Votive stele with male figure in profile holding lance from Sulcis 6th century B.C. tufa, 55 × 37 cm Cagliari, Museo Archeologico Nazionale

Votive stele with female figure holding disc to breast, from Sulcis 3rd century B.C. trachytic tufa 21.2 × 14.4 cm Cagliari, Museo Archeologico Nazionale

Votive stele with figure holding ankh from Sulcis 3rd century B.C. trachytic tufa 12.6 × 12.3 cm Cagliari, Museo Archeologico Nazionale

*Votive stele
with female figure
holding disc to breast
from Sulcis
5th-4th century B.C.
trachytic tufa
82 × 33 cm
S. Antioco, Biggio
Collection*

*Votive stele with
cruciform
figure, from Nora
6th-4th century B.C.
sandstone
43.4 × 29.7 cm
Cagliari, Museo
Archeologico
Nazionale*

geometrical shapes is immediately obvious. The latter are limited to baetyls, single or more rarely double; the lozenge, the bottle idol and the sign of Tanit are all absent. With such a large output, this requires some explanation: evidently the advent of the Greek-type human representations prevented the development of the geometrical designs, which appear rougher and more elementary in character. Consequently the baetyl iconography must be considered the oldest in this production,

which has a first stage lasting from the early 6th century B.C. to halfway
through the 4th. At this point Greek influence intervened and characterized the output until the end, around the 1st century B.C. In the earlier
stage the human representations show both men and women, most often
depicted frontally because of a typical reluctance at Sulcis to use passant
figures. The male figures include the walking Egyptian, and the female
ones the woman with hands to her breast, clasping a long flower or (the
most frequent) with a disc on her breast, first in the Punic version and
then in a Greek adaptation. Also characteristic of Sulcis is the figure wearing a long robe carrying a stola in the left hand and in his right the
Egyptian sign of life, the *ankh*, often enlarged to suggest the sign of Tanit
(hence, probably, its popularity).

Other various and independent iconographies in the last stage show the full
predominance of Greek influence: thus, for example, the woman wearing a
wide pleated garment raising a cup in her left hand while proffering another with her right. Animal images are also typical of Sulcis craftsmanship,
with some seventy examples representing a passant ram (rarely a bull). This
iconography is linked to an equally typical typology, the arched top, and

Votive stele with female figure holding "sign of Tanit" from Sulcis 3rd-2nd century B.C. marble and sandstone 52 × 41 cm Cagliari, Museo Archeologico Nazionale

was applied to small-sized stelae during the last stage of production at Sulcis.

About 150 stelae come from Monte Sirai, the inland fortress founded by Sulcis. Dependence on Sulcis is quite obvious here, though the stelae are rougher and more summary. Geometrical patterns remain rare and limited to baetyls; the prevalent figure is that of the woman with disc on her breast. The presence, although minor, of frontal male figures, the woman with hands on breasts or holding a lotus flower or stola and *ankh*, and the passant animal fully confirms dependence on Sulcis.

The general simplification typical of popular workshops did however lead to certain variations. One example is an engraved figure with a head of abnormal size, trapezoidal body, and threadlike arms upraised. Another interesting type is the stylized image of a woman with a child on her right side at shoulder-level: this is probably a folk representation of the Greek *kourotrophos* motif, a woman with a child in her arms.

Chronologically, the Monte Sirai stelae can be dated between the 4th and the 2nd centuries B.C., the period when the *tophet* in which they were dedicated was in use.

Another stele production centre in Sardinia was Tharros, although there is no comparison with Sulcis in terms of quantity. There are about 300 stelae from the 6th to the 4th century B.C. The major feature at Tharros is the presence of some examples of unusual dimensions. Three of them are 180 cm high, making them the tallest known in the Punic world. They have bases with Egyptian mouldings between two projecting listels, and plinths in the form of truncated pyramids, also ending with Egyptian mouldings between two listels. The upper parts are thrones with backs, with two perfume-burners on the sides and a series of steps in the middle, surmounted by the image of worship, a more or less rounded baetyl. Unique at Tharros are also certain cubical thrones with footstools at the front, derived from Eastern statuary.

As for the actual stelae, as at Nora and Carthage they are prevalently devoid of figures. The baetyl is very common, single, double or triple, with a central projecting element. Also present are the lozenge, the bottle idol and the sign of Tanit, sometimes in an unusual version. Human figures are rare, but some are unusual: thus, the engraved stele bearing the image of a young child before a priest. Similarly outstanding are the "multimedia" examples, that is, human figures in valuable stone lodged in stelae of more common material.

Votive stele with walking animal and astral symbols from Sulcis 3rd century B.C. tufa, 25 × 15 cm S. Antioco Museo Comunale

A number of important problems arise with the Tharros stelae. First there is the numerical disproportion between the stelae (about 300, as we have said) and the urns (several thousand), so it can no longer be said that each stele recorded a sacrifice. In all probability, the *tophet* was also used as a burial place for children who died of natural causes and for whom no stele would have been made. Then there is the problem of the function of the monumental cippi: these may commemorate sacrifices of particularly important infants, or perhaps exceptional sacrifices connected with particularly dramatic events.

Votive stele with lozenge from Tharros 5th-4th century B.C. sandstone, 70 cm Cagliari, Museo Archeologico Nazionale

Still in Sardinia, certain groups of stelae are later and more highly developed, so that their Phoenician heritage appears weaker. Cagliari has yielded a number of large, two-sided stelae, with a stylized human face carved on both sides. Other stelae come from Castelsardo, and like the previous ones date from the Punic-Roman period and have funerary connotations: the engraved heads of the deceased are roughly stylized on long necks and surrounded by palm fronds. Viddalba and Tergu have also yielded late stelae, of the funerary type, while Sant'Imbenia and Porto Torres have left two examples which although late are closer to Punic models: the first with a baetyl in an engraved frame, the second with a naked figure, arms at sides, in a simple frame.

Votive stele with stylized figure, from Monte Sirai 1st century B.C. tufa 38 × 19.7 cm Cagliari, Museo Archeologico Nazionale

Very few stelae have come to light in Iberia: one from Cartagena with a large figure in the field, a cuspidal one from Villaricos with a relief triangle at the top, and more importantly, one from Ibiza with pediment and acroterium, and in the niche a frontal figure with a beard and a long tunic, raising his right arm in the classic gesture of adoration while his left hand, holding a stola, is folded across his chest. This is a funerary iconography we already know from Carthage; therefore Iberia's fundamental lack of traditional-type votive stelae remains.

Terra-cotta Figures
Anna Maria Bisi

Clay is one of the most economical and malleable raw materials that nature offers, and because it requires a relatively simple process of refining and firing, it can be readily used to create all manner of objects — either shaped by hand, turned on the potter's wheel or moulded. The coroplastic figurines of the ancient Near East are the outcome of thousands of years' experience of working with these three techniques. Production was widespread throughout the Syro-Palestinian regions, and in the course of time, as the various cultural groups became more specialized, certain types of clay figure came to have specific functions in the ambit of funerary, cult, and votive practices.

Recent findings in the region of Sarafand-Sarepta on the Phoenician coast, and at Tel Qasile and Tel Shiqmona in northern Palestine, along with the older but no less noteworthy discoveries of material at Akhziv and Sidon, have signalled the presence of a quantity of coroplastic types along the Levantine coast over a span of time ranging from the 12th-11th century B.C. (notably those unearthed at the Philistine sanctuary at Tel Qasile) to the age of Persian supremacy (second half of the 7th century B.C. to the second half of the 4th century B.C.). These figures, which became highly sought-after in the western Phoenician colonies, include the bell-shaped nude female figure modelled on the potter's wheel, and the "pregnant woman", whose striking resemblance to other figures which have appeared at Tyre, Akhziv and Sarepta, and in the older Carthaginian tombs, has led scholars to believe that Phoenician moulds were imported by Carthage, especially since this kind of figure has not been traced elsewhere in the West. Other specimens recovered are figurines of the so-called "nude goddess" or pregnant woman clasping her breasts, statues of Bes, and other small female figures mounted on shield-shaped plaquettes; the headdresses, jewellery and attire of the latter show a marked Cypriot influence.

Cyprus in fact played a seminal role in circulating coroplastic figurines of Canaanite and Phoenician origin throughout the colonial centres of the West. From the 8th century B.C., as the colonists' presence in Cyprus grew more substantial, Phoenician forms and iconographic features found their way into local coroplastic products which had been thriving since the Early Bronze Age. The new figurines depicted nude or clothed female figures, with their arms either crossed below the breasts or bearing gifts; and tympanists, with their instrument propped against their chest, or, in the case of the figures turned on the wheel, at their side. In the latter variant the details are hand-modelled; although this was the established technique used on the

Female statuette with hands holding breasts from Akhziv 8th-6th century B.C. terra-cotta, 18 cm Paris, Musée du Louvre

Statuette bearing lamp on head from Larnaca 8th-7th century B.C. terra-cotta, 23.7 cm Nicosia, Cyprus Museum

Mould and stamp depicting hunting scene from Kythrea 7th century B.C. terra-cotta 6 × 10 cm Nicosia, Cyprus Museum

island, it was nevertheless also influenced by the new culture introduced by the Phoenicians. This second group of figurines, with cylindrical bodies

shaped on the wheel, includes a number of examples carrying a lamp on the head, or with facial features and clothing summarily marked in with dark paint (more rarely in two colours, red and black), recalling the decorations on local pottery. Both the turned and moulded figurines were found in sanctuaries (the Kamelarga sanctuary at Kition, Ayia Irini, Idalion, and Arsos), and date from Archaic Cypriot I and Archaic Cypriot II (700-475 B.C.).

The typologies and special features developed by the Phoenicians in the Iron Age emerge even more clearly in the Phoenician West. The two main techniques used in the Levantine workshops are adopted in the West as well: that of modelling the statues on the potter's wheel, with details added by hand, and that of moulded figures. The figurines made in western Phoenicia display a Hellenic influence which in the East appears only with the onset of the Persian age (significant examples of this are the terracotta statues found at Kherayeb and off the coast of Shavei Zion, south of Tyre). This is a phenomenon which goes beyond the limits of a craft category and involves deeper and more complex socio-cultural relations. In the West, Greek influence had been present since the Archaic period, with terracotta objects imported mainly from the Siceliot centres (Selinus, Agrigentum, Gela, and Megara Hyblaea). The diffusion of this influence is attested by the Carthaginian

Statuette of Bes portrayed with serpent's tail, from Sulcis 4th-3rd century B.C. terra-cotta, 14 cm S. Antioco, Biggio Collection

figurines of the 7th-6th century B.C. found among funerary accessories and at *tophets*. The latter have almost exclusively yielded male and female figurines with tapering bell-shaped bodies turned on the wheel and separately modelled heads.

The facial features, painted details (sometimes resembling "braces" across the chest, typical of the stele "bottle idols"), and the lamp on the head, make them strikingly similar to Cypriot prototypes. On the other hand, the necropoli have produced a very broad variety of terra-cotta objects, largely

*Statuette of pregnant woman
from Syria
8th-7th century B.C.
painted terra-cotta
approx. 20 cm
Paris, Musée du Louvre*

*Female figure
from Amathus
7th-5th century B.C.
painted terra-cotta, 35 cm
Limassol, District Museum*

of the moulded type, including plaquettes with nude or clothed goddesses resembling the Astarte figurines from Syro-Phoenicia; goddesses seated on high-backed thrones wearing a tall *kalathos* and a long veil over their shoulders; tympanists similar to the type coming from Asia Minor; female figures offering up doves; plus the "pregnant woman" figurines mentioned above. From the 5th century B.C. a number of figurines with outstretched arms appear (found from the same period in Sidon), inspired by the figures common in the Siceliot sanctuaries consecrated to the two goddesses of the Eleusinian cult, Demeter and Kore; other finds include draped female figurines carrying an infant or a vessel on their shoulder, female musicians, and incense burners in the form of a female head, peculiar to the closing phase of Punic Carthage. A number of hand-modelled terracotta figures from Carthage complete this picture of North African coroplastic figures (which culminated in the large cult statues of the Neo-Punic sanctuaries of Thinissut and Korba — these, too, show evidence of Siceliot models but with curious remnants of Egyptian themes, such as the lion-headed goddess of Thinissut). The Carthage figurines included the two funerary groups portraying an individual carrying out an ablution or libation in a rectangular basin, and one making bread; they are reminiscent of, respectively, Cypriot prototypes dating from the 7th-6th century B.C. and Phoenician prototypes from Akhziv (8th century B.C.). Punic-Phoenician Sicily, together with Ibiza, offers the largest collection of terracotta figures in the Greek manner. While Sicily's closest and longest lasting ties were in fact with the neighboring colonial Greek world, Ibiza's Hellenized figures were mainly the product of mediation through the Siceliot world. The largest number of pieces come from the strata dating from the 6th and 5th centuries B.C. at the *tophet* in Motya; but sporadic examples have turned up at the Bagno dell'Acqua sanctuary at Pantelleria, and the necropolis in Palermo; in addition specimens dating from the Hellenic period have been found in Soluntum, Eryx and Lilybaeum, as well as in Selinus, dating from the period when the city was under Carthaginian rule (409-250 B.C.). The terracotta figurines from Motya are mainly female figures, representing divinities or gift bearers, recurrent motif of the sanctuaries dedicated to Demeter. While some of these figurines were imported, others were manufactured locally — especially those in the form of a seated goddess with veil hanging down from the *kalathos*, and so-called "seed necklaces" (multiple strands of pendants modelled on the Athena Lindia cult object, originating from the figurines of the Rhodian colony of Gela, and found in all the sanctuaries dedicated to Demeter and Kore in Grecian Sicily); the specimens also include curly-haired heads imported from the Italiot settlement of Medma, votaries offering up piglets (a sacred animal used in Eleusinian rites), tympanists, draped statuettes with naked infants held against the

Female statuette with disc from Amathus 8th century B.C. painted terra-cotta 24.2 cm Limassol District Museum

Head of votive statuette with
crown of feathers, from Bithia
3rd-1st century B.C.
terra-cotta, 15 cm
Cagliari, Museo Archeologico
Nazionale

Statuette of Bes
found at Cagliari
4th century B.C.
painted terra-cotta, 20 cm
Cagliari, Museo Archeologico
Nazionale

Lion-headed female statuette
from Thinissut
1st century A.D.
terra-cotta, 130 cm
Tunis
Musée de Nabeul

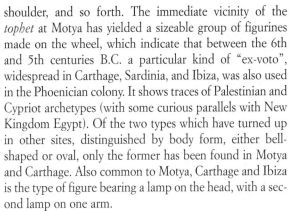

shoulder, and so forth. The immediate vicinity of the *tophet* at Motya has yielded a sizeable group of figurines made on the wheel, which indicate that between the 6th and 5th centuries B.C. a particular kind of "ex-voto", widespread in Carthage, Sardinia, and Ibiza, was also used in the Phoenician colony. It shows traces of Palestinian and Cypriot archetypes (with some curious parallels with New Kingdom Egypt). Of the two types which have turned up in other sites, distinguished by body form, either bell-shaped or oval, only the former has been found in Motya and Carthage. Also common to Motya, Carthage and Ibiza is the type of figure bearing a lamp on the head, with a second lamp on one arm.

Female bust with kalathos from Ibiza 5th century B.C. painted terra-cotta, 50 cm Ibiza, Museo Arqueológico • p. 436

Coroplastic figurines patterned on Hellenized figures modified by Siceliot craftsmen underwent a second period of development between the 4th and 3rd centuries B.C. with the introduction of the head-shaped incense burners bearing a perforated *kalathos* with fruit, wheat sheaves and birds. From Selinus and Lilybaeum these incense burners reached Carthage, Sardinia, Greek Spain (Ampurias), and Punic Spain, whence they were transmitted to the later inland Iberian civilization between Alicante and Murcia.

Again, it was Hellenic Sicily that inspired at least some of the moulded terracotta figurines made in Sardinia in the Punic-Phoenician period. The basic form was not unknown in ancient times, as can be seen from a number of figurines found at Nora and Cagliari, and this influence grew during the Hellenistic period. Together with the cloaked female figures with various attributes and the tall *kalathos* headdress, the tympanist with instrument propped to one side and billowing veil, and the women holding an infant on their left shoulder, a number of unusual examples of incense burners have been found, made in the workshops in Tharros. These specimens show a gradual development away from the Siceliot models, as the headdress becomes more rectangular, clearly influenced by the stone altars also produced locally; in one case, paralleled in Carthage, a young Heracles complete with Nemean lionskin has replaced the woman's head.

Statuette of Bes with head in form of vessel from Agrigentum 4th century B.C. terra-cotta 30.5 cm Agrigento, Museo Archeologico Regionale • p. 437

While the tombs of Nora and Tharros have yielded moulded figurines from the Archaic period that echo Phoenico-Cypriot models (e.g. the nude goddess cupping her breasts, and the goddess with torso resembling a mummy, complete with Egyptian hairstyle), the group of turned statuettes found in Sardinia has provided the most original designs. The male ithyphallic figurine with cylindrical body and pointed beard uneartked at Monte Sirai, and the small bearded kead from *Sulcis* derive from Cypriot prototypes from the Archaic period, though they do show certain atypical features that distinguish them from the main group — a hundred or more statuettes, either whole or in fragments, discovered at the tem-

Kernophoros *female head incense
burner found in Sardinia*
4th-3th century B.C.
*terra-cotta, 12.4 cm
Sassari, Museo Nazionale G.A. Sanna*

Kernophoros *female head
incense burner found in Sardinia*
4th-3th century B.C.
*terra-cotta, 11 cm
Sassari, Museo Nazionale G.A. Sanna*

*Statuette of female deity
bearing* kalathos *from Tharros*
4th century B.C., terra-cotta, 22 cm
Sassari, Museo Nazionale G.A. Sanna

Bell-shaped votive statuette with hand on throat from Bithia 3rd-1st century B.C. terra-cotta, 21 cm Cagliari, Museo Archeologico Nazionale

ple at Bithia dedicated to a healing divinity. Bithia (and also Tharros, though only in sporadic examples) has furnished both the body types already found at Ibiza — bell-shaped and oval — but compared with the latter there is a far wider range of stylistic features and techniques in the treatment of the faces (shaped by hand, and then detailed using the point of a stick) and the arms, gesturing to the parts of the body already healed or for which healing is implored.

Two other elements confirm the importance of the group of votive figures from Bithia — on the one hand, the date of origin (3rd to 1st century B.C.), showing how long this production continued in Sardinia, accounts for some of the variations within the basic canons of this type. On another level, the application of shield-shaped plaquettes for some of the faces, and the lively folk manner revealed in the singular expressiveness of the heads, whose realism at times verges on caricature, have been correctly likened to the technical and stylistic solutions typical of nuraghic bronze-work, which was a rich source of inspiration for the coroplastic figures of Bithia.

Local craftsmen probably also made one of the rare hand-modelled terra-cotta figures that have been found in the Punic world, the nude (and perhaps pregnant) woman, in the former Castagnino Collection in the Cagliari Museum, although the total nudity of the figure (alluding to fecundity) is more akin to the Phoenician and Cypriot coroplastic tradition.

The role of Spain in the development of coroplastic figures is a singular one — partly due to the apparent absence of any examples whatsoever in the most ancient settlements of the Andalusian coast (with the sole exception of a hand-modelled pyramidal incense burner with small Egyptianizing male figures at the corners, which was fished out of the bay of Cadiz), and partly because of the massive concentration of production on the island of Ibiza from the 6th century B.C. to the end of the 2nd.

We can safely say that all the main typologies used in the Punic world are present in Ibiza, and with a highly varied range of original solutions testifying to the imaginative skills of local coroplasts. There are also a number of other types previously encountered in the West only in sculpture and stone relief (such as the male figures in advancing position, wearing the Egyptian-style kilt, with one arm bent across the chest, which have been pieced together from fragments recovered from the Isla Plana sanctuary).

Isla Plana itself (which today is part of the mainland and the site of one of the oldest colonial settlements) has furnished votive figures with torso turned on the wheel; these date from the Late Archaic period (6th to 5th century B.C.), and are very like those of Carthage and Motya.

The figures from Ibiza come either in bell-shaped form (the most widespread in the Punic world) with an open base and arms crossed over the chest or extended to support one or two lamps, while another lamp is positioned on

Plaquette of female figure
with hands on breasts
from Nora
6th-5th century B.C.
terra-cotta, 17 cm
Cagliari, Museo
Archeologico Nazionale

Incense burner
with figures
from Cadiz
7th-6th century B.C.
terra-cotta, 64 cm
Cadiz
Museo de Cadiz

Plaquette with mummified
female figure from Tharros
6th century B.C.
terra-cotta, 25 cm
Cagliari, Museo
Archeologico Nazionale

Bell-shaped votive statuette from Bithia 3rd-1st century B.C. terra-cotta, 20 cm Cagliari, Museo Archeologico Nazionale

Bell-shaped votive statuette with hands on belly from Bithia 3rd-1st century B.C. terra-cotta, 17 cm Cagliari, Museo Archeologico Nazionale

Bell-shaped votive statuette of woman with child from Bithia 3rd-1st century B.C. terra-cotta, 17 cm Cagliari, Museo Archeologico Nazionale

Bell-shaped votive statuette with hands covering eyes from Bithia 3rd-1st century B.C. terra-cotta, 20.5 cm Cagliari, Museo Archeologico Nazionale
• p. 438

Bell-shaped votive
statuette
with lamp on head
found at Ibiza
5th century B.C.
terra-cotta, 25.8 cm
Ibiza, Museo
Arqueológico

Egg-shaped votive
statuette
found at Ibiza
5th century B.C.
terra-cotta, 24.7 cm
Ibiza, Museo
Arqueológico

Egg-shaped votive
statuette
with necklace
found at Ibiza
6th century B.C.
terra-cotta, 21 cm
Barcelona, Museo
Arqueológico

Bell-shaped votive
statuette
with hands to breast
found at Ibiza
6th century B.C.
terra-cotta, 20.8 cm
Barcelona, Museo
Arqueológico

Enthroned deity found at Ibiza 5th-4th century B.C. terra-cotta, 13 cm Ibiza, Museo Arqueológico

the head, or in the oval form with the base sealed by an applied clay plaquette; here one arm is curved downwards towards the sex (all the figures are male) and the other bent upwards. This second type is further characterized by a cord necklace, sometimes adorned with a central pendant, and a low headdress, a motif which sometimes appears in the first series as well.

The figures found in Ibiza's other cult site (the cave sanctuary of Es Cuyram) constitute a typologically homogeneous group even though they were produced from the 4th century B.C. down to Roman times. The group comprises moulded female figurines truncated below the bust with a tall conical headdress of the Siceliot variety and a cloak resembling bird's wings meeting across the chest; here there is often a symbol such as a lotus, disc and crescent moon, or caduceus. Despite the Hellenized appearance of the faces, the terra-cotta figures from the Cueva d'Es Cuyram follow an iconography prevalent in Carthage in Hellenistic times, which in turn drew on Egyptian themes (the goddesses Isis and Nephthys with wide wings protecting the deceased).

But the group that is most representative of Ibizan coroplastic figures both quantitatively and by the sheer variety of types and range of influences developed, is without doubt the hundreds of moulded terra-cotta figures coming mainly from the large urban necropolis of Puig des Molins, and to a lesser extent from the cemeteries of the hamlets scattered throughout the island.

From the end of the 6th century to midway through the 2nd century B.C., the workshops in Ibiza produced a vast number of terra-cottas; the influence of the Phoenico-Cypriot tradition gradually yielded to that of the colonial Greek figures, predominantly from the Siceliot centres. It is often difficult to establish how much time elapsed between the circulation of models from Asia Minor among the western Greek colonies (e.g. the figure with a dove-shaped vase and high diadem, draped in a chiton and cloak) and their arrival in the Punic milieu of Ibiza. However, in the case of the goddesses on plinths, or seated on a throne and wearing a tiara adorned with applied disc-shaped rosettes and "seed necklaces," produced in the workshops at Gela, Agrigentum, Syracuse, and Selinus between the 5th and 4th centuries B.C., the chronological gap between their arrival in the Greek colonies and the circulation of examples made in Ibiza was probably relatively short. Furthermore, very few were produced with imported moulds: generally speaking, the well-worn moulds from Siceliot settlements underwent substantial alterations, including the insertion of local features (huge pierced ears and stumps for arms added by hand; frequent summary finishing touches using the point of a stick, simplification of the headdress and ornaments, etc.).

Statuette of enthroned female with dove and goblet found at Ibiza, 5th-4th century B.C. terra-cotta, 22 cm Ibiza, Museo Arqueológico

When the coroplastic figures from Ibiza are not conditioned by imported models (as in the case of the moulded statuettes portraying gift bearers found at the necropolis of Puig des Molins), domestic tastes are given free rein in the intricate plant motifs incised into the clothing, the abundant and somewhat "baroque" detailing of headdresses and personal adornment (necklaces, earrings, diadems), which curiously seem to coincide with features of Iberian statues found inland.

The necropolis at Puig des Molins has also supplied several dozen four-sided or round plaquettes with motifs either in relief or incised that differ from other terra-cotta figures. They do, however, show certain affinities with a group of other objects with motifs scored into the surface (thought to have been used as moulds for cakes having a funerary and symbolic value), found in Carthage, Sicily, and Sardinia. Apart from the unique and intriguing incidence of a rectangular plaquette bearing a rampant Egyptian sphinx alongside a sacred tree (an image which vaguely recalls themes of the Phoenician ivories from the 8th century B.C.), the finds in Ibiza have included ithyphallic Silenus figures, images of Bes, a god on horseback with

Postern in the Punic walls at Tharros

Votive statuette of youth
with inscription
from the Temple of Eshmun
at Sidon, 4th century B.C.
marble, 35 cm
Beirut, National Museum

Crouching lion from Byblos
6th-4th century B.C.
basalt, 42 × 68 cm
Paris, Musée du Louvre

*Female statue
from Monte Sirai
7th century B.C.
sandstone
40 × 20 cm
Cagliari, Museo
Archeologico
Nazionale*

Female sarcophagus
discovered
near Amrith
4th century B.C.
roseate marble
55 × 210 cm
Paris, Musée
du Louvre

Detail of female sarcophagus
from Cadiz
5th-4th century B.C.
alabaster, 83 × 218 cm
Cadiz, Museo de Cadiz

Fragment of a panel featuring a crouching winged sphinx from Aradus 6th-5th century B.C. alabaster, 61 cm Paris, Musée du Louvre

*Stele of
Yehawmilk
from Byblos
5th century B.C.
limestone
130 × 56 cm
Paris, Musée
du Louvre*

Mould featuring Bes from Ibiza 4th century B.C. terra-cotta, 34 cm Ibiza, Museo Arqueológico

Plaquette featuring Silenus from Ibiza 6th-5th century B.C., terra-cotta 23.5 cm Barcelona, Museo Arqueológico

Plaquette with winged sphinx and palmette from Ibiza 6th century B.C. terra-cotta, 12 cm Madrid, Museo Arqueológico Nacional
• p. 439

rounded shield and Corinthian helmet (which is comparable to Carthaginian specimens from the Archaic period), and above all zoomorphic motifs (fish, dolphins, and insects) and plant motifs, often interwoven with geometric patterns.

Unlike the coroplastic figures of Carthage and Motya, those originating in Ibiza, very popular on home soil, do not seem to have circulated outside the Balearic Islands, whether in the form of moulds or of finished products, though the more typical categories of figure such as the female busts with applied limbs and the statuettes turned on the wheel from Isla Plana, or those patterned after Siceliot models (the head-shaped incense burners) did have some influence on the products of certain Iberian centers of the nearby coast of western Spain (the Albufereta de Alicante and the Serreta de Alcoy).

The specialization that can be noticed in the western coroplastic figures, compared with those of the Phoenician homeland, is further confirmed by a number of cult objects that fall outside the categories of material discussed so far. These are the clay aediculae in use during the first centuries of the Iron Age in Phoenician coastal towns such as Akhziv. These aediculae imitate a kind of temple furniture the origins of which can be found in an example from Kamid el-Loz in the Beqa'a valley (dating from the Late Bronze Age). These pieces were well received in Phoenician-influenced Cypriot circles (a number of small temple models with little niches housing divine figures or baetyls have been found in the tombs of Amathus). In the West, on the other hand, Egyptian-style aediculae have been found exclusively on the stone stelae of the *tophets*. Together with the import of water basins produced in Selinus and Agrigentum, the finds at Motya have provided rectangular shaped clay *arulae* with moulded scenes of felines and griffins fighting (dating from the 4th century B.C.) inspired by models produced in Himera (Sicily) dated one century earlier. In the Punic world, this kind of *arulae* is found exclusively at Kerkouane and Cape Bon, brought from northwest Sicily via Carthaginian trade.

*Female statuette
on plinth
from Ibiza
4th-3rd century B.C.
terra-cotta, 40 cm
Barcelona, Museo
Arqueológico*

*Female statuette
with three-tiered
necklace, from Ibiza
5th-4th century B.C.
terra-cotta, 36 cm
Barcelona, Museo
Arqueológico*

*Female statuette
wearing nose-ring
from Ibiza
4th century B.C.
terra-cotta, 32.5 cm
Madrid, Museo
Arqueológico National
• p. 440*

*Female statuette
from Ibiza
4th century B.C.
terra-cotta, 33 cm
Ibiza, Museo
Arqueológico*

*Fragment of statuette
with one arm to breast
from Ibiza
4th-3rd century B.C.
terra-cotta, 22 cm
Madrid, Museo
Arqueológico Nacional*

*Circular stamp
with two ibises
from Carthage
6th-5th century B.C.
terra-cotta, diam. 10.8 cm
Carthage, Musée de
Carthage*

*Circular stamp with
palmette and lotus
flowers, from Tharros
6th century B.C.
terra-cotta, diam. 10.3 cm
Sassari, Museo Nazionale
G.A. Sanna*

*Circular mould
with geometric patterns
from Olbia
4th century B.C.
terra-cotta, diam. 13.6 cm
Sassari, Museo Nazionale
G.A. Sanna*

Naiskos *with deity astride*
a pair of lions
from Sidon
5th century B.C.
painted terra-cotta, 6 cm
Paris, Musée du Louvre

Naiskos *with female figure*
from Nicosia
6th century B.C.
painted terra-cotta
11.5 × 10 cm
Nicosia, Cyprus Museum

Arula *with griffins*
fighting horse
from Motya
6th-5th century B.C.
terra-cotta, 14.4 × 24 cm
Palermo, Museo
Archeologico Regionale

*Female bust with fawn
from Ibiza
5th-4th century B.C.
terra-cotta, 26.5 cm
Barcelona, Museo
Arqueológico*

Masks and Protomes
Antonia Ciasca

Masks and protomes, usually made of terracotta, are well-known products of Phoenician craftsmanship, thanks especially to the large number of finds in the western Mediterranean. The Italian archaeological term *maschera* (mask) is used to denote modelled representations of the face with apertures for eyes and frequently for the mouth as well. Protome denotes a representation of the face usually without apertures, and the upper part of the bust.

Most of the masks found in the western regions have come to light during tomb excavations — a fact which underlines their fundamental link with the theme of death. In the eastern regions however they have often been found in sanctuaries as well as in necropoli. They have rarely been discovered in other contexts. Although masks were used throughout the ancient world in cultic practices, they have been found in such great numbers in Late Bronze Age and Early Iron Age sites along the coastline of the Near East that they constitute one of the distinguishing elements of Phoenician crafts and culture. One of the peculiarities of Phoenician masks is the fact that they are nearly always made of nonperishable materials like terra-cotta. There are occasional exceptions, for instance the bulls' skulls used for rituals in the great Phoenician temple of Kition in Cyprus. Protomes are even more widespread, since they were in use throughout the Greek world and have been found in a vast range of forms and styles in tombs and sanctuaries, particularly in the colonies in Sicily and Magna Graecia.

Funerary mask from Phoenicia 5th-4th century B.C. gold, 16 cm Paris, Musée du Louvre • p. 473

There are various views about the exact function of masks and protomes. Since they represent deities, the protomes have been seen as votive offerings for sanctuaries and tutelary images in tombs. The apertures for eyes and mouth in the masks suggest that they were used by living people. Life-sized masks could have been worn by priests or devotees in religious ceremonies (for example, those found at Gezer and Tel Qasile in Palestine, those from Cyprus, and the famous masks from the Artemis Orthia sanctuary in Sparta). The smaller ones could have been placed on images or statues. It has been suggested that the masks of the *tophet* of Motya were used to cover the face of sacrificial victims. Sepulchral masks are seen as having had a fundamentally apotropaic function.

In the Near East numerous masks, sometimes of stone, have been discovered along the coastline. They date back as far as the Late Bronze Age in Palestine, and have also been discovered in Syria (Meskene, Tell Hadidi). Life-sized masks have been found at Hazor and Gezer (Palestine), sometimes with distorted features in the so-called "grotesque" style, also found in the West.

With the Iron Age, masks become more common. There is a mask (late 12th-early 11th century B.C.) from the Philistine sanctuary of Tel Qasile (Palestine), which came to light along with zoomorphic types. There are also examples from Tel Shera (10th century) and Hazor (8th century) in Palestine. Masks have been discovered dating from the 9th century onwards along the

Female mask from the necropolis at Akhziv 8th-7th century B.C. painted terra-cotta Jerusalem Bronfman Archaeological Museum

Male mask from the necropolis at Akhziv 7th-6th century B.C. painted terra-cotta Jerusalem, Israel Department of Antiquity Museum

whole length of the Phoenician coast. The mask from Tyre (c. 850 B.C.) is one of the few to have been found in an urban context. A miniature mask (8th century) came to light in a child's tomb at Khaldé near Beirut. Others come from tombs at Akhziv (late 9th to 7th century), from Sheikh Abaroh near Sidon, from Amrith, and from Sarepta. A number have also passed through antiquarians' hands into museums and collections throughout the world.

There is evidence that masks were also used in Cyprus, a natural stopping place between the Asiatic coast and the Aegean. Enkomi has yielded fragments of specimens from sanctuaries and various urban locations of the Late Bronze Age. From the sacred area of Kathari at Kition there is a mask from the early 11th century. Masks from a later period are found in all the main centres of population, in Phoenician sanctuaries and tombs and in tombs where Phoenician and Cypriot cultures combine (Larnaca, Kourion, Amathus, Idalion, Marion, Limassol, and others).

The masks that have come to light both in Asia and in Cyprus are typologically relatively uniform. Of the small number of male "grotesque" masks (Hazor, Gezer, Amrith, Akhziv, Cyprus), it has been suggested that some may be iconographically connected to the Mesopotamian demon Humbaba. The male masks are very varied in type. They are made on a potter's wheel (see, for example, the polished surface and marks of the wheel inside), and are often painted. Some pieces are analogous in form to portrait funeral masks (Hazor, Khaldé), and occasional masks, like the carefully made and strongly plastic example from Akhziv, are close to major sculpture.

In the long-bearded male masks, the way in which hair and beard are represented with carefully fashioned spikes and ringlets (Sheikh Abaroh, mask from the Guimet Collection in the Louvre) and moulded decorations (Toronto mask) evince a folk tradition. Female masks are few, and come mainly from Akhziv. They are mainly of Egyptian inspiration. It should be added that Cypriot workshops made similar cult objects, without apertures, more plaques than masks, in flat relief and decorated with bright colours. They follow the typology of the male masks mentioned above.

In conclusion, the Asiatic coast and Cyprus share the same typology, covering "grotesque", bearded and Egyptianizing masks. In style, however, they vary greatly. It is not likely that a subdivision can be suggested on the basis of the production of long-active workshops; these are one-off pieces made by local potters, which quite often are of very modest cultural standards, even if sometimes the immediacy of representation is striking. Unlike the more prestigious Phoenician craftwork in ivory, bronze and jewellery, few show any awareness of formal conventions from other countries. This is not so much the case in Cyprus, where there was a direct contact with the grand tradition of pottery making, and also, to a lesser extent, in certain places in Phoenicia. Good examples are the Egyptian hair styles we find on the female masks from Akhziv and on the fragment from Amathus, and the bearded Larnaca mask with its Egyptian locks like circular appendages at the temples (Ashmolean Museum, Oxford). The Larnaca mask is sculptural in feeling, while a mould-pressed female mask from Idalion (Louvre, Paris) may be compared with refined carved ivories. The protomes are few, always female and generally made with moulds, and show an Asiatic influence which has become altogether generic and overlaid with influences from the Greek world.

The western material is more homogeneous than the eastern. Masks and protomes have been discovered in many Phoenician colonies: Malta, Carthage, Utica, Bizerta, Motya, Sardinia, Ibiza. There is a single mask from Cadiz. The earliest go back to the 7th century B.C. and continue, with typological and stylistic variations, throughout the archaic and classical periods up to their integration into regional production in the Hellenistic period.

At Carthage male and female protomes and male masks have been discovered. Unlike in the Near East, female protomes are more numerous than male. The few "Egyptianizing" type protomes are all alike: a mass production obviously from a single model with final touches added by hand. They date from the mid-6th century to its end, and follow a typology and style rarely found in objects of other materials (jewellery, for instance). Direct Egyptian influence is evident, for example, in the standardized funeral masks.

Mask in shape of bull's head from Amathus
6th century B.C.
painted terra-cotta, 10.2 cm
Limassol, District Museum

Bearded head from Amathus
6th century B.C.
painted terra-cotta
12.1 cm
Limassol, District Museum

*Grotesque mask
from Kourion
6th century B.C.
terra-cotta
12.9 cm
Nicosia, Cyprus
Museum
• p. 474*

There are numerous Carthaginian protomes of the type called "Graeco-Phoenician", and they offer a very wide range of variations on the theme. The rendering of the face, in particular, is evidence of different cultural levels. Some show a clear influence from the Ionic and Rhodian traditions of minor sculpture. Others give only the slightest hint of the Egyptian-type funeral mask. Others again show massive forms recalling the rounded archaic sculptures of the Sicilian tradition. The "lower level" workshops concentrate attention on details such as the circlets decorating the veil, and not on the fundamental structure. They follow the same costume-types and figurative conventions — these latter often Egyptian in inspiration. Color (red and black) plays an important role.

In the second half of the 6th century and in the 5th century, protomes generally described as "Hellenizing" are produced. Often they are no more than imitations, stamped from imported terracotta moulds and mass-produced, with a few finishing touches.

The earliest examples from Carthage are male masks (7th century). There are many "grotesque" masks, categorized as "negroid" (1st Cintas group) and "grinning" (2nd and 3rd Cintas groups). There are only a few specimens of the former, which exemplify a form and technique soon to fall into desuetude: a use of plain, flat surfaces recalling work in other materials such as wood, a polished finish as on pottery, and so on. With the "grinning" type — much more common than the others — a standard format is used with exaggeratedly grotesque features. Some are virtuoso pieces (see in particular the precision of outline in the lamellar curves at the corners of the mouth). There are holes for inlaid jewels and little triangular spikes on the chin and upper lip. Colour is used (on the teeth, for example) to bring out the grotesque character of the masks. Notwithstanding some discrepancy of opinion, this production may be dated from the 7th century to the 4th-3rd century B.C. (with the introduction of some variants). At the end of the "grotesque" tradition comes the great Carton chapel mask from Carthage, found in an archaeological layer of destruction attributed to the Roman invasion of 146 B.C.

The series of masks from the settlement on the southwest slopes of the Byrsa (2nd century B.C.) shows a different character and function, due evidently to influence from the Greek theatrical tradition.

There are certain unique pieces which do not belong to any series; for example, a male mask (4th century B.C., Louvre, acquired from the antiquaries market), showing the influence of Greek classical sculpture with elements of a clearly African-Punic character superimposed (headdress with "scales"). The few masks (5th Cintas group) dating from the 3rd-2nd century B.C. found at Carthage are of the Greek Silenus-type, cast from matrices which have been considered archaic in form.

Female protome from Motya 6th century B.C. terra-cotta, 15 cm Motya, Museo Whitaker

There are few male protomes from Carthage (4th Cintas group). One of these shows the use of standardized matrices of the type that is also recurrent in the Graeco-Phoenician series. Others from Carthage and Utica are related only typologically.

Grinning mask from Carthage 7th-6th century B.C. terra-cotta 19.5 cm Paris, Musée du Louvre

In Sicily discoveries for the most part have been limited to Motya, and come from the little votive chapel and the *tophet*. There is a strong typological and stylistic relationship with Carthage, even though the few pieces found at Motya may not be really representative. The seven protomes from the Egyptian-style series are so similar to the pieces from Carthage that they could even be from the same workshop. A fragment of a "Graeco-Phoenician" protome carries the usual headdress with horizontal front, appendages at the temples, circlet decorations, and so forth. The modelling of the face suggests Rhodian influence. The only mask (2nd Cintas group)

*Negroid mask
from Carthage
7th-6th century
B.C.
terra-cotta, 19 cm
Tunis, Musée
du Bardo
• p. 475*

is also closely related to the Carthaginian group although it exhibits some peculiarities (absence of decoration). The technique used for the teeth and the mouth with its round apertures at the corners, is identical, as are the enormous ears with pierced lobes. A fragment of a male protome from the same source repeats the typical convention of centrally parted beard and obvious touching up at the sides of nose and mouth.

From this same sanctuary come the remains of female protomes which are clearly imitations of Sicilian prototypes from the late 6th and the 5th centuries B.C., with the usual Punic addition of pierced ears and a mouth aperture. Other small fragments indicate the activity of workshops of profoundly different cultural levels and tastes.

Sardinia has yielded masks and protomes analogous to those described above for Carthage with regard to typology and chronology. Most pieces come from necropoli, though some have come to light in sanctuaries. From Tharros and Sulcis come female protomes of the Egyptian type, closely corresponding to pieces of the same period from Carthage and Motya. They differ, if only slightly, in the elements that are added (eyeballs, eyelids) or remodelled after removal of the piece from the mould (nose). The paucity of

411

Grinning mask
from Motya
6th century B.C.
terra-cotta, 20 cm
Motya, Museo Whitaker

Grinning mask
from San Sperate
6th-5th century B.C.
terra-cotta, 18 cm
Cagliari, Museo
Archeologico Nazionale

Grinning mask
from Tharros
6th century B.C.
terra-cotta, 17.5 cm
Sassari, Museo Nazionale
G.A. Sanna

Grinning mask
from Ibiza
5th-4th century B.C.
terra-cotta, 13.5 cm
Barcelona, Museo
Arqueológico

*Bearded protome
from Monte Sirai
6th-5th century
B.C.
terra-cotta, 14 cm
Cagliari, Museo
Archeologico
Nazionale*

examples and their exact resemblance to each other confirms the likelihood that they come from the same workshop in the southern Mediterranean. A protome from Tharros, perhaps cast from a later mould, is the only one that shows any variance, for the simplified details of its headdress.

The male masks are relatively numerous and varied in typology. There are many "grotesque" masks of the 2nd Cintas type, even if many of the Sardinian pieces do not conform to this group. One of the best examples comes from San Sperate (Cagliari); it resembles others from Bou-Mnijel in Tunisia and from Motya, and could have been produced by the same workshop (the handling of volumes, the cleanness of line, the thin lines around the mouth, and so forth are in fact very similar). The San Sperate mask has rich decoration stamped on it (rosettes, sun and uraeus, small disc and crescent) which indicates a familiarity with techniques used for other materials (jewellery). Other examples of this group come from Tharros. The "grotesque" series also contains masks clearly made by more modest workshops, for instance a piece

413

from Tharros, handmade, in rough clay, lacking polish and showing evident hesitations in the incision of the lines.

Silenus-type masks (5th Cintas group) have been discovered at Sulcis and Tharros dating from the 5th-4th century B.C. They come from different moulds, and share only a general iconography of the type going back to Greek archaic sculpture, and exhibit a wide range of variants. Some are simply mechanical imitations.

Of the few male protomes, a fragment from the sanctuary of Monte Sirai shows a direct relationship to the male and female "Graeco-Phoenician" series from Carthage and Motya. The Santa Gilla (Cagliari) male protome is completely outside the typologies of Punic tradition, and therefore can be presumed to be the work of a Sicilian artisan.

The Cadiz region of western Spain has yielded a single male protome (probably 5th century B.C.); found in a tomb, it is of the negroid type with a smooth Egyptian-style cap of hair, and is not related to the types described above. The masks and protomes from Ibiza are from the late 5th and the 4th centuries B.C. As regards typology, it should be noted that these are only a very small part of the island's prodigious production in terracotta which favors other forms, such as full figures, heads, busts, plaques, head-shaped incense burners, and so forth.

A few female protomes are of "Graeco-Phoenician" type from Carthage. The greatest similarity lies in the obvious finishing by hand (for example, pierced ears), while the Egyptian-style headdress with semicircular appendages at the temples and circlet decorations is seldom employed. It does appear in a fragment that, however, may not have been of local production. In these pieces, only the face — based on an Ionic or Rhodian prototype — is made from a mould, while the bust is usually a plain plaque. Some, which lack the wide bands alongside the neck, could represent the

Female protome from Tharros 6th century B.C. terra-cotta, 14 cm Cagliari, Museo Archeologico Nazionale

Female protome from Sulcis 6th century B.C. terra-cotta, 32 cm Cagliari, Museo Archeologico Nazionale

*Plaquette in form
of human head
from Sulcis
5th century B.C.
painted
terra-cotta, 10 cm
Cagliari, Museo
Archeologico
Nazionale*

*Mask depicting
Silenus
from Sulcis
5th century B.C.
terra-cotta, 25 cm
S. Antioco
Museo Comunale*

*Mask depicting
Silenus
from Tharros
5th-4th century
B.C.
terra-cotta, 24 cm
Cagliari, Museo
Archeologico
Nazionale*

male type. The moulds vary little. The output of contemporary workshops less prone to use mechanical reproduction techniques is vast and highly original, and these maintain the typically Punic taste for added jewellery. Many protomes to the contrary can be classed as mere imitations of Sicilian prototypes from the 5th century; they were produced in series and show no signs of having been touched up.

The rather infrequent "grotesque" masks have little in common with those from the southern Mediterranean. Two alone show a clear influence from prototypes of the 2nd Cintas group. Other grotesque types are generic. More common are the Silenus masks (and protomes), usually cast from Greek-style moulds with touching up and additions. Few take up the conventions typical of the African tradition (for example, the centrally parted beard).

There is a long-bearded male series made in workshops which show little external influence. Some pieces are particularly striking due more to the attention given to design motifs (hair-spikes, moustache, beard) than to the general effect of form and volume. Lastly, a few masks of different size and quality seem to have been inspired by Greek theatrical masks.

In conclusion, protomes and masks have a ritual function in the Phoenician colonies analogous to that of the coastal Near East. The vogue for the

415

female protome, to the contrary, is essentially a western phenomenon, born of a contact with the Greek colonial world, whence are borrowed both the general typology and often the style. Reference to oriental figurative traditions, when they occur, are restricted to costume, and come exclusively from an Egyptian repertoire of a somewhat stereotyped kind. The same thing may be said of the Silenus masks, whose popularity is evident not so much from their numbers as from the variety of moulds used.

The western protome and mask typologies developed along the Tunisian coastline and in western and southern Sicily. Phoenician settlements in Libya and Egypt (little known until recently) could have played an important role on account of their familiarity with Egyptian tradition. Excavations up to now show that the Iberian Peninsula and the adjacent African coastline (western Algeria, Morocco) are excluded. Production and distribution of these objects is limited to that part of the Phoenician world which includes the central, or rather central-southern, Mediterranean coasts. Not by chance the western production — such as that of Sardinia and Ibiza — occurs in territories where there was a strong historical link with Carthage.

Bearded mask
from Ibiza
4th century B.C.
terra-cotta, 19 cm
Ibiza, Museo
Arqueológico

Negroid mask
from Cadiz
4th-3rd century B.C.
terra-cotta, 17.5 cm
Cadiz, Museo
de Cadiz

Bearded head
from Cadiz
6th-5th century B.C.
terra-cotta, 19 cm
Cadiz, Museo
de Cadiz
• *p. 476*

Female head
from Ibiza
5th century B.C.
terra-cotta, 24 cm
Madrid, Museo
Arqueológico Nacional

Female protome
from Ibiza
5th-4th century B.C.
terra-cotta, 22 cm
Barcelona, Museo
Arqueológico

Female protome
from Ibiza
5th-4th century B.C.
terra-cotta, 19.5 cm
Ibiza, Museo
Arqueológico

Jewellery
Giovanna Pisano

Jewellery is one of the most important and interesting products of Phoenician and Punic craftsmanship, although in some cases we should perhaps speak of art rather than simple artisan production. The craft was fostered by commerce in metals along the Mediterranean trade-routes, and is linked with the ancient and rich artistic tradition which had existed in Syria and Palestine before the Phoenicians. Byblos of the 3rd and 2nd millennia B.C. offers a good example with pectorals and gold pendants with repoussé or enamel cloisonné work, in which Egyptian influence predominates, providing the essential link between pre-Phoenician and Phoenician products. From a later period, the jewellery of Tell el-Ajjul (ancient Gaza) and Ras Shamra (ancient Ugarit), anticipate typologies and motifs that were used during the first millennium B.C. (the Phoenician period).

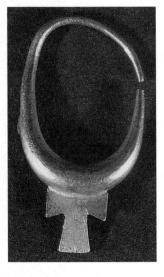

Earring with crux ansata from Carthage 7th-6th century B.C. gold, 3.1 cm Paris, Musée du Louvre

An essential homogeneity, or rather a deep-rooted traditionalist tendency, sometimes makes it difficult to distinguish between pieces made in the eastern and those made in the western Mediterranean when they come to light at Carthage or in the colonies. Further, the custom of hoarding and passing down jewellery from generation to generation makes precise dating a problem: even when the pieces are discovered on a datable site, it is easier to establish the date of use than the date of manufacture.

As regards materials, the jewellery is mostly made of gold, which stands the test of time. Silver was also used, but in this case erosion has taken its toll and fewer pieces have remained. Bronze pieces also appear. Precious stones and multicoloured glass were used in various ways mainly in the making of bracelets and necklaces, often with the above mentioned metals. The techniques most commonly employed are granulation, filigree-work and embossing, generally to be found on earlier pieces.

The most common motifs are of a magic or religious nature. They are mainly of Egyptian inspiration, though sometimes other sources are drawn on. There is a striking preference for designs from the world of plants and animals like the palmette, the lotus flower, the rosette, and the scarab, falcon, sphinx, griffin and lion. Geometrical motifs are also used, while the human figure is less common, with the sole exception of the female figure or half-bust (protome), which was a fertility symbol.

left
*Scarab in
haematite in
a gold and silver
mount from
the Luynes
Collection*
7th century B.C.
1.7 × 1.3 cm
*Paris, Bibliothèque
Nationale*

right
*Scarab in red jasper
on gold and silver*
8th century B.C.
1.68 × 1.25 cm
*Paris, Bibliothèque
Nationale*

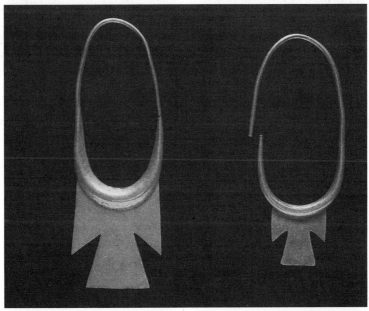

Earrings with crux
ansata
from Tharros
7th-6th century B.C.
*gold, 5.9 cm
and 5.1 cm*
*Cagliari, Museo
Archeologico
Nazionale*

left
*Cylindrical amulet
case from Carthage*
7th-6th century B.C.
gold, 3 cm
*Paris, Musée
du Louvre*

right
*Crested ring
from Carthage*
5th-4th century B.C.
gold-plated bronze
diam. 3.5 cm
*Tunis, Musée
du Bardo*

419

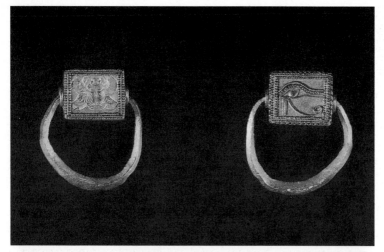

*Swivel ring with eye of Horus and winged beetle
7th-6th century B.C.
gold, 1 × 1.2 cm
Tunis, Musée du Bardo*

*Scarab with staff-shaped mount depicting Isis and the young Horus
6th-5th century B.C.
cornelian and gold, 3.5 cm
Tunis, Musée du Bardo*

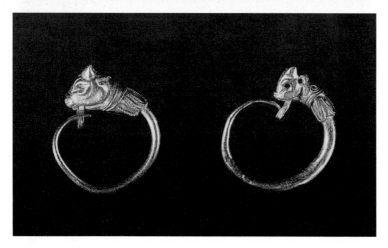

*Earrings featuring ox-head
4th century B.C.
gold, diam. 2 cm
Tunis, Musée du Bardo*

*Crested ring
from Carthage
6th-5th century
B.C.
gold, diam. 3 cm
Tunis, Musée
du Bardo*

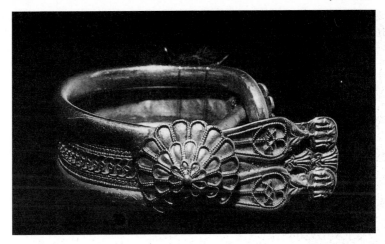

Examples from the eastern regions are gold crescent-shaped earrings and those of silver in the form of a leech or elongated rod, and basket-type pendants that have been found in nearly all settlements of the Phoenician diaspora of the 7th and 6th centuries B.C. The *crux ansata* types, unlike examples from the Phoenician West, have narrow, equilateral arms, making them more like the well-known Egyptian symbol of life (*ankh*), from which the *crux ansata* is derived. There are the rings with a rounded bezel-corner (*en cartouche*) setting, which clearly evoke the Egyptian scroll motif and bear delicate Egyptian-style designs.

Already in the second millennium B.C. Cypriot jewellery shows close links to that of coastal Syria and Palestine. During the course of the first millennium B.C. this tie to the Phoenician homeland remained constant, while at the same time the island transmitted to the West forms and motifs which became characteristic of the colonial milieu. There are numerous earrings in the form of an upturned nail with a rounded head or a head formed of a number of tiny granules soldered together in a cluster and fixed to the base of the little shaft. These types can be dated to the 7th and 6th centuries, as can a series of pendants in the form of a female protome, a disc with central boss, a lotus flower, a palmette — all types which recur throughout the various western Phoenician centers.

Jewellery has been found in tombs at Carthage from as far back as the 7th century B.C. The nature of the site itself suggests that magic values were attributed to the material, and in fact there is a constant choice of motifs imbued with symbolic significance when they appear in Phoenician and Punic art. Many pieces are of gold and a lesser number silver. There are earrings with pendants in the form of elongated drops embellished sometimes with granulation, a basket, or a *crux ansata*. The bracelets are made of plates of metal embossed with winged scarabs and palmettes.

The rings have a rectangular bezel which may be fixed or rotating and have rounded or sharp edges, engraved with complex Egyptianizing scenes in horizontal sequence, which follow precise narrative conventions in the juxtaposition of single elements. Individual subjects derived from these composite scenes, maintaining the same iconographic inspiration, appear on rings of a later, different type (c. 5th century B.C.), such as those with a stirrup bezel. There are many necklaces, showing a large range of combinations of beads of diverse shapes in gold and semi-precious stones (particularly cornelian) and coloured glass, with gold and silver pendants. There remains the doubt as to whether these necklaces have been reconstituted correctly, though it is probable that they do come quite close to the original composition of the individual components. Most interesting among the pendants are those in the form of a leech bow, since their form and iconography show links to the votive stelae. These pendants combine a fairly fixed typology with a decorative syntax rich in luministic and chiaroscuro effects achieved through skilful handling of various techniques including granulation and embossing, combined harmoniously to set off the religious motif which is the central distinguishing component. There are many pieces in the form of a down-turned crescent moon clasping between its horns a gold or gem-studded disc set with an *udjat*-eye or *ib*-heart in gold or cornelian, examples of the transposition of the amulet into the sphere of jewellery.

Shrine-shaped pendant with "bottle idol" and uraei from Carthage 6th century B.C. gold-plated silver 2.3 × 1.5 cm Paris, Musée du Louvre

Of equal magic and religious significance is the pendant made of a circular sheet decorated with a relief band with ends raised towards the central boss. Carthage, among innumerable other examples, has produced one with an engraved inscription that makes it amongst the oldest known (8th or even 9th century B.C.). Amulet cases decorated with a protome of a sacred Egyptian animal are typical pieces. They are usually in gold or silver, but later ones are in bronze or lead. Where they have remained intact, the rolls inside are made of the thinnest leaf, and bear engraved designs of Egyptian origin and sometimes inscriptions inspired by magic formulas. Their diffusion is probably due to Carthage's rise to power in the western Mediterranean.

The work of a later date becomes, in a sense, standardized and conditioned by foreign ideas. These ideas penetrate the Punic (no longer Phoenician) cultural world without completely altering the original core, which remains true to the old figurative canons imbued with religious and cultural implications. A proof of this is the appearance and diffusion even in jewellery of the "sign of Tanit."

From Rachgoun, Tangier and Mogador in Africa come important pieces very similar in character to those from Carthage.

From Malta, apart from several silver pendants with disc and central boss, mention should be made of the fragment of a silver bracelet with traces

*Necklace with
beads
and amulets
depicting
Ptah-patecus
and eye of Horus
from Kerkouane
3rd century B.C.
faience and other
materials
Tunis, Musée
du Bardo*

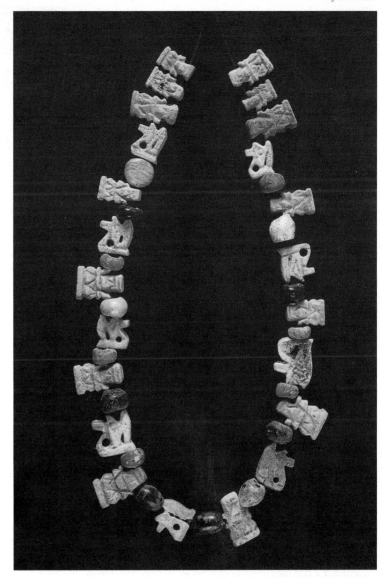

of gold plate embossed with narrative decorations in the Egyptian iconographical convention: two rampant griffins flanking a sacred tree formed
of stylized lotus flower volutes alternating with palmettes below a winged
sun-disc with uraei. The jewellery found in Sicily cannot compare in number with that of Sardinia and Carthage. The typologies of the pieces from
Palermo and Motya are limited. All are in silver, save a very few in gold.
There are earrings in a simple leech-shape with pendants in the form of
baskets, acorns or the *crux ansata*. There are also signet-rings with scarabs
in faience, pendants of the leech bow type or with the Tanit symbol and
an *amphoriskos* motif adapted from coloured glassware.

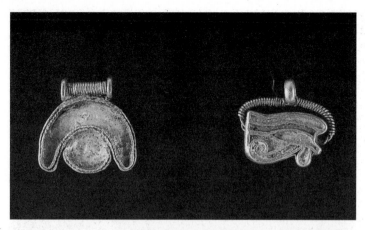

Pendant depicting crescent and disc from Carthage 7th-6th century B.C. gold, 1.6 × 1.7 cm Carthage, Musée de Carthage

Pendant depicting eye of Horus from Carthage 5th century B.C. gold, 1.4 × 1.7 cm Carthage, Musée de Carthage

Shrine-shaped pendant with "bottle idol" and uraei from Carthage 6th century B.C. gold, 2.2 × 1.5 cm Carthage, Musée de Carthage

Earring with crux ansata *from Carthage 7th-6th century B.C. gold, 4 cm Carthage, Musée de Carthage*

Medallion pendant with winged solar disc and uraei from Carthage 7th-6th century B.C. gold, diam. 1.9 cm Carthage, Musée de Carthage

Embossed medallion pendant with inscription from Carthage 7th century B.C. gold, diam. 1.8 cm Carthage, Musée de Carthage

*Necklaced
with beads
and pendants
from Carthage
7th-6th century
B.C.
gilded silver
35 cm
Carthage, Musée
de Carthage*

The Tanit symbol and *amphoriskos* motif were in all probability imported from Carthage as they were used in a period of mutual exchanges
brought about by the contacts between Carthage and Sicily (in particular Motya). The other jewellery is from the "archaic" period (7th and
6th centuries B.C.) before Carthaginian expansion, and is likely to have
come from the East or from Tharros, although it is not impossible it
came from Carthage as well.

Tharros has proved the richest source as regards quantity and quality
for jewellery, as well as for the other *athỳrmata* in Sardinia. The term
athỳrmata covers scarabs, amulets, etc. The fact that they are enclosed
in mounts or bear clasps, etc. qualifies them as jewellery, and in the
broad sense as metallurgy.

Among the earrings there are some complex pieces with leech-shaped
body terminating with stylized bird protomes, and various pendants in

425

the form of a Horus falcon and an elongated drop, linked by two rings. Each of these pieces is unique in its delicate colouring, achieved through the skilful application of various techniques such as embossing, granulation and filigree, which bring out the details of the work, and allow them to be dated to the 7th century B.C. In other earrings of this type a basket replaces the elongated drop pendant. Other simpler versions have one pendant only of the type mentioned above or a *crux ansata*. It should also be pointed out that, unlike Carthaginian jewellery, that of Tharros is mostly in silver. Given silver's tendency to oxidation, it is likely that what has been recovered up to now represents only a fraction of the original quantity manufactured in Sardinia.

Several hair-rings in gold on a silver or bronze core follow the typology of the rod-earrings with tapered ends twisted together in spirals or bent into hooks or knots. Both types are from a later period (5th-2nd centuries B.C.) when work was carried out using mass production methods and lower standards of workmanship: the result of a homogeneous process of evolution in Phoenician craftsmanship, linked to important political changes that brought new and different cultural influences.

As regards bracelets, there are two probably incomplete pieces made up of gold plaques narrowing towards the extremities and joined with hinges made from tiny flattened cylinders housing a pin. One has a winged scarab with a hawk protome on the central plaque, palmettes with volutes on the middle plaques, and lotus flowers on the external ones. The other bracelet shows the variant of two smaller plaques in the centre embossed in this case as well with scrolled palmettes. It should be pointed out that these pieces have an outstanding decorative style, and like other jewellery of this period (7th-6th century B.C.) must be considered works of art.

There are no parallels for these pieces in the Phoenician diaspora, and it has been suggested that they were imported from the Near East. This hypothesis does not rule out the existence and development of a rich local craft tradition, indirectly confirmed not only by the quantity and quality of the material, but also by the local production of jasper scarabs whose gold and silver mounts do not appear to have come from outside Tharros. One bracelet alone retains its original form. It is composed of two ribbed bands overlaid in a spiral and bent at the ends into hooks which bear variously shaped ornaments and a crescent moon-and-disc pendant (the disc would have been set with sand-core glass or a semiprecious stone).

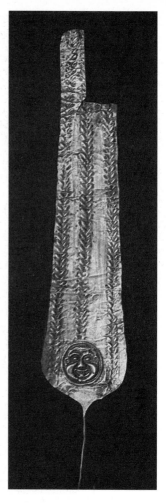

Lamina with gorgoneion from Nora 5th century B.C. gold, 2.6 cm Cagliari, Museo Archeologico Nazionale

426

*Earring with
drop-shaped
pendant
and falcon
from Tharros
7th-6th century
B.C.
gold, 10 cm
Cagliari, Museo
Archeologico
Nazionale*

*Earring with
drop-shaped
pendant
from Tharros
7th-6th century
B.C.
gold, 6.9 cm
Cagliari, Museo
Archeologico
Nazionale*

Most of the rings are of silver or gold-plated silver. Some have a rectangular, square, round or oval mount for a scarab or semi-precious stone, engraved with traditional Egyptian and Phoenician motifs (griffins, falcons, palmettes). Those of the 5th century B.C. onwards, though they comply with the general cultural matrix, are enriched with foreign motifs (negroid protome, kneeling warrior), and must be seen as peripheral.

As regards necklaces, as well as the bronze and silver twisted type with hook-and-eye clasp and with glass "eye" beads, there are necklaces composed of gold ornaments, semi-precious stones and glass in all the usual shapes, and also pendants. Among the motifs used for the pendants there is the Horus falcon, the rosette, the Tanit symbol, the chrysalis. The pendants in the shape of the goddess with hands on breasts and the female protome with *klaft* headdress are particularly interesting. They are in fact two typical examples of the "image cul-

Necklace with amulets depicting Ptah-patecus and, in the centre, Nefertum 7th century B.C. sand-core glass central amulet 5 cm Rome, Museo Archeologico di Villa Giulia

ture," which corresponds (chronologically too) with the female protome and the terra-cotta figurine traditions. Such also is the rendering in faience of the *udjat*-eye, in conformity with its traditional amulet form, or of the acorn, or of the open lotus flower resting on volutes, or the fan-leafed palmette. All these and other motifs are faithfully reproduced in jewellery and ivory work. We have already seen amulet cases among the Carthaginian pieces. Here there are cases in the form of a plain or fluted cylinder bearing a falcon, lion or ram protome, and others with a double protome. Some cases are in the form of a short pillar with pyramidal top, clearly evoking the stone cippi of Tharros.

As regards other jewellery in Sardinia, apart from scattered finds, the pieces discovered at Olbia and Monte Luna (Senorbì) are worth mentioning. From Olbia comes a necklace composed of 18 pieces of sand-core glass, including five human and two animal protomes as central elements. Carthaginian influence, or possibly provenance, seems likely. The jewellery found in the tombs of Monte Luna is equally important. Among the objects in gold, silver and bronze, there are leech-shaped earrings and others in the form of a small rod with plain or

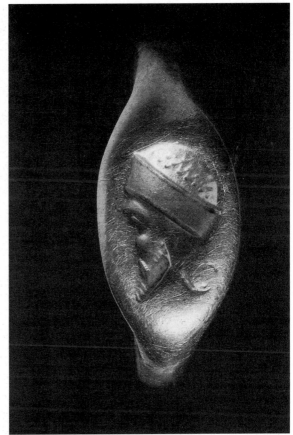

Ring with "sign of Tanit"
from Monte Luna
4th-3rd century B.C.
gold, diam. 1.3 cm
Cagliari, Museo
Archeologico Nazionale

Ring depicting
falcon Horus
from Tharros
7th-6th century B.C.
gold, diam. 2.3 cm
Cagliari, Museo
Archeologico Nazionale

Ring with male bearded
head and headdress
from Tharros
7th-6th century B.C.
gold, 1.9 cm
Cagliari, Museo
Archeologico Nazionale

Ring bezel with griffins
and palmettes
from Tharros
7th-6th century B.C.
gold, diam. 2.3 cm
Cagliari, Museo
Archeologico Nazionale

twisted ends, pendants inlaid with scarabs, rings with stirrup bezels inscribed with single motifs like the "sign of Tanit," the *udjat*-eye, the female protome. There are gold beanshaped ornaments, feathers in gold and silver foil, bracelets worked in various ways. Of the latter there is an example of artistic worth and refined craftsmanship, consisting of gold chains linked at the ends by two cylinders, with an acorn-shaped pendant decorated with granulation.

It has been suggested that this piece was imported from Magna Graecia, and that the rings came from Carthaginian workshops or from Sicily either directly or via Carthage. The date of this jewellery — from the last half of the 5th to the 3rd century B.C. — could indicate a new influx of trade to Sardinia around the end of the 5th century, although considering the period it seems very unlikely that products from Tharros were not being used. As things stand, then, the jewellery of Monte Luna should be considered as an importation, a case apart from the other Sardinian finds, which mostly come from Tharros.

In the Iberian Peninsula, where the most important mines of precious metals (particularly gold) for the jewellery craft were situated, recent excavations on the south coast have added to the hitherto rather meager evidence from Cadiz and Ibiza alone. From Trayamar come leech-shaped earrings, pendants and necklace beads and rings with rotating bezels of the familiar Phoenician type. Of particular interest for its similarity to pieces from Carthage of the same period (7th century), is a disc-pendant decorated with granulation and embossed with a motif common in the colonies: a winged sun-disc above a larger disc with crescent moon, with below an *omphalos* flanked by two uraei with falcons on their heads. These pendants appear to come from the same artistic milieu, but it seems unlikely that they were made locally.

The case of some important groups of jewellery dis-

Bracelet depicting winged beetle palmettes and lotus flowers from Tharros 7th-6th century B.C., gold 12.8 × 3.4 cm Cagliari, Museo Archeologico Nazionale

Necklace with acorn pendant from Monte Luna gold, 24.8 cm Cagliari, Museo Archeologico Nazionale
• p. 477

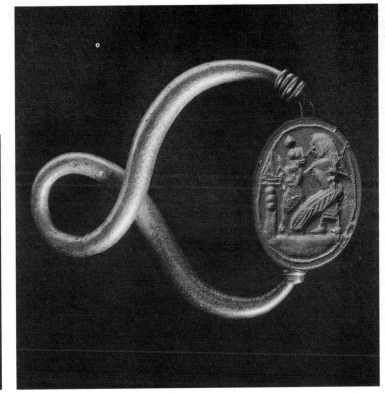

Earring with falcon and basket pendants from Tharros 7th-6th century B.C.
gold, 7.6 cm Cagliari, Museo Archeologico Nazionale

Scarab mounted in gold with Isis and Horus from Tharros 5th-4th century B.C.
green jasper 1.5 × 1.3 cm Cagliari, Museo Archeologico Nazionale

covered at Aliseda, El Carambolo and Ebora — in the hinterland far from contact with the Phoenicians — is different. The repertoire of ornamentation places these pieces within the ambit of orientalizing art: the primary influence is Phoenician — strong from the 7th century B.C. onwards — but a number of other influences, from Greek to Etruscan, may be observed in these local designs, and the jewellery has a decorative exuberance which is well supported by the precious virtuosity of the workmanship.

Among the treasures of Aliseda there is a gold belt of which 62 pieces have remained intact. They are decorated with the common oriental motifs of the man wrestling with a rampant lion, the griffin and the stylized two-volute palmette, all executed more schematically than the models but with a clarity and an intensity of effect achieved by the combination of embossing on a background of granulation. There is also a linked diadem, made up of rectangular plaques each embellished with four rosettes made of knurled wire rolled up and inserted in circular hinges, and hung with bundles and strings of globules with chain pendants finishing in triangular plaques with rich borders surrounding a palmette, rosettes and concave bosses.

The earrings are of the leech-shape but swollen and ringed by a flowery sunburst embellished with lotus blooms and palms flanked by

431

heraldic falcons. The bracelets are flat, decorated with openwork spirals and finish in palmette attachments where lotus flowers are embossed on a background of varied granulation. The necklaces have gold stamped double pendants in the shape of discs, crescents, cylindrical cases either plain or bearing an animal protome, and many-shaped ornaments, all of which show the development of an independent provincial taste based on original Punic typologies. Rings and seals complete the group.

The El Carambolo treasure is composed of 21 pieces in gold, all highly unusual in their richness, originality of form and geometrical decoration, devoid of figurative expression. The treasure came to light all at the same time, and on the basis of the ornamentation can be divided into two groups. The first group includes a pectoral, two bracelets and eight plaques decorated with alternating bands of hemispheres and rosettes in cells separated by ribbed wires. The second group contains a pectoral, a necklace and eight plaques decorated with little hemispheres alternated with strings of rings. The most important piece is the necklace made of a double chain ending in a biconical loop with eight small chains carrying seven ring- or seal-pendants decorated in filigree with stylized geometrical and floral motifs.

The Ebora treasure is made up of about a hundred small gold pieces which form a large hinged diadem with symmetrical triangular end-plates, and a number of necklaces, bracelets, and various pendants. Interesting here is the use of the granulation technique, and the introduction of a purely local element in the development of foreign themes. The issue of the influence of Phoenician forms on indigenous craftsmanship is also illustrated by certain pieces discovered in Portugal.

Pendant with female protome from Tharros 7th-6th century B.C.

gold, 2.9 cm Cagliari, Museo Archeologico Nazionale
• *p. 478*

Pendant with female figure with hands on breasts from Tharros 6th-5th century B.C.

gold, 3.3 cm Sassari, Museo Nazionale G.A. Sanna
• *p. 479*

*Votive stele
featuring priest
and child, found
at Carthage
4th century B.C.
stone, approx.
118 × 15 cm
Tunis, Musée
du Bardo*

*Stele featuring
male figure
and winged
disc from
Umm el-Amed
3rd-2nd century
B.C.
marble
85 × 22 cm
Paris, Musée
du Louvre*

opposite page
Votive stele with open hand "sign of
Tanit", caduceus, and ram above
from Carthage
2nd century B.C.
limestone, 26.5 × 15 cm
Paris, Bibliothèque Nationale

Votive stele with female figure
holding a lotus flower
from Monte Sirai
4th-3rd century B.C.
tufa, 55.5 × 35 cm
Cagliari
Museo Archeologico Nazionale

Female bust with kalathos
form Ibiza
5th century B.C.
painted terra-cotta, 50 cm
Ibiza, Museo Arquelógico

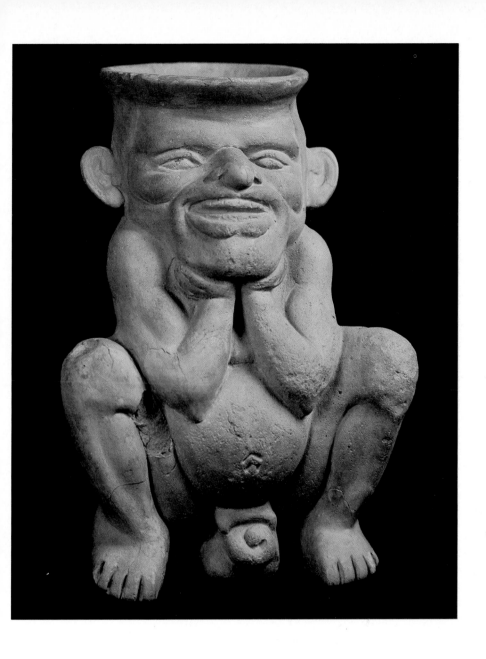

*Statuette of Bes with head
in form of vessel
from Agrigentum
4th century B.C.
terra-cotta, 30.5 cm
Agrigento, Museo
Archeologico Nazionale*

Bell-shaped votive statuette
with hands covering eyes
from Bithia
3rd-1st century B.C.
terra-cotta, 20.5 cm
Cagliari, Museo Archeologico Nazionale

*Plaquette with winged sphinx
and palmette, from Ibiza
6th century B.C.
terra-cotta, 12 cm
Madrid, Museo Arqueológico Nacional*

Female statuette wearing nose-ring, from Ibiza 4th century B.C. terra-cotta 32.5 cm Madrid, Museo Arqueológico National

left
*Drop-shaped pendant
from Sulcis
6th-5th century B.C.
gold, 2.1 cm
S. Antioco, Collezione Biggio*

right
*Amphora pendant
from Tharros
6th century B.C.
gold, 2.5 cm
Cagliari, Museo
Archeologico Nazionale*

left
*Stud with two corollas from
Tharros, 6th-5th century B.C.
gold, diam. 1.9 cm
Sassari, Museo Nazionale
G.A. Sanna*

right
*Pendant with eye of Horus
from Tharros
7th-6th century B.C.
gold, 1.2 × 1.8 cm
Cagliari, Museo
Archeologico Nazionale*

left
*Embossed medallion
with geometric designs
from Tharros
7th-6th century B.C.
gold, diam. 1.25 cm
Sassari, Museo Nazionale
G.A. Sanna*

right
*Pendant with palmette and
lotus flower from Tharros
5th-4th century B.C.
gold, 1.5 cm
Sassari, Museo Nazionale
G.A. Sanna*

right
*Crested ring
from Tharros
4th-3rd century B.C.
gold, diam. 2 cm
Sassari, Museo Nazionale
G.A. Sanna*

*Chrysalis pendant
from Tharros
7th-6th century B.C.
gold, 4.3 cm
Cagliari, Museo
Archeologico Nazionale*

*Amulet case
with protome of falcon
from Tharros
7th-6th century B.C.
gold, 4.3 cm
Cagliari, Museo
Archeologico Nazionale*

*Amulet case
with protome of ram
from Carthage
7th-6th century B.C.
gold, 5.2 cm
Tunis, Musée du Bardo*

*Amulet case
with protome of lion
from Tharros
7th-6th century B.C.
gold, 3.9 cm
Cagliari, Museo
Archeologico Nazionale*

*Amulet with figure
of Horus and Anubis
and fragments of gold
leaf from the tomb
of Ghain Klieb
in Rabat, Malta
7th-6th century B.C.
gold, 2.5 cm
La Valletta
National Museum
of Archaeology*

*Gold, cornelian
and rock crystal
pendants
from Tharros
7th-6th century
B.C.
2.4-1.3 cm
Sassari
Museo Nazionale
G.A. Sanna*

*Gold and cornelian
pendant
from Tharros
6th century B.C.
1.5 cm
diam. 1.6 cm
Sassari
Museo Nazionale
G.A. Sanna*

*Gold-mounted
amulet showing
eye of Horus
from Tharros
6th-4th century B.C.
sand-core glass
1.4 × 1.1 cm
Sassari
Museo Nazionale
G.A. Sanna*

From a tomb at Sines on the Atlantic coast come a number of leech-shaped gold earrings surrounded by a sunburst of fourteen spheres embossed with two-faced protomes from which spring lotus flowers. Though the formulation is simpler and less baroque, this piece is clearly a product of the same cultural background as the Aliseda pendants. In the group there is also a necklace made of sixteen plaques embossed on a matrix with rampant winged griffins and upturned palmettes around a rosette. Again, the motifs recall the jewellery of Aliseda.

Baião, another site on Portuguese soil, has yielded finds, including a necklace, a diadem and four earrings stamped with a Phoenician-type palmette with indented volutes and a flat, leech-shaped form sunk within a border of T-shaped motifs (presumably stylized lotus flowers). Here again an orientalizing cultural background is evident, although it is not possible to say where these pieces were made. What is important, however, is the continuing discovery of sites on the Atlantic coast of the

443

Iberian Peninsula. Though sporadic, they all help to shed light on the character of influence of Phoenician and Punic civilization in the ancient history of the Mediterranean countries.

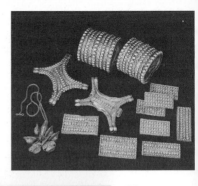

The treasure of El Carambolo
7th century B.C.
gold
Madrid
Museo Arqueológico Nacional
• *p. 480*

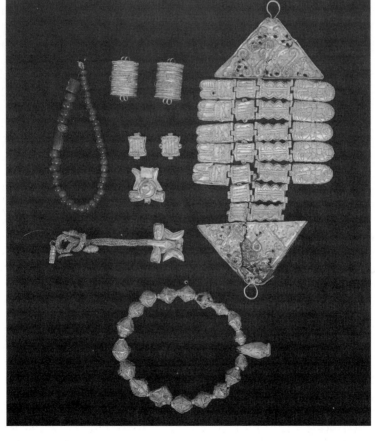

The treasure
of Ebora
7th century B.C.
gold
Madrid, Museo
Arqueológico
Nacional

Scarabs and Amulets
Enrico Acquaro

The frequent discovery of scarabs and amulets in Phoenician and Punic tombs in the East and the West is the most obvious evidence of the prestige enjoyed by Egyptian magic in the Phoenician world. Not only were these objects imported from Egyptian production centres, such as Naucratis and Memphis; their high value as auspicious funerary accompaniments was also reflected by local imitation. The adoption and reworking of Egyptian amulet types and designs in the Phoenician world is the best illustration of how the symbolic value of these objects was recognized throughout the ancient Mediterranean, from prehistory to late Roman times.

The universal adoption of the scarab as a symbol connected to regeneration in this life and in life after death, and also as a seal, demonstrates the extent of Egyptian influence on Phoenician culture from its origins in the Levant. This influence prevailed despite competition from Paleo-Syria and Mesopotamia (which does emerge in significant but isolated points in the same material culture).

Having lost its Egyptian role as a vehicle for political and religious propaganda, the scarab was widely used in the Mediterranean outside the Phoenician world, from Persia to Rhodes, Crete, Greece (Eleusis, Mycenae, Sparta, Perachora), Etruria, Cumae, Pithekoussa, Syracuse. In some cases, scarabs are found as votive offerings or foundation deposits in the sacred enclosures of Byblos, Lachish, Kition, Mycenae and in the temples of Artemis Orthia at Sparta, and Hera Acraia and Hera Limenia at Perachora. But more importantly it is a fundamental component of the grave goods of Mediterranean tombs of all eras, from the first orientalizing period to Roman times.

The Phoenician market's demand for scarabs as protective amulets with a specific meaning (the inscriptions or designs carved into the oval base) shows constant attention to the magical connotations of the iconographies. Thus, hieroglyphic compositions indicating names of divinities (Ra, Amun, Horus, Ptah, Maat) or names of pharaohs (who in the original Egyptian belief were protected by hieroglyphs) were selected more for the ideographic component of the hieroglyph than its phonetic value. Often Egyptian designs are accompanied by inscriptions in the Phoenico-Punic alphabet which identify the scarab's owner and give the magic interpretation of the designs reproduced. The materials used in the production of scarabs were preferably steatite and faience with green and blue glaze, although examples of carved semi-precious stones such as jasper, cornelian, agate, rock crystal and onyx are not lacking. Western workshops utilized the latter materials, and in Greece, Etruria and Punic Sardinia took up the scarab motif and gave it a new figurative repertory in which the Egyptian tradition is combined with themes from Near Eastern, Greaco-Oriental, Magna Graecian and Etruscan mythology.

In the earliest Egyptian examples and in later steatite and faience copies the gold or silver setting follows the Egyptian model of an oval ring. In western production, the mounts have the complexity and richness of workmanship and composition typical of the orientalizing style of Etruscan goldsmithing and of the Phoenician jewellery tradition. The mounts, in gold, silver or gold-plated bronze, are frequently versatile and demonstrate that the scarab was not meant to be worn as a ring, but to be strung on a necklace or used in different amulet compositions.

The Punic master engravers at work in Tharros from the late 6th to the 3rd century B.C. reached a high technical level and achieved an extremely original interpretation of the magic and apotropaic powers of the scarab. The preferred material was a dark green jasper mined from Sardinian deposits known since nuraghic times, a choice which determined the style of the whole production. Carving into a thicker core created a massive type of scarab; in Egyptian examples and imitations in steatite and faience the scarab is usually flat with linear engraving (where present) outlining the insect's back, the space between the elytra, the legs and eyes. The master carvers of Tharros conform to the Etrusco-Ionic tradition in the way the back is cut, often resulting in a relief effect, particularly in the legs and the thorax area. The technique used — linear incisions and globular form — is typically western.

At Tharros, a remarkable skill is demonstrated in the uncontrived application to the basic oval shape of designs borrowed from very different sources, ranging from the Near Eastern ivories to Magna Graecian pottery, from Paleo-Syrian glyptics to Ionic coinage.

The motifs — the enthroned figure, Isis nursing Horus, the god Bes battling with various beasts, mythical Heracles carrying out his labours, a cow giving suck to a calf, numerous sacred animals in the Egyptian tradition (falcon, uraeus), the satyr and Silenus — create a rich array of designs united in their ritual function by the magic message underlying them all. Here Punic art appears in its full maturity, capable of offering to the pre-Roman central and western Mediterranean world a prestigious new interpretation able to hold its own against the best results of Hellenism and the initial orientalizing synthesis of Etruscan art.

The other amulets used by Phoenicians and Carthaginians in their funeral rites follow the path established by the scarab. Drawn from Egyptian sources, carved or impressed in bone, faience or steatite, they reproduce recurrent motifs in that civilization's mythology. The eye of Horus, Horus as a child, Isis the nourisher, Shu, Ptah-patecus, Khnum-

Scarab with three stylized figures from Tharros 7th-6th century B.C. steatite, 1.9 cm Sassari Museo Nazionale G.A. Sanna

Scarab depicting Silenus and inscription 6th century B.C. rock crystal 1.73 × 1.39 cm Paris Bibliothèque National

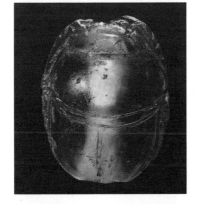 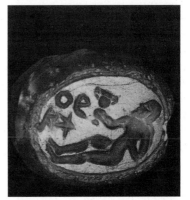

Scarab depicting figure and winged sphinx 7th-5th century B.C. steatite 1.6 × 1.2 cm Sassari Museo Nazionale G.A. Sanna

Ra, Ra, Bes, Anubis, Thoth, Taweret, the monkey, the ram, the hare, the lion, the cat, the sow with or without her young, the crocodile, the falcon are all typical figures which accompany Phoenician and Punic burials, both cremations and inhumations.

In this case as well, Phoenician and Punic religious requirements determine the choice of symbols both for their broad magic connotations and their place in a particular ritual context. Thus, the selection of amulets for funerary applications tends to exclude those specifically related to Egyptian eschatology and ritual, such as the large scarabs of the heart, reproductions of the vital organs of the body (heart, lungs), and of royal and priestly attributes (the red and white crowns, ostrich feathers, knot of Isis, ritual pectorals), and of particular symbols, such as the square and the ladder.

Amulets found in urns containing the cremated remains of sacrificed children draw upon the usual sources, but the choices are specifically related to the children's world, from Silenus masks to Horus as a boy, or lead miniatures of oil lamps, tripods, knives and plates. Magic value is also attributed to shells, often set in silver, such as the cowries carved to resemble more closely the female genitals with their life-giving powers of fertility.

Scarab depicting Isis and Horus from Tharros 4th century B.C. green jasper 1.7 × 1.2 cm Cagliari, Museo Archeologico Nazionale

For their amulets, then, the Phoenician and Punic peoples chose motifs suitable for particular rites from the repertory of Egyptian magic symbols. However, they also included symbols which had originated in their own culture, such as the so-called "sign of Tanit."

Certain amulet types emerge in which the link with Punic art is more explicit. Conceding historical and artistic dignity to a category which was not reserved for the use of the ruling class, and going beyond a generalized distinction according to types, we can perceive a number of basic cultural choices which influenced the design of Punic amulets.

The juxtaposition of human and animal elements in Egyptian sacred iconographies was too widely known in the major arts to allow originality in the transposition to the miniature scale of the amulet. However, the Phoenician amulets of animal totemic divinities often combine anthropomorphic and zoomorphic elements with great freedom.

Particularly interesting in this context are the amulets which depict a uraeus. Though occasionally the treatment of the head is naturalistic, most suggest other animal forms, particularly the dog.

The zoomorphic transposition found in the sphinx and in the monkey-headed figures, and related variants, is analogous. In the sphinx type, in fact, the anthropomorphic head of the animal undergoes transformations which range from a return to zoomorphic qualities (leonine and/or canine, for example) to a more precise characterization in human terms, sometimes linked to a representation of the god Bes.

More complex is the hybridization that occurs in the iconography of amulets with the monkey-headed figure. "Anthropomorphic" nature itself undoubtedly contributes to this continous osmosis between the human and the animal. The integration of man and animal may take the form of a "human" bearing, as in the type of the dog-headed enthroned

left
*Amulet with
"sign of Tanit"
from Ibiza
6th-5th century B.C.
ivory, 2.3 cm
Ibiza, Museo
Arqueológico*

right
*Amulet depicting
cippus
from Sardinia
6th-4th century B.C.
steatite, 1.6 cm
and amulet
depicting right hand
from Tharros
6th-3rd century B.C.
bone, 1.07 cm
Sassari
Museo Nazionale
G.A. Sanna*

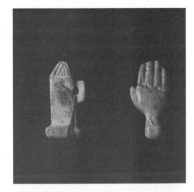

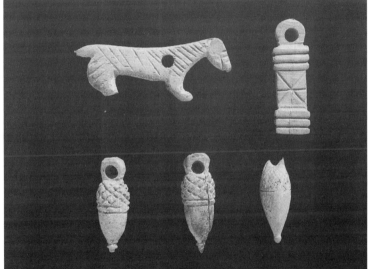

*Amulets depicting
dog, cippus and
acorn
from Villaricos
6th-3rd century B.C.
bone, approx.
1.7-3.05-2.5 cm
Madrid, Museo
Arqueológico
Nacional*

*Amulets of arms
with hand
forming sign
of female genitals
and feet
from Villaricos
6th-3rd century
B.C., bone
approx. 3-2 cm
Madrid, Museo
Arqueológico
Nacional*

449

Scarab with seated lion
uraeus and protome of Bes
from Tharros
6th-5th century B.C.
green jasper, 1.7 cm
Sassari, Museo Nazionale G.A. Sanna

Scarab depicting mummified
Isis and Osiris
from Tharros
6th century B.C.
green jasper, 1.7 cm
Sassari, Museo Nazionale G.A. Sanna

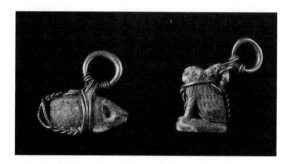

Amulet depicting fish entwined
in gold, from Tharros
7th-4th century B.C.
faience, 1.1 cm
Sassari, Museo Nazionale G.A. Sanna

Amulet depicting cat entwined
in gold, from Tharros
7th-4th century B.C.
faience, 1.2 cm
Sassari, Museo Nazionale G.A. Sanna

figure, while in other cases an essentially human figure assumes a zoomorphic pose.

The iconography of the Egyptian and Egyptianizing amulets adopted by the Phoenician culture often undergoes a series of modifications, additions, and variants for exclusively figurative reasons. The Phoenician amulet thus presents a measure of iconographic and stylistic independence that though modest and sporadic cannot be ignored. Nor can the usual objections to an artistic evaluation of products considered "routine" stereotypes be maintained in the face of this more careful and up-to-date analysis.

Instead it is instructive and opportune to take precisely these modest products as a point of departure for a general understanding of values of aesthetic taste as the expression of a society in all its varied classes and cultural experiences. It is therefore possible to rediscover these values by analyzing the figurative decoration of the entire category. Among the numerous starting points that come to mind, that of the vulgarization and banalization of the designs seems the most significant.

Scarab with enthroned Isis
and incense burner
from Tharros
5th century B.C.
green jasper, 1 cm
Sassari, Museo Nazionale G.A. Sanna

Scarab depicting figure armed
with shield and lance
from Tharros
5th-4th century B.C.
green jasper, 1.5 cm
Sassari, Museo Nazionale G.A. Sanna

Scarab depicting
Bes among
animals
from Tharros
5th-4th century
B.C.
green jasper and
gold, 1.6 cm
Cagliari, Museo
Archeologico
Nazionale

The religious subject matter reproduced on amulet is subjected to a series of adaptations and modifications characterized by a consistent demand for vulgarization. This holds for both the original Egyptian products and the Phoenician imitations. In synthesis, there are two figurative values affected by this requirement: on the one hand, the interpretation of religious themes in more broadly anthropological terms relating them to daily experience; on the other hand, the banalization of the original ritual significance, towards an increasingly abstract and inclusive interpretation.

There are various amulets which demonstrate the vulgarizing trend, ranging from faience plaques to representations of Isis nursing her child.

In the plaques the iconography of the cow with calf seems to be the most influenced by this trend. The beast, with or without calf, in more than one instance seems to be the result of an attentive observation of nature; the dimensions, the proportion of the limbs, and the specific characteristics of the breed take on an importance that eclipses the magical connotations. In other words, it is the beast of burden or farmyard animal which emerges in a concrete way from the remnants of a more high-flown iconographic tradition.

The figure of Isis nursing the child Horus is endowed with analogous values of human ordinariness compared with the original cult formulation. The relationship between mother and son is treated with such familiarity and the rendering is so sketchy that all mythological identification seems to have been lost, leaving only a general maternal theme.

*Amulet depicting crowned uraeus, from Tharros
7th-4th century B.C.
talc, 1.08 cm
Sassari, Museo
Nazionale G.A. Sanna*

*Amulet depicting falcon
from Tharros
7th-4th century B.C.
steatite, 1.9 cm
Sassari, Museo
Nazionale G.A. Sanna*

*Amulet depicting cat
from Tharros
7th-4th century B.C.
talc, 1.6 cm
Sassari, Museo
Nazionale G.A. Sanna*

*Amulet depicting bearded
winged sphinx
from Tharros
7th-4th century B.C.
talc, 1.4 cm
Sassari, Museo
Nazionale G.A. Sanna*

*Amulet depicting
hare from Kition
5th-4th century B.C.
faience, 1.1 cm
Larnaca, District
Museum*

*Amulet
depicting bull
looking backwards
from Tharros
7th-5th century B.C.
ivory, 1.1 cm
Sassari, Museo
Nazionale
G.A. Sanna*

*Amulet depicting horn
from Tharros
7th-5th century B.C.
bone, 3.1 cm
Sassari, Museo
Nazionale G.A. Sanna*

*Amulet depicting Ptah-patecus
from Ibiza
5th-4th century B.C.
faience, 3.05 cm
Ibiza, Museo Arqueológico*

*Amulet depicting monkey
from Tharros
5th-4th century B.C.
ivory entwined in silver, 2 cm
Cagliari, Museo
Archeologico Nazionale*

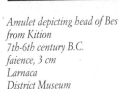

*Amulet depicting head of Bes
from Kition
7th-6th century B.C.
faience, 3 cm
Larnaca
District Museum*

*Amulet depicting Ptah-patecus
from Tharros
5th-4th century B C.
faience, 2.5 cm
Sassari, Museo
Nazionale G.A. Sanna*

*Amulet depicting
Horus-Ra
with crown
from Tharros
4th-3rd century
B.C.
faience, 4.5 cm
Sassari
Museo Nazionale
G.A. Sanna*

The second manifestation of the vulgarizing trend seen in the amulets especially involves complex compositions of juxtaposed elements usually found in single types. In this context the magic and compositional complexity of the figure of Ptah-patecus (with crocodiles, falcons on his shoulders, scarab resting on his head, Isis and Nephthys at his side and behind him Isis nursing the child or his own repeated figure) is of some interest.

In fact the Ptah-patecus summarizes and brings into the stream of his own iconography the various elements that surround him: the lateral divinities, which in some cases blend into the wave form of the uraei, together with the falcons on his shoulders, compose a single vertical sequence which is distinguishable from Ptah-patecus' body only by the vertical arrangement of the suspension rings.

The linear representation of the scarab's back which in the best examples appears over Ptah-patecus' head exemplifies a certain ornamental exoticism not lacking in interest. Essentially linear solutions of the Ptah-patecus type are found in examples where the complex composition achieves a clear and suggestive synthesis in the skilled cross-hatching of short incisions. The clean, fresh handling is very striking, capable of repeating with precision the complex iconography of three-dimensional examples without neglecting any of the most minute details.

*Plaquette depicting cow and calf
from Ibiza
5th century B.C.
steatite, 1.4 cm
Ibiza, Museo Arqueológico*

The application of this linear decoration to a number of animal heads also shows a good level of craftsmanship. The symbolic function progressively blends into a more generalized decorative intention, which in its total freedom from any naturalistic constraint attains extremely attractive results.

Frequent reference has been made to the relationship between primary iconography and amulet iconography, and the consequent problems of transposition and adaptation. The reduction in size and the standardized serial production of the amulets required selection and synthesis of

*Scarab depicting female figure on horseback
from Ibiza
5th-4th century B.C.
green jasper, 1.45 cm
Madrid, Museo Arqueológico Nacional
• p. 513*

*Scarab depicting Isis nursing Horus
from Ibiza
5th-4th century B.C.
green jasper, 1.8 cm
Madrid, Museo Arqueológico Nacional*

*Scarab depicting Heracles with bow
from Ibiza
5th-4th century B.C.
green jasper, 1.6 cm
Madrid, Museo Arqueológico Nacional
• p. 513*

the principal themes. The craftsman called upon to satisfy the demand for amulets worked in the context of what today would be called a mass market, according to his own particular taste and selective capacities, following the figurative examples that surrounded him. The relationship thus established between the manufacture of amulets, humble in their material and destination, and the major categories gave rise to variants and adaptations.

One of the most instructive revelations in this respect comes from an examination of the amulets in relation to two of the so-called major craft categories: terra-cotta masks and carved ivories. Comparing the terracotta masks with the mask-type amulets, and the ivories with the plaque amulets with the suckling calf motif, we see that while the miniature masks do not seem far from the larger scale versions, the designs on the composition plaques, though similar in theme, differ greatly in concept from the realizations on ivory or bone panels and plaques.

Since such a difference cannot be attributed simply to the use of different materials we may conclude that the terracotta masks and the amulets belonged to a similar cultural area, while the refined work in ivory and bone served a market with somewhat different cultural requirements and commercial circuits. All this confirms the independent development of the masks, and the fundamentally elite circulation of ivories, deriving to a large extent from Near Eastern and diverse western markets.

Scarab depicting female figure
astride a bull
from Ibiza, 5th-4th century B.C.
green jasper, 1.40 cm
Madrid, Museo Arqueológico
Nacional
• *p. 513*

Scarab depicting warrior figure
from Ibiza
5th-4th century B.C.
green jasper, 1.1 cm
Madrid, Museo
Arqueológico Nacional

Ivory and Bone Carving
Maria Luisa Uberti

Carved ivory and bone objects make up one of the most important categories of Phoenician and Punic craftsmanship. However, without resorting to specific analyses, it is difficult to distinguish with certainty between the two types of material: ivory, precious and rare, was found in Asia Minor as well as in neighbouring Africa, though not widely available. It was soon substituted, or at least used in parallel applications, by bone, less valuable but easier to find. For this reason, ivory will be the term generally used here to indicate both materials, in accordance with a now accepted practice in this field.

Phoenician ivory carving continues a Syro-Palestinian craft that as early as the Bronze Age had achieved results of exquisite technical skill, reflecting an ancient Near Eastern tradition. A comparative analysis of finds made at Tell Atchana (Alalakh), Ras Shamra (Ugarit), Tell ed-Duweir (Lachish), and Tell el-Mutesellim (Megiddo) provides the most accurate record, in terms of both culture and chronology, of the range of Phoenician production spanning the period from the 13th to the 7th century B.C. This continuity of tradition applies to both form and decoration; however, with the passing of time, among the various concurrent cultural components of the iconographic repertory of the carved ivories, it is possible to perceive a deepening of the Egyptian influence, as the Aegean element declined.

Fan handle with four female figures from Nimrud 8th century B.C. ivory, 13.2 cm London, British Museum

Evidence of true Phoenician artifacts of the last centuries of the 2nd millennium B.C. is scarce; however, this seems to be due to the current state of research rather than a genuine shortage. This is supported by recent finds at Kamid el-Loz, discussion of which follows shortly.

A small plaque with zoomorphic decoration in low-relief found in the tomb of Ahiram of Byblos can be dated to the 8th century B.C. and depicts a bull being attacked by a griffin and a lion, a motif of clearly Mycenaean derivation, but whose manneristic style anticipates some works found at Megiddo and Nimrud. Another ivory find at Byblos, generally dated to the Late Bronze Age, is a pyxis lid with carved decoration: a band with opposing pairs of confronted griffins encircles an eighteen-petalled rosette.

From Kamid el-Loz, an inland Phoenician centre in the Beqa'a valley, comes a group of ivories datable between the 14th century and the close of the 2nd millennium B.C. These include: statuettes in the round (a god seat-

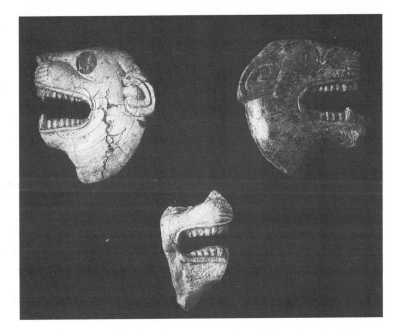

*Lions' heads
from Bernardini
tomb
at Praeneste
7th century B.C.
ivory, 3.8-4.7 cm
Rome, Museo
Archeologico
di Villa Giulia*

ed on a stool, in the Egyptianizing style; a female lyre player), mirror- or tool-handles in the shape of acrobats, human faces, pyxides with free-standing zoomorphic decorations, large ornamental pins, boxes, rosettes in bone, buttons, spoons, gaming boards with carved decoration (hunting scenes). It is therefore a repertory that recalls the typology of the 2nd-millennium pieces, which will reappear in Phoenician ivories of the Iron Age. Stylistically the local interpretations again incorporate Egyptian iconographic influences alongside those more strictly Canaanite, where different elements of Hittite, Aegean, Egyptian and Syrian cultures had already been assimilated into a new language.

The typological and iconographic variety presented by the Megiddo ivories, datable to between 1350 and 1150 B.C., is essential for understanding Phoenician ivories in the strict sense. Megiddo appears to be culturally tied to the artistic expression of the northernmost Phoenician cities, distinguished by a pronounced similarity to the Canaanite tradition. The finds, about 300 examples, include plaques with openwork or low-relief carving; containers for unguents and cosmetics, combs, spoons, mirror-handles, small boxes (one of singular beauty is carved from a single block of ivory with representations of sphinxes and lions in high-relief on the sides), gaming boards in the shape of shields (the game of the 58 holes or "dogs and jackals").

The plaquettes or panels were applied to sacred or domestic furnishings: altars, thrones, stools, beds, tables. Their use as temple and palace wall decorations is hypothetical: the suggestion arises from biblical documentation on Solomon's temple and king Ahab's "house of ivory." They are decorated with motifs representing plants (palmettes and lotus flowers), animals (griffin, sphinx, cow, ram, dog), deities and human beings. One of the most interesting is a carved scene with figures in procession paying homage to a royal personage seated on a throne with winged sphinxes, which recalls the scene on Ahiram's sarcophagus and raises the question of the circulation of cartoons.

The most important lots of the Phoenician era were found in Nimrud, Samaria, Zinjirli, Arslan Tash and Khorsabad, all geographically located outside of Phoenicia proper. The material seems to be a result of direct diffusion (importation of either the finished product or of the artisans), or indirect (as in the case of war booty). The finds from Sarepta, few in number but qualitatively important (for example, the fragment of an Egyptianizing female head), are lacking in specific chronological references, and indicate that the role of that Phoenician centre was minor in terms of the category's widespread diffusion; at the same time they confirm that the lack of evidence for this material is merely a reflection of the current state of research.

The ivories of Nimrud, an Assyrian city not far from Mosul, have been divided into two groups named after the archaeologists who discovered them in the 19th century: the Layard group and the Loftus group. The former comes from the northwest palace of Ashurnasirpal II (883-859 B.C.). This group, thanks to a resumption of excavations by M.E.L. Mallowan in 1949, now includes numerous elements making up the ornamentation of beds or a throne, and pieces sculpted in the round. The panels are in both high- and low-relief and openwork carving, with motifs defined by R.D. Barnett (who conducted the first study of the Nimrud ivories) as Phoenician.

Plaquette with winged griffin from Nimrud 8th century B.C. ivory, 11.7 cm Brussels, Musées Royaux d'Art et d'Histoire • p. 514

The subject matter includes: the "woman at the window"; two youths tying back a papyrus; a youth holding in one hand a lotus flower, with the other raised in salute or benediction; the birth of Horus; a grazing deer; a passant lion; a lion devouring an African in a field of papyri (richly inlaid with lapis lazuli and cornelian and partially covered with gold leaf); a cow giving suck to a calf; a pair of opposing passant sphinxes, with glass inlay and gold leaf according to a composite technique which reappears in the panel with two seated Egyptians with sceptres, face to face before a cartouche bearing hieroglyphs which read '*iwbnwre*; and, lastly, two female protomes, one of such fine workmanship that it merits the name "Mona Lisa."

The religious connotations which accompanied these themes are "absorbed" by their ornamental purpose. This may also be observed in other categories, for instance the composition and stone scarabs — which often share the iconographic repertory of the ivories — and glass pendants. But the iconography may seem less mysterious to present-day observers than to those for whom the panels were made, since nearly all of them can be placed in the religious context of Egyptian mythology and iconography; on the other hand, the "woman at the window" motif represents a version

Plaquette depicting winged sphinx with human head from Nimrud 8th century B.C. ivory, 4.9 cm Brussels Musées Royaux d'Art et d'Histoire

Plaquette with winged sphinx from Nimrud 8th century B.C. ivory, 12.9 cm London, British Museum

of what in the classical period will be the Aphrodite *parakyptousa*, the *prospiciens* Venus.

The Layard group seem to have been brought to Nimrud by Sargon II (721-705 B.C.) as booty from the sack of Hama, but this does not preclude an earlier dating of the pieces. The appearance of the same inscription on another ivory from Shalmaneser Fort has given further support to R.D. Barnett's suggestion that the name *'iwbnwre* should be deciphered as Ia'u-bi'di, King of Hama, defeated by Sargon at the battle of Qarqar in 720 B.C. Furthermore, a number of shells have an inscription in Hittite hieroglyphs with the name of Urkhilina, Great King, the king of Hama defeated by Shalmaneser III in 850 B.C. And finally, the names of Hama and of Laash, a province in the Hama kingdom, have been documented written in Phoenician characters. At all events, the group includes pieces which seem to come from Assyrian, or Syrian, workshops as indicated by the style and iconographic motifs.

The Loftus group comes from the southeast palace, a series of structures later recognized as temples dedicated to Nabu and his wife Ezida. The group is of Syrian manufacture, perhaps from Hama where very similar ivories have been found. M.E.L. Mallowan's reopening of excavations has not only made possible a better understanding of the buildings in terms of their functions, but also led the scholar himself to identify the site where the Loftus ivories were discovered as an area separate from that of the temple complex. This area is called the "burnt palace"; Sargon started the construction in 712 B.C. but at the time of his death in 705 it was still unfinished.

The palace seems to have been plundered and burnt down around 614-612

Panel depicting Assyrian king and courtesan from Nimrud 8th century B.C. ivory, 15 cm London, British Museum

Crowned female head from Nimrud 8th century B.C. ivory, 4.2 cm London, British Museum

B.C. Mallowan discovered hundreds of pieces there that reiterate and expand upon the Loftus repertory.

The inscription "To Milkiram" carved on an ivory in a cartouche has suggested that this was the name of a king of Tyre who lived towards the mid-8th century B.C.

The Loftus and "burnt palace" groups include the following types: ciboria, small bowls, female heads in the round, handles or a sort of sceptre modelled as nude female figures, small shallow dishes for cosmetics supported by nude female figures, animals in the round. Panels and plaquettes are not lacking. The decorations on the sides of the ciboria revolve around the themes of man and lion in struggle, processions of musicians, walking female figures holding flowers. Geometrical and floral motifs usually border the figures.

The greatest ivory treasure, accumulated by Assyrian kings in the course of the 9th and 8th centuries B.C. at Nimrud, was discovered at the so-called Shalmaneser Fort. Among the most noteworthy articles are panels probably belonging to a throne, carved in openwork with figures of lion-headed gods wearing rich necklaces and a solar disc beside a sacred tree; panels with a cow giving suck to a calf; a scalloped openwork panel portraying a passant winged sphinx with a frontal face and elaborate pectoral. In the round examples found at the Shalmaneser Fort depict Syrians and Nubians bearing tribute such as monkeys, lions, ibexes. Other finds attest composite techniques with polychrome glass inlays. Two panels bear fragmentary inscriptions, one of which is identical in content to that on an ivory from

Backrest of throne found in tomb 79 at Salamis 8th century B.C. ivory, wood and gold dimensions of figured plaques 23 × 3.5 cm Nicosia, Cyprus Museum

Arslan Tash: "To our lord Hazael." The other, more lengthy inscription, perhaps commemorates the spoils taken "from a great king."

The ivories of Arslan Tash (ancient Khadatu) are similar to the Layard group. They are a homogeneous collection of the Phoenician school. One of them bears an inscription commemorating "our lord Hazael," like the Nimrud ivory. It is believed that the Hazael in question was a king of Damascus, probably a contemporary of Shalmaneser III (858-824 B.C.), attested by Assyrian sources, so the ivories must date from around the mid-9th century B.C. Perhaps the ivories were tribute paid by Bar-Hadad III, son of Hazael, to Adad-nirari (809-782 B.C.); or, more likely, they were part of the spoils taken by Tiglath-pileser III in the sack of Damascus in 732 B.C., since Arslan Tash was one of his residences.

The motifs depicted on the panels include: the woman at the window; the cow giving suck to a calf; the birth of Horus; two facing male figures before a sacred tree represented by overlapping palmettes; two winged rams facing a sacred tree with volutes; two seated winged sphinxes with pectorals, full face; grazing deer. These panels in Phoenician taste, inspired by the Egyptian iconographic tradition, can be seen in contrast to two others which seem to be more closely related to Syrian workshops: one, in low-relief, with a border of two entwined branches, depicts a passing bearded figure facing frontally; he wears a long tunic, and his hands rest on his abdomen. The other shows a figure with flowing curly beard wearing a kilt, standing on a podium in walking position.

Ivories adorning the house of Ahab (869-850 B.C.) in Samaria seem to be

*Plaquette
depicting woman
at window
from Nimrud
8th century B.C.
ivory, 8 cm
Brussels
Musées Royaux
d'Art et
d'Histoire*

of Phoenician craftsmanship; this is not surprising since Ahab's wife Jezebel was a Tyrian princess. More than 500 fragments have been found, some of them inscribed with Phoenician characters on the reverse, perhaps to facilitate their assembly. Some scholars believe that the panels do not relate to Ahab's reign, but date from the 8th century B.C. Many of the pieces are distinguished by polychrome glass inlays.

The carving techniques employed are openwork, low-relief and high-relief. The panels show Horus on a lotus flower; two winged female figures bearing discs, kneeling in front of a *djed* column; Heh, the Egyptian deity representing "thousands of years"; passant winged sphinxes; scenes of calfs and lions in struggle; palmette friezes; the woman at the window. Compared to the Layard and Arslan Tash groups, the Samaria pieces are closer to the canons of the Egyptian iconography which inspired them.

Apparently also of Phoenician craftsmanship are the ivories found on a site lying between Sargon II's royal palace in Khorsabad and the temple of Nabu, for which they were perhaps made. These, too, seem to be panels whose function was to decorate furnishings now lost. Nine of the finds depict the woman at the window; three show two winged goddesses flanking the sacred tree; fourteen show the passant winged sphinx with full-view face, plus one fragment also with passant sphinx. As at Arslan Tash, Samaria and Nimrud, there are also floral motifs that present varying degrees of complexity and stylization.

The 8th-7th century B.C. ivories uncovered at Zinjirli (Sam'al) in the state of Yaudi are also of Phoenician manufacture. Some of them — plaques with

Panel depicting lion devouring Etiopian from Nimrud 8th century B.C. ivory, gold and precious stones 10 × 10 cm London, British Museum
• *p. 515*

Egyptianizing figures — were furniture decorations, probably part of a throne with lions. Others show motifs with varying stylistic influences (Egyptianizing, Assyrian and Syrian) along the same lines as all the works found at Nimrud primarily inspired by Syrian manufacture. The few finds from Tell Halaf also seem to have been influenced by the same models.

Thus the Phoenician and Syrian craftsmen carved ivories for inlay in wooden furnishings for the entire eastern Mediterranean basin, perhaps producing them *in loco*, or at least in part exporting them to destinations ranging from Crete, Athens, Samos, Lindos and Cyprus to the royal Assyrian courts of the upper Tigris.

Subdividing the production into groups and identifying a series of Phoenician as opposed to Syrian style seems to be a valid and useful approach, especially considering the close continuity of this work with respect to the Late Bronze Age Canaanite tradition. The Phoenician craftsmen of the Iron Age adapted the tradition and developed a form which is predominantly Egyptian not only in its iconography, but also in its stylistic inspiration, with the limits and virtues which an independent school implies. The qualities of this school are confirmed in other categories which seem to have used the same "cartoons" as models.

The development of these schools, then, results from an ancient Near East tradition; the parallel activity of the Syrian and Phoenician workshops does not prevent us from seeking in the latter an indirect or at least secondary expression of the Phoenician coastal centres. I think we can agree with R.D. Barnett when he says that the 9th and 8th centuries B.C. should be called the Ivory Age of the Levant, and that in these two centuries the ivory carving craft was one of the main industries, distinguished by a vast and luxurious trade in coffers and furnishings with workshops probably located in all of the most prosperous cities of Syria, Phoenicia and Palestine.

The ivories discovered at Salamis in Cyprus have close links with Phoenician work. They can be dated from the late 8th to early 7th century B.C. and probably were part of the royal tomb furnishings, especially tombs nos. 77 and 79. The latter has yielded a throne, now reconstructed, inlaid with ivory panels of exceptional beauty. Of these, two small plaques stand out for their openwork on both sides with inlays of blue and brown glass; one represents a composite lotus flower with palmette; the other shows a passant winged sphinx with double crown and palmette.

Other panels have been reconstructed in three tiers, as the headboard of a bed; they present the god of life, Heh, alternated with the sacred palm; the papyrus; confronted wingless male sphinxes facing the sacred palm. Unfortunately other pieces are known to us only from their impressions in the ground. However the Cypriot finds are extraordinary examples of Phoenician ivory work, with traces of gold leaf in addition to the polychrome glass inlays mentioned. They constitute a fundamental document in terms of typology, and give important clues to the use of similar panels found in Nimrud, Arslan Tash, Samaria, and the earlier ones of Megiddo.

Salamis has also yielded ivory objects carved in the round, including an incense burner, made up of a base which carries three series of corollas with leaves turned outwards, and resting on three outward curving legs. The incense burner is similar in type to others in bronze of the same period, from Cyprus, Sardinia and Spain. It is difficult to establish whether the Cypriot ivories are the product of local Phoenician craftsmanship or imported, but this does not alter the fact that they are among the finest technical and stylistic examples of the material found in the East.

Fan handle with two female figures from Nimrud 8th century B.C. ivory, 13.2 cm London, British Museum

Ivory documentation from Carthage seems to be less substantial; the oldest pieces (7th century B.C.) continue eastern production. The smaller quantities of western finds can be explained by the different social context: in the East the material is closely linked to the life of the upper classes, directly or indirectly connected with the palace; in the West, the evidence at the current stage of research seems to be related to a demand for exotic and valuable objects as status symbols. These were domestic or religious emblems that accompanied the journey to the other world, or votive offerings, expressions of particular well-being. Clearly this applies to real ivory; the case is entirely different for the more commonplace objects in bone: tools, rosettes, buttons and small items pertaining to women's cosmetics.

Two Carthaginian mirror handles and a plaquette of the 7th century B.C. recall designs already existing in the East; the handles are female figures in the round with hands to breast, wearing Egyptianizing headdresses and long robes with a fringed belt; the plaque is carved using the openwork technique and represents a rampant stag, passant, among palmettes and a "tree of life." While these finds are evidence of the survival of ivory carving in the West, rather than local products they seem to be imports from the East, considering also the discovery of analogous material in Sardinia and Malta.

Carthaginian combs suggest a different set of considerations, since they differ from the eastern prototypes. The finds include examples with one row of teeth only, and others with two opposite rows divided by a central strip which often has semicircular notches on both short sides, a feature that is also present in Spanish combs. The decoration is usually Egyptianizing in theme, but the technique used is intaglio, sometimes on both sides, instead of low-relief. Among the motifs are: on one side, a dove perched on a crouching sphinx in front of lotus plants; on the other, a bull among lotus plants; two female figures facing the sacred palm; two opposing griffins lying before the sacred palm; a figure in a horse-drawn chariot. This is an iconography with Assyrian or perhaps Persian suggestions. Carthaginian combs do not appear before the 6th century B.C.

Pyxis depicting procession of musicians from Nimrud 8th century B.C. ivory, 7 cm London, British Museum

Possibly imports from the East are a miniature trilobate oinochoe, a seated winged sphinx and a spoon with handle in which plant and animal motifs are merged. The series of amulets, spoons, hairpins, cosmetic cases and so forth made of bone appear to be local products, chronologically spanning the entire Punic phase at Carthage.

The ivories found in Malta come from the area of the ancient temple of Juno at Tas Silg. Cicero's orations against Verres bear testimony to a great quantity of ivory objects which Massinissa returned to the temple after his soldiers had looted it, commemorating the event with an inscribed plaque. The archaeological discoveries have once again confirmed the accuracy of the sources. Among the ivories found, all in a fragmentary state, are an approximately life-sized ear, perhaps part of a statue now lost; a

Plaquette with palmettes from Nimrud 8th century B.C. ivory, 6.2 cm Brussels, Musées Royaux d'Art et d'Historie

right hand with part of the forearm; a fragment of neck with mane, probably part of a lion sculpted in the round; a knob turned on the lathe, perhaps the end of a scepter. Particularly elegant and finely worked is a palmette with stem attached to a sort of semi-pilaster with Aeolian capital, bearing traces of gold leaf; this seems to have been imported from the East, like the other finds mentioned, and presents typological and stylistic analogies with the finds of Arslan Tash, Samaria and Nimrud. It has been dated to the 7th-6th century B.C. Finally, other finds include plaquettes with Punic inscriptions, fragments of small boxes, discs, and so forth.

Evidence from Sicily is still of little interest, consisting of amulets, discs, rosettes, hairpins and so forth. The situation is very different in Sardinia, which offers a range of ivory and bone production that is noteworthy for both typology and iconography. Worthy of mention are the plaquettes belonging to a coffer discovered in a tomb of the Nora necropolis whose Etruscan provenance bears witness to the trade relations between Punic Sardinia and Etruria during the 5th century B.C.

Monte Sirai has yielded two figured bone plaques, together with a number of rosettes and discs. One of the plaques is of specifically Phoenician type, carefully carved on one side with a decoration of palmettes. The other has a triangular shape, into which is fitted a face falling grotesquely onto the chest of a deformed figure, perhaps the god Bes; the arms with tightly clenched fists are visible. Some bone fragments belonging to a single object suggest the existence of a third plaque carved in the shape of a lying sphinx; this would be typologically similar to an Ibizan sphinx dating from the 6th century B.C. The resemblance between these two sphinxes suggests a similar date for the Monte Sirai find, or possibly the 5th century B.C., following the chronology of the two other plaques.

Recent finds of ivory at Tharros have enlarged our knowledge of the repertory of the Punic-Phoenician era, focusing attention on the composite cultural traits that distinguished this category in Sardinia. Contacts with the East, Etruria, Carthage, Iberia and, in later years, the Hellenistic world are attested by some of these ivories, which appeared on the Tharros market as the sort of refined, exotic luxury items that enjoyed a particular demand there, especially between the 7th and 5th centuries B.C. However, alongside these objects are others which were presumably designed to satisfy a modest demand with less costly local products requiring less technical expertise, but not lacking in original expression.

Typological categories documented are: ciborium lid with carved geometrical designs in eastern style; two plaquettes for furnishings, decorated with gorgon heads (one still bears the traces of reddish-brown paint); pendants in the shape of male heads, narrow and tapering at both ends, one of which is very similar to an Ibizan piece; these recall gemstone carvings; a plaquette of Egyptian inspiration, certainly imported from the East, carved with female figures in profile bearing musical instruments; standing female figures in the round (the size suggests that they were amulets), which for technique and style seem to be importations from the Near East; plaquettes with zoomorphic decoration, both in intaglio (clearly related to Iberian production) and in relief, with motifs that, as in the case of Nora, indicate importation from Etruria; a handle belonging either to a tool or a mirror, now lost, of rare technical perfection and exquisite sculptural sensibility

Plaquette depicting Horus as a child on lotus flower from Nimrud 8th century B.C. ivory, 5.6 cm Brussels, Musées Royaux d'Art et d'Historie

Plaquette depicting male figure and lotus flower from Nimrud 8th century B.C. ivory, 10.8 cm London, British Museum • p. 516

Cow giving suck to a calf
8th century B.C.
ivory, 5.7 × 9.8 cm
Paris, Musée du Louvre

Deer
8th century B.C.
ivory, 5.5 × 10 cm
Paris, Musée du Louvre

467

suggesting a high level of craftsmanship such as that of the East; a palmette, carved on both surfaces with thirteen petals arranged fanlike around a lotus flower superimposed over a button and topped by a double-voluted calyx.

Another Eastern import is the openwork palmette, topped by a voluted calyx decorated with carved sepals,whereas a palmette bearing traces of decorations in sea-green enamel suggests Carthaginian mediation. The ivory and bone finds at Tharros also include: hairpins (sometimes with the head in the shape of a Venus Anadyomene, evidence of continuing market demand throughout the Hellenistic-Roman ages, indicating that the city was in contact with both the Punic and non-Punic worlds); spoons; pots for unguents and cosmetics; dice; parts of musical instruments (?); discs, rosettes, buttons. The Tharros ivory evidence, covering a timespan from the 7th to the 2nd century B.C., reflects the centre's involvement in the main trade currents which from the East touched all the great emporia of the Punic West, with or without Carthaginian mediation.

The material from Spain is abundant and raises a number of questions. The first is the provenance of the ivories: most of them are from areas involved in the Phoenico-Punic expansion, but not necessarily of Phoenico-Punic character — El-Acebuchal, Alcantarilla, El-Bencarron, Cruz del Negro, La Joya (Huelva), Medellín, Osuna, Setefilla, Villaricos; those from the lower Guadalquivir area make up the Bonsor Collection.

Two plaquettes carved in the shape of couchant sphinxes have been found: one, in ivory, at Ibiza; the other in bone in the area of the Iberian *oppidum* of Mastret (Gerona). The latter was probably winged. The chronological contribution that could have been made by the Iberian find in hypogeum no. 23 of the 1923 excavation has been annulled by the appearance in the same hypogeum of heterogeneous material probably belonging to different layers of deposits. The two pieces, probably imported from Carthaginian workshops, date from the 6th century B.C. Another small bone plaque representing a winged sphinx in relief also comes from Ibiza and was certainly designed for a wooden furnishing. This plaque is probably of Etrurian importation, from workshops active in the 5th century B.C.

The Spanish ivories cover the following types: plaquettes for furniture, ciborium lids, combs, bowls or cups. The carved motifs are reminiscent of the eastern repertory: geometrical designs; plants (palmettes and lotus flowers); animals (lions, hares, ibexes, kids, griffins, gazelles); human figures

Mirror handle depicting female figure from Carthage 3rd-2nd century B.C. ivory, 16 cm Carthage, Musée de Carthage

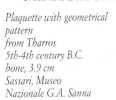

*Plaquette depicting
female figure
from Tharros
6th-5th century B.C.
ivory, 4 cm
Sassari, Museo
Nazionale G.A. Sanna*

*Plaquette with geometrical
pattern
from Tharros
5th-4th century B.C.
bone, 3.9 cm
Sassari, Museo
Nazionale G.A. Sanna*

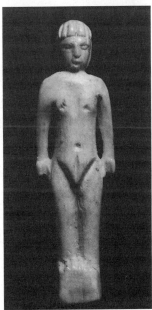

*Female statuette
from Tharros
7th-5th century
B.C.
ivory, 4.3 cm
Sassari, Museo
Nazionale
G.A. Sanna*

(hunters and warriors). In the combs, these motifs can appear in heraldic opposition facing a sacred palm tree. The timespan proposed for this production is the 7th-5th century B.C.

The most significant problem, still a subject of heated scholarly debate, revolves around the true nature of these products: are they the result of Phoenician or of Punic workmanship? Or should they be considered part of the phenomena of orientalizing art? Again, the answer is not unequivocal. Detailed comparisons with eastern work (and a recent reinterpretation of the floral and plant motifs of these ivories is of particular interest in this context) have now made it certain that the products are of Phoenician craftsmanship; less certain, and in my opinion still open to debate, is the identification of the workshop sites. In fact, to exclude the idea of importa-

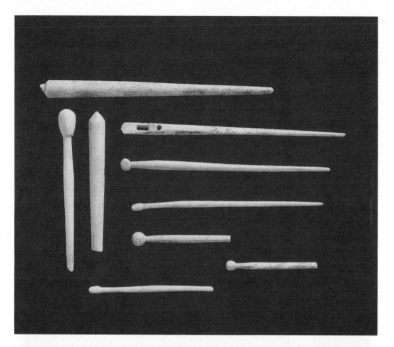

Objects in bone and stone
from a tomb at Villaricos
6th-3rd century B.C.
Madrid, Museo
Arqueológico Nacional

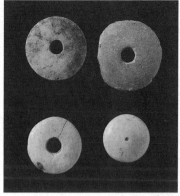

tion in favour of the hypothesis of immigrant Phoenician craftsmen itinerant in Spain limits our understanding of Iberian craftsmanship. Today, the most reliable suggestion seems to be that of stratification: an initial group with links to eastern artisans (working *in loco* or in the homeland) datable to the early 7th century B.C.; a second group in which the eastern tradition blends with local developments already towards the end of the same century; a third group, 6th-5th century B.C., in which the local element, at least stylistically, predominates.

In the end the Greek world with its Hellenistic *koiné*, starting again from the East and plying the same routes already opened to trade by the Phoenicians from the coast of Canaan westward, replaced the Phoenicians, imposing new forms and decorations in a category of craftsmanship that Greece itself had learned from the Near East.

Bronzes
Enrico Acquaro

In the Phoenician and Punic world two main categories of bronze work stand out for their interest: the statuettes and the so-called votive razors. They take on importance in two separate phases: at the beginning of western Phoenician culture and during late maturity. While the production of statuettes, based on a Syro-Palestinian tradition of the late 3rd millennium B.C., continues through to the Early Iron Age (12th-11th century B.C.) providing valuable evidence of the earliest Phoenician presence in the West, the razors were closely linked to Carthage and were a prestigious object by means of which that culture transmitted its values between the 7th-2nd century B.C.

A limited number of basic statuette types were in use in the Phoenician workshops at the end of the 13th century B.C.: the smiting god; the enthroned god with Egyptian crown; the benedictory figure; the woman with heavy chain ornaments. Cyprus plays a pivotal role in the diffusion particularly of the smiting god and benedictory figure types. Both designs derive from Egyptian prototypes; the former is more influenced by ancient Syro-Palestinian tradition, while the latter bears a more lasting Egyptian imprint. The Cypriot role as intermediary between the East and the West is important, considering also the cult objects, tripods and composite candelabra that the island itself produced and exported to the West. Sicilian evidence is limited to the discovery in 1955 of a bronze statue of the smiting god type, 36 cm high, found offshore at Selinus. The god, believed to be Reshef, wears a conical headdress ending in a button like protuberance. From the sides sprout two wings that extend the length of the headdress; they probably represent stylized ostrich feathers of the white crown of Osiris. Two deep cavities, originally filled with another material, perhaps faience or metal, represent the eye sockets. The eyes and the nose are very pronounced. The neck fits into well-formed square shoulders.

The statuette is so corroded that it is impossible to be certain whether the chest and arms are nude, as comparisons with similar statuettes would suggest. The trunk from the waist to the groin shows the traces of a kilt. The right arm is raised to head level; the hand is closed, and probably held an attribute, perhaps a club as can be guessed from the hollow made by the closed fist; the left forearm is extended, and the end part of the hand is missing. The feet have clearly modelled toes; the left leg is projected forward. There are two protuberances on the soles of the feet which probably served to fix the statuette to a base.

Male statuette from Kition 8th century B.C. bronze, 10 cm Limassol, District Museum

Funerary mask
from Phoenicia
5th-4th century B.C.
gold, 16 cm
Paris, Musée du Louvre

Grotesque mask
from Kourion
6th century B.C.
terra-cotta, 12.9 cm
Nicosia, Cyprus Museum

Negroid mask
from Carthage
7th-6th century B.C.
terra-cotta, 19 cm
Tunis, Musée du Bardo

Bearded head
from Cadiz
6th-5th century B.C.
terra-cotta, 19 cm
Cadiz
Museo de Cadiz

Necklace with acorn pendant
from Monte Luna
4th century B.C.
gold, 24.8 cm
Cagliari
Museo Archeologico Nazionale

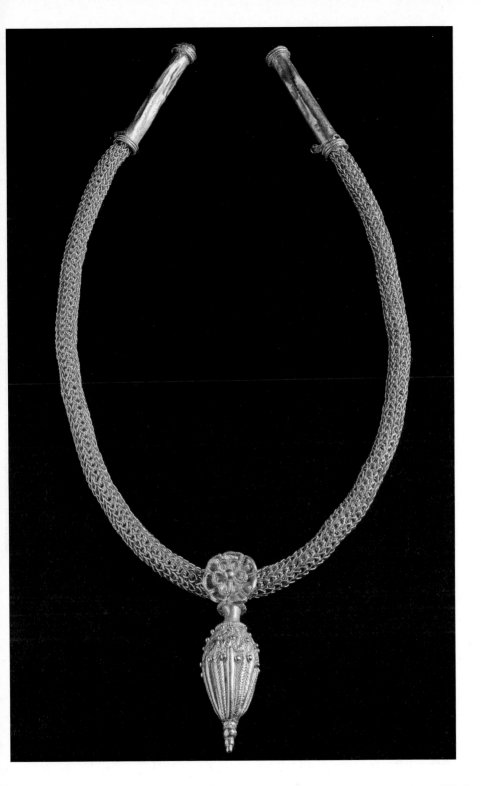

Pendant with female protome
from Tharros
7th-6th century B.C.
gold, 2.9 cm
Cagliari
Museo Archeologico Nazionale

Pendant with female figure
with hands on breasts
from Tharros
6th-5th century B.C.
gold, 3.3 cm
Sassari, Museo Nazionale G.A. Sanna

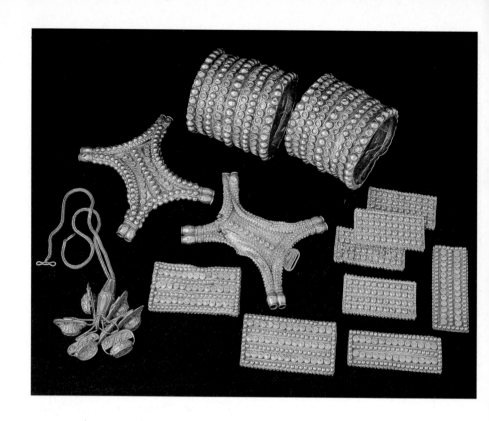

The treasure
of El Carambolo
7th century B.C.
gold
Madrid
Museo Arqueológico Nacional

Male statuette
from Lefkoniko
7th century B.C.
bronze, 21 cm
Limassol, District
Museum

The figure of the god bears a close resemblance to similar Syrian-made statuettes of the Late Bronze Age discovered at Byblos (14th-13th century B.C.). Probably brought west by the Phoenicians, the Sicilian bronze is evidence of the advent of Near Eastern presence in which the Phoenician ascendancy is apparent.

In Sardinia, discoveries dating from a slightly later period than the Selinus bronze come from the area of the Flumenelongu di Alghero nuraghe, from Olmedo and from the holy well of Santa Cristina di Paulilatino. The first two are of the benedictory figure, a Phoenician variant of the Syrian smiting god motif; the third shows a seated figure. These bronze statuettes are clear evidence of the renewal of relations between the nuraghic milieu and the Near East, following the decline of the Mycenaean empire. That the Cypriot intermediary was important is demonstrated by the bronze tripod discovered at Santadi (Cagliari), a local product made copying Cypriot models of the 12th-11th century B.C.

Equally clear is the Phoenician contribution to the iconography of the nuraghic bronze statuettes, even if recent discovery of the broad range of the stone statuary of Monte Frama points to the acquisition of a more complex and varied dynamics for Sardinian statuary in general. On the contrary, the Phoenician inspiration behind the two bronze statuettes (6th century B.C.) unearthed at Monte Sirai is evident. Probably locally produced, they show two seated figures; one is in the act of pouring a liquid from a pitcher held in the left hand into a patera (a shallow bowl without handles used in libationary rites) held in his right, poised on his knee. The other figure is intent upon playing the lyre.

As far as Spanish material is concerned, especially important is the recent discovery at Cadiz of two smiting god-type statuettes. The two specimens squarely enter into the above-mentioned Syrian production of the 14th-13th century B.C., taken up by Crete in the 12th-11th century B.C., as do the following pieces: a bronze statuette of a benedictory figure now in the Madrid Archaeological Museum showing a Cypriot influence of the Early Iron Age, a benedictory figure statuette from Merida, now in the possession of the Hispanic Society of New York, a statuette from Seville, which repeats the smiting god motif and a bronze of the same type in the Saavedra Collection, which is more local in style. The first three bronzes mentioned belong to the category of Near Eastern products introduced to the Iberian peninsula by the Phoenicians, who were penetrating the area from Cadiz along the Malagan coast to the Guadalquivir basin.

El Carambolo (Seville) has yielded a female figure, interpreted as Astarte, with a Phoenician inscription carved on the base. The statuette can be dated no later than the 7th century B.C., and stands 16.5 cm high. It repre-

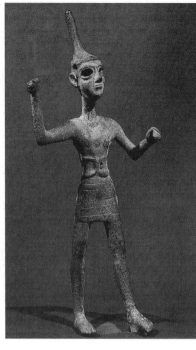

Statuette of deity
from Syria
18th-17th century B.C.
bronze, 12.3 cm
Paris, Musée du Louvre
• *p. 517*

Statuette of deity
from Tortosa
18th-17th century B.C.
bronze, 29 cm
Paris, Musée du Louvre

Statuette of deity
from Selinus
10th-9th century B.C.
bronze, 36 cm
Palermo
Museo Archeologico Regionale

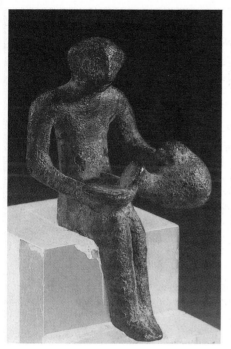

Male statuette with jug and bowl
from Monte Sirai
6th century B.C.
bronze, 5.4 cm
Cagliari
Museo Archeologico Nazionale

Statuette of lyre-player
from Monte Sirai
6th century B.C.
bronze, 5.8 cm
Cagliari
Museo Archecologico Nazionale

Statuette of seated female figure
from Santa Cristina
da Paulilatino
11th century B.C.
bronze, 8.6 cm
Cagliari
Museo Archeologico Nazionale

sents a nude seated female figure; the right hand and left arm are missing. A wig held to the forehead by a band falls in two symmetrical strips along the neck, over her breast and down her back in small rectangular locks, leaving the ears visible. The ears are portrayed nearly frontally, the eyebrows rendered in relief in a pronounced arch, the eyes almond-shaped, the nose fleshy with large, pierced nostrils. The lips are thick with sinuous curves, but not joined at the corners; to their sides are two barely hinted at dimples. The face shows particularly turgid modelling, with slightly protruding cheekbones and a small chin. The shoulders are well formed; the right arm is resting against the chest with the forearm extended forward and slightly raised. The breasts are pronounced, the belly is protruding with a large navel; the joined legs are separated by a deep incision; the feet rest on a plinth, open at the base, with an inscription on the front. Traces of an original support appear under the legs. A product of Phoenician centres of northern Syria, the statuette shows some of the forms of the Egyptian statuary of the New Kingdom.

Statuette of Astarte with inscription from El Carambolo 7th century B.C. bronze, 16.5 cm Seville, Museo Arqueológico

The category of Phoenician and Syrian statuettes, in which the Cypriot element is increasingly evident, was one of the first cultural stimuli brought by Phoenician presence in the West. The resulting influence on the Sardinian and Spanish native cultures is particularly interesting, from the nuraghic bronzes to the Tartessian statuary of the 7th-6th century B.C.

Few products of Punic craftsmanship can demonstrate the artistic freedom of the West compared with the Eastern homeland as conclusively as the so-called votive razors do. The originality of the typological renderings and the deliberate use of design to emphasize eschatological functions already explicit in the form, are clear indications of the category's independence from the Egyptian and Aegean models, which are present but largely superseded by being put to a new and exclusive use.

Found in the main Punic funerary sites, from Iberia to North Africa to Sardinia, razors from the 7th to 2nd century B.C. are evidence of a religious cult which assigned to them the symbolic task of the purifying depilation of the corpse, and perhaps also of the persons who came into contact with it. Placed beside the deceased, these bronze objects supposedly acted as collectors of the impurities drawn out of him and those who piously handled his body. But perhaps there is more to it than this: the razor may have been a symbol of the hope of purity, a tangible guarantee to ease the passage into the other world. Hence the appearance on the two surfaces of engravings which initially were geometric and underlined the progression of forms. Later, in the examples from the late 4th-3rd century B.C. (the middle phase of their documented appearance) they present more complex designs which show a certain artistic sophistication.

It is clear that these representations had the purpose of identifying and

*Statuette of deity
from Cadiz
8th-7th century
B.C.
bronze and gold
13 cm
Madrid, Museo
Arqueológico
Nacional*

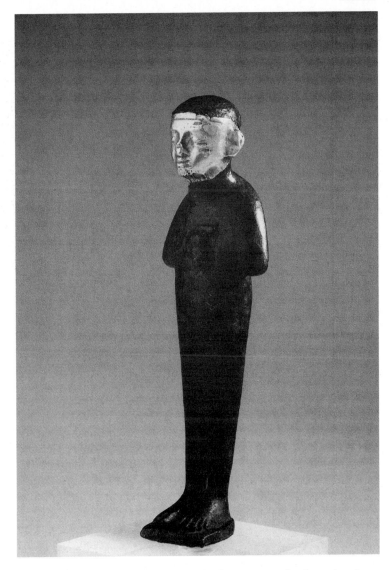

intensifying the object's eschatological value. It must also be pointed out that here the generically life-giving motifs of the prestigious Egyptian magic tradition have evolved in the direction of a doctrine of human redemption of Heraclean origin.

Like the Carthaginian examples from the S.te Monique necropolis, the engraved razors of this period present a skilled intermingling of zoomorphic renderings and mythological motifs. The swan's neck with the plastically rendered beak and wide curve becomes an elegant return to engraving and harmonizes a possible contrast between the two techniques used.

The scarcity of votive razors compared to the impressive quantities of other objects unearthed in the Punic necropoli suggests that their sym-

bolic power must have been reserved for a particular social group. In fact the Punic inscriptions on two of the razors, in addition to providing us with the name of the object, *mglb*, at least in the case of one of them indicate the possibility that the individual being commemorated was a priest of Astarte.

The razors were élite symbols of an undoubtedly exclusive ritual. Examples of razors in iron have been found from the 2nd century B.C. Evidence of a set of funerary beliefs based on ritual repetition, these amulets show that despite its deliberate traditionalism the doctrine could also incorporate new elements.

An analysis of the razors by geographic area identifies Carthage as the main production centre; Sardinia and Spain only rarely produced different, autonomous types.

An analysis by area should start from a definition of the types and designs of the category. The razor has a generally rectangular shape, long and thin; the longer sides are usually rectilinear and parallel; one of the shorter sides

opposite page
*Statuette of
walking figure
from Cadiz
7th century B.C.
bronze, 26.3 cm
Cadiz, Museo de
Cadiz*
• p. 518

*Statuette of figure
in high tiara
from Cadiz
7th century B.C.
bronze, 33.5 cm
Cadiz, Museo
de Cadiz*

*Statuette of
walking figure
from Cadiz
7th century B.C.
bronze, 36.5 cm
Cadiz, Museo de
Cadiz*

*Statuette of deity
from the
Near East
16th-11th century
B.C.
bronze, 26.5 cm
Beirut
Archeological
Museum
American
University*

widens into a crescent shape, with a more or less pronounced curve; the opposite side is narrowed and lengthened into a plastic form, usually doubling back to the main element; occasionally the handle is positioned in the centre of the main element.

In the later examples, the handle is shaped like a swan or ibis; the ends, whether zoomorphic or not, are always divided. In the swan's neck version, incisions open like a fan on the bird's shoulder, representing the remiges and adding naturalistic value to the modelled neck. A small hole, or sometimes a protruding ring, for hanging the razor is usually placed at its centre of gravity, at the level of the bird's shoulder. The size of the razor varies from 4 to 21 cm in length.

The iconography develops from the 4th century B.C. on, and is concentrated on the central part of the razor, and secondarily on the crescent-shaped handle. The motifs are all of religious character and based on magical themes. Among the divinities represented are Isis nursing Horus, Horus-Ra, young Horus, Melqarth, Reshef, Heracles, Hermes, Scylla. The animals (swan, boar, dove, bull, dolphin, griffin, hippocampus, lion) and plants (palm-tree, palmette, lotus flower, rosette) are also related to a magic symbolism which groups iconographic ideas from different traditions (Egyptian, Phoenician, Greek, Etruscan).

Votive razor with sphinx from Kerkouane 4th century B.C. bronze 13 × 4.7 cm Tunis, Musée du Bardo

The entire range of the production of Punic Sardinia closely follows the North African models. The only razor that suggests some stylistic autonomy, now in the Cagliari museum, has a handle representing two swan's necks of different sizes; the smaller one rests on the shoulder of the larger; the body of the latter is rendered with engraving that varies from a light scratch to a deep incision. The hollows for the eyes and the shape of the brow are naturalistically accurate.

Compared with the Carthaginian and Sardinian models, the Spanish manufacture, especially that of Ibiza, shows a certain independence. In the latest period elements of the cultural substratum emerged. From the very first examples, the razors of Punic Spain show a more varied composition. The serration at the internal shoulder and the angle formed by the handle and shoulder, is accompanied by at least one variant: the serration underlines the part opposite that of the eyelet even when the handle, following the line of one of the long sides, displaces the motif from its usual position. The razors without serration also display variants based on the alignment of the handle with the shoulder. Following a considerable development in the 5th century B.C., in the 4th-3rd century B.C. the shapes recapitulate for the most part the previous types: the zoomorphic version of the handle is the only variant. A razor from Ibiza now in the Madrid Archaeological Museum dates to the beginning of the 3rd century B.C. Judging by its

*Votive razor
depicting
a female figure
with drum
on one side
and Horus falcon
on the other
from Ibiza
3rd century B.C.
bronze, 17 cm
Madrid, Museo
Arqueológico
Nacional*

iconography and type it seems to have been imported from Carthage, and it is the only one of the Ibero-Punic razors in which the eyelet for suspension is external.

In conclusion, most of the examples of razors found in the Punic world can be traced back to Carthage. The first typological models originated in this City, as did the main technical and iconographical details which over the centuries modified the original designs, creating notable variants. The two Punic provinces which also produced razors, Spain and Sardinia, developed differently, in line with the local culture. In Sardinia bronze razors remained a production fundamentally extraneous to the indigenous environment throughout. Therefore the artisans depended directly on the models adopted in Carthage and also borrowed designs from the more autonomous Punic-Iberian production.

The early Spanish output suggests a certain autonomy, perhaps because of a decline in North African manufacture, but from the beginning of the 4th century B.C. it once more copies Carthaginian designs although with some late local influences.

Votive razor
with mummified Osiris
from Sardinia
4th-3rd century B.C.
bronze, 8.8 cm
Cagliari, Museo Archeologico
Nazionale

Votive razor depicting
seated figure
from Sardinia
3rd-2nd century B.C.
bronze, 11 cm
Cagliari, Museo Archeologico
Nazionale

Votive razor depicting figure
with gorgoneion
from Sardinia
3rd-1st century B.C.
bronze, 7 cm
Cagliari, Museo Archeologico
Nazionale

Metal Bowls
Sabatino Moscati

Bowl decorated with rams beside a tree from Kirmanshah (?) 8th century B C. bronze diam. 17 cm London, British Museum

The embossed bowls of gold, silver and bronze bearing elaborate decorative designs are limited in number but testify to a refined, elegant craftsmanship. Strangely enough, none have so far been found in the area or period of historical Phoenicia. There are immediate precedents in the surrounding region, however, at Ugarit, and like the ivories, their diffusion — from Assyria to Cyprus, from Greece to Italy — can only be explained in terms of a parallel spread of Phoenician craftsmanship. The hypothesis has been put forward that Cyprus was the major production centre, considering the particular profusion and consistency of finds made there, but for the reasons given above this suggestion is not necessarily true.

The bowls discovered at Nimrud in Assyria come from the same palace of

Sargon II that yielded the ivories. The most reliable date for them is the 8th century B.C. The bowls have a number of common features which illustrate both their variety and their fundamental originality: the rosette in the centre, the decoration of concentric bands with human, animal and geometrical designs, the latter also serving as dividing strips. Like the ivories, they display Phoenician and Syrian stylistic components.

In the simpler bowls ornamental motifs prevail, with no development of narrative designs. The motifs are mainly geometrical, as in a bowl ornamented only with a large rosette: a smaller central rosette is surrounded by a triple circle of linked rings separated by pointillé work.

The evolution from simple to elaborate decoration can be seen in another bowl bearing an eight-pointed star with rosettes in its centre and between the points. Around this broad circular area is a series of narrow concentric bands, with processions of little animals. The space is divided by rays in the form of schematic two-faced figures.

A more elaborate type features a central rosette with geometrical motifs and an outer band or bands with animal and human designs. Examples include a bowl with an outer frieze depicting rams facing one another on either side of the sacred plant; another where the middle frieze depicts facing birds of prey devouring a prostrate hare; a bowl with a middle frieze representing men transfixing lions with spears; another with an outer frieze showing an archer facing backwards on a chariot during a lion hunt; and yet another with an outer frieze of aediculae with two winged griffins crowned by a double Egyptian tiara facing a tall papyrus stem surmounted by a winged scarab.

Bowl decorated with griffins and winged scarabs from Nimrud 8th century B.C. bronze diam. 21.8 cm London, British Museum
• *p. 519*

The Egyptian origin of most of these motifs is obvious but often the designs have been reworked for decorative purposes. In the last case, however, there is no elaboration: the lines and proportions of the winged griffins are fully Egyptian, and the scarab has two wings instead of four, according to the original iconography. We may also observe that the bowls, like other "minor" products, are often the vehicle by which the "major" iconographic motifs passed from Egypt to Mesopotamia: thus, the lion-hunting archer looking backwards from his chariot.

Human figures are also to be found in the central rosettes. In one case, the image is of two people facing each other while they hold a third, central figure by his arms and strike him. This bowl also bears two concentric bands with animal and human figures. In another bowl, we see the deformation of the rosette, probably an intermediate stage before its disappearance. The bowl has four female faces in the centre including a lenticular motif, surrounded by stylized representations of mountains. On the outside, there is a series of probably divine figures without any dividing bands.

In another bowl, a deformed rosette of an ovoidal, lenticular shape is surrounded by hills stylized in the form of a star with figures of goats and trees in low relief in its concavity. Another bowl has no rosette at all: the

Bowl decorated with female faces
and stylized mountains
from Nimrud
8th century B.C.
bronze, diam. 21.9 cm
London, British Museum

Bowl decorated with plant motifs
and inscription from Nimrud
8th century B.C.
bronze, diam. 17.8 cm
London, British Museum

Bowl decorated with stylized mountains
and goats from Nimrud
8th century B.C.
bronze, diam. 24.5 cm
London, British Museum

whole surface is covered with struggling figures and lions, and there is no articulation of space into concentric bands, nor any subdivision into sectors.

Bowls found in Cyprus, which may have been made locally by groups of Phoenician craftsmen who had settled on the island, have been classified into three categories: 8th century, 7th century and 6th century B.C.

The major representative of the first group is a silver bowl from Amathus. In the center is a small rosette with three concentric bands around it showing, from the inside outwards, a series of sphinxes with outspread wings; Egyptian gods and the winged solar scarab on altars; figures of Horus on the lotus flower and stylized palms with two Asiatic-type figures at the sides; and Assyrian-type warriors attacking a turreted city from the right while, on the left, Egyptian-like figures climb a ladder to conquer the walls, or fell trees.

An example of the second group is bowl no. 4554 in the Cesnola Collection. In the center, a four-winged genie spears a lion standing on its hind legs. Surrounding this design is a narrow circular band and a broader one, sepa-

Bowl decorated with hunting
scene, from Ugarit
15th-14th century B.C.
gold, diam. 19 cm
Paris, Musée du Louvre

Bowl decorated with hunting
scene, lion, and winged figure
from Nimrud
8th century B.C.
bronze, diam. 21.4 cm
London, British Museum

494

rated by a plaited motif. The inner one shows a procession of cows, sphinxes, horses and an archer, set among small trees. The outer band has various juxtaposed motifs: griffins, sphinxes and rampant goats beside sacred plants, the pharaoh slaying the enemy, the hero transfixing the griffin.

There are two other outstanding bowls in the second Cyprus group. One, no. 4556 in the Cesnola Collection, is a fragment: it shows the pharaoh in the centre slaying the enemy, and battle scenes on friezes all around him. The other comes from Idalion and is now in the Louvre: in the centre is a geometrical frieze with rosettes and floral motifs. The middle frieze has alternate designs showing the hero attacking the monster and the voluted sacred plant. The outer frieze displays a procession of horses, archers, soldiers, camels and chariots interspersed with floral decorations.

Characteristic of the third Cyprus group is a bowl with the typically Egyptian iconography of the pharaoh slaying his enemies in the central circle. Two concentric friezes are separated by a series of small rings; the first shows a procession of griffins and sphinxes with their feet on the heads of slain enemies, while the outer one displays the repeated scene of a hero fighting a lion or a griffin. Another bowl in this group has animal figures both in the centre and in the concentric friezes.

The spread to Greece of this type of work is documented by a bowl from Olympia which has a large central rosette displaying an eight-pointed star with smaller rosettes

Bowl depicting pharaoh slaying enemy and hunting scene from Idalion 7th century B.C. silver and gold, diam.19.5 cm Paris, Musée du Louvre
• *p. 520*

Bowl with processions of animals, from Praeneste 7th century B.C. gold and silver 13.7 cm Rome, Museo Archeologico di Villa Giulia
• *p. 553*

between the points. There is only one outer frieze, divided into four sectors separated by motifs of gods surmounted by winged discs. Two opposite sectors display banquet scenes, with a figure on a stool and another standing before him. Of the remaining two, one depicts three musicians and the other, two men fighting a griffin.

Before we move on to evidence from the West, we should note that recent studies have allowed us to include three examples from Iran in the Phoenician category. The first is very similar to the Idalion bowl and shows a procession of musicians paying homage to a seated female figure. The iconographic details of both bowls are also similar. The second and third ones resemble some of the Nimrud bowls in the central rosette and the single band with five passant bulls.

An unexpected wealth comes from Italy. Six bowls from Praeneste, four from Cerveteri, one from Pontecagnano near Salerno, and one from Macchiabate near Sibari; and a fragmentary bowl from Vetulonia which resembles them. The most famous Praeneste bowl has the motif of the pharaoh slaying his enemies in the centre. The surrounding frieze displays four symmetrically arranged boats carrying gods and winged scarabs, divided by four figures in lotus flowers arranged like palmettes. The fully Egyptian inspiration of this bowl is evident, although the hieroglyphs on it

make no sense and are purely ornamental. On the other hand, the owner's name, Eshmunazar ben Ashto, is written in correct Phoenician.

A second bowl from Praeneste has a more composite style. The central medallion shows two Egyptian warriors walking in front of an Asiatic prisoner and trampling on other prisoners. The middle band depicts a procession of horses with birds flying above them. The outer frieze has warriors and Assyrian chariots in battle and hunting scenes with Egyptian echoes.

A third Praeneste bowl looks like an almost spherical cauldron, with six heads of serpents added at a later date. A central medallion in the bottom shows a lion with its paws on a prostrate person. An inner band depicts agricultural and hunting scenes, while the second and third bands bear warrior scenes. The whole is in the Egyptian style.

The examples from Praeneste, like the others, probably come from Cerveteri, where other bowls have been found. In the central rosette of the most important one, two lions are mauling a bull. The inner band bears various war and hunting scenes in an environment featuring cypresses and papyrus flowers. The outer band displays rows of warriors amid palmettes and birds. The Cerveteri bowls are not in a good state of preservation, nor are the surviving Vetulonia fragments — showing a procession of quadrupeds — which probably derive from them.

Bowl depicting "day of the hunter" processions of animals and fighting scene from Praeneste 7th century B.C. silver and gold diam. 19 cm Rome, Museo Archeologico di Villa Giulia

496

Lebes with serpent protomes processions of animals and warriors from Bernardini tomb at Praeneste 7th century B.C. silver and gold diam. 19 cm Rome, Museo Archeologico di Villa Giulia

The two examples from Pontecagnano and Macchiabate are noteworthy. They were probably independent of the Cerveteri output and imported via Magna Graecia.

In the central rosette of the Pontecagnano bowl is the pharaoh slaying his enemy in the presence of two gods. There is only one outer band, divided into four symmetrical areas with a design of papyrus plants with Horus on the lotus flower alternating with a galloping horse.

The Pontecagnano bowl dates from the 7th century B.C., while the Macchiabate one must have been made in the previous century. In the centre, a small rosette with a geometrical design is circumscribed by a series of Phoenician palmettes. There are six concentric bands. From the inside to the outside, they depict a series of hares, hawks, figures (some of them with animal heads, representing divine creatures of Egyptian inspiration), goats, bulls, and buds alternating with lotus flowers.

It had long been thought that all of these bowls from the West might not be Phoenician in origin, but rather "orientalizing" work, that is, adaptations or imitations produced by local craftsmen. Today's theory has it that they really are Phoenician, like the oldest ivories in the West, which have a great deal in common with the bowls. We shall have more to say about this orientalizing phenomenon later on.

497

Bowl depicting pharaoh slaying
enemy, papyrus boats
with egyptianizing figures
and inscription
from Bernardini tomb
at Praeneste
7th century B.C.
silver, diam. 19.5 cm
Rome, Museo Archeologico
di Villa Giulia

Skyphos *depicting animal*
and human figures
from Bernardini tomb at Praeneste
7th century B.C.
bronze, 14.6 cm
Rome, Museo Archeologico
di Villa Giulia

499

Painting
Maria Giulia Amadasi Guzzo

Of the very few examples of Phoenician painting that have survived, nearly all belong to the Hellenistic period. As with Greek painting, the presence of decorated pottery cannot compensate for the basic lack of archaeological evidence and literary sources. The evidence that has come to light in both the homeland and colonial areas is almost entirely confined to painted decorations on the walls of tombs. We can only guess as to whether Phoenician houses also bore mural decorations, perhaps on the lines of those discovered in the provincial houses of the Assyrians (e.g. Tell Ahmar), dating from the 8th century B.C., and in the local dynasts' houses dating from the 2nd millennium B.C. The use of painted decorations on votive and funerary stelae, or on various craft objects such as ostrich eggs, gives an idea of how widespread this practice was despite the little that remain. Traces of paint have also been found on stone sculpture (such as the famous sarcophagus of King Ahiram), and on terra-cotta figures (painted details appear on many of the statuettes to denote clothing and specific iconographic features), and there is widespread use of inlay in ivory work. From this we can infer that the Phoenicians, like other cultures of the ancient world, also enjoyed polychrome figurative art. The sum total of these fragments of data is, however, insufficient to give us a clear picture of painting in the Phoenician domestic and colonial worlds.

As in Egypt and in the Syrian examples mentioned above, Phoenician painting must have been a form of colored-in drawing, with the main emphasis on the outline. Imitating the development in the Greek world, some examples from the Hellenistic period show an autonomous use of paint, partly freed from outlines. But already in the preceding period, the painting on the stelae recovered in Motya (Sicily) and the painted decoration found on ostrich eggs show a blend of the two forms of representation (color and outline). The design seems to be developed on one plane, with no spatial effect.

Evidence of the Phoenician style of funerary wall painting has been found mainly in underground burial chambers in the area of Sidon. These tombs were explored by E. Renan in the 19th century, and later by G. Contenau, and date from the 3rd century B.C. onwards. The walls of the sepulchral chambers are mainly decorated with plant motifs: intertwining patterns of garlands, flowers, and petals. The occasional zoomorphic and anthropomorphic motifs also appear, though they are much rarer. The colours are bright, with a preference for red and green. Similar motifs have been found elsewhere in Phoenicia, dating from the 2nd and 1st centuries B.C. Tombs discovered in the region of Tyre (el-Awwatin, Djel el-'Amad) have revealed frescoes depicting events from Greek mythology (Heracles and Alcestes,

The end wall of a tomb showing painted decorations in the necropolis of Djebel Mlezza near Kerkouane 4th-3rd century B.C.
• *p. 554*

The left wall of the same tomb showing painted decorations including altar and cockerel in the necropolis of Djebel Mlezza 4th-3rd century B.C.

501

the torture of Tantalus, the rape of Persephone, the ransoming of the body of Hector, Heracles and Cerberus), in a style that is a continuation of Late Greek Hellenism.

The remaining examples of wall paintings in tombs are all in the West. For Carthage, we have only a report (from L. Delattre) of remnants of paintings in red, observed in the so-called Rabs and Douïmès necropolis sectors. A number of painted funeral chambers have been identified in the region of Cape Bon. This is the site of a famous tomb, whose discovery was published by P. Cintas in 1939, in the necropolis of Djebel Mlezza. The chamber, which is reached via a shaft, is decorated on all but the entrance wall with red ochre applied directly to the rockface.

Internal view of the "Tomb of Sid" with painted decorations in the necropolis of Tuvixeddu Cagliari 4th-3rd century B.C.

At a height of about 80 cm on the three walls there is a running frieze of inverted and upright triangles joined at the apex, which create the effect of decoration with unpainted rhomboids. Above this decorative band, on the left-hand wall as one enters, is depicted a construction mounted on a stepped base (probably a mausoleum); to the left of this an altar is depicted, and on the right above there is a cockerel. On the right-hand wall there is a similar composition, but minus the bird. On the back wall is depicted a stylized city with crenellated buildings, perhaps surrounded by an enclosing wall (also with battlements); a niche tapering into a point is represented on the right, and inside it the so-called "sign of Tanit" crowned by a crescent moon; above right there is another cockerel. All these scenes have been interpreted (notably by M.H. Fantar) as having an eschatological function, narrated sequentially. The sloping roof bears traces of outline decorations of triangles and rhomboids, similar to the frieze painted in colour along the walls of the chamber. The monument described has been dated to the 4th-3rd century B.C. Phoenician elements are the sign of Tanit, and also the typology of the buildings depicted — the paintings lack perspective and proportion (the cockerel is larger than the house in the central scene), and the portrayal of individual details is painstaking but not realistic (the cockerel's feet and the architectural features). Here and in most of the monuments described below, only the outlines of the figures are painted; the lower decorative bands and the cockerels create a chromatic effect.

Elsewhere in the Tunisian region, a number of tombs have decorations in red ochre. There is still doubt as to their date, and as to whether they can be attributed to Punic-Phoenician culture. Particularly interesting in a tomb at Kef el-Blida is the representation of a ship, and (on the spectator's right) a figure armed with a two-edged axe and shield, and another figure who appears to have been struck down (perhaps 1st century A.D.). Despite the use of a single color for this fresco, the technique is pictorial rather than graphic — the images are rendered largely with patches of color creating an effect of immediacy.

Ships also decorate the walls of tombs at Djebel Behlil (Cape Bon) and in the Ued Magasbaia region. A tomb near Djebel Chouchou has yielded the

Walls showing pictorial decorations in the "Tomb of the Uraeus" in the necropolis of Tuvixeddu Cagliari 3rd century B.C.
• *p. 555*

painting of a figure standing before a small construction on a stepped plinth, perhaps an altar. Another scene depicting this kind of stepped construction has been found by M.H. Fantar on the left bank of the Ued Sedjnane. The figures have been interpreted as symbolic, connected to funerary beliefs which we can only guess at.

There is no record of tombs with decorated walls in Sicily, though paintings of a similar nature have been found on the walls of a cave near Palermo, the Grotta Regina (at Monte Gallo), which was used as a sanctuary. The scenes, accompanied by a series of Punic inscriptions, are painted on the rock with a black bitumen-based substance. Given their poor state of preservation, it is impossible to tell whether the inscription and paintings are connected. However, a link has been confirmed in the case of one drawing of a ship with a Neo-Punic inscription alongside. B. Rocco has interpreted this as an invocation to the goddess Isis, and suggested a connection with the "Navigium Isidis" celebration, which according to Apuleius took place in Corinth; but this is only conjecture.

Judging by the form of the surviving letters, these drawings and inscriptions

503

may have been executed between the 4th and the 2nd-1st centuries B.C. (the dating must be approximate because of the poor state of preservation). The images include ships, male figures with helmets, two horses, and a number of other figures that seem to be animals. The uneven surface of the cave walls obviously affected the work so that the outlines are broken here and there. However, in some cases we may perhaps see the influence of the graphic style current in the Hellenistic period, particularly in the profile view of the horses' eyes. One of the male figures shows that the technique of portraying the body frontally and the head in profile was still in use (cf. the "Tomb of Sid" in Cagliari). The inscriptions in the grotto consist largely of devotees' requests for benediction (the deity invoked is Shadrapa). Like the inscriptions, the drawings have no consistent form but seem to have been made at different times by the visitors themselves.

Interesting examples of Punic funerary wall painting have been found in Sardinia at Cagliari, in the necropolis known as Tuvixeddu or S. Avendrace. In 1868 and later in 1912, F. Elena and A. Tamarelli had already reported the existence of tombs (still visible) with red-colored geometrical decorations. Recently (1973 and 1981) two tombs were found with pictorial decoration that is unique in the Phoenico-Punic world. They depict scenes largely corresponding to Phoenician iconographical tradition.

The shaft tomb discovered in 1973 ("Tomb of Sid") has a series of decorations painted directly on the rock walls of the funerary chamber. Below ceiling level runs a frieze, partially preserved, made up of two superimposed *guilloches* in red ochre, with traces of blue colouring inside the design. This band is "supported" by pillars drawn in red ochre with voluted capitals; on each of the three walls of the chamber (excluding the entrance wall) is a rec-

Funerary shrine with banquet scene between columns from Marsala 3rd-2nd century B.C. painted tufa 96 × 62 cm Palermo, Museo Archeologico Regionale

Funerary shrine with banquet scene from Marsala 3rd-2nd century B.C. painted tufa 67 × 49 cm Palermo, Museo Archeologico Regionale

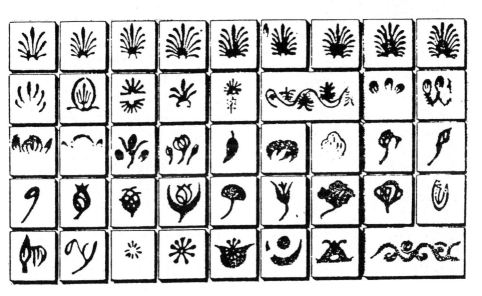

Varieties of pictorial design used in the decoration of ostrich eggs

tangular niche containing three baetyl symbols painted in red. The niche is framed above and along the sides by parallel lines in dark red, and below by a band of triangles and rhomboids in red and blue (cf. the Djebel Mlezza tomb). On the right-hand wall, to the left of the niche, there is a bearded figure with a helmet, brandishing a lance. This figure has been identified as Sid by F. Barreca after comparison with the iconography found at Antas (hence the name ascribed to the tomb). The date proposed is 4th-3rd century B.C.

In the second tomb, excavated in 1981 (known as the "Tomb of the Uraeus"), on the upper part of the side walls there is a frieze composed of alternating palmettes and lotus flowers, painted in dark red on plaster and framed by two bands of the same color. The back wall is decorated with a frieze edged with a red band below, depicting a winged uraeus in the centre, with a plant motif on either side (lotus flowers with a central palmette and volute); on either side is a *gorgoneion* with schematically drawn snakes instead of hair. On the basis of the pottery found there, the tomb has been dated to the end of the 4th century B.C. As in the preceding case, here as well the decoration takes the form of colored drawing rather than true painting. Alongside the typical Phoenician iconography (baetyls, winged uraei), there are motifs common in the Italic world. M. Canepa has pointed out that the design of palmettes and lotuses finds its closest parallel in the Apulian pottery of the second half of the 4th century B.C.

For the paintings on stelae, excavations at Motya (Sicily) have yielded various examples from the 6th to mid-5th century B.C. Specimens in the Late Hellenistic style have been found in Phoenicia itself, and also in Sicily, at Lilybaeum.

Pedimented stelae with representations of the deceased painted on a plaster ground in Late Hellenistic style have come to light in the necropolis at Sidon and are dated to the 2nd-1st century B.C. (the surviving inscriptions are in Greek). Stelae found in strata V-III of the *tophet* at Motya have decorations painted in red; the iconography includes baetyls and clothed female figures in frontal position. Here there is no distinction between colored areas and outline, but probably there were details that have now faded away. A series of scenes (mainly banquets, but some offertory rites) painted on funerary stelae from Lilybaeum (Marsala) dating between the 2nd century B.C. and 1st century A.D., have been linked to Late Hellenistic painting "done in popular provincial circles" (R. Bianchi Bandinelli). Together with the iconography of Greek origin (the inscriptions are also in Greek), there are the symbols typical of Punic stelae: raised hands, the sign of Tanit, the caduceus.

Characteristic of the Punic world, but probably Phoenician in origin (as attested by finds in the Near East), are the decorated ostrich eggs. Examples have come to light in Carthage, Sardinia, southern Spain and Ibiza. The custom covers a long time span, from the 7th to the 2nd century B.C. We can distinguish between geometrical decorations and representations of masks, with large eyes outlined in black and cheeks marked in red. These articles were often included in the grave goods because of the symbolic value attributed to the egg and the apotropaic meaning of masks and the eye.

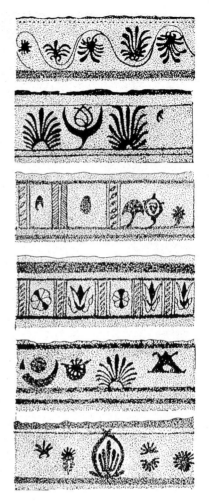

Decorative designs often used on ostrich eggs in Ibiza

I have already mentioned the widespread use of paint on relief and free-standing sculpture, in stone or in terra-cotta. When the colour has been applied on a ground of stucco, the work can be considered as "painting": this is the case, for instance, of the sculptures that adorned the mausoleum identified by A. Di Vita at Sabratha (3rd century B.C.). Fragments of coloured stucco, with geometric and plant designs in green, yellow, red and blue, have come to light in Spain at Almuñecar; their purpose and date are not yet clear.

According to F. Barreca, the decorations of the underground sanctuary of San Salvatore at Cabras (Sardinia) show traces of painting of Punic origin; the sanctuary was used uninterruptedly from nuraghic times through to the Late Roman period and the remains have been attributed to the Constantinian period. The artistic tradition exemplified in Northern Africa

*Decorated
ostrich egg
from Ibiza
5th-4th century
B.C., 13.6 cm
Ibiza, Museo
Arquelógico*

in the funerary paintings of Tripolitania, and in the large mosaics of Tunisia, Algeria and part of Morocco (3rd-4th century A.D., but perhaps also early 5th century A.D.), is connected with the Hellenistic style.

Ostrich Eggs
Sabatino Moscati

The shells of ostrich eggs discovered in Egyptian and Mesopotamian tombs of the 3rd millennium B.C. and in Mycenaean tombs of the 2nd are the eastern forerunners of one of the most commonly found funerary objects of the Punic world. Indeed, so many have been found that the ostrich egg can be considered peculiar to the Phoenicians, although not exclusive (there are a number of Etruscan examples, to be seen in the context of the orientalizing trend). Not all the Punic finds of ostrich eggs are of the funerary type, for examples have also been discovered in civil dwellings in Spain (e.g. El Carambolo, Almizaraque and Toscanos).

Fragment of ostrich egg painted and cut in the form of a mask from Carthage 7th-6th century B.C., 4.2 cm Carthage, Musée de Carthage

M. Astruc's investigation reveals that as early as the 7th century B.C. these eggshells, with their obvious symbolical value, were deposited in tombs at Carthage — since the very dawn of history, man has always identified the egg with the principle of life, the continuity of generations, and by "sympathetic" magic its deposition in a tomb was a sure promise of the seed of life. The custom of including these shells in funerary deposits at Carthage continued until the 2nd century B.C., with periods of greater or lesser frequency. Thus, though we have meagre evidence from the 7th century B.C., we may say that the custom became fashionable in the 6th, making its social connotation as the offering of a luxury item less obvious. The fashion dwindled in the centuries that followed but flourished once more in the 3rd century B.C., finally dying out completely in the 2nd.

The most painstaking classification of the remains, however, will never give us a true picture of the real extent of this particular Punic practice of religious piety. All attempts to identify and quantify the material are frustrated by the fragmentary nature of the finds, which are sometimes little more than dust, a logical consequence of the intrinsic fragility of the eggshell and its inability to resist chemical reactions that disintegrate calcium, its basic component.

Alongside M. Astruc's far-reaching, thorough investigation, the recent research by E. Acquaro aimed at updating and defining characteristics of the Sardinian finds in this category, allow us to establish certain typological and iconographical features by which we can identify production centres. This identification, essential for an investigation of the craft, also becomes interesting from the historical and economic standpoints. The ostrich eggs were definitely supplied from North Africa acting as the middleman market for neighboring regions. The fragility of the eggshells made them luxury goods meeting the demand of an elite market, which became smaller and more refined the farther away it was from the source. One can identify two basic types, based on the final use of the eggs: masks and receptacles. The masks have an apotropaic value, while the receptacles have a more general symbolical value. The mask typology seems to be the more frequent, at Carthage at least.

Fragment of ostrich egg painted and cut in the form of a mask from Carthage 5th century B.C. 10 cm Carthage, Musée de Carthage

Fragment of ostrich egg with painted eye from Carthage 5th century B.C. 10.2 cm Carthage, Musée de Carthage

After the most archaic representations on smallish pieces of unevenly cut shell, in which black is used to outline the faces and draw the large eyes and eyebrows, and red is used for the nose, mouth and two spots on the cheeks, the masks developed more specific iconographies. The convex form of the quarter shell was used for a pseudo-realistic representation of the face, which stands out with expressive vivacity from a background which may be as shiny as ivory or as opaque as chalk. The details of the face are the same, but their rendering is more realistic, with the addition of long, carefully drawn eyelashes, black hair in a festoon or in a series of spirals on the forehead, and a red band below the mouth marking the bottom of the face. The details reveal the original contribution of individual craftsmen to the common pattern: in one mask, for instance, the mouth is drawn by two intersecting rather than by overlapping lines.

As for the receptacle type, for Carthage Astruc lists twelve whole shells perforated at the top, three shells cut at three-quarters of their height, and three cup-shaped shells, cut about half way up. The whole eggshells are not decorated, but four of them have a series of small holes arranged irregularly around the opening, suggesting the application of a rim in some other material. The second type, the shells with the top third cut away, were richly painted when they were found, but the decoration has almost completely faded away by now.

The drawings made at the time of their discovery show geometrical and floral patterns in ochre, pale blue and black. There is a similar decoration on the cups, i.e. the half shells.

The different iconographical repertoire on the irregular fragments and quarter shells on the one hand, and on the various types of receptacles on the other, seems to relate to different funerary functions. The geometrical and floral designs on the receptacles symbolize the concept of life (palmettes and lotus flowers for example) while the frontal face with large eyes is the most mature and expressionistic realization of the apotropaic value of "masks."

Besides Carthage, other necropoli in North Africa have also yielded ostrich eggs. Outstanding are the tombs of Djidjelli and Gouraya, with a rich series of the receptacle type with undecorated whole shells and three-quarter shells. The Gouraya examples, found in tombs dating from the 3rd-2nd century B.C., are interesting for the iconographical repertoire painted on the three-quarter shells. The geometrical and floral motifs, similar to those found at Carthage, do not exclude use of human and animal representations: a winged female figure, a male (carrying a bow perhaps) and an advancing ostrich enliven Phoenico-Punic iconographical influences with a popular stylistic language. Carthage and Gouraya were definitely two main centres of manufacture in North Africa, in a position to export their precious shells throughout the Punic settlements.

In Sicily as in Malta, the fact that eggshells are so perishable does not allow us to go beyond the statement that, here too, there was widespread use of these objects with their symbolic religious value. We have numerous fragments on which the thin red lines of decoration no longer have any iconographic significance. The type of mask painted on quarter shells has not been found. In Sicily and Malta, and as we shall see, Sardinia, there must have been direct links with the North African markets and definitely with Carthage.

In Sardinia, recent work on examples found at Cagliari and Bithia has given us much fresh information on both typology and iconography. Almost whole shells have been found, others that are cup-shaped and also examples of the painted-mask quarter shells. The twenty or so fragments found in the

Fragment of ostrich egg painted and cut in the form of a mask from Cagliari 5th-4th century B.C., 10 cm Cagliari, Museo Archeologico Nazionale

Cagliari necropolis of Tuvixeddu and in the Tharros burial grounds, already known to M. Astruc, seem to belong to this latter type, in both its archaic and more evolved varieties. Previously this interpretation was purely hypothetical due to the bad condition of the finds, but it has now been confirmed in E. Acquaro's work on six shells from the Tuvixeddu necropolis, four recovered during careful cleaning of already known tombs and two from a private collection. The first four recall the Carthaginian masks of the more developed type, both in their red and black colours (now badly faded into reddish and brownish) and in the similar treatment of the facial details: the wavy hair, enormous eyes framed by long lashes and eyebrows, the band that closes the face at the bottom. The four fragmentary masks (now restored) were found in a hypogeum-type burial chamber painted in a style that dates it to the 4th-3rd century B.C. Since there is no correlation with the other contents of the tomb, the dating of the masks to around the 5th-4th century is based on typological and iconographical characteristics. Comparative study also reveals that some of the Cagliari masks were imported from Carthaginian workshops, demonstrating the ability of the African city to meet the requirements of both the domestic and the overseas markets.

The two fragmentary examples from a private collection, which also come from the Tuvixeddu tombs, have masks originally painted in red and black, also now reddish and brownish. They probably come from Carthage as well, and have been dated to the 6th and 5th centuries B.C. respectively. Beyond the interesting fact of masks painted on ostrich eggshells, therefore, one of them is also very early evidence of the Punic presence in Cagliari.

Of exceptional importance for this category in Sardinia are three ostrich eggshells found during recent excavations in the Bithia necropolis. Typologically, they are all different: one is a cup, with the hole for emptying the egg off-center at the bottom, decorated with plaited motifs in brown arranged obliquely; another is a cup with a red-brown band painted 3.2 cm

Fragment of ostrich egg painted and cut in the form of a mask from Cagliari 5th-4th century B.C., 9.2 cm Cagliari, Museo Archeologico Nazionale

from the rim; and the third is a shell minus its top, with a composite decoration.

The cup with the hole at the bottom and plaited motifs is thought to come from a Carthaginian workshop, because of the composition of the design, and the cup with the uniform red band probably has the same provenance. In the case of the third find, the shell with its top cut away, the type of decoration in yellow ochre and its style recall the complicated designs of the receptacle-shells from Gouraya: four metopes framed vertically by bands with geometrical motifs and horizontally by smooth, figured bands. Inside the metopes is the motif similar to the one known as the "sign of Gouraya," also linked with the "second sign of Villaricos."

The most likely hypothesis is that this might be a product imported from Gouraya, but as Acquaro has pointed out, this does not exclude the possibility of "a subsequent intervention of Sardinian craftsmanship that took over the task of elaborating a painted decoration." So for Sardinia too, as for certain Iberian examples, we may think that besides the direct importation of finished products, there was also an import of raw materials, subsequently decorated on the local markets. The historical, economic and artistic implications of this hypothesis are so vast that further studies and, above all, new finds will be needed to confirm or disprove it.

In Iberia (the richest of the Punic colonies in this category of craftsmanship) evidence includes all the known types but there is a certain predominance and variety of the receptacle, and a paucity of examples of the mask type. A recent study by M.P. San Nicolas Pedraz has reassessed the whole Iberian repertoire, updating it and defining it in typological, iconographical, chronological, technical and artistic terms. It is interesting to note that there are very few examples of engraving along with painting in decoration. A true engraving technique was probably used only on four Etruscan examples from Vulci, and in other cases what we see is the slight furrow left by the application of paint which has now faded. In fact in the Punic repertoire, with very few exceptions, we have only painted decoration. The colour range seems to include deep red-ochre, light red-ochre, pale blue, grey-blue, greenish-blue and black. The 802 shells found in Iberia are a reflection of a widespread funerary custom. But although most of the finds were made in necropoli, examples have also been found in private dwellings: in the back of a hut at El Carambolo, on the Toscanos farm, and in a house at Almizaraque. Most of the material comes from Villaricos and Ibiza, but there are also examples from Carmona, Almuñecar (Laurita necropolis), Huelva (La Joya necropolis), Toscanos (Jardín necropolis) and Ibiza (San José and Isla Plana necropoli).

The most common type is the three-quarter shell, cut straight or serrated. Also common is the whole eggshell, perforated at both top and bottom. The cup types are fairly frequent, sometimes pierced at the bottom (the two

*Scarab depicting
female figure
astride a bull
from Ibiza
5th-4th century
B.C.
green jasper
1.40 cm
Madrid, Museo
Arqueológico
Nacional*

*Scarab depicting female figure
on horseback, from Ibiza
5th-4th century B.C.
green jasper, 1.45 cm
Madrid
Museo Arqueológico Nacional*

*Scarab depicting Heracles
with bow, from Ibiza
5th-4th century B.C.
green jasper, 1.6 cm
Madrid
Museo Arqueológico Nacional*

opposite page
Plaquette with winged griffin
from Nimrud
8th century B.C.
ivory, 11.7 cm
Brussels, Musées Royaux
d'Art et d'Histoire

Panel depicting lion
devouring Etiopian
from Nimrud
8th century B.C.
ivory, gold and precious stones
10 × 10 cm
London, British Museum

*Plaquette
depicting male
figure and
lotus flower
from Nimrud
8th century B.C.
ivory, 10.8 cm
London, British
Museum*

Statuette of deity
from Syria
18th-17th century B.C.
bronze, 12.3 cm
Paris, Musée du Louvre

opposite page
Statuette of walking figure
from Cadiz
7th century B.C.
bronze, 26.3 cm
Cadiz, Museo de Cadiz

Bowl decorated with griffins
and winged scarabs
from Nimrud
8th century B.C.
bronze, diam. 21.8 cm
London, British Museum

*Bowl depicting pharaoh slaying
enemy and hunting scene
from Idalion
7th century B.C.
silver and gold, diam.19.5 cm
Paris, Musée du Louvre*

*Ostrich egg cut in the form
of a bowl
with geometric decorations
from Ibiza
5th-4th century B.C.
7.6 cm
Ibiza, Museo Arqueológico*

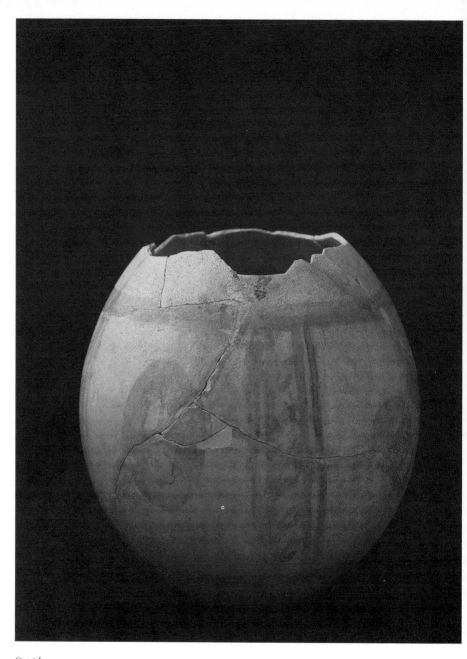

Ostrich egg
cut in the form of a vase
with plant decorations
from Ibiza
5th-4th century B.C.
13.5 cm
Ibiza, Museo Arqueológico

522

types recently identified at Bithia). There are only three examples of painted masks on quarters or fragments, all from Ibiza.

The forms of decoration are varied: horizontal geometrical dividing motifs; vertical geometrical dividing motifs (especially in the type with the metope); mostly floral motifs for a decoration between horizontal bands (various types of palmette, lotus flowers, rosettes, and also a few sun discs on crescent moons, the sinuous serpentine and so on); motifs painted in the metope are mostly phytomorphic, as above, but also zoomorphic (deer, cocks, birds), divine (the eye of Horus) and symbolic (the "second sign of Villaricos," similar to the "sign of Gouraya").

Comparisons with North African production, especially in the case of the whole eggshell devoid of decoration (which can be dated to the 6th century B.C.) and the cup and mask types, suggest importation. The very wide range of decorations on the shells cut one third the way up had prompted M. Astruc to think of local work on imported material. The hypothesis has recently been reassessed very carefully by M.P. San Nicolas Pedraz on the basis of the most recent studies and finds, his conclusion being that it remains an hypothesis awaiting confirmation or disproval. What is certain is the far-reaching capacity of the North African workshops to export a category of art based on a raw material that only they could procure conveniently.

Coins
Enrico Acquaro

Due to differences in the economic, political and cultural climate, there is a marked variance between the coinage used in the eastern and western regions of Phoenician civilization. Phoenicia and Carthage both started to mint coins towards the mid-5th century B.C., more than a century after the first issues of coinage in Asia Minor and Greece. However, this tardy integration into an already evolved monetary system had different aspects in the two areas. The monetization of the cities of Phoenicia had its own role in the Persian world, while that of Carthage from the outset offered an alternative to the Greek system in Sicily, maintaining this strong political function through to the war with Rome.

The first coins minted in Sidon are in silver, stamped on a Phoenician blank around 450-435 B.C. On the obverse there is a warship with triangular sail, on the reverse either a Persian king bending a bow or a chariot, charioteer and royal passenger (perhaps the Persian king). This latter motif predominates throughout the period of independent coinage, and during the reign of Baalshamin II (395-375 B.C.) a third figure is added, following the chariot on foot. Some have seen this as the king of Sidon in high priest's robes. During the reign of Baalshamin I (435-430 B.C.) the turreted fortifications of a city form a backdrop for the ship, and there are two lions on the reverse side. In this period for the first time the kings' initials appear in Phoenician characters. These abbreviations are typical of coins minted in Sidon until its conquest by Alexander the Great in 332-331 B.C. The abbreviations are omitted on only two occasions, both moments of crisis, namely the aftermath of the rebellions of 365-364 and 352 B.C., when the city was for a few years under the sway of Mazaios, satrap of Cilicia, who set an Aramaic legend on the local coin types together with an abbreviated date code.

In the reign of Abdashtart I (375-362 B.C.) a bronze series was added to the silver, repeating the same designs. The coinage of Sidon thus develops within the structures of the Persian Empire, is directly affected by the empire's crises, and claims its own particular "national" distinction from its role as a base for the imperial fleet.

Tyre was another city engaged in marine activities, and acquired monetary autonomy with the minting of a silver series. However, the coin-types of Tyre are not strictly Persian. Constant recourse is made to Egyptian motifs, such as the owl with flagellum and sceptre (reproduced on most of the reverse sides, which is in no way related to the owl of the prestigious Attic coinage).

The first phase of the Tyre coinage occurs between 435 and 400 B.C. The motifs are the dolphin and murex-shell, and later a deity on a seahorse. The first bronze coins were issued between 377 and 357 B.C., using the

*Coin with ship
on obv.
and chariot with
statue of
deity on rev.
minted in Sidon
400-332 B.C.
silver, 25.72 g
Paris, Bibliothèque
Nationale*

*Coin with deity on
winged
hippocampus
on obv.
and owl, scepter
and flabellum
on rev.
minted in Tyre
400-332 B.C.
silver, 13.27 g
Paris, Bibliothèque
Nationale
• p. 557*

*Coin with bearded
head of
deity on obv.
and ship and
inscription on rev.
minted in Aradus
350-332 B.C.
silver, 10.55 g
Paris, Bibliothèque
Nationale*

types of the small silver denominations, such as the satyr's head, ram, dolphin, murex-shell and cedar tree.

Like Sidon, Tyre was caught up in the rebellion of the Phoenician towns in 352 B.C., though with more lasting effects for the coinage: the Phoenician standard was replaced by the Attic one, though the types remained unaltered. The change in coin weights had far-reaching consequences, allowing Tyre to enter a wider commercial circuit of countries where Attic coinage was current, such as Palestine, the Arab towns and Egypt.

The coinage of Aradus does not give a clear picture of the role the town played during Persian domination. On the one hand the adoption of the Persian standard for early issues of coins links Aradus more closely than Tyre and Sidon to the Persian community, while on the other hand the types used are furthest from the Achaemenid range.

The town's first silver coins go back to 420-410 B.C. The obverse shows the half-human, half-fish sea-god, the reverse a warship. In the issues of 380 and 350 B.C., the motif on the obverse changes, though without losing the Hellenistic style already evident in the sea-god, and becomes a bearded deity facing to the right. During these years the first bronze coins were minted, using a variety of motifs: the prow of a warship, the satyr, scorpion, fish and tortoise.

The restoration of Persian power put an end to the minting of bronzes which had increased during the years of rebellion. Realignment with the Persian system affected both weights (the reinstatement of the Persian blank in substitution for the Attic one which had been in favor during the years of rebellion) and motifs, closer to those of the early issues. The last autonomous series minted in Aradus was the silver issue of Gerashtart (339-338 B.C.), with the date of the reign on the reverse.

Byblos minted coins on the Phoenician blank in 425 B.C. Those in silver bear on the obverse the motif of a sphinx with double Egyptian crown, sand on the reverse a stylized double lotus flower, or, in the lower denominations, a lion. The next series, dating from 410-375 B.C., has a warship on the obverse and the motif of a vulture perched on a deer on the reverse. Some innovations appear with the reign of Elpaal (375-365 B.C.): on the obverse a murex-shell, and on the reverse a lion attacking a deer or an ox. The reverse also bears the legend *mlk gbl*, "king of Byblos," in use until 332 B.C.

The coinage issued in the Phoenician towns in the pre-Alexandrian period and that of Cyprus have much in common. The first issues minted at Kition at the end of the 5th and beginning of the 4th century B.C. illustrate this particularly well. The silver coins, minted on a Persian blank, have the crouching lion motif on the obverse, and a blank reverse. In later issues the lion motif is duplicated on the reverse side, with a *crux ansata*.

In 479 B.C., during the reign of Baalmilk I, coins are minted with a Heracles with club and bow on the obverse, and this motif is typical of all the issues minted at Kition until the end of the Phoenician dynasty in 312 B.C. In Azibaal's reign (449-426 B.C.) a new motif comes into use alluding to the Persian victory over the Greeks: a lion attacking a deer.

Dating from Milkyaton's reign (392-361 B.C.) and Baalram's interregnum are the bronze coins attributable to the Kition mint. They use the same types as the silver coins. During the reigns of Milkyaton and Pumayyaton (361-312 B.C.), the last Phoenician sovereign of Kition, gold denominations were issued. These are the only coins of the Near East whose legend is stamped in Phoenician characters.

Minting in the Phoenician colonies of the western Mediterranean developed independently of the eastern cities. The motifs employed have, as we shall see, little in common with those of the East — a fact which once again

Coin with Heracles-Melqarth with leonté on obv. and lion slaying a deer on rev. minted in Kition 361-312 B.C. gold, 4.8 g Paris Bibliothèque Nationale

Coin with head of Kore on obv. and standing horse on rev. minted in Carthage 310-270 B.C. gold, 7.33 g Tunis, Musée du Bardo

Coin with head of Kore on obv. and horse, disc and uraei on rev. minted in Carthage 260-240 B.C. gold, 10.36 g Tunis, Musée du Bardo
• p. 558

reflects the different trade and political alliances of the two regions. Carthage was the natural political and economic center of the monetary system. The series of military campaigns in the provinces which helped to found the Carthaginian empire were consolidated by the imposition of a single monetary system.

The colonization of Sicily gave the Carthaginian metropolitan mints their first stimulus. The earliest Carthaginian series, dating from 410-390 B.C., was issued in silver and bears the forequarters of a horse with a Nike on the obverse, and on the reverse a palm-tree. This issue, stamped on an Attic blank, is related to the conflict between Segesta and Selinus in 416 B.C., which brought about the Carthaginian invasion of Sicily, concluded in 396 B.C. The war in Sicily gave rise to a number of prestigious issues minted there, reflecting the successes and failures of the Carthaginian campaign.

The Carthaginian mint started issuing regularly in the mid-4th century B.C. The Phoenician blank was adopted. This choice reflects a monetary economy geared not only to the western regions, but looking eastwards as well. Coins are minted in gold and electrum; a first series in bronze completes the range. The same motifs are adopted for gold and bronze coins: a Kore's head, a galloping horse, a standing horse, a standing horse before a palm, a palm-tree. Minting in silver starts at the beginning of the 3rd century B.C. with a coin bearing a Kore's head on the obverse and on the reverse a backward-glancing horse before a palm-tree. With the defeat of Carthage in the first war against Rome, minting in gold and electrum declines in favour of the commoner silver, base silver (an alloy with low silver content) and bronze. The same motifs are used through to the fall of Carthage in 146 B.C.: a Kore's head, and a horse standing or glancing backward with letters or various symbols.

The issuing of Punic coins in Sicily is a complex affair related to a continuous interplay with the Greek systems. Alongside the minting in Phoenician towns such as Motya and Panormus which begins around 480 B.C. with legends in both Greek and Punic, coins are also stamped in Sicily under the direct control of Carthage.

Dating back to the 6th century B.C., the Greek issues in Sicily, starting with the Ionic settlements in the southwest of the island, became a model for early coinages in the Phoenician towns. The prestige of the 5th-century silver issues minted in Syracuse was such that its types were adopted both on the coins of the colonies and those issued under Carthaginian control.

At the start, the mints at Motya and Panormus adopted the Euboean-Attic weight system in line with the silver issues of Syracuse, Agrigento, Selinus and Gela. In the first issues in silver and bronze, motifs like the gorgon's head and the palm, from Himera and Selinus, appear alongside others such as the youth on horseback and the head of Arethusa, from Himera and Syracuse, and the dog beneath a small head of a woman and the dog savaging a deer from Segesta. In 405 B.C. motifs from Agrigento (the eagle, the crab) and from Syracuse (the human head, the frontal view of a crab) replace the types from Segesta. The first coins in silver to be minted at Panormus utilize the motifs of the dog with woman's head on the obverse and a woman's head with legend both in Greek and in Punic (*SYS*) on the reverse. Motifs used at Syracuse around 410 B.C. (the head of Arethusa, the quadriga) are from Segesta, and Punic alone is used for the legend. Bronze coins are first issued in 430 B.C. and take their model from Himera: a cockerel, with the legend *SYS*.

Carthage's political and military operations in Sicily are reflected in the silver issues which use the Euboean-Attic blank. The coins bear either the Panormus-type head of Arethusa and quadriga or the head of Arethusa-

Coin with head of Kore on obv. and backward-looking horse on rev. minted in Carthage c. 264 B.C. bronze, 5.76 g Tunis, Musée du Bardo

Coin with head of Kore on obv. and standing horse behind palm-tree and letters on rev. minted in Carthage 350-320 B.C. bronze, 22.6 g Tunis, Musée du Bardo

Coin with head of Kore on obv. and standing horse behind palm-tree on rev. minted in Carthage 350-320 B.C. silver, 18.7 g Tunis, Musée du Bardo

Coin with head of Heracles-Melqarth with leonté on obv. and equine protome palm-tree and inscription on rev. minted in Sicily 300-280 B.C. silver, 16.93 g Tunis, Musée du Bardo

Kore and equine protome with a palm, or the Heracles-Melqarth with lion-skin, equine protome and palm. Custodians of the temple of Melqarth — the stronghold of Carthaginian power in Sicily — seem to be behind the issues minted between 320 and 289 B.C., which bear the Punic legends "Melqarth's elect", "people of the field", "the rulers" and, later, Melqarth-Heracles iconography. There are some further issues in bronze which are clearly of Punic origin but of uncertain mint, and reflect the political situation of pre-Roman Sicily. Such are the coins with a palm on the obverse and a Corinthian-type Pegasus on the reverse — linked, clearly, with Timoleon's campaign in Sicily. Others may not even be of Sicilian origin, such as the series with on obverse and reverse respectively a palm and equine protome, a Kore's head and equine protome, or a human head among ears of corn and a galloping horse.

It was with the first Punic issues in bronze that Sardinia entered into the monetary circuit of the Mediterranean. The first step was in adopting the Carthaginian denomination as well as minting a first issue with a Kore's head on the obverse, equine protome on the reverse. Later series were characterized by the Sardo-Punic motif of a back-ward-glancing horse or a horse with a palm, directly reflecting the economic and political crisis that took hold of Sardinia between 264 and 241 B.C., the year of the battle of the Aegates and the peace with Rome.

238 B.C. saw the Carthaginian abandonment of Sardinia (coin with a head of Kore on the obverse and ears of corn on the reverse, issued both in high and low denominations). In the period 241-238 B.C., in fact, Sardinia set the symbol of its role within the general political scheme on the coins stamped in its mints. One may indeed see the choice of the reverse-side motif (innovative in its triplication of the traditional Punic iconography) as a concession to the local element, and the explicit recognition of Sardinia's clearly defined role as granary of Carthage. The subsequent series in gold and bronze, which have a Kore's head on the obverse and a standing bull facing right on the reverse, and the series in *potin* (yellow copper) and in bronze with a crowned male head on the obverse and a standing bull facing right before a long-stemmed ear of corn on the reverse, symbolize the achievement of Punic Sardinia's political autonomy within the Carthaginian world. These two issues are generally assigned to 216 B.C., and are to be seen in relation to the long years of rebellion and repression on the island starting in 236 B.C. and reaching a climax in 215 B.C. with the Hampsicoras revolt.

The dating of these two issues to the year of the battle of Cannae and Hannibal's establishment of his winter quarters at Capua (215 B.C.) together-er with the novel choice of motifs vis-à-vis traditional Punic themes, reflect a general change of Carthage's policy during the Second Punic War, and above all the Barcae's new strategies.

Coin with head of Kore on obv. and standing horse on rev. minted in Carthage mid-4th to early 3rd century B.C. gold, 9.51 g Cagliari, Museo Archeologico Nazionale • p. 559

The electrum coins minted in Campania under Carthaginian control reflect the same policy respecting Tyrian institutions (as in the early colonization of Sicily) but with a clearer Italic component. The coin with a double-faced woman's head on the obverse and Zeus riding in a quadriga driven by a Victory on the reverse is attributed to a mint in Capua. This issue, like parallel issues in silver and in bronze bearing a Kore's head and horse or equine protome coming from mints in Campania and in the South of the peninsula, is related to the events of Hannibal's Italian campaign between 218 and 202 B.C.

Coin with head of Kore on obv. and horse behind palm-tree on rev. minted in Sardinia 264-241 B.C. bronze, 10.38 g Cagliari, Museo Archeologico Nazionale

Here again the science of numismatics contributes its own clear testimony to our understanding of history. The famous winter spent in idleness at Capua — that favorite butt for the rhetoric of ancient authors — appears, just as modern historical research has shown, as one of the most delicate and vital moments of the Italian campaign, with military action and corrosive political and economic strategies working side by side in an attempt to break the already wavering Italian front. Certainly, however, the issues minted under Hannibal, and their economic and political credibility, cannot have been a novelty for the peoples of the southern Italy where Punic currency had been used since the first Carthaginian campaigns in Sicily.

Finally, the issues in the Punic tradition from the island of Pantelleria (Roman Kossyra) — key to Carthaginian military control of the Straits of Messina — show yet another facet of Punic monetary influence in ancient Italy. The few known denominations show, as with the Maltese issues, how Punic motifs kept their favour even in the later issues with legends in Latin. The motifs are a bust of Isis crowned by a Victory on the obverse and on the reverse a laurel or myrtle wreath surrounding the inscription. The legend is Iranim, the name of the island in Punic — completely different from the later Roman name and the subsequent Latin inscription.

The first issues on the island — usually dated from around 217 B.C., the year of the Roman occupation — bear witness to the vitality of the Punic cultural tradition even in the absence of a political and administrative presence. This tradition, softened by the more general Egyptianizing connotations of the figure of Isis, was seen by Rome as a harmless local culture quite devoid of any threat of Punic competition in a political or economic sense. In this marginal case a Punic element of religious iconography became part of a broadly Italic culture that Rome inherited in its mission for political unification.

Successful mineral exploitation in the Iberian Peninsula is responsible for the high quality series of coins minted there between 238 and 206 B.C. Two issues can be identified. The first is to be associated with regular mints like Cadiz, Ibiza and Sexi. The other can be traced to mints with sporadic pro-

Coin with head of Kore on obv. and standing horse on rev. minted in Carthage mid-4th to early 3rd century B.C. gold, 7.45 g Cagliari, Museo Archeologico Nazionale

Coin with head of Kore on obv. and horse behind palm-tree on rev. minted in Carthage mid-4th to early 3rd century B.C. gold, 3.6 g Cagliari, Museo Archeologico Nazionale

Coin with head of Zeus Hammon on obv. and elephant and inscription on rev. minted in Numidia and Mauritania Giuba I 60-46 B.C. bronze, 12.37 g Milan Civiche Raccolte Numismatiche

Coin with head of Kore on obv. and equine protome on rev. minted in Sardinia 264-241 B.C. bronze, 15.8 g Cagliari, Museo Archeologico Nazionale
• p. 560

Coin with head of Kore on obv. and equine protome and letter on rev. minted in Sardinia 300-264 B.C. bronze, 5 g Cagliari, Museo Archeologico Nazionale

Coin with head of Kore on obv. and three sheathes of wheat and letters on rev. minted in Sardinia 241-238 B.C. bronze, 7.2 g Cagliari, Museo Archeologico Nazionale

Coin with head of Kore and caduceus on obv. and three sheathes of wheat on rev. minted in Sardinia 241-238 B.C. bronze, 3.4 g Cagliari, Museo Archeologico Nazionale

Coin with head of Kore and letter on obv. and bull with star and letter on rev. minted in Sardinia c. 216 B.C. bronze, 4 g Cagliari, Museo Archeologico Nazionale

*Coin with head
of Kore on obv.
and bull with
star on rev.
minted in
Sardinia
c. 216 B.C.
bronze, 4.8 g
Cagliari, Museo
Archeologico
Nazionale*

*Coin with head
of Heracles
with leonté
on obv.
and tuna fish
and inscription
on rev.
minted in Cadiz
237-206 B.C.
bronze, 5.5 g
Milan
Civiche Raccolte
Numismatiche*

*Coin with head
of Heracles
with leonté and
club on obv.
and two tuna
fish and
inscription
on rev.
minted in Cadiz
306-245 B.C.
bronze, 14.7 g
Milan
Civiche Raccolte
Numismatiche*

*Coin with Bes
on obv.
and inscription
on rev.
minted in Ibiza
2nd-1st century
B.C.
bronze, 7.7 g
Ibiza, Museo
Arqueológico*

duction like Ampurias and Saguntum. The probable (though not proven) thesis that all the coins not actually attributable to precise mints — that is to say the gold, silver and bronze coins that are stamped on the Phoenician blank — come from Carthage, has led to their designation as "national" issues.

The most common motifs are a Kore's head and a head of Heracles-Melqarth with lionskin or laurel wreath on the obverse and on the reverse a horse with or without a palm-tree, or an elephant. Coins from Cadiz and Ibiza display more autonomy, with on both sides motifs like the tunny fish and the god Bes corresponding to local economic and religious themes.

Glass
Maria Luisa Uberti

It is an ancient tradition of skill and diverse techniques that has given us pre-Roman (or, as art history has it, "Phoenician") glassware — those fragile creations of elegant form enriched with lively polychrome decoration. Like any fundamental discovery made by man, since antiquity it has acquired its share of legends.

We know now it would be anachronistic to attribute the invention of glass to the Phoenicians as did Pliny the Elder (*Nat. Hist.*, XXXVI, 190-199) and other ancient authors. And yet Iron Age archaeology has shown how, from the 7th or 6th century B.C. onwards, the Levantine coast in general, and in particular Phoenicia, witnessed a proliferation of workshops with craftsmen able to apply the technical processes discovered in Mesopotamia in the 3rd millennium B.C.

Unguent flask in shape of deity kneeling before a vase probably from Etruria 7th century B.C. sand-core glass 10.14 cm Brussels, Musées Royaux d'Art et d'Histoire

According to recent studies, the glass-making industry was handed down from the Mesopotamians to the Egyptians, and thence (particularly in the case of maiolica or faience) to the towns of the Levantine coast, following cyclical processes of flux and reflux dependent on historical and political circumstances.

It has not, however, proved altogether easy to identify glass-making centres in Phoenicia. According to interesting recent studies by D.B. Harden and D. Barag, the resuscitation and flowering of this craft during the Iron Age (7th-6th century B.C.) can be traced to the arrival of a Mesopotamian glassmaker on the island of Rhodes, perhaps at Camiros. The resulting acquisition of technical expertise, together with the chemical properties of Phoenician sand particularly suited to glass-making, gave rise to the belief among contemporary geographers and naturalists that the Phoenicians were the inventors of this complex and sophisticated craft.

Since the glass-making process is the same in both eastern and western Mediterranean centres, we can begin with a review of techniques so as to present below only the typologies found in the various areas of production in the Phoenician diaspora.

Traditional practice and experimental research show that glass is the complex product of the fusion of various substances such as silica, calcium carbonate and sodium and potassium alkalis. As "Phoenician" glass-making illustrates, the outcome of the process can be varied by differing the degree of fusion of the paste or by adding other ingredients, such as, for instance, enamel. Among these variants are frit, a

Unguent flask amphoriskos
from Cyprus
sand-core glass, 6.5 cm
Larnaca, District Museum

siliceous paste obtained at low firing-heat where fusion does not reach vitrification; faience, a maiolica-type siliceous paste; and opaque fused glass. Glass made with a potassium alkali has a lower melting temperature than when it is sodium-based.

Most ancient glass is a mixture of silicate, calcium and sodium, and is much more plastic than the potassium-based type. It is most regrettable that "Phoenician" glass — and especially those examples discovered in the western Mediterranean — has not as yet been subjected to chemical analysis nor have tests been run on western sand-types. It is rather surprising to hear hypotheses of "local" products when as yet there is no justification for more than a typological and technical comparison with glass-making in the eastern Mediterranean, since at least until the 5th century B.C.

Jug in shape of female head from Ugarit 14th-13th century B.C. sand-core glass 16 cm Paris, Musée du Louvre

it is more realistic to think in terms of importation from that area rather than of local production.

The natural colour of glass is blue or greenish-blue. The other colours used in the lively decorations of twisted threads of glass in alternating colours and patterns starting from the base, are obtained by mixing in metal and mineral oxides, with varying results according to the percentage used. Pale blue is obtained by adding copper oxide (or cobalt oxide, though it is not certain that this was used in ancient times); green with iron oxide, light yellow with iron oxide, bright yellow with an antimony compound, white with tin oxide.

In Phoenician times, one of the most common techniques for making unguent flasks and pendants was the so-called "core-formed" technique. The damp core was modelled into the desired shape, wrapped in a piece of cloth, fixed to the end of a cane and submerged in a crucible of molten glass. The whole was then rolled on a flat piece of stone or metal so as to obtain a smooth and consistent surface. Finally, the core was extracted. Decorated pendants required more frequent immersion and touching up, and could also be made by using moulds. The rim, handles and base of unguent flasks were modelled separately and probably applied with pincers. Decoration was added in threads in alternating colours on the still hot and molten form.

In the Phoenician period unguent flasks followed the typology of the Greek vase, as indeed their names show (*alabastra, aryballoi, amphoriskoi, oinochoai*) and evolved along the same lines. Furthermore they appear to have been used in the same areas as Attic pottery. These forms, produced by the core-formed technique, continued to be used until the discovery of glass-blowing. Although the types were Greek, the unguent flasks are part of a craft tradition originating in Mesopotamia. D.B. Harden, as mentioned above, hypothesized that the technical skill able to give new life to a craft almost lost during the

first half of the Iron Age came from Assyria. This impulse was picked up not only in the Aegean Islands but also, it is believed, on the Syro-Palestinian coast in various towns that had chosen the profitable glass industry. The widespread diffusion of these tiny, precious objects, from the Black Sea all the way to the farthest point of the western Mediterranean, is significant proof of the vital, profitable market they served.

Beside the core-formed pieces of glass — unguent flasks, pendants or necklace trinkets — there are objects in faience: seals, amulets and scarabs. One has the impression of workshop furnaces ablaze all through the 6th and 5th centuries. Although this industry must have offered high profits, the workmanship it called for was highly refined and demanding, with long and complicated

Unguent flask
alabastron
*from the Near
Orient area
2nd-1st
century B.C.
sand-core glass*
*12.6 cm
Brussels, Musées
Royaux d'Art
et d'Histoire*

*Unguent flask
left* amphoriskos
centre alabastron
and right
oinochoe
*from the
Barberini tomb
at Praeneste
4th-3rd
century B.C.
sand-core glass*
*14 cm, 6.5 cm
7.7 cm
Rome, Museo
Archeologico
di Villa Giulia*

manufacturing techniques, requiring specialized craftsmen, and slow production rhythms in terms of raw material preparation and product realization; in short, it was a technology even more complex than that of the metal industry. Not without reason are the figured pendants, seals and scarabs often classed as jewellery. And scholars have seen this polychrome glassware as the best alternative for precious stones, which were not always easily and cheaply found. From the main towns of Phoenicia come polychrome unguent flasks dating from the mid-6th to the late 1st century B.C. All three of the groups recognized by Harden as typical of Mediterranean core-formed glassware have been documented. The first group dates from the mid-6th to the beginning of the 4th century; the second from the beginning of the 4th to the 3rd century; and the third

Unguent flask oinochoe
from Tharros
7th-6th century B.C.
sand-core glass, 8.2 cm
Sassari, Museo Nazionale G.A. Sanna

Unguent flask
alabastron
from Phoenicia
5th century B.C.
sand-core glass
14 cm
Paris, Musée
du Louvre

Unguent flask
amphoriskos
from Phoenicia
5th century B.C.
sand-core glass
9.5 cm
Paris, Musée
du Louvre
• *p. 593*

group from the 3rd to the late 1st century. Quite similar, but broader is the range of material found in Cyprus, some of it in centres not usually considered Phoenician. Within these typologies there are variants determined by the natural evolution of the corresponding vase forms and, perhaps, the influence of new centres of production.

Unfortunately even today, the problem of identifying the production centres remains unsolved. While it is acceptable and correct to speak of Levantine or Syrian and Palestinian workshops (and therefore Phoenician), it is not possible to identify their exact location, except for a few individual cases where it is known that polychrome pendants were made with the core-formed technique, and it is fairly safe to assume that unguent flasks were also produced there. The oldest group is also the most homogeneous, as can be seen in the decoration and the careful working of the tiny goose-bill handles designed to take the string by which the miniature vase was slung from the waist or neck. The most usual background colour is an opaque greenish-blue or, more rarely, white. The lip and spirals are in orange, yellow, white and blue. These latter are on the shoulders (and sometimes neck) and on the lower part, forming zig-zag, festoon and feather patterns. The unguent flasks with an opal-white background and purple-red decoration are particularly refined and elegant. This combination of colours, although rarer than others, does not indicate a different period of production: examples are an *alabastron* from the first group and an *oinochoe* from the third, both preserved in the Beirut museum.

The impression that there is not one excavation site (and this is especially true of necropoli) that does not yield at least one unguent flask, either whole or fragmentary, is confirmed by the finds of pendants: these, which really fall under the heading of jewellery and on account of their religious connotations are iconologically to be considered amulets, have come to light in all the eastern Phoenician towns, and particularly in Cyprus.

It is in fact only recently that this curious category of glass has come under scientific scrutiny. An interesting outcome of this work has been the recovery of objects formerly overlooked in excavation reports and the recognition of a craft common to both Phoenician and eastern Greek workshops, at least in the Archaic period. As far as locating these workshops is concerned, apart from the known centers at al-Mina and on the island of Rhodes, the number of objects discovered in Cyprus, very similar in type to finds in Phoenician, suggests the existence of not one but a great many centers along the Syria-Lebanon-Palestine coast and in Cyprus already active by the mid-7th century, continuing through to the 3rd-2nd century B.C.

The types of pendants found in Phoenicia are the following: demon heads (Aradus, Byblos, Tyre); male human heads with smooth hair and beard (Byblos) and with added headband (Sidon); male heads with curly hair and long vertically grooved beards (Umm el-Amad); male heads with locks of hair and beard in a fan-like arrangement (Sidon). Among the finds from Cyprus, nearly all the types are represented (demon, human, animal). They come to us from various sources, some from private collections. Worthy of mention (among many) is the necropolis of Salamis, known for its splendid ivory furnishings. These heads have been interpreted as a representation either direct or symbolic of the main deities, Baal Hammon and Astarte-Tanit. Remaining within the category of core-formed jewellery, necklace-beads with impressed or raised spirals and "eyes," and the rarer tapered cylinders with impressed circular and spiral decorations enjoyed widespread popularity.

In the field of maiolica technique (an almost pure siliceous paste with either mono- or polychrome-glass enamel), Kition's faience serves as a fine example for the eastern regions. There are plaques, amulets and scarabs, that is, the sort of Egyptianizing objects which the literature

Bearded head pendants 4th-3rd century B.C. sand-core glass 6 cm Carthage, Musée de Carthage

542

Sand-core glass necklace with beads and pendants from Carthage 4th-3rd century B.C. Paris, Musée du Louvre
• p. 594

often calls simply "Phoenician", suggesting that the Phoenician mercantile circuits were mainly responsible for their diffusion. One of the most interesting pieces is a vase in the form of a squatting woman with a plant-like headdress, in rigid frontal position on a pedestal decorated with a lion's head. On her shoulders is a sack with a child emerging from it; she holds a kid on her knees. Two openings, on the woman's head and the lion's mouth, are connected by a narrow passage. The particular iconological attributes of this piece — called by E. Lagarge and J. Leclant "une fiole pour eau de jouvence" — are of eschatological interest, placing it in a class of vases decorated with human and animal forms made in Levantine workshops as well as at Naucratis, which seem to have been much sought after in trading-centres of the Punic West, above all at Carthage, although there are examples from pre-Roman Italy as well. Also from Cyprus there is a small faience *alabastron* decorated with animal figures very similar to those on a vase of the same type from Motya.

The series of unguent flasks from Carthage and North Africa in general includes examples from all three pre-Roman Mediterranean groups for typology and date. Color and decoration are the same as well. These facts suggest that at least the pieces from the first and second group were imported: it is more difficult to determine the provenance of the third group, as a local workshop could have existed, though there is no concrete evidence.

Among the core-formed pieces are a great many necklace beads in the form of spheres or tapered cylinders. The range of figured core-formed pendants from Carthage is striking for the lavish workmanship these tiny, precious masterpieces display, with their colours highlighting the iconographic details. At Carthage pendants have been found of many types: demon's head; male negroid head with smooth headband; male head with smooth beard and hair; male head with curly hair and smooth or grooved beard (there are four examples from Sidi Yahia as well); male head with curly hair and smooth, narrow, pointed beard; female head with headdress or twisted hair; small monochrome ram's head; large polychrome ram's head; dove; cockerel; dog; small cylindrical trinket stamped with a human mask. These pieces date from the mid-7th to the 2nd century B.C., although it is unlikely that any workshops were operating at Carthage before the 4th century.

We have already mentioned the extensive series of small faience vases of human and animal shape imported from Phoenicia and the Levant in the 7th and 6th centuries B.C. From a technical point of view these belong to the category of New Year vases and are thus iconologically linked with the idea of rebirth: this analysis is supported by the fact they were found in tombs and temples (Sicily, Greece, Rhodes). Other Egyptianizing objects in faience are plaques, amulets and scarabs.

A recent cataloguing of polychrome unguent flasks from Sicily shows a repertoire (above all from Motya and Birgi) containing pieces from all three pre-Roman Mediterranean groups, hence dating from the mid-6th to the 1st century B.C. The decoration and colouring are also classical. The Sicilian products have been found in areas of known Punic influence and also where contact with the Punic world was short-lived or merely a question of cultural overlap.

Figure pendants have also come to light in Sicily alongside necklace beads decorated with inset or raised threads and spirals. Their geographical distribution is much the same as for the unguent flasks. The types include the demon head (Soluntum, Eryx, Syracuse); male human head (sometimes negroid) with smooth hair and beard (Syracuse and the Palermo area); male head with curly hair and smooth beard (Birgi, Eryx); male head (sometimes two-faced) with curly hair and beard and flowing moustache (Montagnola di Marineo-Palermo, Gela, Aidone-Enna, Birgi); female head with headdress (Pizzo Cannita, Eryx); two-faced monochrome female head with hair in long parallel tresses similar to a type found in Sardinia and Ibiza (Selinus, Birgi, Motya?); polychrome ram's head (Birgi, Agrigentum, Megara, Hyblaea).

Faience vases have also come to light in Sicily. Two are of particular interest: one (from Motya) is an *alabastron* with animal and plant decoration, and is very like one found in Cyprus (see above). The other (from Palermo), is mug-shaped and has Egyptian-style decoration with warriors and plants of the Bocchoris type, very similar to a piece discovered in Etruria. Moulded unguent flasks also reached the Sicilian towns. From the Malophoros sanctuary at Selinus comes an example in the form of a crouching male figure; two others with crouching female figures come from Syracuse. The origin of these pieces, and of the faience amulets and scarabs of the same period, raises the same questions as the Carthaginian production (see above), and that of Sardinia and the Iberian Peninsula.

Sardinia has yielded abundant evidence of small polychrome glass unguent flasks, and figured pendants; in faience moulded vases, plaques, scarabs and amulets have been found. The polychrome'glass unguent flasks from Nora and those recently discovered at Tharros (now in the museums of Cagliari, Sassari and London), together with the single pieces which have sporadically come to light in other areas under Punic influence, show that also in Sardinia the usual typologies were favoured (*alabastra, aryballoi, oinochoai, amphoriskoi*) throughout the periods relative to the three pre-Roman Mediterranean groups, though they mostly come from the first (mid-6th to early 4th century

Bearded head pendant from Olbia 4th-3rd century B.C. sand-core glass 2.9 cm Sassari, Museo Nazionale G.A. Sanna

Ram head pendant from Tharros 7th-6th century B.C. sand-core glass 1.7 cm Sassari, Museo Nazionale G.A. Sanna

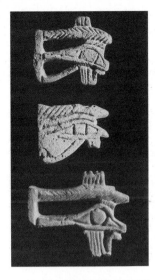

Amulets showing "eye of Horus" from Sardinia 6th-4th century B.C. faience, 3-2.10 cm Cagliari, Museo Archeologico Nazionale

Pendant with double female protome from Sulcis 4th-3rd century B.C. glass, 2.2 cm S. Antioco Collezione Biggio

B.C.). The colours and decoration are of the usual sort.

While omitting here a discussion of the hundreds of "eye" beads which once made up necklaces, now long disintegrated, for anthological purposes we will simply note that Sardinia, and Tharros in particular, also produced a range of less widely distributed objects such as the small, tapered cylinders with pressed thread decoration of the fleur-de-lys or lotus types, belonging to the Eastern tradition.

The figure pendants discovered at Tharros are numerous and varied, and amplify the range of types known from the exceptionally large and lively pieces of the Olbia necklace. The pendant types (including the examples from Tharros now in the British Museum and the Louvre) are as follows: demon head (Tharros); male negroid head with curly locks of hair and smooth beard (Cagliari, Tuvixeddu necropolis); male head with curly hair and beard (Tharros, Olbia); female human head with curly hair or hair wrapped in a headdress (Tharros); two-faced monochrome female head with long tresses of wavy hair of the type found in Sicily and Ibiza (Tharros, Sulcis, Cagliari, Tuvixeddu necropolis); polychrome ram's head (Tharros); dove and cockerel (Olbia); a monster combining human and animal features (Tharros); spool-shaped with human mask (Monte Luna-Senorbì).

In faience, apart from the innumerable amulets and scarabs (of these latter a few are in monochrome glass), we should mention: a seal of oriental provenance with a Thutmose cartouche between two feathers; a moulded unguent flask of the *aryballos* type, decorated with a human head in the jaws of a lion; a modelled unguent flask with a crouching female figure in an urn from the Sulcis *tophet*, and a similar unguent flask which some have attributed to Tharros, now in the Gouin Collection. These two latter pieces belong to the "rebirth" type of unguent flasks mentioned in connection with Cyprus.

In the ancient world these unguent flasks were considered precious both for the workmanship lavished on them and for their contents (balsamic oils, perfumes), and were luxury items imported from the eastern Mediterranean for an elite market. They are decorated with the brownish dotted or linear patterns which characterize not only Sardinian production but also that of Sicily, Carthage, Cyprus and the Levant in general, as well as non-Hellenic Italy. Also in faience there is an oil-lamp or bowl with a relief pattern of animals round the rim, found in the Tuvixeddu necropolis at Cagliari; though of a later period, it was imported from the same region, possibly even from Egypt. Sardinia maintained its contacts with the East even when it became a

province of Rome, thanks to the lengthy survival of a highly consolidated cultural influence. It is thus that the discovery in Syria of blown glass re-established the link between the Oristano (Cornus) region and the coast of Sidon, giving new vigour and continuity to the "Phoenician" glass-making tradition that for its excellence in quality had become a legend in the classical sources.

"Iron Age" glass reached as far as the Iberian Peninsula, both in areas of proven Punic influence and in Spanish and Greek towns (e.g. Ampurias). Here again we note its parallel route, interesting for the socio-economic implications, with Attic pottery. From Ibiza comes the most numerous series of coreformed polychrome glass unguent flasks in all the usual types: *alabastra, aryballoi, oinochoai, amphoriskoi*. The alabastron type is the most common, and the pieces generally belong to the first two pre-Roman Mediterranean groups, and above all to the first.

In Spain another Phoenician glass-making technique of Mesopotamian origin is documented: that of cutting the solid mass when cold. This was less frequently used because of the technical difficulties involved. An example of this type of glass — formally linked to metalwork — comes from La Aliseda and bears indecipherable hieroglyphics. This inscription has led to the suggestion that the piece was imported from Phoenicia during the orientalizing phase, no later than the 7th century B.C.

Various types of figure pendants reached Ibiza, including the usual "eye" beads with inlaid or raised threadlike decorations. The following

Necklace with beads and pendants in sand-core glass found in tomb 24 in the necropolis of Fontana Noa 4th-3rd century B.C. Cagliari, Museo Archeologico Nazionale

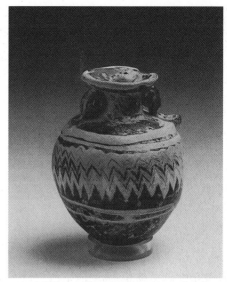

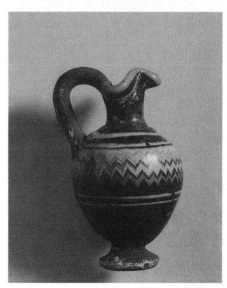

top, left
Unguent flask
amphoriskos
from Tharros
6th-4th century B.C.
sand-core glass, 7.6 cm
Sassari, Museo Nazionale
G.A. Sanna

top, right
Unguent flask aryballos
from Tharros
6th-4th century B.C.
sand-core glass, 6.1 cm
Sassari, Museo Nazionale
G.A. Sanna

below, left
Unguent flask aryballos
from Ibiza
6th-4th century B.C.
sand-core glass, 5 cm
Ibiza, Museo Arqueológico

below, right
Unguent flask oinochoe
from Ibiza
5th century B.C.
sand-core glass, 6.9 cm
Ibiza, Museo Arqueológico

Unguent flask alabastron
from Ibiza
5th century B.C.
sand-core glass, 6.9 cm
Ibiza, Museo Arqueológico

Unguent flask alabastron
from Ibiza
4th century B.C.
sand-core glass, 11.5 cm
Ibiza, Museo Arqueológico

forms are represented: demon head; male head with smooth hair and beard, or hair fastened by a twisted headband; male head with curly hair and smooth beard; male head with curly hair and beard (found in Majorca in a two-faced version); male head with curly hair and small pointed beard; female head with headdress; monochrome two-faced female head with long undulating parallel tresses; pool-shaped necklace beads with male mask; phalli.

The only faience unguent flask is an *aryballos* from Ibiza with a pharaonic cartouche undoubtedly imported from the eastern Mediterranean. The same area also produced the faience amulets and scarabs found in Ibiza and throughout the Iberian Peninsula. These pieces all date from the same period, but may not have been used until some time after their production, as was often the case with luxury goods. Faience lends itself to storage, being harder and stronger than opaque glass.

One of the problems of "Phoenician" glass is always establishing when and from where glassware was imported. We must be cautious in attributing to local industry a craft which requires not only technical expertise (which can be brought by immigrant craftsmen) but also and more importantly specific equipment and raw materials combined in the correct proportions, areas in which we still have no information.

From Sidon to the Northern Adriatic

The finds from Roman Aquileia of the 1st and 2nd centuries A.D. have much in common with pieces from the East and throw light on the continuity of the Phoenician and more specifically "Sidonian" glass tradition. In imperial times the term "Sidonian" referred to the products of workshops in both Syria and Palestine; in fact classical authors employed the notion of "Sidonian glass" rather as we speak of "Venetian glass."

The technique of glass-blowing was invented in Syria, perhaps on the Levantine coast, towards the end of the 1st century B.C. It is not known how it occurred, but the consequences were revolutionary, and the glassware of the northern Adriatic coast shows it clearly. Mass production quickly established itself alongside the production of luxury goods, and found its outlet in all classes of society. Aquileia, the Po estuary and adjoining hinterland are among the areas of the Roman Empire which have received the closest attention of modern research. On the basis of the abundant glassware found in the region of Aquileia, it had long been presumed that there had been a glass industry there. The discovery of signed pieces (for example, *Sentia Secunda facit Aquileiae vitra...*) and great numbers of unfinished pieces along with production waste of matching chemical composition proved the fact.

The brilliant suggestion made by D.B. Harden in his first analyses of glassware that the blown glass pieces signed by the Sidonian craftsman Ennion were made locally following his emigration to the North of

Italy (maybe even to Aquileia itself), has been confirmed by the discovery of pieces signed by glassmakers working in Aquileia. Another confirmation is the fact that certain elegantly carinated pieces of very thin, beautifully coloured glass from the 1st and 2nd centuries A.D. are related in type and technique to the Yahmur glassware of Sidon with polygonal body decorated with relief motifs.

Clear signatures proved beyond doubt that the glass-blowing technique originated in the workshops of Sidon: the oldest known bear not only the maker's name but also his nationality, "Sidonian." Ennion, Artas, Ariston, Eirenaios, Nikon and Jason are among the best known. The pieces by Ennion of Sidon found in the northern Adriatic region are somewhat dull and stereotyped compared with examples of his work made in the East. It is the craft of an old man, but served to hand on the eastern tradition and pave the way for the Venetian glass of the future.

There are wonderful pieces of moulded blown glass by Ennion, with geometrical and plant decorations and inscriptions in Greek. It is interesting from a socio-historical point of view to map the sites in which his signed works have been found. They follow the trade route's determined by natural marine currents that linked the Levant and the Adriatic since the earliest times: starting from Phoenicia we can trace their diffusion to Cyprus, perhaps even Rhodes, then to the Grecian peninsula and the Dalmatian coast, and finally to the northern Adriatic and its hinterland.

Different types of glass bear Ennion's signature: one- or two-handled bowls, narrow-necked vases, cups and *amphoriskoi*. For anthological purposes we would draw attention to a one-handled bowl in sea-blue glass found at Cavarzere in the Adria region. It is in the same mould as a piece by Tremithus of Cyprus with the inscription ΕΝΝΙωΝ ΕΠΟΙ-ΗCEN and MNH <C> ΘΗ Ο ΑΓΟΡΑΖωΝ in four lines. There are two deep-blue two-handled bowls from the same place (Cavarzere), and an amber-coloured two-handled bowl from Bagnolo near Modena, and a similar example bought in Venice and now belonging to the Metropolitan Museum with the inscription ΕΝΝΙωΝ ΕΠΟΙΗCEN MNHCΘΗ Ο ΑΓΟΡΑΖωΝ in three lines.

Typologically similar examples — though with an error in the inscription — were found at Borgo San Donnino near Parma (white opal glass), at Fondi Urbanetti near Aquileia (blue) and at Carezzana near Vercelli (luminous green). The light blue bowl was found along with a coin from the reign of Claudius dated 46 A.D. Transparency and variety of colours here combine with elegance of form: this high-quality northern Adriatic glass has lost none of its iridescence, and some have supposed this due to a secret formula unknown in the other Roman domains. In imperial times the names of the typologies were the same for both ceramics and glass; in the classical sources glass vessels have the same names and uses as those made of metal and pottery.

Necklace with circular and cylindrical beads from Ibiza 5th-4th century B.C. sand-core glass bead diam. 3.1 cm Madrid, Museo Arqueológico Nacional

The high demand for products from the East was probably one of the factors responsible for the establishment of a local production in the 1st century A.D., encouraging the immigration of Syrian, or rather "Sidonian" craftsmen to the towns of the northern Adriatic Sea.

A type of carinated unguent flask, shaped like a truncated cone with sharp upper and lower edges (M.C. Calvi, Group B) seems to fit into the "Sidonian" range. This type could derive from forms used in metalworking, though there is no direct evidence. It appears to belong exclusively to the Aquileia region, the Veneto and the Po valley, and this opinion is supported by the type of material, a brilliantly coloured, very thin glass characteristic of the elegant and refined craftsmanship of the Aquileian glassmakers. The profile of this piece recalls examples of Cypriot pottery and also certain "Sidonian" bottles found at Yahmur (Syria) with their characteristic polygonal body and moulded relief pat-

Bowl made in Syria (?)
found in the Bernardini tomb
at Praeneste
7th century B.C.
sand-core glass, 7.5 cm
diam. 10.4 cm
Rome, Museo Archeologico
di Villa Giulia

*Bowl with processions
of animals, from Praeneste
7th century B.C.
gold and silver, 13.7 cm
Rome, Museo Archeologico
di Villa Giulia*

*The end wall of a tomb
showing painted decorations
in the necropolis of Djebel Mlezza
near Kerkouane
4th-3rd century B.C.*

554

*Walls showing pictorial
decorations in the
"Tomb of the Uraeus"
in the necropolis of Tuvixeddu
Cagliari
3rd century B.C.*

Ostrich egg
cut in the form of a vase
with metope pattern
from Bithia
7th century B.C.
14 cm
Cagliari
Museo Archeologico Nazionale

Coin with deity on winged hippocampus on obv. and owl, scepter and flabellum on rev. minted in Tyre 400-332 B.C. silver, 13.27 g Paris Bibliothèque Nationale

Coin with head of Kore on obv. and horse, disc and uraei on rev. minted in Carthage 260-240 B.C. gold, 10.36 g Tunis, Musée du Bardo

Coin with head of Kore on obv. and standing horse on rev. minted in Carthage mid-4th to early 3rd century B.C. gold, 9.51 g Cagliari, Museo Archeologico Nazionale

*Coin with head
of Kore on obv.
and equine
protome on rev.
minted in
Sardinia
264-241 B.C.
bronze, 15.8 g
Cagliari, Museo
Archeologico
Nazionale*

terns. This type appears to have been started at the time of Ennion and to continue through into the 2nd century A.D.

These unguent flasks can reach levels of great refinement in the polychrome and gilded examples also attributed to workshops of the Aquileia region. Other pieces (such as M.C. Calvi, Type L) also recall Syrian types from the end of the 1st or early 2nd century A.D.

What we have given here is only an outline of a much larger question with significant historical, economic and artistic implications. The craft with which we have been dealing is certainly one of the "lesser" arts in terms of size, but "great" in terms of artistic expression. The tradition of "Phoenician" glass is the forerunner of the famous "Venetian" glass whose beauty and technical brilliance have been acclaimed through the ages.

Pottery
Piero Bartoloni

Phoenician pottery as it evolved both in the homeland and in the western colonies has never been the subject of the sort of detailed study accorded to Greek pottery in general, and Attic in particular. This is largely due to the quality and external appearance of the objects, which indeed do not compare to the much more striking Greek products. Furthermore, it should be kept in mind that research not only in this particular field, but also in the whole of Phoenician and Carthaginian artistic expression and craftsmanship has only recently been awarded its rightful independent status. In reality the damaging effects of a *damnatio memoriae* are apparent in some respects even today in the unhistorical attitude which would deny this civilization a real capacity for independent artistic expression. In fact pottery is not only the primary key for an interpretation of a people's customs, but also, in this case, its chromatic variations and evolution serve as a fossilized guide to the history of Phoenician and Carthaginian civilization.

Moreover, two tendencies are prevalent in this particular field of learning: one depends on purely aesthetic criteria and is applied primarily in the eastern sphere, first to Cypriot and then to Phoenician culture; the other focuses on the formal aspects in the evolution of pottery and has found its main applications in the study of western developments. In the eastern sphere, the study of the decoration is foremost, overshadowing form in the identification of classes for the purpose of establishing chronological categories. On the other hand, in the study of what is inappropriately called the "colonial" world, there is a greater interest in the individual forms and each phase of their evolution because this is the key to a correct chronological ordering of the objects. In the "colonial" milieu the decorative aspect is in fact secondary, and appears very sobre compared with the much richer and more varied decoration of the eastern Phoenician world.

The pottery used in the Phoenician city-states is clearly a direct descendant of Late Bronze Age products of Syro-Palestinian craftsmanship. The migration of peoples which took place at the dawn of the Iron Age in the Near East contributed to the formation of regional cultures of which pottery is but one aspect. As mentioned, the decorative aspect of this type of pottery is paramount; because of this, a similar form decorated in different ways is classified separately according to the color of the paint or the slip which covers it partially or completely. Many categories can be distinguished: pottery painted with red or black paint, or decorated with a geometric pattern in both colors, or with black paint on a red background, or, lastly, with white paint on a bare background; slips may be red, glossy red (more common), and black and white (less common); there are also untreated forms,

*Mushroom-lipped
jug from
Amathus
8th century B.C.
clay, 22 cm
Limassol, District
Museum*

both with and without slip coatings and totally devoid of paint. Differences in shape are rare and mainly limited to the presence of the handle or the divided base.

Forms commonly used in the Near East can be divided into pottery for domestic use, and commercial and funerary ware. These three classes should not be thought of as definitive and absolute; naturally, while a particular form may be found primarily within a specific context, this does not preclude the possibility that it was sometimes used for different purposes. The best example of this are the large commercial amphorae: mainly used for transport by sea or over land, they also had a domestic use as contain-

*Open vessels
for domestic
and funerary use*

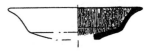

Cups

Plates

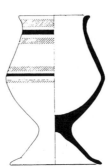

Beaker

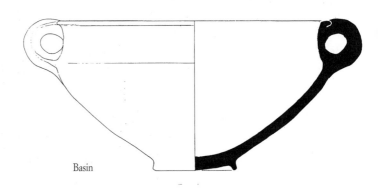

Basin

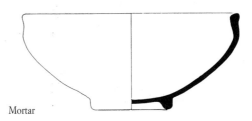

Mortar

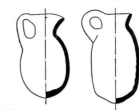

Dippers

Biconical amphora

Jug with carinated neck

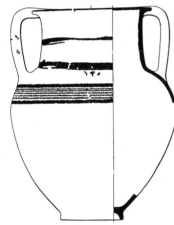

Krater

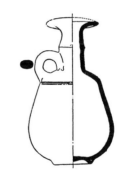

Wide-rimmed jug

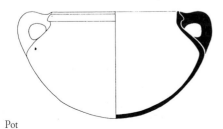

Pot

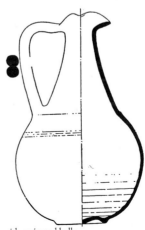

Jug with carinated belly

ers for water or foodstuffs, and a funerary use as ossuaries and sepulchral urns for children.

In a brief review of the forms, starting from the earliest, the first to be considered are the open ones, including a vast range of cups. These for the most part have a flat base, incurved rim or hemispherical or carinated sides. The plates have quite a deep concavity and a thickened or furrowed rim, and seem to be less common. The drinking goblets are set on a high foot, with large cups which sometimes have two or four handles; the mortars have a semi-circular rolled rim. In this category of open forms only the cups have a funerary function. In all respects similar to those described above, they served as grave goods or as lids for ossuaries.

The range of closed shapes is much greater and more diverse; it comprises for the most part vases with handles, such as amphorae, drinking-bowls, cooking pots and jugs. The first group includes containers of biconical shape with horizontal handles or with an oval body and a streamlined neck; these were also used as ossuaries. More numerous are drinking-cups with openings of varying width and a neck that is either straight or of a truncated conical shape; these too are frequently found in burial areas. Among the cooking utensils, which are not recorded in the tomb hoards, the most common type has two handles and a rim moulded in relief to support a possible lid, or the single-handled type with a bulging rim. The juglets known as "dippers" usually have a pointed base and are unglazed; the larger ones include containers with a carinated neck and a short bulging rim. A similar type is equipped with a wide horizontal rim, and was used as an unguent vase, especially in graves. Last to be mentioned are the jugs with a spherical or hemispherical body and a lowered shoulder, divided by carination in imitation of metal prototypes.

Forms not included in the classification given above include: the so-called "pilgrim flasks" with asymmetric body and long neck, with two stirrup-type handles or four looped handles; the hollow biconical stands designed to support containers with a pointed or rounded base; finally, open shell-shaped lamps with a single spout.

The great commercial amphorae date from an earlier period and are an obvious hold-over from the Late Bronze Age. The types found have an ellipsoidal body, extended neck and vertical handles attached at the widest part; at a later date appear amphorae with a subcylindrical body tapering to a point at the base, with either a short neck or none at all, a rolled rim and handles attached near the carinated shoulder.

In parallel with these items of Phoenician manufacture and mould are imported wares, coming either from neighbouring centres, such as Samaria (mainly open, red slip coated shapes), or Philistia (pottery with polychrome decoration), or from places farther afield such as Cyprus and the emporia of Euboea. Lastly, there are local imitations which are either based on contemporary imported forms, or on the more ancient Mycenaean legacy.

The objects of western origin are similar to the eastern Phoenician type at least up to the end of the 8th century B.C. Then new shapes deriving from

opposite page
Jug with trifoil rim found in tomb 302 in the necropolis at Amathus 8th century B.C. painted clay 25 cm Limassol, District Museum

other areas, such as Cyprus, become prominent. Imported and imitative wares also appear, whose origin or inspiration are from more westerly centres such as Greece and the Greek islands, Sicily, and territories settled by the Phoenicians themselves such as Sardinia and the Iberian Peninsula.

From the late 7th century B.C., western pottery begins to diverge in both form and type. Thus there are differences between wares produced in the same period but in different geographical areas. Comparison within the same area must also take into account the stylistic choices of the single fabrics, particularly with regard to decoration. The clays used differ as well: for example, North African kaolin is primarily reddish in colour and contains calcareous elements, while Sardinian kaolin has a predominantly orange colour and is rich in quartz and mica. However, although the forms become differentiated and acquire increasingly marked regional characteristics, they are still fairly close to their eastern Phoenician prototypes until the end of the 6th century B.C. This period (late 6th century B.C.) is marked by Carthage's conquest and absorption of the Phoenician trading stations and cities. The independent courses of development in ceramic forms come to a halt, accompanied by the sudden disappearance of receptacles which up to that moment had been in general use, such as the dippers mentioned above and the little pear-shaped jugs used as unguent vases. The product range changes quite radically and in many cases Carthaginian forms replace the old ones. At the same time Etruscan and Graeco-Oriental wares, previously widely traded and consequently much copied, vanish from the market. The fact that they are replaced by materials produced in Attica is not just a matter of fashion trends: it is clear evidence of new and more profitable alliances.

Like the pottery of the ancient Phoenician cities following the Macedonian conquest, these wares undergo a slow but continuous process of change until the Roman conquest of the Carthaginian empire. They gradually shed their ancient Phoenician characteristics, and in the end are totally absorbed by the unifying Hellenistic influences.

Thus, it is easy to see the difficulties inherent in making a full assessment of Phoenician and Carthaginian pottery, which are compounded by the wide provenance of the materials and by the cultural and commercial contacts with the non-Phoenician Near East, mainland Greece and its colonies and the various indigenous civilizations which created or copied these wares.

It is impossible to summarize here in a few lines all the regional aspects of Phoenician and Carthaginian pottery of the West. This is particularly true of the single developments of each form since, as noted above, each region elaborated on the original forms in a different way, and within the regional context, each fabric had its own distinguishing traits. The commercial amphora is a case in point, important because of its close link with trade but often misinterpreted. The cities of Phoenicia offer two main pro-

Pilgrim flask

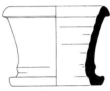

Support

Sea-shell lantern

Pyxis in Mycenaean manner

totypes already described in brief above. While in the homeland the type with a narrow carinated shoulder soon became predominant and followed a well-defined path of development, the slightly earlier type, from the Late Bronze Age, had less success.

On the other hand, there is abundant evidence that the exact opposite happened in the western colonies. After a swift diffusion of the carinated shoulder form throughout all the Phoenician settlements of the central and western Mediterranean, in the early 7th century B.C. the type seems to have disappeared or at any rate to have evolved in an obscure way, leaving very scarce material evidence. At the same time, by contrast, the type with the ellipsoidal body became predominant and widely used over a long period of time, assuming a rope-like appearance and certain distinguishing elements, such as a very short neck or none at all. These are the features which enable us to identify its place of origin.

With the end of the 7th century B.C., each region develops its own characteristic and distinctive forms diverging from the original sack-like shape. A good example is in Sardinia, where the sack-shaped amphora is transformed first by a lengthening of the sides and then, in the 6th and 5th centuries B.C., a narrowing at the centre; in time it becomes torpedo-shaped and gradually finer and slimmer. At the same time in the Balearic Islands it very quickly acquires the shape of two truncated cones, which lasts right up to the Roman conquest of the archipelago, and there are several even later examples. At Carthage the torpedo-shaped type is preferred; but this variant has a rim perpendicular to the sides and no shoulder. In the Hellenistic period, together with imitations, an amphora with bell-shaped mouth and stem base prevails, and is well-documented in the archaeological findings.

*Pots with lids
from Carthage
4th-2nd century
B.C.
clay, 6.2 cm
diam. 9.5 cm
5 cm
diam. 7.5 cm
Tunis, Musée
du Bardo*

*Pot with lid
from Carthage
4th-2nd century
B.C.
clay, 5 cm
diam. 18 cm
Tunis
Musée du Bardo*

*Pot with ring handle
from Carthage
4th century B.C.
clay, diam. 12 cm
Tunis, Musée du Bardo*

top, left
*Amphora with carinated shoulder from San Sperate 6th-5th century B.C.
clay with carving
20 cm
Cagliari, Museo Archeologico Nazionale*

top, right
Amphora with metope pattern found in the thopet *at Sulcis 8th-7th century B.C., painted clay
16 cm
Cagliari, Museo Archeologico Nazionale*
• p. 596

*Mushroom-lipped jug from Paniloriga 6th century B.C. painted clay with carving 32 cm
Cagliari
Museo Archeologico Nazionale*

*Jug with trifoil rim from Paniloriga 6th century B.C. painted clay with carving 25 cm
Cagliari
Museo Archeologico Nazionale*

*Mushroom-lipped jug from Paniloriga 6th century B.C. painted clay with carving 30 cm
Cagliari
Museo Archeologico Nazionale*

8th century B.C.

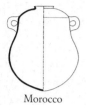  

| Morocco | Sardinia | Spain | Spain |

End of 8th century B.C.
Start of 7th century B.C.

| Ischia | Carthage | Lazio | Carthage |

| Sardinia | Malta | Malta | Ischia |

Start of 7th century B.C.
Carthage

| Carthage | Carthage | Carthage | Carthage |

*Globe-shaped
amphora
from the necropolis
at Rabat, Malta
7th century B.C.
painted clay, 20 cm
La Valletta
National Museum
of Archaeology*

*Globe-shaped
amphora
7th-6th century B.C.
clay, 15 cm
La Valletta
National Museum
of Archaeology*

*Incense burner
with two cups
from Malta
7th century B.C.
clay, 9 cm
diam. 14 cm
La Valletta
National Museum
of Archaeology*

573

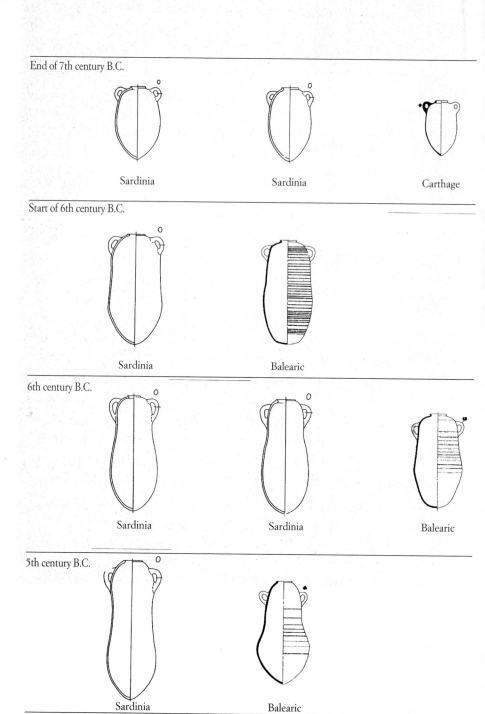

End of 7th century B.C.

Sardinia — Sardinia — Carthage

Start of 6th century B.C.

Sardinia — Balearic

6th century B.C.

Sardinia — Sardinia — Balearic

5th century B.C.

Sardinia — Balearic

*Funerary amphora
from the necropolis
at Rabat, Malta
7th century B.C.
painted clay, 42 cm
La Valletta, National Museum
of Archaeology*

575

4th century B.C.

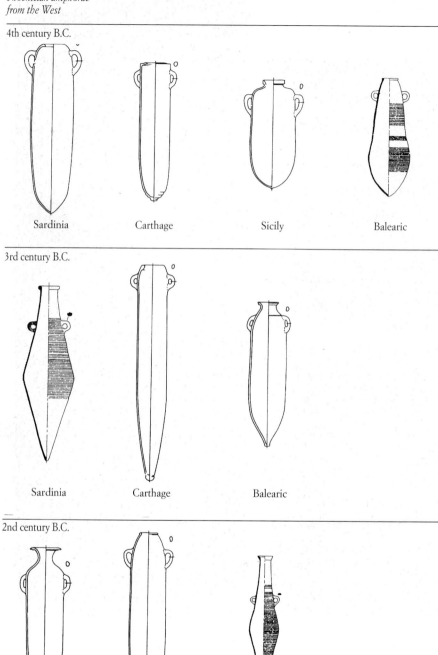

Sardinia   Carthage   Sicily   Balearic

3rd century B.C.

Sardinia   Carthage   Balearic

2nd century B.C.

Carthage   Sardinia   Balearic

Jar from Ibiza
3rd-2nd century B.C.
clay, 32.9 cm
Ibiza
Museo Arqueológico

Jar from Ibiza
6th-3rd century B.C.
painted clay, 31.5 cm
Madrid, Museo
Arqueológico Nacional

Loutrophoros *from Ibiza*
4th century B.C.
painted clay, 54 cm
Madrid, Museo
Arqueológico Nacional

Jug with trifoil rim
from tomb 19B in the necropolis
at Almuñecar
7th century B.C.
clay, 17 cm
Granada, Museo Arqueológico

Part IV   The Phoenicians and the World Outside

Substrata and Adstrata
Sabatino Moscati

The far-reaching spread of the Phoenicians over a vast geographical area inevitably involved a multitude of different encounters with other peoples and cultures. And the relations ensuing from such encounters inevitably influenced many aspects of Phoenician civilization. In our discussion of the phenomenon, a distinction must be made between the effect of *substrata*, that is, civilizations already existing in the areas where the Phoenicians appeared and spread, and the effects of *adstrata*, that is, civilizations adjacent to Phoenician settlement; this phenomenon will be examined from both sides, that is, the influence exerted by others on the Phoenicians and the influence exerted by the Phoenicians on others.

Beginning with the substrata, a general distinction should be drawn between the homogeneous homeland substratum, that is, the Syro-Palestinian civilization of the 3rd-2nd millennium B.C., and the heterogeneous substratum of the Mediterranean diaspora; furthermore, consideration must be given to the different effect of the substrata, depending on the cultural level, which was higher in Cyprus and lower in North Africa, for example.

But a more complex problem concerns the adstrata: Egyptian civilization, for instance, was an adstratum, especially for Carthage; but it originally contributed to the Phoenician substratum in the Syro-Palstinian area. Cypriot civilization, in turn, was a matter of substratum for the Phoenician conquest of the island, but when that conquest spread only to a part of the island, it became a matter of adstratum.

The only real adstratum was Greek civilization, which the Phoenicians and Carthaginians came up against throughout the whole span of their historical expansion; and it was by far the most decisive factor, active and not receptive, in pratically all the manifestations of the phenomenon, with effects that varied (and hence, analysis of them varies, too) with different places and times. As for Roman civilization, which evolved from the Hellenistic *koiné*, its encounter with Punic civilization occurred at the end of the historical period mainly in Africa. By and large, it took the form of a re-utilization by the Romans of Punic structures and installations in Africa, or the ultimate expression of cults that had developed in various forms from the pre-Punic period onwards.

One special case is the meeting between the Punic and Etruscan civilizations. Its historical base has long been formulated, but only in recent years has its

Ornamental plaquette from a royal bed featuring Hazael king of Damascus (?) found at Arslan Tash 9th century B.C. ivory, 17.8 cm Paris, Musée du Louvre
• p. 597

Map of Oriental imports in the Aegean Sea 11th-7th century B.C.

Thasos

Thermos
Delphi
Ptoion
Lefkandi
Eretria
Ithaca
Perachora
Eleusis
Athens
Smyrna
Chio
Olympia
Aegina
Anavyssos
Samos
Ephesus
Argos
Sunion
Miletus
Sparta
Rheneia/
Delos
Amyklai
Paros
Seraglio
Ialysus
Kamiros
Lindos
Fortetsa
Cave of Mt. Ida
Teke

Black painted Attic amphora from Tharros 6th century B.C. clay, 24.3 cm Cagliari, Museo Archeologico Nazionale

effect on craftsmanship been fully realized. In fact, as we see especially in Etruscan finds in Sardinia, it was a long-distance relationship, in the form of trade and commerce. So if Etruscan civilization can be called an adstratum, it is only in a very broad, conventional sense. And yet, conventions aside, the fact remains that the phenomenon was quite peculiar in itself, and will be dealt with in a separate chapter.

Our analysis can begin with an examination of the effect of the substratum in the Near East. Phoenician civilization has been seen to be essentially the outcome of a historical continuity that centered on the coastal regions, in the face of the dwindling predominance of the Assyrians in the northeast and of the Egyptians in the southwest, with the affirmation inland of the new nations of the Hebrews and Aramaeans. The phenomenon should therefore be investigated in the context of the diaspora, starting with North Africa, where the indigenous substratum (the so-called Libyan civilization) emerges in specific cases, as in Latin-Libyan inscriptions and the funerary tumuli of Medracen and the royal mausoleum of Mauritania (the so-called "tomb of the Christian"). On the whole, the phenomenon took place at a late date, as can be seen particularly in the stelae, in which popular features of the Libyan substratum are integrated only when the original inspiration is weakened by changing circumstances.

The religious milieu shows particular sensitivity to these influences. It has been pointed out that even though the cult of sacred stones (the baetyls that were to live on in cippi and stelae, for instance) was unknown in the Phoenician East, it became widespread in the indigenous sacred stone worship of Africa. The same can be said of the cult of water springs. As for sacred animals, the development of the bull and ram iconographies can be linked with the environment, and other animals often appearing on North African stelae (but not on others) can also be associated with local cults: fish, for example. One significant case is the mask. Alongside types of possible eastern and Greek origin, we have others (the negroid ones) in which the African influence is undeniable. Regarding the funerary cults, the Libyan tumuli and their survival in mausoleums have already been mentioned. Moving on to the Mediterranean colonies, one typical adstratum effect in Sicily can be seen in the Selinus stelae. The rough examples with one or two heads can apparently be associated by typology with the Punic environment: this is confirmed by an identical stele from Marsala; and Selinus itself had its Punic stage. In certain examples, there are definite traces of Greek influence. But in any case, the rough nature of the workmanship seems to be a popular form of elaboration, or rather, popular influence in a monumental category which is very probably wholly Punic.

Amulet representing Sekhmet from Sardinia 6th-5th century B.C. semi-precious stone, 5.4 cm Cagliari, Museo Archeologico Nazionale

Unlike the work done for other regions, the problem of the indigenous substratum in Sardinia, the nuraghic substratum, has been thoroughly examined by G. Lilliu, who defined it in terms of "influence" and "interference." In fact, as we have already seen in the case of Cyprus, it is possible to speak of a substratum for that part of the island that was occupied by the Phoenicians and Carthaginians, but since occupation was not total there is also an adstratum when it comes to relations between the already settled Phoenicians and Carthaginians on the one hand and the independent nuraghic peoples on the other.

The most interesting question involves the bronzes. In the past, it was thought that the rich Sardinian production influenced the scanty, late Phoenician material known. More recently, however, Phoenician evidence has been extended both by the examples from Monte Sirai, which date back to the 7th-6th century B.C., and by the 9th-century Paulilatino examples. Thus, the relationship seems to have been reversed. Since Sardinian production developed from the 7th century B.C. on, it may be deduced that the Phoenicians imported the art of bronzework — well known in the East — into Sardinia, giving the Sardinian peoples their initial inspiration. Moreover, it was a purely typological inspiration, because the originality of the Sardinian images is as full as it is undeniable.

One very interesting phenomenon to observe in Sardinia are the stelae, especially because there are so many of them. The rougher examples, the non-decorated cippus types and the baetyl types, can be immediately excluded from our discussion, for they are part of the Phoenico-Punic tradition, within which lies their full explanation. The problem becomes somewhat different when, on the basis of the "cartoons," local craftsmen stepped in with simplifications, schematizations and, indeed, incomprehension. Thus at Monte Sirai, in the Sulcis colony where fairly rough work was done by native craftsmen, there are examples of stelae on which simple intaglio designs take the place of relief work, the aedicula disappears, and the iconography is reduced to the human figure sketched in with a few impressionistic lines and with manifest deformations. Even more distant from the Punic models, although still reflecting the initial ispiration, are the stelae from such places as Viddalba, Tergu, Castelsardo, Alghero and Porto Torres. Rather late chronologically speaking, the very name conventionally attributed to them — Sardo-Punic — suggests a form of local elaboration so advanced that it has quite forgotten the remote models.

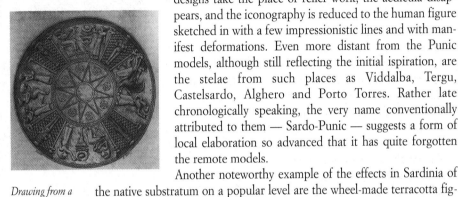

Drawing from a bronze plate showing worship scenes processions of musicians and figure slaying griffin from Olympia 8th century B.C. Athens, National Museum

Another noteworthy example of the effects in Sardinia of the native substratum on a popular level are the wheel-made terracotta figurines from Bithia. There is no doubt about the Punic models for this category: they have been found from Africa to Sicily, were sporadically produced in other centres in Sardinia (Nora, Tharros) and are widely attested in Iberia. But the Bithia case is special, for hundreds of them have been discovered, and the vivacious, rough workmanship of the local craftsmen is very obvious. They may also have been influenced by the Sardinian bronzes. Whatever the case, however, if the large group of Bithia terracottas is quite distinct from any other, that can only be due to the effect of the popular substratum.

In Iberia, certain rare stelae (from Cartagena, Villaricos and Ibiza) can undoubtedly be taken as local elaborations of a genre that is noted above all for its absence. In Iberia, too, the action of the local substratum is very lively, and involves high-prestige articles, such as jewellery and ivories. The problem here is more complicated than elsewhere, because it implies the convergence of other elements (Greek, Etruscan) and causes a phenomenon of symbiosis that is called "orientalizing." This will be discussed later.

Passing now to the effects of adstrata, the most important one for Phoenician culture was Egyptian civilization, and the more our knowledge increases, the more apparent it becomes how important that effect was. One fine meaningful example is the iconography of the Motya stelae in which, in certain cases (the advancing naked man, the two figures facing each other), Egyptian influence seems to be direct, full and uncontrasted without there being any evidence of an intermediate route. In these circumstances, the relationship with Egypt is an essential factor for an understanding of Phoenician craftsmanship. First and foremost, we may say that the relationship became decisive at the

very moment when the Phoenicians stepped into the limelight of history. Elsewhere it has been mentioned that 1200 B.C. is the approximate time when the Egyptians began to step up their expansion in and influence on the coastal cities of the Syro-Palestinian area. A great deal is owed to H. Frankfort for having demonstrated that after the passage of the "Peoples of the Sea," the inland cities of Syria-Palestine turned mainly towards Mesopotamia for a reconstruction of their civilization, while the coastal cities turned to Egypt. Two categories of craftsmanship provide particular evidence of this phenomenon: the ivories and the metal bowls. Two groups of ivories can be compared: one from the 14th-13th century B.C., with examples from Alalakh, Ugarit, Byblos, Lachish and above all Megiddo, the other from the 9th-8th century B.C., with examples from Samaria, Zinjirli, Arslan Tash, Salamis, Khorsabad and above all Nimrud. The comparison is enlightening, for it reveals a remarkable continuity of traits, and it demonstrates the affirmation in the second group of a much greater Egyptian influence while other features decline, such as the Aegean influence that dominated at Ugarit in the splendid example of the "goddess of the savage beasts." It is interest-

Plaquette showing griffins and sacred tree from Nimrud 8th century B.C. ivory 14.3 × 13.8 cm London, British Museum

Scarab with enthroned figure inside aedicula from Tharros 5th century B.C. cornelian and gold, 1.8 × 1.5 cm Cagliari, Museo Archeologico Nazionale
• *p. 598*

Usciabti with mr hoes in his hands from Sulcis 11th century B.C. terracotta, 9.5 cm S. Antioco Collezione Biggio

ing to add that Egyptian influence also extended to the iconography in Phoenicia of statues and reliefs, because ivory work in Egypt developed very little.

In the metal bowls, as well, there is a Syro-Palestinian production from the 14th-13th century B.C., the most outstanding examples being the two gold bowls from Ugarit. In it, there is a convergence of the most diverse influences: Mesopotamian, Anatolian, Aegean and, of course, Egyptian. Bowls from the 9th-8th century B.C., on the other hand, for which the major centres were again at Nimrud and Cyprus, reveal the growing influence of Egypt, but not so much as in the ivories, because the Mesopotamian and Aegean tradition remained more vital. Furthermore, the spread of these articles throughout the Greek and Italian worlds brings us once again to the problem of the orientalizing style, which will be dealt with separately.

One phenomenon distinct from those previously discussed is the direct influence of Egypt on Carthage and the western area. Especially in light of the research of J. Vercoutter, it appears to be a reflection of a separate effect in time and opposite in space compared with what passed through Phoenicia. The effect becomes explicit above all in direct imports from Egypt to Carthage and the western colonies. One typical example concerns the amulets, for their Egyptian manufacture can be proved: the same material, same technique, same iconography, same style. But that is not all: the Carthaginian and western amulets evolve along the same lines as Egyptian ones, so there can be no doubt about their originating in Egypt.

A somewhat similar case involves scarabs. Here, the many examples found in Phoenicia make it possible to deduce an indirect route, from Egypt to the Phoenician cities and subsequently to the West. But in most cases, what we have said of amulets can be applied to scarabs: in the earliest stage, the 7th-6th century B.C., featuring examples in faience, there are identical materials, technique, iconography and style in Egypt and Carthage. There is also an analogous evolution in time, in the presence and absence of types and motifs according to the various periods. One can also determine their exact place of origin: Naucratis was the major production and export centre, even though it was not necessarily the only one, because a series of designs with Ptah and Sekhmet suggests Memphis as their place of origin.

All this having been said, it may be added (and this is where I disagree with Vercoutter) that the fact of importation does not exclude that of imitation. With the amulets especially, the faience was definitely worked at Carthage, and the mediocre quality of some examples suggests the work of local craftsmen. We have proof in the amulet-cases in precious metal, inside which there are occasionally thin sheets of metal bearing misconstrued

Egyptian motifs and even Punic inscriptions. The earliest scarabs (7th-6th century B.C.) were characterized by the use of faience, followed in the 4th-3rd century B.C. by a production characterized by dark-green jasper, mainly in Sardinia. In this latter case, therefore, there seems to be an inverse movement between Carthage and the colonies to the one usually accepted. The question must now be posed as to whether the large-scale practice of importing specific craft categories from Egypt to the Punic world and subsequently imitating them was restricted to craftsmanship alone, or if a parallel transfer took place with concepts and beliefs. It undoubtedly did, since a selective process applied to imported or copied material is evident. They are articles associated with magical functions, and the proof is both positive and negative. With amulets, preference is given to the *udjiat*-eye, the uraeus, the Ptah-patecus and others which have typically magical connotations; in the same way, amulets like the heart scarab, the four sons of Horus and others with typical funerary connotations are avoided. In other words, this is precious evidence of the Punic world's dependence upon Egypt for superstition and magic, and such dependence is clearly expressed in the craftsmen's decisions.

Scarab with Heracles-Melqarth struggling with bull from Ibiza 5th-4th century B.C. green jasper 1.8 × 1.4 cm Barcelona, Museo Arqueológico

One last consideration should be made in this section on Egypt concerning the route taken by concepts and iconographic motifs from Egypt to the Punic West. It is traditionally held that the route went from Egypt to Carthage and from there to the colonies, but this theory is now open to debate on a number of points.

We have already mentioned the Sicilian stelae, in which the Egyptian influence came in directly, without a stopover in Carthage. Vercoutter has maintained a similar thesis for the amulets and scarabs: the trade between Naucratis and Carthage must at the most have been indirect, inasmuch as the Egyptian objects moved on to Sicily. It is therefore on this island that we have to seek the fundamental link in the chain.

The contribution of Cyprus to Phoenician civilization has long been well known. Indeed, we may say that it has been assessed in many of its aspects that are both correlated and distinct: in the first place, the developments and divergences that characterize the imposition of Phoenician civilization on Cyprus; secondly, the real or presumed Cypriot origin of certain features of religion and art which spread through the Phoenician world; and thirdly, the function of Cyprus as a go-between in the passage of Phoenician civilization from East to West. Until a few years ago, these factors led us to attribute great importance to the Cypriot contribution to Phoenician culture and civilization.

Following this pattern of consideration, stress was laid first on the presumed Cypriot characterization of certain features of writing, language, pantheon and pottery; and secondly, on presumably Cypriot features in certain forms of production, such as the Proto-Aeolian capitals, the motif of

opposite page
Statuette of figure with timpanum from Amathus 6th century B.C. painted terra-cotta 13.6 cm Limassol, District Museum

Statuette of figure donning bull's mask from Amathus 6th century B.C. painted terra-cotta 13.2 cm Limassol, District Museum

Amulet representing Ptah-patecus on crocodiles from Carthage 5th-4th century B.C., faience 4.9 cm Carthage, Musée de Carthage

Amulet representing Ptah-patecus from Carthage 6th-4th century B.C., faience 5.3 cm Carthage, Musée de Carthage

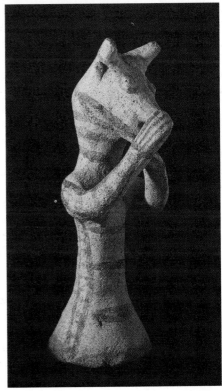

587

the so-called temple boy in stelae, the headgear and clothing of the tambourine-girl in terracotta statuettes and so
on, plus the alleged Cypriot origin of such articles as
bowls, statuettes such as those from Sidon and divine figures like Pumay; and thirdly, the intermediary function
exerted by Cyprus, along with its own contributions, in the
passage of terracotta figurines, masks and so on from East
to West. From this set of supposed relations there emerged
a kind of "pan-Cypriotism" in the assessment of Phoenician and Punic civilization.
More recently, our growing knowledge has reduced the
scale of that pan-Cypriotism. First of all, it has been seen
that where nothing or very little is known as yet about true
and proper Phoenician production, there is no real reason
for attributing a decisive role to Cyprus. Furthermore, in a

series of cases, the presence of similar evidence in other areas of the
Phoenician diaspora (the ivories and metal bowls, for example) renders theories of their Cypriot origin uncertain and not even probable. And this is all
the more true when (as with the ivories and metal bowls mentioned above,
as well as the socalled Proto-Aeolian capitals) a preceding or parallel tradition in the Syro-Palestinian area can be identified.

*Group with
Demeter and
Kore
from Kherayeb
3rd-2nd
century B.C.
terra-cotta
15.2 cm
Beirut, National
Museum*

One can safely talk of Cypriot origins only when the elements considered
are by their very nature extraneous to the Phoenician world and the Syro-
Palestinian world that preceded it. Examples can be taken from religion:
until there is proof to the contrary, the cult of Pumay is one such; in art,
another such is the temple-boy. For the rest, there is no doubt that Cyprus
offers us numerous elaborations and specializations of Phoenician traditions, and it did carry out the essential function of intermediary; but this can
be said of other regions, and may be considered as belonging to the natural evolution of each part of the Phoenician world, without it being necessary to deduce which came first and when.
The dominant adstratum in the West, as in the East somewhat later, was
Greece. Its influence was very extensive in art and craftsmanship, involving
every sector of production. The phenomenon of Hellenization, later to be
flanked by Romanization, was constant, from stelae to sarcophagi, from terracotta figures to masks and yet other genres. It may be stated that in the
whole span of Phoenico-Punic production, the Greek influence made itself
felt in the earliest stage (7th-6th century B.C.), was consolidated in the second stage (5th-4th century and onwards) and successively became predominant in most areas.
The examples of this are so many that reference to the articles on the various craftwork genres is sufficient. However, one particularly significant case
should be recalled: the Sulcis stelae, which show the massive influence of
Greek iconographies in the 4th century B.C., both in the frames and in the
images within the frames. These iconographies drastically pull the curtain
down on the Phoenico-Punic repertoire, totally annihilating it in some cases

Statuette of female figure with seed necklace from North Africa 4th-3rd century B.C. terra-cotta 18.5 cm Tunis, Musée du Bardo

(the geometrical designs, for instance) or adapting it so much that it changes completely. It is interesting to note that careful analysis reveals Carthage as the place of origin of the artisan-bearers of the Hellenizing art. That shows a direct passage from Africa to Sardinia without a stop-off in Sicily, from which, however, the Greek influence spread to Carthage.

It sometimes happened that the massive advent of Greek influence ran parallel with and did not overlap Punic production. This occurred when Punic culture was sufficiently well established and enjoyed a certain geographical independence, as at Motya, for instance. The abundant production of terracotta figurines of the Greek type there (enthroned goddess with veil, enthroned goddess with bead necklace, Demeter with piglet, and others) flanked Punic models without influencing or conditioning them. This was juxtaposition rather than interpenetration. By and large the same may be said of the large-scale production of terracotta figurines at Tharros in Sardinia.

There was interpenetration in religion, however, and it was mostly a one-way process, from the Greek world to the Phoenician world and not the other way round (acceptance in Graeco-Roman environments of Phoenician cults like the worship of Astarte and Eryx was merely sporadic). Representative of the Hellenization of Phoenician religion was the well-known oath made by Hannibal in the treaty with Philip V of Macedonia in 215 B.C., related by Polybius. The text mentions obviously Punic divinities or divinities with Phoenician equivalents in Greek guises: Zeus must be Baal Hammon, Hera is Tanit, Apollo seems to correspond with Reshef, Heracles with Melqarth and so on, with some uncertain cases, but definitely a general trend to adapt the Punic to the Greek.

An interesting historical testimony regarding the introduction of Greek cults in the Punic world is the tale related by Diodorus Siculus (XIV, 63, 1) about how the Carthaginians accepted the cult of Demeter and Kore. Having laid siege to Syracuse in 396 B.C., Himilco ordered his soldiers to destroy the sanctuary of the two goddesses that stood close to the city. For the Carthaginians, there followed a series of defeats which they associated with the sacrilegious deed. Hence, they decided to dedicate a solemn celebration at Carthage to the two goddesses, offering sacrifices "according to the Greek rites." And the Greek aristocracy residing in Carthage was charged with administering the divine services. As we see, this was true and proper "adoption" of foreign divinities which were thereafter acknowledged as such. And figuring alongside this adoption is the large-scale production of terracotta figurines representing Demeter and Kore.

In the Roman period, we come down to a religious syncretism attested by

Statuette of figure with plumed tiara from Genoni 5th-3rd century B.C. bronze, 13 cm Cagliari, Museo Archeologico Nazionale

recent discoveries in Sardinia. Here, the raised temple of Antas, near Iglesias, definitely belongs to the Roman age. Also Roman is the divine name Sardus Pater that appears in the inscriptions. But the area around the temple has yielded Punic inscriptions in which the god Sid is mentioned repeatedly. There must, therefore, have been a succession (and a successive identification) of cults here: a god from nuraghic Sardinia, evidently the greatest because of the form that his name assumed in the Roman period, was replaced by the Punic god Sid when the Carthaginians moved in and occupied the place of worship. And in their turn, the Romans reinstated the local divinity and gave him the name Sardus Pater.

Phoenicians and Egyptians

Sergio Pernigotti

Pectoral belonging to King Ip Abi Shemu found at Byblos 18th century B.C. gold, cloisonné and gemstones 4.3 cm Beirut, National Museum

Relations between ancient Egypt and the peoples and civilizations that appeared and developed in the geographical area which, broadly speaking, we can call Syria-Palestine, are extremely ancient, dating back to a far earlier period than the one in which the Phoenicians first made their appearance in the history of the Near East. As is well known, it is only from around 1200 B.C. that one can properly speak of a truly autonomous and identifiably Phoenician civilization in the coastal cities of the area.

It may at first seem unusual to speak of relations between Egypt and the Syro-Palestinian world in a period as remote as two or three thousand years B.C.: Egyptian civilization is traditionally defined as an "oasis civilization," largely closed to outside relations and influence. While it is true that up to around the middle of the 2nd millennium B.C. this definition does apply fairly well to certain Egyptian characteristics, it can be accepted only with a number of reservations and some substantial corrections.

In fact, of the three geographical areas contiguous to the country, only Libya seems to have been completely cut off from Egypt, at least judging from the historical documents available today. Relations with Nubia were determined by its special importance to the Egyptians as the "gateway to Africa", to be left open and practicable at all times, whether by friendly persuasion or armed force. Relations with the ancient Near East, on the other hand, were continuous right from the pre-dynastic era and had a regularity and importance that far exceeded those with the other two geographical areas.

First of all naturally there were commercial relations, but it is very difficult to decide which way the trade actually moved and to distinguish what was really imported from the goods used to pay for the imports. It is also difficult to assess the volume of trade, which always had the enormous distances and natural obstacle of the deserts to contend with.

However, in the wake of the commercial relations, very different and much more important connections were established. Passing through Syria and Palestine, Egypt was able to make contact with the remote world of Mesopotamia. In fact the rise of urban civilization in the Nile valley, the move to unify North and South under a single sovereign and even the appearance of hieroglyphic writing were due to the influence of the Mesopotamian world on Egypt. The rich archaeological evidence shows that relations between the two civilizations were very close and important. However, there can also be no doubt that Egypt's indebtedness to its eastern neighbours gradually diminished as we enter the era of recorded history. Egyptian civilization then took on unmistakable characteristics of its own which ultimately excluded outside influences felt to be extraneous. This process was evident in the attachment the Egyptians always showed towards their own traditions, which should be interpreted as a desire to preserve the values of the past intact because of their prestige, rather than as a kind of lazy conservatism produced by geographical isolation.

External relations were never entirely peaceful. Already during the reign of the Pharaoh Den of the 1st dynasty the sources mention a "first turn in beating the Easterners," i.e. the first Egyptian victory against peoples who may well have been the inhabitants of the desert areas between the Nile Delta and Palestine who periodically moved towards the great pastures and abundant water of the delta when their wells ran dry and famine was rife. These border clashes with "those who live on the sand" were a constant feature of Egyptian foreign policy towards the East, as was trade with Syria and Palestine, and with the city of Byblos in particular. Abundant archaeological evidence in the form of Egyptian objects found particularly in Byblos and distributed continuously throughout the entire 3rd millennium B.C., is sufficient proof of this. This situation probably remained essentially unchanged during the long period of crisis commonly known as "the first intermediate period," the only difference being that there was probably a gradual increase in the numbers of "Asiatics" entering the delta area as the structure of the Egyptian state weakened. It was only during the 12th dynasty, with the building of the so-called "walls of the prince," that the situation was brought under control, and normal relations with the coastal states (with Byblos always foremost among them) were reestablished, if only for a short period. This seems to be proved by an increase in the number of Egyptian objects found in Phoenicia and elsewhere in the Syro-Palestinian area.

The occupation of Egyptian territory by the Hyksos must have started in the same way, with slow progressive infiltrations into the delta area. Whatever we may conclude about the real extent of this so-called "invasion" and the origin of the invaders, there can be no doubt that the presence of people coming from the Syro-Palestinian area ("Canaanites"), must have been of enormous importance. The arrival of these "princes from foreign lands" (this would seem to be the true meaning of the ethnic term "Hyksos" in Egyptian) may be seen as an episode, albeit on a much larger scale and on a more permanent basis, of the long history of infiltrations into Egypt and exoduses towards Palestine on the part of Semitic peoples which is well known from the vivid accounts of it given in the Bible.

With the establishment of the New Kingdom in Egypt after the successful war of liberation against Hyksos domination, the question of Egypt's rela-

Medallion with king Ip Abi Shemu's name inscribed in a cartouche found at Byblos 18th century B.C. gold, cloisonné and gemstones diam. 7.1 cm Beirut, National Museum
• p. 599

Ornamental plaquette from a royal bed depicting the birth of Horus found at Arslan Tash 9th century B.C. ivory, 8.5 cm Paris, Musée du Louvre

Unguent flask
amphoriskos
from Phoenicia
5th century B.C.
sand-core glass
9.5 cm
Paris, Musée
du Louvre

Sand-core glass necklace
with beads and pendants
from Carthage
4th-3rd century B.C.
Paris, Musée du Louvre

Pilgrim flask
found in tomb 17 at Alaas
11th century B.C.
13.5 cm, diam 12 cm.
Nicosia, Cyprus Museum

Amphora with metope pattern
found in the thopet at Sulcis
8th-7th century B.C.
painted clay, 16 cm
Cagliari
Museo Archeologico Nazionale

opposite page
Ornamental plaquette
from a royal bed featuring Hazael
king of Damascus (?)
found at Arslan Tash
9th century B.C.
ivory, 17.8 cm
Paris, Musée du Louvre

Scarab with enthroned figure
inside aedicula, from Tharros
5th century B.C.
cornelian and gold, 1.8 × 1.5 cm
Cagliari
Museo Archeologico Nazionale

Medallion with king
Ip Abi Shemu's
name inscribed in a cartouche
found at Byblos
18th century B.C.
gold, cloisonné and gemstones
diam. 7.1 cm
Beirut, National Museum

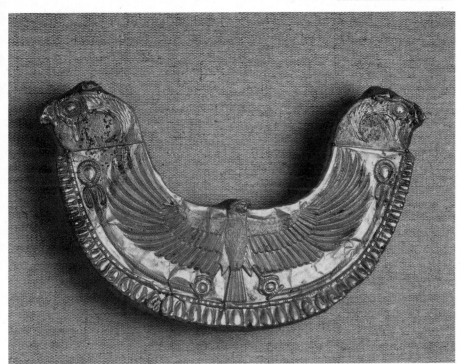

King Ip Abi Shemu's pectoral with ends in form of falcon's head and decorated with falcon bearing two palmtrees found at Byblos 18th century B.C. gold, 20.5 cm Paris, Musée du Louvre

opposite page Throne with cylindrical base found in the Barberini tomb at Praeneste 7th century B.C. bronze, 92 cm diam. 50 cm Rome, Museo Archeologico di Villa Giulia

tions with Phoenicia came to be seen in a completely different light. The bitter experience of foreign occupation had taught the Egyptian rulers that for the safety of their country it would be necessary to confront any enemy force in Palestine, far away from the delta itself, instead of committing the error, which in the past had been fatal, of waiting for the aggressors to reach the Suez isthmus.

Thus Egypt's Phoenician policy was an aggressive one, the intention being to ensure direct or indirect control, through the use of buffer states, of the main routes leading from Mesopotamia and Asia Minor to Egypt.

This policy, aimed at safeguarding the military security of the country, was followed by a watchful presence designed to maintain the status quo. By now Egypt had abandoned all vestiges of its tradition as an "oasis" closed to contact with its neighbors. Its armies and officials were present and active in the Palestine area and the country was open to eastern influences which it willingly embraced in the religious field as well. The already vast pantheon of Egyptian gods was further enlarged by the arrival of numerous Syro-Palestinian divinities in the Nile valley.

The abundance and consistency of the archaeological evidence again shows that this was a period of long-lasting and closely cultivated foreign relations. Long periods of armed peace resulting from the extensive military campaigns of Thutmose III alternated with sudden outbreaks of war, especially under the pharaohs of the 19th dynasty, when the system of buffer states came under attack by the Hittite armies. The wars culminated in a battle outside the walls of Kadesh, in which Rameses II and Muwatallish the Hittite deployed their best troops and the pharaoh won a great and, in many respects, decisive victory. In spite of the continuous efforts of Merneptah, son and successor of Rameses II, in Syria and Palestine the period immediately following the age of the great soldier-kings of the 19th dynasty saw a gradual retrenchment and an increasingly defensive stance on the part of Egypt.

In fact, the period that corresponded to the 20th dynasty in Egypt (c. 1200-1085 B.C.) proved crucial to the whole of the ancient Near East, shaken by the incursions of the "Peoples of the Sea", a motley crowd of different races who reached the coasts of the Nile Delta where they were finally defeated by the army of Rameses III in the eighth year of his reign.

While on the one hand these dramatic events virtually eliminated the Egyptian presence in Syria and Palestine and marked the end of Egypt as a great power, restricting it to its own immediate territory and, at least apparently, producing a withdrawal into the "oasis" culture of previous times, on the other hand they proved decisive in establishing a recognizably "Phoenician" civilization with clearly defined features of its own in the coastal settlements. Thus it is only from this time onwards that we can properly speak of relations between Phoenicians and Egyptians: the whole of the previous period, though essential for a correct understanding of what followed, is to be viewed as a kind of prehistoric period as far as the contacts between the two civilizations are concerned.

The main features of Phoenician civilization were beginning to emerge clearly against the background of general ferment and expansionist tendencies of the Near East. At this important stage of its history, it found itself confronting a country, Egypt, that was in decline for both external and internal reasons and whose image, though not yet completely tarnished, was nowhere near so bright as in the glorious days of the New Kingdom.

A vivid picture of this phase of the relationship between the two civilizations is given by an Egyptian papyrus containing a text, perhaps a historical romance, known as the *Story of Wenamon*. The Egyptian Wenamon was officially sent to the Phoenician coast to purchase timber for a barque consecrated to the god Amun. The ship on which Wenamon made the journey was captained by a certain Mengebet, almost certainly a Phoenician.

This work, besides possessing outstanding literary qualities, is of fundamental importance as a reflection of the general historical situation, especially the economic reality. The story is set at the start of the long period of crisis that lasted from 1085 to 664 B.C., when Egypt was governed first by members of the powerful Theban priesthood of the god Amun, then by dynasties of Libyan origin and finally succumbed, prior to the "renaissance" of the 26th dynasty, to Ethiopian domination, interrupted by two Assyrian invasions.

At home the nation was on the verge of collapse, divided as it was between two centers of power, Thebes and Tanis, at opposite ends of the country, while on the international scene it had to be content with sharing preeminence. Wenamon's journey is a faithful reflection of this situation. The envoy sailed for the East on a ship captained by a Phoenician and was welcomed with respect by the prince of the city of Dor. During his stay in this city, however, he was robbed of the gold and silver he brought with him to buy the timber. The prince of Dor refused to compensate him for his loss and so Wenamon resolved to take the law into his own hands. After a brief call at the port of Tyre, he reached Byblos, traditionally the focal point of trade between Egypt and Phoenicia, and here he robbed the coffer of the ship he had travelled on, thus recovering part of the money stolen from him.

His stay in Byblos, however, was not fortunate. While he was vainly seeking to embark for Egypt, Sekerbaal, the prince of the city, sent envoys every day ordering him curtly: "Get out of my port!" When he finally found a ship ready to take him back to Egypt, Wenamon discovered that the prince's attitude toward him had changed: a local priest in a trance had advised him to treat his Egyptian guest with greater respect. And so Wenamon was summoned to court. He describes his meeting with Sekerbaal thus: "I found him seated in his room; he had his back to a window so that the waves of the great sea of Syria seemed to break behind his neck."

Despite the priest's trance, the welcome given to Wenamon was, to say the least, chilly: Sekerbaal consented to have the timber cut and delivered only after a long series of insults, accusations, bargaining and consultation of the documents in the official files, and even then only on condition that Egypt should first send him payment. During his stay in Byblos poor Wenamon had to put up with insults and insinuations of all sorts: in the earlier times, when Egyptian ambassadors were backed by a powerful army, they would obviously never have been treated like this.

But Wenamon's misfortunes did not end here: he was chased to Cyprus by a fleet of ships seeking revenge for the money stolen from their coffer. In Cyprus his adventures came to a sudden end since the final part of the papyrus was missing. What did fate have in store for him? Despite all his misfortunes there can be no doubt that he managed to return to Egypt, since his story is told in the form of a "report" to his superiors.

The picture given by Wenamon's story is certainly a sad one compared to the prestige that Egypt had enjoyed in Syria and Palestine a few centuries earlier. It is not, however, quite so tragic as may appear at first sight. It is true that Egypt, as this important literary document shows, had lost much of the prestige it had enjoyed during the 18th dynasty; nevertheless it remained a country full of vitality and the cities of the Nile Delta still traded intensively with the mercantile centres of Phoenicia; certain details in the story of Wenamon indicate the existence of specific trading agreements. And despite everything, the Egyptians still appear to have kept their spirit of adventure, enterprise and courage intact.

It was the survival of this adventurous spirit that allowed Wenamon to return to Egypt, as we can suppose he did despite the fact that the last part of the papyrus is missing. The happy ending to the story must have been a solace to Egyptian readers of the 21st dynasty. Seen next to such a valuable literary document, the archaeological evidence appears scant indeed. The few, but important exceptions are two alabaster vases with the cartouche of Rameses II, found in the tomb of Ahiram, king of Byblos; fragments of another vase bearing the name of the same king; and a small plaque with the name of Rameses IX, all dating back to the same period as the story of Wenamon. Apart from these isolated cases, however, the existence of relations between Phoenicia and Egypt can only be deduced from indirect sources. Such sources however indicate that although trade between the two countries had undoubtedly slackened, political connections remained. This is the real meaning of the precious news that there was an Egyptian princess in Solomon's harem. Such an honor had never before been bestowed upon any sovereign.

Scarab showing figure and inscription 7th century B.C. agate, 3.2 cm Paris, Musée du Louvre

Archaeological evidence for the first half of the 1st millennium B.C. is very discontinuous. Most of it refers to two very different historical periods: the Libyan era (22nd and 23rd dynasties: 950-730 B.C.) and the 26th "Saite" dynasty (664-525 B.C.). During the latter period the amount of evidence increases considerably. During the intermediate period, which included the 24th dynasty with only one "native" sovereign, and the 25th characterized by Ethiopian domination and the two Assyrian invasions, hardly any archaeological evidence is to be found in Phoenicia, a fact which to a certain extent is explained by the serious internal crisis that afflicted the country.

The start of the 23rd dynasty was marked by the energetic policies of the Pharaoh Sheshonk I (the biblical Shishak) who, like many of his glorious predecessors, led a victorious military campaign against Jerusalem. The Bible is quite explicit (I *Kings*, XIV, 25-26): "And it came to pass in the fifth year of King Rehoboam that Shishak king of Egypt came up against Jerusalem. And he took away the treasures of the house of the Lord and the treasures of the king's house; he even took away all." The victory and the immense booty captured must not only have improved Egypt's financial position, but also restored much of the country's prestige, especially in the eyes of the princes of Byblos.

The archaeological evidence clearly shows that some form of relationship between Egypt and Phoenicia had been resumed. Proof of this lies in the extent and importance of the surviving materials. These include fragments of royal statues, such as those of Sheshonk I and Osorkon I (where alongside the Egyptian hieroglyphs are to be found Phoenician inscriptions in the names of the Byblian kings Abibaal and Elibaal) and that of Osorkon II, also from Byblos. There is also a whole series of alabaster vases: these include a vase found in Samaria bearing the name of Osorkon II, others brought to Assur by Esarhaddon's soldiers after they sacked Abdi-Milkuti's palace in Sidon (one of these is in the name of the future Pharaoh Takelot

III), and the famous exemplars found in the necropolis of Almuñecar in Spain, also bearing the names of the "Libyan" sovereigns Osorkon II, Sheshonk II and Takelot II. The possibility of the latter's coming directly from Egypt may be ruled out; as has been authoritatively argued, they must have been imported into Spain after remaining in cities along the Phoenician coast for varying lengths of time.

Not much else can be added to the list and it must also be remembered that we are talking about a span of some two hundred years, a period when Phoenician expansion toward the West had become a reality. Thus although the evidence shows that trading relations had been resumed after the hostilities of Sheshonk I's reign, it must also be admitted that they cannot have been as intensive as in previous times and that the traces they left behind in the archaeological sites so far explored in Phoenicia and Egypt are relatively few.

The situation changed considerably during the 26th dynasty: after the serious crisis of Ethiopian domination and two Assyrian invasions, Egypt regained its unity under the enlightened, energetic leadership of Psammetichus I, prince of Sais. During this period the progress of relations between Phoenicia and Egypt can easily be followed thanks to the many and varied documents available, ranging from classical and Egyptian sources to archaeological evidence. The latter, compared with the sources of the immediately preceding centuries, is unusually plentiful and is not confined only to the presence of Egypt in Phoenicia: there is also unmistakable evidence of Phoenicia in Egypt.

After using the second Assyrian invasion as a means to eliminate Ethiopian influence and drive the Cushite monarchs back into Nubia, the founder of the 26th dynasty, Psammetichus I, succeeded in weaving a clever web of diplomatic relations with the other potentates still present in Egypt. In a relatively short time he had dominated the princes of the Nile Delta and reigned supreme in the whole of Egypt.

In his skillful operation designed to rebuild the country, Psammetichus I did not scruple to use the services of Ionian and Carian mercenaries who had originally come to the Nile Delta as pirates and robbers. The pharaoh was impressed by their military efficiency and promptly used them against his enemies at home and abroad, allowing them to settle in Egypt.

This was a door through which foreigners could enter Egypt. Not only Greeks and Carians were able to settle, but also people of Semitic origin, some of whom were certainly Phoenicians. A passage of the letter of Aristeas, whom there is no reason to doubt, informs us that the Egyptian army included Semitic elements among its ranks; this is confirmed by inscriptions found on the statue of one of Psammetichus' generals, by name Djed-Ptah-iuf-ankh, whose titles included "commander of the Aamu" and "leader of the foreign contingents." There is no doubt that the term "Aamu" refers to Asiatics and it is equally certain that among them there were soldiers speaking Semitic languages. It can also be safely assumed that some of these were Phoenicians, especially in the light of what we know

about the army of Psammetichus II, who must have merely continued a tradition started by his illustrious forebear.

One of the logical consequences of Psammetichus I's policy of restoring the structures of the state was an active military presence in Palestine and Phoenicia. This fits with Herodotus' account of the 29-year-long siege of Ashdod, and the discovery of fragments of Egyptian statues at Arvad.

It must also be remembered that Psammetichus I probably founded the city of Naucratis in the Nile Delta, not far from Sais: the city was a center for trade with the Greeks but it seems unlikely that Phoenician trade was excluded. Although Naucratis is first mentioned only several decades after the reign of Psammetichus I, it is highly probable that trading activities with both Greeks and Phoenicians began much earlier, to justify the city's foundation around 620 B.C. What is certain is that before long, the unmistakable merchandise produced in the workshops of Naucratis and other cities in the Nile Delta (the so-called "Naucratis junk") was to be found almost everywhere along the Mediterranean coasts.

It is certain that the first merchants arrived in Egypt in the wake of the first Greek, Carian and Phoenician mercenaries: the soldiers opened up the road and the merchants soon followed along it. Theirs was not just a temporary stay: Herodotus wrote that during his journey to Egypt (c. 450 B.C.), at Memphis he found not only the descendants of the Greek and Carian mercenaries but also a whole Phoenician district: "Around this temple (i.e. the temple of Hephaestus-Ptah) live Phoenicians from Tyre, and the whole district is called 'the Tyrian quarter'". It is interesting that the word used by Herodotus for the district, here translated as "quarter," is *stratópedon*, a word with a definitely military connotation.

The trend toward closer relations with the Phoenician world continued during the reign of the son and successor of Psammetichus I, Necho, who managed to create a kind of short-lived empire in Syria and Palestine during his military campaigns to defend the Assyrians against the Babylonians. This empire undoubtedly included the cities of Phoenicia, as demonstrated by the fragment of a relief found at Sidon, on which the last part of the pharaoh's name seems to be inscribed.

*Urn with Egyptian hieroglyphic
inscription, fragment of plate
and scarab with hieroglyphic
inscription, found in tomb 16
at Laurita-Almuñecar
9th-8th century B.C.
alabaster, clay, faience and gold
Granada, Museo Arqueológico*

Necho's Asiatic empire was extremely short-lived and finished tragically with the battle of Carchemish in 605 B.C. His close relationship with Phoenicia, however, is confirmed by two further episodes, now generally accepted as being factual.

The first of these is the famous circumnavigation of Africa carried out by Phoenician sailors on Necho's order. They sailed from the Red Sea, rounded the Cape of Good Hope and after an adventurous voyage lasting three years, during which at one point they had "the sun on their right," they returned to the ports of the Nile Delta via the Mediterranean and the Red Sea. The project failed since the technical difficulties were enormous, but it shows Necho's interest in finding a solution to the problem of communications between the Mediterranean and the Red Sea (the circumnavigation of Africa was also an attempt to solve the same problem).

The objectives of this policy were primarily commercial, so Phoenicians were undoubtedly involved. Greeks also played a part and apparently were entrusted with the building of triremes, a number of which were placed in the Red Sea.

Military and trading relations between Egypt and Phoenicia must have been very close during this period, as is shown by a papyrus written in Aramaic (or perhaps Phoenician?) found at Saqqarah, in which a certain prince Adon asks the pharaoh for urgent military assistance.

Direct evidence regarding the Phoenicians also appears in Egypt during the short reign (595-589 B.C.) of the third king of the 26th dynasty, Psammetichus II. During the military campaign conducted by the sovereign in the third year of his reign against Nubia, his army consisted of a division of Egyptian soldiers plus a kind of "foreign legion" composed of mercenaries of Greek, Carian and Semitic origin, some of whom must certainly have been Phoenicians.

An impressive document of this military expedition is provided by the graffiti carved on the legs of the huge statues of Rameses II on the façade of the temple at Abu Simbel in Nubia. In most cases the soldiers simply wrote their names as a souvenir of their visit and the Phoenician names among them are easy to identify.

The longest of the graffiti is written in Greek: it is worth quoting it in full since it sheds light on the composition of the Egyptian army sent to fight against Nubia: "When King Psammetichus came to Elephantine, those who sailed with Psammetichus, son of Theocles, wrote these things: they journeyed beyond Cherchis for as far as the river would allow; the foreigners were led by Potasimto and the Egyptians by Ahmose."

This not only confirms the existence of a "foreign legion" but also gives us the name of its commander, an Egyptian general named Potasimto, well-known to Egyptologists through various monuments from his tomb.

For the remaining sovereigns of the 26th dynasty there is no longer such plentiful and explicit evidence of relations between Egypt and Phoenicia, now mostly based on peaceful trading.

During the reign of Apries, classical sources speak of an expedition against

Sidon and naval battles against the Tyrians. As for Ahmose, his successor, only two tokens have survived: the fragment of a sistrum handle and a vase found at Sidon, possibly his votive offerings. The first mention of Naucratis occurs during the reign of Ahmose, although as we have seen the city was probably founded more than fifty years previously. There is no doubt that

there were Phoenicians among the Greeks who lived in the trading centre and it is highly probable that their number increased during this period: Ahmose concentrated all trade with the Greek world in Naucratis, and the Phoenicians, in their traditional role as freight merchants, had excellent opportunities to do business there.

All this is confirmed by a later fact: during the 30th dynasty King Nectanebo I introduced a 10 percent levy on customs operations, a sign that business for the Greek and Phoenician merchant was going so well that the pharaoh took the opportunity of ensuring a share for the Egyptian state coffers as well.

Façade of the temple of Abu Simbel Egypt

In 525 B.C. Egypt was conquered by Cambyses and became a satrapy of the Persian Empire. It regained its independence for a while, but when Alexander the Great arrived in the valley of the Nile, the country he was about to conquer was merely one province of a huge empire.

The country's new situation, however, did not interfere with its relations with Phoenicia; on the contrary, the connection between the two countries almost certainly became closer and more intense. There were in fact no longer any political or military barriers to interfere with trade; both countries were now satrapies of the Persian Empire.

It is therefore no surprise that in Phoenicia we find real or imitation Egyptian sarcophagi used to bury eminent local figures, or a widespread use of decorative patterns of Egyptian inspiration. Moreover, Darius I successfully completed work on the canal between the Nile and the Red Sea and this must have pleased the Phoenicians, long interested in improving communications between the Red Sea and the Mediterranean.

By now, however, Egypt and Phoenicia were part of a much larger political game, and apart from an occasional reassertion of authority they were reduced to pawns moved by masters with very different interests to their own. The 5th century B.C. saw the conflict between the Persian king and the Greek world. Like all the other satrapies in the Persian Empire, Egypt and Phoenicia were forced willy-nilly to take the side of the ruler. This is the reason why whenever there were anti-Persian outbreaks in Egypt, the Egyptians came closer to those Greeks who were fighting against their traditional enemy.

The Phoenician cities tried several times to turn the Egyptian revolts against the Persians to their own advantage, especially during the 30th dynasty, but these were only brief interludes before the Achaemenid yoke again pressed heavily on Egypt and the entire Syro-Palestinian area.

The arrival of Alexander the Great after the bold, though vain attemps by

Tyre and Gaza to stand in his way, and the support given him by other Phoenician cities and Egypt itself, marked the beginning of a completely new era in the history of the whole region. The foundation of Alexandria brought definitive changes in trade relations and even greater changes followed the foundation of the Hellenistic kingdoms around which the fortunes of the Phoenician cities and Egypt were soon to revolve.

Phoenicians and Etruscans

Enrico Acquaro

The Phoenicians and the Carthaginians are often mentioned by classical authors in relation to other Mediterranean peoples. The similarities they refer to, over and above the military alliances formed from time to time in the West, concern ethnic, institutional and political affinities. Thus, Thucydides (6, 2, 6) recalls how the Phoenicians were able to retreat in the face of the Greek colonists in western Sicily, "reassured by the alliance of the Carthaginians" (which archaeological data proves to have been based also on their common Oriental origin). Thus various authors, such as Plato (*Eryxias*, 399 and 400b), Nicholas of Damascus (*FGrHist*, 90F 103z-7-9) and Jerome (*Chron.a Abr.*, 1303), cite as a valuable example of a premonetary system the use in Sparta, Rome and Carthage of a conventional leather object. Thus Polybius (6, 43, 1) mentions the perfect organization of Carthage, the only non-Greek city to stand comparison with the institutions of Crete, Sparta, Mantinea, Athens and Thebes.

There can be no doubt, however, that the relationship of Carthage with

Mineral deposits along the central Tyrrhenian coast of Italy

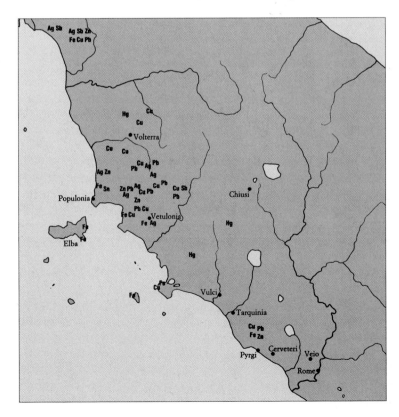

Etruscan cities was particularly close and important, even more so if we extend it to include the whole of the Phoenician world, of which Carthage was the supreme political expression.

The commercial and political interests which set both the Carthaginians and the Etruscans against the Greeks of the West were similar. This does not, however, mean that the two peoples were united simply to combat the Greek threat, those alliances and interrelations so often recorded by classical sources in the various theatres of war in the Mediterranean area. There was also a deep mutual understanding of which all Greeks were well aware. In this respect, Aristotle is unequivocal (*Politica*, 3, 9, 1280a): the Etruscans and the Carthaginians are held up as an example of how two peoples can control their own historical destinies in unison.

It is against this background of mutual understanding that the historical facts concerning common military operations should be viewed: the naval battle of Alalia, for example, fought around 540 B.C. by united Carthaginian and Etruscan forces, probably mercenaries, against the Phocaeans who had established themselves in Corsica (Herodotus, 1, 166), and the simultaneous defeat of the Etruscan and Carthaginian forces by Syracuse, at Himera and at Cumae in 479 B.C. To this may be added the fact that Etruscan mercenaries fought in the Carthaginian armies against Agathocles in the military operations of 311-310 B.C. (Diodorus, 19, 106; 20, 11) .

The points of contact in the Etrusco-Carthaginian entente, however, went far beyond this, as became evident from a detailed reexamination of the vast amount of archaeological evidence found in the pre-Roman Mediterranean area. The spread of material culture indicated a high degree of commercial and economic interpenetration, confirming the close understanding that existed between the two peoples. The reexamination of archaeological data that eventually led to this reconstruction of the facts was prompted by the research conducted since 1956 in the area of the Etruscan sanctuary of Pyrgi and the ancient port of Caere

(Cerveteri). In addition to the obvious importance of the finds, these discoveries are significant because the data they yield fall into a precise historical context.

Ancient manuscripts in fact tell us that Pyrgi, a town on the Tyrrhenian coast, was the main port of Caere and the site of the sanctuaries of Apollo of Leucothea and Ilizia. In 384 B.C. Dionysius of Syracuse, engaged in battle against the Etruscans and the Carthaginians, occupied and destroyed the sacred area and made off with an extraordinarily rich booty, an indication of the enormous wealth accumulated in the sacred place: 1, 500 silver talents, along with a sizeable number of prisoners. In 1956, the area was identified as being indeed along that coast, between the Roman (later medieval) city of Santa Severa and an Etruscan burial ground.

Important features of the discovery were the exceptional size of the sanctuary, totally unknown in any other part of Etruria, and the uncovering of two temples dedicated to the worship of Astarte-Uni and Apollo-Suri, dating from the first half of the 6th century B.C. These temples went through various phases of rebuilding, survived the Syracusan plunder and remained intact until the first half of the 3rd century B.C.

However, the most significant discovery was made in 1964: three gold plaques, two inscribed in Etruscan and one in Phoenician, which were found in a hiding-place made out of rubble. The plaques, which date back to approximately the same period as the original foundations of one of the temples, had been piously concealed there after the Roman conquest in 270 B.C. and the subsequent demolition of the temples, together with the gold nails of the temple door and an inscribed bronze tablet.

Detail of handle found in the Barberini tomb at Praeneste 7th century B.C. bronze and silver 21 × 8.5 cm Rome, Museo Archeologico di Villa Giulia

The main text is inscribed in two parallel versions, in Etruscan and in Phoenician. The king of Caere, Thefarie Velianas, perhaps in gratitude for a prayer answered, establishes the cult of a goddess known as Uni in Etruscan and Astarte in Phoenician. The cult of Leucothea and Ilizia was therefore only a late form of worship practiced in the sanctuary, which continued with the institution of sacred prostitution, closely linked to Astarte, until the latter part of the period.

The Pyrgi plaques, which constitute the earliest contemporary documentation of the historical events they refer to, are eloquent proof of the presence of the Carthaginians on the Latium coast. The very fact that an Etruscan ruler should have dedicated a place of worship of such importance to the Phoenician goddess Astarte and devoted at least a part of it to the practice of sacred prostitution, characteristic of this goddess, speaks for itself.

The Pyrgi discoveries are a clear confirmation of the active interpenetration in Etrusco-Punic relations mentioned by Aristotle. However, the place where this closely-woven network of interchange can most easily be seen is in fact the largest island in the Tyrrhenian Sea (once known as Sardinian Sea or Etruscan Sea), namely Sardinia. Rather than the Etruscan vases imitated from Corinthian work, or isolated finds such as ivory and sculptures from the rich Carthaginian necropoli, it is the evidence we find in Sardinia that gives us a clear idea of the degree of inter-penetration between two production systems. The real substance and great economic importance of the coexis-tence of Phoenicians and Etruscans in the Tyrrhenian Sea was based on the Phoenician interest in, and subsequent colonization of Sardinia. A wide-range analysis of trade relations between Sardinia and Etruria is therefore an indispensable key to understanding the real dynamics of the relationship between the Etruscans and the Carthaginians.

Its geographical position and rich deposits of metals (cop-per, silver, lead, iron, tin) had made Sardinia a busy Mediterranean trade centre since the 15th century B.C., when their preurban settlements took on an urban charac-ter and the nuclei of the future historical cities took shape.

At this stage we find the earliest evidence of relations between Sardinia and the Etruscan cities, consisting mainly of bronzes dating to the late 10th-early 9th century B.C.

Throne with cylindrical base found in the Barberini tomb at Praeneste 7th century B.C. bronze, 92 cm diam. 50 cm Rome, Museo Archeologico di Villa Giulia
• *p. 600*

In the 9th century and throughout the 8th century B.C. trade was brisk between the northern seaboard of Etruria (especially Vetulonia, which acted as a link with the other cities) and the area of the Gulf of Asinara, between Olbia and Cala Gonone, in Sardinia. From this period date the Sardinian archaeological finds of Laerru, Ploaghe and Forraxi Nioi, and the important discoveries of fibulae belonging to the Villanovan area of Bologna, Latium and Campania. In Etruria nuraghic material has been found mostly in Vetulonia and Populonia, but also in other sites, such as the necropoli of Bologna and southern Etruria; nuraghic influences have been identified in the pottery from Vetulonia and Populonia, related to the Sardinian production of *askoi*.

The finds from this period relate to an exchange of luxury goods between Etruscans and Sardinians, on a basis of political and economic equality. Initially, at least, the Phoenician element already present in Sardinia appears to have been excluded from this commerce. The increase in the Phoenician population in the 7th century B.C. brought about a change in Sardinian trading practices: imported goods gradually disappear from the nuraghic sites and more Etruscan and Greek items are found in the Phoenician cen-ters on the southern and western coasts. Most of the items come from Caere, but considering the wide scale of Mediterranean trade at that time, other Etruscan cities were probably also involved.

From the end of the 7th century B.C., Etruria regularly imported pottery, first from Corinth and then from eastern Greece. During the same period there is also evidence of contact with Greece in Sardinia: wooden statuettes have been found at Nora, Sulcis and on the nuraghic site of Sa Testa, near Olbia. The material probably reached the latter via the Phoenician colonies, where the combination of Greek and Etruscan wares is constantly found.

A great deal of *bucchero* ware has been found on Phoenician sites; commercial amphorae are rare and in the style of the 6th century B.C. Examples of Etrusco-Corinthian pottery include cups with winged creatures and also *alabastra* and *aryballoi* used as oil-bottles. Greek pottery is represented by Corinthian vases, nearly all of them small.

The rare Attic vases date back to the early 6th century B.C.; the Tyrrhenian amphora from Tharros is the oldest, though not the only example. Other finds have been made at Tharros, Nora, Bithia and Sulcis, and at inland sites such as Monte Sirai, San Sperate, Paniloriga: they consist of amphorae, cups and *lekythoi*, dated to the 5th century B.C.

Greek pottery is frequently found throughout the whole Punic Mediterranean area, though the quantity and quality vary. At Carthage, for example, so far more Corinthian than Etruscan pottery has been found; in Sardinia there are very few Greek items but a great deal of Etruscan material.

After a comparison with other Mediterranean centres, the existence of different trading routes for Corinthian pottery has been suggested: it is possible that Carthage, Sicily and Taranto imported directly from Corinth whereas Sardinia, the South of France and Spain received the wares via Etruria. Differences also emerge within the Etruscan pottery trading circuit: Sardinian imports are different from those of Gaul, where purchases of pottery appear to have been particularly selective; Carthage has the same type of imports as Sardinia.

The lack of archaeological evidence regarding Greek settlements on the island and the hypothesis of Etruscan mediation of imports conflict with classical sources, indicating that Greek colonies existed prior to Phoenician ones in Sardinia. The colonization legend seems to have originated in circles having an economic interest in the island during the period following the Carthaginian conquest; these were probably Athenians of the 5th century B.C., when sporadic Attic visits to the island appear plausible.

Close links between Phoenicians and Etruscans are also revealed by finds other than pottery. There are three bone plaques, dating to the 5th century B.C., from the necropolis of Nora, with relief carvings of animal-like figures: these and twenty others were part of a chest imported from Etruria and, in all probability, from Tarquinia. From Tharros comes a bone plaque with a hare crouching on the right-hand side, and a figurine carved in the round also of bone. These two finds are of Etruscan origin: the small plaque, similar to one found at Nora, is connected to Tarquinia; the figurine is similar to one found at Marsiliana d'Albenga and belongs to the Etruscan orientalizing production. Plaques of the same type have been found at Bologna, together with zoomorphic carvings also found at Tharros and Nora, and bone and ivory gaming dice similar to those found in Etruscan and Punic burial grounds. These items are all part of a commercial circuit linking the production centres to the trading and import centres and prove the existence of markets for both routine and luxury wares.

Gem carving in Etruria during this period was of high quality, with many elements of Attic origin. Thanks to the close trading links existing between

Etruria and Punic Sardinia, Tharros absorbed this orientalizing style and adapted it in designs for the locally produced green jasper scarabs.

Recent studies have tended to refute the idea that the Etruscans were the only intermediaries by suggesting that trading took place on a wider scale, and that at least some of the imports are the result of direct trade with centers in eastern Greece or were brought in via Marseilles. If this is true, the finds in the Phoenico-Punic centres of Othoca and Neapolis could be an indication of direct contact between Greek cities and Sardinia. The battle of Alalia in 540 B.C. was in fact a successful attempt by Etruscans and Carthaginians to stop the Greeks who were threatening to take over their trading routes.

Punic-Etruscan trading must have followed two main routes: to the north passing by the eastern coast of Corsica, the island of Elba and the peninsula of Piombino; to the south touching the southernmost islands of the Tuscan archipelago. Phoenician and Punic settlements found on the central and northern coasts of Sardinia (Dorgali is the latest discovery) were presumably stopping-off points along the route. Once the Etruscan products reached the large towns on the Sardinian coast, they entered the island's own trading circuit which distributed them to inland centers, as demonstrated by the finds at Monte Luna (Senorbì), San Sperate, Monastir and Monte Sirai.

The foundation of Alalia by Greek colonists was a serious threat to the hegemony of Carthage and caused the trading connection between Etruria and Carthage to become a more practical political and military agreement. Alalia lay on the route joining the Straits of Messina to the South of France, via Campania, Latium and Etruria, with stopping-off points in Corsica. At this moment of radical political change, almost no imports appear to have reached the Phoenician centers in Sardinia: Etruscan pottery disappears and Corinthian and eastern Greek pottery is very rare, although Attic items can be found.

The battle of Alalia, or of the Sardinian Sea, was the opportunity the Etruscans and Carthaginians were looking for to eliminate their Greek rivals from the Tyrrhenian area; after the battle Alalia and the whole of Corsica fell under Etruscan influence. Etrusco-Carthaginian control of the

Mediterranean was thus reestablished and relations between the two parties were probably facilitated by the fact that their citizens could reside in each other's countries.

The first treaty between Carthage and Rome in 509 B.C., described by Polybius (3, 22), merely confirmed the spheres of influence that had previously been established with the Etruscans; at the end of the 6th century B.C. Carthage was the political and commercial power which controlled trading relations with the Italian world. From 510 B.C. onwards (the period when the sanctuary of Pyrgi was founded) a high concentration of imported items reappears in Sardinia. Most of them are examples of Attic pottery, reaching the island through Etruria.

From this period onwards, Etruria was controlled more and more from Rome, which gave political unity to the Hellenistic cultural *koiné* dominating the Mediterranean. The memory of the close entente that had existed between Carthage and Etruria, and briefly returned during Hannibal's war, was entrusted to the historians of the new peoples who converged in the Roman-dominated Mediterranean. Finally that memory led to a recollection of the Etruscan and Punic origins of some of the first imperial dynasties of Rome.

The "Youth of Motya"
Vincenzo Tusa

The archaeologist's work, although always fascinating, often has a monotonous side to it. Hundreds, even thousands of potsherds come to light as soon as the excavator's pick breaks into the ground, and all these fragments have to be examined and understood because they make history, our history, the history of mankind: this is the obscure, routine side of the job.

Sometimes, though, the monotony suddenly disappears and is replaced by enormous enthusiasm and satisfaction. This happens when the earth yields some rare piece of man-made evidence that sheds a bright light on our precursors. And our enthusiasm and satisfaction are all the greater when the object is a work of art in the truest sense of the word. A discovery with these qualities repays us for all the obscure, routine effort and, I would like to say, the real difficulties we meet with in our profession.

This is the case of the statue discussed here.

It was found on the island of Motya in October 1979 by a team of archaeologists from the Faculty of Punic Antiquities of Palermo University.

Statue of youth from Motya 5th century B.C. marble, 180 cm Motya, Museo Whitaker

The statue represents a young man, in its present state 1.81 m high; the feet are missing, so the figure was taller than usual. The arms are also missing, but their position can be reconstructed. The right arm was raised and held a spear, or was perhaps raised higher to display a flower — or laurel — wreath, or some other symbol. The left arm was folded; the hand, with outspread fingers, is thrust into the side (the modelling shows an exceptional plastic feeling). The head is turned slightly to the left, the forehead framed by a triple row of round, "snail" curls, which continue, divided into a single and a double row, on the lower part of the nape. Only the ears are exposed: these are clearly shaped, as we can see from the left ear, better preserved than the other.

Unfortunately the face is badly chipped in most areas, perhaps because of all the stones that surrounded it. The nose, cheekbones, lips and chin are particularly damaged, but this does not prevent us from appreciating the extremely high quality of the work. The soft, delicate treatment of the different facial planes, the harmony of proportions of its various parts, and the pathos that pervades the figure are evident at first sight, but appear even more striking after careful, protracted observation. In my opinion these are the main qualities that make this statue one of the highest testimonies of Greek culture in general.

Continuing the description, the top of the head is only roughly carved and contrasts strongly with the refined workmanship of the rest.

Five bronze pivots (the two back ones remain; the place of the others is marked by three holes, one in the centre and two on either side) prove that the head was covered by a bronze headdress, perhaps a laurel wreath, probably connected with the function represented by the youth.

The most striking element, however, is the ankle-length garment that covers the figure entirely, except for the arms and a small area of the chest. The feet, as I have mentioned, are missing, but were visible and perhaps naked, since the robe ends clearly above them. The garment is very heavy, richly gathered with close pleating; the folds are particularly numerous in front below, forming a mass with a slight wave movement. The necessary weight of such an ample robe is hardly evident, because the fabric is skillfully rendered with very fine, light pleats which give it movement, outlining the body in its remarkably sinuous posture.

These qualities are even more evident on the back, where the surface of the robe is almost smooth, interrupted only by the belt that clasps the figure at chest-height, and by a few folds caused by the movement of the limbs and the body itself. Above, at the height of the right arm, there is a small rectangular hollow, like a stamp impressed a few millimeters into the surrounding surface. We do not know whether this was a particular symbol or a motif used as the artist's signature.

The right leg is languidly extended forward, and from the knee bent slightly back again. The left leg, on which most of the weight rests, is straight and set a little behind the body. This attitude determines the rhythm of the whole figure, resulting in a series of muscular contrasts which create a charming, harmonious composition.

The anatomy of the body is clearly in evidence, outlined by the soft, almost floating garment: from the very pronounced buttocks to the genitals, knees, calves, the robe emphasizes the various parts of the body, making the vitality of this youth appear almost more vibrant than if he were nude.

Together with the robe a particular element attracts our attention: this is the wide sash-belt, perhaps made of leather or purple fabric in the original model, which the youth wears round his chest: two strings cross at the back and are tied in front, at the centre of the chest, where they were held by a metal stud which today has disappeared but is indicated by two large, deep holes which fixed it to the marble.

Who does this statue represent? where was it placed? what was its function? to which period of Greek sculpture can we attribute it? It is not simple to give an exact, full answer to these questions. However, I shall try to provide an answer, if only hypothetical, bearing in mind particularly the place where the statue was found, a Phoenico-Punic settlement, and the garment the figure is wearing, which is certainly Phoenico-Punic. The long, heavy robe with the sash round it was a costume often worn by priests, but the youth of the subject and his whole bearing rule out this interpretation. Considering the position of the body and particularly the arms, I think this may be the idealized figure of the young man (the patron or perhaps his son?) who rode with the driver in the chariot: after victory in a race, he performed a lap of honour with his right hand raised and holding a laurel crown or similar attribute.

If this is so, the statue would have been designed to remind the Motyans of an illustrious fellow-citizen, the winner of a race. If the original site of the statue was not far from the place where it was found, near the remains of the large Motyan sanctuary, it may have stood in an open space that was probably part of a wide urban road or square.

The dating of this statue has created various arguments among scholars. One opinion, which however considers neither the head of the statue nor the costume it is wearing, attributes it to mid-Hellenism, i.e. the 3rd century B.C. However, I have no doubt whatsoever — and here the majority of scholars who have considered the statue agree with me — that it should be dated around 470-460 B.C. This is clearly proved by the head, which can only belong to the "severe" period of Greek sculpture, and the costume which, as I have said, is Phoenico-Punic ("The Carthaginians kept their eastern costume which made them immediately recognizable in Italy and Greece. Like the peoples of Phoenicia, they wore a wide tunic which was ordinarily ankle-length. Sometimes it fell loose and sometimes it was caught by a belt, often hidden under the folds of the tunic," S. Gsell; "The Carthaginian national costume, of Phoenician origin, used neither toga nor cloak. It consisted of a straight, ankle-length tunic, which was very wide..." S. Moscati) answers those who argue that in the "severe" period, a similar costume was inconceivable in Greek sculpture.

In conclusion, this was probably a statue commissioned by a rich Motyan from a Greek artist.

Apart from these scholarly investigations and interpretations, the statue certainly represents an outstanding work of art, exceptional not only for its great aesthetic value but also for the historical and human message it brings to us: it may be considered a symbol of the meeting between the Greek and Phoenico-Punic civilizations — the two elements that for several centuries determined the history of the Mediterranean, that history which is "our history."

Orientalizing Art
Sabatino Moscati

There is a large group of objects on the borders of
mainstream Phoenician artistic production; in some
respects it can be legitimately included in the main
body of objects, yet at the same time it can be considered a class in itself, having been produced by others
under Phoenician influence. For this group of objects

the term "orientalizing art" has been coined. This is clearly a makeshift definition, especially since it is restricted to that part of the production considered to be exclusively Phoenician in style.
Substantially, the question should be seen in terms of an alternative classification concerning not so much the place of origin as the contents of the various genres or groups of objects. Exactly what is Phoenician and what, on
the other hand, is the product of workshops in which the Phoenician component is only one among others, and not necessarily even a direct influence? The objects of this alternative are mainly the jewellery, carved ivory
and bronzes found in Iberia, and also the bowls and ivories found in Italy
in non-Phoenician contexts; thus the issue becomes one of definition: of
local production, the artisans, and where they came

*Ivory plaquette
featuring
kneeling warrior
flanked by a
winged griffin
and a lion
from Carmona
6th century B.C.
New York
The Hispanic
Society
of America*

from. In recent times, the subject has been further
developed in Italy, following the increase in our
knowledge. The question asked was: is there anything in the finds made in Phoenician centres that
can be defined as orientalizing art?
Leaving consideration of the single categories aside
in favor of an overview, we note a clear pattern of

evolution in research and opinions. Initially, very simply but rather superfi-
cially, practically all the related material was attributed to Phoenician art.
An evolution in characteristics could be perceived, but it was considered to
be within the framework of Phoenician craftsmanship, the consequence of
the far-reaching diaspora of the artisans and not of the intervention of extraneous factors.

*Ivory comb
decorated
with lion
and hare
from Carmona
6th century B.C.
New York
The Hispanic
Society
of America*

Subsequently, and it seems, by some form of reaction, opinions were
reversed. The intervention and contribution of foreign craftsmen was
acknowledged, and the non-Phoenician environment in which many of the
products appeared was confirmed. Virtually all the material in question was
classified as "orientalizing," that is, as belonging to a non-Phoenician art
(influenced by the Phoenician, but not exclusively). The remarkable thing
about this was that the opinion gained support as our knowledge improved,
especially as regards Spain, so that the increasing amount of material corresponded to a decreasing attribution to the Phoenician world. Today, espe-

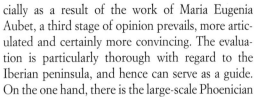

Ivory comb decorated with winged griffins slaying gazelles, from Carmona 6th century B.C. New York, The Hispanic Society of America

cially as a result of the work of Maria Eugenia Aubet, a third stage of opinion prevails, more articulated and certainly more convincing. The evaluation is particularly thorough with regard to the Iberian peninsula, and hence can serve as a guide. On the one hand, there is the large-scale Phoenician penetration along the south coast of the peninsula, and hence, the certainty that Phoenician craft workshops were established on Iberian soil (instances of importation aside). There is, therefore, no doubt that some of the products can be considered wholly Phoenician. On the other hand, there is the diffusion via trade of Phoenician objects much farther inland than in the occupied region. This means that these products were received by the local craftsmen who assimilated them, re-elaborated them and mixed them with other influences, thus creating the phenomenon of orientalizing art.

There seems to be a rather different situation with the jewellery and ivories. The jewellery in the recently discovered coastal centres such as Trayamar, is independently Phoenician, but there is little of it which indicates that it was imported. However, such centres as La Aliseda, Cerro de Carambolo and Ebora, richer and more complex, lie outside the Phoenician area, a fact which leads us to see there a convergence of Phoenician and local elements. If, therefore, we have to talk of orientalizing art, there is no doubt that the Phoenician component here is much more evident than elsewhere. But perhaps it is altogether a different case: Phoenician artisans may have settled inland and operated there. If this is so, the elaboration would have to be partially or entirely attributed to them.

Decorated stand from the Barberini tomb at Praeneste 7th century B.C. ivory, 8.2 cm Rome, Museo Archeologico di Villa Giulia

As for the carved ivory of Carmona, Aubet's work suggests a stratification in time that cannot be applied to the jewellery. A first group is posited as the work of Phoenician artisans who emigrated to Iberia and were active early in the 7th century B.C. In the case of these craftsmen, we can safely talk of provincial art, but still in a Phoenician environment. A second group of ivories is interpreted as showing of local acclimatization in the second half of the same century. A third group appears to be purely local and is dated to the 6th and 5th centuries B.C.

It is clear that the details of a thesis like this, based mostly on stylistic features, are open to debate, but it does demonstrate that an evolution did take place, and in the direction indicated.

Having defined its terms, the question of orientalization can be extended to other categories of craftwork. This has been done, in Iberia in particular, and especially for the bronzes. A number of female statuettes from a tomb at Cástulo, cast in the round, suggest an Egyptian, and hence Phoenician connotation, on account of a series of features: the Hathor hairstyle, the head crowned with a lotus flower, the arms crossed over the chest and holding an open papyrus. These statuettes could be the products of local orien-

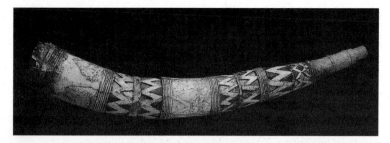

Decorated tusk from the Barberini tomb at Praeneste 7th century B.C. ivory and amber 40.5 cm Rome, Museo Archeologico di Villa Giulia

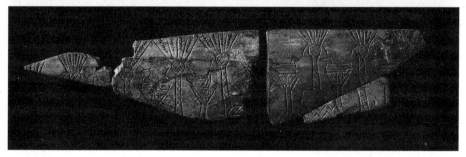

talization, but they could equally be imports from Phoenicia or Cyprus. The characteristic bi-conical jugs with a palmette at the lower join of the handle, also in bronze, are also obviously influenced by the Phoenicians, but because of the sites in which they were found they are in all probability locally made, and may therefore be classified as examples of orientalizing art. The distribution of discoveries is remarkably indicative of their diffusion: from the lower valley of the Guadalquivir to the mid-valleys of the Guadiana and Tagus, and as far as the upper Duero. And it is no less significant that this diffusion coincides in substance with the "silver route" of the Roman age.

Certain belt plaques can also be classified in the same way. The best-known one comes from Sanchorreja and depicts a winged lion, its head covered by a tiara, resting on a calyx palmette and facing a sacred tree with lotus leaves and flowers.

One true revelation for orientalizing art in Iberia is a recently discovered monument, the scope of which surpasses Phoenician inspiration and links up with the Syrian and Anatolian area. It is the funerary monument found at

Plaquettes depicting ritual scene on a papyrus boat and plant motifs from the Bernardini tomb at Praeneste 7th century B.C. ivory, 4.6 × 8 cm 4.3 × 7.3 cm Rome, Museo Archeologico di Villa Giulia

*Crouching lion
from the
Barberini tomb
at Praeneste
7th century B.C.
ivory
2.4 × 6.1 cm
Rome, Museo
Archeologico
di Villa Giulia*

*Lion and female
figure from the
Barberini tomb
at Praeneste
8th century B.C.
ivory
5.4 × 13.5 cm
Rome, Museo
Archeologico
di Villa Giulia*

Pozo Moro in the province of Albacete, about 200 km from the south coast. The monument bears lions projecting on the sides and has friezes in relief representing mythological scenes of the Syro-Phoenician or Neo-Hittite type. In all probability, this is a funerary monument made for some royal personage, and is highly indicative of the Eastern influence on Iberian art.

Moving across to Italy, ivories and metal bowls have been found in places completely outside the orbit of Phoenician colonization. We must therefore explain their Phoenician components in terms of trade and the trade routes. Once again, credit goes to Aubet for her in-depth research on the ivories. They come from Praeneste and, as in the case of the Carmona ivories from Iberia, should be divided into different periods. A first group seems to be Phoenician and obviously imported. A second group is Syro-Anatolian, also imported. A third group can be considered orientalizing, that is, indigenous workmanship inspired by imported examples.

This assessment gives rise to a number of considerations. First, it is interesting to see reflected here at Praeneste the distinction between a Phoenician group and a Syrian group, typical of the Near East; it provides

*Comb clasp
with zoomorphic
decoration
from the
Bernardini tomb
at Praeneste
7th century B.C.
gold
6.3 × 16.5 cm
Rome, Museo
Archeologico
di Villa Giulia*

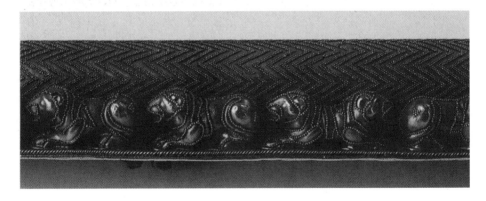

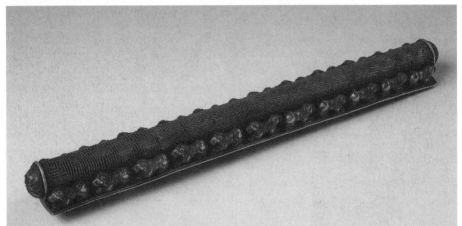

*Cylindrical comb clasp
with detail
of zoomorphic decorations
from the Bernardini tomb
at Praeneste
7th century B.C.
gold, 19.6 cm
Rome, Museo Archeologico
di Villa Giulia*

further confirmation of the Phoenician character of the work. Secondly, there is an obvious parallel with the situation in Iberia: first comes the Phoenician material (with ethnic penetration in Iberia, with trade in Italy), and then local developments follow. Finally, for the arrival and distribution of Phoenician products in Italy, a comparison with the ivories and metal bowls indicates Cerveteri as the major center.

The bowls were found in various places: Praeneste and also, as already mentioned elsewhere, Cerveteri, Pontecagnano and Macchiabate near Sibari. Aubet's investigation identifies the bowls as primarily Phoenician, and they do not diverge significantly from Eastern examples. Therefore they must be Phoenician imports, again distributed from Cerveteri. In the case of the Macchiabate bowl, however, we may imagine direct or indirect importation via the Ionian Sea without going as far as Etruria.

As we have said, the whole question of orientalizing art comes up again with finds in the localities of Italy. This is particularly so in Sardinia, where an analysis of the statue discovered at Monte Sirai recalls the Vulci centaur. The most complex case is Tharros, where the scarabs and ivories in particular display a series of iconographies suggesting Etruscan influence, probably absorbed during the most intensive phase of commercial relations, in the 4th century B.C. In other words, in this case there seems to be a late orientalizing art, probably further developed at Tharros.

A more in-depth assessment is yet to come. Meanwhile, however, the picture is becoming increasingly complex.

Detail of a bronze caldron showing protome of griffin Rome, Museo Archeologico di Villa Giulia

The contrast between Phoenicia and the orientalizing centers falls away, since the orientalizing phenomena did not result merely from the development of Phoenician themes outside their own area, but also from a secondary action of a return to these themes. All in all, in the light of the most recent studies, orientalizing art appears as a very interesting phenomenon of evolution or interference on the fringe of Phoenician production, along frontiers which are not always clear but illustrate a vital osmosis among the civilizations of the ancient Mediterranean world.

The Phoenicians as Seen by the Ancient World
Federico Mazza

Closely examined, the destiny which history has reserved for the Phoenicians is a singular one indeed, both as regards their role in the events taking place along the coastal strip of their eastern homeland and in the great adventure of their expansion throughout the Mediterranean, where Carthage was in a position to receive the prestigious legacy of Tyre, and to acquire sufficient power to become a rival on equal terms first with the Greeks and then with the Romans. It was a "singular" destiny for the following reason: by the almost unanimous consensus of the ancients the Phoenicians were given credit for the invention of alphabetic writing, or at least for having introduced it and spread it among the other peoples of the Mediterranean; nonetheless we are able to learn very little, and in some cases unfortunately nothing, directly from them about the events which were milestones in their path through history and through civilization.

At first sight this statement might appear to conflict with the fact that we possess tens of thousands of epigraphic documents, chiefly from Carthage and its territory and also, but to a lesser extent, from Phoenicia proper and its colonies. This should not obscure the facts; the great limitation of their contribution soon becomes all too clear, once the overall votive-funerary scope and the generally repetitive and stereotyped nature of its formulas have been observed. Therefore the conspicuous mass of epigraphic evidence available has no bearing on the amount of information that can actually be obtained from it, particularly as regards variety.

Illustration of a votive stele with ship and hand from Carthage 2nd century B.C. limestone 44 × 18 cm Carthage, Musée de Carthage

The restricted range and monotonous structural uniformity of these texts sets strong limitations on their possible usefulness. Fortunately these limitations are not absolute, at least for certain kinds of data, such as titles, public offices, institutions or trades; and, to a far greater degree, names of divinities and persons, which are important not only in themselves, but also for the light they shed on the complex relationship existing between man and the sphere of the divine. But the ray of light projected by this documentation irremediably excludes a whole range of information which would be basic to any attempt to make a better "reading" and interpretation of the most significant aspects of this civilization.

Limited, therefore, in terms of those indispensable instruments of knowledge which are direct sources, we depend to a vast extent on indirect sources, Egyptian, Near Eastern and, above all, the information which comes down to us from the Greeks and Romans, who were forever in competition with the Phoenicians and Carthaginians, if not indeed locked in bitter struggle.

This state of affairs is rendered even more regrettable by the fact that there is evidence of the existence, in various Phoenician cities, of archives and collections of official documents, including explicit references to a tradition of historiography. Another obstacle to the reconstruction of the basic outlines of the thought and culture of this people, besides the almost total loss of temple and palace archives, is the disappearance of a huge patrimony of literary works. Among these were religious and philosophical works, some of them the fruits of currents of thought which in Carthage, for example, must have developed under the influence of Greek metaphysics; then there were treatises on geography, political and legal writings, and manuals of a technical and educational nature, such as Mago's celebrated manual on agriculture, held to be of fundamental importance by the Romans — so much so that, according to Pliny (*Nat. Hist.*, XVIII, 5, 22), the senate issued a decree to this effect: "...with a single exception it laid down that his twenty-eight books should be translated into Latin, in spite of the fact that Cato had already written his treatise; and that the task should be undertaken by persons instructed in the Punic language; the person who got the best part was D. Silanus, a personage of noble origins."

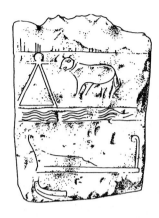

Illustration of a votive stele with "sign of Tanit" from Carthage 2nd century B.C. limestone 21 × 16 cm Carthage, Musée de Carthage

With the exception of a few surviving passages, this work unfortunately shared the oblivion which almost symbolically was the fate of the libraries of Carthage. After the fall of the city (still according to Pliny) these were given away to the African princes, with a gesture which says much about the foresight of Rome concerning the destiny reserved for the cultural legacy of its detested enemy. Faced with this situation, in many respects discouraging, there is no choice but to turn to the information offered by indirect sources, always bearing in mind the intrinsic risks and difficulties which arise from the distortions inherent in all evidence of this kind, as well as in the manner in which it has been transmitted to us.

Exemplary in this respect is the fate of the so-called "Annals" of Tyre, long quotations from which appear in the works of Josephus. A critical examination of them makes obvious the extreme improbability that whole passages taken from the archives of Tyre could have reached Josephus without considerable changes, and through him have come down to us. Recent studies have in fact shown that what we have is really only the result of a Greek adaptation of material that was certainly Phoenician in origin, but by that time third hand. What is more, the writer was not interested in the text itself, but simply concerned to transmit some information contained in it.

Nor are the assertions of Josephus himself any more reassuring; according to him (*Ant.*, VIII, 55) letters and copies of official documents "...are preserved to this day, not only in our books, but also among the Tyrians, so that any who wish to ascertain this exactly, if they apply to the officials of the Tyrian archives, will find there that things are in accord with what we have said." Furthermore (*Contr. Ap.*, I, 107): "Among the Tyrians, for a great many years, there have been written documents publicly compiled and archived with great care, referring to memorable events which have occurred among them and among others."

Rather than being a guarantee of an objective reference to a documentary legacy checked at source, these assertions turn out to be a rhetorical expedient, with an implied polemical edge which also casts doubt upon other cases where references to "Punic books" — in which, as we are told by Saint Augustine (*Epist.*, XVII, 2), "...according to very learned persons, many wise things were contained" — raise the suspicion that the authors were using a fiction in order to give greater credibility to their own ideas, or give them the charisma and nobility of an ancient tradition.

The question thus arises as to what general opinion we should form about the value and importance of the indirect sources, especially classical ones, in our attempt to understand what the ancient world thought, both positively and negatively, about the Phoenicians.

Undoubtedly the answer is they make an enormous and indispensable contribution, even though we must be constantly aware of the two basic characteristics which constitute the limits of their objectivity. On the one hand there is notable discontinuity in the phases of history they concentrate on. The Greek and Latin authors, as in fact is only natural, gave the greatest space to the long wars in which the Phoenicians and Carthaginians were in conflict first with the Greeks, both of the mother country and of Sicily, and then with the imperial power of Rome. Concerning these phases we therefore have far more widespread and detailed information, partly because it is very close in time, or even contemporary, and there is more direct interest in the events narrated. For other aspects or sectors of Phoenician civilization, on the other hand, and particularly for the most ancient period, our evidence is sporadic and inconclusive, leaving vast gaps that are nearly always impossible to bridge by other means . On the other hand, the often extremely prejudiced slant inevitable in this type of documentation must be kept in mind, in order to see our data more correctly, beyond the distortions of opportunism and propaganda. Especially in classical authors, this is directly due to the fact that they were in the opposite camp, so that it was only natural that they should put in a bad light — or sometimes openly disparage — their commercial rivals, not to mention the treatment reserved for their political and military adversaries, who became the butts of every sort of accusation.

Nevertheless, it is also true that in certain cases more positive or even openly eulogistic attitudes are not lacking, for example concerning the power of Carthage at the time of the Punic Wars, or certain aspects of the figure of Hannibal. But even here we have to be on our guard against an approach which in fact, by subtle and devious ways, pursues the same propagandistic

*Illustration of
a bronze bowl
with decoration
in concentric
friezes from
the necropolis
at Macchiabate
near Sibari
8th century B.C.*

ends: that is, implicitly stressing one's own merits or attenuating one's faults by praising the greatness and skill of the enemy.

Even with these limitations and conditions, magnified by the lack of an adequate body of direct information which undoubtedly would have contributed to a more balanced picture, we may now set out on an anthological journey through the opinions which, in various epochs and various circumstances, the ancients expressed about certain aspects of Phoenician and Punic civilization, and its role in the development of history in the Mediterranean.

If we were forced to put total faith in the judgments of the two Greek historians Plutarch and Appian on the character of the Carthaginians, our journey would certainly get off to a shaky start. Plutarch in fact writes (*Praec. ger. rei publ.*, III, 6): "They are a coarse, gloomy people, submissive to those who govern them, but despotic toward those who are governed by them. They are abject in moments of fear but ferocious in anger, inflexible in their decisions and rigid to the point of caring nothing for the joys and pleasures of life." And he is echoed by Appian (*Lib.*, VIII, 62): "The Carthaginians are cruel and arrogant towards everyone when their fortunes are prospering, but when things go against them they are very servile."

In any case, it should be kept in mind that such decidedly negative statements, though made so long after the fall and destruction of Carthage, are among the most explicit expressions of the anti-Phoenician tradition which, with many ups and downs and the evidence of authors both great and small, goes back to the very dawn of Phoenician civilization, and of its relations with the other peoples of the Mediterranean theatre.

"Ups and downs" because the portrait of ancient opinion given by our sources appears contradictory. It oscillates between admiration and contempt, unconditional praise for certain gifts and gratuitous abuse, to the point of the most scurrilous accusations. However, this remains within a climate of opinion conditioned from the start by that vein of suspicion and underestimation which the Greeks cultivated towards cultures differing from their own, a product of those peoples whom in any case they defined as "barbarians."

The Homeric poems provide the first authoritative example of this ambivalent attitude, giving a series of images regarding the earliest contacts between the Phoenician peoples and the Greek world. On account of the enormous and profound legacy bequeathed by the Homeric epics to the subsequent classical literary tradition, these images became almost emblematic in portraying or stigmatizing aspects of the civilization of a people which often crystallized into stereotyped commonplaces. Thus, in the *Iliad* we begin to learn about one of the favourable qualities unanimously ascribed to the Phoenicians, that is, their highly refined skill in craftsmanship (*Il.*, VI, 288-95):

"Hecuba descended into the fragrant store-room
Where lay the many-hued robes, the work of Sidonian
Women, which Alexandros himself, like unto a god,
Had brought from Sidon, sailing the broad sea,
At the time when he brought back Helen of noble lineage.
Hecuba chose one, gave it as a gift to Athena,
The largest and loveliest in design and colours,
It shone like a star..."

And further on (*Il.*, XXIII, 740-45):
"The son of Peleus at once set out prizes for the foot-race,
An embossed silver mixing-bowl, which contained six measures
But in beauty far exceeded all others, on earth,
Since it was wrought by the famous craftsmen of Sidon;
Phoenicians had borne it over the misty seas,
Displayed it in the harbors, given it as a gift to Thoas."

This was a gift appreciated equally unconditionally on the other side of the eastern Mediterranean where, at the time of the alliance between Hiram of Tyre and Solomon, the latter was forced to rely on Phoenician builders and craftsmen for the great construction works he had promised, first and foremost the building of the Temple of Jerusalem itself. The Phoenicians were hired with no regard to expense, so much so that the Old Testament tells us (*I Kings*, 5, 6) that Solomon will pay Hiram's workmen: "...according to all that thou shalt appoint: for thou knowest that there is not among us any that can skill to hew timber like unto the Sidonians." Famous, also, was the

Two examples of motifs decorating ostrich eggs left, a Ibiza specimen 4th-3rd century B.C. right, a Villaricos specimen 6th-5th century B.C.

Wavelike motif and foliate frieze repeated on late stelae from the Carthage tophet

master craftsman whom Solomon summoned specially from Tyre (*I Kings*, 7, 13) because he was: "...a worker in brass: and he was filled with wisdom, and understanding, and cunning to work all works in brass." The Old Testament gives long lists of his prodigious accomplishments in adorning and finishing the structure and furnishings of the Temple (*I Kings*, 7, 40-45).

Returning to the Homeric poems, the *Odyssey* offers us a picture which grows broader and more varied as we come to the historical period which witnessed a widening of the horizon with regard to relations and trading between the Mediterranean peoples. It is therefore not long before an atmosphere of antagonism and competitiveness arises which later becomes the root cause of judgments often vitiated by partiality, preconceived distrust, and hostility.

In the first part of the work the Phoenicians are still seen in an objectively positive light, and Ulysses in flight from Crete thus describes the help they gave him (*Od.*, XIII, 271-86):

"At once I boarded a ship, and the admirable Phoenicians
I begged, and offered them a copious part of the booty.
I begged them to give me a passage, leave me ashore on Pylos
Or in beautiful Elis where the sons of Epeius govern.
But instead they were driven here by the violence of the wind,
However much they fought it; but they did not betray me.
Driven astray down here, therefore, we arrived by night...
"And here sweet sleep received me, because I was exhausted,
But they, taking my riches out of their hollow vessel,
Laid them where I was lying, on the sand; and then,
Setting sail for well-populated Sidon, they departed."

The Phoenicians are therefore thought of as people worthy of admiration, who do everything in their power to keep their bargains and promises, and who are honest with regard to the possessions of a foreigner whom they could very easily have robbed. But already in the following books certain standards

633

of judgment emerge which were destined to have a negative impact on the reputation of this people throughout the remainder of its history.

It is in the words of Ulysses that we first come across the cliché of the crafty, grasping Phoenician merchant (*Od.*, XIV, 287-300):

"Then there came a Phoenician man well practised in deceits,
A thief who among mankind had brought off many an evil deed.
He tricked me with his cunning, and took me with him until
We arrived there in Phoenicia, where he had his goods and houses...
"He embarked me on the Libyan route in a ship which ploughs the waves,
Hatching plots, so that I would help him transport the cargo
But in fact so as to sell me, and make a packet of money."

The picture is filled in with details in the subsequent story told by Eumaeus. He too has happened across people of the same sort (*Od.*, XV, 415-26):

"One day there came some Phoenicians, famous navigators,
Rascals, with a host of knick-knacks in their black ships.
Then, in my father's palace there was a Phoenician woman,
Tall, beautiful, and skilled at splendid needlework...
"Then somebody enquired who she was and where she came from,
And she spoke at once of her father's lofty dwelling:
'I glory in having been born in Sidon abounding in bronze,
And am the daughter of Haribans, immeasurably rich.'"

These Phoenicians then offer to take her back by a stratagem to the house from which she had been kidnapped by pirates from Taphos, and she accepts, offering to pay her passage (*Od.*, XV, 448-53):

"... and I will bring gold, as much as I can lay my hands on;
And another reward as well I can offer you:
A son of my master's, brought up in the palace and young,
Easy to sell, and he trots behind me everywhere;
I will bring him on the ship and he will make you earn
An enormous profit, wherever you may go among foreigners."

What has so far emerged from these passages in the Homeric epics makes it possible to point out a series of behavioral elements and types more or less explicitly preconceived in terms of ethics or values. These constitute the key coordinates around which, in subsequent centuries, the reputation of the Phoenicians was destined to revolve, together with the image of things peculiar to their civilization.

Thus we have mention of their skill as craftsmen, considered supreme in many fields, and of their undisputed fame as great navigators; but also of their notoriety as cunning, dishonest merchants, sometimes even unscrupulous kidnappers and slave traders.

Concerning the skill of the Phoenicians in crafts and technologies the judgment was always positive and laudatory. We have already mentioned the high esteem with which the Old Testament refers to the expertise of a Phoenician craftsman engaged on work connected with Solomon's building projects. Of this man, Josephus (summarizing other data belonging to the biblical tradition) states (*Ant.*, VIII, 76) that: "He was expert in every kind of work, but

Illustration of a wall relief from Sennacherib's (705-681 B.C.) palace depicting the sack of a Phoenician city

particularly in the working of gold, silver and bronze." An expertise which Phoenician craftsmen in general demonstrated also in other spheres, since the same author tells us, expanding somewhat upon the biblical text (*Ant.*, VIII, 69) that: "The entire construction of the temple was carried out with the highest degree of skill, by the use of stones cut so precisely, and joined together so accurately and in so refined a manner, that to the observer they appeared without mark of chisel or other implement. The entire fabric seemed put together on its own rather than by means of implements."

Explicitly favorable judgements, or at least implicit recognition, can be found for a whole range of crafts and industrial activities. For example, the 5th-century B.C. Athenian poet Hermippus, in a passage lauding the outstanding products of Mediterranean countries, mentions Carthage and its "many-colored carpets and cushions". This is an indication of the excellence of a craft raised to such heights as to merit a treatise of its own, now lost. This was the work of Polemon, a learned Greek who at the beginning of the 2nd century B.C. devoted a whole opus to the types of fabric to be found at Carthage.

In any case, the Phoenicians had excelled in this craft since time immemorial, as we have seen from the words of Homer, and remarkable examples of it were also found in other Phoenician colonies. Malta, for example, as we are told by Diodorus (V, 12, 2), "possesses craftsmen skilled in every kind of work, the most important of which are those who spin flax into linen, which is of a wondrous lightness and softness."

It is common knowledge that this skill in craftsmanship reached its apogee in the art of dyeing fabrics with a unique crimson or purple color ("Tyrian purple"), and these fabrics were enormously popular for many centuries all over the Mediterranean, becoming — as we would say today — a status symbol, a sure sign of wealth and refined taste.

From time to time Assyrian monarchs would embark on military expeditions as far as the Mediterranean and the coasts of Phoenicia. Their avowed intent of conquest and power was often accompanied — under the guise of exacting tribute — by their need to acquire raw materials and luxury goods. In their inscriptions frequent mention is made of precious apparel and coloured fabrics. For example, Ashurnasirpal II (883-859 B.C.) wrote thus in his annals: "At that time I conquered the whole of Mount Lebanon and reached the Great Sea of the land of Amurru. I washed my armor in the deep sea and made offerings to the gods. The tribute from the kings of the seacoast, Tyre, Sidon, Byblos, Makhalata, Maisa, Kaisa, Amurru, and Aradus which is an island in the midst of the sea: gold, silver, tin, copper, bronze vessels, garments of colored wools, linen garments... These I received as their tribute and they prostrated themselves at my feet."

Some two centuries later, in another incursion against the Phoenician cities, Ashurbanipal (668-626 B.C.) reveals the continuing interest in this characteristic and much sought-after product: "Gold, woollen fabrics dyed in purple or violet hues... these I imposed on them as annual tribute."

Tyre, in particular, enjoyed the reputation of queen of cities with regard to this craft, as reported by Pliny (*Nat. Hist.*, IX, 60, 127): "The best purple dye in Asia is found in Tyre." Strabo, who visited the city at the time of Augustus, speaks of the great number and importance of the Tyrian purple industries (XVI, 2, 23): "...In fact the purple dye of Tyre has proved itself to be the best from every point of view. The molluscs are gathered near the shore and everything needed for the manufacture is easily obtainable. Although the vast number of factories making the purple dye renders the city unpleasant to live in, on the other hand it has made it extremely prosperous, thanks to the supreme skill of its inhabitants."

In the whole classical world, therefore, the idea of the purple dye and of the fabrics coloured with it was always connected with the image of luxury and became a symbol of civil and religious power; in Roman times it was reserved for the emperors and the highest members of the senate and the priesthood, partly because it cost so much. Pliny relates that Cornelius Nepos recorded the fact that in his time "...double-dyed Tyrian purple fabric was impossible to buy for less than 1000 *denarii* per pound" (*Nat. Hist.*, IX, 63, 137).

It might be useful at this point to cite what in some ways is an extreme example, in order to call attention to the reputation and high consideration in which this typical product of Phoenicia was always held: centuries later,

Illustration of various types of murex

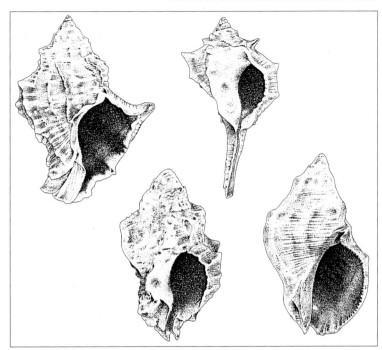

Theodosius II, Roman emperor of the East (401-450), established in his famous Code (*Cod. Theodos.*, X, 20, 18; 21, 3) that numerous state officials "should be sent to the Phoenician purple dye factories for specific periods of time so that, by means of the close vigilance of these officials, any fraud may be prevented... Every person, of whatever sex, rank, calling, profession or family must abstain from the possession of this type of product, which is reserved solely for the Emperor and his Family."

Until the very last stages of the ancient world, therefore, the fame of insuperable excellence of the technique which the Phoenicians had made into an art survived intact. Classical authors themselves had already made it into a myth which had its origins in Tyre, perhaps following ancient Phoenician legends. Tyrian purple was in fact directly connected with Heracles, the Greek equivalent of the Phoenician Melqarth, founder and god of the city, who had been the first to discover and use it in order to give a love-pledge to a beloved nymph called Tyro. During a walk upon the beach this nymph had been so entranced by the wonderful colour released by the juices of a mollusc that she rejected even the advances of Heracles until such time as he should give her a garment dyed with this purple.

The beaches of Phoenicia were famous not only for the "discovery" and development of the art of dyeing fabrics with purple. In the opinion of classical authors, in fact, their sands were particularly suited also to the manufacture of glass. Strabo (XVI, 2, 25) confirms this in precise terms: "Between Acco and Tyre there is a beach of dunes which produces the sand employed for making glass. It is said that the sand is not subjected to fusion

on the spot, but transported to Sidon to undergo that process. Some maintain that the Sidonians also have a supply of this vitreous sand." Pliny adds
(*Nat. Hist.*, XXXVI, 65, 190-91): "The part of Syria on the borders of
Judaea, which is called Phoenicia, has a marsh at the foot of Mount Carmel
which is called Cendevia... The sands around it extend for no more than
five hundred paces, but for many centuries it was the only area in which
glass was produced." He goes on (*Nat. Hist.*, XXXVI, 66, 193): "Sidon was
at one time renowned for these products, especially on account of the fact
that the first glass mirrors were produced there."

Pliny's belief that the Phoenicians deserved total credit for the invention of
glass is certainly excessive, since the technique was known earlier in other
parts of the Near East, particularly in Egypt. All the same, they brought the
technique to such a pitch of excellence and showed such skill in working
transparent glass, that this opinion does have some measure of justification.
But the Phoenicians were not given credit for particular skill only in the
refined techniques of top-level craftsmanship. Such skill was recognized also
on other occasions when they were called upon to display outstanding practical sense and organizational ability. An example is to be found in
Herodotus, when he refers to the use of Phoenician workers for the excavation of a canal across the isthmus joining Mount Athos to the mainland, during the campaign of Xerxes against Greece (VII, 23): "Thus the barbarians
proceeded with the work of excavation, having divided up the area by
nations... All the laborers, however, with the exception of the Phoenicians,
had to do twice the work because of the continual slipping of the sides of the
channel. And it was obvious that this was bound to happen, because they
had kept the same width at the top as at the bottom of the canal. The *Tools for*
Phoenicians, on the other hand, displayed particular ability in this as in other *glass-making*

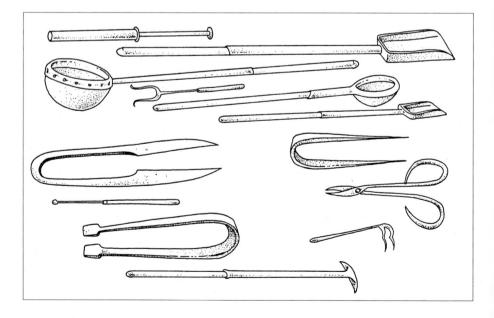

Drawing of a late stele from the Carthage tophet featuring a boat

works. In fact, as soon as they had their part assigned to them, they began to dig the canal starting with a width double what it should have been, gradually decreasing it as the work proceeded, in such a way that when they reached the bottom their channel was equal in width to all the others." However, the most typical image of the Phoenicians, which implied and exalted all the other gifts for which they were famous, was the one which showed them as indissolubly bound to the sea, masters of its routes and secrets, both as expert navigators and explorers and as capable and astute merchants.

"One day there came the Phoenicians, famous navigators," says a line in Homer, with a single lapidary judgment consecrating a fame that was never usurped, and was the opinion universally held from shore to shore of the Mediterranean, in the East as in the West.

Even King Solomon, having enlarged his dominions as far as the Red Sea and realizing the need to equip himself with a fleet adequate to the requirements of more extensive trading, was obliged to have recourse to the technical and nautical skill of the Phoenicians (*I Kings*, 9, 27): "Solomon made a fleet of ships in Ezion-geber, which is beside Eloth, on the shore of the Red Sea, in the land of Edom. And Hiram sent in the fleet his servants, mariners who had knowledge of the sea, with the servants of Solomon."

Also in the Bible we find a passage which — even in the passion of Ezekiel's diatribe against an idolatrous people, prophesying the fall of Tyre and the end of her extraordinary opulence at the hands of the armies of Babylon — raises a solemn lament in which the city itself appears transfigured in the allegorical image of a ship of exceeding beauty, as if the prophet wished to cast the mantle of dream over the memory of a prosperity doomed to perish (*Ezekiel*, 27, 3-9): "O Tyrus, thou hast said, I am of perfect beauty. Thy borders are in the midst of the seas, thy builders have perfected thy beauty. They have made all thy ship boards of fir trees of Senir; they have taken cedars from Lebanon to make masts for thee. Of the oaks of Bashan have they made thine oars; the company of the Ashurites have made thy benches of ivory, brought out of the isles of Chittim. Fine linen with broidered work from Egypt was that which thou spreadest forth to be thy sail; blue and purple from the isles of Elishah was that which covered thee. The inhabitants of Zidon and Arvad were thy mariners: thy wise men, O Tyrus, that were in thee, were thy pilots. The ancients of Gebal and the wise men thereof were in thee thy caulkers: all the ships of the sea with their mariners were in thee to occupy thy merchandise." Thus, although within a framework that foretells its destruction, Ezekiel's lament gives an excellent picture of the image of the fundamental relationship of the Phoenicians with the sea, a relationship considered to be an insuperable model.

This judgment was substantially shared even by the Greeks, who were certainly not apt to lavish praises and appreciation on the qualities and conquests of civilizations which differed from theirs.

"To a supreme degree the Phoenicians were the first to plough the seas," is stated by a Homeric scholium (*Schol. Il.*, XXIII, 744), giving in a certain sense the measure of an opinion which considered the Phoenicians undisputed masters of long-distance navigation and of the exploration and colonization of lands at the very confines of the known world, and even beyond. These words of Herodotus (I, 1) could be considered indicative: "They say that having arrived from the sea which is called Eritrean upon the coasts of this one [the Mediterranean], and having established themselves in the territory where they still live, the Phoenicians undertook long voyages and, transporting merchandise from Egypt and from Assyria, betook themselves to many parts." The same could be said for these words of Strabo (I, 3, 2): "The sea-power of Minos is on the lips of all, as is the maritime skill of the Phoenicians, who ventured far beyond the Pillars of Hercules, and founded cities both there and at a halfway stage, on the coast of Libya, not long after the events at Troy."

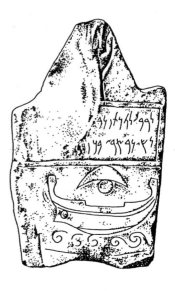

Although they are projected onto a plane of pseudo-history his words are significant and echo the recognized ability of the Phoenicians — as early as the beginning of the 1st millennium B.C. — to reach the furthest regions of the western Mediterranean and the Atlantic coasts of Spain and Africa; this appears to be substantially supported, beyond any questions of strict chronology, by the convergent opinions of the ancients who, from Diodorus to Strabo himself, from Pliny to Velleius Paterculus and yet others, testify to the great antiquity of many colonies in the West.

Drawings of late stelae from the Carthage tophet featuring boat and the bow of a ship

Along the same lines are the later records of those exceptional explorations of unknown regions which, in the 5th and 4th centuries B.C., saw Phoenician ships commissioned by the Pharaoh Necho to achieve the circumnavigation of Africa, or reach the coast of West Africa as far as the Gulf of Guinea under the Carthaginian Hanno, or again under a Carthaginian, Himilco, sail up the Atlantic coasts of Spain and France, perhaps even reaching the British Isles. In this context Tyre once again emerges as the city worthy of symbolizing all this renown: "Tyre... illustrious on other occasions for its progeny, she who gave life to Leptis, Utica and this famous rival, Carthage hungry for conquests, she who founded Cadiz beyond the inhabited world," writes Pliny (*Nat. Hist.*, V, 19, 76). Quintus Curtius is of the same opinion: "Founded by Agenor, she was for a lengthy period mistress of the sea, and not only in her own coastal waters, but wherever her fleets could reach... In any case, her colonies spread over the whole world: Carthage in Africa, Thebes in Boeotia, Cadiz on the

Ocean. I think that, as they sailed the open seas and often landed in places unknown to others, the Tyrians wisely chose the sites which could best welcome their numerous children."

Audacious voyages to discover new lands and the foundation of colonies are interwoven in the Phoenician tradition from very ancient times. These two characteristics have a common denominator which constitutes the third basic aspect of the image of this people: the constant and prevalent commercial incentive.

From the beginning the ancients could appreciate this disposition, but it is interesting to note how, in our sources, objective understanding of the phenomenon is in many cases flanked — sometimes in such a way as to pervert it completely — by a vision conditioned by partisan positions, often denigratory. These should be interpreted with the reservations necessary for any indirect source, especially when this expresses the point of view of an author belonging to a world which saw the encounter with the civilization of the Phoenicians in terms of competition, or even bitter conflict.

"The Phoenicians invented trade": this statement of Pliny's (*Nat. Hist.*, VII, 57, 199) is certainly too categorical to be correct, but it does grasp the essence of a fact which Diodorus expresses more clearly (V, 20, 1): "Since ancient times the Phoenicians have made continual journeys for reasons of trade, have established numerous colonies in Libya and no less numerous ones in the western regions of Europe. Since their undertaking worked out perfectly according to their intentions, they acquired enormous riches, and began to navigate beyond the Pillars of Hercules, in the sea which men call Ocean." And again (V, 35, 1-5): "The country [of the Iberians] has the finest and most numerous silver mines... The natives do not know the use of it, while the Phoenicians, who were experienced in trade and had understood what it was, bought the silver in return for small quantities of other merchandise. So that the Phoenicians, transporting the silver to Greece and Asia and to other peoples, acquired great riches... Thus, carrying on this type of traffic for a long time, they prospered greatly and founded many colonies, some in Sicily and the neighbouring islands, others in Libya, Sardinia and Iberia."

These observations led Diodorus to a reflection which is almost a general comment (V, 38, 3): "The Phoenicians therefore, it would seem, from ancient times were skilled in making discoveries for their own profit."

A conclusion certainly in harmony with the substance of the phenomenon and with the image existing of it also outside the Greek world, as we see clearly in Isaiah's prophecy of the overthrow of Tyre (*Isaiah*, 23, 2-8): "Be still, ye inhabitants of the isle; thou whom the merchants of Zidon, that pass over the sea, have replenished. And by great waters the seed of Sihor, the harvest of the river, is her revenue; and she is the mart of nations. Be thou ashamed, O Zidon: for the sea hath spoken, even the strength of the sea, saying, I travail not, nor bring forth children, neither do I nourish up young men, nor bring up virgins. As at the report concerning Egypt, so shall they be sorely pained at the report of Tyre. Pass ye over to Tarshish; howl, ye inhabitants of the isle. Is this your joyous city, whose antiquity is of ancient days? Her own feet shall carry her afar off to sojourn. Who hath taken this counsel against Tyre, the crowning city, whose merchants are princes, whose traffickers are the honourable of the earth?"

It is plain that such an outstanding, undisputed ability to discover new sources of wealth, to turn them to profit, to be present nearly everywhere, in the most varied areas of trade and supplies, with the possibility — in certain periods the exclusive possibility — of being the contact between economic spheres which were otherwise non-communicating, so as to exploit shrewdly the various advantages... all this undoubtedly made the Phoenicians fearsome rivals to anyone, and particularly to the Greeks.

The result was a direct, intense confrontation, including recourse to what we would today call unfair methods of competition, particularly by propaganda — negative of course — against the Phoenician antagonist, in a series of attempts to damage his image with the suspicion and stigmatization of aspects deliberately shown in a bad light; and from here it is only a step to downright slander.

A repertoire of criticism was not lacking, and they did not have to look far to find it. The Homeric tradition, with all the weight of its prestige, had already indicated the main negative points, together with unconditional appreciation of the skill in craftsmanship and maritime expertise of the Phoenician people. In this way expressions such as "skilled in deceit", "rascal", "weaver of swindles", "cunning fellow", along with the execrated practice of kidnapping women and boys to be sold as slaves, increasingly became clichés which accompanied the image of the Phoenicians, especially the merchants. This was also the fruit of the Greek world's preconceived distrust of "barbarians" and models of behaviour expressed by civilizations and cultures differing from their own, as mentioned above.

As early as Herodotus we can say that a zenith was reached in this respect since he even seems to accept the mythical Phoenician "rape" of the women of Argos, among whom was princess Io, daughter of King Inachus, as the ideological justification for the profound hostility between the Greeks and the peoples of Asia (I, 1): "The wise men of Persia assert that the prime responsibility for this discord goes back to the Phoenicians... Having landed at Argos, therefore, they displayed their wares. Four or five days later, when nearly all their goods had been sold, it is said that a number of women went down to the seashore, among them the king's daughter... When they were close under the bows of the ship, intent on purchasing the wares which pleased them most, the Phoenicians suddenly dashed at them, urging each other on. Most managed to escape, but Io and others were carried off. Having put them aboard, the Phoenicians set sail for Egypt."

The image of the Phoenician merchant as represented in the sources naturally oscillated according to which aspect was being stressed at the time, depending on the evolution of the role he played in the system of commercial and economic relations, which underwent profound changes in the Mediterranean during the course of the 1st millennium B.C., and the greater or lesser degree of conflict existing between him and his Greek or Roman counterparts.

G.C. Picard, an assiduous student of Phoenician and Punic civilization, once pertinently remarked that: "For the Greek historians of the 5th and 4th centuries the Carthaginian is no longer a merchant rolling in money, a thief and a bit of a pirate, but a ferocious warrior, an arch-enemy capable of the worst atrocities."

There are, however, statements which, though still substantially unfavorable, depict the Phoenician merchant in colors less harshly denigratory and more good-naturedly ironical. A fragment attributed with some uncertainty to Aristophanes (Fr. 957 Kassel-Austin) reads: "I am becoming a true Phoenician: with one hand I give and with the other I take away."

Here we have the elements of one of the many variations on the theme of the Phoenician and his all-important relationship to trade and profit, a theme that enjoyed great popularity in both Greek and Latin comedy.

In fact, with the moderation of the harsh political and military conflict between Phoenicians and Greeks which had divided the Mediterranean both east and west into zones which were often mutually out of bounds, the age of Alexander the Great, characterized by conquests and the resulting diffusion of Hellenism, together with the introduction of new trends in style and taste brought from the far away East, helped to create conditions favoring a return of the Phoenician and Carthaginian merchants. The traditional heterogeneity of their cargoes ("...carrying every sort of trifles in their black ships," as Homer was the first to note), put them in the best position to satisfy the eclectic and esoteric tastes of the markets in the new Hellenistic kingdoms, from the Egypt of the Ptolemies to the Syria of the Seleucids, and even Greece itself.

It was in this spirit, then, that *The Carthaginian* becomes the subject and title of two Greek comedies, one by Alexis and the other by Menander. Unfortunately they are both lost, but we can get an idea of them from the

Drawing inspired by the bronze doors of Shalmaneser III's (858-824 B.C.) palace at Balawat showing the city of Tyre

Poenulus by Plautus, who undoubtedly used them as a model and mined them for material.

It is probably in the context of the altered climate described above that we should view the portrait of the merchant Hanno, presented with an irony free from any real partisan hatred, in spite of the fact that the comedy was staged in the midst of the hostilities between Rome and Carthage. Amusement and caricature prevail over slander and denigration (*Poen.*, vv. 975-76): "But what bird can this be, arriving here in his tunic? Perhaps they snaffled his coat at the public baths."

Even when use is made of the hackneyed clichés of the anti-Phoenician repertoire, it is done with the sense of calm self-confidence of one who, having sufficiently understood the proverbial Punic craftiness, is now able to make a joke of it without fear of somehow falling into a trap (*Poen.*, vv. 112-13): "Besides, this fellow knows every language, but cunningly pretends not to: he is a true Carthaginian, and what more need one say?" And further on (*Poen.*, v. 1125): "Our Carthaginian is a proper rogue: he winds everyone round his little finger." Further proof of an attitude which is far from malevolently hostile comes from Plautus himself, in the admission that in fact the Greeks and Romans also practiced the slave trade in women and children.

An essentially analogous tendency is found in Polybius, who is keen to demonstrate that he has not become involved in partisan interpretations of events between Carthage and Rome, and makes an explicit declaration of impartiality in describing these events and of objectivity with regard to the images of the contenders. He exposes the limitations of their respective sources, Philinus of Acragas and Fabius Pictor (I, 14, 1-5): "...who did not report the truth, as they ought to have done... Philinus, on account of the favor and unconditional sympathy he felt for the Carthaginians, holds that they did everything for the best, wisely and with valor, and the Romans not; Fabius, on his part, behaved in precisely the opposite manner. In other aspects of life such partiality might be permissible, because a righteous man ought to be favorable toward his friends and love his country... But when he takes on the role of historian, he must forget all that, and must often approve and greatly eulogize the enemy, when the facts require it, and often, on the other hand, blame and censure those he loves most, when the errors of their actions render it necessary. "

In accordance with this position, the image of the Carthaginians which emerges from the narrative of the Greek historian does not seem to be distorted by factious hostility or the hatred born of prejudice. Thus we find ample testimony to the courage and skill of the Carthaginian seamen (I, 27, 7-11): "The Romans, seeing the Carthaginians drawn up in a thin line, attacked the center... At once the Carthaginians stationed in the center fell back, according to orders received, in order to scatter the enemy formation... When it seemed to the Carthaginians that the first and second naval squadrons [of the Romans] were sufficiently far from the others, and they saw the signal hoisted in Hamilcar's ship, all at once turned back and attacked their pursuers. The battle raged: the Carthaginians were far superior in the speed with which they encircled, in the swiftness of their advance and the haste of their retreat." Or, on another occasion (I, 51, 3-6): "The Carthaginians gradually showed their superiority because of the many advantages they had throughout the conflict. Not only were their ships much faster than those of the Romans, thanks both to the excellence of their construction and to the training of their crews, but also in their favour was the space they had for maneuver, having drawn up their battle-line towards the open sea. If, therefore, one of their vessels was hard pressed by the enemy, it escaped by withdrawing into the open sea, thanks to its speed, and then, putting about, it rammed the opposing vessels in the bows or amidships; for in the pursuit they [the Romans] pressed too far ahead, and in their attempts to turn back they were hampered by the weight of their vessels and the lack of skill among the crew. Thus they [the Carthaginians] struck one after another, and many were sunk."

A skill and experience which Polybius ascribes to the Phoenicians' profound link with the sea, passed on to the Carthaginians, who (I, 20, 12): "Since the times of their ancestors held undisputed dominion over the sea", and who (VI, 52, 1): "...build and equip better ships, because this experience is their inheritance from ancient times, and they have practiced the art of navigation more than any other people." This was a tradition so unanimously recognized that even long after the end of Carthage and her power, it remained in certain figures of speech (Festus, *Tyria maria*): "Tyrian waters: a saying which has become proverbial, for the Punic people, originating in Tyre, were so powerful on the sea that navigation was dangerous for all other mortals."

But the point of view of Polybius, and his determination to adopt a position as objective as possible toward the Carthaginians, is best exemplified by the picture he has given us of the man who was in a sense their symbol, Hannibal (IX, 22, 8-10; 24-26 *passim*): "Some, it is true, maintain that Hannibal was very cruel, others assert that he was miserly, and it is not easy to establish the truth... In fact not few, but very many, are the things which men are forced to say and do against their natural inclinations, partly because of the influence of their friends, partly due to the diversity of circumstances which present themselves... He, indeed, found himself in very varied and exceptional circumstances, and had close counsellors very different from himself in character, so that it would be hard to judge his character from his conduct in Italy... It is said that the acts of cruelty attributed to Hannibal in Italy were in fact the work of Hannibal Monomachus... It seems, however, that Hannibal was extremely miserly, and that he had in Mago a counsellor who was stingier still... and I have had particular evidence on the matter from Massinissa, who gave me proof of the miserliness of all Carthaginians in general, and particularly of Hannibal and of Mago, known as the Samnite... Besides, Hannibal's nature was exposed to, and often adapted itself to, the insistence of his friends, but even more frequently yielded to objective situations... Therefore he found himself forced to openly abandon certain cities... With some of these, indeed, he went so far as to violate treaties... As a result of this he was sometimes accused of ruthlessness, at other times of cruelty, because violences and massacres were in fact committed, and pillage also, by the soldiers who abandoned the towns... It is therefore very difficult to assess the true character of Hannibal, both because of the influence which his counsellors had over him, and because of what was imposed upon him by objective circumstances. In any case, his reputation for avarice was prevalent among the Carthaginians, that for cruelty among the Romans."

The tragic and exhausting conflict with Rome could not fail to negatively influence general opinion regarding the Carthaginians (who in the end succumbed) and the image of them created by their contemporaries. This is especially true of those who, ignoring the example of Polybius, had no intention of applying themselves to a careful sifting of the sources and traditions in an attempt to gain an objective assessment, or of those who had ideological motives for taking sides.

Thus, if on the one hand authors such as Plautus, Cornelius Nepos or Virgil himself do not reveal tones that ally them to the chorus of the most ardent proponents of anti-Punic propaganda, we find a very different language in other writers, from Cicero to Livy and the Greek historians of the Imperial age, such as Plutarch and Appian.

Cornelius Nepos, for example, brings the biographical side of Roman historiography fairly close to the models and the moralistic intentions of the Hellenistic tradition, leaving us a "positive" image of Hannibal, according to the canons of the pro-Hannibal scholastic tendency (*De excell. duc.*, XXIII, 1): "...it cannot be denied that Hannibal was as superior in ability to all other commanders as the Roman people was in valour to all other nations. Indeed, each time he came into conflict with them in Italy, he emerged the victor. And if the envy of his fellow-citizens at home had not weakened his forces, it seems certain that he would have been able to defeat the Romans. But the envy of many proved able to vanquish the courage of a single man."

In Cicero, on the other hand, we see the total re-emergence of practically the whole range of traditional accusations and slanders, though presented not in harshly polemical tones but with the skilled and subtle rhetoric worthy of the style of this great writer. Thus, for example, the fraudulent character of the Carthaginians is reasserted while pretending to justify it by an extrinsic cause (*De lege agr.*, II, 35, 95): "The Carthaginians are led to fraud and lying, not by their nature, but because of the situation of their country; since through their ports they have relations with many merchants and foreigners of diverse origins, and the thirst for profit impels them towards deceit." Or else we see him projecting a negative light on them by allowing it to filter between the lines of some pseudo-historical notions, such as (*Rep.*, II, 4, 9): "... among the Barbarian peoples, none of them previously had any naval traditions except the Etruscans and the Phoenicians, the first as merchants, the second as pirates"; or again (*Rep.*, III, fr. 3): "It

Drawing of coin minted in Spain with bearded head on obv. and elephant with karnak *on rev. 237-218 B.C. 14.61 g*

was the Phoenicians with their trifles and their merchandise who into Greece first introduced greed, luxury and the unbridled desire for everything," thus giving new vigour to another of the cardinal points of the anti-Punic polemic, that is, the luxury of the Carthaginians as corrupt and corrupting, as opposed to the Roman ideal of austere parsimony, exalted by Livy as the vital sap of the greatness of Rome (*Proem.*, 11): "...where such great and durable honor was enjoyed by poverty and parsimony, that the less one had the less one desired." Until, in the end, the polemic comes out into the open when Cicero declares (*Pro Scauro*, XIX, 42): "All the records of the past and all historical traditions have borne witness that the Phoenician people is the most deceitful. As regards their heirs, the Carthaginians, the many Punic rebellions, the treaties violated and broken, demonstrate that this ethnic trait has in no way been attenuated."

Back into the forefront, then, comes the picture of the Phoenician as a cheat and a traitor, which we find re-echoed in so much literature, both verse and prose, reduced to the level of an overworked commonplace of which we have numerous, significant attestations.

Livy, for example, contrasting it proudly with the honour of the Romans, several times stigmatizes the *punica fides* which, at least on one occasion, is put practically on the same level as Greek wiliness (XLII, 47, 7): "These are the characteristics proper to the Romans, who have nothing of the duplicity of the Carthaginians, nor of the wiliness of the Greeks, among whom it is considered more worthy of praise to deceive the enemy than to overcome him by force."

With the same decision we find reproof for the systematic, proverbial breaking of one's word, as for example in connection with an episode in the battle of Lake Trasimene (XXII, 6, 11-12): "The following day, since apart from everything else they were suffering from extreme hunger, they surrendered, because Maharbal, who had pursued them through the night with all his cavalry forces, gave them his word that, if they would lay down their arms, they would be allowed to go, clad only in their shirts. This promise was respected by Hannibal with Punic conscientiousness, so they were all thrown in chains." Or again, the equally proverbial cruelty and perfidy of the Carthaginians which, among so many other negative traits, we find almost symbolically summed up in Livy's description of Hannibal, where the positive aspects, attributed to him solely on the purely extrinsic plane of his physical endowments, are amply counterbalanced and annulled by the far more serious moral defects ascribed to him (XXI, 4, 5-9): "He had the greatest degree of audacity in confronting dangers, and in these dangers the greatest circumspection. No labor could weary his body or cast him down in spirit. He could bear heat and cold equally well; his eating and drinking

647

were regulated by natural desire and not by pleasure; his times of waking and sleeping were not distinguished by day and night; what was left over when everything was done was devoted to repose; this was not favored by a soft bed or by silence; very often he was seen lying on the ground wrapped in a soldier's cloak between the guard-posts. He was not distinguished, among those of his own age, for the excellence of his attire; on the other hand his weapons and his horses were of the best. He was the greatest, whether on foot or on horseback. In battle he was in the foremost rank; after the battle he was the last to withdraw. These virtues of his were equally matched by his defects: inhuman cruelty, more-than-Punic perfidiousness; nothing for him was either true or sacred, he had no fear of the gods, no valid oath, no scruples."

The authority of Livy could, with this, hardly escape giving new impetus to the anti-Punic position, contributing to the falsification of the judgment on an entire people and its civilization, which was increasingly crystallizing into an image fed on prejudices and commonplaces.

So here is Valerius Maximus, intent on being an encyclopaedist, brilliant, superficial and by no means innocent of nationalistic partisanship, who without any critical sense of his own re-echoes (VII, 4, 4) the concept of "that Punic craftiness notorious throughout the terrestrial globe."

And Silius Italicus, following the tradition of Livy and Virgil, writes (*Pun.*, III, 231-34):

"First, with the banners, marches the youth of Carthage, of Tyre,
with agile limbs, though bereft of the beauty of tall
stature, but skilled in deceiving and ever ready to prepare
stratagems in the dark."

Not to speak of Appian, in whom we read (*Lib.*, VIII, 62-64): "The Carthaginians... break treaties as soon as they have made them. They have neither respect for their agreements nor regard for their oaths... The acts perpetrated by Hannibal himself in war, with stratagems and broken oaths... even at the cost of his own allies, destroying their cities and massacring their soldiers who were in his service, would take too long to list... What treaty, what oath, have they not trodden under foot?"

A final passage from Livy, referring to the speech of the consul on the occasion of a Capuan delegation after the battle of Cannae, shows us another aspect which, in the opinion of classical authors, constituted a characteristic feature of the Carthaginians: ferocity and inhuman cruelty (XXIII, 5, 12-13): "This rabble of soldiery, already cruel and ferocious by nature and custom, has been rendered more cruel still by their leader himself, by building bridges and dykes with stacks of human bodies and, disgusting to relate, habituating them to feeding off human flesh. What man born in Italy would not hate to see, and to have as masters, those men nourished by such iniquitous meals, while for us it is sacrilege even to touch them; and to beg for our rights from Africa and from Carthage?"

How different and how distant this appears from the attitude of Polybius, who on this subject made great efforts not to fall into the temptation of demonizing the adversaries of Rome (IX, 24, 4-7): "When Hannibal decided to undertake the expedition from Spain into Italy, he realized at once that the greatest difficulty confronting the enterprise resided in the provision of victuals... In fact it seemed impossible to traverse that route, because of its length and the many savage, barbarous peoples who lived in the regions which would have to be crossed... Hannibal known as Monomachus expressed his opinion, maintaining that he could see only one way in which they could reach Italy... They had to accustom the army to feeding on human flesh. Hannibal could make no objection to the boldness and efficacy of this opinion, but he could induce neither himself nor his friends to entertain such a plan."

Nevertheless, the motif of the barbarous cruelty of the Phoenicians and Carthaginians is not solely linked to and dependent on the savage episodes which took place in the course of the Punic Wars. It came from much further back, and had been amplified by the classical tradition which developed around the subject of the clash between Greeks and Phoenicians, especially during the violent conflicts which took place in Sicily. It had thus long taken on the aspect of an established literary theme, nourished on the one hand by the horror of killings and ritual massacres (such as the one ordered by Hannibal, son of Gisco, who in 409 at Himera had the throats of three thousand prisoners slit on the very spot where his grandfather Hamilcar had met his death after the great Carthaginian defeat of 480), or the slaughter of five hundred people at Carthage when Agathocles was besieging the city in 310; and also nourished, on the other hand, by execration for the practice of human sacrifice, especially that of children.

In such a context there developed the picture passed down to us by Greek and Roman authors, particularly concerning the ferocity and cruelty on a human and religious level of a people with barbarous and "primitive" cultic practices considered aberrant, and therefore already repudiated by the contemporary culture of the classical world.

In a passage of Cleitarchus, a Greek historian of the end of the 4th century B.C., quoted in a scholium to Plato (Rep., 337 A), we read that: "The Phoenicians, and above all the Carthaginians, who worship Cronus, when they want something important to happen, promise that if they get their wish they will sacrifice a boy to the god. Indeed, they have a bronze statue of the god with the hands palms upwards and stretched over a brazier, into which the child falls. When the flames envelop the body the limbs contract and the mouth contorts into a grimace, until the body falls into the brazier. This kind of grimacing smile is called sardonic, because they die laughing." This is the most ancient account of the practice of these sacrifices, and can be seen in connection with another item of information concerning the detail of the so-called "sardonic laugh", in a certain sense amplifying the "barbarous" dimension of the custom, as opposed to the customs of the Greeks (Schol. Hom. Od., XX, 302): "Those who dwell in Sardinia, of Carthaginian origin, have a barbarous custom, very different from that of the Greeks. On certain established days they sacrifice to Cronus not only the most handsome of their prisoners, but also old people who have passed seventy years of age. To those offered in sacrifice, weeping seems shameful and cowardly, while laughing seems brave and beautiful. For this reason a laugh simulated in painful circumstances is called sardonic."

But the most famous and vivid accounts of this dramatic rite come from two great Greek historians, Diodorus Siculus and Plutarch. The occasion of the siege of Carthage by Agathocles of Syracuse in 310 is thus described by Diodorus (XX, 14, 4-6): "They [the Carthaginians] then became convinced that Cronus was wrathful against them, because, whereas in the most ancient times it had been their habit to sacrifice to this divinity the very noblest of their sons, more recently they had adopted the habit of sacrificing children who had been bought and brought up in secret. Furthermore, when they made an enquiry, they discovered that some of those who should have been sacrificed might have escaped... In their anxiety to make amends for their omission, they chose two hundred of the noblest young boys and sacrificed them publicly while no less than three hundred others, feeling themselves suspected, chose to be sacrificed of their own free will. These people in fact had a bronze statue of Cronus, stretching out its hands palms uppermost and sloping downwards in such a way that every boy placed on them rolled down and fell into a pit full of fire."

Plutarch completes the picture with other details (*De Superstitione*, 13): "The Carthaginians... used to sacrifice their sons to Cronus, and those who had no sons bought them from the poor as if they were lambs or birds. The mother stood and watched without tears or groans; if she had wept or uttered a lament she would have been dishonoured, without preventing the sacrifice. The place was filled with the sounds of those who, in front of the statue, beat drums and tympani, so that shrieks should not be heard."

Paradoxically, though, these new details added by Plutarch to the accounts of Cleitarchus and Diodorus, particularly that of the mother who watches the rite impassively, seem to indicate — as recent research has suggested — an attempt to rationalize, in a context in which weeping was forbidden, the otherwise incomprehensible motive for a laugh connected with an atrocious death. The suspicion that the classical authors who speak of them in reality had no direct knowledge of these rites appears all the more founded: in fact all the greatest historians, from Herodotus to Thucydides, from Polybius to Livy, do not even mention them. It is therefore likely that in the few descriptions which have come down to us, echoes of legends and gossip, combined with negative propaganda aims, induced the writers to give such a dark picture of the cultural phenomena of a world that was felt to be completely foreign. The image of Phoenician and Punic civilization given by ancient writers was, as we have seen, not always negative or vitiated by distortions due to misunderstandings or prejudices. Before closing this rapid anthological survey at least one other important aspect remains to be mentioned. This concerns judgments on the constitution of Carthage.

The interest which classical authors, especially Greek, invested in the com-

Drawing of a terra-cotta "grinning" mask found in the Carthage necropolis

parative study of various forms of institutions is truly remarkable. It may be seen in the perspective of the need to find an ideal model of government which would enable them to achieve a social and political stability strong enough to overcome the precarious and uncertain conditions which, especially during the 4th century B.C., characterized Greek political life. This gives particular significance to the generally positive judgment that emerges from the classical sources, which once again provide our main evidence of basic aspects of Phoenician and Punic civilization.

In the testimony passed on to us by Strabo (I, 4, 9), Eratosthenes was among the first to leave us a favorable opinion of Carthaginian institutions: "In his later works Eratosthenes disapproves of the principle of a bipartite division of the human race into Greeks and barbarians, and of the counsel given to Alexander, to treat the Greeks as friends and the barbarians as enemies. It is better, he maintains, to take virtue and dishonesty as the criteria of division. Indeed, many of the Greeks are bad people, while many of the barbarians have a refined civilization, such as the Indians or the Aryan peoples, or again, the Romans and the Carthaginians, whose institutions are truly admirable."

The passages devoted to this subject by Aristotle and Polybius are even more telling. In an erudite analysis of the various political systems of his day, the former states that (*Polit.*, II, 8, 1): "The Carthaginians appear to have a good constitution, with many features superior to those of others,

651

and particularly similar to that of the Spartans. Indeed, in truth, these three constitutions — the Cretan, the Spartan and the Carthaginian — are analogous to one another and very different from all others. In Carthage many of the institutions are good, and the proof that its constitution is well founded is the fact that the people remain spontaneously faithful to their own system of government and — something worthy of note — there has never been either a civil uprising, or a tyranny."

Finally, Polybius once more takes up the concept (VI, 43, 1) according to which "nearly all writers of history have told of the fame acquired by the states of Sparta, Crete, Mantinea and Carthage, on account of their virtue," and tries to grasp the underlying meaning of a historical development faced with the decisive test of the confrontation with Rome (VI, 51, 1-5): "It seems to me that originally, in its general lines, the constitution of the Carthaginians was well conceived... On the whole, then, the structure of the state was very similar to that of Rome or Sparta. But at the time when the Hannibalic war began, the Carthaginian constitution was in a situation different from and inferior to that of Rome... In fact, simply because Carthage reached its period of greatest power and prosperity earlier than Rome, at the time of the struggle against the latter it was already in a phase of decadence, whereas Rome was in its greatest splendor, at least as far as its form of government was concerned."

Unfortunately, in spite of the flattering general opinion which emerges from the words of Eratosthenes, Aristotle and Polybius, and the basic importance of their contribution, there still remains the difficulty of understanding the nature and evolution of ideological structures and institutions about which the voice of the protagonists themselves is silent. From some points of view, indeed, the comparative studies made by the ancients on the political systems of the Mediterranean world, which have contributed to what knowledge we do have, may in themselves represent a further screen between us and understanding; for, as Sabatino Moscati has acutely observed, taken as a whole we also note "a certain levelling out which they perform, an unconscious accentuation of the analogies which today conditions our judgment."

Now that this brief journey through the opinions of classical authors is coming to a close, what can be said about the basic outlines of the image of Phoenician and Punic civilization that emerges from them?

Without doubt, we are faced with a highly contradictory situation due both to the lack of balance in the chronological distribution and in the very nature of the sources, and to the perspective which characterizes them, and which frequently oscillates between two opposite tendencies. On the one hand, in fact, there is the tendency to praise the gifts and conquests of the Phoenicians to the point of mythicizing them, in many cases raising them to the level of a proverbial fact or a literary motif; on the other is the tendency to run them down and denigrate them, in some cases stigmatizing aspects and modes of behavior of a different culture and making them the object of a bitter, self-interested propaganda campaign.

Illustration of decorations on a ivory bowl from Nimrud now conserved at the British Museum of London

As we have seen, this mainly occurs with those statements — the most numerous and significant — which apply to the moments of direct confrontation with the civilizations of Greece and Rome, so that the resulting overall picture could hardly be anything but partial and unilateral. None the less, it has left us a lively summary in the words of the Roman scholar Pomponius Mela (I, 12): "The Phoenicians were an intelligent people who prospered both in peace and in war. They were outstanding in literature and other arts, in mercantile and military navigation, and in the government of an empire."

Dido and Her Myth
Sergio Ribichini

The adventures of the Carthaginian queen are familiar to us particularly from Virgil's account in the *Aeneid*, where the daughter of Belus, also known as Elissa, kills herself for love and revenge, leaving a curse on the future of Rome. But the tradition concerning the life of the first queen of Carthage certainly preceded the Augustan age and was one of the stories connected with the migration of the Phoenicians toward the Mediterranean West.

In its earliest form, as recounted by Justin and other Greek and Latin writers, the myth described the arrival in Africa of Phoenicians coming from Tyre, led by Elissa, sister of King Pygmalion. The princess, heir to the throne together with her brother before the people elected the latter as sole sovereign, had married her maternal uncle, Acherbas, who was priest of Heracles-Melqarth and extremely rich. When Pygmalion had his uncle murdered in order to get possession of his fortune, Elissa managed to flee with a group of faithful followers and her husband's riches, which were saved by a stratagem. The exiles stopped in Cyprus, where they gained the support of the priest of Jupiter in the colonization effort they were about to undertake in the West, and also abducted eighty women as brides for Elissa's young followers.

Having arrived in Africa with her people, in order to obtain sufficient land for them to live on at least for a while, the queen again used cunning. She concluded a bargain with the inhabitants for the purchase of as much land as could be covered by an ox-hide; she then cut the hide into thin strips which could be laid around the whole hill of the promontory of Carthage. The citadel was subsequently called "Byrsa," a Punic word which in Greek means "ox-hide."

The reception given to the fugitives by the local inhabitants was favourable and soon a flourishing trade arose between them. Thereupon it was decided to found Carthage, and the land was obtained in exchange for a tax to be paid annually to the local inhabitants. During the building of the city, first an ox's head came to light, considered an unfavorable omen, and then the head of a horse was found, interpreted as a symbol of courage and power.

After these events, when the city built by Elissa had already become rich and powerful, the local king Iarbas summoned ten of the most prominent Carthaginian citizens and asked to marry their queen, threatening them with war. Impelled by the situation, the dignitaries tricked the queen into giving her word that she would marry Iarbas. But they never had more than her promise to wed, because Elissa asked for three months to give her answer and during that time she erected a funeral pyre for sacrifices in honour of the deceased Acherbas. After immolating a great many animals, the queen climbed on the pyre and stabbed herself to death with a sword, declaring that she would thus be rejoining her husband. Her subjects, according to Justin, elevated her to the rank of a deity, preserving her cult until the destruction of Carthage.

The problems posed by this narrative, known from the ancient writers with only a few variants, are of several sorts: from the origin of the tradition to the chronology of the events narrated, from the structure of the story to the validity of its various parts. All these are overshadowed by the question of how the original material has been reworked to fit classical mythology.

A number of elements appear to be definitely of Phoenician origin — for example, the names, and particularly that of the heroine. It seems certain that "Dido" was originally a sobriquet, which was added to and subsequently replaced the earlier name Elissa as a clarification, with various etymological explanations already in ancient literature. Timaeus of Tauromenius says that Dido meant "wanderer." Servius suggests the etymology virago, "virile woman," a title used for the queen after her death on the pyre. Eustathius claims instead that the name meant "murderer of her husband" or "responsible for his death," according to an epithet attributed to her in Libya. Finally, the name Dido may derive from an original Punic word analogous to the Hebrew *dd*, "breast." As for Elissa, which is found in Phoenico-Punic nomenclature as *Elishat*, Timaeus states that the Greek word corresponding to the Phoenician name was *Theiosso*, which seems to mean "the consecrated one."

Besides the names, a number of specific leitmotifs in the tale seem to reflect original Phoenician traditions, such as the suicide of the heroine by fire, which can be connected to a particular Carthaginian myth ideology. The various stages of the journey to North Africa with the halt in Cyprus probably reflect real, specific Phoenician colonization movements. That the writers who narrated these events had a good knowledge of the Phoenician environment is also evident from their mention of the cult of Heracles-Melqarth at Tyre.

Finally, associated with Elissa's adventures we also often find a precise dating for the foundation of Carthage, at the end of the 9th century B.C. However, we must be very aware of the mythical character of the story, which means it can have no certain and direct application to the earliest history of the Phoenicians in the West. Rather, it tells us about the time and the worlds in which it was narrated and had effect. By separating the myth of Elissa-Dido from historical questions about the foundation of Carthage, it is easy to identify a number of possible "readings" of these events, which mix and reflect, besides the original viewpoint (perhaps), the more obvious one of Greek and Roman culture toward Phoenician "otherness."

There seem to be two leitmotifs in the tale. First, the endogamic marriage of the heroine with her maternal uncle, which is seen as negative although it is of capital importance throughout the story. Already at the very beginning, the union between Acherbas (brother-in-law of the deceased king) and Elissa (heir to her father's throne) is presented as a threat to the power of the reigning sovereign, to the extent that Pygmalion murders his uncle/brother-in-law. Then during the voyage, the kidnapping of Phoenician women in Cyprus in fact marks the refusal of the future Carthaginians to intermarry with African women. Finally, Elissa's suicide on the pyre confirms the rejection of exogamous marriage by the queen's reunion with her deceased Phoenician husband. Comparative studies have shown that precisely these elements (marriage between kin and ritual suicide), which Greek morality rejected, were often applied in classical mythology to personages thought to be of Phoenician origin (the parents of Adonis, Side, Heracles-Melqarth), reflecting the Greek conviction that these were "normal" practices among the Phoenicians.

Another recurrent and equally criticized motif is deception, by which Elissa flees from Tyre with the riches of Acherbas, obtains land in Africa, accepts the will of her subjects but then avoids the marriage with Iarbas. Deceptions and tricks are repeated and underlined with puns implying a negative judgment on the conduct of the Phoenicians and Carthaginians, considered swindlers and liars, kidnappers of women, violators of their word. From Homer to Plautus and the Fathers of the Church, this was a cliché that repeatedly invited the Greeks and Romans to mistrust these rival merchants and colonizers.

With these particular connotations the myth of Elissa reads very clearly, particularly if we consider it in parallel with the story of the foundation of Rome. We need only recall the adventures of Aeneas, exiled and widowed like the Tyrian princess, but prepared to marry the daughter of the Latin king although forced by this to go to war. Then there is the fact that the foundation of Carthage is entrusted to a woman who is a "man-hater," capable of assigning Aeneas to a weak, effeminate role, and who steals or rents the land for her people, while the founders of Rome are the descendants of the hero, emphatically virile and full owners of the land they plough. We may also compare the measurement of the space of Carthage using strips of oxhide with Romulus's refusal to mark the boundaries of the territory of Rome in order not to preclude the expansionist aims of its people. And we should compare particularly the omens drawn from the discovery of the skulls of an ox and a horse at the moment when Carthage was founded, and those derived from the discovery in Rome of a human head in the foundations of the temple to Jupiter on the Campidoglio: while the Carthaginian omens in both cases suggest subjection as the fate of the city, the Capitoline discovery sanctions without a shadow of doubt the supremacy of Rome over the Punic world.

Altogether, comparison with the classical traditions relating to the foundation of colonies and cities leads to the conclusion that many elements of the story of Elissa-Dido, although perhaps part of the Punic tradition, have been reworked in the version of the myth that has reached us. This is due to Carthage's specific position as a subordinate antagonist, first of Greek trade and colonial expansion and then, more decidedly, of the imperial destiny of Rome.

Did the Phoenicians Land in America?
Maria Giulia Amadasi Guzzo

Map of South America showing the city of João Pessoa

All cultures that present a degree of development and complexity higher than that of neighboring ones, pose the question of their origin. The simplest answer is that of an arrival from outside. It would be impossible to exclude the pre-Columbian cultures of Central America from this kind of reconstruction, and several scholars have sought to establish a link between them and the Near East. Evidence for such links is mainly derived from certain inscriptions presumed to be Phoenician, but whose authenticity remains doubtful.

Within this framework the most sensational supposed discovery, which gave rise to animated discussion, became public in 1874, when the director of the National Museum of Rio de Janeiro, Ladislau Neto, published the copy of a Phoenician inscription said to have been unearthed near Parahaiba, the modern João Pessoa, in northern Brazil, not far from the Atlantic coast. This copy had been sent to the Brazilian Historical and Geographical Institute in 1872 with an accompanying letter the signature of which was never identified. After its publication by Neto, the inscription was declared a forgery by eminent Semitists, and by the end of the 19th century had been forgotten.

In 1968, the inscription was examined again by an authoritative Semitist, Cyrus H. Gordon, known primarily for his research on the language and script of Ugarit. Gordon published the newly edited document and made strong claims for its authenticity. The "rehabilitation" of the inscription was validated by a few terms and constructions, which were documented on the basis of discoveries made after 1874, especially in Ugarit.

The content of the inscription is as sensational as its discovery in Brazil; owing to the regularity of the signs, it is fairly easy to read and had already been interpreted in the 19th century. It should be recalled, however, that discordant readings, due partly to differences between the first and second copy, have been found in the translation proposed by the various scholars who have grappled with the text. The following translation is proposed by C. H. Gordon: "We are Sons of Canaan from Sidon, the city of the king. Commerce has cast us on this distant shore, a land of mountains. We set [sacrificed] a youth for the exalted gods and goddesses in the nineteenth year of Hiram, our mighty king. We embarked from Ezion-geber into the Red Sea and voyaged with ten ships. We were at sea together for two years around the land belonging to Ham [Africa] but were separated by a storm [lit., 'from the hand of Baal'] and we were no longer with our companions.

So we have come here, twelve men and three women, on a ... shore which I, The Admiral, control. But auspiciously may the exalted gods and goddesses favor us!"

Map of the main sea streams showing the presumed route of the Phoenician ship that voyaged to Parahaiba

So by a truly felicitous chance the text which has survived would be one which recounts the arrival of the small group of Phoenicians who seemingly started (a mere fifteen of them!) the growth of Meso-American cultures. This is by no means the only reason for doubting the authenticity of the inscription, whose original was never recovered. The arrival of a craft, aided by favorable currents, on the northern Brazilian coast after a voyage from the Atlantic coast of equatorial Africa (about 3,500 km) cannot be ruled out by geographers, in a purely theoretical way. Long and dangerous crossings in traditional craft have been attempted by modern man to prove similar hypotheses. But the success of such voyages is not sufficient to transform these hypotheses into certainties. However, in the case in point too many elements pertaining to the inscription belie its authenticity, regardless of any theoretical assumption.

On the whole, and in spite of Gordon's assertions, every element of the Parahaiba inscription may be interpreted on the basis of the knowledge of the Phoenician world available in the 19th century and partly in antithesis to what we know today. First of all, the overall structure of the inscription, whose narrative scheme is in the first person plural, has never been substantiated by any Phoenician document at our disposal. It tallies, however, with accounts of voyages known to be of Phoenician source, and especially with the famous account of the African circumnavigation accomplished by the Carthaginian Hanno around 425 B.C., which we know from its Greek version, supposedly a translation from the original Phoenician. This account, whose publication dates back to 1533, was edited in 1853 in a way that remains valid to this day. It could, then, have been known and used by the supposed forger.

The occasion of the voyage round Africa during which the Phoenician craft became separated from the rest of the expedition is equally well-known. It concerns a voyage of circumnavigation promoted — according to Herodotus — by Pharaoh Necho in the 6th century B.C. and accomplished within three years by a Phoenician fleet. In the inscription Ezion-geber is given as the port of departure; from there, ships sailed on the famous voyages towards Ophir at the time of King Solomon. The name of the king is Hiram, contemporary to Solomon and David in the Bible, but also mentioned in classical sources as king of Tyre in the 5th century B.C. So many coincidences within a single document, confirming what was already known, but in different periods, from the Bible and the classical authors! But in what kind of writing and language? As has been pointed out by contemporary Semitists, the flow of the signs is distinguished by a regularity which is unusual in Phoenician inscriptions. The perpendicular character of the script, in particular, differs from the slanted version we have come to recognize as Phoenician; besides, the shape of single letters is often chronologically incongruous and sometime opposed to the Phoenician 6th-centu-

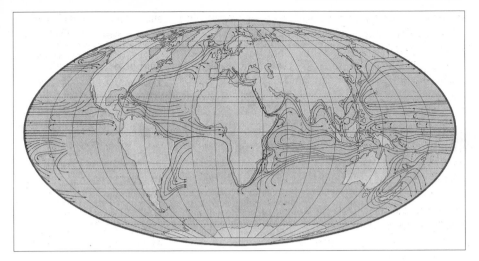

Copy of the Parahaiba Phoenician inscription published by C.H. Gordon

ry script, although the paper in question has been assigned to that period. On the other hand the signs correspond well to those in alphabetical tables of the l9th century, when the chronology of Phoenician documents and the development of the script were less known than today. The text is written in a language as perplexing as the script. Each word shows a correspondence with Hebrew and on the whole (in spite of the disagreement about interpretation, which would surely have amused the text's modern author!) the paper is clear and comprehensible, unlike any other Phoenician inscription of that length. However the spelling and use of words and syntax do not always correspond to what we know about the Phoenician language.

On the basis of these discrepancies the inscription had been assumed to be false already in the 19th century, for these differences cannot be attributed to a supposed mixed dialect spoken in Ezion-geber, but rather to the ignorance of the Phoenician language on the part of the author. The latter seems to have a cultured background; he certainly knew biblical Hebrew and had some knowledge of Phoenician history. He must have consulted works on the Phoenician language (these were available in fairly large numbers around 1870) and for signs he must have resorted to the alphabetical tables. The resulting document was bound to cause a sensation; however, it did not then and does not now succeed in appearing authentic.

Both the name of the inventor of the Parahaiba inscription and his aims have remained unknown; however we may take quick look at the atmosphere in which the forgery occurred. In the 19th century Phoenician studies were taken up with enormous interest in the wake of important discoveries: in 1844 the Marseilles Tariff, a lengthy document recording the amounts due to the clergy and to the offerers for different sacrifices; in 1855 the inscription of Eshmunazar, king of Sidon, whose epigraphic characters partly inspired our forger; in 1868 the famous stele of Mesha, written in Moabite, whose contents show various correspondences with the Old Testament. It was precisely during those years that E. Renan accomplished his mission in Phoenicia and prepared a corpus of Semitic inscriptions which included Phoenician examples. This fervor of studies and discoveries led to a series of epigraphic forgeries, and the Parahaiba inscription fits admirably among them.

The emperor of Brazil at the time was Pedro II, erudite and especially steeped in the study of Semitic languages. One of the scholars in Pedro's retinue may have wished to gratify him with some sensational discovery in his kingdom; or the sale of a false inscription may have been planned with the connivance of a scholar. Perhaps, after being refuted by Semitists, the inscription was hidden (or had it never been engraved on stone at all?). All that remained were the copies through which Neto himself tried to retrace the original and track down the perpetrator of the forgery. It is said that he had reached some sort of conclusion, but the whole thing was allowed to lapse into oblivion. More than a century has gone by and those who could have thrown light on this event are long dead. It is certain that the forger did not profit financially from the affair, but his exploit is remembered and arouses interest and polemical debate to this day.

General Bibliography

General bibliography
Maria Teresa Francisi

For a detailed bibliography refer to the special section published in *Rivista di Studi Fenici*. The following abbreviations are used here:

AC = *Archeologia Classica*
ACFP I = *Atti del I Congresso Internazionale di Studi fenici e punici, Roma 5-10 novembre 1979, I-III, Roma 1983*
AEA = *Archivo Español de Arqueología Annales*
ESC = *Annales Economies Sociétés Civilisations*
BCA = *Beni Culturali e Ambientali*
BCH = *Bulletin de Correspondance Hellénique*
CahT = *Les Cahiers de Tunisie*
CB = *Cahiers de Byrsa*
MANL = *Memorie dell'Accademia Nazionale dei Lincei*
NBS = *Nuovo Bullettino Archeologico Sardo*
NSc = *Notizie degli Scavi di Antichità*
OA = *Oriens Antiquus*
PEQ = *Palestine Exploration Quarterly*
RANL = *Rendiconti dell'Accademia Nazionale dei Lincei*
RDAC = *Report of the Department of Antiquities of Cyprus*
RSF = *Rivista di Studi Fenici*
SE = *Studi Etruschi*
SicArch = *Sicilia Archeologica*
SS = *Studi Sardi*

Phoenician Civilization

On Phoenico-Punic civilization in general:
G. Contenau, *La civilisation phénicienne*, Paris 1949
S. Moscati, *Tra Cartagine e Roma*, Milano 1971
Id., *I Fenici e Cartagine*, Torino 1972
V. Tusa, La civiltà punica: Popoli e civiltà dell'Italia antica, III, Roma 1974, pp. 9-142
S. Moscati, *I Cartaginesi in Italia*, Milano 1977
E. Acquaro, *Cartagine: un impero sul Mediterraneo*, Roma 1978
S. Moscati, *Il mondo dei Fenici*, Milano 1979
D. Harden *The Phoenicians*, Harmondsworth 1980
S. Moscati, *Il mondo punico*, Torino 1980
G. Garbini, *I Fenici. Storia e religione*, Napoli 1980
S. Moscati, *Cartaginesi*, Milano 1982
Id., *L'enigma dei Fenici*, Milano 1982
AA. VV., *Fenici e Cartaginesi in Italia: Bollettino d'Arte*, 31-32 (1985), pp. 1-96
S. Moscati, *Italia punica*, Milano 1986

On specific aspects of the Phoenico-Punic question:
AA.VV., *The Role of the Phoenicians in the Interaction of Mediterranean Civilizations*, Beyrouth 1968
AA.VV., *Ricerche puniche nel Mediterraneo centrale*, Roma 1970
S. Moscati, *L'enigma dei Fenici*, cit.
AA.VV., *Atti del I Congreso Internazionale di Studi fenici e punici, Roma 5-10 novembre 1979, I-III*, Roma 1983
AA.VV., *Studia Phoenicia*, I-IV, Leuven 1983-86

On Mediterranean expansion and the historical events:
S. Gsell, *Histoire ancienne de l'Afrique du Nord*, I-IV, Paris 1921-24
AA.VV., *L'espansione fenicia nel Mediterraneo*, Roma 1971

A. Montenegro Duque, *Historia de España, I. España preromana*, Madrid 1972
A. Parrot - M. Chéhab - S. Moscati, *Les Phéniciens. L'expansion phénicienne. Carthage*, Paris 1975
G. Bunnens, *L'expansion phénicienne en Méditerranée*, Bruxelles 1979
S.F. Bondì, in E. Gabba - G. Vallet, *La Sicilia antica*, I, 1, Napoli 1980, pp. 163-218
F. Barreca, *La Sardegna e i Fenici: Ichnussa*, Milano 1981, pp. 350-417
F. Decret - M. Fantar, *L'Afrique du Nord dans l'antiquité*, Paris 1981
H.G. Niemeyer (ed.), *Phönizier im Westen*, Mainz 1982
AA.VV., *Fenici e Arabi nel Mediterraneo*, Roma 1983

On Carthage in particular:
C. Picard, *Carthage*, Paris 1951
B.H. Warmington, *Carthage*, London 1960
M. Fantar, *Carthage, la prestigeuse cité d'Elissa*, Tunis 1970
AA.VV. *New Light on Ancient Carthage*, Ann Arbor 1980
G. and C. Charles-Picard, *La vie quotidienne à Carthage au temps d'Hannibal*, Paris 1982
S. Lancel, *La colline de Byrsa à l'époque punique*, Paris 1983
W. Huss, *Geschichte der Karthager*, München 1985

On Hannibal and his military campaigns:
G. Charles-Picard, *Annibale, il sogno di un impero*, Roma 1968
G. De Beer, *Hannibal. Ein Leben gegen Rom*, München 1970
W. Görlitz, *Hannibal Eine politische Biographie*, Stuttgart 1970
G. Brizzi, *Studi di storia annibalica*, Faenza 1984
AA.VV., *Studi annibalici (in occasione del XXII centenario): Rivista storica dell'antichità*, 13-14 (1983-84), Bologna 1985

On navigation:
P. Bartoloni, *Le figurazioni di carattere marino rappresentate sulle più tarde stele di Cartagine*. I-II: *RSF*, 5 (1977), pp. 147-64; *RSF*, 7 (1979), pp. 181-91
M.C . De Graeve, *The Ships of the Ancient Near East (c. 2000-500 B.C.)*, Leuven 1981
J. Desanges, *Le point sur le "Périple d'Hannon": controverses et publications récentes: Enquêtes et documents*, 6 (1981), pp. 11-29
H. Frost, *La réconstruction du navire punique de Marsala: Archeologia*, 170 (1982), pp. 42-50

On industry and commerce:
J. Pirenne, *A propos du droit commercial phénicien antique: Bulletin de l'Académie Royale de Belgique*, 41 (1955), pp. 586-614
M. Ponsich - M. Tarradell, *Ganum et industries antiques de salaison dans la Méditerranée occidentale*, Paris 1965
W. Culican, *The First Merchant Venturers. The Ancient Levant in History and Commerce*, London 1966
J. Doumet, *Étude sur la couleur pourpre ancienne et tentative de reproduction du procédé de teinture de la ville de Tyr décrit per Pline l'Ancien*, Beyrouth 1980
G. Falsone, *Struttura e origine dei forni da vasaio di Mozia*, Palermo 1981
M. Gras, *Trafics tyrrhéniens archaïques*, Rome 1985
AA.VV. *Il commercio etrusco arcaico. Atti dell'incontro di studio, 5-7 dicembre 1983*, Roma 1985

On the writing and language:
G.R. Driver, *Semitic Writing from Pictograph to Alphabet*, London 1954
H. Donner - W. Röllig, *Kanaanäische und aramaïsche Inschriften*, Wiesbaden 1966-69
M.G. Guzzo Amadasi, *Le iscrizioni fenicie e puniche delle colonie in Occidente*, Roma 1967
J.B. Peckham, *The Development of the Late Phoenician Scripts*, Cambridge (Mass.) 1968
AA.VV., *Le lamine di Pyrgi. Tavola rotonda internazionale*, Roma, 1970
J. Friedrich - W. Röllig, *Phönizisch-punische Grammatik*, Rom 1970

F.L. Benz, *Personal Names in the Phoenician and Punic Iscriptions*, Roma 1972
S . Segert, *A Grammar of Phoenician and Punic*, München 1976
M.G. Guzzo Amadasi - V. Karageorghis, *Fouilles de Kition III. Inscriptions phéniciennes*, Nicosia 1977
F. Bron, *Recherches sur les inscriptions phéniciennes de Karatepe*, Genève 1979
G. Garbini, *Storia e problemi dell'epigrafia semitica*, Napoli 1979
J.C.L. Gibson, *Textbook of Syrian Semitic Inscription. III Phoenician Inscriptions Including Inscriptions in the Mixed Dialect of Arslan Tash*, Oxford 1982
M.G. Guzzo Amadasi, *Scavi a Mozia - Le iscrizioni*, Roma 1986

On the religion in general:
G. Charles-Picard, *Les religions de l'Afrique antique*, Paris 1954
M. Fantar, *Eschatologie phénicienne-punique*, Tunis 1970
H. Gese - M. Höfner - K. Rudolph, *Die Religionen Altsyriens, Altarabiens und der Mandäer*, Stuttgart 1970
G . and C . Charles-Picard, *Vie et mort de Carthage*, Paris 1970
P. Xella, *Problemi del mito nel Vicino Oriente Antico*, Roma 1976
AA.VV. *La religione fenicia. Matrici orientali e sviluppi occidentali*, Roma 1981
S. Ribichini, *Poenus Advena. Gli dèi fenici e l'interpretazione classica*, Roma 1985
AA.VV. *Studia Phoenicia - IV. Religio Phoenicia*, Namur 1986
S. Moscati, *Il sacrificio punico dei fanciulli: realtà o invenzione?*, Roma 1987

On the principal deities:
F. Barreca, *Il tempio di Antas e il culto di Sardus Pater*, n.p. 1975
W.J. Fulco, *The Canaanite God Reṧep*, New Haven 1976
M.H. Fantar, *Le dieu de la mer chez les Phéniciens et les Puniques*, Rome 1977
J. Ebach, *Weltentstehung und Kulturentwicklung bei Philo von Byblos*, Stuttgart 1979
F.O. Hvidberg-Hansen, *La déesse TNT (Tanit). Une étude sur la réligion canaanéo-punique*, I-II, Copenhague 1979

S. Ribichini, *Adonis. Aspetti "orientali" di un mito greco*, Roma 1981
AA.VV., *Adonis. Relazioni del Colloquio in Roma 22-23 maggio 1981*, Roma 1984
M.L. Barré, *The God-List in the Treaty between Hannibal and Philip V of Macedonia: A Study in Light of the Ancient Near Eastern Treaty Tradition*, Baltimore (Maryland) 1984
G.C. Heider, *The Cult of Molek. A Reassessment*, Sheffield 1985

On the myth of Dido in particular:
G. Grottanelli, *I connotati "fenici " della morte di Elissa: Religioni e Civiltà*, 1 (1972), pp. 319-27
A. Borghini, *Episodi di un'archeologia mitica cartaginese: dal rifiuto del bue al suicidio endogamico di Elissa: Studi Urbinati/B3, 58* (1985), pp. 69-100
J. Scheid - J. Svembro, *Byrsa. La ruse d'Elissa et la fondation de Carthage: Annales ESC*, March-April 1985, pp. 328-42
S. Moscati, *La fortuna di Elissa: RANL*, ser. VIII, 40 (1985), pp. 95-98

In the political and administrative organization:
G. Charles-Picard, *L'administration territoriale de Carthage: Mélangés A. Piganiol*, III, Paris 1966, pp. 1257-65
S.F. Bondì, *I Libifenici nell'ordinamento cartaginese: RANL*, ser. VIII, 26 (1971), pp. 653-62
Id., *Istituzioni e politica a Sidone dal 351 al 332 a.C.: RSF*, 2 (1974), pp. 149-60
E. Gonzalbes Cravioto, *La administración local en la Hispania cartaginesa según las fuentes literarias: Unidad y pluralidad en el mundo antiguo. Actas del VI Congreso español de estudios clásicos (Sevilla, 6-11 de abril de 1981)*, II, Madrid 1983, pp. 7-17
S. Ribichini, *Temple et sacerdoce dans l'économie de Carthage: Bulletin archéologique*, 19 (1983), pp. 29-37
Ju.B. Tsirkin, *Carthage and the Problem of Polis: RSF*, 14 (1986), pp. 129-41

On the army and warfare, see particularly:
J.F. Lazenby, *Hannibal's War. A Military History of the Second Punic War*, Warminster 1978

T. Wise, *Armies of the Carthaginian Wars 265-146 B.C.*, London 1982

B. Caven, *The Punic Wars*, London 1983

The Great Areas

On Phoenicia:

D. Baramki, *Phoenicia and the Phoenicians*, Beyrouth 1961

J. Pairman Brown, *The Lebanon and Phoenicia*, I, Beyrouth 1969

On the principal cities of Phoenicia:

P. Montet, *Byblos et l'Egypte*, I-II, Paris 1928

M. Dunand, *Fouilles de Byblos*, I-IV, Paris 1937-73

Id., *Byblos, son histoire, ses ruines, ses légendes*, Beyrouth 1963

E.J. Wein - R. Opificius, *7000 Jahre Byblos*, Nürnberg 1963

J.-F. Salles, *La nécropole "K" de Byblos*, Paris 1980

M. Saghieh, *Byblos in the Third Millennium*, Warminster 1984

J. Jidejian, *Sidon through the Ages*, Beyrouth 1972

M. Chéhab, *Trente années de recherches archéologiques au Liban (Les dossiers de l'Archéologie, 12)*, Paris 1975

N. Jidejian, *Tyre through the Ages*, Beyrouth 1969

J.P. Rey-Coquais, *Arados et sa pérée aux époques grecque, romaine et byzantine*, Paris 1974

M. Dunand - N. Saliby, *Le temple d'Amrith dans la pérée d'Aradus*, Paris 1985

P.J. Riis - M.-L. Buhl (ed.), *Sukas I-VII*, Copenhagen 1970-83

J.B. Pritchard (ed.), *Sarepta. A Preliminary Report on the Iron Age*, Philadelphia 1975

Id., *Recovering Sarepta, a Phoenician City*, Princeton 1978

On the Phoenicions in Cyprus:

E. Gjerstad, *The Swedish Cypnus Expedition. IV. The Cypro-Geometric, Cypro-Archaic and Cypro-Classical Periods*, Stockholm 1948

V. Karageorghis, *Chypre*, Genève 1968

O. Masson - M. Sznycer, *Recherches sur les Phéniciens à Chypre*, Genève-Paris 1972

G. Clerc et al., *Fouilles de Kition II. Objets égyptiens et égyptisants*, Nicosia 1976

V. Karageorghis, *Kition. Mycenaean and Phoenician Discoveries in Cyprus*, London 1976

Id., *Two Cypriote Sanctuaries of the End of the Cypro-Archaic Period*, Roma 1977

Id., *Cyprus. From the Stone Age to the Romans*, London 1982

C. Baurain, *Chypre et la Méditerranée orientale au Bronze récent. Synthèse historique*, Paris 1984

AA.VV., *Cyprus between the Orient and the Occident*, Nicosia 1986

On North Africa:

J. Carcopino, *Le Maroc antique*, Paris 1948

P. Cintas, *Fouilles puniques à Tipasa*, Alger 1949

J. Baradez, *Tipasa*, Alger 1952

P. Cintas, *Contribution à l'étude de l'expansion cartaginoise au Maroc*, Paris 1954

M. Tarradell, *Lixus*, Tetuán 1959

Id., *Marruecos púnico*, Tetuán 1960

A. Jodin, *Mogador, comptoir phénicien du Maroc antique*, Paris 1963

A. Lézine, *Utique*, Paris 1970

P. Cintas, *Manuel d'archéologie punique*, I-II, Paris 1970-78

AA.VV., *Prospezione archeologica al Capo Bon*, I-II, Roma 1973-1983

AA.VV., *Tunisie, 30 siècles de civilisation*, Tunis 1983

M. Fantar, *Kerkouane cité punique du Cap Bon (Tunisie)*, I-III, Tunis 1984-86

On Sicily in general:

B. Pace, *Arte e civiltà della Sicilia antica*, I, Milano 1958

L. Pareti, *Sicilia antica*, Palermo 1959

V. Tusa - E. De Miro, *Sicilia occidentale*, Roma 1983

V. Tusa, *I Fenici e i Cartaginesi: Sikanie*, Milano 1986, pp. 577-631

S. Moscati, *L'arte della Sicilia punica*, Milano 1987

On the single cities:

J.I.S. Whitaker, *Motya. A Phoenician Colony in Sicily*, London 1921

M.O. Acanfora, *Panormo punica, MANL*, ser. VIII, 1 (1947), coll. 197-248

AA.VV., *Mozia I-IX. Rapporti preliminari delle campagne di scavo 1964-1974*, Roma 1964-78

B.S.J. Isserlin - J. Du Plat Taylor, *Motya. A Phoenician and Carthaginian City in Sicily*, I, Leiden 1974

AA.VV., *Lilybaeum: NSc*, ser. VIII, 30 (1976), suppl.

AA.VV., *Lilibeo. Testimonianze archeologiche dal IV sec. a.C. al V sec. d.C.*, Palermo 1984

On coinage:

A. Cutroni Tusa, *Monetazione punica e sua circolazione nell'Italia antica: Popoli e civiltà dell'Italia antica*, III, Roma 1974, pp. 109-116

Ead., *La documentazione numismatica: Atti del colloquio "I Cartaginesi in Sicilia al tempo dei due Dionisi": Kokalos*, 28-29 (1982-83), pp. 213-26

On Malta, Gozo and Pantelleria:

A. Mayr, *Die Insel Malta im Altertum*, München 1909

Id., *Die antike Münzen der Insel Malta, Gozo und Pantelleria*, München 1894

AA.VV., *Missione archeologica italiana a Malta. Rapporti preliminari delle campagne 1963-1970*, Roma 1964-73

A. Verger, *Pantelleria nell'antichità: OA*, 5 (1966), pp. 249-75

J.D. Evans, *The Prehistoric Antiquities of the Maltese Islands: a Survey*, London 1971

On Sardinia in general:

G. Pesce, *Sardegna punica*, Cagliari 1961

S. Moscati, *Fenici e Cartaginesi in Sardegna*, Milano 1968

F. Barreca, *La Sardegna fenicia e punica*, Sassari 1979

E. Acquaro, *Arte e cultura punica in Sardegna*, Sassari 1984

F. Barreca, *La civiltà fenicio-punica in Sardegna*, Sassari 1986

S. Moscati, *L'arte della Sardegna punica*, Milano 1986

On the single cities:

D. Panedda, *Olbia nel periodo punico e romano*, Roma 1952

Id., *L'agro di Olbia nel periodo preistorico, punico e romano*, Roma 1954

AA.VV., *Monte Sirai I-IV. Rapporti preliminari delle campagne di scavo 1963-66*, Roma 1964-67

G. Pesce, *Tharros*, Cagliari 1966

AA.VV., *Ricerche puniche ad Antas*, Roma 1969

G. Pesce, *Nora. Guida agli scavi*, Cagliari 1972

G. Chiera, *Testimonianze su Nora*, Roma 1978
AA.VV. *Tharros I-XIII. Campagne di scavo: RSF, 3* (1975), pp. 88-119; *RSF*, 3 (1975), pp. 213-25; *RSF*, 4 (1976), pp. 197-228; *RSF*, 6 (1978), pp. 66-99; *RSF*, 7 (1979), pp. 49-124; *RSF*, 8 (1980), pp. 79-142; *RSF*, 9 (1981), pp. 29-119; *RSF*, 10 (1982), pp. 37-127; *RSF*, 11 (1983), pp. 49-111; *RSF*, 12 (1984), pp. 47-101; *RSF*, 13 (1985), pp. 11-147; *RSF*, 14 (1986), pp. 95-107; *RSF*, 15 (1987), pp. 75-102
AA.VV., *Monte Sirai 1979-1985. Campagne di scavo: RSF*, 8 (1980), pp. 143-45; *RSF*, 9 (1981), pp. 217-30; *RSF*, 10 (1982), pp. 273-90; *RSF*, 11 (1983), pp. 183-203; *RSF*, 12 (1984), pp. 185-98; *RSF*, 15 (1987), pp. 179-90
A.M. Costa, *Santu Teru - Monte Luna (campagne di scavo 1977-79, 1980-82): RSF*, 8 (1980), pp. 265-70; *RSF*, 11 (1983), pp. 223-34
A. Mastino, *Cornus nella storia degli studi*, Cagliari 1983
R. Zucca, *Tharros*, Oristano 1984
E. Acquaro - C. Finzi, *Tharros*, Sassari 1986

On the Iberian Peninsula:
G. del Olmo Lete - M.E. Aubet, *Los Fenicios en la peninsula ibérica: Aula Orientalis*, 3-4, Barcelona 1985-86

On the single cities:
M.J. Almagro Gorbea, *Excavaciones arqueológicas en Ibiza*, Madrid 1967
H.G. Niemeyer - H. Schubart, *Toscanos*, Berlin 1969
AA.VV., *Tartessos y sus problemas*, Barcelona 1969
AA.VV., *Huelva. Prehistoria y antigüedad*, Madrid 1974
J.M. Blázquez, *Tartessos y los origenes de la colonización fenicia en Occidente*, Salamanca 1975
H.G. Niemeyer - H. Schubart, *Trayamar*, Mainz 1975
M. Tarradell - M. Font, *Eivissa cartaginesa*, Barcelona 1975
AA.VV., *Historia de España antigua. I. Protohistoria*, Madrid 1980
AA.VV., *Almuñécar. Arqueologia y Historia*, Granada 1982
M.E. Aubet Semmler, *El santuano de Es Cuyram*, Ibiza 1982
H. Schubart - G. Maass Lindemann, *Toscanos 1971*, Berlin 1982

J.H. Fernández, *Guía del Puig des Molins*, Ibiza 1983
C. Gómez Bellard, *La necrópolis del Puig des Molins (Ibiza). Campaña de 1946*, Madrid 1984
V.M. Guerrero Ayuso, *La colonización púnico-ebusitana de Mallorca*, Ibiza 1984

The World of Art

For a history of the arts and crafts, besides the general books listed in the first section, see particularly:
G. Perrot - C. Chipiez, *Histoire de l'art dans l'antiquité. III: Phénicie-Chypre*, Paris 1885
P. Cintas, *Manuel d'archéologie punique*, I-II, cit.
S. Moscati, *Il mondo punico*, cit.

For some particularly important collections:
G.C. Picard, *Catalogue du Musée Alaoui. Nouvelle série*, Tunis 1957
E. Acquaro - S. Moscati - M.L. Uberti, *Anecdota Tharrhica*, Roma 1975
Id., *La collezione Biggio. Antichità puniche a Sant'Antioco*, Roma 1977

For the Cypriot components:
A.M. Bisi, *Kypriakà. Contributi allo studio della componente cipriota della civiltà punica*, Roma 1966

For orientalizing art in Spain:
M. Almagro Gorbea, *El Bronce final y el periodo orientalizante en Extremadura*, Madrid 1977

On architecture and town-planning, besides the general works listed in the first section:
H . Frankfort, *The Art and Architecture of the Ancient Orient*, Harmondsworth 1954, pp. 188-201
A. Lézine, *Architecture punique. Recueil de documents*, Paris 1962
Th.A. Busink, *Der Tempel von Jerusalem von Salomo bis Herodes*, Leiden 1970
B. Wesenberg, *Kapitelle und Basen*, Düsseldorf 1971
K. Nicolaou, *The Historical Topography of Kition*, Goteborg 1976
P. Wagner, *Der ägyptische Einfluss auf die phönizische Architektur*, Bonn 1980

On the sacred buildings and tophets:
P. Cintas, *Le sanctuaire punique de Sousse: Revue Africaine*, 90 (1947), pp. 1-80
A. Berthier - R. Charlier, *Le sanctuaire punique d'El-Hofra à Constantine*, Paris 1955
G. Pesce, *Il tempio punico monumentale di Tharros: MANL*, 45 (1961), coll. 333-439
V. Karageorghis, *Two Cypriot Sanctuaries of the End of the Cypro-Archaic Period*, cit.
V. Tusa, *Edifici sacri in centri non greci della Sicilia occidentale: Philias Charin. Miscellanea di studi classici in onore di Eugenio Manni*, Roma 1980, pp. 2125-37
M.E. Aubet Semmler, *El santuario de Es Cuyram*, Ibiza 1982

On the necropolis:
P. Gauckler, *Nécropoles puniques de Carthage*, I-II, Paris 1915
A. Vives y Escudero, *La necrópolis de Ibiza*, Madrid 1917
D. Levi, *Le necropoli puniche di Olbia: SS*, 9 (1950), pp. 5-120
M. Astruc, *La necrópolis de Villaricos*, Madrid 1951
M. Pellicer, *Excavaciones en la necrópolis púnica Laurita, del Cerro de San Cristóbal (Almunécar, Granada)*, Barcelona 1962
M. Ponsich, *Nécropoles phéniciennes de la région de Tanger*, Tanger 1967
A. Tejera Gaspar, *Las tumbas fenicias y púnicas del Mediterráneo Occidental (Estudio tipológico)*, Sevilla 1979
P. Bartoloni - C. Tronchetti, *La necropoli di Nora*, Roma 1981
H. Benichou-Safar, *Les tombes puniques de Carthage. Topographie, structures, inscriptions et rites funéraires*, Paris 1982
F. Molina Fajardo - A. Ruiz Fernández - C. Huertas Jiménez, *Almuñécar en la antigüedad. La necrópolis fenicio-púnica de Puente de Noy*, Granada 1982

On the fortification systems.
A.M. Bisi, *Ricerche sulle fortificazioni puniche di Lilibeo (Marsala)* : *OA*, 6 (1967), pp. 315-18; *AC*, 20 (1968), pp. 259-65
Ead., *Erice (Trapani). Saggi alle fortificazioni puniche: NSc*, ser. VIII, 22 (1968), pp. 272-92

A. Ciasca, *Scavi alle mura di Mozia (campagne 1975-79): RSF*, 4 (1976), pp. 69-79; *RSF*, 5 (1977), pp. 205-18; *RSF*, 6 (1978), pp. 227-45; *RSF*, 7 (1979), pp. 207-27; *RSF*, 8 (1980), pp. 237-52

On the ports:
G. Schmeidt, *Antichi porti d'Italia: L'Universo*, 45 (1965), pp. 225-74
P. Cintas, *Le port de Carthage*, Paris 1973

On the statuary and stone reliefs:
M. Dunand, *La statuaire de la favissa du temple d'Echmoun à Sidon: Festschrift K. Galling*, Tübingen 1970, pp. 61-67
G. Falsone, *La statua fenicio-cipriota dello Stagnone: SicArch*, 10 (1970), pp. 54-61
S. Moscati, *Una testa a rilievo in pietra da Monte Sirai: RSF*, 11 (1983), pp. 219-22
V. Tusa, *La scultura in pietra di Selinunte*, Palermo 1983
V. Tusa, *Il giovane di Mozia: RSF*, 14 (1986), pp. 143-52

On the sarcophagi:
E. Kukahn, *Anthropoide Sarkophage in Beyrouth, und die Geschichte dieser sidonischen Sarkophagkunst*, Berlin 1955
M. Fantar, *Un sarcophage en bois à couvercle anthropoïde découvert dans la nécropole punique de Kerkouane: Comptes-rendus de l'Académie des Inscriptions et Belles Lettres*, 1972, pp. 340-54
E. Porada, *Notes on the Sarcophagus of Ahiram: Journal of the Ancient Near Eastern Society of Columbia University*, 5 (1973), pp. 355-72
R. Corzo Sánchez, *El nuevo sarcófago antropoide de la necrópolis gaditana: Boletin del Museo de Cádiz*, 2 (1979-80), pp. 13-24
R. Fleischer, *DerKlagenfrauensarkofag aus Sidon*, Tübingen 1983

On the stelae in general:
A.M. Bisi, *Le stele puniche*, Roma 1967

On the stelae from Carthage:
M. Hours-Miédan, *Les représentations figurées sur les stèles de Carthage: CB*, 1 (1951), pp. 15-160
M.E. Aubet -J. Ferron, *Orants de Carthage*, Paris 1974

C. Charles-Picard, *Les représentations de sacrifice molk sur les ex-voto de Carthage: Karthago*, 17 (1976), pp. 67-138
P. Bartoloni, *Le stele arcaiche del tofet di Cartagine*, Roma 1976
J. Ferron, *Mort-dieu de Carthage ou les stèles funéraires de Carthage*, I-II, Paris 1976
C. Charles-Picard, *Les représentations du sacrifice molk sur les stèles de Carthage: Karthago*, 18 (1978), pp. 5-116

On the stelae from Cyprus:
V. Karageorghis, *Naïskoi de Chypre: BCH*, 94 (1970), pp. 27-33
V. Wilson, *Excavations at Kouklia (Palaepaphos). The Kouklia Sanctuary: RDAC*, 1974, pp. 139-46

On the stelae from Sicily:
V. Tusa, *Le stele di Selinunte*, Palermo 1976
S. Moscati - M.L. Uberti, *Scavi a Mozia - Le stele*, I-II, Roma 1981

On the stelae from Sardinia:
G. Lilliu, *Le stele puniche di Sulcis (Cagliari): MANL*, 40 (1944), coll. 293-418
S. Moscati - M. L. Uberti, *Le stele puniche di Nora nel Museo Nazionale di Cagliari*, Roma 1970
S.F. Bondì, *Le stele di Monte Sirai*, Roma 1972
G. Tore, *Su alcune stele funerarie sarde di età punico-romana: Latomus*, 34 (1975), pp. 293-318
S.F. Bondì, *Nuove stele da Monte Sirai: RSF*, 8 (1980), pp. 51-70
S. Moscati - M.L. Uberti, *Scavi al tofet di Tharros. I monumenti lapidei*, Roma 1985
P. Bartoloni, *Le stele di Sulcis. Catalogo*, Roma 1986
S. Moscati, *Le stele di Sulcis. Caratteri e confronti*, Roma 1986

On the terracotta figurines and moulds:
M. Chéhab, *Les terres cuites de Kharayeb*, Paris 1951-54
J.H. and S.H. Young, *Terracotta Figurines from Kourion in Cyprus*, Philadelphia 1955
M.E. Aubet, *Los depósitos votivos púnicos de Isla Plana (Ibiza) y Bithia (Cerdeña)*, Santiago de Compostela 1969

M.L. Uberti, *Le figurine fittili di Bitia*, Roma 1973
M. Tarradell, *Terracotas púnicas de Ibiza*, Barcelona 1974
J. Ferron - M. E . Aubet, *Orants de Carthage*, cit.
M.J. Almagro Gorbea, *Corpus de las terracotas de Ibiza*, Madrid 1980
M.P. San Nicolás Pedraz, *Las terracotas figuradas de la Ibiza púnica*, Roma 1987

On protomes and terra cotta masks:
G. Charles-Picard, *Sacra Punica. Étude sur les masques et rasoirs de Carthage: Karthago*, 13 (1965-66), pp. 1-115
W. Culican, *Some Phoenician Masks and Other Terracottas: Berytus*, 24 (1975-76), pp. 47-87
E. Stern, *Phoenician Masks and Pendants: PEQ*, 108 (1976), pp.109-18
G. Chiera, *Una maschera silenica da Sulcis: RANL*, 35 (1980), pp. 505-508
S. Moscati, *Due maschere puniche da Sulcis: RANL*, 35 (1980), pp. 311- 13

On the jewellery:
F.H. Marshall, *Catalogue of the Jewellery, Greek, Etruscan and Roman, in the Department of Antiquities, British Museum*, London 1912
A. Blanco Freijeiro, *Orientalia. Estudio de objetos fenicios y orientalizantes en la Península: AEA*, 29 (1956), pp. 3-51
J.M. De Carriazo, *El tesoro y las primeras excavaciones de Ebora (Sanlúcar de Barrameda)*, Madrid 1970
Id., *El tesoro y las primeras excavaciones en "El Carambolo" (Camas, Sevilla)*, Madrid 1970
G. Quattrocchi Pisano, *I gioielli fenici di Tharros nel Museo Nazionale di Cagliari*, Roma 1974
B. Quillard, *Bijoux carthaginois. I: Les colliers. D'après les collections du Musée National du Bardo et du Musée National de Carthage*, Louvain-La-Nueve 1979
J. Wolters, *Die Granulation. Geschichte und Technik einer alten Goldschmiedekunst*, München 1983
M.J. Almagro Gorbea, *Orfebrería fenicio-púnica*, Madrid 1986
S. Moscati - M.L. Uberti, *Iocalia Punica*, Roma 1987

On the amulets and scarabs:
J. Vercoutter, Les objets égyptiens et égyptisants du mobilier funéraire carthaginois, Paris 1945
P. Cintas, Amulettes puniques, Tunis 1946
P. Bartoloni, Gli amuleti punici del tofet di Sulcis: RSF, 1 (1973), pp. 181-203
S.F. Bondì, Gli scarabei di Monte Sirai: Saggi fenici-I, Roma 1975, pp. 73-98
G. Matthiae Scandone, Scarabei e scaraboidi egiziani ed egittizzanti del Museo Nazionale di Cagliari, Roma 1975
E. Acquaro, Amuleti egiziani ed egittizzanti del Museo Nazionale di Cagliari, Roma 1977
S. Verga, Scarabei e scaraboidi nel Museo Pepoli di Trapani: SicArch, 40 (1979), pp. 27-36
A. Fresina, Amuleti del Museo J. Whitaker di Mozia: SicArch, 43 (1980), pp. 27-50
E. Acquaro, La collezione punica del Museo Nazionale "Giovanni Antonio Sanna" di Sassari. Gli amuleti: RSF, 10 (1982), suppl., pp. 1-46
J.H. Fernández -J. Padró, Escarabeos del Museo Arqueológico de Ibiza, Madrid 1982
J. Boardman, Escarabeos de piedra procedentes de Ibiza, Madrid 1984
R. Giveon, Egyptian Scarabs from Western Asia from the Collections of the British Museum, Freiburg 1985
S. Verga, Scarabei in pietra dura nel Museo Archeologico Regionale di Palermo: RSF, 14 (1986), pp. 153-80

On the ivory and bone objects:
J. Bonsor, Early Engraved Ivories, New York 1928
C. Decamps de Mertzenfeld, Inventaire commenté des ivoires phéniciens et apparentés découverts dans le Proche Orient, Paris 1954
A.M. Bisi, I pettini d'avorio di Cartagine: Africa, 2 (1968), pp 10-73
S. Moscati, Gli avori del santuario di Giunone a Malta: Studi in onore di E. Volterra, VI, Milano 1969, pp. 269-74
E. Petrasch - J. Thimme, Phönizische Elfenbeine, Karlsruhe 1973
R.D. Barnett, A Catalogue of the Nimrud Ivories with Other Examples of Ancient Near Eastern Ivories in the British Museum, London 1975

M. Mallowan, The Nimrud Ivories, London 1978
M.E. Aubet, Marfiles fenicios del Bajo Guadalquivir. II: Acebuchal y Alcantarilla, Valladolid 1980
Ead., Marfiles fenicios del Bajo Guadalquivir (y III): Bencarrón, Santa Lucía y Setefilla: Pyrenae, 17-18 (1981-82), pp. 231-79
R.D. Barnett, Ancient Ivories in the Middle East and Adjacent Countries, Jerusalem 1982
S. Lancel, Ivoires phénico-puniques de la nécropole archaïque de Byrsa, à Carthage: ACFP, 1, III, cit., pp. 687-92

On the bronzes and razors:
G. Charles-Picard, Sacra Punica. Étude sur les masques et rasoirs de Carthage, cit.
E. Acquaro, I rasoi punici, Roma 1971
V. Tusa, La statuetta fenicia del Museo Nazionale di Palermo: RSF, 1 (1973), pp. 173-79
C .A. Di Stefano, Bronzetti figurati del Museo Nazionale di Palermo, Roma 1975
O. Negbi, Canaanite Gods in Metal, Tel Aviv 1976
A.M. Bisi, La diffusion du "Smiting God" syro-palestinien dans le milieu phénicien d'Occident: Karthago, 19 (1980), pp. 5-14
M. Gras - G. Tore, Bronzetti dalla Nurra, Sassari 1981
G. Tore, I bronzi figurati fenicio-punici in Sardegna: ACFP, 1, II, cit., pp. 449-61

On the metal bowls:
E. Gjerstad, Decorated Metal Bowls from Cyprus: Opuscula Archaeologica, 4 (1946), pp. 1-18
G. Markoe, Phoenician Bronze and Silver Bowls from Cyprus and the Mediterranean, Berkeley 1985

On the painting and ostrich egg-shells:
M. Astruc, Supplément aux Fouilles de Gouraya: Libyca, 2 (1954), pp. 9-48
Ead., Traditions funéraires de Carthage: CB, 6 (1956), pp. 29-58
Ead., Exotisme et localisme. Études sur les coquilles décorées d'Ibiza: Archivo de Prehistoria Levantina, 6 (1957), pp. 47-112
D. Olivia Alonso - M. Puya García de Leaniz, Los huevos de avestruz de

los Alcores de Carmona: Homenaje Chicarro, Madrid 1982, pp. 93-111
A. Caubet, Les oeufs d'autruche au Proche Orient Ancien: RDAC, (1983), pp. 193-98

On the coins:
L. Müller, Numismatique de l'ancienne Afrique, I-II, Copenhagen 1861
E. Birocchi, La monetazione punico-sarda: SS, 2 (1935), pp. 64-164
L. Forteleoni, Le emissioni monetali della Sardegna punica, Sassari 1961
G.K. Jenkins - R.B. Lewis, Carthaginian Gold and Electrum Coins, London 1963
G.K. Jenkins, Coins of Punic Sicily, I-IV: The Swiss Numismatic Review, 50 (1971), pp. 25-78; 53 (1974), pp. 23-41; 56 (1977), pp. 5-65; Schweizerische Numismatische Rundschau, 57 (1978), pp. 5-68
L. Villaronga, Las monedas hispano-cartaginesas, Barcelona 1973
E. Acquaro, Le monete puniche del Museo Nazionale di Caglian, Roma 1974
L. Forteleoni, Monete e zecche della Sardegna punica, Sassari 1975
M. Chéhab, Monnaies gréco-romaines et phéniciennes du Musée National, Beyrouth, Liban, Paris 1977
F. Guido, Le monete puniche della collezione L. Forteleoni, Sassari 1977
E. Acquaro, La monetazione punica, Milano 1979
J.W. Betlyon, The Coinage and Mints of Phoenicia. The Pre-Alexandrine Period, Chico (California) 1982
AA.VV., Studi di numismatica punica: RSF, 11 (1983), suppl.

On glass:
A. Giammellaro Spanò, Pendenti vitrei policromi in Sicilia: SicArch, 39 (1979), pp. 25-48
M. Seefried, Les pendentifs en verre sur noyau des pays de la Méditerranée antique, Roma 1982

On pottery:
P. Cintas, Céramique punique, Paris 1950
A.M. Bisi, La ceramica punica. Aspetti e problemi, Napoli 1970
P. Maynor Bikai, The Pottery of Tyre, Warminster 1978
A. Rodero Riaza, Colección de cerámica púnica de Ibiza en el Museo Arqueológico Nacional, Ibiza 1980

J. Ramón, *La producción anfórica púnico-ebusitana*, Eivissa 1981
A. Ribera Lacomba, *Las anforas prerromanas (fenicias, ibericas y púnicas)*, Valencia 1982
P. Bartoloni, *Studi sulla ceramica fenicia e punica di Sardegna*, Roma 1983
P. Maynor Bikai, *The Phoenician Pottery of Cyprus*, Nicosia 1987

The Phoenicians and the World Outside

On the relations between the Phoenicians and the Greeks:
J. Dunbabin, *The Greeks and their Eastern Neighbours*, London 1957
S. Moscati - M. Pallottino, *Rapporti tra Greci, Fenici ed Etruschi ed altre popolazioni italiche alla luce delle nuove scoperte*, Roma 1966
F. Nicosia, *La Sardegna nel mondo classico: Ichnussa*, Milano 1981, pp. 421-76
L.-M. Hans, *Karthago und Sizilien. Die Entstehung und Gestaltung der Epikratie auf dem Hintergrund der Beziehungen der Karthager zu den Griechen und den nichtgriechischen Völkern Siziliens (VI-III Jahrhundert v. Chr.)*, Hildesheim 1983
S. Moscati, *Fenici e Greci in Sicilia: alle origini di un confronto: Kokalos*, 30-31 (1984-85), pp. 1-19

On the relations between the Phoenicians and the Sards:
G. Lilliu, *Rapporti fra la civiltà nuragica e la civiltà fenicio-punica in Sardegna: SE*, 18 (1944), pp. 323-70
F. Barreca, *Sardegna nuragica e mondo fenicio-punico: Civiltà nuragica*, cit., pp. 308-28

On the relations between the Phoenicians and the Egyptians:
J. Vercoutter, *Les objets égyptiens et égyptisants du mobilier funéraire carthaginois*, cit.
R. Stadelman, *Syrisch-Palästinensische Gottheiten in Ägypten*, Leiden 1966
G. Scandone, *Testimonianze egiziane in Fenicia dal XII al IV sec. a.C.: RSF*, 12 (1984), pp. 133-63

On the relations between the Phoenicians and the Etruscans:
M. Pallottino, *Les relations entre les Étrusques et Carthage du VIIe au IIIe siècle avant J.C. Nouvelles données et essai de périodisation: CahT*, 11 (1963), pp. 23-29
J. Ferron, *Les relations de Carthage avec l'Etrurie: Latomus*, 25 (1966), pp. 689-709
F. Canciani - F.W. Von Hase, *La tomba Bernardini di Palestrina*, Roma 1979
M. Cristofani, *Gli Etruschi e il mare*, Milano 1983
P. Bernardini - C. Tronchetti, *La Sardegna, gli Etruschi e i Greci: Civiltà nuragica*, Milano 1985, pp. 285-307
M. Gras, *Trafics tyrrhéniens archaiques*, cit.

On orientalizing art:
M. Pallottino, *Orientalizzante: Enciclopedia Universale dell'Arte*, X, Venezia-Roma 1963, coll. 223-37
M.E. Aubet, *Estudio sobre el periodo orientalizante - I. Cuencos fenicios de Praeneste*, Santiago de Compostela 1971
Ead., *Los marfiles orientalizantes de Praeneste*, Barcelona 1971
B. D'Agostino - G. Garbini, *La patera orientalizzante da Pontecagnano riesaminata – L'iscrizione fenicia. SE*, 45 (1977), pp. 51-62
A. Rathje, *Oriental Imports in Etruria in the Eight and Seventh Centuries B.C.: Their Origins and Implications: Italy before the Romans*, London 1979, pp. 145-83

On the classical sources:
L. Troiani, *L'opera storiografica di Filone da Byblos*, Pisa 1974
H.W. Attridge - R.A. Oden, *Philo of Byblos. The Phoenician History*, Washington 1981
A.I. Baumgarten, *The Phoenician History of Philo of Byblos. A Commentary*, Leiden 1981
S. Ribichini, *Mito e storia: l'immagine dei Fenici nelle fonti classiche: ACFP*, 1, II, cit., pp. 443-48
A. Simonetti, *Sacrifici umani ed uccisioni rituali nel mondo fenicio-punico. Il contributo delle fonti letterarie e classiche: RSF*, 11 (1983), pp. 91-111
H.G. Niemeyer, *Die Phönizier und die Mittelmeerwelt im Zeitalter Homers: Jahrbuch des Römisch-Germanisches Zentralmuseums*, 31 (1984), pp. 1-94

On the traditions and legends:
J. Bermeio Barrera, *Mitología y mitos de la Hispania prerromana*, Madrid 1982

For the Phoenicians in Brazil:
C.H. Gordon, *The Authenticity of the Phoenician Text from Parahyba: Orientalia*, 37 (1968), pp. 75-80

Photo Credits

Piero Bartoloni, pages 501, 554

Giraudon, pages 46, 356

David Lees, pages 79, 100, 160, 224, 234, 236-239, 310, 331-333, 354 (top, right)

Giuseppe Leone, pages 69, 139, 166, 225, 238, 240, 241, 242-250, 352, 362, 370-371, 385, 404, 410, 412, 482 (below), 504, 612

Erich Lessing, pp.: 10, 12, 26, 27, 29, 32, 33, 34-35, 37, 38-39, 40, 42, 44, 58, 61, 75, 84, 86, 87, 136, 140, 144, 148, 150, 155, 170, 197, 198, 206, 207, 208, 210, 211, 213, 222, 257, 312, 314, 316, 319, 320, 323, 324-328, 357, 358, 368, 380, 382, 406, 407, 408, 410, 418, 421, 422, 442, 468, 473, 482, 495, 517, 542, 543, 573, 575, 594

R.E. Nassif, pages 11, 127, 171, 173, 176-178, 230

Gesualdo Petruccioli, pages 375, 441, 502-503, 545, 585, 606

Folco Quilici, pages 21, 205, 233, 235